MEDICAL

MALPRACTICE

LAW

MEDICAL
MALPRACTICE
LAW

ANGELA RODDEY HOLDER, J. D.

*Member of the Bars of South Carolina
and Louisiana*

*Contributor, Law and Medicine Section,
Journal of the American
Medical Association*

Contributing Editor, Prism

Foreword by Milton Helpern, M. D.

A Wiley Biomedical-Health Publication

JOHN WILEY & SONS, New York • London • Sydney • Toronto

Library of Congress Cataloging in Publication Data:

Holder, Angela Roddey.
  Medical malpractice law.
  (A Wiley biomedical health publication)
  Bibliography: p.
  1. Malpractice—United States. 2. Medical laws
and legislation—United States. I. Title.
[DNLM: 1. Jurisprudence. 2. Malpractice. W44 H727m]

RA1056.5.H64   614′.19   74-17221
ISBN 0-471-40615-5

Printed in the United States of America

10 9 8 7 6 5 4 3

To Tom and, with love, for John

FOREWORD

I am very pleased and honored to write the Foreword to this timely book: *Medical Malpractice Law* by a distinguished attorney, Angela Roddey Holder. Mrs. Holder has been a regular contributor on the subject of malpractice to the Law and Medicine Section of the *Journal of the American Medical Association* and *Prism Magazine*, and she is a member of the South Carolina and Louisiana Bars. Her career and her special knowledge of the field of medical malpractice make her eminently qualified for the enormous task she has undertaken in the preparation of this excellent treatise on an increasingly important subject

Whereas the advances in the science and practice of medicine have produced greater complexity and sophistication in the methods used in diagnostic and therapeutic procedures with life-saving and life-prolonging benefits for many patients, they have also brought about an increase in claims of medical malpractice and litigation, which have skyrocketed the cost of malpractice defense.

Mrs. Holder's book systematically discusses all aspects of medical malpractice. She is not concerned with the strategy of the law suit, but with records of actual cases and with what happened when litigation had taken place. The text is factual and objective. Her treatment of the subject is educational and her attitude is not one of indignation suggesting unreasonable abuse of the physician and the hospital. The book does not take sides with either the medical or the legal professions, but describes the problem and outcome in each case, pointing out that the solutions are not uniform in all jurisdictions and in many cases are subject to reconsideration.

The author discusses many topics in which the possibility of malpractice action is in a state of flux. Thus the subjects of the constitutional rights of various groups of patients, of the rights of minors to contraceptive knowledge and abortion, and of voluntarily committed patients are included, making this book the most up to date of its kind. The rights of drunken drivers with regard to incriminating blood tests and of the sick person in legal custody are also discussed.

The book is written in language understandable to the medical student and the physician. It is extremely well documented, but never with loss of clarity. It contains an alphabetical index and a jurisdictional one, both especially valuable for attorneys, as well as a comprehensive bibliography.

This work, a veritable vademecum on the subject of medical malpractice, should achieve a wide circulation and find a place in every law and medical library. In addition, physicians, lawyers, medical and law students, medical examiners, and coroners will find it to be a tremendous storehouse of information on the subject of malpractice, where criminal and civil situations frequently cross paths.

Valuable books like this one only appear from time to time. The author is to be congratulated on this fine work.

MILTON HELPERN, M.D., L. DR.
Chief Medical Examiner,
City of New York,
Ret. Professor Emeritus,
New York University
School of Medicine
Director, Institute of Forensic Medicine
New York Univesity
of the City of New York
Chairman, Committee on
Forensic Medicine
Medical Society of
the State of New York

PREFACE

When a physician accepts a patient for diagnosis and treatment both parties acquire legal rights and legal obligations. These rights and obligations affect every aspect of the physician-patient relationship. Choice of drugs and of diagnostic tests and procedures, use of medical equipment, information given or withheld, and actions of persons subordinate to the physician are among the many facets of the decision and treatment process that may have bearing on a subsequent determination of the legal obligations of the parties. The purpose of this book is to explain the principles of the physician's obligation to his patient from the beginning to the end of the relationship. To suggest ways in which the physician can avoid situations that lead to lawsuits, I discuss those principles of law that apply to the areas of diagnosis and treatment in which difficulties most frequently arise. I hope that when the physician has finished reading the book he will be a bit less confused about the legal system—the context in which these rights and obligations are enforced—and that he will be less in agreement with Charles Dickens's statement that "the law is an ass."

All the examples given in the book are actual cases. Each of the patients was a human being with feelings and with human dignity. I have written this book in the hope that both physicians and attorneys will recognize and respect the essential humanity of all those they serve. People turn to our two great and learned professions in the most frightening moments of their lives. Let us never forget that our licenses to practice are given us in trust; we must serve people and serve them well.

ANGELA R. HOLDER

Rock Hill, South Carolina
June 1974

CONTENTS

CHAPTER I

CREATION

OF THE

PHYSICIAN- PATIENT

RELATIONSHIP

Contractual Relations. The physician–patient relationship is generally considered to be a contractual one, although the contract is usually implied from the actions of the parties and is not often expressed in contract terms. A contract for a physician's services or a contract to buy a car may be very simply defined as "a deliberate agreement between competent parties, upon a legal consideration, to do or to abstain from doing, some act."[1]

Of course, the contractual relationship between a physician and a patient is a very different thing from one involving the purchase of a car. Therefore it is much more difficult to define the existence, nature, and extent of a contract for professional services.

An express contract between a physician and a patient may begin with a specific agreement between the two for treatment. The patient asks the physician to treat him and the physician agrees to do so.[2] For a valid contract to exist, however, there must be mutuality of understanding between the parties as to the terms of the agreement. If a patient asks a physician to undertake treatment of an illness by a particular method, the physician is not obligated to do so, but the patient should be informed that a different method will be utilized.

A laboratory technician at a hospital cut her hand severely on a test tube. She was sent to the emergency room where a resident treated her. She told him if the tendon was cut, she did not want the wound sutured, but wanted the tendon repaired. He sutured the wound and it was later found that the tendon was severed. She did not recover damages because the expert testimony indicated that he had followed the appropriate method.[3]

The patient has the right to accept or reject the proposed contract for the physician's services on the basis of a genuinely informed consent and

1

understanding of the treatment involved, as will be discussed in a later chapter.

The definition of treatment is usually not difficult to determine. By legal definition, it is "a broad term covering all steps taken to effect a cure of an injury or disease, the word including examination and diagnosis as well as application of remedies."[4] A patient consults a surgeon and presents all the symptoms of appendicitis. The surgeon advises him that his appendix should be removed at once. The parties agree and surgery is performed. Postsurgical care is administered until the patient recovers. The "treatment" involved is obvious.

In some situations, however, the definition of "treatment" may be somewhat difficult to determine. In one case the question arose over the refusal of the physician's malpractice insurance carrier to defend an action or pay a judgment obtained by a former patient on the ground that the acts did not involve treatment.

A psychiatrist treated a female patient for a period of several years. In the course of therapy she "fell in love" with him. Instead of dealing with the transference phenomenon as psychiatrists normally do, the psychiatrist took her on trips, engaged in widespread socializing with her, including taking her to parties as his "date," prevailed on her to live on his farm and urged her to invest large sums of money in his business ventures. The patient eventually sued him for malpractice for abusing their relationship. She recovered a judgment. On that issue alone the case went up on appeal. The carrier's refusal to involve itself resulted from its position that such activities were totally unconnected with the practice of medicine. Thus the acts performed were not "professional services" within the meaning of their coverage. The court held the carrier liable. The damage which resulted to the patient was held to have "directly and proximately resulted from the professional services of the defendant" and those acts were therefore covered by his policy.[5]

Another decision also involved a rather liberal definition of the word "treatment."

An osteopath was treating a patient in his office when the treatment table collapsed as the result of a defective safety catch. The patient was injured. His insurance policy was for premises liability and specifically excluded any injury which was the result of "malpractice." The court found that injuries during the course of professional treatment came within the exclusion and therefore the company was not liable for the judgment.[6]

The fact that the patient does not or cannot pay for the services of the physician does not affect the existence of the contract or lessen the physician's liability for negligence thereunder.[7]

A clinic patient was operated on by a resident for removal of his gallbladder. A piece of gauze was left in his abdomen. The defendant was the consultant surgeon who saw the patient before and after the operation but who was not present at all times during surgery. He was not paid for his services and did not expect to be. The court upheld his liability for the resident's error.[8]

Even if treatment is undertaken under an express contract between physician and patient, except in most unusual circumstances, courts do not assume a guarantee or warranty from a physician that he will cure the patient.[9] The only promises the physician is usually held to make are that he has the normal degree of skill, care, and knowledge and that he will use all three in treating the patient. Sometimes, however, a physician does guarantee results. If those results are not obtained, he is liable for breach of warranty even if he has used the highest skill.[10]

A man and his wife were parents of two retarded children. Wishing to avoid another tragedy, the husband had a vasectomy. A third child was born who was retarded and physically handicapped. The wife sued the surgeon for breach of contract because he had assured the couple that the husband was sterile. The court held that she had a good cause of action.[11]

The contractual relationship between doctor and patient may begin with a far less explicit understanding of the treatment relationship than that created by an express contract. In such an instance the contract is held to be "implied." An implied contract is defined as "one not created by the explicit agreement of the parties but inferred by the law as a matter of reason and justice from their acts or conduct, the circumstances surrounding their transaction making it a reasonable, or even a necessary, assumption, that a contract existed between them by tacit understanding."[12]

Actions by either or both the physician and the patient may be held in retrospect to constitute an implied contract which is sufficient to create a relationship between them. Commencement of actual treatment usually suffices to impose a contract and hence a duty upon the physician to follow it through.[13]

A patient was hospitalized for complications from a varicose vein operation which had been performed by one defendant. Gangrene set in. The second defendant, partner of the first, came to see him for the first time and told him that amputation of the foot was immediately required and that he would perform it. The patient consented. The surgeon left. Four days later when neither surgeon had returned or communicated with the patient in any way, he had himself removed to another hospital. The operation was performed there. The court held that a relationship between the second surgeon and the patient existed. Therefore the surgeon was liable for abandoning his patient.[14]

Whether or not a physician–patient relationship has been created by implication is of vital importance in determining whether or not the physician is later obligated to continue to treat the patient. For example, an implied contract may result from a single telephone call.

A man and his wife went to the emergency room of a hospital. He presented symptoms of chest pains and shortness of breath. His wife told the nurse on duty he was having a heart attack. The patient told the nurse that they were members of a prepaid medical group. The nurse replied that the hospital did not take care of patients of that group. She called a physician who was at the hospital at the time and the patient related his symptoms on the phone. The physician told him to go home and call a physician from the medical group in the morning when the group's office was open. The hospital nurse and the physician refused any further attention to the patient. The patient went home and dropped dead. The court held that the jury could have found that the physician accepted the man as a patient at the time he talked to him on the telephone. The verdict in favor of the hospital, ordered by the trial judge, was reversed and a new trial was granted.[15]

Before prescribing medicine over the telephone or advising a person who calls, particularly if the individual and his history are unknown to the physician, prudence would dictate that the physician realize that he has tacitly agreed to take the individual as a patient and follow up on the problem. If he does not wish to do so, the call should be limited to advising the person to seek medical assistance elsewhere. If the stomachache of which the caller complains at 4:00 a.m. turns out 2 hours later to be a ruptured appendix, the fact that the physician and his patient had never actually met would not move most juries in this country to undue sympathy for the physician.

Another case involved a medical school professor who examined clinic patients prior to selecting a few of them to participate in a lecture he was preparing to give at the medical school. He saw the patient's injured knee and in an aside to the resident who was with her, advised that her leg be amputated. The suggestion was forthwith effected. The physician never actually treated the patient, never saw her after that momentary interlude, and did not use her at his lecture. She sued the city for the original injury to her leg and for malpractice at the city hospital. She named the professor one of the parties defendant. In finding him liable, the court said:

> It is not necessary in order to create the relation of physician and patient that he should actually treat the patient. If he makes an examination of the patient, with her knowledge and consent, she believing that the examination is being made for the purpose of treating her, then the relation is created by implication and it is wholly immaterial what the secret object or purpose of the physician was in making it. In the absence of evidence to the contrary, the plaintiff had the perfect right to assume and rely upon the assumption that the physicians who were apparently in charge of the hospital were rightfully there and as such had the authority to examine and prescribe for her; and he will not afterwards be heard to say that he was not connected with the institution and had no authority to examine or treat her.[16]

In a recent decision in a similar situation, however, a court held that no physician–patient relationship existed because the patient had never seen the professor.

A woman had been treated by a surgeon for a prolonged period of time. His diagnosis was ulcerative colitis. The surgeon attended a conference led by a gastroenterologist with a national reputation for expertise in the treatment of the disease. The surgeon presented the woman's case to the conference. The professor gave his opinion, which was shared by most of the physicians present, that surgery was indicated. After it was performed the woman sued the surgeon and the professor, alleging that the operation had been unnecessary and was negligently performed. She claimed that the professor had been negligent in failing to examine her and obtaining sufficient information before making his recommendation. The court dismissed the action. It held that no physician–patient relationship had ever existed, pointing out that the professor had never met, seen, or treated the woman. The decision pointed out that the purpose of the conference was for the exchange of information, not for the treatment of patients. Since the professor could not control the actions of the physicians present and was entitled to assume that they would rely on their own opinions, he did not assume any duty of care for the patients discussed at the conference.[17]

A casual question asked of a physician outside a situation in which a professional relationship would ordinarily be thought to exist, however, does not usually constitute such a relationship. A physician who is backed into a corner at a cocktail party and asked his opinion of various aches and pains by a fellow guest and who replies in an off-hand manner out of simple politeness may undoubtedly be subject to extreme social irritation at the time, but in all probability would not be liable for malpractice as the result of his comments.

A hospital employee stopped the medical director of her hospital in the hall and asked him a question about a medical condition from which she suffered. He replied with a few suggestions and went on his way. She later sued him for malpractice for failing to advise her to have an operation. The court pointed out that the physician–patient relationship is a consensual one in which the patient knowingly seeks the assistance of the physician and he in turn knowingly accepts the person as a patient. In this case the court held that the physician never agreed to treat her or advise her as a physician. "Merely because the defendant was a physician and knew of the condition of the patient would not devolve upon him the duty of rendering to her medical care."[18]

Some physicians never see their patients. Pathologists,[19] for example, usually do not. Radiologists[20] may well never see or communicate with the patients for whom they read Xrays, reports of which are sent to the primary physicians. In these cases, however, it is quite clear that a physician–patient relationship is established.

A pathologist, an employee of the defendant hospital, misdiagnosed a biopsy and advised the surgeon that the patient had cancer of the cervix. A hysterectomy was performed. It was later proved that the diagnosis was incorrect. The hospital was liable for his negligence.[21]

A radiologist may likewise be negligent in reading Xray films and therefore become liable to the patient.

A radiologist did not report a shadow on a film which would have indicated the presence of a kidney stone. At the time the films were taken, the patient was complaining of a backache and a cut on her neck. The radiologist did not report the existence of the shadow because it was outside the scope of the information requested of him. Several months later, the patient underwent removal of the stone and later the entire kidney had to be removed. She sued the hospital which employed the radiologist. The theory of the suit was that earlier diagnosis of her problem would have prevented her subsequent difficulties. The jury found in her favor and the appellate court upheld the award.[22]

In none of these cases was there any actual contact between the physician and his patient and yet courts in all states would hold that a physician–patient contractual relationship may be implied between them.

Right to Refuse to Enter into a Contractual Relation.   A physician in private practice ordinarily has the right to refuse to see a patient, although if he sees him at all in the course of an emergency, he must provide at least temporary care. The refusal is legally permissible even if the situation does constitute an emergency and no other physician is available.[23]

The classic case in this area is **Hurley v. Eddingfield,** decided in 1901 by the Supreme Court of Indiana. The patient had at one time been a patient of the physician's, but the relationship had terminated. When he became ill, he sent a messenger with the physician's fee and told him to bring the physician back with him. The physician refused to come even though it was made clear to him that an emergency existed and no other doctor was available. The patient died. The court pointed out that the physician probably could have saved the patient's life if he had gone and that he was not at that time busy with another patient. He had simply refused to go. However, the court pointed out that the physician–patient contractual relationship is one depending on the assent of both parties and that a license to practice medicine does not compel a physician to contract against his will. He had the right to refuse to see the patient and was not therefore liable for the patient's death.[24]

It should be pointed out that Section 5 of the Code of Ethics of the American Medical Association recognizes the physician's right to choose his patients. It goes on to state, however, that in an emergency he should render service to the best of his ability. Ethics are not, however, enforceable by law in spite of the consequences to the person denied assistance. Furthermore, there is usually adverse public reaction which ensues not only to the physician who has refused to go to the aid of an emergency case, but to the medical profession as a whole.[25]

A physician who is employed by a hospital in the emergency room, is an intern or resident on duty there, or is a staff member who is required by hospital regulations to take his turn on the emergency service does not have the right to refuse to treat an emergency patient. Furthermore, hospital rules requiring staff members to participate in such duty have been upheld by all courts which have considered them. Such requirements are considered reasonable in view of the benefits the physician receives from his hospital staff membership.[26] Not only the physician but the hospital as well may be liable for failure to treat an emergency patient.

A 2-year old girl was sent to the hospital with pneumonia as diagnosed by her pediatrician. He sent a note requesting admission and noted the diagnosis. The intern on duty told her mother that the child did not have pneumonia and sent her home. She died immediately thereafter and the hospital was liable for the intern's failure to treat her.[27]

A patient with a severe gunshot wound in his chest was brought to the hospital. The defendant, on call for emergency cases, came and looked at him. He knew that the patient was in shock but did not institute even rudimentary first aid procedures in spite of the fact that the patient had been in the emergency room for almost 2 hours. The physician ordered him transferred to another hospital. The patient died in the ambulance. The physician was held liable for his failure to treat the patient.[28]

A patient with severe head pains was taken to the hospital. The resident on duty in the emergency room took his blood pressure but attempted no more thorough examination. He told the patient to go home. The man died in the car on his way. Since a neurologist testified that any physician should have recognized symptoms of extreme medical emergency from the objective manifestations exhibited by the patient, the hospital was liable for the resident's negligent failure to treat the man.[29]

On the other hand, if a physician in the emergency room sees a patient and examines him with due care and transfers him to a more appropriate hospital after emergency needs are met, he is not liable for his refusal to treat the patient if something happens after the patient leaves the premises.

The admitting officer at a VA hospital refused to treat a patient because the hospital had no facilities for treating chronic alcoholics. He gave the patient paraldehyde and ordered him transferred to another hospital. He called the admitting physician at the second hospital and told him that he was transferring the patient. He also reported what medication had been administered and warned him to observe the patient closely to be sure that the patient did not vomit and choke. The second physician told him that the patient would be turned over to the police and the VA physician made no objections or comments. The man died in jail from aspiration of vomitus. The court held that the VA physician was not liable for failing to treat the patient. The court pointed out that the physician's only duty had been to deliver him safely into competent hands, which he had in fact done.[30]

Unless some special relationship of such a nature as described in these cases exists, the physician is legally, if not morally, free to keep on driving past an automobile accident.[31] Innumerable physicians report that they are afraid to stop at accidents because they are wary of later malpractice suits, but surveys by the American Medical Association and others actually reveal that no such claims have been reported by physicians.[32] In an effort to induce physicians to render aid at accidents, however, almost all states have now enacted "good samaritan" laws. While these statutes vary widely among the states, all attempt to eliminate recovery of damages for ordinary negligence in the course of medical treatment at the scene of an accident. Most of them exclude "gross negligence." Thus a physician who was on his way home from a cocktail party and considerably under the influence of alcohol would not be protected by the statute if he caused or aggravated injury to an accident victim as the result, not of the emergency circumstances, but of his inebriated condition. Good samaritan statutes vary so widely as to coverage that all physicians would be well advised to consult attorneys on the statute applicable in their home state or in one in which they expect to spend extended periods of time.

If a physician does stop to render assistance at an emergency or agrees to see an emergency patient, he is obligated to use due care as far as possible under the circumstances in treatment of that patient. Of course he is unlikely to have adequate equipment or drugs at the scene of an automobile accident. Therefore he might be able to treat a patient much less skillfully than he would in an emergency room or at his office. The standard, however, which would be applied is that degree of skill, care, and knowledge that the average practitioner would use under the circumstances which have been imposed by the emergency. If that standard is met, the physician could not be found liable even in the absence of a good samaritan law.

The physician must, for example, treat accident victims whom he has agreed to help with common human decency.

A woman, her baby, and her mother-in-law were hurt in an automobile accident. The baby was unconscious. A passing motorist took all three of them to a physician's office after a telephone call in which the physician had agreed to meet them. The physician was rude and told them that there was nothing the matter with any of them. He refused to examine the adults at all, but finally agreed to examine the baby. Although the baby was still unconscious, he told the mother that the child had not been injured. When the baby vomited, the physician told the mother that the child was sick because she had been over-feeding her. He told the mother-in-law to go wash herself because she was a "mess." The women called the baby's father to come and get them, but the physician refused to allow them to wait inside his office until the man arrived. He sent them outside in below-freezing weather until their ride came, in spite of the fact that the baby's clothes were wet with vomit. The father picked them up and took them to the hospital. He had been a medical corpsman in the service and testified that he thought the baby was dead. The adults were treated and released, the baby was treated for shock and a depressed skull fracture and remained in the hospital for a week. The mother sued for damages for "outrageous conduct" and the appellate court held that she had a good cause of action. The court stated that the physician, having agreed to treat them, had the duty to make a good faith effort to provide adequate treatment or advice. The court held that the case should have been submitted to the jury instead of being dismissed by the trial judge because a jury could reasonably conclude that the physician recklessly failed to perform his duty toward the three.[33]

The physician who stops at an accident is not obligated to continue to treat the victims once competent assistance has arrived. He should, of course, remain on the scene until the police and ambulance arrive. In a critical situation where there was no physician on the ambulance, the physician might be obligated to accompany the victim to the hospital, but under no circumstances would he be legally obligated to continue treatment after they reach the emergency room.

In most states, legislation exempts emergency treatment from licensure requirements prohibiting practicing without a state license. Thus a vacationing physician in a state other than the one in which he is licensed may assume, given a genuine emergency, that he is in no real danger of arrest for practicing medicine without a license. The definition of "emergency," however, is interpreted somewhat strictly. As one case indicates, a physician cannot open an office in a state where he has no license and then define as the emergency the acute shortage of physicians in the area.[34]

The physician himself may be injured at the scene of an accident where he has stopped to help victims. The common law "rescue doctrine" was developed to afford recourse to the rescuer as against the original wrongdoers. For example, if a physician stopped to help an accident victim and was injured while he was removing the victim from the car, he would have a valid suit against the driver who caused the accident. If he were injured by another driver who recklessly failed to slow down as he approached the scene, the physician would undoubtedly be able to sue both the original wrongdoer and the driver who ran into him. Contributory negligence, the defense that the damage was caused by the fault of the injured party, is not available to the wrongdoer in a rescue situation. In this case the driver who caused the accident could not say to the injured physician, "If you'd minded your own business and not stopped to help, you wouldn't have gotten hurt, so it was your own fault."[35]

Physicians employed by corporations to care for employees are sometimes injured while treating them. Whether or not the employer is liable depends on the contract between it and the physician.

A physician was under contract to treat injured workmen employed by a large road-building firm. A rock slide occurred during construction. It was established that the slide was the fault of the company's engineers. Two workmen were critically injured and pinned under the rocks. The physician had to go to the scene to treat them. One man was so badly pinned that the physician had to amputate his leg to get him out. On the way to the site of the accident the physician fell and sustained severe injuries to his back, but he kept going until he reached the men. He sued the company for his own injuries and recovered damages. When he contracted to provide professional services, the court said, it was assumed that such services would be provided at the hospital or at his office, not at the scene of injuries. The physician was held not to have assumed the risk of such dangers to himself at the time he made the contract.[36]

If, however, the physician's contract of employment assumes that emergency care will be given at the scene of accidents, he does assume the risk of injury to himself and cannot sue his employer.

A physician who knew that he had cardiac problems was under contract to treat employees of an off-shore diving company. Out-of-office services were to be provided under the contract at a higher rate than those performed in his office. A diver who was employed by the company and who lived in a pressurized tube was partially eviscerated when he flushed a toilet. The company sent a helicopter for the physician. He and a surgeon who was him decided that surgery inside the chamber was necessary. Most of the operation was performed with the physicians on their knees because of lack of space. The operation lasted several hours and the patient recovered. The physicians had to stay in the tube for a protracted period in order to be depressurized. When it was safe, they and their patient were removed to a hospital. The physician had a heart attack shortly after they got to the hospital. The court did not allow him to recover damages from the diving company. It found that he should have known that his heart condition should have precluded such work and therefore he assumed the risk for which he had specifically contracted. He was, in fact, paid at special rates for assuming such risks.[37]

Liability of a hospital for refusing to admit an emergency patient or to give him proper care in the emergency room has been the subject of many cases.[38]

Most courts have held that a private hospital probably does not have any legal obligation to have an emergency room at all, but if it does, it must accept all patients who require its services.[39]

A 4-month old baby was critically ill with diarrhea. His pediatrician was out of town, so his mother took him to the emergency room. The nurse refused to call a doctor and refused to admit him. The baby died. The court found the hospital liable. The opinion stated that as long as there were symptoms consonant with an "unmistakable emergency" which the nurse should have recognized, the hospital was liable for failure to admit the baby.[40]

If the hospital receives any public funds, it may not have any admissions criteria based on race, creed, or color.[41]

Once the hospital has accepted the patient, it must also exercise due care in treatment. If the physician who is negligent is an employee of the hospital, such as an intern, resident, or full-time emergency room physician on salary from the hospital, the hospital is usually liable for his negligence as it would be if a staff nurse or other nonphysician employee was negligent.[42] If the physician is a staff member on rotating call for the emergency room, he is usually considered an "independent contractor," not an employee, and in most states the hospital is usually not liable for his actions. This is due to the fact that courts generally find that hospitals usually cannot control the professional services of on-call staff physicians. Some states, however, seem to be willing to impute his negligence to the hospital.[43]

A 16-year old boy was in a wreck. He was unconscious when taken to the emergency room. He was left without examination or treatment for 45 minutes. An intern did not examine him but took the opinion of several bystanders that the boy was drunk. He ordered the boy removed to another hospital. The boy died from a ruptured liver. The hospital was liable for the intern's negligence.[44]

Another 16-year old boy was hit by a car while riding his bicycle. His mother took him to the emergency room with symptoms of headache and vomiting. The physician serving his turn in the emergency room did not examine the back of the boy's head. He sent the boy and his mother home and the boy died before morning. Autopsy revealed a basal skull fracture. The mother sued both the physician and the hospital for negligence. Expert medical testimony proved her case, but the physician was held to be an independent contractor and the hospital was not liable for his negligence.[45]

Once the patient's emergency needs are met, however, a private hospital does not have to admit a patient who cannot furnish either the requisite deposit or proof of insurance coverage.

A patient was in a wreck almost in front of a private hospital which maintained an emergency room. He was brought in. His blood pressure was taken and Xrays were made. He was kept in the emergency room for about 4 hours. While he was being readied for admission as an in-patient, his wife indicated that she could not pay the deposit. He was moved by ambulance to the city hospital. The court found that the hospital had not been negligent in moving him. It had met his acute needs and his condition was not impaired by moving him to another facility.[46]

It goes without saying, however, that if the hospital is the only one in the community it cannot refuse to admit a patient under those conditions.

A physician under contract to treat prisoners is under an obligation to see sick inmates when called upon to do so. The Eighth Amendment to the United States Constitution forbids "cruel and unusual punishment" and the due process of law clause of the Fourteenth Amendment requires states to adhere to the rights granted in the Eighth. These provisions have been interpreted to mean that a prisoner has a constitutional right to essential medical care.[47]

A suit for violation of any of the prisoner's basic constitutional rights falls under the federal Civil Rights Act, and it has been held in innumerable decisions that these rights have been violated when prison personnel refuse to provide medical care to an obviously sick prisoner.[48]

A prisoner had been shot in the leg prior to being placed in a cell. The custodian of the jail refused to call a physician in spite of the fact that the leg became obviously infected. A judge released the prisoner and he obtained medical attention, but the infection was so widespread that his leg had to be amputated. The court upheld his action against the jailor under the Civil Rights Act.[49]

Once a physician has seen the prisoner and ordered medication or other treatment for him, failure of prison officials to comply with the medical orders and allow the prisoner the medication or treatment indicated also constitutes cruel and unusual punishment.[50]

Of course the treatment must be available before prison officials may be held to have violated the prisoner's rights by failing to provide it.[51] For example, failure to treat a narcotics addict for his addiction during his term of imprisonment is not cruel and unusual punishment.[52]

It is also necessary to prove that the officials knew that the prisoner required medical attention. If there is evidence that no one realized that he was sick, the officials will not be liable for failure to call a physician.[53] If the physician on contract to the prison has a working arrangement whereby he will come when called instead of scheduling regular rounds, he is not liable for any failure to go unless he has been summoned by the jailor and refused.[54]

Courts have made a clear distinction between a denial of care and negligent care. Once the prisoner has been seen and treated by a physician, he is very rarely able to persuade a court that he has been subjected to cruel and unusual punishment. In order to violate a prisoner's constitutional rights, improper medical treatment must be continuing, must not be supported by any competent school of medical practice whatever, and must amount to a complete denial of care. Simple negligence in treatment is not a denial of the constitutionally mandated right to medical care, but is an ordinary tort.[55] Gross negligence may be equated with damage intentionally inflicted and is thus an Eighth Amendment violation.[56]

A prisoner suffered from violent muscle spasms and was transferred to another facility for treatment. He was given tranquilizers and returned to his original prison. The prison physician refused to give him the same medication and substituted another drug which the prisoner claimed did not help his condition at all. The court held that the exercise of faulty judgment by a prison physician did not constitute a civil rights violation and that while the prisoner had a right to medical care, he did not have the right to any type or scope of medical care he desired.[57]

It should be noted that it is not a violation of the right against cruel and unusual punishment to administer proper medical treatment to a prisoner who has religious objections to it.[58]

In other words, the prisoner cannot be the ultimate judge of what medical treatment is necessary and proper for him. In the absence of any factually supported allegations of obvious neglect or intentional mistreatment, the courts place their confidence in the reports of reputable prison physicians that reasonable medical care is being rendered.[59]

No general rule can be stated as to the laws in all jurisdictions in regard to the right of the prisoner to bring an action for malpractice against the physician who was negligent in his treatment. Of course treatment which does not constitute cruel and unusual punishment may still be negligent. Many states deny a prisoner the right to bring any civil action of this type for anything which occurs during his imprisonment. Others permit prisoners to sue as readily as any other patient alleging malpractice. Even where the action is allowed, however, juries are most reluctant to accept the testimony of a convict when his opposing party is the prison doctor.[60] A federal prisoner does have the right to sue the government under the Federal Tort Claims Act for negligent treatment he has received from a prison physician.

A prison physician misdiagnosed a patient's ailment which he thought a minor one. After considerable effort extending over a considerable time, the prisoner's lawyer, who was convinced that his client was seriously ill, arranged for him to be seen by an outside specialist. It was discovered that the prisoner had a brain tumor. Surgery removed the tumor but the result was inevitable blindness. Testimony was introduced that if the surgery had been performed at the time the prison physician should have discovered the tumor his sight would have been saved. The Supreme Court upheld his right to sue the government just as any other patient in a federal hospital may do.[61]

Patients also have the right to refuse treatment if they do not wish to have it. An adult generally does not have to be treated against his will as long as he is reasonably mentally competent.[62] The contract between physician and patient is consensual as to both parties.

An elderly woman, all of whose children were grown, was suffering from a terminal illness. Treatments to prolong her life were both painful and expensive. She asked the physicians to allow her to die in peace by simply ceasing the treatments. To protect themselves from civil actions by her heirs or the possibility of criminal charges, they asked the court to rule on their duty in the matter. The court held that under the circumstances any conscious adult had the right to make the same decision.[63]

Innumerable decisions have involved the right of an adult, conscious Jehovah's Witness to refuse a blood transfusion where such is an absolute medical necessity. Where the patient is pregnant[64] or has small children[65] the courts have usually ordered the transfusion. Where the patient is unconscious and the refusal is given by a relative, also, the courts usually order the blood given.[66] Some states have also held that even though the adult is conscious, knowingly refuses the blood, and has no children whose welfare will be affected, once they are within the hospital for treatment they simply have no constitutional "right to die."[67] On the other hand, courts in several other states have held that a competent adult does have the right to refuse blood transfusions on the grounds of religious conviction even though there is an overwhelming probability that death will result.[68]

With progress in medicine the number of people who survive for years with severe handicaps increases. Whether a young adult who knows that he faces years of existence in a wheel chair or hooked into a kidney machine at a cost which bankrupts his family has the right to refuse treatment on the grounds that he would simply prefer to die has never been answered by the courts, but in all probability a case of this nature will be presented within the next several years. A well-reported movement has begun within the last few years in which many have signed, while in good health, what is called a "living will." These provisions, usually included as clauses or codicils in ordinary wills with a copy given to the physician at the time the document is signed, order the physician not to prolong the person's life by "heroic means" after his intellect has been impaired in case of accident or illness. It is highly unlikely that any court would overturn such a request. The point at which treatment may be terminated without constituting a violation of the patient's rights even if the patient is known not to want life without functional ability to be prolonged is a critical question in law, medicine, and theology at this time. Should a patient whose family assets would be devoured by the expense of maintaining him on a machine and who will die if the machine is turned off have the right to tell the physician prior to that time that he does not wish to be placed on the machine? This is of course essentially an ethical and moral problem for the physician. It is not a legal problem because our legal system in most circumstances would not require the physician to institute heroic measures. After they are instituted it is highly unlikely that any physician would be accused of murder or manslaughter for ceasing the mechanical maintenance of "life."

Parents have no right, based on religious belief or for any other reason, to deny their children adequate medical care. The state has the right to assume guardianship of neglected children and order such treatment as they may require. Parents have always been denied the right to object on religious grounds to blood transfusions where they are necessary to save the child's life.[69] They may also not refuse on religious or any other grounds to comply with state laws requiring inoculations for children entering school.[70] Refusal to permit medical treatment where it is highly desirable, even if it is not necessary to save the child's life, is generally considered to constitute "child neglect" as a matter of law.[71]

A teenage boy suffered from a massive deformity of the face and neck. He was so grotesque he was excused from school attendance and was therefore illiterate. Surgery could correct the condition but could not be performed without blood transfusions. The mother objected on religious grounds to administration of blood and therefore would not consent to surgery. The court held that he was a "neglected child" and ordered the surgery performed.[72]

Simple failure to obtain medical care for a child when it is obviously necessary may, if the child dies, sustain a manslaughter conviction against the parents.[73] It is totally irrelevant that the reason the child was denied medical care was that the parents' refusal to provide it was rooted in religious conviction.

Treatment of a narcotics addict for addiction or for any other relevant medical or psychiatric condition presents peculiar problems in establishment of the physician–patient relationship. Dispensing of narcotic drugs is very strictly regulated by federal and state statutes. A physician who wishes to dispense narcotics must, under the provisions of the 1914 Harrison Narcotics Act,[74] obtain a federal narcotics number. He is required to report the amount of narcotics received and dispensed at intervals determined by the Internal Revenue Service office in his district. The dispensation and use of "dangerous" nonnarcotics such as barbiturates is also regulated by federal law.[75]

Failure to abide by the provisions of these statutes will render the physician subject to criminal prosecution and disciplinary proceedings. There have been numerous cases of criminal prosecution of physicians for prescription of narcotic drugs without proper cause and compliance with applicable statutes in recent years.[76] The constitutionality of these statutory restrictions was upheld by the United States Supreme Court in 1919.[77]

As the addiction problem in this country has grown, new drugs such as methadone have been developed in an attempt to rehabilitate addicts. Since most of those drugs may themselves be subject to abuse, statutes which place very stringent restrictions on their prescription have been enacted and upheld as constitutional.

A physician had used methadone in his private practice to treat addicts. A state statute was enacted which prohibited its use except in specially licensed clinics. One of the physician's addict patients sued to have the law declared unconstitutional. He claimed that it interfered with his right to be treated by the physician of his choice and further denied him the right to privacy and confidentiality. The court upheld the statute.[78]

Statutes which require physicians to report the names of addicts who come to them for treatment have also been upheld.[79]

Thus a physician is absolutely required to know the various statutory provisions involving prescription of narcotics or other dangerous drugs and his relationships with addict patients and to comply with them. Treatment of addicts or dispensing of drugs outside the boundaries of the statutes may well result in the arrest and conviction of the physician. It is altogether probable, however, that a narcotics addict who is seriously ill with a medical or surgical problem may be given narcotics during his hospitalization in order to prevent withdrawal from worsening his physical condition and interfering with treatment for his illness. As soon as his condition allows it, however, measures to reduce his narcotic intake must be instituted.

Thus in terms of the physician–patient relationship, even though a physician is faced with a good-faith request for narcotics or other drugs by an addict, he is in serious danger of prosecution if he supplies them in violation of the law. These statutes are very strictly enforced by both state and federal agencies and careful examination of narcotics reports submitted by physicians is the rule, not the exception.

Third-Party Contracts.   The physician–patient contract may be and frequently is entered into with the physician by a third party on behalf of the patient. Members of a family request the physician to treat other members. Employers arrange for preemployment physical examinations or provide medical care for sick and injured employees. Courts appoint physicians to examine litigants in various types of cases. The police request physicians to perform blood alcohol tests on suspected drunken drivers. In all these cases some party other than the one to be examined or treated requests the physician to act.

An employer's physician who merely performs preemployment physical examinations or the physician for a life insurance company who examines prospective policy holders is not generally considered to establish a physician–patient relationship with the party who is examined.[80]

Xrays at the time of a preemployment physical clearly indicated tuberculosis. No mention of this was made to the applicant, who was hired. Three years later, while still in the company's employ, she became so ill with tuberculosis that she was hospitalized for an extended period. She sued the employer and the physician, but the court held that her only recourse was Workmen's Compensation. The physician's legal duty at the time of the examination was to the employer, not to her. No physician–patient relationship was held to exist; therefore there was no duty to report the findings to her.[81]

A few states, however, have abrogated this rule. In these states courts hold that in spite of the fact that no physician–patient relationship exists with an employment applicant, the physician is still required to use due care in his examination.[82] If a physician at a preemployment physical examination does find evidence of illness and reports it to the person examined and the parties understand that the physician is willing to undertake treatment of the patient instead of sending him to another physician, the physician–patient relationship is created as of that point in time, not as of the time of the examination. If the physician is thereafter negligent, he is liable.[83]

Because of the old common law rule that an employer is not liable for injuries to one employee caused by another unless the employer was negligent in his selection of the injuring party, the right to sue a company physician for malpractice may be denied even if the treatment relationship does constitute a physician–patient relationship.[84] In most states, therefore, if a company physician negligently treats an employee for an illness, the employee's only recourse is an action in Workmen's Compensation, recovery under which is usually substantially less than in a negligence suit.

An employee impaled her finger with a rivet. The medical director of the plant in which she worked treated it. She alleged damage as the result of his negligent treatment and sued him for malpractice. The action was dismissed on the grounds that even if he were negligent, Workmen's Compensation was her exclusive remedy.

An employee injured his back while working on an assembly line. The plant physician advised him that it was a very minor injury and sent him back to work. A few hours later, extensive and permanent paralysis set in. The original injury was discovered to have been quite serious and continuing work had substantially aggravated it. The court held that the employee had no recourse against the physician and was only allowed to recover Workmen's Compensation payments.[86]

Some states, including Missouri[87] and California[88] do allow suits against company physicians. The Federal Employers' Liability Act[89] gives railroad workers the right to sue a railroad if physicians employed either full or part-time treat workers negligently. The Jones Act[90] provides the same liability for a shipowner if a seaman is negligently injured by a ship's surgeon.

Where a physician is asked by a judge to perform a physical or psychiatric examination or to treat a person involved in an action before the court, no contractual relationship of physician and patient is held to exist. Physicians are frequently asked to examine a plaintiff in a personal injury suit in an attempt to resolve conflicts between experts for the plaintiff and the defendant. They report to the trial court, not to the parties to the suit. Therefore, they are undoubtedly absolved of any risk of legal liability even if they negligently misdiagnose a condition.[91] The same rule would undoubtedly apply to a surgeon who operates under a court order to remove a bullet from a suspect's body so it may be used in evidence at his trial. Several recent decisions indicate that such surgery does not violate the prisoner's constitutional rights against search and seizure or self-incrimination and thus the surgeon would be absolutely protected from any suit charging him with violation of the prisoner's constitutional or civil rights.[92] In other jurisdictions, however, courts do hold that surgical removal of a bullet from a suspect's body to use in evidence against him and not for any reason connected with his medical treatment does constitute an infringement of his constitutional rights against unreasonable search and seizure.

Three armed men held up a supermarket. A gun battle with police ensued and one policeman and one robber were killed. Another robber was shot but escaped. A person thought to be the wounded suspect was picked up several weeks later. He was taken to the hospital and Xrays revealed metallic fragments in his buttocks. The police obtained a search warrant and the fragments were removed by a surgeon under local anesthesia. The fragments were identified as parts of police bullets and were admitted in evidence against the accused. He was convicted of the policeman's murder. On appeal the

Indiana Supreme Court held that such an extensive intrusion into his body had constituted a sufficiently unreasonable violation of his constitutional rights to require reversal of his conviction.[92a]

As long as a surgeon in a case such as this operates under a warrant valid on its face, however, he would be immune from a suit charging him with violation of the suspect's civil rights.

A court-appointed psychiatrist who examines an accused person for evaluation of his sanity is also not liable for misdiagnosis. Courts in all states take the position that no physician–patient relationship exists unless treatment is contemplated or given and these examinations are not conducted for that purpose.[93] Furthermore, court-appointed psychiatrists are protected by judicial immunity from liability for malpractice even if the examination is negligent as long as it is conducted in good faith.[94]

Policemen frequently ask physicians to withdraw blood from an arrested person suspected of driving while intoxicated.[95] Although blood tests have been less frequently used since breath and urine tests have become more reliable and widely accepted, they are still used in some circumstances. The physician who knows that treating a patient without consent usually constitutes assault and battery but who is asked by a policeman to take a blood sample from a driver who objects may be quite concerned about his own liability.

The United States Supreme Court has upheld the admissibility of blood tests.[96] The Court ruled that removal of blood by a physician using standard medical procedures in doing so from a conscious person who does not consent, but who does not offer physical resistance, does not violate the suspect's constitutional rights. However, the use of physical force may constitute denial of those rights.

A person under arrest for driving under the influence had been taken to the emergency room for treatment of injuries he had sustained in the accident which led to the arrest. The arresting officer asked a physician to withdraw blood for the test. The physician agreed to do so, but the suspect became very abusive and physically attacked him and the policeman. The policeman and hospital orderlies held the suspect down by force while the physician took the blood sample. The man sued for damages. The court held that the policeman was liable, but that the physician who had played no part in the restraint of the suspect was not.[97]

Should force be necessary to extract blood from a suspect, the physician should not participate in its application. He is probably well advised to refuse to participate at all. The question is largely academic, however, since the use of force undoubtedly renders the test results inadmissible in evidence against the driver in any case, thus defeating its purpose.[98] Blood tests obtained without consent may not be used in evidence against the driver unless the procedure was undertaken incident to an arrest and after the driver had been advised of his rights.[99]

In some jurisdictions a person has the right to have his own physician administer a blood test.[100] In others, however, he does not.[101] It is clear that where the person asks for his own physician and that physician signifies that he is willing to act, the physician requested by the police need not withdraw the sample. In any event, there are no decisions in which a physician has been sued for assault and battery for withdrawing blood from a suspected drunk driver.

A hospital staff attempted to bring an action for a declaratory judgment to determine their civil liability, if any, for performing blood tests. The action arose after a resident at the hospital refused to extract blood from a hostile suspect and was threatened with arrest by the police officer who had asked him to do it. The physicians wanted a determination of their civil liability to a suspect in advance of future requests. The Wisconsin Supreme Court refused to issue a ruling on the grounds that what the physicians requested was an advisory opinion which it was not empowered to give.[102]

Most authorities feel that it is clear that the physician in his office or in the emergency room is not under any legal obligation to perform such tests for the police. Only if he were under contract to the police would he be required to do so.[103]

The question of the admissibility of the testimony of the physician on the results of the blood test depends on the circumstances surrounding the extraction of the blood. Where the relationship was established solely for the purposes of the test, no privilege exists and the physician is free to testify.[104] On the other hand, particularly if the suspect is already a patient of the physician's, if the blood is withdrawn primarily for the purposes of treatment, the physician–patient relationship is usually held to exist and the physician may not testify.[105] In other words, if a suspect is himself injured in an automobile accident and blood is withdrawn primarily for typing for a transfusion or other therapeutic purpose, privilege may exist and the physician may be barred from testifying as to the results of any intoxication test. However, rules as to the existence and application of the physician–patient privilege vary widely from state to state and it is quite clear that no general principles in this area may be drawn.

Family members frequently request that a physician treat one of their numbers. In all cases, the physician–patient relationship is held to exist even though the express or implied contract for treatment was made with a person other than the patient.

The patient may, in fact, be an unborn child. A physician providing care for a patient he knows is pregnant does have a physician–patient relationship with the baby in the sense that he owes the child careful treatment. Until 1946, no court would allow a child, through its guardian, to recover for injuries negligently inflicted before birth, but most states do now allow a suit for prenatal injuries if the child is eventually born alive.[106]

A pregnant woman told her physician that she had been exposed to German measles. He told her not to worry about it and did not give her gamma globulin. The baby was born with serious defects attributable to the mother's contracting the disease. The court allowed the baby to recover damages from the physician.[107]

The unborn child, therefore, once born alive is a legal entity with whom the physician deals and injury to him, if preventable, is equivalent to an injury to any other person. Since the child must be born alive in order to sue, although the mother may have a cause of action in her own right against a wrongdoer who causes her to miscarry, there is no possibility of an action against a physician who has performed an abortion at the request of the mother on behalf of a would-be guardian of the child as long as the child was not born alive.

Of course, young children's parents or guardians are the persons who usually engage the physician for treatment of the child's illness. The duty of care, however, which flows from the physician–patient contractual relationship is owed to the child himself.[108]

Normally, the father, if present, should sign any consent forms for surgery since under the common law rule the father is considered the child's natural guardian. However, where the father is physically absent, either permanently for purposes of any form of medical care or even temporarily out of town in an emergency, the mother may consent. If parents are legally separated or divorced and the mother has physical and legal custody of the child, she is perfectly legally competent to consent to any medical procedure even if the father should object.[109]

A teenage girl was in the legal custody of her mother. The parents were divorced. Her mother arranged for her to have an extremely serious operation for relief of a congenital heart condition. Her father brought an action to stop the surgery because he felt that the procedure was still too experimental and risky. The trial judge attempted to effect agreement between the parents. He ordered the father to suggest names of specialists to whom the mother could take the child for corroboration or disapproval of both the original diagnosis and the recommendation for surgery. The opinion pointed out, however, that in case accord could not be reached, since the mother had legal custody, she would prevail and the surgery would be allowed.[110]

In case of an informal separation, if the father is physically absent, for the physician's purposes he may assume that the mother is in the same legal position as if she had a court order of custody.[111]

Where parents are divorced or separated, the mother assumes primary responsibility for the physician's bill if she is the parent who arranges for medical services. She may then proceed against the father, since he remains liable for his child's necessary expenses even in the absence of a court order for child support.[112] If the mother refuses to pay, however, the physician is justified in billing the father directly.

Medical treatment of children in emergencies without parental consent is considered legally acceptable and parents may not recover damages for treatment without their consent from a physician who administers it.[113] Of course the child may bring an action by his guardian under any circumstances if the treatment is negligent. Other than in emergency cases, however, parents do have a cause of action against a physician for administering nonnegligent care to their young children without their consent.[114]

A 15-year-old boy who lived with his mother was persuaded by his aunt to donate skin for grafts for the aunt's child who had been badly burned. The hospital knew that the child lived with his mother but she was not told of the procedure or asked to consent. Complications developed and the boy was hospitalized for more than 2 months. In addition to the negligence action brought on behalf of the child, the court held that the mother had a cause of action in her own right.[115]

The common law for many years has recognized the concept of "emancipation." This means that the minor, who is usually self-supporting or away from home, is responsible for himself economically and otherwise and his parents have surrendered their parental duty. A married minor, for example, is considered emancipated by law and without any question may consent to medical treatment for himself or his own minor child.[116] Minors who are in military service are of course considered to be emancipated and no parental permission is required.[117] Where a college student is living away from home, even when financially dependent on his parents, medical treatment may generally be administered without parental consent. Where there is an emergency situation such as an appendectomy or an automobile accident which must be dealt with, unless the minor objects to the notification of the parents, it is probably a wise course to follow, but if the physician proceeds to treat him without such consent, it is highly unlikely that a suit will result.

One authority concludes that parental consent may be omitted (a) if the patient is of the age of discretion, by which is meant 15 and older; (b) if the medical measures are taken for the patient's own benefit, meaning that a minor certainly could not be used as a transplant donor without parental permission; (c) if the measures can be justified as necessary by conservative medical opinion; and (d) if there is some good reason why parental consent cannot be obtained.[118] Many states, including Mississippi, Arizona, California, Indiana, Nevada, New Mexico, and Pennsylvania, have enacted special statutes allowing emancipated minors to consent to medical treatment or surgery without parental involvement.[119] Others will doubtless follow suit. In most states even in the absence of statutes courts now hold that the older minor does have the right to consent to surgery or medical treatment and that the parent does not have a cause of action for failing to notify him.[120] There have been no recent reported cases in which any physician has been held liable for treating a minor of 14 years or older without parental consent when the minor has himself consented. If the patient is over the age of 14 the physician in any case should ask for his consent to treatment as well as that of the parent or guardian.

A 17-year old girl went to visit her mother who was a hospital patient. As she was leaving, she slammed her finger in the front door of the hospital. She was taken to the emergency room and minor surgery was performed. The girl was not in shock, was in good physical and mental condition, and gave her consent. There was no allegation that the surgery was improperly performed, but the mother sued on the grounds that she had not been asked for her permission. The court held that the girl was perfectly able to consent for herself and therefore no cause of action would lie against the surgeon.[121]

The same rule has been applied to cosmetic surgery on an 18-year old girl's nose. No recovery by the parent was allowed for operating without his knowledge.[122]

However, if the physician expects to bill the parents for nonemergency medical or surgical treatment performed without their knowledge or consent, he may discover that the parent has the right to disavow financial responsibility.[123] In an emergency the parent remains financially liable for the minor's medical expenses as long as he is contributing to the minor's support.

One area in which this subject frequently arises is the right of a physician to treat a minor for venereal disease without parental knowledge.[124] Most states now have enacted statutes permitting a minor to consent to treatment of venereal disease by himself. It is obvious that any patient with venereal disease constitutes a medical emergency. Although there are no decisions specifically on this point, if the child refuses to inform his parents or implicitly or expressly states that he will leave the physician's office and not obtain treatment at all if his parents are notified, the physician may proceed without consulting the parents. It would appear that the likelihood of a lawsuit in this situation is extremely remote and that the physician who treats the minor with venereal disease without parental consent probably runs less risk of a suit for treating a child than he does if he allows the child to remain untreated. Furthermore, of course, he has a professional responsibility in this matter. The American Medical Association has expressly adopted the position that the physician should not hesitate to treat a child with venereal disease.[125] Its statement of official position indicated that:

> The inability to obtain parental consent to treat a minor for venereal disease should not cause a physician to withold treatment if, in his professional judgment, treatment is immediately required.

> This applies even though such an action might appear to make the physician liable to a technical charge of assault and battery.

> It is of course better if the physician can persuade the minor to inform his parents and thereby provide the necessary consent. But where this is impossible, and it appears that without the physician's promise of confidentiality the youth will probably delay seeking treatment the youth's health is paramount to any other consideration.

Thus it would appear that a physician is entirely justified in applying the doctrine of emergency treatment, considering a minor with venereal disease to be as much of an emergency case as one who has been involved in an automobile accident.

One out of every 19 children born in this country is illegitimate, more than 40% of the mothers of these children are under 19 and a "substantial" number are under 15 years of age.[126] The issue of providing contraceptives to minors is one which is anything but hypothetical in this country at the present time.[127] The Supreme Court of the United States declared in 1965 that restrictions on giving contraceptives to married woman were unconstitutional and in violation of their right of privacy,[128] and in 1972 the Court extended the same privilege to unmarried persons.[129] Both cases involved adult women, however.

On the principle that a minor who is sexually active constitutes a medical emergency, a physician who gives her contraceptives is probably protected from a suit by her parents as long as she was sexually active prior to the request for contraception. In 1968 the American Bar Association's Family Law Section came out strongly in favor of the availability of contraception for all persons who wish it regardless of age. As their report stated:[130]

> In view of the impulsiveness of adolescents as well as the lack of foresight in trust-to-luck against pregnancy observed among sexually mature teenagers, the availability of birth control cannot be thought to be the determinant of whether or not they engage in sex relations. The development of a youthful standard of sexual morality is a matter for the home, the church and the community; it cannot be maintained through ignorance of the availability of birth control.

No physician, of course, is obliged to give contraception or to perform sterilization on any patient if he finds it morally repugnant. However, in no case which can be located has a physician been found liable for giving a teenager contraception.[131] While there does not appear to be any substantial legal risk to the physician who responsibly prescribes contraception for a sexually active minor, there are certain procedures which he should follow to protect himself. Inquiry should always be made as to the feasibility of parental consent. A full case history should be obtained and maintained and the physician should indicate therein that he has considered the patient's total situation. A record should be kept of "emergency" need and the judgement of the physician that pregnancy would constitute a serious hazard. He should make absolutely certain that the minor is clearly aware of any risks, hazards, or problems presented by the method of contraception and she should be required to sign a form indicating that she understands the possible difficulties. Where follow-up care is indicated, it should be insisted upon. It is perfectly obvious that many physicians as a matter of moral principle do not wish to give contraception to their unmarried minor patients and they are under no obligation to do so. However, if the physician's reluctance to provide a teenage girl with contraception is based solely on the fear that he may be sued, this possibility appears to be extremely remote.

It would be extremely unwise, to say the least, for a physician to sterilize an unmarried minor in the absence of parental consent. Due to the irreversible nature of the procedure, the minor alone should not be considered competent to consent.

The United States Supreme Court declared in January 1973 that restrictions on abortions during the first trimester of pregnancy were unconstitutional insofar as they exceeded the requirement that they be performed by a licensed medical practitioner. During the second trimester, the state may require, if it sees fit to do so, that abortions be performed in a hospital or clinic with emergency facilities. During the last trimester, the state has the right to prohibit abortions except where the mother's life or health would be endangered by a continuation of the pregnancy.[132] Since the women involved in the Supreme Court litigation were all adults, the obvious question unanswered by the court is whether or not a minor girl can consent to having an abortion without parental knowledge. There are no cases directly on the subject. Prior to those decisions, however, in the District of Columbia[133] and California[134] courts had held that abortions could be performed on girls who were, respectively, 18 and 20 without parental consent. There is also one decision which indicates that a minor girl may not be forced to have an abortion against her will at the request of her parents.

A 16-year old girl was pregnant. She wished to marry and her mother objected and wished her to have an abortion. She took the child to a gynecologist who, sensibly, refused to abort her without a court order in view of the child's vehement objections to the procedure. The juvenile court held that the mother could not force her to have an abortion, and this conclusion was upheld on appeal to the Supreme Court of Maryland.[135]

Except with a very young girl, for example, one under 14, a physician probably is protected if he performs an abortion on a girl who refuses to tell her parents that she is pregnant. Again, he should urge her to discuss the matter with her parents, but if she refuses to do so, he is protected from any possibility of being sued if he proceeds with her consent alone.[136]

Spouses not infrequently summon medical assistance for each other. Of course a husband or wife is perfectly capable of creating a physician–patient relationship on behalf of the other partner.

If a mentally competent adult has given consent to treatment, it is not necessary to discuss the proposed treatment with the patient's spouse unless the patient voluntarily requests some nontherapeutic procedure which bears on the reproductive system.[137] Where sterilization, abortion, or other such procedures are involved, however, the spouse may have the right to be notified and to prevent the procedure if it is objectionable to him or her.

It should be noted that the Supreme Court did not discuss in its recent decisions the right, if any, of a husband to object to his wife's abortion. There is at least one decision indicating that a man has no right to object if an unmarried woman whom he has impregnated has an abortion, however.[138] An unmarried man is also not usually required to pay for the abortion of a woman who is pregnant by him.[139] Further, a man has no right to object to his wife's abortion if it is genuinely therapeutically necessary.[140]

However, since the Supreme Court decisions there has been one lower court ruling on the subject of a married man's right to object to a totally elective, nontherapeutic abortion. One federal district judge in Florida has held that husbands do not have any legal standing to raise such objections.[141] However, until several appellate courts or the United States Supreme Court rule on this question, it would be extremely unwise for a physician who knows that his patient is married and living with her husband to abort her without her husband's consent unless there is clear evidence to him that the husband is not the father of the child and that the object of the abortion is to keep him from finding out that his wife is pregnant.

It should be noted that even prior to the Supreme Court decisions, in those jurisdictions in which elective abortions were legal, courts held that indigent women had a right to be admitted to public hospitals for abortion.[142] Private hospitals, however, may refuse to allow abortions as long as they are not the only available hospitals in their communities.[143]

Voluntary sterilization is now legal in all states.[144] Since several lower courts have ruled that indigent women have a constitutional right to abortions in public hospitals[145] and in two cases the Supreme Court has ruled[146] that the right to contraception is a constitutional right, it is probable that sterilization is protected under the same principles.[147] Courts have already decided that neither public hospitals[148] nor private hospitals receiving federal funds[149] may adopt regulations forbidding voluntary sterilization on their premises. Private hospitals which do not receive public funds, however, probably are entitled to do so.[150]

Whether or not a given patient should be sterilized upon request, of course, is a matter of medical judgment. The physician's moral or religious objections to sterilization cannot be violated and he cannot be forced to perform an operation he believes is wrong. A physician who has no general objection to sterilization may consider it unwise to sterilize a very young patient. He is not compelled to do so. Until 1969 the American College of Obstetricians and Gynecologists adhered to an age–parity formula, but they now allow sterilization for "anyone legally capable of giving the obstetrician–gynecologist permission to operate on her." Age and parity are, however, still quite relevant factors in medical judgment in any request for sterilization. A married minor would be an adult for this purpose.[151] In the event that an unmarried minor asks to be sterilized, it would be extremely unwise to perform the procedure without parental consent in the absence of extreme therapeutic emergency and, in fact, local counsel probably should be consulted as to the advisability of obtaining a court order.

Several states, including Georgia, North Carolina, and Virginia, have enacted statutes establishing procedures for voluntary sterilization. Most provide for a waiting period prior to elective sterilization and all require consent of the spouse if the patient of either sex is married. With the increasing popularity of sterilization operations as a result of the discovery of the laparoscopy procedure, thus allowing women to be sterilized on an outpatient basis, it is probable that more states will enact legislation to establish procedures for voluntary sterilization. Where such a statute exists, of course, the physician must follow the statutory requirements and it is incumbent upon him to be aware of them.

Except where there is a state statute on the subject, there are no decisions on whether a spouse has the right to veto sterilization on his or her partner. It is highly probable, however, that such a right would probably be declared to exist in an appropriate case. The abortion and contraception cases view the decision to have children or not to have children as one for the couple involved, not the state, but no appellate decisions have determined the rights of the couple in conflict with each other. Presumably this question will be settled in due course, but in the meantime, consent of the spouse should certainly be obtained in order to prevent the physician from being the defendant in a test case.

This, however, assumes that the couple is living together at the time the request for sterilization is made. If the man or woman is legally or informally separated from the spouse and has been for some considerable time, it would appear that he or she should be treated as if he were unmarried, as long as there is no specific statutory conflict. Furthermore, if the person whose spouse refuses to consent to sterilization consults the physician and tells him that he or she is not married, the physician would hardly incur liability if he believed the patient.

Negligent performance of a sterilization operation involves the same principles of professional liability as any other type of procedure. However, in many cases, patients who became pregnant or whose wives become pregnant after sterilization operations have sued the surgeons for breach of contract of his promise to sterilize them even though they did not allege negligence in the performance of the surgery. In some cases, recovery is allowed.[152] Either problem can be averted by requiring a consent form to be signed by both patient and spouse which indicates that they know that there is no absolute guarantee of sterility after the operation.

The customary tests should be run after a vasectomy and the necessity of these tests should be explained to the patient.[153]

Beyond the question of consent by the spouse, however, any mentally competent adult whose surgeon feels as a matter of medical judgment that there is no hindrance to performance of the operation has a right to voluntary sterilization.

While a husband is normally liable for his wife's medical bills, it is highly unlikely that any court would require him to pay for an abortion or sterilization to which he did not consent and about which he was deliberately kept unaware.

In some cases one spouse may discuss the other with a physician who never actually sees the "patient." In that case, however, depending on the circumstances, a contractual relationship between the physician and the person discussed may be held to exist and the physician may thereafter be subject to malpractice liability. For example, there are many cases where a husband or wife, acting with wilful malice, has persuaded a psychiatrist to sign commitment papers on the spouse and the psychiatrist has done so without ever seeing the patient. In all cases, the committed person, once freed, recovered extremely heavy damages from the psychiatrist for both negligence and false imprisonment.[154]

The Physician's Right to Limit the Contract. The physician has the perfect right to make various types of reasonable limitations on his relationship with the patient. The most obvious is the specialist who is treating a patient for an ailment within his field of specialization but refuses to prescribe for another ailment outside his area. For example, if a pregnant patient comes to an ophthalmologist for treatment of an eye infection and brings up obstetrical complaints while she is there, the ophthalmologist is not only legally justified in refusing to advise her, he probably would be subject to severe criticism if he did.

An internist treated a patient for bacterial colitis. The patient did not improve, so the internist sent him to a surgeon. The surgeon diagnosed appendicitis and removed the appendix. The patient sued the internist for abandonment because the internist had refused the patient's request to perform the surgery himself. The court held that the internist did not have to remove appendixes when he had limited his practice to internal medicine.[155]

A physician may limit his practice in other ways as well.

An obstetrician refused a patient's request to plan to deliver her baby at home. She told him that she would hire a midwife to do it and terminated the professional relationship. After she went into labor, complications developed and her husband called the obstetrician at the midwife's behest. The obstetrician again refused to come to the house and deliver the baby and told the husband to bring his wife to the hospital. Six hours later when she was finally brought there, the obstetrician delivered a dead baby. The parents sued him. The case was dismissed. The court pointed out that the dangers of a home delivery to both mother and child were so obvious that the obstetrician was entirely justified in refusing to do it. The opinion pointed out that the obstetrician repeatedly told the patient's husband that he would see her as soon as she got to the hospital.[156]

Physicians may quite properly refuse to see their patients outside the limitations of their own communities.

A woman cut her leg and contacted a physician in the middle of the night. The physician's partner, on call for the medical group, sutured the wound and told her explicitly to return in 2 days for examination. The next day the patient and her husband went on vacation to a town some miles away. While there, her leg gave her difficulties and she called the physician and demanded that he come to the other town and see her. He refused and referred her to a physician there whom he knew. She sued him for refusing to come. The court said that a physician is entirely justified in limiting his practice to his own community.[157]

Except in extreme emergencies, a physician also has the right to refuse to make house calls if his ordinary practice excludes them.[158]

An obstetrician delivered a woman's baby. Several days after she got home from the hospital, she called and indicated that she was having problems. She asked him to make an immediate house call. He told her that he had an office full of patients and could not leave them and told her to come to his office. She became angry, went to another obstetrician's office and sued the first one. The court dismissed the action. The opinion pointed out that the physician had the right to tell her that he could see her only at his office or at the hospital. Since she was well enough to have gone to another obstetrician's office, the court noted that she was also well enough to have gone to the defendant's.[159]

The physician, not the patient, has the right to determine the times and frequency of appointments.[160] He certainly has the right to reasonable time off as long as an adequate, competent substitute is available. If two physicians practice together, for example, and alternate weekends-on-call, a patient has no right to complain if he cannot see the physician he prefers.

A consulting physician who examines a patient at the request of a primary physician but who does not intend to continue to treat the patient certainly is not legally obligated to do so. This should, however, be made clear to both the patient and the primary physician.[161] If this is not done, it is not impossible that the consultant may be later sued for abandonment. A physician who refers a patient to a specialist for treatment generally is held to have relieved himself of any further responsibility to the patient in the absence of an understanding that he will be associated with the specialist in caring for the patient.[162] Again, however, this should be explained clearly to the patient and the specialist in order to avoid any possibility of misunderstanding.

NOTES

1. Smith v. Thornhill, 25 SW 2d 597, Tex 1930.
2. Cartwright v. Bartholomew, 64 SE 2d 323, Ga 1951; Tveldt v. Haugen, 294 NW 183, ND 1940.
3. Suburban Hospital Association v. Mewhinney, 187 A 2d 671, Md 1963.
4. Kirschner v. Equitable Life Assurance Society, 284 NYS 506, NY 1935; Hester v. Ford, 130 So 203, Ala 1930.
5. Zipkin v. Freeman, 436 SW 2d 753, Mo 1968.
6. Harris v. Fireman's Fund Indemnity Co., 257 P 2d 221, Wash 1953.
7. McNevins v. Lowe, 40 Ill 209, Ill 1866; Ritchey v. West, 23 Ill 329, Ill 1860; Barnes v. Gardner, 9 NYS 2d 785, NY 1939.
8. Rule v. Cheeseman, 317 P 2d 472, Kans 1957.
9. "Guarantee of Medical Results," 219 *JAMA* No. 3, page 431, January 17, 1972; Zoterell v. Repp, 153 NW 692, Mich 1915; Hawkins v. McCain, 79 SE 2d 493, NC 1954; Vann v. Harden, 47 SE 2d 314, Va 1948; Marvin v. Talbott, 30 Cal Rptr 893, Cal 1963.
10. Robins v. Finestone, 127 NE 2d 330, NY 1955; Safian v. Aetna Life Insurance Co., 24 NYS 2d 92, NY 1940; Gluckstein v. Lipsett, 209 P 2d 98, Cal 1949.
11. Doerr v. Villate, 220 NE 2d 767, Ill 1966.

12. Landon v. Kansas City Gas Co., 10 F 2d 263, DC Kans 1926; Caldwell v. Missouri State Life Insurance Co., 230 SW 566, Ark 1921; Cameron, to use of Cameron v. Eynon, 3 A 2d 423, Pa 1939.

13. Stohlman v. Davis, 220 NW 247, Neb 1928; Gross v. Partlow, 68 P 2d 1034, Wash 1937; Childers v. Frye, 158 SE 744, NC 1931.

14. McGulpin v. Bessmer, 43 NW 2d 121, Iowa 1950.

15. O'Neill v. Montefiore Hospital, 202 NYS 2d 436, NY 1960.

16. Smart v. Kansas City, 105 SW 709, Mo 1907.

17. Rainer v. Grossman, 107 Cal Rptr 469, Cal 1973.

18. Buttersworth v. Swint, 186 SE 770, Ga 1936.

19. "Biopsies, Part I," 223 *JAMA* No. 12, page 1429, March 19, 1973; "Biopsies, Part II," 223 *JAMA* No. 13, page 1573, March 26, 1973; Valdez v. Percy, 217 P 2d 422, Cal 1950.

20. Harvey v. Silber, 2 NW 2d 483, Mich 1942; Tessier v. United States, 164 F Supp 779, DC Mass 1958; Keene v. Methodist Hospital, 324 F Supp 233, ND Ind 1971.

21. Lundberg v. Bay View Hospital, 191 NE 2d 821, Ohio 1963.

22. Capuano v. Jacobs, 305 NYS 2d 837, NY 1969.

23. Findlay v. Board of Supervisors, 230 P 2d 526, Ariz 1951; Rice v. Rinaldo, 119 NE 2d 657, Ohio 1951; Agnew v. Parks, 343 P 2d 118, Cal 1959.

24. Hurley v. Eddingfield, 59 NE 1058, Ind 1901.

25. Editorial, "The Public Wants a Doctor When They Want Him," 136 *JAMA* 695, March 6, 1948.

26. Yeargin v. Hamilton Memorial Hospital, 195 SE 2d 8, Ga 1972.

27. Barcia v. Society of the New York Hospital, 241 NYS 2d 373, NY 1963.

28. New Biloxi Hospital v. Frazier, 146 So 2d 882, Miss 1962.

29. Reeves v. North Broward Hospital, 191 So 2d 307, Fla 1966.

30. Murray v. United States, 329 F 2d 270, CCA 4, 1964.

31. Chayet, Neil L., *Legal Implications of Emergency Care*, Appleton-Century-Crofts, New York, 1960, Chapter I, "The Duty to Act."

32. 180 *JAMA* 706, May 26, 1962; 189 *JAMA* No. 5, page 390, August 3, 1964; 270 *New Engl J Med*, No. 19, page 1003, May 7, 1964.

33. Rockhill v. Pollard, 485 P 2d 28, Ore 1971.

34. Chayet, *op. cit. supra* at 31, Chapter 7, "Practicing Without a License in an Emergency"; Rilcoff v. State Board of Medical Examiners, 203 P 2d 844, Cal 1949.

35. "The Physician as Rescuer," 223 *JAMA* No. 6, page 721, February 5, 1973.

36. Solgaard v. Guy F Atkinson Co., 491 P 2d 821, Cal 1971.

37. Carter v. Taylor Diving and Salvage Co., 341 F Supp 628, DC La 1972.

38. "Emergency Room Liability," 220 *JAMA* No. 5, page 761, May 1, 1972; "Hospital's Right to Refuse Admission," 213 *JAMA* No. 4, page 673, July 27, 1970; Chayet, *op. cit. supra* at 31, Chapter 3, "Hospitals and Emergency Care."

39. "Hospital Emergency Services and the Open Door," 66 Mich Law Review, page 1455, 1968; Williams v. Hospital Authority of Hall County, 168 SE 2d 336, Ga 1969; Smith v. Children's Hospital of Michigan, 189 SW 2d 753, Mich 1971.

40. Manlove v. Wilmington General Hospital, 169 A 2d 18, 174 A 2d 135, Del 1961.

41. Flager Hospital v. Hayling, 344 F 2d 950, CCA 5, 1965.

42. "Liability for Resident's Negligence," 213 *JAMA* No. 1, page 181, July 6, 1970.

43. "The Darling Case," 206 *JAMA* No. 7, page 1665, November 11, 1968; "The Darling Case Revisited," 206 *JAMA* No. 8, page 1875, November 18, 1968; "Hospital Liability for Physician Negligence," 214 *JAMA* No. 9, page 1755, November 30, 1970; "Negligent Selection of Hospital Staff," 223 *JAMA* No. 7, page 833, February 12, 1973; "Hospital Liability for Staff Negligence," 224 *JAMA* No. 8, page 1225, May 21, 1973; Darling v. Charleston Community Memorial Hospital, 200 NE 2d 149, 211 NE 2d 253, Ill 1965; Pederson v. Dumouchel, 431 P 2d 973, Wash 1967.

44. Methodist Hospital v. Ball, 362 SW 2d 475, Tenn 1961.

45. Cooper v. Sisters of Charity of Cincinnati, 272 NE 2d 97, Ohio 1971.

46. Joyner v. Alton Ochsner Medical Foundation, 230 So 2d 913, La 1970.

47. "Prisoner's Right to Medical Treatment," 216 *JAMA* No. 7, page 1253, May 17, 1971; Ramsey v. Ciccone, 310 F Supp 600, DC Mo 1970; Willis v. White, 310 F Supp 205, DC La 1970.

48. McCollum v. Mayfield, 130 F Supp 112, DC Cal 1955; Hirons v. Patuxent Institution, 351 F 2d 613, CCA 4, 1965; Edwards v. Duncan, 355 F 2d 993, CCA 4, 1966; Tolbert v. Eyman, 434 F 2d 625, CCA 9, 1970.

49. Coleman v. Johnston, 247 F 2d 273, CCA 7, 1957.

50. Sawyer v. Sigler, 445 F 2d 818, CCA 8, 1971; Martinez v. Mancusi, 443 F 2d 921, CCA 2, 1970.

51. Shaffer v. Jennings, 314 F Supp 588, DC Pa 1970.

52. Smith v. Schneckloth, 414 F 2d 680, CCA 9, 1969; New York ex rel Baker v. Narcotic Addiction Control Commission, 297 NYS 2d 1018, NY 1968.

53. Church v. Hegstrom, 416 F 2d 449, CCA 2, 1969.

54. Landsdown v. Worthey, 458 F 2d 485, CCA 8, 1972.

55. United States ex rel Gittlemacker v. County of Philadelphia, 413 F 2d 84, CCA 3, 1969; Bishop v. Cox, 320 F Supp 1031, DC Va 1970; Irwin v. Arrendale, 159 SE 2d 719, Ga 1967; Smith v. Baker, 326 F Supp 787, DC Mo 1970.

56. Ramsey v. Ciccone, 310 F Supp 600, DC Mo 1970.

57. United States ex rel Hyde v. McGinnis, 429 F 2d 864, CCA 2, 1970.

58. Veals v. Ciccone, 281 F Supp 1017, DC Mo 1968.

59. Cates v. Ciccone, 422 F 2d 926, CCA 8, 1970.

60. Sneidman, B., "Prisoners and Medical Treatment: Their Rights and Remedies," 4 *Crim Law Bull* 450, Oct 1968.

61. United States v. Muniz, 374 US 150, 1963.

62. "Right to Refuse Necessary Treatment," 221 *JAMA* No. 3, page 335, July 17, 1972; In re Appointment of a Guardian of the Person of Maida Yetter, Docket # 1973-533 (Pa Ct Common Pleas) Northhampton County, Pa 1973.

63. Palm Springs General Hospital v. Martinez, Fla Cir Ct, Dade Co., Docket # 71-12687, 1971.

64. Raleigh-Fitkin Memorial Hospital v. Anderson, 201 A 2d 537, NJ 1964.

65. Application of President and Directors of Georgetown College, Inc., 331 F 2d 1000, CA DC 1964.

66. Collins v. Davis, 254 NYS 2d 666, NY 1964.

67. Kennedy Hospital v. Heston, 279 A 2d 670, NJ 1971.

68. "Adult Jehovah's Witnesses and Blood Transfusions," 219 *JAMA* No. 2, page 273, January 10, 1972; In Re Brooks' Estate, 205 NE 2d 435, Ill 1965; Erickson v. Dilgard, 252 NYS 2d 705, NY 1962; "Jehovah's Witnesses and Blood Transfusions," 195 *JAMA* No. 6, page 303, February 7, 1966.

69. Hoener v. Bertinato, 171 A 2d 140, NY 1961; People ex rel Wallace v. Labrenz, 104 NE 2d 769, Ill 1952; State v. Perricone, 181 A 2d 751, NJ 1962; In re Clark, 185 NE 2d 128, Ohio 1962.

70. McCartney v. Austin, 298 NYS 2d 26, NY 1969.

71. In re Karwath, 199 NW 2d 147, Iowa 1972.

72. In re Sampson, 317 NYS 2d 641, NY 1970.

73. "Child Abuse and the Physician," 222 *JAMA* No. 4, page 517, October 23, 1972; Craig v. State, 155 A 2d 684, Md 1959; People v. Pierson, 68 NE 243, NY 1903; State v. Clark, 261 A 2d 294, Conn 1969; Eaglen v. State, 231 NE 2d 147, Ind 1967; People v. Edwards, 249 NYS 2d 325, NY 1964.

74. 26 USCA Sections 4701–4736, 4773.

75. 21 USCA Sections 301–392.

76. Coolahan v. Maryland, 270 A 2d 669, Md 1970; United States v. Warren, 453 F 2d 738, CCA 2, 1972; Massachusetts v. Miller, 282 NE 2d 394, Mass 1972; United States v. Ramzy, 446 F 2d 1184, CCA 5, 1971; Arizona v. Marcus, 450 P 2d 689, Ariz 1969; White v. United States, 399 F 2d 813, CCA 8, 1968.

77. United States v. Doremus, 249 US 86, 1919.

78. Blinder v. California, 101 Cal Rptr 635, Cal 1972; California v. Anderson, 105 Cal Rptr 664, Cal 1972.

79. Felber v. Foote, 321 F Supp 85, DC Conn 1970.

80. Battistella v. Society of the New York Hospital, 191 NYS 2d 626, NY 1959; Riste v. General Electric Corporation, 289 P 2d 338, Wash 1955; Jines v. General Electric Corporation, 313 F 2d 76, CCA 9, 1962; Metropolitan Life Insurance Co. v. Evans, 184 So 426, Miss 1938.

81. Lotspeich v. Chance Vought Aircraft Corporation, 369 SW 2d 705, Tex 1963.

82. Beadling v. Sirotta, 176 A 2d 546, NJ 1961; Union Carbide and Carbon Corporation v. Stapleton, 237 F 2d 229, CCA 6, 1956.

83. Rannard v. Lockheed Aircraft, 157 P 2d 1, Cal 1945.

84. "The Physician as Fellow Servant," 223 *JAMA* No. 10, page 1203, March 5, 1973.

85. Bergen v. Miller, 250 A 2d 49, NJ 1969.

86. Jones v. Bouza, 160 NW 2d 881, Mich 1968.

87. Wilson v. Hungate, 434 SW 2d 580, Mo 1968.

88. Hoffman v. Rogers, 99 Cal Rptr 455, Cal 1972.

89. Federal Employers' Liability Act, 45 USC Section 51.

90. Jones Act, 46 USC Section 688; "Liability of Company for Ship's Surgeon," 215 *JAMA* No. 8, page 1381, February 22, 1971; DeZon v. American President Lines, 318 US 660, 1943.

91. "Appointment of Independent Medical Expert," 216 *JAMA* No. 1, page 207, April 5, 1971.

92. Webb v. Texas, 467 SW 2d 449, Tex 1971; Creamer v. Georgia, 192 SE 2d 350, Ga 1972.

92a. Adams v. State of Indiana, 229 NE 2d 834, Ind 1973.

93. "Compulsory Psychiatric Examination," 220 *JAMA* No. 9, page 1277, May 29, 1972; Massey v. State, 177 SE 2d 79, Ga 1970; People v. Lowe, 248 NE 2d 530, Ill 1969.

94. Cawthon v. Coffer, 264 So 2d 973, Fla 1972.

95. "Liability for Administering Blood Test," 217 *JAMA* No. 1, page 119, July 5, 1971.

96. Schmerber v. California, 384 US 757, 1966.

97. California v. Kraft, 84 Cal Rptr 280, Cal 1970.

98. California v. Kraft, 84 Cal Rptr 280, Cal 1970.

99. California v. Superior Court, 493 P 2d 1145, Cal 1972.

100. Couch v. Rice, 261 NE 2d 187, Ohio 1970; New York v. Seaman, 315 NYS 2d 743, NY 1970.

101. Fallis v. Department of Motor Vehicles, 70 Cal Rptr 595, Cal 1968.

102. Waukesha Memorial Hospital v. Baird, 173 NW 2d 700, Wisc 1970.

103. Chayet, *op. cit. supra* at 31, page 60.

104. Washington v. Kulijis, 422 P 2d 480, Wash 1967; Iowa v. Bedel, 193 NW 2d 121, Iowa 1971.

105. Ragsdale v. Arkansas, 432 SW 2d 11, Ark 1968; Couch v. Rice, 261 NE 2d 187, Ohio 1970.

106. "Prenatal Injuries," 214 *JAMA* No. 11, page 2105, December 14, 1970; "Liability for Mental Anguish," 217 *JAMA* No. 6, page 869, August 9, 1971.

107. Sylvia v. Gobeille, 220 A 2d 222, RI 1966.

108. Domina v. Pratt, 13 A 2d 198, Vt 1940; Swank v. Halivopoulous, 260 A 2d 240, NJ 1969; Koury v. Follo, 158 SE 2d 548, NC 1968; "Parental Consent to Treatment of a Minor," 200 *JAMA* No. 1, page 273, April 3, 1967.

109. "Mother's Right to Consent," 213 *JAMA* No. 8, page 1393, August 24, 1970.

110. Durfee v. Durfee, 87 NYS 2d 275, NY 1949.

111. Burge v. City and County of San Francisco, 262 P 2d 6, Cal 1953.

112. Yarborough v. Yarborough, 290 US 202, 1933; Hachat v. Hachat, 71 NE 2d 927, Ind 1947; Porter v. Powell, 44 NW 295, Iowa 1890.

113. Luka v. Lowrie, 136 NW 1106, Mich 1912; Sullivan v. Montgomery, 279 NYS 575, NY 1935.

114. Zaman v. Schultz, 19 Pa D & C 309, 1933.

115. Bonner v. Moran, 126 F 2d 121, CA DC 1941.

116. Bach v. Long Island Jewish Hospital, 267 NYS 2d 289, NY 1966.

117. Swenson v. Swenson, 227 SW 2d 103, Mo 1950.

118. Shartel, Burke and Plant, Marcus, *The Law of Medical Practice*, Springfield, Illinois, C C Thomas, 1959, page 26.

119. Miss Code Sections 7129-81 et seq; Ariz Rev Stat Sections 44-132, 44-133; Cal Civ Code Section 34.5; Ind. Stat. Ann Section 35-4407; Nev Rev Stat Section 129.030; New Mex Stat Ann Section 12-12-1 et seq.

120. Sullivan v. Montgomery, 279 NYS 575, NY 1935; Lacey v. Laird, 139 NE 2d 25, Ohio, 1956; Gulf and Ship Island RR Co. v. Sullivan, 119 So 501, Miss 1928; Bishop

v. Shurly, 211 NW 75, Mich 1926; Smith v. Seibly, 431 P 2d 719, Wash 1967; Bakker v. Welsh, 108 NW 94, Mich 1906.

121. Younts v. St. Frances Hospital and School of Nursing, 469 P 2d 330, Kans 1970.

122. Lacey v. Laird, 139 NE 2d 25, Ohio 1956.

123. Poudre Valley Hospital District v. Heckart, 491 P 2d 984, Colo 1971.

124, "Treating a Minor for Veneral Disease," 214 *JAMA* No. 10, page 1949, December 7, 1970.

125. *AMA News*, April 17, 1967, page 4.

126. "Family Planning and the Law," Report on Family Planning, Family Law Section, American Bar Association, *Family Law Quarterly*, December 1967, pages 103–108.

127. "Minors and Contraception," 216 *JAMA* No. 12, page 2059, June 21, 1971.

128. Griswold v. Connecticut, 381 US 479, 1965.

129. Eisenstadt v. Baird, 405 US 438, 1972.

130. *Op. cit. supra* at 126.

131. "Birth Control, Teenagers and the Law," by Harriet F. Pilpel and Nancy F. Wechsler, in *Family Planning Perspectives*, Vol. 1, page 29, 1969.

132. Roe v. Wade, 410 US 113, 1973; Doe v. Bolton, 410 US 179, 1973.

133. In re Boe, 322 F Supp 872, DC DC 1971.

134. Ballard v. Anderson, 484 P 2d 1345, Cal 1971.

135. In re Smith, 295 A 2d 238, Md 1972.

136. Gibbs, Richard F., "Therapeutic Abortion and the Minor," 1 *J Leg Med*, No. 1, page 36, March–April 1973.

137. Rosenberg v. Geigin, 260 P 2d 143, Cal 1953; Nishi v. Hartwell, 473 P 2d 116, Hawaii 1970; Kritzer v. Citron, 224 P 2d 808, Cal 1950; Barker v. Heaney, 82 SW 2d 417, Tex 1935; Rytkonen v. Lojacono, 257 NW 703, Mich 1934.

138. Jones v. Smith, 278 So 2d 239, Fla 1973.

139. B. v. S., 335 NYS 2d 131, NY 1972.

140. O'Beirne v. Superior Court of Santa Clara County, Sup. Ct. Cal, December 7, 1967.

141. Coe v. Gerstein, Case No. 72-1842-Civ JE (DC Fla, Aug. 14, 1973); cert. den. US Sup. Ct, Docket No. 73 1157, 1974.

142. Doe v. General Hospital of the District of Columbia, 434 F 2d 423, CCA DC, 1970.

143. Stewart v. Long Island College Hospital, 296 NYS 2d 41, NY 1968.

144. Parker v. Rampton, 497 P 2d 848, Utah 1972; Jessin v. County of Shasta, 79 Cal Rptr 359, Cal 1969.

145. Doe v. General Hospital of the District of Columbia, 434 F 2d 423, CCA DC, 1970.

146. Griswold v. Connecticut, 381 US 479, 1965; Eisenstadt v. Baird, 405 US 438, 1972.

147. "Voluntary Sterilization," 225 *JAMA* No. 13, page 1743, September 24, 1973; "Voluntary Sterilization of Women as a Right," Forbes, Peter R., 18 *DePaul Law Review*, Nos. 2 and 3, page 560, Summer 1969; "Right to Sterilization," 227 *JAMA* No. 9, page 1151, November 26, 1973.

148. Hathaway v. Worcester City Hospital, 475 F 2d 701, CCA 1, 1973.

149. Taylor v. St. Vincent's Hospital, USDC Mont, November 1, 1972.

150. Ham v. Holy Rosary Hospital, Docket No. 1 4910, Mont Dist Ct, Custer County, Feb 13, 1973.

151. Smith v. Seibly, 431 P 2d 719, Wash 1967.
152. Custodio v. Bauer, 59 Cal Rptr 463, Cal 1967; Doerr v. Villate, 220 NE 2d 767, Ill 1966; Jackson v. Anderson, 230 So 2d 503, Fla 1970.
153. "Vasectomies," 217 *JAMA* No. 13, page 1943, September 27, 1971; Lane v. Cohen, 201 So 2d 804, Fla 1967.
154. "Erroneous Commitment," 219 *JAMA* No. 10, page 1389, March 6, 1972; DiGiovanni v. Pessel, 250 A 2d 756, NY 1969; Sukeforth v. Thegan, 256 A 2d 162, Maine 1969; Karjavinen y. Buswell, 194 NE 295, Mass 1935; Dunbar v. Greenlaw, 128 A 2d 218, Maine 1956; Kleber v. Stevens, 241 NYS 2d 497, NY 1963.
155. Skodje v. Hardy, 288 P 2d 471, Wash 1955.
156. Vidrine v. Mayes, 127 So 2d 809, La 1961.
157. McNamara v. Emmons, 97 P 2d 503, Cal 1939.
158. Nash v. Meyer, 31 P 2d 273, Idaho 1934; Urritia v. Patino, 297 SW 512, Tex 1928; Saunders v. Lischkoff, 188 So 815, Fla 1939.
159. Rogers v. Lawson, 170 F 2d 157, DC CA 1948.
160. Dabney v. Briggs, 121 So 394, Ala 1929.
161. Podvin v. Eickhorst, 128 NW 2d 523, Mich 1964.
162. Engle v. Clarke, 346 SW 2d 13, Ky 1961.

CHAPTER II

THE

DUTY

OF CARE

General Definition of the Term "Due Care." Once a physician–patient relationship has been established, the physician is obligated to diagnose and treat the patient's illness or injury with "due care." Failure to do so constitutes "negligence" for which the patient may recover monetary damages.

All negligence actions are a species of "tort" law, which is defined as "a violation of a duty imposed by general law or otherwise upon all persons occupying the relation to each other which is involved in a given transaction."[1] Negligence in particular is defined as "the omission to do something which a reasonable man guided by those ordinary considerations which ordinarily regulate human affairs, would do, or the doing of something which a reasonable and prudent man would not do."[2] All negligence actions are therefore predicated on the allegation that the party who claims damage was owed some duty by the other and that the duty was breached, causing injury. In any automobile accident litigation, for example, the plaintiff claims that the defendant owed all others on the road a duty to drive safely and that he breached that duty, thus causing the accident. If a customer in a store buys a soft drink and, after drinking half of it, discovers a worm in the remainder, he will allege when he sues the manufacturer that there was a duty owed to all customers, himself included, to bottle drinks without impurities and that breach of the duty injured him by making him sick.[3]

The standard used by courts in determining whether or not there has been a breach of duty in any negligence action is the "reasonable man" rule. If the reasonable, prudent man would have avoided the difficulty, the defendant will be held to have been negligent. On the other hand, if the reasonable man would have acted in the same way the defendant acted, no negligence can exist as a matter of law even though the plaintiff's injury may be quite genuine. As A. P. Herbert wrote, describing the reasonable man: "This excellent but odious character stands like a monument in our Courts of Justice vainly appealing to his fellow-citizens to order their lives after his own example."[4] For example, in an automobile accident on an icy highway, the defendant may be held to be negligent even if he was driving at the posted speed at the time that he skidded into the plaintiff's car. The reasonable, prudent driver would have slowed down on the ice. On the other hand, a reasonable, prudent man would not anticipate that a small child would suddenly run out onto an interstate highway in a deserted rural area. If this situation occurred, the driver would be unlikely to be found negligent even if he ran over the child.

These basic principles of negligence law are applied in cases in which a patient alleges that a physician has in some manner been negligent in diagnosing or treating the patient's complaint, but in any type of professional negligence action against a professional person, including physicians, lawyers, architects, and others, the concept of "the reasonable man" becomes the "duly careful member of the profession." Two old and very famous decisions in cases which alleged that physicians had been negligent established the definition of medical negligence which is now accepted by the courts of all states.

As early as 1898 the highest court in New York established the basic definition of medical negligence in *Pike v. Honsinger*.[5] The patient had been kicked in the knee by a horse and claimed that the defendant had set it in a negligent manner, resulting in a failure of the bones to unite. The court said:

> The law relating to malpractice is simple and well settled, although not always easy of application. A physician and surgeon, by taking charge of a case, impliedly represents that he possesses, and the law places upon him the duty of possessing, that reasonable degree of learning and skill that is ordinarily possessed by physicians and surgeons in the locality in which he practices, and which is ordinarily regarded by those conversant with the employment as is necessary to qualify him to engage in the business of practicing medicine and surgery. Upon consenting to treat a patient, it becomes his duty to use reasonable care and diligence in the exercise of his skill and the application of his learning to accomplish the purpose for which he was employed. He is under the further obligation to use his best judgment in exercising his skill and applying his knowledge. The law holds him liable for an injury to his patient resulting from want of the requisite skill and knowledge or the omission to exercise reasonable care or the failure to use his best judgment. The rule in relation to learning and skill does not require the surgeon to possess that extraordinary learning and skill which belong only to a few men of rare endowments,

but such as is possessed by the average member of the medical
profession in good standing. . . . The rule of reasonable care
and diligence does not require the use of the highest possible
degree of care and to render a physician and surgeon liable,
it is not enough that there has been a less degree of care than
some other medical man might have shown or less than even
he himself might have bestowed, but there must be a want of
ordinary and reasonable care, leading to a bad result.

The Supreme Court of Indiana expanded on this definition in 1938.
Adkins v. Ropp[6] involved a patient who had lost the sight of one eye. He
claimed that the defendant had been negligent in removing a foreign body
from it and the eye had then become infected as the result of the negligence. The defendant argued that the infection was an unavoidable result
of the original injury. That court said:

When a physician and surgeon assumes to treat and care for
a patient, in the absence of a special agreement, he is held in
law to have impliedly contracted that he possesses the reasonable and ordinary qualifications of his profession and that he
will exercise at least reasonable skill, care and diligence in his
treatment of him. This implied contract on the part of the
physician does not include a promise to effect a cure and
negligence cannot be imputed because a cure is not effected,
but he does impliedly promise that he will use due diligence
and ordinary skill in his treatment of the patient so that a cure
may follow such care and skill, and this degree of care and
skill is required of him, not only in performing an operation
or administering first treatments, but he is held to the like
degree of care and skill in the necessary subsequent treatments
unless he is excused from further service by the patient himself,
or the physician or surgeon upon due notice refuses to further
treat the case. In determining whether the physician or surgeon
has exercised the degree of skill and care which the law
requires, regard must be had to the advanced state of the profession at the time of treatment and in the locality in which
the physician or surgeon practices.

In law, negligence is not by any means limited to situations involving
carelessness. For example, a physician who does not have the training to
perform a given procedure or who does not ask for the necessary information on which to make a diagnosis may be extremely careful as he deals
with the patient and in fact his care may meet the highest possible stand-

ards, but he may still be negligent if he does not refer the patient to a specialist.

Thus, simply put, the physician must have adequate knowledge and skill and use it with adequate care in his dealings with a patient. "The reasonably prudent physician or surgeon, acting under the same circumstances" is the standard by which his conduct will be judged.

An electrocardiogram made when a patient complained of chest pains indicated possibly serious cardiac abnormalities. The physician did not tell the patient anything about the results, nor did he prescribe rest or any treatment. A week later when the chest pains recurred and were worse, the patient called him and the physician told him to go to the hospital. He did not, however, tell him to go in an ambulance, so the patient walked down several flights of stairs and rode to the hospital in his car. Examination revealed that he had had a heart attack several days before. Open heart surgery was required to repair the damage. He sued and recovered damages from the physician. The court held that a duly careful, reasonably prudent physician would have told his patient about the electrocardiogram results and would have hospitalized him immediately.[7]

Application of the Principles of Due Care. Certain factual situations are quite common in medical malpractice suits. Thus there are general guidelines from many judicial decisions as to what acts constitute due care as a matter of law in many areas.

The obvious first step in determining due care is consideration of the amount of skill possessed and used in treating the patient. A physician may be liable either for failure to know what he is doing, if a reasonably prudent physician would have known, or he may be liable if he knows what to do, but for some reason does not do it carefully or omits doing it at all. "Skill and knowledge" as discussed in the definitions of due care usually includes the former, "diligence" the latter. A physician may, for example, be liable in negligence if he is remiss in his obligation to realize that he is not capable of treating the patient and should therefore send him to a specialist. A physician whose native language is not English would probably be found liable if his difficulties with the language prevent him from reaching any understanding of the patient's complaints and as a result he administers the wrong treatment no matter how skillfully he applies it. Both of those problems would involve lack of skill. Failure to visit a hospitalized patient sufficiently frequently to keep aware of his problems, on the other hand, would constitute lack of diligence.

Nonphysicians who attempt to treat diseases, once they come within the boundaries of the practice of medicine, are held to the same standard of skill and knowledge as a physician. A chiropractor, for example, is judged by the knowledge of other chiropractors as long as what he is doing does not involve the practice of medicine. If he ventures into diagnosis or treatment of a medical problem, the law requires him to be as knowledgeable and able to treat the patient as a physician would be. If he cannot comply with this standard, he cannot later defend himself on the ground that he did not know what he was doing because of his lack of education.

A chiropractor applied a cast to a fractured wrist. It was too tight and damage resulted. He was found negligent and the usual standards for physicians were applied.[8]

A patient's symptoms clearly indicated appendicitis. The treatment by a drugless healer included enemas and laxatives. The patient's wife asked the healer to call a physician and he refused. The wife eventually contacted a surgeon but peritonitis was already present when the patient got to the hospital. The patient died. The court held that once he left the confines of his limited practice, the healer was required to adopt and use with due care generally recognized medical treatment.[9]

Since there is frequently less than unanimous opinion in the medical profession on the best method of treating a given problem, a physician is generally free to adopt the one of several alternative treatments he thinks best.[10] As long as the course of treatment chosen is one which is accepted by a "respectable minority" of the medical profession, the courts regard it as an approved one.[11]

A physician did not administer a relaxant drug to a patient prior to an electroshock treatment. A fracture resulted. At the time of the incident there was honest disagreement among recognized psychiatric experts as to the side effects risk of the medication. The court held that failure to give the medicine was not negligent.[12]

A patient's laryngeal nerves were injured during a thyroidectomy. The patient claimed that if another method of performing the operation had been used, the injury could not have occurred. No claim was made that the physician had not been careful in using the method he employed. Since both methods were recognized as acceptable the court held that no negligence had occurred.[13]

Where the alternate methods are recognized by reputable physicians, use of one over the other does not constitute negligence even if hindsight clearly indicates that the one not used probably would have produced a better result.[14]

Experimentation which is undertaken for the knowledge of the physician instead of the treatment of the patient is not, however, within the same category. A physician whose method is either unknown to or disapproved by his peers might well find himself presumed to be negligent if the patient suffers damage, particularly if he did not follow the usual methods of treatment prior to the use of his own innovations.[15] Use of an unproven method of treatment which damages the patient is usually considered negligent even if it is carried out with the highest possible degree of care.[16]

Of course the degree of innovation which is legally acceptable is largely determined by the patient's condition. If the ailment is not serious, presumably negligence would be found if innovation in treatment causes damage of any sort. On the other hand, where the patient is critically ill or not responding to the usual treatments for the condition from which he suffers, use of unproven methods might well be justified as long as the patient or his family understands that the treatment is unproven and the consequences thereof are not predictable.

A teenage boy died as the result of an unorthodox orthopedic procedure. His parents had consented to the surgery but were not told that it was experimental. The surgeon was found liable for his failure to disclose that fact to the parents.[17]

A patient with a broken arm was treated by use of a metal cast, which the surgeon removed weekly, and massage. At the end of the treatment, the arm was useless. The court held that such a radical departure from the normal methods of orthopedics constituted negligence.[18]

A patient broke his ankle. A year of treatment by standard methods did not result in any improvement. Several physicians advised him to have it amputated. Another surgeon performed an unorthodox operation. Eighteen months later the ankle was amputated. The court held that under the circumstances the new and unorthodox procedure was justified as last resort and all that had resulted from its failure was what would have happened sooner without it.[19]

Due care may require the prudent and careful physician to consult with other medical practitioners in many situations.[20] He may, for example, be required by principles of good medical practice to contact for information or instructions a physician who has previously treated the patient.

An elderly woman broke her hip. Her family physician, a general practitioner, referred her to an orthopedic surgeon, who inserted a nail in the fracture. The orthopedist took over her care while she was in the hospital but returned her to the supervision of the family physician when she was dismissed. The general practitioner knew that the orthopedist's instructions during hospitalization excluded weight-bearing, but he made no inquiry of the orthopedist as to instructions for himself or the patient at the time of dismissal. She walked on the affected leg since she had had no instructions to the contrary. The device broke and further surgery became necessary. She sued the family doctor. The court found that he failed in his duty of due care when he did not consult with the orthopedist as to instructions in the case.[21]

A patient had had a piece of bone removed from his nose and his optic nerve was unprotected. He consulted another physician a considerable time after surgery for treatment of asthma. He told the second physician about the nasal surgery and the name of the surgeon who had performed it. The second physician did not call the surgeon to inquire about the operation or any of its effects. During his treatment of the asthmatic condition, the optic nerve was damaged and the patient lost the sight of that eye. The court held that the physician's failure to consult with the prior surgeon before beginning treatment constituted negligence.[22]

In some cases, the physician may be obliged by the principles of due care to consult with another physician on his diagnosis or plan of treatment even though the second physician is not asked to take over responsibility for the case. Innumerable decisions discuss the necessity of consultation when a diagnosis is uncertain.

An 11-year old boy, a service dependent, was seen at a base dispensary and a diagnosis of appendicitis was made. Since the dispensary did not have surgical facilities, he was sent to a service hospital in the area. The physician who saw him at the hospital was an ear, nose, and throat specialist. Although the child's mother gave him the diagnosis sheet from the dispensary and requested surgical consultation, he refused to call a surgeon. He sent the child home. Later the same night the mother took the child back to the hospital and he was seen by an intern. The intern also refused to call a surgeon and again the mother made repeated requests that he do so. When the physicians at the dispensary were advised of this, they contacted a surgeon at the hospital themselves. The surgeon examined the boy and operated, but the appendix had ruptured and the child had peritonitis. The court held that the failures to consult a surgeon on the case, since one was immediately available, was negligence, especially in view of the original diagnosis and the mother's repeated requests.[23]

Consultation on treatment may also be required if the physician knows or should know that his methods of dealing with the case are proving ineffectual.[24]

After an operation in 1952, a surgeon knew that the patient's wound drained constantly but did nothing about it. In 1961 the patient's children took her to a specialist, who removed a sponge from the incision. The court held that the surgeon was negligent in failing to consult with someone in the face of abundant evidence that something was wrong.[25]

In some situations the physician has the duty to refer the patient to a specialist for diagnosis or treatment and to allow the specialist to take over the case.[26] If a physician who is not a specialist in the field of the patient's illness knows or should know that treatment by a specialist is reasonably available and would benefit the patient, he is negligent if he does not advise the patient of that fact.[27]

A man was struck by a car and knocked unconscious. The physician on call to the local police department came to the accident scene and looked at him but made no examination. He did not turn him over. He told the policemen that the man was drunk and not injured. The man was taken to jail and remained almost unconscious for several days while in a cell. His family finally got him removed to the local hospital but he died of a massive skull fracture. The court held that the physician should reasonably have anticipated that there would be head injuries when anyone is struck by a car and failure to refer him to a hospital was negligent.[28]

However, before a nonspecialist can be found liable for failure to refer a patient, the circumstances must be such that the duly careful generalist should have known that a problem existed which he was not equipped to solve.[29]

Symptoms of a simple and widespread eye ailment were virtually identical to glaucoma. The general practitioner who treated the patient for the common complaint did not realize that glaucoma was present until severe and permanent damage to eyesight had occurred. The court held that he was not liable for his failure to refer the patient since his original diagnosis was reasonable.[30]

A great many cases in which it was alleged that the nonspecialist was liable for failure to refer involved fractures.[31] In general, if an orthopedist is readily available, a general practitioner would be well advised to make referrals in all cases of suspected broken bones.

A physician who knows what is wrong with the patient and exactly what treatment is necessary may have an obligation to refer the patient to a hospital which has better facilities or equipment than are locally available.[32]

A general practitioner attempted to remove a foreign object from a patient's eye. Symptoms presented evidence of a detached retina, but he did not have the instruments necessary to make a conclusive diagnosis. By the time the patient consulted a specialist her vision was permanently damaged. The court held that the general practitioner was negligent in failing to send her to someone who had the specialized instruments required.[33]

A patient was Xrayed after an automobile accident. It was agreed by him and the physician that if any fractures were discovered, he would be sent to the university teaching hospital for treatment. A lateral Xray of the vertebrae was not possible because of lack of the necessary Xray equipment. There were in fact fractures which would have been discovered by such an Xray. The court held that the physician was negligent because he failed to advise the patient that all Xrays necessary for a complete evaluation could not be made locally.[34]

In an emergency, of course, a different factual situation is presented. A physcian in a small hospital might in fact be considered negligent if he sent a patient to a larger hospital if the patient's condition would be jeopardized by the move. In that situation, good and careful medical practice would require only that the physician do the best he could with whatever equipment he had at his disposal.

In most cases, if a physician refers a patient to a duly qualified specialist of whom there is no reason to suspect negligence and the first physician's involvement with the case terminates at that time, any negligence by the specialist is not imputed to him and he is not liable for it.[35] When the referring physician continues to participate actively in the care of the patient, however, he may be jointly liable with the specialist.[36] If his assistance is entirely directed by the specialist, as in a situation in which he assists in surgery planned and carried out by the specialist, or if the specialist assumes all decision-making responsibility, however, the referring physician probably would not be liable even if he continued to visit the patient in the hospital or involved himself in other cooperative ventures to that extent.[37] The controlling factor, therefore, in any question of joint liability in a referral situation is the extent of participation by the referring physician in diagnosis and treatment.

One of the most important duties a physician owes his patient under the general concept of due care is his obligation to keep abreast of new developments in medicine.[38]

A hospital was liable for the negligence of one of its staff physicians who set a fractured leg in an emergency. The physician admitted at the trial that he had not read a book on orthopedics in 10 years, but he had not asked for consultation when obvious postoperative signs of difficulties developed.[39]

Medication permanently affected a patient's eyesight. Medical literature had contained numerous articles indicating the possibility of such a side effect but the physician who prescribed it had not read any of the articles. The court found that he was negligent in failing to keep up with and be aware of developments in the field.[40]

What may be accepted as the most advanced practice of medicine or surgery at one time in a physician's career may be swiftly outdated by new discoveries and advances and it is his obligation to render treatment to his patients based on adequate understanding of those new developments.

A common defense to an allegation by a patient that the physician has been negligent is a showing that customary and approved practice in the community was followed. Where a physician can show that he has followed the practices and treatment methods commonly employed by his local peers, he is usually not considered negligent.[41]

However, in recent years courts have begun to realize that the local custom itself may be negligent and if it is, the fact that the negligence is widespread is no defense.[42]

A patient went into shock following surgery. The surgeon did not visit him for 12 hours. Although he showed that the local custom was to deal with this problem by telephone, he was still found liable for the patient's death.[43]

A patient fell during Xrays. The radiologist was not aware that part of her complaint was "dizzy spells." Even though local custom did not make history-taking the radiologist's responsibility, the court held that he had been negligent in failing to question her.[44]

Therefore, while adherence to the usual practice by which the local medical community deals with a problem is ordinarily a good defense to a charge of negligence, "everybody does it" is no excuse if "it" is in fact a sloppy or careless practice.

Due care obligates a physician to follow up on his patient's progress.[45] He must be sure, for example, that his patient understands his instructions pertaining to medication, restrictions on activities, return visits, and the like.[46] If the patient is a child or young adolescent, of course, the physician must communicate instructions to the parent as well as to the child.[47] If the patient is senile or otherwise incompetent, instruction must be given to a family member or other responsible adult.[48] If the patient has difficulty with English, the physician must present the instructions until he is sure that they have been understood.[49] If there is any question of illiteracy, oral instructions corresponding to any written ones, such as those on medication labels, must be given.

In particular, if any medication is prescribed which might affect a patient's ability to drive a car or to participate in similar activities in which the physician knows or should know that he is likely to be engaged, the physician is absolutely obligated to explain this to him. If a patient becomes drowsy as a side effect of medication while driving, falls asleep at the wheel, and has a wreck, not only will he have a malpractice suit against the physician, but any other persons who are injured would have an action against the physician as well.[50]

A bus driver, whose occupation was known to his physician, received allergy medication which made him very drowsy. This side effect was indicated in the manufacturer's material which was available to the physician, but he did not warn his patient of the possibility. The driver went to sleep at the wheel of the bus. He and all the injured passengers collected damages from the prescribing physician.[51]

If instructions are given and the patient disobeys them, of course he and not the physician is at fault when his condition does not improve.[52] It should be remembered, however, that a sick or frightened person may not be capable of the same kind of common sense, judgment, and intelligence he exhibits when he is well. For that reason, in order to prevent any misunderstanding in the patient's mind about what he has been told to do or to refrain from doing, a physician should make a habit of having patients repeat instructions back to him to be sure they understand.

A physician is also obligated to pay attention to patients' compaints. Failure to listen to what a patient is trying to tell him about any symptoms or changes in condition could result in the physician's remaining unaware of early indications of serious problems. While obvious schedule disruptions would occur if a physician tried to talk to all patients who call him at his office, telephoning a drug store to prescribe medication on the basis of what an office assistant tells him the patient says his symptoms are is potentially dangerous for that reason. A better practice is for the physician himself to return the call when he has time to talk to the patient.

Another type of failure to communicate with and listen to the patient which may result in serious consequences is a failure to take an adequate medical history or to make reasonable inquiries about the circumstances of the illness.[53]

A diagnosis was made on admission to the hospital that a patient suffered from delirium tremens. In fact the patient was almost a teetotaler. After death an autopsy revealed a massive subdural hematoma. Since the physician who made the diagnosis could have made immediate inquiries about the patient's drinking habits from members of the family who were at the hospital, failure to do so was held to be negligent.[54]

A patient was a barbiturate addict. She had been hospitalized for treatment of the problem. She continued to take large quantities of Nembutal after she was released and her family physician advised her husband to have her readmitted. She told the admitting physician that she took Nembutal. Her husband asked to talk to the physician, but the physician refused to speak to him, so he left an empty Nembutal vial on the physician's desk. Although the physician had the name and telephone number of the family doctor, he did not call him about the case. He made a diagnosis of schizophrenia. The patient died several days later of barbiturate withdrawal. The physician was found negligent for having failed to take a proper history or to make reasonable and proper investigations of the circumstances leading to the patient's admission.[55]

A man made threats against his wife and their family physician. The physician, the family's minister, the local sheriff, and other persons concluded that he was psychotic and he was committed to the state mental hospital. Shortly afterwards he was transferred to a Veterans Administration hospital. He told the psychiatrist at the VA hospital that he had no hostility toward his wife and denied that he had ever threatened her. The psychiatrist believed him and concluded that the wife, not the husband, was the one with mental problems. The psychiatrist arranged for his release and got him a job at a nearby ranch. The ranch owner was told nothing of the patient's history. The man left the ranch, went back to his home town, and killed his wife. The administrators of the wife's estate brought suit alleging that the psychiatrist had been negligent in releasing the man. The court found that most of the information which the psychiatrist had chosen to ignore were matters of objective fact which he could have verified or disproven in a very few minutes by telephone calls before making the assumption that his patient was truthful. This failure to verify facts was considered a failure to use any care or judgment whatever and the administrators recovered damages.[56]

Of course all patients do not recover from their problems. Physicians are neither magicians nor insurers of their patients' good health. Some conditions refuse to respond to all known methods of treatment and some patients exhibit idiosyncratic reactions to established and accepted methods of cure. The legal definitions of due care and negligence are such that no inference of negligence is raised from the fact that a patient's condition did not improve. A poor result is never sufficient in and of itself to establish negligence by a physician or surgeon.[57] As long as the treatment was proper, there is no malpractice regardless of the outcome of the patient's illness.

A very old decision[58] from the Minnesota Supreme Court gave an excellent summation of the legal principles to be applied in case of bad result:

> Physicians and surgeons deal with progressive inductive science. On two historic occasions, the greatest surgeons in our country met in conference to decide whether or not they should operate upon the person of the President of the United States. Their conclusion was the final human judgment. They were not responsible in law, either human or divine, for the ultimate decree of nature. The same tragedy is enacted in a less conspicuous way every day in every part of this country.

A physician is also not liable for an honest error of judgment.[59] The law does not demand infallibility of any physician. If he complies with recognized standards, a simple error will not subject him to liability. In retrospect he may realize that his judgment was wrong, but as long as it was reasonable, he is not liable.

A patient was burned during Xray treatments. In finding that there was no negligence, the court said:

> Physicians and surgeons must be allowed a wide range in the exercise of their judgment and discretion. In many instances

there can be no fixed rule to determine the duty of a physician
but he must often use his own best judgment and act accordingly. By reason of that fact, the law will not hold a physician
guilty of negligence even though his judgment may prove
erroneous in a given case, unless it be shown that the course
pursued was clearly against the course recognized as correct
by the profession generally.[60]

While liability for misdiagnosis will be discussed in a later chapter, diagnostic errors are the best examples of decisions involving the "error of
judgment" concept.

A 32-year old married woman gave every symptom of fibroid tumors of the
uterus. Two pregnancy tests were negative. When the defendant made the
incision to begin a hysterectomy he discovered that she was pregnant and
terminated the surgery. The patient miscarried and sued him. The court found
that due care had been used in arriving at the diagnosis and therefore the
surgeon was not liable.[61]

A diagnosis of ectopic pregnancy was made. When emergency surgery
began, it was discovered that the patient had a normal pregnancy and acute
appendicitis. The surgeon removed her appendix, her recovery was normal,
and she delivered a healthy child at term. She later sued because she had not
given permission for removal of her appendix. The court declined to find the
surgeon at fault for going ahead with the procedure and implied that the
woman was an ingrate.[62]

In both cases, of course on the basis of the symptoms presented the
diagnoses were reasonable, if incorrect. By contrast, in several cases similar to the first one in which no pregnancy tests were made and no investigation of the possibility of pregnancy was carried out, the physicians were
liable for negligent misdiagnosis.[63]

The Locality Rule.   Until quite recently, as a matter of law comparison
was made of the due care exercised by the particular physician in reference to that of other physicians in his geographical area. The standard test
was "that degree of care which other physicians exercise in the same or
similar communities." The skill and knowledge of a physician were compared only to other physicians in the same geographical area on the theory
that physicians practicing in isolated rural areas, for example, should not
be expected to be as well trained and up-to-date as a physician in an

urban environment.[64] This rule does remain strictly adhered to in a few states,[65] but it has been completely abrogated in others and, in general, even where it is still theoretically accepted it has been modified.[66] In most jurisdictions today, the local standard of practice is considered only one factor presented for the jury's determination and is not in and of itself determinative of the presence or absence of negligence.[67]

Most states now make the comparison on the basis of the "professional area," those centers to which a patient can be easily transferred for treatment, as opposed to the strict geographical area.[68] There is no longer any reason why a small-town physician cannot practice at the level of competence of his urban counterpart. As early as 1940 the Supreme Court of North Dakota pointed out[69] that with the advent of rapid transportation and communication, horizons of physicians have been widened and even the physician in the smallest village now has access to all medical journals, opportunities for continuing education, and larger medical centers to which he may refer patients. The intellectual borders of the physician's community have been extended far beyond those remotely conceivable a century ago when the locality rule was devised and when it was both fair and reasonable.

Some courts in fact have adopted the position that the old interpretation of the locality rule gives rural physicians an undue and unfair advantage over urban physicians. In one decision,[70] the Supreme Court of Washington pointed out that the small-town physician should not enjoy a legal advantage not given to other small-town tort defendants and should not be able to rely on being "a little more careless" there. The decision pointed out that small-town residents who drive cars and cause automobile accidents are not allowed greater latitude for either carelessness or incompetence than urban drivers enjoy when sued for damages.

A recent decision involving alleged negligence in setting a fracture exemplifies the modern trend away from the locality rule:

> Reasons for the more narrow rule which might have obtained in times past, where transportation was difficult, medical schools and hospitals often inaccessible, and doctors licensed to practice with little or no formal training no longer have any validity. Medical practitioners frequently receive a part or all of their educations in states other than the one in which they settle to practice. . . . There are doubtless areas of medicine where knowledge of proper treatment is limited geographically by prevalence of the disease or by reason of special facilities for study, but the human race has suffered from broken bones for as long as it has been in existence.[71]

Many states which still apply the locality rule in some form to general practitioners have abrogated it completely as to specialists and assume that a specialist will adhere to national standards. Even as to general practitioners, however, the general trend is away from any geographical considerations at all and this may be anticipated to continue in the future.

The Specialist's Standard of Care. While the general practitioner is held to the standard of care of "the reasonably careful and prudent physician," a specialist is required to adhere to the standard of the "reasonably careful and prudent specialist" in his field.[72] The "average specialist in the same field at the same time," not "the average physician" is the specialist's equivalent of "the reasonable man."[73] This rule has been accepted in all jurisdictions and applied to all specialties. The Supreme Court of North Carolina succinctly stated the universal principle in a 1966 decision.[74] The suit involved an obstetrician who had failed to diagnose an ectopic pregnancy.

> A physician who holds himself out as having special knowledge and skill in the treatment of a particular organ or disease or injury is required to bring to the discharge of his duty to the patient employing him as such specialist not merely the average degree of skill possessed by general practitioners but that special degree of skill and care which physicians similarly situated who devote special study and attention to the treatment of such organ, disease, or injury ordinarily possess, regard being had to the state of scientific knowledge at the time.

Thus the standard to which a specialist must adhere is quite a bit broader than that which courts consider reasonable to expect from a nonspecialist.[75]

A resident in obstetrics and gynecology was allegedly negligent in performing a circumcision. In the course of the trial, he testified that he had performed between 600 and 800 circumcisions prior to the one which was involved in the suit. The court therefore held that he would be considered a specialist even though he had not completed his training. In comparing the standard required of a specialist with that of a general practitioner, the court stated: "It would not seem at all unreasonable to hold him to a higher standard of care than that required of a general practitioner, although he has only completed one-third of his residency. The difference between the duty owed by a specialist and that owed by a general practitioner lies not in the degree of care required but in the amount of skill required. It would stand to reason that one who had performed between 600 and 800 circumcisions would, and should, be expected to have more skill in performing such operations than would a general practitioner."[76]

The result of the differing standards of course means that in a given situation a specialist may be found negligent, whereas a general practitioner who did the same thing would not.

A pediatrician was caring for newborn twins. He ordered them placed in incubators and wrote orders for the administration of oxygen. More oxygen than he ordered was given, but he did not follow up on the orders and therefore did not discover it for some time. Both babies were almost blinded as a result of retrolental fibroplasia. Although it was clear that there would have been no damage if his orders had been correctly followed, the court found that he was liable for his delay in discovering the error. The court conceded that the community standard of practice did not indicate any custom of checking on nurses and that a general practitioner who had not investigated would not have been liable for his failure to discover the situation. The theory of the decision was that a specialist should have known that the standard practice was not adequate to protect the babies, whereas a general practitioner would not be expected to know.[77]

Even a specialist is not presumed to guarantee that his patient will get well. As long as he observes the required standard of care, neither a specialist nor a general practitioner is liable for an error of judgment.[78]

Courts in most states have now completely abandoned the locality rule in regard to the standard of care required from a specialist. The specialist is increasing assumed to adhere to national standards in his field and numerous decisions have pointed out that the usual reason a patient consults a specialist in the first place is to have his problem treated by someone who is abreast of all advances.[79]

A patient was paralyzed after receiving a spinal anesthetic during delivery. The anesthesiologist was held to a national standard of knowledge of the method of administration of an anesthetic substance, not the local one which was applied to nurses and nonspecialists who administered anesthesia.[80]

A psychiatrist gave a telephone order for discharge from the hospital of a patient shortly after the patient had an electroshock treatment. He did not see the patient. He also ordered a prescription for a heavy sedative to be taken home by the patient. He did not warn either the patient or the patient's wife about the strength of the drug. The patient was so confused and sedated when he got home that he set himself on fire with a cigarette, did not wake up, and was critically burned. The court applied the national standard, not local practice, as to the method of evaluating the patient for discharge from the hospital and in failing to warn of the properties of the drug. Conceding that either or both might not have constituted negligence if a general practitioner had done them, the court nonetheless held that a specialist was presumed to be aware of national standards and hence required to meet them.[81]

A pediatrician failed to make a standard PKU test on a newborn. The baby had the disease and the delay in diagnosis caused permanent impairment. Evidence that such tests were not made in the community's hospitals was not disputed, although the parents showed that they were in general use throughout the country. The court held the pediatrician to the national standard and found him negligent for failing to make the test.[82]

Since eminent specialists often disagree on the merits of a particular treatment, of course failure to follow majority opinion as to a given method does not presume a specialist to be negligent. The respectable minority rule within the members of the specialty will control.

Proximate Cause. Even if a patient can prove that a physician or surgeon did not meet the required standard of care, he cannot recover damages unless he can also prove that the negligence caused him injuries which would not have occurred in its absence. Even if there is clear-cut proof of misdiagnosis, for example, the patient must prove that his condition was worsened by the error before a jury can, as a matter of law, award him pecuniary compensation. This requirement of proof between cause and effect is known as the legal concept of "proximate cause."[83] No matter how negligent the physician may have been, harm must be shown to have resulted before damages may be awarded.[84]

A child had Perthes disease in one leg. The defendant, by mistake, put the cast on the other leg. No harm was proved to have occurred as a result of the error, so no damages were awarded.[85]

Where a patient is so ill or so severely injured that death may be imminent, if negligence occurs in the course of treatment and the patient dies, damages will not be awarded unless the survivors who bring the action can prove that the deceased probably would have survived in the absence of the malpractice. In many cases, particularly those in which patients have been critically injured in automobile accidents, this may in fact be quite difficult to prove.

An automobile accident victim sustained severe head injuries and was taken to the nearest hospital. The general practitioner who saw him did not attempt to give him rudimentary first aid or treat his shock. He ordered him sent by ambulance to a hospital many miles away which had a neurologist on its staff. The patient died in the ambulance. The court agreed that failure to deal with shock was negligence, but in the absence of any evidence that the head injuries would not have caused the patient's death in any event, the verdict in favor of the physician was required as a matter of law.[86]

If the initial injury or illness is not considered life-threatening, however, the causal connection between severe damage or death and negligence is correspondingly easier to demonstrate.

A patient died after a tonsillectomy. Evidence indicated that the cause of death was probably the manner in which the anesthetic had been administered. Since there is rarely a substantial likelihood of death after having one's tonsils out, the court assumed that there was a causal connection between the negligence and the death, even in the absence of exact and specific proof of what had gone wrong.[87]

Delay in diagnosis may also be negligent and yet not be established as the proximate cause of damage to the patient. In innumerable fracture cases, in particular, a great many of which involved fractured hips, the problem was not discovered until long after the original evaluation of the injury. In numbers of these cases, the physicians have submitted evidence that a high percentage of such fractures never heal properly even with an immediate diagnosis. Courts have therefore been reluctant to conclude that the delay caused the outcome.[88]

An automobile accident victim fractured a cervical vertebra. The fracture was not discovered for 2 months. A bone graft was necessary. The patient sued the physician for his failure to discover the fracture immediately. At the trial, defense witnesses testified that the treatment would have been the same and the graft would have been necessary if the fracture had been discovered immediately. Since the delay caused no worsening of the patient's condition or any difference in the type of treatment required, the court held that no proximate cause existed.[89]

Where delay does complicate the method of treating the problem or worsen the patient's condition, however, proximate cause can be proved.

A surgeon suspected from postoperative symptoms that he had left a sponge in a patient after a mastectomy. He did not Xray the area or give the patient any indication that he knew why her wound continued to drain. She moved to Great Britain and he sent her records to her new physician without any indication of his suspicions. The wound became seriously infected and another operation performed in England by another surgeon revealed the sponge. Since the infection could have been prevented by earlier removal of the sponge, the court held that there was a causal connection between the negligent failure to investigate the problem and the patient's damage.[90]

Since the sick or injured patient has something wrong at the time he consults the physician, numerous decisions involve attempts to determine if the poor result of treatment was caused by the physician's negligence or the preexisting condition of the patient. Before any patient can recover damages, he must eliminate his condition as the probable cause of the failure to recuperate fully.

An automobile accident victim had a broken leg. By mistake, the cast was put on the wrong leg and the error was not discovered for 10 days. Since the residual stiffness of the leg was as likely to have been caused by the accident itself as it was by the error, no proximate cause of damage was shown against the orthopedist.[91]

After a hysterectomy damage' was discovered involving the patient's left ureter. The patient alleged that it was sewed or crushed during surgery. Evidence for the surgeon indicated that the condition was as likely to be a natural swelling following surgical interference. The court held that no proximate cause was shown.[92]

Where there may be two or more causes for a bad result of treatment, the jury is charged with the responsibility of choosing between them. However, there must be factual evidence, not merely surmise, if negligence is alleged to have played a part in the patient's condition. Although proof beyond a reasonable doubt is not required in order to allow the patient to recover damages, he does bear the burden of proving all the facts which he alleges indicate negligence. The defendant, in most cases, does not have to prove that he was not negligent. The evidence presented by the plaintiff must be "substantial" and causation must be shown to be at least a "reasonable probability" before damages can be awarded.[93]

Proof of Negligence.   Since the standard of care in suits against medical practitioners is the reasonably careful physician or surgeon, specialist or not, in most cases the plaintiff is required to prove both that standard and the defendant's deviation from it by the use of expert testimony. Expert testimony is given by another physician. If the case involves a specialist, the expert witness is usually, but not always, from the same speciality. He explains to the court and the jury what the standard of care should be in the situation at hand and gives his opinion on how well the defendant met the standard. If a physician wishes to defend on the grounds that he was not negligent, he usually presents expert medical witnesses of his own to rebut the testimony of the plaintiff's experts. If he wishes to present an affirmative defense, that is, if he wishes not only to deny that he was negligent, but to show that the plaintiff caused the problem himself or to make some other affirmative response to the charge, he is required to bear the burden of proving such a defense and almost always would use expert witnesses to do it. Since a jury of laymen is not considered competent to know the standard of care in a complex matter of medical diagnosis or treatment or whether the defendant complied with it, as a matter of law the jury usually cannot render a verdict against a physician without expert testimony on behalf of the plaintiff indicating that the expert believes the defendant to have been negligent.

A physician's own statements contemporaneous with the event or in court on cross-examination indicating that he was negligent can in some cases be substituted for the requirement of an expert witness for the plaintiff. In some states the defendant may be asked on cross-examination what the standard of care in the situation should have been.

Some areas of negligence are so obvious that courts have held that laymen can understand them without expert help and therefore no expert witness is required. This is the doctrine of *res ipsa loquitur*—the thing speaks for itself.[94]

Where the accident is one which does not usually occur in the absence of negligence, the apparent cause was within the exclusive control of the physician, and the patient could not have contributed to the difficulties, the doctrine may be applied. This rules out most cases of misdiagnosis, since such may occur without any lack of due care.

The usual example of the use of *res ipsa loquitur* in a malpractice case is one in which a sponge or other foreign object is left in a patient's body during surgery. The jury is considered qualified, without the necessity of expert explanation, to conclude that something is wrong when a sponge is left. Furthermore, in these cases the surgeon is in control of the instrumentalities and it can hardly be the patient's fault.[95] Paralysis after spinal anesthesia is another common situation in which expert testimony is not usually necessary to prove negligence.[96] The risks of more complicated medical procedures, such as laminectomies which may result in paralysis, are usually not considered sufficiently obvious, however, to allow a jury to infer negligence from the event itself.[97]

In most states in a case in which *res ipsa loquitur* is utilized, the jury may, but is not required to, infer negligence from the mere existence of the situation.[98] In a few jurisdictions, however, presentation of a *res ipsa loquitur* situation raises a presumption of negligence, meaning that the jury is obliged to find in favor of the plaintiff unless the physician presents a satisfactory explanation other than negligence of how the event occurred.[99]

NOTES

1. Coleman v. California Friends Church, 81 P 2d 469, 470, Cal 1938.
2. Schneider v. Little Company, 151 NW 587, 588, Mich 1915.
3. Boyd v. Coca Cola Bottling Works, 177 SW 80, Tenn 1915.
4. A. P. Herbert, *Misleading Cases in the Common Law*, pp. 12–16, Methuen Press, London 1927.
5. Pike v. Honsinger, 49 NE 760, NY 1898; "The Standard of Care, Parts I, II, and III," 225 *JAMA* No. 6, page 671, August 3, 1973; 225 *JAMA* No. 7, page 791, August 13, 1973, 225 *JAMA* No. 8, page 1027, August 20, 1973.
6. Adkins v. Ropp, 14 NE 2d 727, Ind 1938.
7. Armstrong v. Svoboda, 49 Cal Rptr 701, Cal 1966.
8. Wallace v. LaVine, 97 P 2d 879, Cal 1940.
9. Kelly v. Carroll, 219 P 2d 79, Wash 1950.
10. Peddicord v. Lieser, 105 P 2d 5, Wash 1940; Gielskie v. New York, 200 NYS 2d 691, NY 1960.
11. McHugh v. Audet, 72 F Supp 394, DC Pa 1947; Dahl v. Wagner, 151 Pac 1079, Wash 1915.
12. Foxluger v. New York, 203 NYS 2d 985, NY 1960.
13. Di Fillipo v. Preston, 173 A 2d 333, Del 1961.
14. Bruce v. United States, 167 F Supp 579, DC Cal 1958; Blankenship v. Baptist Memorial Hospital, 168 SW 2d 491, Tenn 1942.
15. Baldor v. Rogers, 81 So 2d 658, Fla 1955.
16. "Alternative Medical Procedures," 212 *JAMA* No. 2, page 385, April 13, 1970.
17. Fiorentino v. Wenger, 272 NYS 2d 557, NY 1966, rev'd on other grounds, 227 NE 2d 296, NY 1967.
18. Davis v. Wilmerding, 24 SE 2d 337, NC 1943.
19. Miller v. Toles, 150 NW 118, Mich 1914.
20. "Duty to Consult," 226 *JAMA* No. 1, page 111, October 1, 1973.

21. Largess v. Tatem, 291 A 2d 398, Vt 1972.

22. Langford v. Kosterlitz, 290 Pac 80, Cal 1930.

23. Steeves v. United States, 294 F Supp 446, DC SC 1968.

24. Akins v. Novinger, 322 F Supp 1205, DC Tenn 1970; Manion v. Tweedy, 100 NW 2d 124, Minn 1959.

25. Osborne v. Frazor, 425 SW 2d 768, Tenn 1968.

26. "Duty to Refer Patient to Medical Specialist," 204 *JAMA* No. 8, page 281, May 20, 1968; "Referral to a Specialist," 211 *JAMA* No. 11, page 1911, March 16, 1970.

27. Logan v. Field, 75 Mo App 594, Mo 1898; Benson v. Dean, 133 NE 125, NY 1921.

28. Ramberg v. Morgan, 218 NW 492, Iowa 1928.

29. Manion v. Tweedy, 100 NW 2d 124, Minn 1959.

30. Wohlert v. Seibert, 23 Pa Sup Ct 213, 1903.

31. "Duty to Refer Patient to Orthopedic Specialist," 204 *JAMA* No. 7, page 249, May 13, 1968; Morgan v. Engles, 127 SW 2d 382, Mich 1964; Doan v. Griffith, 402 SW 2d 855, Ky 1966; Tveldt v. Haugen, 294 NW 183, ND 1940; Rahn v. United States, 222 F Supp 775, DC Ga 1963.

32. "Duty to Refer to Larger Hospital," 224 *JAMA* No. 12, page 1687, June 18, 1973.

33. Smith v. Mallinckrodt Chemical Works, 251 SW 155, Mo 1923.

34. Wilson v. Corbin, 41 NW 2d 702, Iowa 1950.

35. "Liability of Referring Physician," 204 *JAMA* No. 3, page 273, April 15, 1968; Wallace v. Yudelson, 224 Ill App 320, 1927; Harwick v. Harris, 166 So 2d 912, Fla 1964.

39. Arshanasky v. Royal Concourse Co., 283 NYS 2d 646, NY 1967.

37. Floyd v. Michie, 11 SW 2d 657, Tex 1928.

38. "Failure to 'Keep Up' as Negligence," 224 *JAMA* No. 10, page 1461, June 4, 1973.

39. Darling v. Charleston Community Memorial Hospital, 200 NE 2d 149, 211 NE 2d 253, Ill 1965.

40. Reed v. Church, 8 SE 2d 285, Va 1940.

41. Gresham v. Ford, 241 SW 2d 408, Tenn 1951.

42. Lundahl v. Rockford Memorial Hospital Association, 235 NE 2d 671, Ill 1968; Incollingo v. Ewing, 282 A 2d 206, Pa 1971.

43. Morgan v. Sheppard, 188 NE 2d 808, Ohio 1963.

44. Favalora v. Aetna Casualty Co., 144 So 2d 544, La 1962.

45. "Follow-up Procedures," 212 *JAMA* No. 1, page 223, April 6, 1970.

46. Miles v. Hoffman, 221 Pac 316, Wash 1923; Beck v. The German Klinik, 43 NW 617, Iowa 1889.

47. Sharpe v. Pugh, 155 SE 2d 108, NC 1967.

48. Steele v. Woods, 327 SW 2d 187, Mo 1959.

49. Krusilla v. United States, 287 F 2d 34, CCA 2, 1961.

50. Whitfield v. Daniel Construction Co., 83 SE 2d 460, SC 1954.

51. Kaiser v. Suburban Transportation System, 398 P 2d 14, Wash 1965.

52. Merrill v. Odiorne, 94 Atl 753, Maine 1915; Reis v. Reinard, 117 P 2d 386, Cal 1941; Williams v. Marini, 162 Atl 796, Vt 1932.

53. "Failure to Take Medical History," 226 *JAMA* No. 4, page 509, October 22, 1973; Burke v. Miners' Memorial Hospital, 381 SW 2d 758, Ky 1965; Hart v. Van Zandt, 399 SW 2d 791, Tex 1965.

54. Chasco v. Providence Memorial Hospital, 476 SW 2d 385, Tex 1972.

55. O'Neil v. New York, 323 NYS 2d 56, NY 1971.

56. Merchants National Bank v. United States, 272 F Supp 409, DC ND 1967.

57. Teig v. St. John's Hospital, 387 P 2d 527, Wash 1963; Williams v. Chamberlain, 316 SW 2d 505, Mo 1958; Lane v. Calvert, 138 A 2d 902, Maryland 1958.

58. Staloch v. Holm, 111 NW 264, Minn 1907.

59. Leighton v. Sargent, 27 NH 460, 1853; Eckleberry v. Kaiser Foundation Northern Hospital, 359 P 2d 1090, Ore 1961.

60. Blankenship v. Baptist Memorial Hospital, 168 SW 2d 491, Tenn 1942.

61. Hoglin v. Brown, 481 P 2d 458, Wash 1971.

62. Barnette v. Bachrach, 34 A 2d 626, CCA DC 1943.

63. Pugh v. Swiontek, 253 NE 2d 3, Ill 1969; Jarboe v. Harting, 397 SW 2d 775, Ky 1965.

64. Marchlewski v. Casella, 106 A 2d 466, Conn 1954.

65. Lockart v. Maclean, 361 P 2d 670, Nev 1961; Correia v. United States, 339 F 2d 596, CCA 1, 1964.

66. Sinz v. Owens, 205 P 2d 3, Cal 1949.

67. McGulpin v. Bessmer, 43 NW 2d 121, Iowa 1950; Blair v. Eblen, 461 SW 2d 370, Ky 1970.

68. Pederson v. Dumouchel, 431 P 2d 976, Wash 1967.

69. Tveldt v. Haugen, 294 NW 183, ND 1940.

70. Douglas v. Bussabarger, 438 P 2d 829, Wash 1968.

71. Murphy v. Little, 145 SE 2d 760, Ga 1965.

72. "Standard of Care for Specialists, Parts I and II," 226 *JAMA* No. 2, page 251, October 8, 1973; 226 *JAMA* No. 3, page 395, October 15, 1973.

73. Lewis v. Read, 193 A 2d 255, NJ 1963; Rule v. Cheeseman, 317 P 2d 472, Kans 1957; Dinner v. Thorp, 338 P 2d 137, Wash 1959.

74. Belk v. Schweizer, 149 SE 2d 565, NC 1966.

75. Carbone v. Warburton, 91 A 2d 518, 94 A 2d 680, NJ 1953; Barnes v. Bovenmyer, 122 NW 2d 312, Iowa 1963.

76. Valentine v. Kaiser Foundation Hospitals, 12 Cal Rptr 26, Cal 1961.

77. Toth v. Community Hospital at Glen Cove, 239 NE 2d 368, NY 1968.

78. Crovella v. Cochrane, 102 So 2d 307, Fla 1958; Price v. Neyland, 320 F 2d 674, CA DC 1963.

79. Hundley v. Martinez, 158 SE 2d 159, W Va 1967.

80. Brune v. Belinkoff, 235 NE 2d 793, Mass 1968.

81. Christy v. Saliterman, 179 NW 2d 288, Minn 1970.

82. Naccarato v. Grob, 180 NW 2d 788, Mich 1970.

83. "Proximate Cause, Parts I, II, and III," 218 *JAMA* No. 9, page 1479, Nov. 29, 1971; 218 *JAMA* No. 10, page 1617, Dec. 6, 1971; 218 *JAMA* No. 11, page 1761, Dec. 13, 1971.

84. Morse v. Moretti, 403 F 2d 564, CA DC 1968.

85. Reder v. Hanson, 338 F 2d 244, CCA 8, 1964.

86. Black v. Caruso, 9 Cal Rptr 634, Cal 1960.

87. Whitfield v. Whittaker Memorial Hospital, 169 SE 2d 563, Va 1969.

88. Mayo v. McClung, 64 SE 2d 330, Ga 1951; Moore v. Tremelling, 78 F 2d 821, CCA 9, 1935; Kuhn v. Banker, 13 NE 2d 242, Ohio 1938; Carrigan v. Roman Catholic Bishop, 178 A 2d 502, NH 1962.

89. Rudick v. Prineville Memorial Hospital, 319 F 2d 764, CCA 9, 1963.

90. Dietze v. King, 184 F Supp 944, DC Va 1960.

91. Deckard v. Sorenson, 2 Cal Rptr 121, Cal 1960.

92. LePrince v. McLeod, 171 So 2d 189, Fla 1965.

93. Brown v. Hughes, 30 P 2d 259, Colo 1934; Barham v. Widing, 291 Pac 173, Cal 1930.

94. "Res Ipsa Loquitur, Parts I–VII," 221 *JAMA* No. 5 page 537, July 31, 1972; 221 *JAMA* No. 6, page 633, Aug 7, 1972; 221 *JAMA* No. 10, page 1201, Sept. 4, 1972; 221 *JAMA* No. 11, page 1329, Sept. 11, 1972; 221 *JAMA* No. 12, page 1441, Sept. 18, 1972; 221 *JAMA* No. 13, page 1587, Sept. 25, 1972; 222 *JAMA* No. 1, page 121, Oct. 2, 1972.

95. Mondot v. Vallejo General Hospital, 313 P 2d 78, Cal 1957.

96. Seneris v. Haas, 291 P 2d 915, Cal 1955.

97. Gray v. Grunnagle, 223 A 2d 663, Pa 1966.

98. Huffman v. Lindquist, 234 P 2d 34, Cal 1951; Pendergraft v. Royster, 166 SE 285, NC 1932.

99. Carruthers v. Phillips, 131 P 2d 193, Ore 1942.

CHAPTER III

MISDIAGNOSIS

Misdiagnosis of a patient's condition is the cause of a substantial proportion of all malpractice suits. The others, of course, allege that the diagnosis was correct, but somehow the treatment was negligent or inadequate. Misdiagnosis may involve either of two situations: (*a*) the physician fails to discover a disease which the patient has or (*b*) he tells a patient who is free of disease that he has a condition from which he does not actually suffer.

The standard of care required in diagnosis is the use of the same degree of skill, care, and knowledge as would be used by the average prudent physician with his training in the same geographical area.[1] In one case[2] the court defined malpractice as follows:

> Malpractice may consist of lack of skill and care in diagnosis as well as in treatment. A patient is entitled to a thorough and careful examination such as his condition and attending circumstances permit with such diligence and methods as are usually approved and practiced by physicians of the same school of medicine, judgment, skill and under similar circumstance.

In any area of medicine, therefore, in which a diagnosis cannot be made with mathematical certainty and precision, which includes virtually all, the simple fact that a misdiagnosis has occurred does not impose liability.[3] A physician who has used the skill and care of those reasonably careful physicians who were discussed in Chapter II is therefore not liable if he makes a mistake or an error of judgment in a diagnosis. The question of liability usually revolves around whether or not the physician used the usual and customary inquiries, examinations, and tests to determine the nature of the difficulty, and if he did, he has a good defense to any lawsuit.

Incomplete Information from Patients.   Obviously, the physician cannot diagnose a condition properly if he has no reason whatever to suspect its existence. If the patient or some member of his family is capable of describing the illness and for some reason omits relevant information which the doctor would reasonably expect him to volunteer, the physician is not liable if he makes a mistake. He cannot be assumed to be a mind reader.

A small child ingested a quantity of aspirin. The child's father took him to the emergency room and told the attendants in the emergency room that the child had taken aspirin. They specifically told him to advise the physician of that fact. The father, however, made no mention of this and the diagnosis was that the child had flu. The child died shortly thereafter and the parents sued. The court held that the father could not recover for the alleged misdiagnosis since the physician could hardly have been blamed for not knowing what the father never told him.[4]

The mother of a 15-month old patient had the flu. In the late afternoon the father brought the child to the hospital and told the family physician who had treated the mother that morning that she was sick. He did not tell him that the child had eaten aspirin. The physician concluded that the child had the flu as her mother did. The child died. However, in this case, unlike the first one, the child was hyperventilating and exhibiting other objective symptoms of aspirin poisoning at the time she was brought into the hospital. It was therefore determined that the doctor should have been warned that some other problem might have been present.[5]

The difference in these two decisions illustrates the point of liability. A physician is not negligent if he misdiagnoses a case because material matters are withheld if his observation of the patient does not indicate to the duly careful physician that the information he has received is either inaccurate or incomplete. If his observations do not coincide with the information, however, he is responsible for making a reasonable investigation to resolve the conflict. At that point he would be, and to use the example of the second case above was, negligent if he did not pursue specific inquiries.

The physician usually has the right to assume that the patient is telling the truth in most circumstances. If a woman denies having had sexual intercourse, for example, a physician will not be liable if he does not immediately diagnose that she is pregnant.[6]

Other decisions have involved failures to take adequate history of the present illness and in several the physicians have been found liable.

A patient was diagnosed at one hospital as having a possible appendicitis. No beds were available, however, so he was transferred by ambulance to another hospital with a sheet indicating the diagnosis. The receiving physician did not read the sheet, ordered an enema, and sent him home. He was later taken to a third hospital where his ruptured appendix was removed, but he died of peritonitis. The court held that the physician was negligent in failing to read the transfer sheet or ask any questions of the patient or those with him about the diagnosis.[7]

A physician is, of course, also required to ask appropriate questions designed to elicit all necessary and relevant information and may not merely rely on information the patient volunteers. During the history-taking, the physician should be particularly on his guard to ask questions designed to elicit information on any allergies the patient may have. Not only may the information be helpful in establishing a diagnosis, but, far more importantly, it is absolutely necessary to discover if a patient is allergic to any medication which the physician may prescribe.[8]

It is now clear that it is incumbent upon a physician who is about to administer penicillin, tetanus antitoxin, or any other drug to which an allergy or other form of adverse reaction is statistically likely to inquire about any previous difficulties with the drug.[9] Where the patient who knows he has an allergy is given the medication, the physician will be liable for the reaction.[10] However, where the patient denies knowledge of any previous reaction, if questioned appropriately and such a reaction occurs, the physician is not usually liable.[11]

Of course nonnegligent failure to take a history does not render the physician liable for misdiagnosis. In an emergency situation, for example, where the patient is unconscious, the physician would be negligent in waiting until the patient could talk and tell him the circumstances of the illness or accident before he proceeded with treatment which is apparently appropriate in view of the discernible symptoms.[12]

As was discussed in the preceding chapter, whether or not a physician has an obligation to consult prior hospital records is determined by the facts of the case. Where the illness necessitating the admission is relevant to an earlier sickness, of course the physician must avail himself of such information.[13] Where the illness is totally unrelated, however, earlier charts would be considered relevant only if the reasonably careful physician or surgeon would think so and obtain them.

Furthermore, information received from another physician must be duly considered. If a physician has a patient who has been seen by another physician and he knows the diagnosis given by that physician, he must be extremely careful before he discards it.[14] However, in referral cases, the physician or surgeon to whom the patient is referred is not ordinarily required to make an independent diagnosis. The requirements of ordinary care are fulfilled by accepting the diagnosis of the referring physician, assuming that there is nothing in the patient's condition to put the specialist on notice that an erroneous diagnosis has been made.[15] If the patient's symptoms indicate that the original diagnosis might be incorrect, however, the specialist is obliged to make his own evaluation prior to initiating treatment.[16] Therefore, failure to take a history where a reasonably careful physician would do so or to make reasonable inquiries of the patient or a family member or to examine earlier records which causes a misdiagnosis as the result of incomplete data does constitute negligence if the result is damage to the patient.[17]

Careful Examinations. A patient is entitled to an ordinarily careful and thorough examination such as the circumstances, the condition of the patient, and the physician's opportunity for examination permit.[18] The most usual cause of litigation arising from misdiagnosis is the allegation that the physician did not make a careful physical examination of the patient. If this is proven, and if the patient has been damaged by this failure, the physician will be liable. In many cases, the evidence has presented indications of negligent failure to examine patients with due care.

A 7-year old boy was a diabetic. About a year after his condition was discovered, his mother discovered that his urine contained a considerable amount of glucose. Several hours later, she found the child unconscious and in a cold sweat and rushed him to the physician's house. The physician looked at him, took his pulse, and advised her that the child was in a diabetic coma. He did not make any tests or examine the boy for more than a very few minutes. The child then began to convulse and the defendant washed his stomach out with a solution of soda water. Some hours later, the boy was rushed to the hospital where he was found to be suffering from profound insulin shock. At some time prior to admission, he also had had a cerebral hemorrhage. The result was severe and permanent brain damage. The court found that the physician was liable for failure to conduct a proper examination and to make a urine test.[19]

A patient developed acute abdominal pains. She was the wife of a military officer and he took her to the base dispensary. The physician examined her for 10 minutes and told her she had a virus. He did not perform a rectal examination. She died 8 hours later of a strangulated intestine. Expert testimony for the plaintiff indicated due care would have required a rectal examination on the basis of the symptoms presented and the experts agreed that prompt surgery would have saved her life. The court held that since no condition can be validly ruled out simply because it is unlikely, due care demands much more than a cursory examination.[20]

The patient was a pregnant woman. She complained of acute stomachaches. Her physician, the defendant, made a house call and gave her a penicillin shot. A few hours later, she grew worse and fainted every time she got out of bed. Her husband called the physician again and was told to give her aspirin. The third time he called the physician, he was told to "quit bothering him." Two hours later when her husband took her to the emergency room at the nearest hospital, the patient was dead on arrival. She had bled to death from a ruptured tubal pregnancy. The court held that the physician was liable for failure to make an adequate examination on which to base his diagnosis.[21]

Decisions involving psychiatrists have alleged that misdiagnosis of a person's mental condition was made after a totally inadequate evaluative examination.

A woman's husband told a psychiatrist that she was in need of commitment. He came to the house to talk to her and gave her an injection. He made no effort to make an examination and the woman, in fact, did not know that he was a psychiatrist. When she regained consciousness, she was in his mental hospital. She was given electroshock treatments over her objections. At the trial of her suit against the psychiatrist, testimony was introduced to the fact that she had never been mentally ill. The court held that the psychiatrist was liable both for negligent misdiagnosis and for false imprisonment.[22]

Physicians should be extremely reluctant to commit a patient whom they have not seen at the time of the commitment.[23]

A 73-year old woman was committed to a mental institution on a petition signed by her husband and two physicians. One of the physicians certified that he had seen and examined her 4 days before the date of the certificate, but in fact he had seen her for the last time many months ago. The court held him liable for misdiagnosis.[24]

A duly careful physician will examine the patient with the necessary thoroughness possible under the circumstances. If a physician is attempting to give emergency treatment outside a hospital, the courts would not expect him to use the same degree of care in examination as he would be expected to employ within it. For example, if a physician sees a neighbor's child fall out of a tree and receive a serious head injury and administers attention to that, no court would fault him for not realizing that the child's arm was fractured as well. Thus, as long as the physician complies with recognized medical standards which would be exercised by similar physicians in similar circumstances, he will not be liable if he fails to discover something during the examination.

The variety of illnesses in which suits have been filed alleging negligent examination cover all fields of the practice of medicine and surgery.[25]

A patient died of a subdural hematoma a few hours after being seen and released from a hospital emergency room. The symptoms of pain and nausea should have alerted the examining physician to the necessity of a complete examination, but one was not given. The court held that his heirs had a good cause of action.[26]

A man became ill while driving his car and got out to vomit. A policeman arrested him for drunkenness. He went into spasms in his cell and the defendant was called. He saw the man twice, 5 minutes each time, and advised the police that he was drunk. The man died a few hours later. Autopsy revealed that he had no alcohol in his blood and had died of a coronary occlusion. The court found that the examination was so cursory as to constitute negligence.[27]

A patient was released from a mental hospital and killed his wife. His threats toward her and others were widely known in his home town and were the reason for his commitment. The psychiatrist believed him when he denied making the threats and did not call anyone in the home town to investigate the facts. The court found that this failure to verify any facts was sufficiently below the standard of due care as to render his diagnosis negligent.[28]

A man was bitten on the arm by a coyote. The defendant treated the bite. Some days later, his leg began to pain him and the defendant diagnosed rheumatism and prescribed treatment. He eventully had to have his leg amputated because of septicemia from the bite. The court found that the failure of the physician to examine the patient carefully was negligence. However, the court found insufficient the evidence that the septicemia could have been prevented if the proper care had been given and it thus reversed the jury's verdict for the plaintiff.[29]

Use of Appropriate Diagnostic Tests.   Failure to utilize the appropriate tests on which a correct diagnosis could be based has been the subject of innumerable decisions.[30]

The patient had a hysterectomy. During the operation, her ureter was sutured. When symptoms of kidney problems developed, the defendants did not pursue the idea noted on the chart than an IVP should be performed. They did not consult a urologist or do anything but give her antibiotics for their presumptive diagnosis of an infection. Six days after surgery, an IVP finally revealed the problem, but the ureter was damaged and the patient eventually lost her kidney.

In this case, the court reviewed the argument that an error of diagnosis need not indicate negligence, but held:

> There is a vast difference between an error of judgment and negligence in the collection of factual data essential to arriving at a proper conclusion or judgment. If the physician, as an aid to diagnosis, does not avail himself of the scientific means and facilities open to him for the collection of the best factual data from which to arrive at his diagnosis, the result is not an error of judgment, but negligence in failing to secure an adequate factual basis upon which to support his diagnosis.[31]

This is the general rule in all states. Such obvious aids to diagnosis as Xrays, pregnancy tests, and biopsies are universally recognized as so necessary and routine that failure to employ one where it might be indicative of the patient's condition is extremely likely to result in a finding of negligence.

Many cases have dealt with undiagnosed pregnancies.[32] Generally, failing to use standard tests to confirm or deny a possible pregnancy indicates a lack of due care in diagnosis.[33] If a false negative result occurs, however, the physician is not usually held liable for relying on results of the test.[34]

A woman's condition was diagnosed as a fibroid tumor. No tests for pregnancy were made. When surgery began, it was discovered that she was pregnant. The court held that the diagnosis had been negligent.[35]

A 32-year old married woman had symptoms of a fibroid tumor. Two different types of pregnancy tests were given and both were negative. When the incision was made for the hysterectomy, the surgeon discovered that she was pregnant and terminated the operation. She had a miscarriage and sued. The court held that he had used all available methods of diagnosis which would be utilized by a duly careful physician and thus he was not negligent in making his diagnosis.[36]

It should be carefully noted, however, that an ectopic pregnancy is a definite medical emergency.[37] If a physician suspects that one is possible, he is not negligent if he proceeds to surgery without waiting for pregnancy tests to be performed even if he is proved incorrect.[38]

While most decisions involve failure to recognize pregnancies, in some cases women are told that they are pregnant when in fact they have another medical problem. If tests are used, the physician is again free to rely on their results even in the case of a false positive.[39] If he has not, however, used tests, he may be liable for negligent misdiagnosis.[40]

An unmarried woman had a fibroid tumor. Without using any tests, the physician diagnosed pregnancy. He not only told her that she was pregnant, he told several of her relatives. He was found liable for negligent misdiagnosis and for breach of confidential information.[41]

Also, there may be situations in which a physician or surgeon should determine whether or not a woman is pregnant before performing surgery or treating her for an unrelated condition. In those cases as well the physician will be liable if he does not use standard tests in evaluating the patient's condition.

A patient had gall bladder disease. She was also pregnant but did not know it. No pregnancy test was made and she had a miscarriage following surgery. The court held that it was negligence to proceed with elective surgery without testing her for pregnancy, since the treatment would have been different and nonsurgical if the physician had known of her condition.[42]

Of course, in an emergency such as suspected appendicitis, a surgeon is justified in operating on a woman without waiting for the results of a pregnancy test.[43]

Failure to take Xrays can lead to misdiagnosis of a patient's condition. On the other hand, overuse of Xrays does involve certain hazards.[44] If the symptoms presented by the patient are such that it is not standard practice to order Xray films, it is not negligence if films are not made.

An elderly patient was recuperating from a stroke. He fell out of bed and fractured his hip. Xray films were taken but did not disclose the fracture. The problem remained undiagnosed for some time. The court held that there was no failure of due care. The patient's symptoms were consistent with his earlier known ailments, so his physician was not on notice that there was anything else wrong with him.[45]

A patient was in an automobile accident and the defendant saw him in the hospital emergency room. No Xray films were taken and the defendant did not realize that he had a fractured rib and punctured lung. Another physician made the diagnosis the following day. The patient proved negligence in diagnosis, but he did not prove damage because of the brief period of delay.[46]

A patient complained of back pains. A neurosurgeon and an orthopedic surgeon concurred with her physician's diagnosis of sciatica. Several weeks later, she broke her leg. Surgery was necessary. At that time, it was discovered that she had osteomyelitis. She sued on the grounds that no Xrays had been taken at the time of her complaints, but the court found that in the absence of any showing that on the basis of the symptoms presented a reasonable doctor would have taken Xrays, she could not recover.[47]

Thus it appears that a physician is not liable in negligence for failing to take Xrays in a given situation unless it is shown that, according to the usual practice in his locality, the circumstances presented were such as to require the doctor, in the exercise of the skill and care with which he was charged, to make an Xray examination.[48]

Hip and leg fracture cases constitute a large number of the suits alleging that failure to make Xrays led to complications.[49] Failure to take Xrays for a suspected hip fracture after an elderly person has a fall may very easily result in a misdiagnosis. Whether or not failing to discover the condition constitutes negligence depends on the circumstance.

An elderly man already incapacitated by a stroke had a fall. His physician did not take Xrays. Eleven days later, at his family's insistence, he was taken to the hospital. Routine Xrays were made there and the fracture was discovered. The court held that the failure to take Xray films was negligence of the variety that did not require proof by expert testimony. The opinion stated that with a patient of this age, any physician should realize that a fracture was more than possible after a fall. It further held that negligence in the collection of factual data on which a diagnosis is based is not "an error of judgment," but negligence.[50]

The same conclusion might be applied to many cases involving children.

A small child fell down some steps. He complained of pains in his knees, so Xrays were taken. Further Xrays would have shown his hip fracture, which went undiagnosed for some time. The court held that a cause of action existed and therefore the question was sent to the jury.[51]

Another frequent source of litigation is failure to Xray head injuries.[52]

A 16-year old boy was hit by a truck. He was taken to the emergency room. Xrays were made, but no one even looked at the back of his head, which was the area where the blow was received. The physician did not check his vital signs and told his mother to take him home. He died as a result of a skull fracture. It was held that the diagnosis was negligent.[53]

A patient was found unconscious and clad only in his underwear. He was lying on the lawn of the hotel at which he had been staying. He was taken to the hospital where no medical history or Xrays were taken. The intern told police he was drunk and the patient was removed to the jail. He was found dead in his cell 4 hours later. Autopsy revealed a massive skull fracture. The court found that dismissing him from the hospital without Xrays was negligence.[54]

A patient fainted in a service station and hit his head on the cement floor. He had seen the defendant surgeon about a year prior to the incident with complaints of fainting spells. The defendant assumed that this was another attack and made no Xrays, although a very incomplete history of the accident was given to him. By the time his wife picked him up at the hospital, the patient was completely incoherent. She took him to another hospital where Xrays were taken and a diagnosis of intracranial clots was made. He died before treatment could be started. The court held that an adequate history of the incident would have put the defendant on notice of the seriousness of the problem. Therefore he was negligent for having failed to realize that an Xray was necessary.[55]

Several cases, most of them quite old, deal with failure to use Xrays to locate and assist in removing a foreign body from the eye.[56] The rarity of these cases in recent years would seem to indicate that it has become far more standard practice to use Xrays in this situation.

A patient told a physician that he had been hit in the eye by a broken spring and that there was something in it. No Xrays were made and the physican diagnosed a scratch on the cornea. Another physician took Xrays and discovered a piece of steel in the eye. Expert testimony indicated that a complaint of that nature should have required taking diagnostic Xrays, and the physician was liable.[57]

Another patient was hit in the eye by a nailhead. The physician examined the eye, using only a magnifying glass, and found a corneal laceration. He instructed the patient to wash his eye out. The patient finally consulted another physician, who discovered the object. By that time, however, the patient had lost all sight in the affected eye. The court held that the physician should have suspected the existence of a foreign body and taken Xrays to help locate it, particularly since he had an Xray machine available in his office for immediate use. He knew or should have known that prompt diagnosis would have alleviated the problem.[58]

Diagnosis of tuberculosis is, of course, another area in which Xrays are vital. In most cases where tuberculosis is not discovered, Xrays have been made but are either apparently unread or misinterpreted.[59]

A patient lived in the house with several family members who had active tuberculosis, of which her physician knew. He did make Xrays and concluded that she had "smouldering tuberculosis," but he did not tell her. Several months later she became acutely ill. She sued and it was held that she should have had immediate treatment. The physician was liable.[60]

Where Xrays have been taken for any reason and indicate the possible existence of tuberculosis, the radiologist is obliged to report that fact to the physician, regardless of the primary purpose of the Xrays. The physician is thereafter obliged to act on the report.[61] He must advise the patient of the possibility of the disease and order further diagnostic tests which would confirm or disprove the radiologist's opinion.

Thus, in many types of illness or injury, Xrays are an essential part of the data required for a proper diagnosis. Where such a situation exists, failure to obtain films thus becomes a question of negligence. Few, if any, courts would consider it to be an "error of judgment" in any of the situations discussed above.

Where a reasonably careful physician or surgeon would conclude, on the basis of the patient's symptoms, that a biopsy would be indicated, failure to advise that the procedure be performed may constitute negligence.[62] Failure to recognize a malignant neoplasm where one is in fact present can, of course, result in the patient's death or serious incapacity. For that reason, when these cases occur, either because no biopsy was performed or because a biopsy was performed, but the report of the results mistakenly indicated that no malignancy was present, the juries' verdicts tend to be extremely high.

A dentist suffered from radiation dermatitis. In 1958 the defendant performed a biopsy and reported that no malignancy existed. In 1962 a malignancy of the lymph node was discovered, and shortly after it was discovered that the patient had a malignant growth on his finger. Finally, cancer was discovered in his armpit. His entire arm was amputated and, with it, his livelihood. After the first malignancy was identified, it was discovered that the diagnosis of the 1958 biopsy had been in error. The malignancy had been in existence at that time. The plaintiff received substantial damages.[63]

A patient had numerous ailments, including several lumps on her neck. The defendant examined the lumps in September 1964, but did not consider a biopsy necessary. The patient consulted another physician in December 1965, after having seen the defendant at intervals during the year. The second physician ordered an immediate biopsy. At that time, a diagnosis of lympho-sarcoma was made. Expert testimony at the trial indicated that failure to have arranged for a biopsy at the time the lumps were first examined constituted negligence. Further testimony indicated that if a prompt diagnosis had been made, the treatment of the condition would have been far easier.[64]

A number of these cases have involved misdiagnosis of breast cancer.[65] An error in the evaluation of a biopsy can have extremely serious consequences when any disease is present, but where there is evidence that due care was not used in making the diagnosis that a breast malignancy is not present, the consequences to the patient are very likely to be exceedingly serious.

A patient had a lump in her arm. A biopsy was performed at the defendant hospital in 1963. The specimen was reported to be nonmalignant. In 1966, she developed a lump in her breast and another in her arm. Not only were those diagnosed as malignant, but reexamination of the slides from the first biopsy showed that an error had been made and the malignancy had existed at that time. She recovered extremely heavy damages.[66]

On the other hand, an error in the evaluation of a biopsy which results in a serious and unnecessary operation or an incorrect diagnosis that an inoperable malignancy exists also virtually guarantees heavy damages for the plaintiff. There are obvious serious physical and emotional consequences to the patient of being told incorrectly that malignancy is present. While presumably it is "better" to diagnose a malignancy which does not exist than it is to fail to discover one which actually does exist, in either case the patient unquestionably has been harmed by the error.

During an operation to discover whether or not the patient had cancer of the breast, the immediate report from the pathologist was that the frozen section removed from the breast was malignant. Twenty minutes later, a corrected diagnosis that no malignancy was present and that the previous one had been in error was rushed to the operating room. The defendant, however, continued the surgery and finished removing the breast. Expert testimony for the plaintiff indicated that surgery could have been halted after the second report was received, although the defendant claimed that the operation was almost completed by the time the error was discovered. The surgeon was found negligent.[67]

A patient was told, on the basis of laboratory reports, that he had Hodgkin's disease. When his physician treated him for 10 years and realized that his patient continued to feel fine and have no further symptoms, he checked on the tests. The laboratory's original diagnosis was established to have been incorrect. The patient sued the laboratory, but the court held that the statute of limitations had run.[68]

A physician may also be likely to be found negligent if he performs radical surgery for a suspected malignancy without ordering a biopsy first, except in a very serious emergency situation. If his opinion is wrong and the surgery later proves to have been unnecessary, he will be found negligent.

A hysterectomy was performed without a biopsy to determine the exact nature of the plaintiff's illness. There was no pathologist in the community and, although there was no emergency, the defendant did not advise his patient to go to another city where one would be available. The hysterectomy itself was performed in an allegedly negligent manner. Expert testimony for the plaintiff at the trial indicated that there had been no reasonable medical evidence of cancer at the time of the surgery. The hysterectomy had been unnecessary. She received substantial damages.[69]

Other types of surgical tests are also necessary in some cases to make a proper diagnosis of the patient's complaint. Where the test carries serious inherent risk, it becomes a matter of medical judgment whether or not the patient, whose condition is best known by the physician, should be subjected to the procedure. Therefore, the more complicated and dangerous the test may be, the less likely it is that a court will find that a physician was negligent in failing to perform it. If, however, the patient's condition is quite serious, of course a physician would be much more likely to be held liable for failing to have ordered a fairly dangerous test than if the condition was no more serious, at worst, than the test itself.

A patient's executor sued on the grounds that failure to perform an arteriogram had been negligence. The patient had accompanied his younger brother to the hospital for suturing. He fainted in the emergency room while his brother was being sewed up and hit his head on the floor. He was examined by a general practitioner and a neurologist. The following morning his condition became much worse. The neurologist prepared to perform an arteriogram and called a neurosurgeon, but the patient developed breathing difficulties and the procedure was not performed. Several hours later, the neurosurgeon operated but found no evidence of a hematoma. The patient died. Autopsy revealed the presence of a large epidural hematoma. There was evidence that it would have been discovered if the arteriogram had been performed. The patient's survivors sued on the grounds that failure to perform the arteriogram was negligent and caused the death of the patient. The court recognized the fact that in a small percentage of cases an arteriogram has adverse effects and held that the physicians were well within the reasonable exercise of their professional judgment to conclude that this was one of them. Therefore, the court found that in this case failure to perform an arteriogram was not negligence and that there was no liability on the part of the physicians.[70]

In an emergency situation, misdiagnosis which leads to the conclusion that surgery is not required may also result in liability. For example, there have been several cases alleging negligence in failure to discover the necessity of performing a Cesarean section or in unduly delaying the decision to perform one, by which time the patient or the baby had sustained damages.[71]

A patient in her mid-30's had had two stillborn babies. She was determined to have her third child by Cesarean and the osteopath who managed her prenatal care agreed. He told her that he would arrange for an obstetrician to perform the surgery. He did arrange for the obstetrician to deliver the baby, but failed to tell him that he felt a Cesarean was indicated. The baby was born dead after an extremely lengthy labor. Expert testimony indicated that the baby would probably have lived if the Cesarean had been performed. The osteopath was held liable for damages for breach of contract as well as for negligence. The court held, after considering the protracted discussions on the subject between the parties during the pregnancy, that the agreement to provide a surgeon to perform the operation was an essential element of that particular contract for prenatal care.[72]

A woman was a diabetic. Her baby, which was extremely large, died during delivery. She sued the physician, and the court held that she stated a good cause of action. Expert testimony indicated that any diabetic mother ran a very high risk of having an abnormally large baby. The defendant should have been aware that the possibility existed and prepared for the fact that a Cesarean might well be necessary.[73]

Where placentas have detached before delivery, juries quite frequently return verdicts indicating that it is negligent to fail to perform a Cesarean and that the diagnosis should have been obvious to the attending physician.[74]

In short, under some circumstances, failure to perform a Cesarean may violate normal standards of skill and care which a duly careful physician should employ in treating his obstetrical patients.[75]

The same principle of liability would be applicable to a misdiagnosis which prevented the necessary performance of any emergency surgery. For example, failure to diagnose appendicitis might well be negligent if standard practice was not followed and the delay caused a rupture and peritonitis.[76] However, several decisions have indicated that no liability will ensue for misdiagnosis of appendicitis if standard tests are run and normal results are obtained.[77]

Failure to perform an electrocardiogram is not usually considered to be as clearly negligent as is failure to perform an Xray in the case of a suspected fracture.[78] However, where there is a known heart defect, failure to take an electrocardiogram might be considered negligence if objective symptoms of heart disease are present.

A workman sued his employer's physician. In 1943 when he was examined at the preemployment physical, the physician realized that he had a heart murmur which indicated the existence of a lesion. He was not told about it and was approved for heavy work. In 1948 he became incapacitated and a firm diagnosis of cardiovascular syphilis was made. He did not recover damages, however, because all his testimony supported the defendant's contention that the heart condition was progressive and the result would have been the same whether he had worked or not.[79]

A physician who fails to use ordinary laboratory tests in diagnosing a patient's condition may also be liable for negligence. There are an infinite variety of suits in which allegedly negligent misdiagnoses occurred as the result of failure to use or act upon routine laboratory tests.

A pediatrician did not routinely make PKU tests of newborn infants. One baby was permanently brain-damaged before his condition, which would have been disclosed by the test, was discovered when he was several months of age. It was held that the pediatrician was liable for the misdiagnosis. The test was in general use throughout the country, was simple, and was accurate and he was negligent in having failed to avail himself of it as a routine diagnostic measure.[80]

The patient came to the physician with a swelling on his knee and other symptoms. He examined the patient's knee, took his history, and then gave him an injection. The patient became quite ill and expert evidence showed that the usual practice in that area was to make an Xray study, a blood test, and a biopsy. All of them were routinely required in similar situations by physicians in that area; therefore the court upheld the jury's finding that the physician had been negligent.[81]

In several cases physicians were liable for misdiagnosis of a condition which was actually diabetes.[82]

A patient was diagnosed as having the flu. The physician ordered his admission to the hospital but did not see him for 20 hours. When he finally ordered blood and urine tests to be made, the patient was already critically ill and died almost immediately thereafter. When an autopsy was performed, the cause of death was given as severe diabetic acidosis. There was expert testimony for the plaintiff that tests should have been ordered immediately on admission to the hospital in view of the symptoms presented and that failure to recognize the existence of diabetes was the proximate cause of the patient's death.[83]

After a routine physical examination, a patient's urine test report indicated diabetes, but the physician apparently did not read it. Several months later, the patient became unconscious, he was admitted to a hospital, and his condition was discovered. Shortly thereafter he had a series of strokes. The court conceded that the physician had been negligent in failing to diagnose the diabetes, but held that no causal connection had been proved between the failure to treat the patient for diabetes and the onset of the strokes.[84]

Of course, as was pointed out in the preceding chapter at some length, a physician has an obligation to keep up with the advances in medicine. If he has failed to use tests, procedures, or other aids to diagnosis which are in current use at the time he sees the patient because he is unaware of their existence or availability, he would, of course, be liable for his failure to do so.

Erroneous interpretations of laboratory tests may also result in liability for the primary physician.

A 13-year old girl was in a hospital under the care of the defendant. Routine urine tests were made, but there was an erroneous report that her urine was negative for glucose. Relying on the report, the defendant treated her for anorexia nervosa. She died and it was discovered that she died of an undiagnosed diabetic condition. A cause of action was allowed.[85]

A physician was caring for a newborn baby. He knew that the mother was Rh— and that the father was Rh+. When the baby was born, it developed jaundice and tests were carried out. The results of the tests were incorrect and indicated that nothing was wrong. The physician did not order a retest, a new hemoglobin test, or a Vandenburg test. Within a week, symptoms of irreversible brain damage were obvious. Expert witnesses for the plaintiff testified that on the basis of what the physician knew before the child was born about the blood incompatibility and on the basis of the obvious symptoms presented by the baby, he should have realized that the results of the tests were in error. He was therefore responsible for further investigation. The court held that a physician will be liable for a mistaken diagnosis when that mistake results from a failure to comply with the recognized standards of medical care and upheld the jury's verdict for the plaintiff.[86]

If, as in the preceding cases, objective symptoms indicate that there is a possibility of error in laboratory test results, a physician who does not investigate this conflict may himself be liable. If, however, the results of the tests are reasonably consonant with his understanding of the patient's condition, if an error is made, the hospital and the physician in charge of the laboratory would presumably be the only parties liable. The treating physician usually would not.

Regardless of the primary physician's liability, however, misinterpretation of test results which causes a misdiagnosis of the patient's condition will probably constitute negligence on the part of the physician who made the error if the patient suffers damage. Liability would be the same if the report erroneously indicated that a serious disease was present when it was not or if an actual disease was not discovered.[87]

It is also clearly negligence on the part of the physician making the test report or hospital employees to fail to transmit promptly and properly the medical information and test results to the primary physician.[88] If there is a delay in transmission of the findings to the primary physician or he never receives the test results at all and the patient is thereby damaged, the hospital and the physicians responsible will undoubtedly be liable.

A radiologist did not report a shadow on an Xray film which would have indicated the presence of a kidney stone. At the time the Xray films were taken, the patient's complaints included a backache and a cut on the back of her neck, and the Xray films were taken to assist the physician in the diagnosis of those two problems. A shadow was apparent in the area of her right kidney, but the radiologist made no report of it since it was outside the scope of the information requested of him. Several months later, the patient developed a kidney stone which was surgically removed. Several years later, the entire kidney had to be removed. The patient sued the hospital which employed the radiologist. Her theory was that early diagnosis of the presence of the kidney stone would have prevented the subsequent difficulty. The court held that failure to transmit the information about the shadow had been a proximate cause of the worsening of the subsequent kidney disease, and the radiologist was therefore negligent.[89]

A patient collected $300,000 in damages for false imprisonment from a governmental hospital. He had been unwarrantedly incarcerated in a mental hospital for 19 years because of incomplete records. The patient was supposed to have been released in 1949, but the psychiatrist in charge of his case never made the appropriate notations on his chart so that the discharge could be processed. All the psychiatric notes indicated that the patient was severely disturbed and he was classified as "very hostile" because he kept insisting that he was hospitalized by mistake. The court held that failure to keep proper notes of his case and transmit them properly was the sole and only cause of his continued medically unwarranted detention. During the years in the hospital, he had been disciplined and beaten by hospital personnel and other patients, apparently for doggedly insisting that he was supposed to be released. The courts found "the grossest negligence" in his treatment.[90]

A child had had a biopsy performed. There was considerable question about the diagnosis and a definite difference of opinion among the pathologists who saw the slides. The defendant was to have had the slides sent to another laboratory where they would be read by experts on the type of malignancy in question. The slides were not sent until months after the patient's mother was assured that they had been. The child died shortly thereafter, and the court upheld a finding of negligence in failing to transmit the slides promptly.[91]

While on vacation a woman injured her ankle. The defendant treated her on the basis of a radiologist's report that her ankle was sprained and that no fracture was present. When she was released from the hospital, she went home and was treated by her family physician after telephone discussions with the defendant. After her departure the radiologist called the defendant and told him that he had made a mistake and that the ankle was fractured. This information was not transmitted to the family physician. Her ankle was permanently deformed and the defendant was held liable. The court found that he had been negligent in failing to transmit the corrected diagnosis.[92]

Therefore, when laboratory tests are necessary for a diagnosis, it is of utmost importance, not only in terms of the patient's welfare, but in terms of the legal liability of the hospital or physicians involved that all information pertaining to test results and all other medical records be kept up-to-date and transmitted properly to those persons who are supposed to receive them. Failure to do so may result in very serious consequences to the patient and a resultant finding of negligence against those who caused the delay.

In summation, a physician is not negligent simply because he has not made a correct diagnosis of his patient's illness or injury. The general rule is that a doctor is not liable for an error of judgment in diagnosis as long as he has complied with recognized medical standards and used due care. If he has performed or ordered all the accepted tests and procedures which a reasonably careful physician would consider appropriate, has taken into consideration all the relevant symptoms, and has made a careful evaluation of the patient's past and present illness history, he is not legally negligent simply because he is wrong. For example, once he has received all possible test results, there may be two, three, or even more plausible, reasonable explanations for the patient's condition. Choosing a differential diagnosis at that point has become solely a matter of medical evaluation and judgment. If the physician is wrong, he will not be liable.

The mother of a 5-year old child told a surgeon she was sure her child had appendicitis. The defendant examined the child and ordered laboratory tests and Xrays. Because the child's throat was very red and her white blood count was not elevated, he considered the possibility of appendicitis, but concluded that she had tonsillitis and prescribed accordingly. The child's appendix ruptured and her parents sued. The court held that the error was an honest mistake of judgment, not negligence. All available data had been collected and considered. The court pointed out that a physician is not held to insure the correctness of his diagnosis.[93]

A child had his appendix out. While recuperating, he developed chicken pox. The combination of symptoms masked the fact that he had developed peritonitis. The court held that the physician was not negligent in failing to differentiate the peritonitis from the "normal" symptoms of the other two conditions and that he had used due care and good judgment in caring for the child.[94]

Courts recognize that medicine is still as much of an art as it is a science and they also recognize that it is not possible to make diagnoses of many illnesses with absolute precision. In a given case, it may well be that no physician, no matter how eminent, could have made the correct diagnosis or, even if the correct diagnosis had been made, that the patient would have had a better chance for recovery. Therefore, as one court has said, "A physician is not liable in negligence for a misdiagnosis unless it was clear that the course pursued was clearly against the course recognized correct by the profession generally."[95]

Proximate Cause.   Before a physician can be liable for misdiagnosis, it must be established that the misdiagnosis in fact caused damage to the patient. Even if the physician's diagnosis is incorrect, his treatment may be as suitable for the actual ailment as for the one he incorrectly diagnosed. Since the patient is not only required to show that the misdiagnosis constituted legal negligence, but also that its effects damaged him in some way, no recovery will be allowed if the treatment is right for the wrong reasons.

A patient's broken hip was diagnosed as a strained muscle. The physician ordered complete bedrest. Experts testified that complete bedrest was also the accepted treatment for hip fractures. The plaintiff could therefore not prove that he had been injured and no damages were allowed.[96]

A workman injured his foot on the job. The defendant took Xrays and told him no fracture was present. He diagnosed a sprain, strapped the foot, and told him to use crutches. A year later at an examination for Workmen's Compensation, Xrays revealed fractures which had healed in correct alignment. The patient sued, but the physician was not found liable. Expert testimony indicated that the treatment given was proper for fractures as well as sprains.[97]

Of course, where a misdiagnosis is not followed by appropriate treatment, the patient probably will be damaged. Most of the cases where the treatment was considered appropriate are those in which a fracture was not discovered, usually due to the fact that no Xray was made. If bedrest is prescribed for a fracture, generally speaking, the patient can show no particular damage.

It is clear, however, that compensable injury in a misdiagnosis case may consist only of extension of the period of pain and suffering or other disability. The physician may be liable even though the patient eventually recovers completely if his negligent error prolonged the recuperative period of the patient.[98] In other words, before a patient can recover damages for misdiagnosis, he is obliged to show that he would have received better results in a shorter length of time from proper treatment than he did from the treatment prescribed by the defendant.[99]

A delay in diagnosis, particularly in acute surgical cases, may, of course, make the patient's condition far more serious than it would have been if it had been properly diagnosed, and therefore in these cases the question of damages is not usually hard to establish. Such cases, for example, involve fairly clear-cut symptoms of appendicitis where a misdiagnosis was made and the patient very soon thereafter developed peritonitis.

However, a surgeon who concludes in good faith that a patient's condition will be best served by a "wait and see" approach or a physician who adopts the same attitude toward the decision to send the patient to a surgeon is not negligent. The criteria are the same as are required in any other professional activity—the reasonable standard of care. As long as such a delay occurs under circumstances where the reasonable practitioner would do the same thing, no negligence is present even if damage results. In fact, it should always be remembered that rushing into surgery might well expose either the surgeon or the referring physician to a liability action if the operation turned out to be unnecessary.[100] However, where the reasonable practitioner would have performed immediate surgery, a physician is negligent if he fails to do so.

A 10-month old boy fell from a highchair and hit his head. He vomited for several days and one of his eyes crossed. The general practitioners who had taken care of him told his mother that he had a virus. She talked to them numerous times and they kept assuring her that there was nothing really wrong with the child. When he showed no improvement, she took him to a pediatrician in another town who immediately diagnosed a subdural hematoma. Surgery followed to correct the condition, but the child was permanently blind in one eye. Expert testimony indicated that prompt diagnosis of the problem would have saved the child's eye. Plaintiff's experts also testified that a general practitioner should have recognized a situation in which intracranial pressure was present.[101]

As long as the doctor has, however, availed himself of standard diagnostic procedures and still has not absolutely pinpointed the diagnosis, a delay of surgery is not likely to result in a finding of negligence.

It should be further noted that sometimes a physician is obliged to refrain from taking action. Where the treatment for a condition is more serious than the condition itself, the physician would be remiss in his professional obligation if he pursued the matter.

A neurosurgeon diagnosed a patient's condition as a brain tumor. The patient had been referred by her ophthalmologist. The neurosurgeon performed a craniectomy in order to locate the tumor. This operation resulted in paralysis of the patient, but did not locate the tumor. A year later, another neurosurgeon located the tumor which was in a position where it would have been inoperable in any case because the patient could not have survived the surgery. In a suit against the first surgeon, the court held that although the defendant had not located the tumor, he could not have removed it if he had. In spite of the fact that the patient had authorized its removal before surgery, indications to a surgeon that the authorized procedure would kill the patient obliges him not to pursue that course of action. In this case and in many others, of course, the duty of care is to inaction.[102]

In these cases, of course, the patient can show no proximate cause. If the correct diagnosis had been made, the treatment still would have not been possible because of the high risk of harm to the patient which would have ensued if effective treatment had been carried out.

Diagnosis of Non-Existent Disease.   The foregoing portion of this chapter has dealt with the physician's failure to discover a genuine medical problem. He either does not think that there is anything wrong with the patient or he recognizes that a medical problem exists, but diagnoses it as being of another type. The converse of this situation occurs when a physician tells a healthy patient that he is suffering from a disease. The effects of this type of misdiagnosis are usually not as severe. Although damages have been very large where unnecessary surgery has been performed on patients, it is far better in terms of legal liability to tell a patient that she has cancer and remove her breast when she does not, than fail to discover that she has cancer in time to save her life.[103] There seem to be almost as many cases where physicians have concluded that patients suffered from serious diseases which they did not actually have as there are cases where a serious disease was overlooked. However, the same rules of due care apply.

A surgeon is theoretically liable for "unnecessary surgery," but there are very few successful actions in this area.[104] If the diagnosis has not been negligent, surgery is not usually considered legally "unnecessary." By this it is meant that it is perfectly evident to both surgeons and lawyers that frequently the preoperative diagnosis is not confirmed when surgery is performed. The patient's problem may well be caused by an entirely different illness altogether. The occurrence of this situation does not indicate negligence on the part of the surgeon unless he has not used standard procedures and tests in arriving at his preoperative diagnosis.[105]

A child choked on peanuts and lost her voice. The surgeon hospitalized her and waited 3 days to see if spontaneous improvement occurred and then operated. He did not find the peanuts, and the child died of unavoidable postoperative complications. In finding that the surgeon had not been negligent in deciding to perform the operation, the appellate court concluded that a surgeon, in determining if an operation is necessary, can only be guided by such information as he can gain without the operation. He is not liable for an honest mistake; he is only liable if he is unskilled in his diagnosis. In other words, the surgeon did not become liable when, upon performance of the surgery, his preliminary diagnosis was discovered to be incorrect. He had used acceptable skill and care in arriving at it.[106]

An 8-year old patient was seen by her pediatrician after a minor accident. On examination, he discovered a swelling in her side and suspected a hernia. He advised the patient's mother of this possibility and recommended that the child be seen by a surgeon. The surgeon concurred with the pediatrician's diagnosis and advised surgery. After the operation had commenced, the presence of a fatty pad, but no hernia, was revealed. The surgeon then obtained the mother's permission to check for a hernia on the other side of the abdomen, but nothing was found there either. No damage to the child resulted except for two small scars. At the trial, the surgeon admitted that his original diagnosis had been proven incorrect, but denied that he had been negligent. He contended that his preoperative conclusions were reasonable under the circumstances, and pointed out that they had been agreed to by the pediatrician. He also testified that fatty pads of that type were extremely rare. The trial court directed a verdict for the surgeon and an appeals court upheld it. The opinion of the appeals court indicated that an incorrect diagnosis cannot be held to be negligence without a clear showing of failure to use due care.[107]

Where the diagnosis of either a medical or surgical condition is not based on proper tests, however, and the patient is hospitalized, operated on, or subjected to mental anguish, and in fact has no disease at all or a less serious disease than that diagnosed, the physician may very well be liable. Quite a few cases in the area have involved unjustified diagnoses of breast cancer, as was discussed in an earlier portion of this chapter. Tuberculosis has also been the subject of misdiagnosis in one very famous case.

A job applicant was referred to the defendant physician for a preemployment physical examination. There was a diagnosis of active tuberculosis, so employment was denied. After submitting to exhaustive tests elsewhere, it was established that the patient in fact did not have and had never had tuberculosis. The court allowed recovery.[108]

Some eye operations present peculiar problems. A recent cataract surgery decision illustrated the surgeon's dilemma. If he advises surgery when others might regard it as unnecessary, he runs a legal risk; on the other hand, if he refuses to operate when others might have gone ahead, he would run an equal risk.

A surgeon advised a patient that he would go blind if he did not have cataract surgery. Apparently, however, he did not make clear to the patient what the postoperative restrictions would be. The patient checked into the hospital and found out how much would be involved. He left the hospital and went home. He sued the physician for deceit for advising an unnecessary operation. At the trial several expert witnesses for the plaintiff testified that he did not have cataracts to begin with and implied strongly that no reputable physician would have advised surgery. Others testified for the defense. The court held that since these were two opposing medical schools of thought on the subject, the jury of laymen could not be asked to choose between them. No recovery was allowed.[109]

Unnecessary surgery which results from either a negligent diagnosis or a mistake will render the surgeon liable.

A patient was admitted to the hospital with a complaint of injuries to his foot. While he was there, a scalene node biopsy was performed. He alleged that the operation had been totally unnecessary because no neck or chest ailment ever existed or was complained of that required any surgery at all. The appellate court held that he stated a cause of action.[110]

Several cases have involved chart mix-ups which resulted in operations on the wrong patient. In all cases of mistaken identity, liability is automatic and the only question is the amount of damages.[111] At the very least, a hospital is presumed to have an adequate system of patient identification. Surgeons are required to make absolutely sure that they are performing the right operation on the right patient.

Extremely high verdicts have been allowed by juries in several recent cases involving hysterectomies which were later proved to have been unnecessary.

The patient had an ovarian infection and a cyst. In attempting to alleviate the problem, a surgeon performed a hysterectomy. The patient developed peritonitis following the operation. At the trial several gynecologists testified that the surgery should not have been performed while the infection was acute and that the infection should have been treated with antibiotics. Most of the plaintiff's medical experts also testified the condition might well have been cured by drugs and that surgery might not have been necessary. The court held that a question of fact was presented and should be determined by the jury.[112]

After a hysterectomy was performed, the pathologist found the organs to have been normal. In addition to the fact that the surgery was allegedly unnecessary, a fistula had developed. The patient collected heavy damages since the court also found that she had not in fact ever consented to a hysterectomy.[113]

Because of the implications of removal of the reproductive organs, unnecessary hysterectomies, where proved to have been based on negligent misdiagnoses, generally have resulted in very high verdicts.[114]

On the other hand, recovery of damages for unnecessary appendectomies is quite rare.[115] Because it is almost impossible to make an absolutely certain diagnosis that appendicitis is present and any delay may result in a rupture of the appendix and consequent peritonitis, the general medical opinion appears to be that when in doubt, surgery should be performed. There is an obvious difference between removal of the useless appendix and the removal of reproductive organs or some other part of the body, aside from the fact that the inherent risk of an appendectomy is far lower than that of most other types of surgery. It is generally considered perfectly proper to perform an appendectomy for diagnostic purposes. There are, therefore, frequent cases in which the appendicitis is discovered to be less than acute, or in some of them, totally nonexistent. No recovery for unnecessary surgery for appendectomy cases in and of itself can be found. However, there are several cases in which the diagnosis of appendicitis followed by an appendectomy turned out to be incorrect and the patient had another disease which went untreated as the result of the appendicitis diagnosis.

A child whose appendix was removed upon presentation of the usual symptoms eventually was discovered to have had an intestinal obstruction from which peritonitis eventually resulted. In suing for damages for misdiagnosis, the plaintiff's parents charged that the diagnosis of the plantiff's appendicitis was negligent in and of itself and the surgery which followed was negligent because it was unnecessary. In denying liability, however, the court held that with the patient's symptoms as they were, the diagnosis was reasonable and well within the range of reasonable medical judgment.[116]

A patient thought she was pregnant and she appeared at her family doctor's office with the symptoms of appendicitis. He correctly diagnosed the fact that she had appendicitis, but incorrectly told her that she was not pregnant. She told him that she would not submit to surgery if she were. The surgeon correctly removed her inflamed appendix, but established during surgery that she was pregnant. She made a normal recovery and eventually delivered a normal child. In finding the physician was not guilty of malpractice in misdiagnosing her pregnancy, the court held that his diagnosis complied with the normal standards of practice which could be expected. Since her appendicitis could have become acute in the later stages of her pregnancy resulting in very serious consequences to both herself and her baby, she had no cause for complaint.[117]

Iatrogenic Disorders. Iatrogenic disorders are psychiatric complications caused solely by the diagnosis of the physician.[118] In other words, a patient who has been incorrectly informed that he or she is suffering from a dread disease develops psychological or psychiatric symptoms as a result and is in fact made ill. In the rare cases where this can be proved, recovery can be found.

A patient was suffering from bursitis in her right shoulder. She received a series of Xray treatments from the defendant radiologists. After the third treatment, she experienced nausea. She told one of the radiologists about it before he administered the next treatment. He prescribed certain pills which she took. At the conclusion of the sixth treatment, she still had a pain in her right shoulder and one of the radiologists suggested that if the pain continued, she should come back again. The pain persisted and 3 days later the patient returned. After the Xray treatments her shoulder began to itch, it turned pink, then red, and blisters formed. Scabs formed and lasted several months and one lasted several years. Her condition was eventually diagnosed as chronic radiodermatitis. She consulted her attorneys and was prepared to file suit against the radiologists for her dermatitis. Her attorneys sent her to a dermatologist for examination. Unfortunately for the radiologists, the dermatologist advised the patient to have her shoulder checked every 6 months because the area of the burn might become cancerous. She then enlarged the malpractice suit and asked for damages in case she developed cancer. She introduced on the issue of mental anguish the testimony of a neuropsychiatrist to the effect that she was suffering from a severe cancerphobia, that is phobic apprehension that she would ultimately develop cancer at the site of the radiation burn. The neuropsychiatrist further testified that the patient might have permanent symptoms of anxiety. She recovered damages.[119]

In another recent case, however, damages for cancerphobia were denied.

A woman had two lumps in her breast. At the time of biopsy the surgeon removed one of them. He assured her that the biopsy was negative and that the lump which remained in her breast was also highly unlikely to be malignant. She claimed in the suit that the retained lump caused her to suffer anxiety and that he should have removed it as well. The jury brought in a verdict for the patient, but it was dismissed by the trial court. On appeal the trial court's decision was affirmed. The higher court pointed out that every physician the woman consulted assured her that she did not have cancer and that she had no cause for concern. The court said the present case could be distinguished from the one above where a physician's negligence actually produced a potentially cancerous condition and might have permitted cancer to develop unchecked. Affirming the lower court's decision, the court found that the woman did not demonstrate that her fear of contracting cancer was either reasonable or attributable to negligence.[120]

Other cases have also denied recovery.

A physician erroneously told his patient that she had active tuberculosis. His diagnosis was held to be reasonable under the circumstances. He was also held to have made it in good faith. In denying the patient's suit for mental anguish, the court pointed out that if the doctor had been correct but had not told the patient, he would have been negligent. The court stated that she would have had a cause of action only if the diagnosis had been made without due care, had been unreasonable, or was not well-founded or if he had acted in bad faith. In this particular fact situation none of those conclusions was justified.[121]

An obstetrician told his pregnant patient that he could not hear the baby's heartbeat and that he was "concerned." He told her to come back in a week. She leaped to the conclusion that he meant that her baby was dead. She went the next day to another obstetrician who told her there was no cause for alarm and who cared for her throughout the rest of her pregnancy. She sued the first obstetrician for damages. The court dismissed her claim, holding that she had suffered no damages. She had, in fact, been the sole cause of her own anxiety.[122]

Therefore, as long as the diagnosis that the patient is in fact suffering from some serious complaint is based on a reasonable probability which would have been arrived at by a duly careful physician, the doctor is not liable if the patient does not in fact have the disease. The same standards apply as in any other misdiagnosis situation. It is extremely unlikely that without any actual physical damage, recovery would be allowed simply for mental anguish. However, where surgery is clearly unnecessary, the simple pain and suffering of unnecessary exploratory surgery might very well result in damages.

This chapter has dealt with liability for misdiagnosis. It has been seen that where a physician either fails to realize that the patient has a serious medical problem or thinks that a medical problem exists when it does not, he is not liable for any good faith errors of judgment or mistakes. As long as the physician has made the diagnosis on the basis of all reasonably available information, he is not liable if he is wrong. Courts do not require a physician to guarantee the correctness of his diagnosis or, as will be seen in the next chapter, the success of his treatment.

NOTES

1. Alden v. Providence Hospital, 382 F 2d 163, DC CA 1967; Pearce v. United States, 236 F Supp 431, DC Okla 1964; Booth v. United States, 155 F Supp 235 (Ct Cl 1957).
2. Wheatley v. Heideman, 102 NW 2d 343, Iowa 1960.
3. "Misdiagnosis Without Fault: Part I," 219 *JAMA* No. 7, page 967, Feb 14, 1972; "Misdiagnosis Without Fault: Part II," 219 *JAMA* No. 8, page 1127, Feb. 21, 1972.
4. Johnson v. St. Paul Mercury Insurance Company, 219 So 2d 524, La 1969.
5. Rewis v. United States, 369 F 2d 595, CCA 5, 1966.
6. McHugh v. Audet, 72 F Supp 394, DC Pa 1947.

7. Mulligan v. Wetchler, 332 NYS 2d 68, NY 1972.

8. "Physician's Liability for Drug Reactions," 213 *JAMA* No. 12, page 2143, Sept 21, 1970.

9. "Liability for Penicillin Reaction," 212 *JAMA* No. 11, page 2015, June 15, 1970; "Tetanus Antitoxin Reactions," 224 *JAMA* No. 4, page 559, April 23, 1973.

10. Yorston v. Pennell, 153 A 2d 255, Pa 1959; Stokes v. Dailey, 85 NW 2d 745, ND 1957; Snyder v. Pantaleo, 122 A 2d 21, Conn 1956; Agnew v. Larson, 185 P 2d 851, Cal 1947.

11. Tangora v. Matanky, 42 Cal Rptr 348, Cal 1964; Campos v. Weeks, 53 Cal Rptr 915, Cal 1966.

12. Burke v. Miners' Memorial Hospital, 381 SW 2d 758, Ky 1964.

13. O'Neil v. State, 323 NYS 2d 56, NY 1971; Schwartz v. United States, 230 F Supp 536, DC Pa 1964; Collins v. Meeker, 424 P 2d 488, Kan 1967.

14. Steeves v. United States, 294 F Supp 446, DC SC 1968; Just v. Littlefield, 151 Pac 780, Wash 1915.

15. Maercklein v. Smith, 266 P 2d 1095, Colo 1954; In re Johnson's Estate, 16 NW 2d 504, Neb 1944.

16. Bugg v. Security Benevolent Association, 112 P 2d 73, Kans 1941.

17. "Failure to Take Medical History," 226 *JAMA* No. 4, page 509, October 22, 1973.

18. Saunders v. Lischkoff, 188 So 815, Fla 1939.

19. Domina v. Pratt, 13 A 2d 198, Vt 1940.

20. Hicks v. United States, 368 F 2d 626, CCA 4, 1966.

21. Smith v. Shankman, 25 Cal Rptr 195, Cal 1962.

22. Maben v. Rankin, 358 P 2d 681, Cal 1961.

23. "Erroneous Commitment," 219 *JAMA* No. 10, page 1389, March 6, 1972.

24. DiGiovanni v. Pessel, 250 A 2d 756, NY 1969.

25. "Heart Attacks," 223 *JAMA* No. 3, page 365, Jan. 15, 1973; "Improper Release from Mental Hospital," 220 *JAMA* No. 6, page 897, May 8, 1972; "Failure to Diagnose Infection," 220 *JAMA* No. 2, page 321, April 10, 1972; "Foreign Bodies in the Eye," 218 *JAMA* No. 3, page 495, Oct. 18, 1971; "Lung Cancer," 222 *JAMA* No. 7, page 877, Nov. 13, 1972.

26. Reeves v. North Broward Hospital District, 191 So 2d 307, Fla 1966.

27. Johnson v. Borland, 26 NW 2d 755, Mich 1947.

28. Merchants National Bank v. United States, 272 F Supp 409, DC ND 1967.

29. Anderson v. Nixon, 139 P 2d 216, Utah 1943.

30. "Failure to Make Diagnostic Tests," 210 *JAMA* No. 1, page 213, Oct. 6 1969; Smith v. Yohe, 194 A 2d 167, Pa 1963.

31. Clark v. United States, 402 F 2d 950, CCA 4, 1968.

32. "Misdiagnosis of Pregnancy," 218 *JAMA* No. 13, page 2013, Dec. 27, 1971; "Mistaken Diagnosis of Pregnancy," 202 *JAMA* No. 10, page 249, Dec. 4, 1967; "Failure to Diagnose Normal Pregnancy," 202 *JAMA* No. 8, page 375, Nov. 20, 1967.

33. Smith v. Wright, 305 P 2d 810, Kan 1957; Pugh v. Swiontek, 253 NE 2d 3, Ill 1969; Jarboe v. Harting, 397 SW 2d 775, Ky 1965.

34. Crovella v. Cochrane, 102 So 2d 307, Fla 1958.

35. Greenwood v. Harris, 362 P 2d 85, Okla 1961.

36. Hoglin v. Brown, 481 P 2d 458, Wash 1971.

37. "Failure to Diagnose Ectopic Pregnancy," 202 *JAMA* No. 9, page 213, Nov. 27, 1967.

38. Barnett v. Bachrach, 34 A 2d 626, CA DC 1943.

39. Stephenson v. Kaiser Foundation Hospital, 21 Cal Rptr 646, Cal 1962.

40. Peterson v. Hunt, 84 P 2d 999, Wash 1938; Patterson v. Marcus, 265 Pac 222, Cal 1928; Kleinman v. Armour, 470 P 2d 703, Ariz 1970.

41. In re Johnson's Estate, 16 NW 2d 506, Neb 1944.

42. Paulson v. Stocker, 4 NE 2d 609, Ohio 1935.

43. Barnett v. Bachrach, 34 A 2d 626, CA DC 1943.

44. "Non-negligent Failure to Take Xray Films," 219 *JAMA* No. 9, page 1259, Feb. 28, 1972.

45. Carrigan v. Roman Catholic Bishop, 178 A 2d 502, NH 1962.

46. Robinson v. Gatti, 184 NE 2d 509, Ohio 1961.

47. Hall v. Ferry, 235 F Supp 821, DC Va 1964.

48. Dietze v. King, 184 F Supp 944, DC Va 1960.

49. "Hip Fractures," 219 *JAMA* No. 5, page 659, Jan. 31, 1972; Gonzales v. Peterson, 359 P 2d 307, Wash 1961.

50. Smith v. Yohe, 194 A 2d 167, Pa 1963.

51. Calvaruso v. Our Lady of Peace Roman Catholic Church, 319 NYS 2d 727, NY 1971.

52. "Roentgenograms of Head Injuries," 222 *JAMA* No. 5, page 613, Oct. 30, 1972.

53. Cooper v. Sisters of Charity, 272 NE 2d 97, Ohio 1971.

54. Bourgeois v. Dade County, 99 So 2d 575, Fla 1957.

55. Rostron v. Klein, 178 NW 2d 675, Mich 1970.

56. "Foreign Bodies in the Eye" 218 *JAMA* No. 3, page 495, Oct. 18, 1971.

57. Kosak v. Boyce, 201 NW 757, Wisc 1925.

58. McBride v. Saylin, 56 P 2d 941, Cal 1936.

59. "Misdiagnosis of Tuberculosis," 219 *JAMA* No. 4, page 561, Jan. 24, 1972.

60. Vigil v. Herman, 424 P 2d 159, Ariz 1967.

61. Maertins v. Kaiser Foundation Hospital, 328 P 2d 494, Cal 1958.

62. "Biopsies: Part I," 223 *JAMA* No. 12, page 1429, March 19, 1973; "Biopsies: Part II," 223 *JAMA* No. 13, page 1573, March 26, 1973.

63. O'Brien v. Stover, 443 F 2d 1013, CCA 8, 1971.

64. Cullum v. Seifer, 81 Cal Rptr 381, Cal 1969.

65. "Breast Cancer," 222 *JAMA* No. 13, page 1713, Dec. 25, 1972.

66. Lipsey v. Michael Reese Hospital, 262 NE 2d 450, Ill 1970.

67. Valdez v. Percy, 217 P 2d 422, Cal 1950.

68. McQuinn v. St. Lawrence County Laboratory, 283 NYS 2d 747, NY 1967.

69. Gist v. French, 288 P 2d 1003, Cal 1955.

70. Solorio v. Lampros, 82 Cal Rptr 753, Cal 1969.

71. "Liability for Cesarean Section," 214 *JAMA* No. 4, page 809, Oct. 26, 1970.

72. Stewart v. Rudner, 84 NW 2d 816, Mich 1957.

73. Dinner v. Thorp, 338 P 2d 137, Wash 1959.

74. Thomas v. Ellis, 106 NE 2d 687, Mass 1952.

75. Wilson v. Martin Memorial Hospital, 61 SE 2d 102, NC 1950.

76. Steeves v. United States, 294 F Supp 446, DC SC 1968.

77. "Misdiagnosis of Appendicitis," 212 *JAMA* No. 10, page 1763, June 8, 1970.

78. Sagall, E. L. and Reed, B. C., *The Heart and the Law*, Macmillan Co., New York, 1968, page 136.

79. Brown v. Scullin Steel Company, 260 SW 2d 513, Mo 1953.

80. Naccaroto v. Grob, 180 NW 2d 788, Mich 1970.

81. Fortner v. Koch, 261 NW 762, Mich 1935.

82. "Diabetes: Part I," 223 *JAMA* No. 4, page 471, Jan 22, 1973; "Diabetes: Part II," 223 *JAMA* No. 5, page 591, Jan. 29, 1973.

83. Hill v. Stewart, 209 So 2d 809, Miss 1968.

84. Albright v. Powell, 147 SE 2d 848, Ga 1966.

85. Kern v. Kogan, 226 A 2d 186, NJ 1967.

86. Price v. Neyland, 320 F 2d 674, CA DC 1963.

87. Lundberg v. Bay View Hospital, 191 NE 2d 821, Ohio 1963.

88. "Failure to Transmit Medical Information," 213 *JAMA* No. 13, page 2351, Sept. 28, 1970.

89. Capuano v. Jacobs, 305 NYS 2d 837, NY 1969.

90. Whitree v. New York, 290 NYS 2d 486, NY 1968.

91. Jeanes v. Milner, 428 F 2d 598, CCA 8, 1970.

92. Welch v. Frisbie Memorial Hospital, 9 A 2d 761, NH 1939.

93. Sinkey v. Surgical Associates, 186 NW 2d 658, Iowa 1971.

94. Riggs v. Christie, 173 NE 2d 610, Mass 1961.

95. Carter v. Ries, 378 SW 2d 487, Mo 1964.

96. McBride v. Roy, 58 P 2d 886, Okla 1936.

97. Goedecke v. Price, 506 P 2d 1105, Ariz 1973.

98. Sibert v. Boger, 260 SW 2d 569, Mo 1953.

99. Weatherman v. White, 179 SE 2d 134, NC 1971; Hall v. Bacon, 453 P 2d 816, Idaho 1969.

100. "Delay of Surgery," 216 *JAMA* No. 9, page 1527, May 31, 1971.

101. Levermann v. Cartall, 393 SW 2d 931, Tex 1965.

102. Huttner v. MacKay, 293 P 2d 766, Wash 1956.

103. "Unnecessary Mastectomies," 206 *JAMA* No. 1, page 199, Sept. 30, 1968.

104. "Unnecessary Surgery," 213 *JAMA* No. 10, page 1755, Sept. 7, 1970; "Recent Decisions on Unnecessary Surgery," 222 *JAMA* No. 12, page 1593, Dec. 18, 1972.

105. Martin v. Parks, 165 So 2d 220, Fla 1964.

106. Kelly v. Hollingsworth, 181 NW 959, SD 1921.

107. Doerr v. Movius, 463 P 2d 477, Mont 1970.

108. Beadling v. Sirotta, 176 A 2d 546, NJ 1961.

109. Sims v. Callahan, 112 So 2d 776, Ala 1959.

110. Bryson v. Stone, 190 NW 2d 336, Mich 1971.

111. "Mistaken Identity," 221 *JAMA* No. 7, page 747, Aug. 14, 1972.

112. Copeland v. Robertson, 112 So 2d 236, Miss 1959.

113. Hundley v. St. Francis Hospital, 327 P 2d 131, Cal 1958.

114. "Hysterectomies," 217 *JAMA* No. 10, page 1439, Sept. 6, 1971.

115. "Misdiagnosis of Appendicitis," 212 *JAMA* No. 10, page 1763, June 8, 1970.

116. Rogers v. United States, 216 F Supp 1, DC Ohio 1963.

117. Jaeger v. Stratton, 176 NW 61, Wisc 1920.

118. "Iatrogenic Disorders," 200 *JAMA* No. 13, page 237, June 26, 1967.

119. Ferrara v. Galluchio, 152 NE 2d 249, NY 1958.

120. Winik v. Jewish Hospital of Brooklyn, 293 NE 2d 95, NY 1972.

121. Kraus v. Spielberg, 236 NYS 2d 143, NY 1962.

122. Morgan v. Aetna Casualty Company, 185 F Supp 20, DC La 1960.

CHAPTER IV

INCORRECT

OR

INADEQUATE

TREATMENT

The definition of negligence in treatment is the same as that in diagnosis. After determining what is wrong with the patient, the physician or surgeon is obliged to use that degree of skill and care in treating him as would be exercised by the average reputable physician of the same school of practice in the same locality. As was discussed in Chapter II, a physician usually is not held to guarantee a cure. When he undertakes to treat a patient, all he agrees to do is to use diligence and ordinary skill.[1] If the patient does not improve or dies, or if an unexpected and untoward result occurs in the course of treatment, the physician is not liable. The results of any treatment may vary under the best of circumstances, skill, and care, from excellent to very poor. No inference of negligence is ever drawn from the fact that a patient dies or does not get well.

In *Derr v. Bonney*[2] the alleged negligence involved a failure to set a fractured ankle properly. The court's definition of negligent treatment is an excellent statement of the general definition of a physician's legal responsibility in treatment:

> (1) An individual licensed to practice medicine is presumed to possess that degree of skill and learning which is possessed by the average members of the profession in the community in which he practices, and it is presumed that he has applied that skill and learning with ordinary and reasonable care to those who come to him for treatment; (2) The contract which the law implies from the employment of a physician or surgeon is that the doctor will treat his patient with that diligence and skill just mentioned; (3) He does not incur liability for his mistakes if he has used methods recognized and approved by those reasonably skilled in the profession; (4) Before a physician or surgeon can be liable for malpractice, he must have

done something in the treatment of his patient which the recognized standard of medical practice in his community forbids in such cases or he must have neglected to do something required by those standards. (5) In order to obtain a judgment against a physician or surgeon, the standard of medical practice in the community must be shown and further, that the doctor failed to follow the method prescribed by that standard; (6) It is not required that physicians and surgeons guarantee results, nor that the result be what is desired; (7) The testimony of other physicians that they would have followed a different course of treatment than that followed by the defendant or a disagreement of doctors of equal skill and learning as to what the treatment should have been does not establish negligence.

In other words, the physician who accepts a patient for treatment holds himself out as qualified to make a careful diagnosis and plan of treatment and to use good judgment in carrying that treatment out. He does not hold himself out as a miracle-worker or as a magician. He is not, in short, liable simply because his treatment produces a poor result.[3]

A physician may make a warranty that he will in fact cure the patient and if so, he will be liable for breach of contract if the patient is not cured, whether or not he was negligent.[4]

A man's hand was burned by an electric wire and the defendant agreed' to perform an operation to remove the scar tissue and to graft skin from the patient's chest onto the affected hand. During discussions with the patient's father before the operation the defendant said, "I will guarantee to make the hand a 100% perfect hand." While no negligence in performance of surgery was alleged, the condition of the hand was not greatly improved. The defendant was held liable for breach of contract including a promise to cure.[5]

In several decisions surgeons had assured patients who were scheduled for vasectomies or tubal ligations that they would be sterile after surgery. When pregnancy occurred, the patients sued, not for negligence, but for breach of the sterilization contract. Where such an assertion can be proved, they have collected damages even though no negligence was shown.[6] Since the parents of the unplanned child ask damages for mental anguish, physical damage to the mother, and all expenses of raising the child to adulthood, large amounts of money are invariably involved. It is also highly unlikely that a court would require a pregnant woman to have an abortion in order to mitigate damages.

A druggist negligently dispensed tranquilizers instead of the oral contraceptives prescribed. The patient became pregnant and gave birth to a
healthy child. She sued the druggist. The court held that she stated a good
cause of action and that she had not been obliged to mitigate damages by
having an abortion or by surrendering the child for adoption. The court held
that requiring either action would be unreasonable.[7]

Any gynecologist, urologist, or general surgeon who performs sterilization
operations should not only explain to the patient and his or her spouse that
no guarantee of sterilization can be made, the surgical consent form should
include a specific statement to that effect.

A physician is required to tell a patient or family member if his treatment is not beneficial.[8] Although the courts do not assume that if a patient is not cured, the physician has been negligent, if the physician knows
that treatment is ineffective he is obligated to adopt one of several alternatives. If a specialist would facilitate the patient's recovery, as discussed in
Chapter II, he must make a referral. If another course of treatment would
appear to be more beneficial than the one being used, the physician must
adopt it.[9]

It may well be that any treatment would be ineffective. The patient may
have a disease, such as a cold, from which he will recover in due course
without treatment. If antibiotics or any drug with a potential for serious
adverse reaction is prescribed where they are useless for a disease from
which the patient will inevitably recover without treatment and a drug reaction occurs, the physician will be liable for not having "left well enough
alone."[10] The patient should simply be told that "nature will take its
course" and that no treatment is necessary.

The converse situation, of course, involves the terminally ill patient. In
this case, it may be good medical judgment to continue ineffective treatment to keep the patient unaware of the facts, but if so, his spouse, parent,
or some responsible adult in his family must be told the truth.

In order to make a proper evaluation of whether or not treatment is
effective, the physician is obliged to heed the patient's complaints. If a
patient can show that he tried to tell the physician something but was ignored and if he had been heard with proper attention the results would
have been better, a jury is altogether likely to be sympathetic.[11]

A patient's ankle was broken and the defendant applied a cast. The patient
told him the cast had slipped, but he paid no attention and did not Xray.
The bones misaligned. The defendant was liable.[12]

A high school boy fractured his ankle at football practice. It was set by the the defendant. Six months later he complained of pain but was ignored. The physician did not Xray and therefore nonunion of the bones was not discovered. The physician was liable.[13]

A patient broke her arm and the physician applied a cast. She complained that it was too tight but no examination was made. He went on vacation for 2 weeks. She complained almost daily at his hospital during his absence. Technicians applied heat, but she was not seen by any other physician. When the cast was removed, a piece of plaster about-the size of a cigarette was found to be embedded in her arm, causing permanent disability. A cause of action was stated.[14]

Insufficient or too infrequent visits to allow the physician to keep abreast of the patient's progress may also constitute negligence.[15]

In the early years of this century, a child had scarlet fever, frequently a fatal disease at that time. Despite three separate pleas from the parents, the physician refused to come the day after he had first seen her. When he eventually responded, she died a few minutes after his arrival. He admitted to the parents that if he had come earlier he could have saved the child's life. He was found negligent.[16]

A patient had had congestive heart failure for which his physician had treated him. When another attack occurred, he was told to go to the hospital. The physician called in orders for Xrays and electrocardiograms. He did not, however, visit the patient for 3 days although he saw other patients in the same hospital each day. When the physician finally saw him, he realized that the patient was in critical condition and ordered oxygen, but the patient died. The court held that the widow stated a cause of action.[17]

Some treatment, of course, carries with it certain inherent risk, even if administered with greatest care. While the question of informed consent and other matters of patient-information will be dealt with in a later chapter, the question of liability for such inherent risk, if an untoward result occurs, is a very important one.

An adult patient had suffered from a mastoid condition since early childhood. Immediately after a mastoidectomy her face was paralyzed. A second operation revealed that the seventh cranial nerve had been severed. There was clear evidence of considerable bone necrosis and therefore the court agreed with the surgeon's allegations that the outcome had been an unavoidable accident.[18]

As long as the patient is told about inherent and unavoidable risks prior to administration of treatment, in the absence of negligence he cannot recover damages if an unfortunate result occurs.[19] Where a patient undergoes Xray treatment, for example, he assumes the risk of Xray burns as long as no negligence is present.[20]

A diabetic had elective surgery on his leg. Although great care was used, an infection set in and the leg was amputated. The patient admitted that the surgeon had discussed at great length all the unavoidable risks attendant upon any surgery on a diabetic patient. The court held that he could not recover damages for the unfortunate result.[21]

Most medical treatment which is held to be negligent involves one of two situations: either the physician does not follow the standard practice in treating the condition, meaning that he administers incorrect treatment, or he undertakes to administer proper treatment, but does it in an inadequate or incorrect manner.

A physician who carefully follows standard and accepted procedures will not be held negligent whatever the outcome of the case. As long ago as 1871 the highest court of New York said, "Where the case is one as to which a system of treatment has been followed for a long time, there should be no departure from it, unless the surgeon who does it is prepared to take the risk of establishing by his success the propriety and safety of his experiment."[22]

"Standard practice," however, is extremely hard to define in some cases. There may well be no standard practice for dealing with the medical or surgical problem from which a given patient suffers.

A patient consented to a heart transplant. The surgeon explained to him and to his wife that if death appeared imminent, a mechanical heart substitute would be used. The risk of the procedure was very carefully explained and the patient signed a special consent form indicating that he was aware that the mechanical heart had never before been used. His condition deteriorated and the mechanical device was used, followed by a transplant. The patient died the day after surgery. His wife sued. The court held that the wife had to prove negligence by expert testimony. Since the defendant was one of very few surgeons in the world who had ever performed the transplant operation and since there was absolutely no precedent for use of a mechanical heart, no one could testify to the standard practice. A verdict for the surgeon was ordered by the court.[23]

More usually, medical opinion as to the proper treatment of an illness is divided. There may be two, three, or even more methods of treatment of a given problem, all of which are advocated by eminent medical authorities. If the treatment given is in accord with a recognized system, it is not negligence to use it.[24] If a physician can show that he has used a method which is approved by at least a respectable minority of medical opinion, the plaintiff must then be able to show that the method itself was applied in a negligent manner. This is true even if hindsight would indicate that another method might have produced better results.[25]

A surgeon used acetrizoate in performing an aortogram. The patient–plaintiff was paralyzed after the test and Xrays revealed that some of the solution had escaped from the aorta. The solution was used, at that time, in about half the aortograms performed in the country. The defendant testified that he used it instead of another, less toxic substance because it permitted better pictures to be made. The court held that the surgeon had the right to use his best judgment in choosing an agent recognized by a large number of his peers without having negligence imputed to him.[26]

If a patient's condition or the nature of his illness or injury is such that the usual and accepted method of treatment would present unusual hazards to him, a departure from it is not considered negligence.

A child with Down's syndrome was a resident of a state institution. She had heart and lung problems and developed cataracts on both eyes. Her mother requested eye surgery on numerous occasions and the surgeon in charge of the case refused. He felt that her physical ailments made the administration of anesthesia too dangerous and that she would also rip off the bandages. The child's mother removed her from the institution and surgery was successfully performed elsewhere. She sued for negligent delay of surgery. The court found for the institution and its surgeon. The court held that the defendant had a right to the use of his best medical judgment since he could show that other physicians agreed with him.[27]

If established treatments have been less than successful and the patient's condition is sufficiently serious to necessitate an unproven approach, it is not generally considered negligence to employ it.[28] As long as the physician can justify innovative treatment techniques as being in the best interest of his patient and not as a procedure to elicit research information for himself, the physician will not be negligent if he uses a nonapproved method.[29]

Recent press reports indicated that large groups of public health service patients were denied any treatment of syphilis for a period of many years simply to allow the physicians to study the effects of untreated syphilis. The survivors of the experiment and the heirs of those who died presumably would be exceedingly likely to recover damages.[30]

In a situation in which a patient had a known allergy to tetanus antitoxin, a physician would be negligent if he administered it even if the standard practice would be to do so. The risk of tetanus would be less likely than the risk of serious harm from the injection.[31]

Deviation without excuse from standard practice, however, indicates negligence in most cases. It usually indicates either that the physician did not know the correct method of treating the condition or that, although he knew it, he carelessly failed to utilize it.

A physician failed to sterilize his instruments or wash his hands before performing minor office surgery. The patient developed an infection. He recovered damages.[32]

When a newborn baby was discharged from the hospital, the defendant pediatrician noted a swollen area on his hip. He merely told the baby's mother to change a gauze pad. When pus formed, the mother called and reported it but he gave no new instructions. He twice refused to see the child. A week later the baby was critically ill with a staphylococcus infection. Since standard practice would have been to obtain a culture and administer antibiotics before releasing the child from the nursery, the court held that the unjustified deviation constituted negligence.[33]

As had been discussed in the chapter on diagnosis, a physician is obliged to keep up with advances in medical treatment. The standard practice, of course, changes as developments in medicine progress.[34] If a physician is unaware of recent developments in treating a particular complaint, he may well be liable if use of an outmoded method damages the patient.[35]

There are an infinite variety of decisions in which negligent medical or surgical treatment has been alleged. No comprehensive survey is possible, but examples will be given from several fields of surgery and medicine. The subject of injury from therapeutic agents is discussed in greater length in the following chapter.

Surgical Negligence.   Some surgical situations constitute unavoidable accidents. Where, either during or after an operation, an untoward result occurs, it may well be held that no negligence existed because the most careful surgeon could not have avoided the complication. An example of one type of case in which this conclusion is reached fairly frequently is that of the appearance of a vesicovaginal fistula following hysterectomy.[36]

Symptoms of a vesicovaginal fistula did not appear until some days following a hysterectomy. The patient sued and alleged that the cause of the injury was the puncture of her bladder during the operation. The court refused to find the surgeon negligent. The testimony of all the other physicians who had been present during the operation indicated that there was no evidence of a cut in the bladder at that time. Since there was no immediate escape of urine, the court held that it could not have occurred at that time.[37]

In another case where the leakage first became apparent 10 days following surgery, the court refused to hold that the surgery was the inevitable cause of the fistula. The court said that the condition could not be legally attributed to the surgery alone and stated that the occurrence of a rare complication does not raise a presumption that it was caused by negligence.[38]

Unavoidable accidents may occur in any type of surgery in which the physician is proceeding with due care. If some form of difficulty occurs he is not liable as long as he deals with it promptly, efficiently, and carefully.

One of the worst types of untoward incidents during surgery is cardiac arrest.[39] If the patient's preoperative condition contraindicates surgery and the operation proceeds as scheduled, the occurrence of cardiac arrest is generally attributable to negligence.[40]

However, if the problem occurs during surgery under circumstances in which there had been no way to anticipate its likelihood, if the surgeon acts promptly to cope with the problem, he is not considered negligent.

Cardiac arrest occurred during delivery of a baby. After protracted labor, the patient had been prepared for a Cesarean section by the administration of a spinal anesthesia, but delivered normally. The obstetrician had the patient's chest open and was massaging her heart within 1 minute after the arrest occurred. The court held that he had met all standards of care in the emergency presented to him, and no inference of negligence would be imputed.[41]

A child had cardiac arrest and resulting brain damage during a tonsillectomy. A suit was filed against the anesthesiologist. The jury returned a verdict for the defendant and it was upheld on appeal. The appellate court approved the trial judge's charge to the jury that although due care must be used in an emergency, less time is available for thought and contemplation as to alternatives than exists in a nonemergency situation.[42]

It is obvious that any surgeon, regardless of specialty, is obliged to know what to do instantly in case of a cardiac arrest. He would be negligent if he wasted time by attempting to locate another surgeon to deal with the problem. Therefore, delay regardless of the specific nature of the surgeon's training, will be considered negligent.

A 6-year old boy with a slightly elevated temperature was admitted to the hospital for elective eye surgery. He ran a low fever all night before surgery and was very restless. When cardiac arrest occurred during the surgery, the ophthalmologist did not feel competent to open the child's chest; so he waited for another surgeon to help him. The delay caused severe brain damage. The court found negligence in the way the emergency was handled, as well as negligence in performing surgery at all.[43]

Another form of difficulty which may result without regard to the type of surgery involved is the situation in which the wrong operation is performed.[44] Either a patient undergoes surgery intended for another patient or the correct patient undergoes surgery on the wrong part of the body. While, as will be seen in a later chapter, operating without the patient's consent is considered assault and battery, most courts allow these cases to be tried as negligence actions. Once the facts are proved, negligence is automatic and the only question to be determined is the amount of damages which will be awarded.[45]

A serviceman's wife was admitted to a military hospital for surgery. She understood that the operation would be performed on her left knee and signed a consent to that specific effect. For some reason, the operation was on her right knee. She recovered damages.[46]

However, in most of these cases, the surgeon has some reason to believe that he is performing the right operation. All these cases could be prevented if written consents were requested before surgery and were made a part of the operative record which the surgeon saw before he began.

A man thought he was going to be circumcised. A vasectomy was performed instead. The patient and his family physician had had several discussions over the telephone about the procedure, which was only referred to by either party as "the operation," which the patient thought meant circumcision. The patient's wife had talked to the physician about a vasectomy and the physician assumed that that was "the operation" the patient meant. As a result of this breakdown in communication, the physician told the surgeon to whom he referred the patient to perform a vasectomy. At no time prior to surgery did the surgeon talk to the patient, merely relying on what the family doctor told him. No written consent forms for any type of surgery were signed by either the patient or his wife. When the surgeon asked the general practitioner about consent forms, he was told that they had been signed and were in the physician's office. The court held that the patient had a good cause of action in negligence against the family physician. However, as to the surgeon, the court held that he had had every right to rely on the family doctor's word. Since there was no allegation that the vasectomy had been improperly performed, no cause of action existed against the surgeon.[47]

Injury to a part of the body other than that on which surgery is performed is a frequent cause of negligence suits. In most of them, the surgeon will be held liable. While he does not guarantee successful outcome of the surgery performed, most courts hold that there is an inference of negligence when something untoward happens to a part of the patient's body which is not involved in surgery.

A patient's buttocks were burned during delivery. The antiseptic solution applied before delivery had dripped onto the rubber sheet on which she lay and had collected in puddles underneath. She recovered damages.[48]

Allegations of negligence in performance of diagnostic surgery are by no means unknown. While, as was discussed in the preceding chapter, a physician is obliged to use all reasonable tests to make a careful diagnosis of his patient's condition, there is a calculated risk involved in such procedures as myelograms, aortograms, and gastroscopic examinations. Therefore the surgeon should carefully consider whether the patient's condition makes it necessary or if the condition is such that at worst it is less likely to create permanent difficulties than performance of the diagnostic procedure may cause. If the use of this type of test is not justified in terms of calculated risk even if it is performed in a careful manner, the surgeon may very well be liable for having performed it at all if an unavoidable result occurs.

Numerous cases have involved perforation of the esophagus during esophagoscopies and gastroscopies.[49] Negligence in these perforation cases is held to occur only when the physician has not met the required standards of due care.

Where resistance was encountered during a gastroscopy but the physician attributed it to cardiospasms and continued, perforation of the esophagus resulted. The court found no evidence of negligence. The decision specifically pointed out that there was no presumption of negligence merely because the medical care terminated in an unfortunate result.[50] There was no evidence that it might not have occurred even though proper skill was used.

During a gastroscopy the physician lifted the patient up to show an intern how to tell if the tube was in the right position. The movement of the patient's body caused a perforation of his esophagus. The physician was liable for the damage.[51]

Untoward results occur in a small percentage of cases involving angiograms and aortograms. In most of these cases, the surgeons have not been found negligent because experts are in agreement that untoward results occur in some of these cases in spite of the fact that the physicians involved have used the highest standards of skill, care, and knowledge.[52] However, it is extremely important that the patient be aware of any inherent risks. While the surgeon may not be liable if the patient is aware that he is undergoing a procedure which is not entirely safe, if he is not so informed, although the untoward result was unavoidable, the surgeon may be liable.[53]

Pyelograms are extremely valuable aids in making diagnosis of conditions involving the kidneys, ureter, and bladder. However, some adverse reaction to these tests have been noted.

An experienced and qualified radiologist subcutaneously injected a substance into the patient's hip before a pyelogram. Before the injection was attempted, the physician had asked her whether she had ever had hay fever or asthma or whether she knew if she was sensitive to the drug and she answered in the negative. As a result of the injection, an iodine granuloma appeared. The appellate court held that the plaintiff stated a cause of action.[54]

Cystoscopic examinations may also involve unexpected results. The most frequent difficulty is an infection which occurs after the procedure is completed and in those cases the urologist may very well be liable.[55] However, cystoscopic examination is considered sufficiently safe so that a physician confronted with a problem where one should be used is more likely to be negligent for failure to advise that a cystoscopic examination should be performed than he is to run a risk of being sued as the result of injury. In one case a patient consulted a physician who told him he had an enlarged prostate. Two years of treatment went by before a cystoscopic examination was made. By that time the patient had an inoperable malignant tumor of the prostate. He died, and a malpractice suit followed. The physician was found negligent in having failed to order a cystoscopic examination.[56]

Therefore, where some form of surgical diagnostic procedure is indicated, a physician's failure to utilize it means that a physician may be liable for negligent misdiagnosis. On the other hand, if the procedure is advised and performed, an unanticipated accident of some sort occurs, and the patient is left in a condition worse than his original one, the physician may also be found negligent. However, in all these cases, courts apparently assume that as long as the patient gives an informed consent and understands any dangers of the procedure, the surgeon is not liable in the absence of specific negligence in performance.

Various surgical specialties encounter specific problems common only to their own branch of surgery. Generally speaking, however, the standard of due care prevails in all of them regardless of the nature of the surgery performed.

Obstetrics and gynecology is a fertile field for damage suits. Of course, one reason is that the obstetrician is involved with two patients, mother and baby, instead of one, as is true in other surgery.[57] Several decisions have involved injuries to the baby which occurred during or immediately after delivery. Several cases have involved brain and spinal damage caused by negligent use of forceps. In these cases, if the negligence can be proved, the mother or baby has a good case.[58] In some cases babies' arms and legs have been fractured during difficult deliveries.

If a forceable delivery is necessitated by a serious threat to the life of either mother or child, a broken bone is a calculated risk, and the physician is not liable if it occurs. In the absence of such a life or death emergency, however, this type of injury to the infant would undoubtedly be enough to allow the jury to infer negligence.[59]

Evidence indicated that a Cesarean should have been performed, but was not. The baby's oxygen supply was cut off and brain damage resulted. The obstetrician was held liable.[60]

A baby's face was severely cut when the incision was made to perform a Cesarean. The court held that the allegation of the fact was sufficient to state a cause of action.[61]

A baby was blinded in one eye by forceps trauma. The court held that negligence might be inferred from the unusual character of the injury.[62]

Injuries to the mother occurring during delivery generally involve rather common situations. For example, sponges or needles have been left in patient's bodies. However, this subject will be discussed in detail in the following chapter. Injuries to a part of the patient's body other than that involved in the obstetrical area have also occurred.

A patient's shoulder was broken at some point during labor or delivery after she was returned to her room. She had convulsions when she developed eclampsia after delivery. There was no evidence that she had fallen in the labor or delivery room or when she returned to her own room. Because of her condition she had been watched almost constantly during the entire period. The court found that whatever its cause, the fracture had not resulted from negligence or trauma and therefore the obstetrician was not liable.[63]

Gynecology involves the same type of injuries as are usual in obstetrics, including foreign objects left in patient's bodies. Several cases involving complications of gynecological surgery have involved injuries to the patient's body other than the area on which surgery was performed, and in these cases, liability is virtually automatic.

After gynecological surgery, the patient's arm was paralyzed from unknown causes. The court held that a paralyzed arm is so extraordinary after a hysterectomy that an inference of negligence was raised.[64]

Dilation and curettage is, of course, a very common gynecological procedure. There are almost no decisions in which negligence has been alleged in this procedure.[65] In general, the cases on this subject involve standard allegations of surgical malpractice, such as patients who were burned.[66] Because of the frequency of this procedure, determining the standard practice in performing it would not be at all difficult and, therefore, any departure from standard practice would subject the gynecologist to presumptive liability.

Vasectomies are another area of surgery in which few cases have been decided.[67] Since the operation is a very simple one, only one case can be found in which there was an allegation of negligence.

For economic reasons a patient chose to have a vasectomy performed in the surgeon's office instead of the hospital. He died of a hemorrhage immediately following surgery. The court held that a cause of action was stated.[68]

Generally speaking, cases involving any type of sterilization operation are much more likely to involve an action for breach of contract to make the patient sterile than of negligence in the manner in which the operation was performed.

Orthopedics is an area in which probably more cases have been filed than any other type of surgery. This is undoubtedly due to the number of fractures set in this country every year compared to other types of surgery. The orthopedist's liability exposure is correspondingly greater than most other types of surgeons.

Where a cast is put on in such a manner that the patient is harmed, the orthopedist may very well be liable.[69] Where a physician applies a cast to a fracture, he is legally obligated to do so in keeping with the standards of skill and care which can be reasonably expected of him. Numerous courts have made the point that physicians must not only set a fracture properly, but due care requires them to be aware of any symptoms of circulatory problems or infection thereafter. If these should arise, the physician is obligated to deal with them promptly and efficiently. If the patient offers evidence of a failure to do so, a cause of action is stated.[70]

A patient complained that his cast was causing extreme pain, but the physician went on vacation without any effort to deal with the patient's problems. There were also obvious symptoms of infection. The patient, a high school football player, eventually lost his leg. The jury found that the physician's failure to investigate the complaint was negligence.[71]

A 4-year old child's arm was broken. When the cast was removed, it was found that the child had Volkmann's Contracture. The physician maintained that the injury was caused by an injury to the vessel at the time of the break. Since there was evidence that the pulse was good after the injury, however, the court upheld the jury's decision that the cast had caused the injury.[72]

Several tight cast cases have specifically held, in keeping with the general rule, that where the physician possesses and exercises the requisite degree of care, he is not responsible for the occurrence of a bad result.

After a cast on the patient's arm was removed, Volkmann's Contracture was discovered. Several physicians other than the defendant, who had applied the cast, had seen the patient during the time when the cast was worn, and none of them detected any trouble. The court held that no negligence could be assumed.[73]

Another type of liability claim made against orthopedists is that a fracture has not united. Nonunion of a fracture is not usually considered a matter which can be determined to be negligence without expert testimony, as long as the orthopedist does not ignore obvious signs of difficulty.[74] Courts are aware that nonunion can occur in a certain number of cases without any negligence whatever.[75]

The patient was injured in an automobile accident and, among other injuries, fractured her left femoral shaft. The defendant performed an open reduction and put the leg in a cast. He told her not to walk on it. She then developed traumatic psychosis and her husband eventually committed her to a mental hospital while the cast was still on her leg. By the time she was released, nonunion had occurred. She claimed that the physician in the mental hospital had told her to walk on the cast and that it was the defendant's responsibility to have given orders to allow her to remain off it and to have visited her in the mental hospital although he was not its staff. The court refused to find the defendant negligent. He had no right, much less a duty, to assume this type of responsibility at a hospital with which he was not affiliated.[76]

Infections following fractures are by no means unknown. In general, courts take the position that the infection can result from a variety of causes, including the original injury. It is therefore extremely difficult for a patient to collect damages from an orthopedist if an infection occurs.[77] However, if the orthopedist does not treat an infection when it occurs, he may well be liable.

A patient's arm was broken. There was an improper reduction. The wound drained and a screw which had been used in the surgery fell out. The defendant did nothing about it even when his own Xray films indicated a serious problem existed. In this particular case, the court found the physician liable for the infection. The court pointed out that even if the infection had been unpreventable, the methods that the defendant used to deal with it were such that negligence could be found without expert testimony.[78]

Gas gangrene is, of course, a complication which is at least conceivable, if not probable in fracture cases.[79]

A patient was knocked down by a car and broke her leg. The accident happened on a Saturday. The defendant orthopedist set the leg, put a cast on it, and admitted the patient to the hospital. By the next afternoon she could not move her toes, but the hospital did not notify the physician. He did not make rounds on Sunday and neither did his partner. They also did not see her the following morning, although the hospital finally called the orthopedist's partner later in the day. By the time she was seen, gangrene had set in and the leg had to be amputated. She sued both orthopedists and the hospital. Expert witnesses testified that the patient's condition was attributable to a failure to put a bivalve in the cast at the first sign of difficulty and that her problem was irreversible after the first 12 to 16 hours. The experts further testified that the orthopedists had been negligent in failing to see her by that time. There was no evidence that the original injury had caused either nerve or vascular damage. The court held that she stated a cause of action.[80]

A great many of these cases, however, have indicated that gas gangrene is an unavoidable complication of fractures and unless the patient can show some specific negligence in the manner in which the cast was applied or postoperative treatment was carried out, he is not likely to recover damages.[81]

"Surgical error" of course, is quite often the subject of malpractice suits. Two cases involving gall bladder surgery are relevant as examples. The patients' common bile ducts were severed. In both cases postoperative symptoms indicated that something was wrong, and in neither case did the surgeon investigate it. They were both found liable.[82]

The "slip of the knife" surgical error will very frequently result in liability and, in fact, liability is usually inevitable without some evidence indicating a medically acceptable excuse for the outcome.

A woman's right ureter was sutured in two places during a hysterectomy and the surgeon was found liable.[83]

The patient's spinal accessory nerve was crushed with a hemostat during removal of a lymph node in the neck. The surgeon was found liable.[84]

During an operation for inguinal hernia the patient's spermatic cord was cut. The surgeon was liable.[85]

Where a patient's recurrent laryngeal nerve is damaged during thyroid operations, the courts generally apply the concept of surgical error and find the surgeon liable.[86] However, some cases have held that damage of this type during a thyroidectomy is an inherent risk of the procedure and without proof of specific negligence, the patient cannot recover damages.[87]

It should be emphasized, however, that the mere fact that a surgical procedure ends in a bad result does not automatically indicate in any situation that an inference of negligence may be made. No presumption of negligence is raised simply because a result is rare, but if there is evidence that the condition is extremely rare and an allegation is made of surgical error, the combination of the two factors may be enough to send the question to the jury.[88]

Because of the very serious consequences, including blindness, of untoward results in an eye operation, patients who have suffered them are quite likely to file suit.

A patient had had two cataract operations. The first was successful. A detached retina occurred after the second. The patient claimed that the second operation was negligently performed, causing a loss of vitreous fluid. The loss of fluid in turn allegedly caused the detachment. The court rejected the claim since the patient did not furnish any evidence to show a casual connection between the loss of fluid and the retina problem.[89]

It is extremely important, particularly in any eye surgery, that the patient be made aware of any foreseeable risk of blindness.

The plaintiff was for many years aware that she had a corneal disease in both eyes. She consented to a corneal transplant in her left eye. Prior to undergoing surgery, both her referring ophthalmologist and the surgeon who performed the operation told her that she could not lose her sight. After the operation she was, in fact, blind in the affected eye and her other eye, for no demonstrable reason, improved. She sued. No allegation of negligence in the performance of the surgery was alleged. She asked for damages on the grounds that the surgery was unnecessary, not that it was negligently performed. However, there was no evidence which showed that if she had known of the possible risk of blindness, she would have refused to undergo the surgery.[90]

Plastic surgery presents psychological problems which are usually absent in other types of surgery. Some of the persons who seek to have cosmetic surgery performed are generally unhappy about their social life and consider themselves unattractive solely as a result of their physical problem. If the surgery does not prove to be a panacea for these problems, it may very well be that this type of patient would have serious adjustment traumas when he realized that his difficulties were caused by more factors than his looks. This type of emotional reaction to an encounter with any kind of medical or surgical treatment not infrequently leads to allegations that the physician, not the patient, is at fault. When personality problems of which the patient is presumably unaware are blamed on a cosmetic deficiency, removal of the deficiency may actually increase the extent of the problem. This sort of patient is the one who is generally quite hard to please under any conditions, and if there is any excuse for doing so, can become quite litigation-minded with little difficulty.

Surgeons who perform cosmetic operations should therefore be aware of the psychological undercurrents which exist in these cases.

Of course the same standards of due care apply in cosmetic surgery as in any other part of surgery.

The defendant performed cosmetic surgery on the excessively pendulous breasts of a 50-year old woman. After surgery, two lumps developed that very probably were malignant, although no differential diagnosis had been made at the time of the trial. Furthermore, one breast was obviously larger than the other one, the patient was terribly scarred, and her nipples were far above the normal position. The patient submitted photographs of her chest to the court and jury during the trial and the court agreed with the jury's conclusion that she had been horribly disfigured. She recovered $115,000.00 in damages.[91]

An exotic dancer, otherwise known as a stripper, also had cosmetic breast surgery. An infection which presumably was the result of negligence occurred after the operation. She collected $38,500.00 in damages because she showed that as a result of the infection and the scar, she was completely disabled from continuing her usual employment.[92]

A professional entertainer has cosmetic surgery on her nose which she considered too long to be attractive. The surgery was improperly performed and two further operations were required. After the third operation her nose looked far worse than it had originally. She was allowed to collect damages for the mental anguish caused by her concern over possible loss of employment and damages for breach of a contract to improve her appearance, as well as the damages normally awarded in malpractice cases.[93]

Surgical hemorrhage is another untoward result which may occur in any type of operation.[94] Generally speaking, merely proving the fact that a hemorrhage occurred does not automatically indicate that the surgeon was negligent.

A patient underwent surgery for an epigastric hernia. He died from a hemorrhage 14 hours after surgery. The autopsy revealed that the bleeding had come from an artery of the liver. The defendant surgeon had tied it off with one ligature which had slipped out of place. The plaintiff, the widow of the deceased, took the position that the surgeon had been negligent because he had not used two ligatures. The court pointed out that post-operative hemorrhage can occur despite the highest degree of surgical care and skill. It further held that no evidence had been shown by the plaintiff which indicated that standard surgical practice would have required the use of two ligatures.[95]

The patient had a hernia operation and had a hemorrhage shortly thereafter. A vessel had been cut. The medical evidence indicated that it was as likely that a ligature had been properly applied but had slipped off than that it was never applied, as alleged by the patient. The plaintiff did not recover damages because he presented no testimony which proved surgical negligence.[96]

While the surgeon may well not be legally liable for the fact that his patient has a hemorrhage, if he does not deal with the situation with speed when it does occur, he may be negligent.

Severe vaginal bleeding occurred after a hysterectomy. Neither the operating surgeon who was the defendant nor his two substitutes who saw the patient during his absence made any effort to find out what the problem was. After she was released from the hospital, still bleeding, a massive hemorrhage occurred. Surgery at that point revealed that the vaginal branch of the uterine artery had been severed during the original surgery. The surgeon was found negligent.[97]

An adult patient had a tonsillectomy. She began to bleed and the surgeon restitched the site. He then left the hospital. The patient had a massive hemorrhage and the physician could not be located. She died. However, because the autopsy revealed that the cause of death was a pulmonary embolism and not the loss of blood, the court held that there was insufficient causal connection between the absence of the physician and the death. Presumably, if the patient had died from the direct result of the hemorrhage, the widower could have recovered damages.[98]

A surgeon who treats a hemorrhaging patient by approved methods and with due care is also not liable if the patient dies or is severely injured. A surgeon must, however, make himself or a substitute available to deal with this situation should it arise. Although he does not have to remain at the hospital with every patient, if a surgeon informs those in charge of his patients where he can be located if there is any possibility of hemorrhage or other postoperative complications, and deals with it promptly and in keeping with approved methods of treatment, he probably will not be liable even if the patient dies. Due care is as ever the key. Courts are aware that unexpected complications occur in any surgery and that the unavoidable risk of hemorrhage does exist.

Medical Negligence. Most cases alleging medical, as opposed to surgical, negligence involve therapeutic agents such as Xrays, drugs, and blood transfusion, all of which will be discussed in the next chapter.

Surprisingly few malpractice suits involve allegations of inadequate or incorrect treatment of heart conditions. Most cases involving cardiologists allege misdiagnosis.

A patient, a dentist, visited the defendant internist because of chest pains. An electrocardiogram revealed abnormal results which could have been due to a heart condition, but the patient was not advised of this, nor was he warned to rest. A week later, the dentist still had chest pains and the defendant administered an analgesic. After an 8-hour delay, the defendant made arrangements for the patient's hospitalization. However, he allowed the patient to walk to his car and be driven to the hospital instead of going in an ambulance. The patient subsequently had an infarction and eventually had to undergo open heart surgery. The court held that the physician had been negligent in failing to hospitalize him.[99]

Differences of opinion as to the proper treatment of heart disease generally preclude successful actions for negligence in treatment of the condition itself, as long as the treatment given is accepted by at least a respectable minority of the profession.

A patient developed severe pains in his chest and was referred to a cardiologist by his general practitioner. He was admitted to a hospital and began to improve rapidly. The cardiologist diagnosed the condition as cardiac insufficiency. At no time during hospitalization was the patient given anticoagulants. Almost immediately after his discharge from the hospital, the patient had another heart attack and died. At the trial, it was alleged that the cardiologist had been negligent because he had failed to prescribe anticoagulant drugs. Expert testimony indicated the possible dangers inherent in these drugs, and the cardiologist testified that he had decided not to use them for this reason. The court held that no negligence had been shown.[100]

A psychiatrist may be liable for negligent treatment if a patient commits suicide if such an event should have been foreseeable.[101] If the patient's actions are such that a reasonably prudent psychiatrist under the circumstances should have anticipated a suicide attempt, the concept of "due care in treatment" requires prevention of the opportunity.[102] The fact that a patient has begun treatment as the result of a suicide attempt renders liability under the concept of "reasonable foreseeability" virtually automatic in all cases. Failure to guard a patient who is threatening to do what he in fact does is sufficiently obvious to make the only question the amount of damages to be awarded.[103]

A woman was admitted to a mental hospital suffering from acute depression. She made two suicide attempts while there and her physician told the head floor nurse after her wrist was sutured for the second time that she was not to leave the ward. The nurse did not note this order on the patient's chart and the patient walked out with no objection from the nurses on the next shift. She left the hospital grounds and ran in front of a car and was run over. She had permanently disabling orthopedic injuries and severe organic brain damage. The jury's award of $275,000 in damages against the hospital was upheld on appeal.[104]

However, if the use of due care in observing the patient and in making the initial diagnosis would not have put the psychiatrist on notice that the patient was suicidal, he is not liable if self-injury occurs.

A patient was admitted to a mental hospital as a voluntary patient. He was suffering from anxiety and depression, but was not psychotic. He gave no indication of any symptoms indicating a desire to hurt himself. While he was outside for a walk a day after receiving electroshock treatments, he climbed a 6-foot wall and jumped to the ground on the other side, injuring himself severely. The psychiatrist was not liable for his injuries.[105]

This result is usually reached when a patient who has never indicated any suicidal symptoms goes beserk.[106]

As more and more mental hospitals make the decision that the advantages of an "open door" policy as a therapeutic concept outweigh the risk of suicide in a given case where no previous attempt at self-destruction has been made, the number of these decisions will increase. However, freedom for a psychiatric patient is a matter of medical judgment on the part of the treating psychiatrist. As long as he is informed about and alert to the patient's condition, it is usually quite difficult to prove lack of due care in what is often considered a calculated risk inherent in modern psychiatry.

It should be noted that if a patient in a mental hospital becomes ill with a physical illness and the psychiatrist does not provide medical treatment, he may be negligent.

The plaintiff's daughter was both psychotic and retarded. She was a patient in a state mental hospital. She became ill with a fever in excess of 101°, but no effort to administer any treatment was made for 4 days. Her temperature at that time rose to 106° and she was taken to a general hospital where medical treatment was given, but she died a few hours after admission. The court found that her mental condition was such that she was under the exclusive control of the defendant hospital and it was liable for failing to treat her illness.[107]

From time to time a patient is released from a mental hospital and assaults another person, resulting in a suit against the psychiatrist by the victim or his heirs.[108] Where there is no evidence that the patient's assault should have been foreseeable with the use of due care by the psychiatrist, no negligence will be found.[109]

A patient had been in a state mental hospital for 12 years without showing any tendencies toward violence. He was given the privilege of going for walks in the neighborhood and attacked the plaintiff, who sued his psychiatrist. The court held that none of the evidence indicated that allowing the patient reasonable freedom had been bad medical judgment in view of the absence of any reason to foresee the risk.[110]

Where a patient is known to be dangerous to himself or others, however, failure to supervise him properly does state a cause of action against the hospital or the psychiatrist.[111]

A mental patient who was known to be violent overpowered an attendant, escaped from the hospital, stole a car, and caused a fatal automobile accident. The state was held liable for having failed to provide a number of attendants in wards containing individuals known to be dangerous sufficient to prevent just such an event.[112]

Thus the same standard of due care is applied in psychiatric treatment as is required for all other fields of medicine or surgery. If the psychiatrist's treatment involves injury when the patient is released, the question is not whether the psychiatrist should have known better, but whether the duly careful psychiatrist, given the facts of the case, would have given the patient the freedom which provided the opportunity for an assault to occur.

If a patient has been voluntarily admitted to a mental hospital and wants to leave, failure to release him if he is not dangerous constitutes negligence in treatment, not negligence in diagnosis. A voluntary patient who has indicated a desire to leave, but who is not in the psychiatrist's opinion capable of functioning without danger to himself or others should be civilly committed in a judicial hearing or released. Failure to do either of the above and retaining the patient against his will is not only negligence, it will support legal actions for false imprisonment and for violation of the patient's civil rights.

A woman in her late 70's was tricked by a relative into going to a mental hospital. She thought she was going to a general hospital for treatment of an abdominal complaint. She signed herself in. As soon as she found out where she was, she asked to go home, but was held for over a year in spite of her daily objections. She finally climbed out a second floor window in spite of her age and physical infirmities and ran to a telephone to call her lawyer. As soon as he found out where she was he had a court order releasing her within an hour. The hospital did not even argue that she was incompetent or ask for a civil commitment. She sued and the court stated that she had cause of actions both for negligence and for false imprisonment. The court did not accept the hospital's contention that she was required to try to escape or be assumed to consent.[113]

If a patient has been involuntarily committed in lieu of standing trial on a criminal offense, at the point where he is not dangerous to himself or others he has a constitutional as well as a legal right to release from confinement.[114] The patient's right to due process of law means that he may not be confined in a mental hospital for a longer time than he would have served in the penitentiary upon conviction.[115] If he is, at that point, still dangerous to himself or others or mentally incompetent, he has the right to demand civil commitment. Unless he is legally insane, however, he has the right to demand trial or release.[116]

A man was charged with a minor offense and committed to a state mental hospital. After a short while the psychiatrist ordered him discharged, but because proper records were not kept his release order was not processed. He proved that he was beaten by hospital personnel because he kept insisting that he was supposed to get out. The chart entries indicated that his insistence that he was there by mistake and that he was being beaten were diagnosed as loss of reality contact. The period of false imprisonment was 14 years, 3 months and 20 days. He recovered $300,000 from the state.[117]

A severely retarded deaf mute was charged with robbery. He could not read or write, so he could not communicate with his lawyers. The judge ordered him committed until he improved. The Supreme Court of the United States held that indefinite commitment of an accused because of his lack of capacity violated his rights to due process of law. The court held that he must be released or hospitalized under a civil commitment, in which he would have far greater rights.[118]

Persons involuntarily committed to mental institutions also have a constitutional right to adequate psychiatric and medical treatment.[119]

In two decisions[120] federal courts found that personnel shortages were so great that treatment programs in state mental hospitals in two states were so inadequate there was no possibility that any of the patients could improve. The court pointed out that using mental hospitals as warehouses for society's problems means that the involuntarily committed patients were serving life sentences for crimes for which they had never been convicted in clear violation of their constitutional rights. The hospitals were ordered to provide treatment meeting appropriate psychiatric standards or release the patients. While no damage suits can be found for negligent failure to treat, except in conjunction with false imprisonment, it is highly probable that a patient who is neither treated nor released could sue and recover large damages for negligence and for civil rights violations.

Medical negligence may include the failure to protect either the patient or a third person from a contagious disease. For example, two recent cases involved successful suits against physicians who were treating tuberculosis patients. They were allowed to remain at home while being treated with medication, and their small children, living in the same household, contracted the disease. In both cases, the physicians were liable.[121]

A man had applied for employment and the corporation's physician had given him a preemployment physical. A chest Xray was positive for tuberculosis, but the physician did not inform him of that fact. The man's wife contracted tuberculosis from him. The court held that she had a cause of action against the corporation.[122]

The neighbor of a smallpox victim asked the physician whether she would be likely to catch it if she helped nurse the patient. The physician assured her that she would not. She offered her assistance to the smallpox victim, caught the disease, sued the physician, and collected damages.[123]

A physician told a parent that, although a child had scarlet fever, there was no danger that the parents would become infected. The parents did catch the disease, sued, and recovered damages.[124]

Needless to say, if a physician who is treating a patient for a communicable disease is the cause of infection of another patient, he may be liable for giving the second patient the disease. In a very old case, a physician was told that if he was attending any smallpox patients, the plaintiff would not employ him. He was in fact doing so, but concealed such activity from the patient, who contracted smallpox from him. The physician was liable.[125]

Thus it may be seen that medical and surgical negligence consist of deviation from standard practice. If the patient who is properly treated by an accepted method or an allowable deviation from an accepted method does not recover or dies, or if the treatment causes a worse condition than that from which the patient originally suffered, the physician or surgeon is still not liable if he carefully used standard practice and treatment.

Follow-Up Care. A physician's responsibility is not concluded when he completes immediate treatment of the patient.[126] A surgeon, for example, has the duty of postoperative care, particularly as long as the patient is in the hospital. If a postsurgical or obstetrical infection occurs, the physician will be liable if he has not visited the patient sufficiently frequently to be aware of it.

A man fractured his arm in a farm accident and went to the emergency room. He saw an intern who called the defendant, an orthopedist. The intern reported that the patient had a compound fracture. The defendant told him to clean the patient's arm, but gave no orders for antibiotics. He did not see the patient himself that day and only a moment before surgery the following day. An infection set in 3 days later and the arm eventually required amputation. The defendant's failure to see the patient at all for 2 days was the basis for the determination that due care had not been used.[127]

If, however, the surgeon has made an effort to make a prompt and careful diagnosis of postoperative complications or infection, he is not liable simply because one occurs.

A patient fractured her ankle and the defendant performed an open reduction. When her temperature went up, he diagnosed and treated her problem as tonsillitis. The infection at the site of the surgery was not discovered for a few more days, by which time her ankle had fused. All the experts agreed that the defendant had opened the cast at the earliest time at which her symptoms indicated the decision was in order. He was held to have used due care.[128]

The physician is required to continue attendance after the immediate treatment is over until, in the exercise of duly careful judgment, he decides that the patient's condition does not demand further visits.

A patient was admitted to the hospital in critical condition about 1:00 a.m. after receiving a gunshot wound of the trachea. The physician arrived shortly thereafter, but rendered only minimal aid. He had been drinking, but there was considerable disagreement among hospital personnel as to his degree of inebriation. When he went home at 3:45 a.m. at a time when all evidence indicated that the patient was experiencing great difficulty in breathing, he had not done a tracheotomy or given a blood transfusion. At about 4:00 a.m., 15 minutes after he left, another physician responded to a nurse's call and instituted emergency measures. He requested that the physician be telephoned to release the patient to his care. After two telephone calls and the loss of about half an hour, the physician grudgingly told the second physician that he could treat the patient. The patient died of shock and blood loss during an operation which started shortly before 5:00 a.m. The court held the physician liable for failure to continue treatment once he had accepted the patient.[129]

Once a physician has undertaken to treat a patient, therefore, he cannot end his professional responsibilities except, first, with the consent of the patient, secondly, by giving the patient notice sufficient to allow him to obtain another physician, or thirdly, when the patient's condition no longer requires it. Errors as to the last, that the patient is no longer in need of treatment, seem to be the most common cause of suits in this area.

A child had a fractured femur. Traction apparatus caused pressure necrosis of her foot. The court held that there was sufficient evidence to show that the attending physician did not come to the hospital and see her often enough to discover the difficulty. He was liable for failing to follow her progress with sufficient care.[130]

If a patient is being cared for at home, the physician of course has a far greater obligation to give careful and specific orders and instructions to untrained helpers than if the patient is being cared for in a hospital.

A patient was seriously ill at his home in the country several miles from the physician's office. He was nursed only by his wife, his daughter, and the wife of a neighbor, none of whom were nurses. His condition deteriorated as the result of the fact that none of the women knew how to care for him. The physician was found to be negligent for having failed to give them proper instructions.[131]

Further, the responsibility of a physician is not concluded when the patient's immediate need is met. Check-up visits to keep abreast of the patient's progress are as vital as the use of due care in performance of the original operation or treatment.[132]

A patient had a hysterectomy. No postoperative pelvic examination was made. The patient's vagina closed, as she discovered when she attempted to have sexual intercourse with her husband a few weeks after surgery. The court found the surgeon negligent for failing to make adequate postoperative examinations.[133]

If tests or other examination reports received by a physician after a patient has left his care indicate that further diagnosis or treatment may be required, a physician who fails to contact the patient, report on the results, and issue instructions for further examination is negligent.

A patient had a Pap smear at a routine physical examination. The laboratory report came back "suspicious for malignancy." The patient had no telephone and moved a few days after the examination. The physician made no effort to trace her when a note to her old address was returned, although he could have done so since he knew how to contact her mother. She made another appointment 5 months later and he told her at that time of the laboratory report. The patient did have a malignancy and major surgery was required. A cause of action was stated against the physician for his failure to pursue efforts to locate her.[134]

If the patient should return for further treatment the physician is obliged to tell him so.

A patient was injured in an automobile accident. He had multiple fractures of the facial bones and the defendant gave him emergency treatment. After a week the man was discharged from the hospital. His face was still too swollen to realign the fractured bones. The defendant therefore did not tell him to consult a specialist in order to have the bones set. As a result of delay, the bones became fused. The patient's face was disfigured and his vision was impaired. The physician was held liable for failing to instruct the patient to see a specialist.[135]

A small piece of steel was imbedded in a patient's eye. He went to the hospital and was seen by a general practitioner, who called an ophthalmologist, the defendant in the case. Xrays were taken, but the steel could not be found. The ophthalmologist claimed that he told the patient to return the next morning, by which time he thought he could locate the fragment. The plaintiff not only denied that he had been told to return, but testified that he asked the defendant if it were necessary to come back and the defendant had told him that it was not. In any case, he did not return to the physician's office. The eye became infected before another physician found the steel. He went blind in that eye. The jury believed the physician's testimony instead of the patient's, but if they had believed the patient the physician would have been liable.[136]

Even when the patient is released from direct supervision by the physician, responsibility and obligations to him do not necessarily cease. If his condition requires continuing self-care, the physician who neglects to explain these matters is negligent. In particular, such matters as any restriction on mobility or activities for patients recovering from fractures must be carefully explained.[137]

A construction workman fell from the third floor level of a building. He was taken to the hospital where fractures of one arm and one leg were diagnosed. The next day Xrays revealed compression fractures of two vertebrae. The orthopedist who treated him did not tell him of the back injuries and did not tell him to restrict his activities. Several years later he sustained severe back injuries while helping another employee lift a heavy object. In a suit against the first physician, the orthopedist who treated him for the second injury testified that it had been negligence to fail to tell the patient of injuries and to warn him to restrict his activities. The court held that a cause of action was stated.[138]

Explicit instructions about medication are also required.

A patient was given ointment for treatment of a skin infection. The ointment caused irritation and burning. It was clear that the practice among physicians in the area was to tell patients to wash off an ointment if it produced irritation, but there was no evidence that any instruction to this effect was given either to the patient or to his family. The court held that failure to give such instructions constituted negligence.[139]

A physician is obligated to give a patient explicit instructions about the possible side effects of any prescribed medication and to make sure the patient is aware of any problems which the medication might cause, such as increasing the effects of the patient's ordinary alcohol intake or complications of combining the drug with any other medication.

A psychiatrist discharged a patient immediately after a shock treatment. He prescribed a heavy sedative but did not warn either the patient or his family about side effects. The man set himself on fire with a cigarette when he went to sleep from the effects of the drug and the treatment. The court held that the psychiatrist's failure to instruct and warn the patient was negligence.[140]

Several decisions indicate that prescribing drugs such as antihistamines, tranquilizers, sedatives, and painkillers which could affect a patient's ability to drive a car without advising him of that fact will leave the physician open to suit not only by the patient, but by anyone else injured in a wreck which the patient causes by going to sleep at the wheel.[141] In addition to whatever specific instructions may be required for a particular patient, the physician should also instruct the patient to report to him any changes in his condition, such as new symptoms or unusual occurrences.[142]

The physician must make his instructions understood to the patient. Therefore, if the patient has any disabilities affecting his comprehension of information, the physician must not merely content himself with giving the type of instructions which he may fairly assume a member of his own family would understand.

A recent immigrant to this country spoke almost no English. He had a serious heart condition and the physician knew that he was employed as a manual laborer. The physician did not communicate well enough with the patient to make the patient understand that he could not return to work, so the patient did so. He had another heart attack and died. The jury verdict in favor of the patient's family was upheld on appeal.[143]

Specifically, if there is any question of the patient's ability to read, either because of functional illiteracy or vision problems, the physician may not merely assume that the patient is able to follow the dosage instructions on medication labels. Oral instructions must be given.

If the patient is mentally incompetent, senile, or otherwise unable to understand instructions, the physician must explain the situation to some other member of the family or deal with the patient in such a way that no instructions need be given.

A woman had varicose vein surgery. While there was no negligence in performance of the surgery, gangrene set in and she eventually lost all the toes on one foot. All the experts at the trial of the negligence suit against the surgeon agreed that a paravertebral block would have been the only proper treatment. The defendant concurred, but testified that the patient refused to consent. Undisputed evidence showed that she was semiconscious for most of the time after surgery, was in acute pain, and was heavily sedated. She testified that she had no recollection of being asked to consent. The surgeon admitted that he had not discussed the problem with her husband, although he had been at the hospital almost every day for long periods of time. The court held that where the patient is not able to understand the necessity of proposed treatment, whether the inability is the result of the illness or not, the physician is legally required to consult the next of kin.[144]

A senile, 73-year old woman was admitted to the hospital with a respiratory problem. Her physician ordered a vaporizer placed in her room. Hospital personnel told her not to get out of bed but did not use bedrails. She became confused, forgot the instructions, and got up to go to the bathroom. She tripped over the vaporizer and burned herself badly. The court held that the nurses, knowing her mental condition, would not have had reasonable cause to believe that she would have remembered what she was told and that the hospital was therefore liable for her injuries.[145]

Where children are involved, even adolescents, it is usually advisable to instruct the parents as well as the child.[146]

In short, the physician takes his patient as he finds him. The fact that the patient is elderly, forgetful, cannot speak English, cannot read, has a hearing problem, or is very young is no excuse for the physician later if the patient is damaged by failing to understand the information imparted by the physician.

A physician, of course, is not liable if a patient understands instructions but refuses to follow them. In that case, any damage is the patient's own fault and is a good defense to a negligence action against the physician.

A small child had a boil on her back. The physician gave her mother explicit instructions on care of the child, but the mother did not follow them. The infection spread and the physician had to administer antibiotics. She died of anaphylactic shock. The jury found the mother, not the physician, to be the negligent party.[147]

A physician who wishes to eliminate any possibility of allegations that he failed to give proper warnings or instructions or was negligent in any way in follow-up care must give attention to basic principles of common sense as well as medical judgment. He must explain instructions to the patient who is before him in light of all the difficulties under which the patient may be functioning, including, quite possibly, the emotional distress and pain inherent in the illness, and until the patient understands them, instructions are not complete. A physician must always bear in mind that he cannot always expect a sick person to conform to the standard of conduct, intelligence, foresight, and comprehension which it is reasonable to expect from someone who is well.[148] Once he has done this, however, he is not negligent if those instructions are not followed.

Therefore, just as was true in determining malpractice in diagnosis, malpractice in medical treatment consists solely of unjustified deviation from standard practice in dealing with a patient's illness or injury. If standard procedures are employed or if there is justified deviation from them, the physician is not liable even if the patient does not recover.

NOTES

1. Adkins v. Ropp, 14 NE 2d 727, Ind 1938.
2. Derr v. Bonney, 231 P 2d 637, Wash 1951.
3. Lane v. Calvert, 138 A 2d 902, Md 1958.
4. "Guarantee of Medical Results," 219 *JAMA* No. 3, page 431, January 17, 1972.
5. Hawkins v. McGee, 146 Atl 641, NH 1929.
6. Doerr v. Villate, 220 NE 2d 767, Ill 1966; Custodio v. Bauer, 59 Cal Rptr 463, Cal 1967.
7. Troppi v. Scarf, 187 NW 2d 511, Mich 1971.
8. Benson v. Dean, 133 NE 125, NY 1921.
9. Baldor v. Rogers, 81 So 2d 658, Fla 1955.
10. Rotan v. Greenbaum, 273 F 2d 830, CA DC 1959.
11. Schwartz v. United States, 230 F Supp 536, DC Pa 1964.

12. Merker v. Wood, 210 SW 2d 946, Ky 1948.

13. Gonzales v. Peterson, 359 P 2d 307, Wash 1961.

14. Livingston v. Portland General Hospital Association 357 P 2d 543, Ore 1960.

15. "Abandonment: Parts I–IV," 225 *JAMA* No. 9 page 1157, August 27, 1973, 225 *JAMA* No. 10, page 1285, Sept. 3, 1973, 225 *JAMA* No. 11, page 1429, Sept, 10, 1973, 225 *JAMA* No. 12, page 1571, Sept. 17, 1973; "Desertion, Abandonment and Neglect of Patient," 199 *JAMA* No. 8, page 245, Feb. 20, 1967; Johnson v. Vaughn, 370 SW 2d 591, Ky 1963.

16. Tadlock v. Lloyd, 173 Pac 200, Colo 1918.

17. Levy v. Kirk, 187 So 2d 401, Fla 1966.

18. Calhoun v. Fraser, 126 SW 2d 381, Tenn 1938.

19. Natanson v. Kline, 350 P 2d 1093, 354 P 2d 760, Kans 1960.

20. Hales v. Raines, 141 SW 917, Mo 1911; Ballance v. Dunnington, 217 NW 329, Mich 1928.

21. Mainfort v. Giannestras, 111 NE 2d 692, Ohio 1951.

22. Carpenter v. Blake, 60 Barbour 488, NY 1871.

23. Karp v. Cooley, 349 F Supp 827, DC Tex 1972.

24. "Alternative Medical Procedures," 212 *JAMA* No. 2, page 385, April 13, 1970.

25. Bruce v. United States, 167 F Supp 579, DC Cal 1958.

26. Ball v. Mallinkrodt Chemical Works, 381 SW 2d 563, Tenn 1964.

27. Davis v. New York, 315 NYS 2d 82, NY 1970.

28. Miller v. Toles, 150 NW 118, Mich 1914; Jackson v. Burnham, 39 Pac 577, Colo 1895; Allen v. Voje, 89 NW 924, Wisc 1902.

29. Fortner v. Koch, 261 NW 762, Mich 1935.

30. *New York Times*, May 9, 1973, page 54.

31. Davie v. Lenox Hill Hospital, 81 NYS 2d 583, NY 1948.

32. Lanier v. Trammell, 180 SW 2d 818, Ark 1944.

33. Aurelio v. Laird, 223 NE 2d 531, Mass 1967.

34. Reed v. Church, 8 SE 2d 285, Va 1940; Powell v. Risser, 99 A 2d 454, Pa 1953.

35. McCandless v. McWha, 22 Pa 261, Pa 1853; *See* McCoid, Allan H., "The Care Required of Medical Practitioners," pages 39–45, *Professional Negligence*, Roady, Thomas G. and Anderson, William R., Eds., Vanderbilt University Press, Nashville, 1960.

36. "Liability for Vesicovaginal Fistula," 212 *JAMA* No. 6, page 1113, May 11, 1970; Dees v. Pace, 257 P 2d 756, Cal 1953.

37. Modrzynski v. Lust, 88 NE 76, Ohio 1949.

38. Silverson v. Weber, 372 P 2d 97, Cal 1962.

39. "Cardiac Arrest," 216 *JAMA* No. 13, page 2217, June 28, 1971.

40. Bradshaw v. Blaine, 134 NW 2d 386, Mich 1965.

41. Dunlap v. Marine, 51 Cal Rptr 158, Cal 1966.

42. Linhares v. Hall, 257 NE 2d 429, Mass 1970.

43. Quintal v. Laurel Grove Hospital, 397 P 2d 161, Cal 1964.

44. "Mistaken Identity," 221 *JAMA* No. 7, page 747, Aug. 14, 1972; "Mistaken Procedures," 226 *JAMA* No. 8, page 1053, Nov. 19, 1973.

45. O'Grady v. Wickman, 213 So 2d 321, Fla 1968.

46. Lane v. United States, 225 F Supp 850, DC Va 1964.

47. Maercklein v. Smith, 266 P 2d 1095, Colo 1954.

48. Woronka v. Sewall, 69 NE 2d 581, Mass 1946.

49. "Liability for Esophageal Perforation," 216 *JAMA* No. 8, page 1399, May 24, 1971.

50. Demchuck v. Bralow, 170 A 2d 868, Pa 1961.

51. Newman v. Spellberg, 234 NE 2d 152, Ill 1968.

52. "Angiograms," 213 *JAMA* No. 2, page 349, July 13, 1970.

53. Salgo v. Leland Stanford Board of Trustees, 317 P 2d 170, Cal 1957; Bowers v. Talmage, 159 So 2d 888, Fla 1963.

54. Horace v. Weyrauch, 324 P 2d 666, Cal 1958.

55. Moore v. Belt, 212 P 2d 509, Cal 1949.

56. Silvers v. Wesson, 266 P 2d 169, Cal 1954.

57. "Liability for Obstetrical Injuries," 217 *JAMA* No. 7, page 1015, August 16, 1971; "Birth Injuries," 219 *JAMA* No. 1, page 129, Jan. 3 1972.

58. Scott v. McPheeters, 92 P 2d 678, Cal 1939.

59. Korman v. Hagen, 206 NW 650, Minn 1925; Brooks v. Serrano, 209 So 2d 279, Fla 1968.

60. Stetson v. Easterling, 161 SE 2d 531, NC 1968.

61. Graham v. Sisco, 449 SW 2d 949, Ark 1970.

62. Larrabee v. United States, 254 F Supp 613, DC Cal 1966.

63. Poor Sisters of St. Francis v. Long, 230 SW 2d 659, Tenn 1950.

64. Horner v. Northern Pacific Benevolent Association Hospitals, 382 P 2d 518, Wash 1963.

65. "Liability in Dilation and Curettage Cases," 218 *JAMA* No. 12, page 1873, Dec. 20, 1971.

66. Beaudoin v. Watertown Memorial Hospital, 145 NW 2d 166, Wisc 1966.

67. "Vasectomies," 217 *JAMA* No. 13, page 1943, Sept. 27, 1971.

68. Dunn v. Campbell, 166 So 2d 217, Fla 1964.

69. "Liability in 'Tight Cast' Cases," 217 *JAMA* No. 12, page 1767, Sept. 20, 1971.

70. Hanson v. Thelan, 173 NW 457, ND 1919; Galloway v. Lawrence, 145 SE 2d 861, NC 1966.

71. Vann v. Harden, 47 SE 2d 314, Va 1948.

72. Rose v. Friddell, 423 SW 2d 658, Tex 1967.

73. Atkins v. Humes, 107 So 2d 253, Fla 1958.

74. Olson v. Weitz, 221 P 2d 537, Wash 1950.

75. Gebhardt v. McQuillen, 297 NW 301, Iowa 1941; Meador v. Arnold, 94 SW 2d 626, Ky 1936.

76. Clark v. Wichman, 179 A 2d 38, NJ 1962.

77. Uter v. Bone and Joint Clinic, 192 So 2d 100, La 1966.

78. Bradshaw v. Wilson, 94 NE 2d 706, Ohio 1950.

79. "Liability for Gas Gangrene," 221 *JAMA* No. 9, page 1083, August 28, 1972.

80. Scott v. Salem County Memorial Hospital, 280 A 2d 843, NJ 1971.

81. Williams v. Vanderhoven, 482, P 2d 55, NM 1971.

82. Guillen v. Martin, 333 P 2d 266, Cal 1958; Yerzy v. Levine, 260 A 2d 533, NJ 1970.

83. Tomei v. Henning, 431 P 2d 633, Cal 1967.

84. Gerhardt v. Fresno Medical Group, 31 Cal Rptr 633, Cal 1963.

85. Haines v. Ebert, 187 NE 2d 522, Ohio 1961.

86. Mayers v. Litow, 316 P 2d 351, Cal 1957; Patrick v. Sedwick, 391 P 2d 453, 413 P 2d 169, Alaska 1964.

87. Di Filippo v. Preston, 173 A 2d 333, Del 1961.

88. Fraser v. Sprague, 76 Cal Rptr 37, Cal 1969.

89. Stundon v. Stadnik, 469 P 2d 16, Wyo 1970.

90. McDermott v. Manhattan Eye, Ear and Throat Hospital, 228 NYS 2d 143, 203 NE 2d 469, NY 1964.

91. Gluckstein v. Lipsett, 209 P 2d 98, Cal 1949.

92. Wangel v. Pangman, Trial Court decision, Los Angeles County, Cal, Docket No. WEC 9141, 1971.

93. Sullivan v. O'Connor, 296 NE 2d 183, Mass 1973.

94. "Surgical Hemorrhage," 220 *JAMA* No. 3, page 453, April 17, 1972.

95. Engle v. Clarke, 346 SW 2d 13, Ky 1961.

96. Scardina v. Colletti, 211 NE 2d 762, Ill 1965.

97. Gist v. French, 288 P 2d 1003, Cal 1955.

98. Michael v. Roberts, 23 A 2d 361, NH 1941.

99. Armstrong v. Svoboda, 49 Cal Rptr 701, Cal 1966.

100. Haase v. Garfinkel, 418 SW 2d 108, Mo 1967.

101. "Liability for Patient's Suicide," 215 *JAMA* No. 11, page 1879, March 15, 1971.

102. Lange v. United States, 179 F Supp 777, DC NY 1960.

103. Meier v. Ross General Hospital, 67 Cal Rptr 471, Cal 1968; United States v. Gray, 199 F 2d 239, CCA 10, 1952.

104. Adams v. State, 429 P 2d 109, Wash 1967.

105. DeMartini v. Alexandria Sanitarium, 13 Cal Rptr 564, Cal 1961.

106. Schwartz v. United States, 226 F Supp 84, DC DC 1964; Frederic v. United States, 246 F Supp 368, DC La 1965.

107. Soto v. New York, 333 NYS 2d 588, NY 1972.

108. "Improper Release from Mental Hospital," 220 *JAMA* No. 6, page 897, May 8, 1972.

109. Fernandez v. Baruch, 244 A 2d 109, NJ 1968.

110. Higgins v. New York, 265 NYS 2d 254, NY 1965.

111. Merchants' National Bank v. United States, 272 F Supp 409, DC ND 1967.

112. Dunn v. New York, 312 NYS 2d 61, NY 1970.

113. Geddes v. Daughters of Charity, 348 F 2d 144, CCA 5 1965.

114. Dixon v. Jacobs, 427 F 2d 589, DC CA 1970.

115. Rouse v. Cameron, 373 F 2d 451, DC CA 1966.

116. "Right to Release from Mental Hospital," 220 *JAMA* No. 10, page 1405, June 5, 1972.

117. Whitree v. New York, 290 NYS 2d 486, NY 1968.

118. Jackson v. Indiana, 406 US 715, 1972.

119. "The Right to Treatment," 220 *JAMA* No. 8, page 1165, May 22, 1972; "The Right to Treatment," 57 *Georgetown Law Journal*, March 1969.

120. Sas v. Maryland, 334 F 2d 506, CCA 4, 1964; Wyatt v. Stickney, 325 F Supp 781, DC Ala 1971.

121. Golia v. Health Insurance Plan of Greater New York, 166 NYS 2d 889, NY 1957; Hofmann v. Blackmon, 241 So 2d 752, Fla 1970.

122. Wojcik v. Aluminum Company of America, 183 NYS 2d 351, NY 1959.

123. Jones v. Stanko, 160 NE 456, Ohio 1928.

124. Skillings v. Allen, 180 NW 916, Minn 1921.

125. Piper v. Menifee, 51 Ky 465, 1851.

126. "Follow-Up Procedures," 212 *JAMA* No. 1, page 233, April 6, 1970.

127. Benzmiller v. Swanson, 117 NW 2d 281, ND 1962.

128. Thibodeaux v. Aetna Casualty Insurance Company, 216 So 2d 314, La 1968.

129. Johnson v. Vaughn, 370 SW 2d 591, Ky 1963.

130. Moeller v. Hauser, 54 NW 2d 639, Minn 1952.

131. Miles v. Hoffman, 221 Pac 316, Wash 1923.

132. "Responsibility for Future Medical Care," 199 *JAMA* No. 9, page 253, Feb. 27, 1967.

133. Wooten v. Curry, 362 SW 2d 820, Tenn 1961.

134. Ray v. Wagner, 176 NW 2d 101, Minn 1970.

135. Doan v. Griffith, 402 SW 2d 855, Ky 1966.

136. Barnes v. Bovenmyer, 122 NW 2d 312, Iowa 1963.

137. Beck v. The German Klinik, 43 NW 617, Iowa 1889; Pike v. Honsinger, 49 NE 760, NY 1898.

138. Martisek v. Ainsworth, 459 SW 2d 679, Tex 1970.

139. Newman v. Anderson, 217 NW 306, Wisc 1928.

140. Christy v. Saliterman, 179 NW 2d 288, Minn 1970.

141. Whitfield v. Daniel Construction Company, 83 SE 2d 460, SC 1954; Kaiser v. Suburban Transportation Company, 398 P 2d 14, Wash 1965.

142. Lemon v. Kessel, 209 NW 393, Iowa 1926.

143. Krusilla v. United States, 287 F 2d 34, CCA 2, 1961.

144. Steele v. Woods, 327 SW 2d 187, Mo 1959.

145. Clark v. Piedmont Hospital, 162 SE 2d 468, Ga 1968.

146. Sharpe v. Pugh, 155 SE 2d 108, NC 1967; Orendino v. Clarke, 402 P 2d 527, Ore 1965.

147. Puffinbarger v. Day, 24 Cal Rptr 533, Cal 1962.

148. Williams v. Marini, 162 Atl 796, Vt 1932.

CHAPTER V

INJURIES

FROM

THERAPEUTIC

AGENTS

The preceding chapter discussed the general principles applicable to alleged negligence in treatment by the physician. Many malpractice suits, however, allege that some therapeutic agent was either inappropriate for the treatment of the patient's problem or that it was negligently administered. This chapter will discuss legal principles involving foreign objects left in patients' bodies following surgery, untoward results of blood transfusions, Xray injuries, anesthesia injuries, electroshock therapy, and injuries and complications from the use of prescribed drugs.

Foreign Objects. The classic example of medical negligence taught to beginning law students is the "foreign object" case. If a surgeon leaves something used during the operation in the patient's body, he will usually be presumed to be negligent. Most courts in this country do not even require proof by an expert witness that such a situation violates normal principles of due care, because a jury of laymen is perfectly able to realize that sponges, towels, knives, and hemostats do not belong in patient's bodies after surgery is completed. However, there are exceptions to this rule and not every case results in a decision for the patient.

After surgery for an ectopic pregnancy, the patient vomited constantly and lost 30 pounds. The surgeon repeatedly assured her that there was nothing wrong with her. Two and one-half years later another surgeon removed a cloth sack 10 inches wide and 18 inches long from the patient's body. The surgeon was found liable.[1]

After gall bladder surgery in a military hospital, a serviceman continued to have pains in his abdomen. After his discharge from the service he was operated on by a private surgeon and a towel 18 by 30 inches was discovered in his abdomen. The military surgeons denied having left it there, but since the towel had "US ARMY" printed on it, in large letters, the government was found to have been negligent.[2]

It is usually true, of course, that physicians are found liable when they leave objects behind in their patients.[3] Sponges, gauze, and other cloth objects are the subjects of many decisions every year.[4]

Failure to have a sponge count made after an operation is completed but before closing sutures are begun is usually, but not always, considered to be negligent.[5] However, if special circumstances indicate that such a count is not standard practice in the type of surgery involved, this inference of negligence may not be drawn.

A patient hemorrhaged after delivery. In order to stop the bleeding the obstetrician packed her vagina with pieces of gauze. Two years later in another operation a piece of gauze was discovered in her abdomen. Experts testified that it was not customary to count sponges used in delivery, since they would be expelled if they were not removed. The obstetrician was not negligent.[6]

If a nurse's sponge count is wrong and as a result one is left behind, the surgeon is not automatically considered absolved from legal responsibility.[7] The surgeon is usually responsible for the negligence of other operating room personnel as "the captain of the ship" and is therefore indirectly liable for the error of the nurse who makes the miscount.[8]

Use of laparotomy pads without metal rings to assist in counting or locating them during surgery or in locating them by Xray if one is inadvertently left behind may well be considered negligence.[9]

Surgical instruments are also sometimes left in patient's bodies. Needles are the most frequent offenders.[10] Forceps and hemostats are also involved in a large number of these cases.[11]

During gall bladder surgery a hemostat 5½ by 2½ inches was left in the patient's abdomen; it was not discovered for approximately 6 weeks. During the operation necessary to remove it, its position required removal of a portion of the patient's small intestine. The court held that leaving the object, in and of itself, constituted negligence on the part of the surgeon.[12]

Drains and tubes which slip into patient's bodies are also common sources of liability suits. Usually negligence is also provable in these cases.[13]

After kidney surgery a drainage tube was inserted. On the tenth postoperative day the surgeon instructed a resident to remove the drain. The resident clipped the tube off at the skin surface and did not remove it. The surgeon was liable for the resident's negligence.[14]

However, in another case the court did not find that the fault lay with the physician.

A 5-year old child's pleural cavity was drained and a tube inserted. The outside end of the tube was pinned to gauze wrapped around the patient's body. The gauze was later removed and the drain fastened to his chest with adhesive. The child's mother denied having disturbed the tube, but it disappeared and could not be found. The physician told her to take the child to the hospital unless she was sure that the drain was not in his chest, but she did not do so. Four years later the tube was discovered during further chest surgery. Since the mother, not the physician, had caused the displacement, he was not negligent.[15]

Miscellaneous objects of unbelievable variety sometimes turn up in patient's bodies and later in court. These include pieces of broken glass,[16] dead insects,[17] an ordinary sewing needle, presumably left in the gauze surgical sponge during manufacture,[18] false teeth knocked out of the patient's mouth during intubation,[19] a piece of rubber glove,[20] and a light bulb which fell out of a surgical instrument during a tonsillectomy.[21]

In one case during nasal surgery, the surgeon dropped two small bones he had removed from the patient's nose into her mouth and they ended up in her lung.[22] In another a capsule containing radium was dropped down the patient's throat.[23] In all these cases the surgeons were found liable.

The general principle of virtually automatic negligence does have exceptions, however. In extremely complex and prolonged surgery, there may be particular situations in which a court may find that a given surgeon was not negligent in leaving something behind.

During an extended operation for removal of a malignant tumor from the patient's lung, a sponge was left. Its presence was revealed by a routine Xray on the first postoperative day and it was removed several days later. The patient made a full recovery. Because of the patient's condition, there had been an unusual amount of blood loss during surgery and 4 quarts of blood had been transfused. Nearly 100 sponges had been used. A nurse reported that the sponge count was correct and the surgeon tried to verify it by visual observation and by feeling for sponges. The court held that under the peculiar circumstances of this operation, negligence would not be presumed.[24]

With that exception, which is rarely presented, virtually the only defense to a case in which a sponge or a hemostat is left in a patient is "surgical emergency." When the patient's condition is such that the procedure must be terminated as quickly as possible, the surgeon may not be liable if he leaves a foreign object in the patient's body.[25]

A child had an operation to repair a severed artery in his foot. The surgeon broke two needles during the operation. While he was attempting to locate them, the child stopped breathing. Surgery was completed as swiftly as possible after the patient was resuscitated. The needles were therefore left in his foot and worked themselves out. The court held that the surgeon had not been negligent in leaving them behind.[26]

A Kelly clamp was left in a patient's abdomen. During a search for it, her condition deteriorated suddenly and the operation was completed immediately. The court accepted the fact that due care had necessitated leaving the clamp behind, but found that the surgeon had been negligent in failing to try to locate it after she recovered from the original operation.[27]

Although courts consider it "common knowledge" to know that a surgeon should be able to see or feel an object the size of a sponge or clamp, reinforced by the undeniable fact that the surgeon is ultimately responsible for keeping an accurate count of the number of instruments and sponges in use, a more complex and less legally clear situation is presented when an instrument breaks and an undetected piece is left in the patient. The primary factual consideration is usually a determination of whether the surgeon was using the instrument correctly at the time it broke, presumably as the result of an inherent defect or simple accident, or whether the problem was the result of the incorrect or negligent manner in which it was being used. Even though the piece may be so small that its absence is unnoticed, surgeons may be liable if they were negligent and caused the break.

Many cases involve broken needles. Some of them break during injections; suture needles have been the cause of numerous suits.[28] Generally speaking, if the needle was being used properly at the time it broke, but hindsight indicates that it was defective in some manner not apparent by ordinary observation prior to use, the dentist, physician, or nurse who was using it is usually not liable.[29] If the needle was improperly inserted, however, liability is altogether probable.[30] Most courts take the position that the mere fact that a needle breaks during an injection or while it is being used to suture a patient is not any indication of negligence in itself, and therefore the patient cannot recover unless he can prove improper use.[31] Some, however, indicate that where a needle has broken it is incumbent on the defendant, if he wishes to avoid liability, to prove that it was not his fault and the burden is on him to show either that the needle was defective or that the break was an unavoidable accident.[32]

Other types of instruments, however, which break during surgery usually do not result in an automatic inference of negligence on the part of the surgeon. In these cases the question of liability usually revolves around whether or not the surgeon acted promptly and properly after the incident occurred.

During a tonsillectomy the rubber tip of a mouth gag broke off and went down the patient's throat. Xrays were taken immediately following completion of surgery. The tip was located and removed from the bronchus. The court found for the surgeon. It held that the breaking of the gag had been an unavoidable accident or the result of a latent defect in its manufacture. Since the surgeon had used due care and good judgment in dealing with the problem he was not liable for the untoward event.[33]

During nasal surgery a chisel was used on the bones involved. The point of the chisel broke and was imbedded in the patient's sinus. Experts testified that the accident was in all probability caused by a latent defect in the chisel and that the fact that the instrument broke did not of itself indicate any lack of due care. The defendant prevailed.[34]

A tonsillotome broke during a tonsillectomy and a part of it went down the patient's throat. The surgeon was not held liable in the absence of any expert testimony as to negligence in use.[35]

Four recent decisions have involved breakage of plastic catheters.

A plastic catheter used for intravenous feeding disappeared into the patient's arm. It was never found and no explanation of how it had gotten broken was offered. Since there was no evidence of mechanical defect and since it was never recovered the court held that the hospital was liable.[36]

Prior to a gall bladder operation a patient was put under "light" anesthesia. He was asleep but his muscles were not relaxed. The nurse who administered the anesthesia attempted to put a tube down his throat and he "bucked" on the table. She did not tell this to the anesthetist. The second anesthetist tried to insert a plastic catheter into the patient's hand and the hand jerked. The tubing broke and a piece $4\frac{1}{2}$ inches long disappeared into his arm. After the gall bladder was removed and before the patient woke up, Xrays were taken and the surgeon made three incisions in his arm to find the tubing before locating it. Infections resulted from the incisions, which in turn caused damage to a nerve in his arm. The court held that the negligence of the first nurse in failing to tell the second anesthetist that the patient was not sufficiently anesthetized to keep him from moving around was the cause of the breakage of the tube. Therefore the plaintiff recovered damages.[37]

While a needle and catheter were being inserted by a nurse to provide intravenous fluids following surgery the tubing broke and a portion of the catheter went into the patient. It lodged in the left atrium of her heart and open heart surgery was required to remove it. A suit was brought against the hospital, the nurse, the manufacturer, and the distributor. The distributor was dismissed prior to trial since it had merely transported the unit. While there was evidence that the nurse had not followed the manufacturer's instructions exactly, the trial jury found that her negligence, if any, had not been the proximate cause of the event and that the defect which had caused the break was the result of the design of the object. The sole defendant against whom the jury returned a verdict was the manufacturer. The appellate decision upheld the jury.[38]

During an unspecified type of operation a 6-inch plastic catheter was broken off in the patient's artery. A second operation did not locate it. The patient sued on the ground that the surgeon had been negligent in using it in such a way that it broke in the first place and that he had been negligent in not being able to find it afterwards. The trial court judgment for the plaintiff was reversed as a matter of law. The court pointed out that in any medical malpractice case there is a presumption that due care had been used and the plaintiff bears the burden of proving lack thereof. In this case the court held that expert testimony would be required to show negligence either as to the fact that the accident happened or that negligence had occurred afterwards. The plaintiff also alleged that the surgeon had not used due care in trying to extract the catheter himself and claimed that he should have called in a specialist in this type of surgery. The court found that this was not negligence.[39]

Instruments used by orthopedists in bone surgery are frequently broken.[40] Obviously, contact with a bone is more likely to result in a broken instrument than is contact with a soft part of the patient's body.

During an operation on the patient's humerus a drill broke and a piece was imbedded in the bone. The court held that the break was as likely to have resulted from an inherent defect in the instrument or from an unavoidable accident as it was from negligence on the part of the surgeon. Without any expert evidence of specific negligence on the part of the surgeon, the court would not hold him liable for having left the object in the patient's body. However, the surgeon did not order Xrays or attempt to locate the fragment and he was therefore negligent in that regard.[41]

During an operation to fuse vertebrae in the patient's back, the wire used for that purpose broke. A small piece migrated to the lower part of the patient's back and caused serious damage. The surgeon had routinely looked at the wire, which was supplied by the hospital, prior to beginning surgery. No visible defect appeared. It separated into smaller pieces than he had anticipated when he began to use it. The court held that no inference of negligence on the surgeon's part could be drawn. The defect in the wire was as likely to be caused by a defect in manufacture as it was to be caused by surgical negligence. In the absence of a showing by expert testimony that there had been negligence in the manner of use or that the defect should have been apparent to the surgeon on visual inspection, he was not liable.[42]

It is quite clear that whether or not the surgeon is liable for having left the foreign object in the patient's body or whether its presence was an unavoidable accident, failure to tell the patient and make efforts, if possible, to remove it is clearly negligent. Concealment of facts in these cases is in itself grounds for a damage suit and negligence need not be proved in order to allow recovery.[43]

During a subtotal gastrectomy performed in a military hospital, a surgical needle broke. The postoperative report indicated that half of it was removed, so clear evidence was presented that the surgeons knew that the other half was not. The patient was told nothing about the incident. A year later Xrays at another government hospital revealed the needle. Physicians at the second hospital advised the surgeons at the first hospital of what they had found, but neither group of physicians told the patient. Five years later a private surgeon found and removed it. The government was liable for concealment by its physician-employees.[44]

During postoperative treatment following gall bladder surgery, the tip of a catheter, about $1\frac{1}{2}$ inches long, did not come out with the rest of the tube when it was withdrawn. Nothing was said to the patient and a year later it was expelled naturally. The patient recovered damages for concealment. The physician was liable for failing to tell the patient the truth even though he was not liable for the fact that the catheter broke.[45]

Where a patient's condition following surgery is very poor, a surgeon may, however, be acting with very good medical judgment if he waits until the patient is better before he tells him that an object has been left.[46]

If a second operation is required to remove the object, the surgeon is usually justified in waiting until the patient's condition improves enough from the first operation to enable him to withstand the second to tell him.[47]

After a gall bladder operation in which a needle broke off in the patient's side, her general condition was very serious. The needle was causing no immediate problems and it was not in an area where an infection would be likely to result. The surgeon waited 6 weeks before he told her. The court found that he had been justified by her emotional and physical condition. His conclusion that a relapse might be caused by the psychological disturbance of finding out about the needle before she could withstand further surgery was held to be well within the range of duly careful judgments.[48]

A patient received a head wound when her husband hit her over the head with a chair. The defendant cleaned and sutured the wound and administered penicillin and tetanus antitoxin. After symptoms of tetanus began, she was admitted to the hospital. While she was being given intraspinal infusions of tetanus antitoxins, she jumped and the needle broke. The physician waited to tell her and to remove the needle until her condition improved, a period of 27 days. The court held that he had used good medical judgment and was not negligent in delaying removal of the needle. He was also not liable for the breakage of the needle.[49]

During colon surgery, a suture needle was left in the patient because his condition suddenly worsened. Use of enough anesthesia to permit a protracted search was considered highly inadvisable. However, the surgeon did not attempt to find the needle later or tell the patient about it although the patient complained of rectal pain for months afterward. The surgeon was found not liable for the breakage of the needle, but he was for his concealment of the facts.[50]

The surgeon may be liable for failing to remove the object even if he was not negligent in having left it in the patient's body.[51] If he has or should have reason to believe that the patient might have a foreign object in his body or if he knows that there is one, he has an obligation to order Xrays or make other suitable efforts to discover its exact location.[52]

If removal of the object presents a greater medical hazard than any risk of leaving it in, however, good medical judgment may require that it remain and, if so, the surgeon is not liable.[53]

A patient had an operation to shorten the femur of his right leg. A drill was used. A $\frac{1}{4}$-inch long segment of the drill bit broke and was embedded in the bone. Expert testimony indicated that the procedure required to remove it would have weakened the bone and presented a greater hazard than leaving it in. The surgeon was held not negligent in leaving it.[54]

Blood Transfusions. A wide variety of problems may result from blood transfusions. Donors may be injured while giving blood. Patients may receive mismatched blood, negligence in the method of administering the transfusion may occur, or the patient may contract serum hepatitis or syphilis from infected blood.

The most usual source of litigation is the situation in which the patient contracted homologous serum hepatitis from blood he received in transfusion.[55] The defendants in these cases are invariably the hospital and the blood bank which supplied the blood ordered by the treating physician. Since the physician plays no role in selection of blood to be used pursuant to his orders, he is not made a defendant in these cases. The problem, of course, is that at the present time there is no effective means of detecting the existence of hepatitis virus in whole blood. Since negligence by definition requires an act or omission which deviates from the recognized standard of care, that which is unpreventable is not considered negligent.

Adequate questioning of donors is, however, imperative, and a blood bank which fails to do so may find itself liable if blood which it has processed is later found to have infected a patient. Drug addicts, for example, frequently donate blood to obtain money to support their habits and their incidence of serum hepatitis is incredibly high.[56]

A patient contracted serum hepatitis. Investigation revealed that he had received 2 pints of blood from the same blood bank. Of the two donors, one gave a fictitious name and address and was never located. The other testified that he was asked no questions of any kind. State requirements for accrediting blood banks strictly specified questions donors were to be asked for the express purpose of preventing transfusion hepatitis. The patient sued both the blood bank and the hospital. The court found that failure to have asked the proper questions constituted negligence as a matter of law by the blood bank. If the hospital knew or should have known that required standards were not being met, the court held that it, too, would be negligent. The question of the hospital's liability was ordered resubmitted to the jury.[57]

However, it is highly unlikely that any court will hold that an inference of negligence can be drawn simply because a blood bank uses paid donors.

A young woman donated blood to the defendant blood bank and was paid $5.00. Three weeks later she became ill. Hepatitis from an unknown cause was diagnosed. Her physician notified the blood bank. It, in turn, notified the hospital which had received the blood and used it, but by that time the patient had already contracted the disease. He sued the blood bank. He argued that since those persons who gave blood for money were so statistically likely to be infected with hepatitis, the use of paid donors should be held to be negligence per se. The court, however, rejected this view. It held that in the shortage of donors which now exists, inducement may be required in order to obtain the necessary amount of blood. Since the donor was questioned carefully and thoroughly and was not an addict or a member of any other high-risk group, the court found that the defendant had not been negligent in accepting her as a donor.[58]

The patient in this case also alleged that the blood bank's failure to use the SGOT test on donated blood was negligence. The court found that at the time the transfusion was given, not a single blood bank in the country used the test and that none of the accrediting organizations required it. Since the test was not in regular use, it was not a departure from customary standards of due care to omit it. Assuming the SGOT test does become standard, it will, of course, constitute negligence to fail to use it. While there are no decisions on the specific point, it is at least arguable that it would now be considered negligence to omit the Australian antigen test.

Until such time as a safe, effective, and economically feasible method of detecting hepatitis in blood is devised, it is highly unlikely that a blood bank or hospital which uses due care in processing of blood and questioning of donors will be found negligent in a transfusion hepatitis case. Since the infection is impossible to prevent, hospitals and blood banks are only required to use such reasonable care as can be expected from institutions of their type.

In one case a donor was sued. She had contracted hepatitis but was unaware of it at the time the donation was made. The court held that since the patient did not allege that the donor knew or should have known she had the disease, she could not be found negligent.[59]

Since negligence can rarely be established and since the patient who contracts serum hepatitis is usually made extremely ill and in numerous cases has died, several years ago suits began to allege not that the blood bank or hospital was negligent, but that because the blood was sold, the sellers violated the implied warranties of fitness for use common to all sales contracts. In 1954 the highest court of New York held that furnishing blood was a service, not a sale. Warranties which would be present in an ordinary sale were therefore inapplicable.[60] The Florida Supreme Court in 1966, however, held that a commercial blood bank was bound by sales warranties.[61] A New Jersey appellate court followed suit in an action against a blood bank and a hospital.[62] In that case, it held that two sales had occurred, one from the blood bank to the hospital and one from the hospital to the patient. However, the Supreme Court of New Jersey remanded the case to the trial court for further findings of fact. While some states refused to follow the concept that warranties applied,[63] others did. Finally, in 1970 the Supreme Court of Illinois held[64] that blood supplied to a patient by a hospital was a sale, not a service. Therefore the hospital was liable for violating its duty to make the blood "fit for use" in spite of the fact that there was no known method of doing so. The New Jersey Supreme Court reached the same conclusion in 1972.[65]

As a result of these decisions state legislatures tried to eliminate the possibility of huge damage suits against hospitals. By the end of 1972, 41 states had enacted statutes providing that furnishing of blood is a service, not a sale. Presumably these statutes will eliminate recovery of damages where negligence cannot be proven. However, in a 1970 decision, the Supreme Court of Pennsylvania held that even if a service and not a sale is involved, warranties of fitness for use might still be held to exist.[66]

Syphilis in a donor can now be easily detected. Therefore few cases involving transmission of that disease in blood have been decided in recent years. If, however, such an event occurred, negligence would be established in all probability.[67]

Mismatched blood, of course, can seriously injure or kill a patient. Most situations which result in a transfusion of the wrong type of blood are caused by a technician's clerical error. If the technician is an employee of the hospital, the hospital is usually liable for the negligence.[68] If the pathologist in charge of the laboratories is the director of the technician's work, he, too, may be liable for the error,[69] but if no direct supervision is involved he usually is not, since it is a clerical, not a medical mistake.

A hospital technician correctly typed a patient's blood as AB. A woman with a very similar name was admitted to the same floor. She had type A blood. Another lab technician put the wrong patient labels on both units of transfusion blood. The first woman received the wrong blood and died. The laboratory technician who had made the error was found liable; but in an extremely unusual decision, the court held that the hospital was not because they had used due care in hiring him.[70]

A patient was admitted to the hospital for a hysterectomy. When the technician took the blood sample she did not mark the name on the tube as was explicitly required by hospital regulations. She also obtained samples from two other patients and confused the tubes. The woman was type O but she was given A blood. She died from the transfusion. The hospital was liable.[71]

Even where no negligence is present, in rare cases hemolytic reactions can occur. In this situation courts do not infer negligence from the fact that the patient died and expert testimony is required to prove it.[72]

Mistyped blood can cause female patients to have life-long problems in child bearing and therefore damages usually are considerable.

A woman's blood was incorrectly typed as Rh+ and she received a transfusion of that type. She was actually Rh—. A few months after recovery from surgery she became pregnant. Her child was a stillborn. No further pregnancy was possible. The hospital was liable for the technician's error.[73]

A woman was Rh— and was given Rh+ blood. No immediate ill effects were noted. Three years later she gave birth to a stillborn child and several years after that she delivered another dead baby. After losing the second baby she underwent exhaustive tests to discover what was wrong and the error was discovered. Although the time for filing suit had expired, the opinion indicated that a timely suit would have resulted in a finding of negligence.[74]

Several cases have attempted to apply the concept of warranties of sale, which had been successfully argued in serum hepatitis cases, to cases where incompatible blood was given. However, where the blood is "wholesome and free of defect" warranties do not apply and, unless negligence can be proved, damages will be denied.[75]

A physician who orders blood is not usually liable for a clerical error made by a hospital technician who mismatches blood, since he has no control over the way the technician performs the assigned duties.[76]

A patient was admitted to the hospital for surgery. Another patient with the same name was admitted the same day. The blood samples were confused and the first received the transfusion intended for the second and died. The trial court dismissed the case against the surgeon, but the appellate court held that since the transfusion had been administered in his presence in the operating room, he was responsible for all persons who acted under his direction.[77]

That case, however, is the only one in which the surgeon was held responsible for negligence which occurred prior to the time the transfusion was begun. In all other cases in which physicians have been found negligent, they themselves were somehow remiss in their use of due care or the error was the fault of people directly under their control.[78]

A surgeon did not order blood for a patient prior to surgery. Hospital regulations required that written orders for blood be submitted before the blood was released for use. During the operation a pint of blood was delivered to the operating room. The anesthetist asked the surgeon if he wanted it given and the surgeon replied in the affirmative. The surgeon, the anesthetist who failed to notice another patient's name on the bottle, and the hospital were all held liable when the patient died from the effects of the incompatible blood.[79]

A patient was recuperating from surgery. The day before she was to go home a nurse and an intern came into her room with blood and apparatus for a transfusion. She told them that her surgeon had not told her that he had ordered blood and asked them who the donor was. They told her that her daughter had donated it. She told them that she did not have a daughter, but they insisted on administering the transfusion. She had a severe reaction. The intern and the nurse were both found negligent, and the hospital, as their employer, was liable.[80]

Failure to administer blood when due care indicates that it is necessary to do so may also constitute actionable negligence. Where an obstetrician or pediatrician knows that parents of a newborn child have Rh incompatibility or where he should know, on the basis of symptoms presented by the baby, that it is affected with erythroblastosis, failure to diagnose the condition immediately and begin exchange transfusions may well constitute negligence.[81]

After a Cesarean section a patient hemorrhaged and died. Expert testimony indicated that the anesthesiologist who was charged wih the responsibility of administering blood had given the patient an entirely inadequate amount. Further, there was testimony that if enough blood had been transfused she would have lived. The court found that a cause of action had been stated against the anesthesiologist and the hospital which employed him.[82]

Negligence may, of course, occur in the administration of blood as it may in any other medical procedure. Where it does, normal principles of liability apply.[83]

An anesthetized patient was returned to his room while a transfusion was being given. The anesthesiologist had inserted the needle and begun administration of the blood. The floor nurse looked at the patient's arm and left an orderly in charge. The needle became dislodged. The orderly tried to summon help, but the nurse came only after a protracted delay. The blood infiltrated the tissues and permanent impairment occurred. The hospital was liable for the negligence of the nurse and the orderly. However, since the transfusion was properly begun and working well when the patient left the operating room the physician who started it was not liable for negligence which occurred after the patient left his care.[84]

A woman was almost 7 months pregnant. Because she was anemic her physician told her to go to the emergency room of the hospital where he administered 1000 cubic centimeters of whole blood. She died of pulmonary edema. Expert testimony indicated that transfusing that much blood into a pregnant woman was negligent. The physician settled the case and the court held that the emergency room nurses had not been negligent in carrying out his orders to continue the transfusion after he began it and left.[85]

After an uneventful delivery, a woman began to hemorrhage and went into shock. The obstetrician pumped blood into the vein of her left ankle. She recovered, but the blood had escaped into the tissues of her leg, which had to be amputated. The physician testified that he knew that such an event might occur but that she was in imminent danger of dying and that he had had to choose between saving her life and the calculated risk to her leg. The court found that he had not been negligent.[86]

A few decisions involve suits by donors who were injured in the course of giving blood.

A blood donor who had given blood at a hospital blood bank developed an infection. She sued and alleged that a contaminated needle had been used. Expert testimony indicated that because no culture had been taken, there was no evidence that the needle was contaminated or, even if it had been, that it was the source of the infection. The hospital was not liable.[87]

A donor fainted after giving blood. He fell and was hurt. The court found that he stated a cause of action against the blood bank for negligence in postdonation care.[88]

At a Red Cross community blood donation drive, a prospective donor told the nurse that she had recently had a baby, that she was anemic and that on one occasion she had been turned down as a donor. The nurse accepted her. She became ill as the result of giving blood. The court held that the Red Cross had been negligent in failing to take a more detailed history from her before accepting her as a donor.[89]

Thus both as to donors and recipients of blood, ordinary principles of due care apply. Standard and customary practice is usually the best evidence that care has been used, but presumably a technician who made an error and mismatched blood could not rely on the fact that failure to be careful was customary in the community. Hospitals and blood banks are not legally responsible in negligence for untoward effects of transfusions where care and skill are used. A physician would be negligent himself if he ordered blood where it was unnecessary, since there is always a calculated risk of hepatitis or hemolytic reaction even when all precautions are taken. Where the condition of the patient is such that these calculated risks must be taken, however, he is also not liable for untoward results.

Xrays.   Numerous cases allege that patients have been burned or otherwise injured during exposure to Xrays made for either diagnostic or treatment purposes. The liability, if any, of a physician, technician, or hospital for injuries from defective Xray machines will be discussed in the next chapter and this discussion will assume that the machine was working properly at the time the injury occurred.

A physician who undertakes to treat or diagnose with Xrays is bound by the usual standard of due care, skill, and knowledge. A radiologist is held to the specialist standard. As in all questions of medical negligence, if due care is used, he is not liable for unfortunate results.[90] He is, however, liable for negligent departure from customary and accepted standards used in exposing patients to Xrays.[91]

A patient who had cervical cancer received Xray treatments without incident. A year later further treatments were indicated. Her stomach was burned so badly that she became addicted to the pain-relieving drugs. She sued the radiologist. There was expert testimony that it was proper to expose a patient to a very high dosage when the malignancy was not halted by a lesser one. The radiologist was not negligent.[92]

An 11-year old boy had a wart on his heel. The defendant attempted to remove it by Xray. The area was severely burned and the boy was crippled. Evidence shows that use of Xrays for this purpose was accepted as proper by other physicians. The dosage was clearly within normal limits. The court held that no negligence could be found and pointed out that all experts agreed that Xray burns sometimes occur in spite of the highest degree of care.[93]

The major problem in trying to establish, on the one hand, if negligence was present or, on the other, if duly careful treatment produced an unavoidable result is that many persons are hypersensitive to Xrays.[94] There is no effective means of predicting with any accuracy whether a patient will be hypersensitive and thus if he should be treated with a lower dosage than would be appropriate for another. Many courts understand that in most situations the radiologist cannot prevent the results of a patient's hypersensitivity.

A patient was burned during diagnostic Xrays. Evidence was presented that some patients are more susceptible to burns than others and that there is no feasible means of predicting which persons are hypersensitive. The court held that negligence could not be inferred.[95]

Some courts, however, hold that the fact of a burn from Xray raises an inference of negligence. In these jurisdictions the defendant must show that the patient was hypersensitive or provide some reasonable explanation of the cause of the burn other than that too much radiation was given.[96]

A patient received Xray treatments for eczema. He was so severely burned that his legs had to be amputated. The court held that the jury could properly find the defendant negligent.[97]

A cancer patient received 160 Xray treatments without incident. She was severely burned on the one hundred and sixty-first. Since all experts testified that any hypersensitivity would have appeared after only a few treatments, the court held that it was reasonable to assume that negligence occurred in the last treatment.[98]

Most courts, however, require specific proof of negligence in administering Xrays before allowing recovery for burns.[99]

A patient had multiple myeloma and radiation treatments were given. Acute radiodermatitis developed. He fell and the area of the lesion was injured. Infection set in and amputation was eventually necessary. The court held that the application of radiation treatments does not lie within the common knowledge of lay jurors and that thus no negligence would be inferred. If the patient wished to prove negligence, he was required to do so by expert medical testimony. Since he had none to offer, he had no case.[100]

Some courts make a distinction between burns from diagnostic Xrays and those sustained during Xray treatments, where the object is, after all, the destruction of tissue.[101] These courts are willing to assume that properly conducted diagnostic Xrays do not produce the extended exposure to radiation which is necessary to cause a burn. If a burn occurs, negligence may be inferred.[102] On the other hand, however, the administration of Xray treatments is so much a matter of medical judgment that the same courts require proof of specific negligence before recovery of damages for burns during treatment will be allowed.[103]

All courts appear to be in agreement, however, that if a part of the patient's body which was not intended to be Xrayed is burned, negligence may properly be inferred.

A patient received Xray treatments on his chin. His arms received severe burns. The court found the physician negligent.[104]

A patient's ear was being Xrayed to remove a wart. His head, face, and neck were severely burned. The court upheld an inference of negligence.[105]

Some courts hold that since the danger of Xray burns during treatment is frequently unpreventable, the patient is presumed to assume the risk of burns from treatment which is given with due care. He does not, of course, assume the risk of negligent treatment.[106] However, before the defendant can successfully argue that his patient had assumed any risk, it must be clear that the patient had been throughly informed on the subject and was in possession of all material facts as to the possibility of burns. The patient's decision to proceed with treatment must be based on a truly informed consent.[107]

Injuries other than burns also occur during the course of the administration of Xrays. In most cases the usual rules of negligence liability apply to this type of incident. Untoward results which have occurred during complicated diagnostic tests using Xrays, such as angiograms, have been discussed in Chapter III.

During a diagnostic Xray the guidelight of the machine came in contact with the anesthetized patient's skin. The Xray technician who placed the tube in position without looking to see if the patient would be burned was held to have been negligent and the hospital was liable for its employee's error.[108]

An Xray technician grasped a patient under the arms to pull him into proper position on the table. The patient had had longstanding back problems and had undergone laminectomy and spinal fusion, although the reasons for the Xrays were not connected with his back problems. His back was badly wrenched and he suffered serious injuries. He was held to state a cause of action against the hospital for the technician's negligence.[109]

A patient was hospitalized for severe abdominal pains which were eventually diagnosed as a ruptured appendix. While under heavy sedation she was taken on a stretcher to the Xray department. The Xray table was raised to vertical. No straps were used to protect the patient from falling. She slumped and broke her ankle. The technician had not examined the patient's chart to find out that she was sedated. She also should have realized from the fact that the patient had been brought in on a stretcher that she was not able to stand or walk. The hospital was liable for the technician's negligence in failing to care for the patient properly.[110]

During preparation of a patient for a lumbar myelogram, the Xray machine's screen was lowered and struck a needle which had been inserted in the patient's spine. The technician had failed to replace a stop-switch on the machine. Fluid escaped from the needle and damaged the patient severely. The court held that the patient could recover damages from the hospital which employed the technician.[111]

During dental Xrays a patient was severely shocked and thrown from the chair when she came into contact with wires from the machine. The court found that the dentist was negligent in the manner in which he used the machine.[112]

A patient was placed on a table for Xrays. The technician forgot about him and he lay on the table for $3\frac{1}{2}$ hours. He thought that the Xray machine was on during the entire time and was terribly frightened by the prolonged exposure. He had serious back problems which restricted his freedom of movement, the reason the Xray films were being made, but finally rolled off the table onto the floor to get out of the way. He was injured. The court held that he stated a cause of action against the hospital.[113]

Thus, radiologists, as all other physicians, are not held to insure the success of treatment or even that injuries received during it will not be worse than the patient's original complaint. All that is required of them and the technicians who work under their direction is adherence to customary and usual standards of skill, care, and knowledge.

Anesthesia.   Anesthesia administration is another area of potential liability. While cardiac arrest was discussed in Chapter IV it should be remembered that it is a problem which is intertwined in most cases with the administration of anesthesia.

As in all cases the anesthesiologist is only required to use due care under the circumstances and is not held to warrant the successful outcome of the procedure.[114] A specialist in anesthesiology is, of course, held to the higher degree of care which is ordinarily expected of specialists in any field.[115]

One possible cause of harm to a patient is explosion of anesthetic gases.[116] The patient may either be burned or he may inhale smoke or flames. If the cause of the explosion is a fault in the anesthetic equipment or insufficient safeguards against static electricity in the operating room, the hospital, not the surgeon or anesthesiologist, is usually the only party liable. If, however, either or both of those individuals fail to do something to protect the patient or in some way cause the explosion to occur, of course they will be personally liable.[117]

During an operation on a patient with lung cancer, the anesthesia, a mixture of cyclopropane and oxygen, ignited and exploded. The patient was seriously injured by flame inhalation. The cause of the accident was finally determined to be static electricity, although there was no electrical equipment in the room from which a spark could have come. The surgeon and anesthesiologist were not personally liable because there was no evidence that the anesthesia had been administered in a negligent manner. However, the hospital was liable because it could not establish that all possible precautions to ground equipment had been taken.[118]

A patient was seriously burned. After nitrous oxide had been administered, there was an explosion inside the facial mask used for the anesthesia. The explosion occurred when a electric cauterizing needle was applied to the patient's face. The court refused to infer negligence on the part of the surgeon in the face of expert testimony that the probable cause was impurities in the gas when it was manufactured. It should be noted that this case was decided in 1923. With a far wider variety of anesthetic agents now available, a surgeon in this situation today undoubtedly would be liable.[119]

On the other hand, surgeons and anesthetists are presumed to understand the combustible properties, if any, of anesthetic agents. If they use equipment which is likely to ignite a fire or explosion they will be liable.

A 9-year old boy died during a tonsillectomy. When the surgeon applied an electric instrument to his face, ether vapors exploded. The surgeon was liable because he had used electrical equipment in the presence of combustible vapors.[120]

Mistakes are sometimes made and the wrong drug given as an anesthetic. Where this is proved and the possibility is eliminated that the proper drug was given but the patient had an idiosyncratic reaction, liability is automatic.[121]

A patient was to have a spinal anesthetic for a hemorrhoidectomy. On the anesthesiologist's tray were identical jars of colorless liquid. One was alcohol, the other, the anesthetic substance, xylocaine. The alcohol was given instead of the xylocaine and paralysis resulted. The anesthesiologist was liable.[122]

Paralysis or leg muscle weakness from spinal anesthesia may result from an unforeseeable, unpredictable allergy to the substance used. This may occur without negligence. Where there is expert testimony indicating that the paralysis was caused by the patient's unforeseeable adverse reaction to the drug, there is no recovery of damages.[123]

Of course paralysis may also occur from negligent administration of the anesthestic and if so, heavy damages are usually awarded. It should be noted that most courts are willing to assume that negligence has occurred from the fact of the result.[124] Any claim of allergic reaction is usually presented as a defense to overcome or rebut this presumption.[125]

A woman had spinal anesthesia for delivery of four children and on no occasion were there any problems. The fifth time she delivered a baby the same anesthetic was used. She was partially paralyzed. The court rejected the argument that she must have had an allergic reaction and pointed out that if she had any sensitivity to the substance it would have been obvious at the first delivery.[126]

An overdose of anesthesia can, of course, kill the patient. Where there is evidence that an overdose occurred as the result of failure to use due care, liability is assured.

A 3-year old died during a tonsillectomy. Expert testimony indicated that the cause of death was an overdose of ether. There was no suggestion that he had any preexisting condition which could have caused his death. The judge charged the jury that in the absence of some explanation or suggestion by the defendants of some causation other than their own negligence, the jury was entitled to find both the surgeon and the nurse–anesthetist liable. The verdict in favor of the surgeon and against the hospital, employer of the nurse, was upheld on appeal.[127]

Where a patient begins to exhibit symptoms such as cyanosis, indicating that too much anesthesia has been given, surgery must be terminated at once. Failure to do so or to recognize symptoms of over-reaction or overdose will be considered negligence even though the anesthetist may not have been at fault in causing the condition.[128]

During a delivery, the defendant, a specialist in anesthesiology, administered a spinal anesthetic. When the patient attempted to get out of bed 11 hours later, she slipped and fell on the floor. Her leg remained numb and weak. Expert evidence indicated that her condition resulted from an excessive dose of anesthesia. The court found the anesthesiologist liable.[129]

If a patient has a preexisting condition which cannot be determined by the use of ordinary care in preoperative examination and death occurs from hypersensitive or idiosyncratic reaction to the drug used, no liability occurs.[130] Several older decisions involved children with enlarged thymus glands who died under ether, for example, and in all these cases the verdicts were in favor of the surgeons. It was then accepted that the condition could not be discovered prior to surgery.[131] However, a part of the legal responsibility of anyone who undertakes to administer anesthesia is to have enough knowledge of the patient's condition to predict reasonably foreseeable problems which are or should be known to a duly careful physician or which would be disclosed by a careful physical examination or questioning of the patient. If such a condition which should have been known causes death or injury when the anesthetic is given, liability is altogether probable.

A dental patient had extremely severe hypertension for which her physician was treating her. Prior to injecting a local anesthetic the dentist did not ask any questions about her physical condition or inquire about medication she was taking. The substance which he used to deaden patients' mouths specifically and clearly stated that under no circumstances should it be used for hypertensive patients. She got up from the chair after her tooth was filled and collapsed on the floor with a stroke. The dentist was liable.[132]

In several cases, surgeons and anesthesiologists have been held liable for proceeding with nonemergency, elective surgery in which inhalation anesthesia was used when the patient had a cold. These cases can easily result in death or cardiac arrest. Since cold symptoms are usually obvious from casual observation of the patient, courts usually find that performance of the surgery was negligent.[133]

A 23-month old child died during an elective operation to correct a foot deformity. Hospital records indicated that the child's poor physical condition had delayed the operation for 2 months, but the baby was still ill when it was performed. She only weighed 16 pounds. Nursing notes the day before surgery indicated the presence of a nasal discharge. The surgeons were liable, not for improper use of anesthetic, but because there was evidence to show that the operation should have been postponed until the child's condition improved.[134]

Choice of anesthetic agent might be altered if the patient's hypertension, heart condition, or kidney problems, to enumerate only a few possibilities, were known to the anesthesiologist or surgeon. It is entirely their responsibility to make a sufficiently careful examination to discover any such conditions. Administration of gas anesthesia which escapes into the patient's stomach can cause very serious injury or death. In cases where insufflation is proved to have occurred, the anesthetist is usually found liable.[135]

Infiltration of injected anesthetic agents into tissues surrounding the area can also cause damage to the patient. This can, of course, occur entirely without negligence.[136]

An infusion of thiopental sodium infiltrated the tissues of the patient's hand for 8 minutes after it was begun. The anesthesiologist did not notice anything until he realized that it was strange that the patient had not gone to sleep. Serious and permanent tissue damage resulted and the patient sued the anesthesiologist for failure to pay attention. However, she did not produce any evidence of what signs, other than her continued consciousness, should have alerted the anesthesiologist to the situation and therefore the verdict for the defendant was upheld on appeal.[137]

In most cases, however, the courts reason that the event would not have happened if the anesthesiologist had carefully observed the site at which the agent was injected.[138]

Endotracheal tubes can damage vocal chords if they are not gently and carefully inserted or if the tube is too big for the patient's throat.[139] If there is evidence that customary practice in selection and use of the tube is followed, however, there is no negligence.[140] Teeth are also frequently knocked out by endotracheal tubes.[141] If due care is used in the insertion of the tube or if there is any mouth condition, such as pyorrhea, which could have been as likely as negligence to have caused the loosening or loss of the teeth, the anesthetist will not be liable.[142] On the other hand, negligent damage to teeth will result not only in a finding of liability, but in some cases, in a finding of a breach of contract to care properly for a hospital patient.[143]

Any use of anesthesia involves at least some degree of calculated risk. Necessary surgery, however, mandates its careful use. All that is required of an anesthesiologist is compliance with customary and accepted practice and standards of due skill, care, and knowledge. These must be applied both in choice of anesthetic agent, bearing in mind the type of surgery involved and the condition of the patient, and in administration once the agent is selected.

Where care has been used, regardless of the outcome, the anesthesiologist will have met all requirements of the law.

Drugs.   Drugs constitute the overwhelming majority of therapeutic agents which are the subject of suits. A drug different from the one prescribed may be given. The proper drug may be administered in a negligent manner. The patient may become addicted to a narcotic. Side effects of various drugs cause innumerable lawsuits against physicians and drug manufacturers. Allergies to drugs, known or unknown, may cause problems. The drug chosen may be the wrong one for the patient's illness. The dose may be excessive. In all these situations the patient may file a suit, but in only a few will liability be automatic. It should be noted that a great many drug-reaction cases involve principles of vicarious liability—the physician's liability for the negligence of another who actually administered or, in some cases, manufactured the drug. These questions will be dealt with in a later chapter and this discussion will concern only those principles of primary liability which involve the negligence of the person who actually administered or ordered the drug.

Where the wrong drug is administered by mistake, liability is automatic as a matter of law.[144]

A heart attack patient was suffering from severe vitamin deficiency. Injections of vitamin B_{12} were prescribed, for which she came to her physician's office. The office assistant gave her an injection of adrenalin by mistake. The physician, summoned from a luncheon to deal with the problem, administered an injection of a tranquilizer to counteract the adrenalin. She became nauseated and fainted on the way to the bathroom. She fell and was seriously injured. She recovered substantial damages.[145]

During a gastric cytology test, a medical technician instilled a solution of 10 percent sodium hydroxide instead of an 0.85 percent chloride solution into the patient's stomach. The two solutions were kept side by side on the same shelf in identical bottles. The patient had a 19-week hospital stay, a substantial portion of his stomach was removed, and he also became addicted to the pain-relieving medication. He recovered $162,500 in damages from the hospital which employed the technician.[146]

Oral administration of medicine intended to be used externally is also clearly negligent.[147] So is injection of a drug which should be given orally.[148] In these cases, all the plaintiff has to prove is that a mistake occurred and the only question remaining is the amount of damages which will be recovered. Since any intelligent housewife is aware that harmful substances should not be kept on the same shelf in her bathroom cabinet with medicines used for her family, courts feel that it is not too much to expect that those physicians who keep drugs in their offices and hospitals make absolutely certain that poisonous or harmful substances are not kept on the same shelf, much less in identical containers, as medications.

In the cases cited above, the drug given caused direct injury to the patient as a result of its own properties. However, where the medication given by mistake itself does not harm the patient, but the patient, deprived of the proper medication for his illness, suffers damage, liability will also be found. While complete coverage of the question of the liability of a pharmacist who makes a mistake in filling a prescription is outside the scope of this text, two recent decisions bear out this principle.

A pharmacist gave a woman tranquilizers instead of the prescribed birth control pills. She was not adversely affected by the tranquilizers but promptly got pregnant. He was liable. Further, the court held that she was not required to have an abortion or to release the child for adoption to mitigate damages.[149]

A patient with a serious cardiac problem received gout medication instead of the prescribed heart drug. She was not harmed by the medication but had another serious heart attack as the result of failure to take the proper heart medication. The pharmacist was liable.[150]

The drug prescribed may be the wrong one for the patient's condition. Which drug should be prescribed for a patient's illness is, of course, a question of medical judgment. Thus, if a respectable minority of the profession adheres to the view that the medication is proper to use in treating the illness, as long as it is not administered in a negligent manner the physician is not liable for adverse reaction or for the fact that the patient does not improve.[151]

However, if the drug is clearly inappropriate, the physician will be liable.

A patient had mumps. The defendant asked her if she were allergic to penicillin and she replied in the negative. He gave her an injection of the drug and she died of anaphylactic shock a few minutes later. The court found that if the drug had been appropriate, the physician would not have been liable, since he made all reasonable inquiries. In the face of unanimous medical testimony that penicillin was totally useless for mumps and that he should not have given it, however, he was negligent for having prescribed it.[152]

Hospitals and, less frequently, physicians have sometimes been allegedly negligent in the manner in which they stored a drug and patients have claimed that it decomposed or became contaminated. If this is proven, negligence is usually automatic. However, unless there is clear evidence that medication which should have been refrigerated or otherwise specially stored was not or there is clear evidence that the medication was used past a certain known date when its efficacy expired, the usual defense in these cases is that the drug was contaminated during manufacture and that the hospital could not have been aware of the contamination prior to using it. In these cases, the manufacturer, not the hospital or the physician, is usually liable.

A patient, who also happened to be a nurse, was given an injection of decomposed morphine and lost the use of the arm in which the morphine was injected. It was established that the head nurse on the floor had determined 6 months previously that the substance had deteriorated and told another nurse to throw it away, but her order was not carried out. The hospital was liable.[153]

The proper drug may be prescribed and given, but the administration may be carried out in a negligent manner. Damage to the patient may be extremely severe and general rules of due care in treatment apply in determining liability. Injections are, for obvious reasons, the most frequent cases in which complaints are made that negligence in administration has damaged the patient.

Failure to sterilize equipment prior to using it for injections was the subject of several older decisions, but with increasing use of prepackaged disposable hypodermic kits, presumably for this very reason, these cases are infrequent. If infection results, liability is virtually assured on proof of failure to sterilize.[154] However, since infections may result from a variety of causes, proof of specific and causal negligence is required to demonstrate that the needle was in fact unsterile and that it, not the patient's preexisting condition, was the proximate cause of the infection.[155]

A patient testified that prior to an injection by a hospital nurse her skin was not rubbed with alcohol. Evidence showed that the needle used had not been sterilized. A staphylococcus infection developed. Medical testimony for the patient indicated that the abscesses which developed were clearly the result of the injection. The hospital was liable.[156]

It should be noted that where prepackaged and presterilized hypodermic kits are utilized and discarded after one use, in case of resulting infection courts will presume that the contamination must have occurred during the manufacturing process and the manufacturer, not the physician or the hospital, will be liable.[157]

Injection of medication intravenously when the prescription was for intramuscular administration can cause death or serious injury. Where this occurs the person who made the error and his employer, such as a hospital, not the physician who ordered the drug, is liable. Furthermore, where a drug is in common use a physician can usually rely on nursing personnel to know how the substance should be injected and even if he does not specify the method of administration, he will not be personally liable.

A combination of penicillin and other drugs was ordered to be injected intramuscularly. A nurse misread the order and injected them intravenously.

The patient had an instantaneous grand mal seizure. The hospital was liable for the nurse's error. Since the physician's orders were correct, however, he was not.[158]

A practical nurse injected penicillin intravenously instead of intramuscularly as ordered. The patient died. The hospital was liable for her negligence.[159]

A physician ordered an injection of Dramamine for a postsurgical patient. He had given the order over the telephone when he received a call that the patient was vomiting. He specified only that it should be given by hypodermic and did not issue any order as to method. The drug was injected subcutaneously and caused a fat necrosis. It should have been given intramuscularly. The court found that there was ample evidence that the staff nurse should have known even without a physician's order how it should have been given. The method was specified in the hospital's nursing manual and the drug was in constant use. The physician was not negligent. The court felt that he had a right to rely on the assumption that a nurse would follow standard practice. The hospital was, however, liable for her negligence.[160]

In the case of an unusual drug, of course, a physician who did not specify the method of administration would be liable if an incorrect one was used.

A 2-year old child had a serious heart condition for which the defendant prescribed a very unusual digitalis compound which was administered orally. When the child was hospitalized, the drug was ordered without any instructions as to method of use. It was injected and the child died. The nurse who gave the injection and the head floor nurse both testified that they had never heard of administering this medication except by injection. The physician was liable for having failed to specify such an unusual method of administering the drug.[161]

Injections into the wrong part of the body may also lead to a negligence suit.[162] However, if no damage results specifically from the error which would not also have occurred if the injection had been given in the proper place, no liability will ensue.

An injection was ordered for the patient's arm, but by mistake a nurse gave it in the patient's hip. An abscess followed. There was no other injury. The court found the hospital not liable for the error. It held that if the injection had been given as ordered, there was no reason to believe that an abscess of the arm would have been less likely. The court held that before recovery of damages would be allowed, the patient had to show that the nurse's negligence caused the abscess, not merely altered the part of the body where it occurred.[163]

Infiltration of injected medication outside the proper area may also cause extremely serious tissue damage.[164] In most cases where this has occurred, an acute emergency existed and infiltration was a calculated risk of immediate administration of a drug necessary to save the patient's life. Thus the courts are willing to assume in these cases that negligence must be proved. Necrosis of tissue frequently results from the administration of Levophed. While this drug is a lifesaver in innumerable cases, infiltration is a well-recognized complication and if use of the drug is not justified by the patient's condition, this result may well be deemed negligent. As long as the patient had constant attention during the infusion and his condition warranted its administration in the first place, courts hold that tissue necrosis is an unavoidable side effect for which no damages can be recovered.[165] However, while the infiltration itself may be unavoidable, failure to recognize and deal with it speedily may result in a finding of negligence.[166]

The single biggest cause of damage from injections is nerve damage when an improperly placed needle hits a nerve.[167] This is particularly common when an injection into the patient's buttock hits the sciatic nerve and causes either a "foot drop" or a more serious paralysis.[168] Where this result occurs in a hospital, the physician is not usually liable for the negligence which occurred in carrying out his orders.[169] Where the physician himself or one of his office employees administers the injection and nerve damage results, he is usually considered responsible.[170]

A child was in the hospital for 24 hours for a tonsillectomy. During that time three different nurses administered five injections. When the child stood up to be dressed before going home it was discovered that his left leg was paralyzed. It was clearly established that one of the injections had penetrated the sciatic nerve. The hospital was liable for the negligence although it was never established which nurse had given the injection which caused the injury. The physician was not liable since he had no control over the manner in which staff nurses carried out his routine orders.[171]

In most cases where this situation occurs, courts have held that the causal connection is so complex that negligence may not be inferred from the simple fact that the event occurred, and proof of specific negligence in the manner in which the injection was given is usually required.[172] There is, of course, always the possibility that the condition of the patient or an unpreventable allergy to the medication, not the method of injection, caused the damage.

Some patients faint after withdrawal of blood or injections and are injured in falls. Assuming that there is no adverse reaction to the substance used and the patient just got "sick to his stomach" at the sight of a needle or his own blood, as long as there was no preliminary indication that this was about to occur, no liability will ensue.[173] The risk is not considered foreseeable under most circumstances.

An 11-year old girl suffered from bronchitis. Her mother took her to the family physician, who gave her a penicillin injection. She was seated on a treatment table. Her mother was in the examining room with her. The physician injected the substance and, while standing near the girl, turned his head to speak to her mother. When the girl moved, they both thought she was getting down from the table, but she pitched forward to the floor, hit her mouth, and suffered injuries. The evidence was clear that the child had not complained, had not changed color, and had given no sign of distress. The court held that the physician was not negligent in failing to realize what was about to happen in time to catch her.[174]

Withdrawal of blood is highly likely to make many patients sick and standard practice usually indicates that the patient ought to be allowed to remain seated for a few minutes after the procedure is completed, especially if the patient appears nervous or says "my own blood makes me sick" and exhibits any symptoms of impending distress. However, where this occurs, unless the patient can prove a community standard of allowing patients to remain seated, he cannot usually recover damages.[175]

Overdosage of medication, whether by design or mistake, can, of course, injure patients. Proper dosage of any medication is a matter of medical judgment. There may be ample and justified reasons why a patient's condition necessitates administration of a dosage in excess of that commonly prescribed or suggested by the manufacturer.[176] However, the physician is presumed by the courts to know the correct dosage and to use extreme caution in exceeding it. If he exceeds it as a matter of ignorance, not deliberate choice, he will assuredly be liable for resulting damage to the patient.

A pediatrician prescribed penicillin and streptomycin in combination for a 9-month old infant. The baby was in the hospital with acute bronchitis and the physician ordered 75 percent of the adult dose. The drug caused permanent nerve deafness. The label on the bottle said in red, capital letters NOT

FOR PEDIATRIC USE. The defendant had not read the manufacturer's package insert which also indicated that it was not to be used for children. He was liable.[177]

A retarded, psychotic patient was transferred to a state mental hospital from an institution for the retarded after several suicide attempts. Large doses of four different tranquilizers were given several times a day and she died 3 weeks later. The toxicologist who performed the autopsy testified that the combinations and amounts of drugs found in her body indicated that she had died of a drug overdose from 5 to 10 times that given in proper clinical use of any of the drugs. The state was liable for the prescribing physician's negligence.[178]

As was discussed in the chapter on misdiagnosis in relation to history-taking, where a drug allergy which is known to the patient or can be pre-determined is overlooked and an adverse reaction occurs, the physician will be liable. It is absolutely incumbent on a physician to make proper inquiries or sensitivity tests to determine, as far as possible, whether an allergy exists.[179] Administration of a medication to which the patient has indicated a known allergy will impose virtually automatic liability as a matter of law.[180]

A patient had been sick on a prior occasion, had been given penicillin, and had developed a rash. His physician had warned him against ever taking the drug again. He gave the patient a note indicating penicillin allergy which the patient kept in his wallet. After involvement in an automobile accident he was brought to the emergency room of a teaching hospital. His history was taken by an intern and he told the intern of the allergy. He also handed the intern the note. The intern did not mention this on the chart. During surgery he remembered it and took the note to the door of the operating room. He gave it to a nurse and told her to tell the surgeon, but she failed to do so. Penicillin was administered both during surgery and after the patient regained consciousness. He told the nurse who was about to administer another injection that he had an allergy, but she insisted on giving it to him. Finally, after several days he flatly refused to be injected at all until he had seen the surgeon, who had not visited him since the operation, and told him about the allergy. The surgeon ordered immediate cessation of penicillin, but the patient had an acute and serious cardiovascular accident. The court held the surgeon liable for all the separate negligent acts of his subordinates.[181]

However, if there is no indication that hypersensitivity exists and there is no skin test or other method of determination, liability will not be imposed.[182]

A patient had an infected finger. The physician asked her if she were allergic to penicillin and she answered in the negative. She told him that she had taken it on prior occasions without problem. He gave her an injection and she dropped dead of anaphylactic shock. Since he had used all known means to determine allergy, he was not liable.[183]

The two most common substances which cause serious allergic reactions are penicillin and tetanus antitoxin (TAT). Questioning, of course, is the only method of determining allergy to penicillin or other antibiotics, but skin tests can reveal allergy to TAT. Failure to administer such a scratch test will, in most cases, be held to be negligent.[184]

Where the test is administered, moreover, the proper time must be allowed to elapse before the skin is observed. Failure to wait long enough after the test before administering the injection is clear evidence of negligence. However, as is true with questions about penicillin, if a scratch test, properly administered, does not produce any indication of allergy, use of the antitoxin is not negligent if an adverse reaction does occur.[185]

All the decisions which have held that anaphylactic shock was unavoidable and not caused by physician negligence make the implicit finding that once it did occur the physician acted promptly in attempting to deal with it. A physician would certainly be negligent if he made no effort to give treatment in this situation even if he were entirely blameless for the fact that it occurred.

Unavoidable side effects of drugs can also injure patients. Generally speaking, a physician is obliged to know exactly what the predicted adverse effects of any drug will be.[186] Prescription of a drug in ignorance of its potential for harm is clear negligence.[187] If there are warnings about the drugs in medical journals which the physician should read or if the manufacturer itself issues warnings, the physician is held to know them whether he actually does or not.[188] He is also bound by any other knowledge which he may have received from any source, including his own experience, about the possibility of side effects.[189] Of course, good medical practice frequently requires administration of a drug in the face of known side effects, and the matter usually is one of calculated risk. If the patient's condition warrants use of the drug and if no other drug is as effective, the physician is not negligent even if side effects do occur. If another drug would, however, be as effective and less potentially hazardous he is legally obliged to prescribe it.

A physician prescribed Stilbestrol for a patient for 3 years. She developed breast cancer. Since he should have known that this drug should never be used in patients with family histories of cancer, the court held that the patient had a good cause of action against him.[190]

One of the more tragic examples of severe side effects which have resulted in any number of decisions has been drug-induced aplastic anemia.[191] These cases involved use of chloromycetin which caused patients' death. In many cases the drug had been prescribed for very minor ailments. After the manufacturer's warnings of the first cases were sent out to physicians and reports of this effect were published in medical journals, all cases found the physicians liable who continued to administer it except for very serious illnesses.[192] Even when the courts concluded in rare cases that it was the only effective treatment for the patient's disease, physicians were held liable for failing to have ordered frequent blood tests and throat cultures while the patient was taking it.[193]

Hundreds of cases involving many types of drugs which cause serious side effects, including death and blindness, are decided each year, of which the aplastic anemia cases are but one example. All drugs, for that matter, have such potential. Aspirin, for example, is capable of causing serious injury to some patients. Briefly stated, however, a physician is held to know that which he ought to know. It is his duty to keep up with reports of injuries from drug side effects and to remember those reports when he decides whether or not potential harm outweighs the drug's usefulness to his patient. If no reports prior to prescription of the drug should have put him on notice, however, he is not liable for a side effect reaction. In the earliest aplastic anemia cases, for example, before the potential for harm was reported, the physicians who administered chloromycetin, even for very minor illnesses, were not liable for the deaths of their patients.[194]

The side-effect potential may not vitiate the need for the drug, but the physician is quite obviously compelled by principles of due care to tell his patient about the more obvious ones. A physician, for example, would be negligent if he did not tell a patient who is taking certain types of tranquilizers or other sedatives that the drug might, when combined with reasonable and expected alcohol intake, create a harmful synergistic reaction. Two decisions involved physicians who prescribed medication which they knew might make the patients sleepy. They did not, however, tell the patients anything about this possibility. The patients fell asleep while driving vehicles and injured themselves and others.[195] In one case, in fact, the patient was a bus driver who went to sleep at the wheel of the bus. He injured not only himself, but a number of his passengers, and the physician was liable for their injuries as well as his patient's.[196]

Furthermore, where there are equally effective alternative solutions to the patient's problem the patient, not the physician, may have the right to choose to take a drug with known side effects or to elect another method of treatment. For example, there have been several cases involving birth control pills. While most of them have involved the manufacturers, not the prescribing physicians, as defendants, before giving a patient a prescription for these pills, it is clearly incumbent on the physician to tell her that some serious side effects have been reported and offer her the choice of pills or another method of contraception, such as an IUD. If she elects the greater contraceptive safety of the pill over the other device and suffers harm from the medication, the physician would not be liable. It should be noted that federal regulations now require contraceptive pills to include package inserts warning the patient herself and presumably these absolve the physician from some potential liability, but if there is any question whatever in his mind of her ability to read and understand these warnings fully, he is obligated to tell her himself and to make sure she understands them. A duly careful physician when prescribing a drug with serious side-effect potential should also specifically tell his patient to report any symptoms to him in order to treat them or change the medication.

The final problem in drug liability is potential addiction of a patient.[197] If a patient is clearly terminally ill, in great pain, or extremely aged, a physician may justifiably prescribe addictive narcotic drugs if no others are available which will give equivalent relief, even if the patient does become addicted. However, in two recent cases addictive drugs were prescribed for younger and less seriously ill patients and the physicians were liable for the outcome.

A woman was suffering from nausea but had no complaint of pain. Her physician gave her morphine injections for 18 months, at the end of which time he was giving her three injections a day. Her husband finally took her to another physician, who diagnosed gallstones. When those were removed, the nausea stopped. The physician was liable for her addiction. Medical evidence showed that at no time had she been in unbearable pain. Use of narcotics to that extent was considered negligent as a matter of law. He was also found negligent for having failed to use reasonable standards of diagnostic care to determine what the cause of the nausea had been.[198]

A patient had, in sequence, two D and C's, a hysterectomy, and an operation to relieve an intestinal obstruction. During all the periods of hospitalization she received large doses of both morphine and Demerol. After her release from the hospital the defendant prescribed morphine for self-injection at any time she requested it. He was liable not only for actual damages, but for punitive or extra, "punishment" damages for her addiction.[199]

It should be noted that in both cases expert witnesses testified for the plaintiffs that the narcotic was not the proper drug for the relief of the problem in the first place, altogether aside from the subsequent addictions. Further, in neither case was a nonaddictive drug used to relieve discomfort before prescription of the morphine. While there are no cases on the subject, if patients who are suffering from extreme pain which cannot be relieved in any other way become addicted to necessary narcotics, the physicians would not be liable as long as the drug was not continued any longer than absolutely necessary and proper steps were taken to deal with the addiction problems as soon as their conditions permitted.

Thus, as we have seen, prescription of any drug carries with it at least the hypothetical possibility that the patient will be injured, in some cases much more seriously than he was by his original illness. The physician does not insure against this. He must simply have the usual and customary degree of knowledge as to the drug's properties and use due skill in prescribing it. Where he knows that a minor problem, such as mumps or a common cold will correct itself without the use of potentially hazardous medication such as antibiotics, he should firmly resist the patient's pleas to "give me something to take." With increasing reports of abuses of tranquilizers and sedatives, he should attempt to establish that the patient's condition genuinely indicates that the prescription is necessary. In these cases taking time to talk to the patient and allowing him to ventilate his worries might eliminate the need for any drug. The fundamental principle here is that physicians should always resist patient pressure to "use a cannon to shoot a gnat."

Electroshock and Other Psychiatric Treatments. With increasing use of medication for psychiatric patients, the necessity for electroshock treatments has apparently decreased. In any event, there are far fewer decisions from the 1960's and 1970's than from earlier decades in which patients alleged that they were injured by the treatments. The discovery and use of muscle-relaxant drugs concomitant with shock therapy has undoubtedly decreased the frequency of fractures sustained during treatments as well, but fractures remain the subject of most negligence suits. While there are a few cases in which patients allege other types of injury during shock treatment, such as nerve deafness,[200] these are extremely rare and fit no particular pattern. The other substantial cause of litigation involving electroshock and similar treatment is allegation of inadequate care during the immediate posttreatment period.[201]

In most cases courts take the position that fractures which occur in the course of electroshock treatments are not indicative of negligence. It is well established that these fractures can occur without negligence and therefore they are usually considered one of the calculated risks of electroshock.[202] In most cases where the patient's condition was such that duly careful psychiatrists would have considered the electroshock treatment warranted and where the treatment is given in accordance with accepted methods, there is no liability for fractures.[203] Most cases in which psychiatrists have been found liable have involved situations in which fractures were unpreventable, but were not diagnosed for some time because of negligent failure to Xray. This is especially likely to be considered negligence if shock treatments continue after the patient complains of pain.[204]

The patient underwent five electroshock treatments and complained of immediate severe pain in his lower back following the first treatment. The psychiatrist administered heat treatments and injections to relieve the pain, but did not Xray. Two days after the patient was discharged by the psychiatrist he went to another doctor who discovered a severe compression fracture of the ninth thoracic vertebra. Evidence of failure to comply with **Standards for Electroshock Therapy** which had been prepared by the American Psychiatric Association and which indicated that Xrays should be made as soon as a patient complains of pain following shock therapy was considered sufficient to state a cause of action on behalf of the patient.[205]

Other forms of psychiatric treatment may also cause fractures and the same principles apply.[206]

A plaintiff was mentally competent, but suffering from severe emotional illness. The psychiatric treatment combined insulin shock therapy with electroshock. There was no serious effort to warn him of any risk involved in either. While undergoing therapy the plaintiff suffered a violent reaction resulting in multiple fractures of the spine. The case was decided primarily on the issue of informed consent and therefore the court never reached the point of determining whether or not the therapy had been administered in a negligent manner before finding the psychiatrist liable.[207]

If therapeutic restraints are necessary they must be safe and they must be applied in a manner which will not injure the patient.[208]

A man entered a mental hospital as a voluntary patient. On the day of admission he decided he wanted to leave. Instead of using ordinary restraints, his psychiatrist ordered six nurses to hold the man down on the floor while the psychiatrist put a tourniquet around the man's neck to cut off the blood supply to his brain. The psychiatrist also forcibly administered ether. Unsurprisingly, the patient died. The hospital was liable.[209]

If the patient is restrained only when absolutely necessary for his own protection and minimal force is used to place him in restraints which are safe and cause the least discomfort possible, the psychiatrist and the hospital will not be liable for unavoidable injury.[210] Since medication is now available to calm and control violent patients, it is far more likely that courts would find liability for injuries from the use of restraints than they would have in the years before the discovery of Thorazine and other tranquilizing drugs.

Since patients are usually dazed or semiconscious atfer electroshock, their capacities to look after themselves may be severely impaired. If posttreatment supervision is not sufficient and the patient is injured, the psychiatrist or hospital is usually liable. The patient, for example, must not be allowed to fall out of bed after a treatment.[211]

A patient who was dismissed shortly after an electroshock treatment fell down stairs on his way out of the hospital and died of a broken neck. The psychiatrist was negligent in releasing him so soon after treatment.[212]

A psychiatrist sent a hospitalized patient home immediately after electroshock treatment because he discovered the patient could not pay his hospital bill. He also prescribed a heavy sedative, but did not warn either the patient or his wife of any possible dangers. The patient, confused from the combination of the drug and the effects of the treatment, fell asleep and set himself on fire from a cigarette. He suffered third-degree burns over a wide area of his body and almost died. The psychiatrist was liable for failing to provide adequate posttreatment care.[213]

On the other hand, if standard and approved practices in restraining and caring for patients after treatment are followed and the patient manages to untie restraints or otherwise injure himself, the psychiatrist or nurse in charge is not negligent.[214]

This chapter has considered some of the many categories of therapeutic agents which have caused damage to patients. In many cases the condition of the patient entirely justified the risk of unpreventable harm and no negligence whatever was found in either choice or administration of the therapy. In others the physican himself was negligent in one respect or the other. Other decisions involved negligence of subordinate personnel in the effectuation of the physician's orders.

In all cases, however, no guarantees of cure or even guarantees that no harm would be done are ever presumed to be given to a patient. As long as standards of care are met, courts will hold that the physician or his subordinate was not negligent.

NOTES

1. Tiller v. Von Pohle, 230 P 2d 213, Ariz 1951.
2. Jefferson v. United States, 77 F Supp 706, DC Md 1948, 340 US 135, 1950.
3. "Foreign Objects Left in the Patient," 195 *JAMA* No. 4, page 275, Jan. 24, 1966.
4. Ales v. Ryan, 64 P 2d 409, Cal 1936; Armstrong v. Wallace, 47 P 2d 740, Cal 1935; Shearin v. Lloyd, 98 SE 2d 508, NC 1957.
5. French v. Fischer, 362 SW 2d 926, Tenn 1962; Bowers v. Olch, 260 P 2d 997, Cal 1953.
6. Landsberg v. Kolodny, 302 P 2d 86, Cal 1956.
7. Key v. Caldwell, 104 P 2d 87, Cal 1940.
8. Grant v. Touro Infirmary, 223 So 2d 148, La 1969; Funk v. Bonham, 183 NE 312, Ind 1932.
9. McLennan v. Holder, 36 P 2d 448, Cal 1934; Rural Educational Association v. Busch, 298 SW 2d 761, Tenn 1956; Martin v. Perth Amboy General Hospital, 250 A 2d 40, NJ 1969.
10. Sugaya v. Morton, 40 P 2d 581, Cal 1935.
11. Long v. Sledge, 209 So 2d 814, Miss 1968.
12. Conrad v. Lakewood General Hospital, 410 P 2d 785, Wash 1966.
13. Champion v. Bennetts, 236 P 2d 155, Cal 1951; Chesley v. Durant, 137 NE 301, Mass 1922.
14. Capps v. Valk, 369 P 2d 238, Kans 1962.
15. Cyr v. Landry, 95 Atl 883, Maine 1915.
16. Pendergraft v. Royster, 166 SE 285, NC 1932.
17. Prewett v. Philpot, 107 So 880, Miss 1926.
18. Johnson v. Ely, 205 SW 2d 759, Tenn 1947.
19. Dohr v. Smith, 104 So 2d 29, Fla 1958.
20. Mondot v. Vallejo General Hospital, 313 P 2d 78, Cal 1957; Hall v. Delvat, 389 P 2d 692, Ariz 1964.
21. Rhodes v. Lamar, 292 Pac 335, Okla 1930.
22. Bennett v. Murdy, 249 NW 805, SD 1933.
23. Jacobs v. Grigsby, 205 NW 394, Wisc 1925.
24. Miller v. Tongen, 161 NW 2d 686, Minn 1968.

25. Benson v. Dean, 133 NE 125, NY 1921; Harrison v. Wilkerson, 405 SW 2d 649, Tenn 1966; Dietze v. King, 184 F Supp 944, DC Va 1960.

26. Steinmetz v. Humphrey, 160 SW 2d 6, Ky 1942.

27. Swanson v. Hill, 166 F Supp 296, DC ND 1958.

28. Ingram v. Poston, 260 SW 773, Mo 1924.

29. Ernen v. Crofwell, 172 NE 73, Mass 1930.

30. Kelly v. Stern, 132 Atl 234, NJ 1926.

31. Williams v. Chamberlain, 316 SW 2d 505, Mo 1958; Houston Clinic v. Busch, 64 SW 2d 1103, Tex 1933.

32. Oleksiw v. Weidener, 207 NE 2d 375, Ohio 1964.

33. Emery v. Fisher, 148 Atl 677, Maine 1930.

34. Tady v. Warta, 196 NW 901, Neb 1924.

35. Passey v. Budge, 38 P 2d 712, Utah 1934.

36. Dickerson v. St. Peter's Hospital, 432 P 2d 293, Wash 1967.

37. Corson v. United States, 304 F Supp 155, DC Pa 1969.

38. Vergott v. Deseret Pharmaceutical Company, 463 F 2d 12, CCA 5, 1972.

39. Shea v. Phillips, 98 SE 2d 552, Ga 1957.

40. Furr v. Herzmark, 206 F 2d 468, DC CA 1953.

41. Kaplan v. New York, 100 NYS 2d 693, NY 1950.

42. Inouye v. Black, 47 Cal Rptr 313, Cal 1965.

43. Percifield v. Foutz, 285 P 2d 130, Nev 1955; Taylor v. Milton, 92 NW 2d 57, Mich 1958.

44. Jackson v. United States, 182 F Supp 907, DC Md 1960.

45. You Goo Ho v. Yee, 43 Hawaii 289, 1959.

46. Mandelbaum v. Weil, 203 NYS 289, NY 1924.

47. Oleksiw v. Weidener, 207 NE 2d 375, Ohio 1964; Kaplan v. New York, 100 NYS 2d 693, NY 1950.

48. Hohenthal v. Smith, 114 F 2d 494, CA DC 1940.

49. Williams v. Chamberlain, 316 SW 2d 505, Mo 1958.

50. Benson v. Dean, 133 NE 125, NY 1921.

51. Bernsden v. Johnson, 255 P 2d 1033, Kans 1953.

52. Dietze v. King, 184 F Supp 944, DC Va 1960; Pasquale v. Chandler, 215 NE 2d 319, Mass 1966.

53. Zanzon v. Whittaker, 17 NW 2d 206, Mich 1945; Van Skike v. Potter, 73 NW 295, Neb 1897.

54. Furr v. Herzmark, 206 F 2d 468, CA DC 1953.

55. "Liability for Transfusion Hepatitis," 211 *JAMA* No. 8, page 1431, Feb. 23, 1970; "Recent Decisions on Liability for Transfusion Hepatitis," 228 *JAMA* No. 6, page 786, May 6, 1974.

56. Holder, James B., M.D., "Serum Hepatitis," 6 *Lawyers' Med J* 79, May 1970.

57. Hoder v. Sayet, 196 So 2d 205, Fla 1967.

58. Hutchins v. Blood Services of Montana, 506 P 2d 449, Mont 1973.

59. Hubbell v. South Nassau Communities Hospital, 260 NYS 2d 539, NY 1965.

60. Perlmutter v. Beth David Hospital, 123 NE 2d 792, NY 1954.

61. Russell v. Community Blood Bank, 185 So 2d 749, Fla 1966.

62. Jackson v. Muhlenberg Hospital, 249 A 2d 65, NJ 1969.

63. Lovett v. Emory University, 156 SE 2d 923, Ga 1967.

64. Cunningham v. MacNeal Memorial Hospital, 266 NE 2d 897, Ill 1970.

65. Brody v. Overlook Hospital, 296 A 2d 668, NJ 1972.

66. Hoffman v. Misericordia Hospital, 267 A 2d 867, Pa 1970.

67. Giambozi v. Peters, 16 A 2d 833, Conn 1940.

68. National Homeopathic Hospital v. Phillips, 181 F 2d 293, CA DC 1950; Redding v. United States, 196 F Supp 871, DC Ark 1961; Callahan v. Longwood Hospital, 208 NE 2d 247, Mass 1965.

69. Davis v. Wilson, 143 SE 2d 107, NC 1965.

70. Mississippi Baptist Hospital v. Holmes, 55 So 2d 142, Miss 1951.

71. Parker v. Port Huron Hospital, 105 NW 2d 1, Mich 1960.

72. Joseph v. Groves Latter Day Saints Hospital, 348 P 2d 935, Utah 1960.

73. Berg v. New York Society for the Relief of the Ruptured and Crippled, 136 NE 2d 523, NY 1956.

74. Olson v. St. Croix Valley Memorial Hospital, 201 NW 2d 63, Wisc 1972.

75. Baptisa v. St. Barnabas Medical Center, 262 A 2d 902, 270 A 2d 409, NJ 1970; Dibblee v. Groves Latter Day Saints Hospital, 364 P 2d 1085, Utah 1961; Gile v. Kennewick Public Hospital District, 296 P 2d 662, Wash 1956; Goelz v. Wadley Institute, 350 SW 2d 573, Tex 1961.

76. Parker v. Port Huron Hospital, 105 NW 2d 1, Mich 1960.

77. Mazer v. Lipschutz, 327 F 2d 42, CCA 3, 1963.

78. "Physician Risk in Blood Transfusions," 205 *JAMA* No. 10, page 177, Sept 2, 1968.

79. Weiss v. Rubin, 173 NE 2d 791, NY 1961.

80. Necolayff v. Genesee Hospital, 73 NE 2d 117, NY 1947.

81. Price v. Neyland, 320 F 2d 674, CA DC 1963.

82. James v. Holder, 309 NYS 2d 385, NY 1970.

83. Sanchez v. Rodriguez, 38 Cal Rptr 110, Cal 1964.

84. Sherman v. Hartman, 290 P 2d 894, Cal 1955.

85. Powell v. Fidelity Casualty Company, 185 So 2d 324, La 1966.

86. Chapman v. Carlson, 240 So 2d 263, Miss 1970.

87. Brown v. Shannon West Texas Memorial Hospital, 222 SW 2d 248, Tex 1949.

88. Boll v. Sharpe and Dohme, Inc., 120 NE 2d 836, NY 1954.

89. Bowman v. American National Red Cross, 241 NYS 2d 971, NY 1963.

90. Gore v. Brockman, 119 SW 1082, Mo 1909.

91. Hess v. Rouse, 22 SW 2d 1077, Tex 1929; Wilkinson v. Harrington, 243 A 2d 745, RI 1968; "Radiation Therapy," 220 *JAMA* No. 13, page 1807, June 26, 1972.

92. Blankenship v. Baptist Memorial Hospital, 168 SW 2d 491, Tenn 1942.

93. Nance v. Hitch, 76 SE 2d 461, NC 1953.

94. Henslin v. Wheaton, 97 NW 882, Minn 1904; Ballance v. Dunnington, 217 NW 329, Mich 1928; Antowill v. Friedmann, 188 NYS 777, NY 1921.

95. Runyan v. Goodrum, 228 SW 397, Ark 1921.

96. Costa v. Regents of the University of California, 254 P 2d 85, Cal 1953; Thomas v. Lobrano, 76 So 2d 599, La 1954.

97. Waddle v. Sutherland, 126 So 201, Miss 1930.

98. Lewis v. Casenburg, 7 SW 2d 808, Tenn 1928.

99. Sweeny v. Erving, 228 US 233, 1913; Gorman v. St. Francis Hospital, 208 NE 2d 653, Ill 1965; Routen v. McGehee, 186 SW 2d 779, Ark 1945.

100. McCarthy v. Boston City Hospital, 266 NE 2d 292, Mass 1971.

101. Ragin v. Zimmerman, 276 Pac 107, Cal 1929.

102. Bennett v. Los Angeles Tumor Institute, 227 P 2d 473, Cal 1951; Evans v. Clapp, 231 SW 79 Mo 1921.

103. Moore v. Steen, 283 Pac 833, Cal 1929.

104. Martin v. Eschelman, 33 SW 2d 827, Tex 1930.

105. Emrie v. Tice, 258 P 2d 332, Kans 1953.

106. Hales v. Raines, 141 SW 917, Mo 1911; Gross v. Robinson, 218 SW 924, Mo 1920.

107. Natanson v. Kline, 350 P 2d 1093, 354 P 2d 670, Kans 1960; Green v. Hussey, 262 NE 2d 156, Ill 1970.

108. Synnott v. Midway Hospital, 178 NW 2d 211, Minn 1970.

109. Austin v. Sisters of Charity of Providence, 470 P 2d 939, Ore 1970.

110. Albritton v. Bossier City Hospital, 271 So 2d 353, La 1972.

111. Beeck v. Tucson General Hospital, 500 P 2d 1153, Ariz 1972.

112. Curley v. McDonald, 160 NE 796, Mass 1928.

113. Caylor v. Virden, 217 F 2d 739, CCA 8, 1955.

114. Whitfield v. Whittaker Memorial Hospital, 169 SE 2d 563, Va 1969.

115. Brune v. Belinkoff, 235 NE 2d 793, Mass 1968.

116. "Res Ipsa Loquitur: Anesthesia," 221 *JAMA* No. 11, page 1329, Sept 11, 1972.

117. Dierman v. Providence Hospital, 188 P 2d 12, Cal 1948.

118. Andrepont v. Ochsner, 84 So 2d 63, La 1955.

119. Wilt v. McCallum, 253 SW 156, Mo 1923.

120. McKinney v. Tromly, 386 SW 2d 564, Tex 1964.

121. Loveland v. Nelson, 209 NW 835, Mich 1926; Lippard v. Johnson, 1 SE 2d 889, NC 1939; Ball Memorial Hospital v. Freeman, 196 NE 2d 274, Ind 1964.

122. Oberlin v. Friedman, 213 NE 2d 168, Ohio 1965.

123. Gravis v. Physicians' and Surgeons' Hospital, 415 SW 2d 674, Tex 1967; Ayers v. Parry, 192 F 2d 181, CCA 3, 1951; Hall v. United States, 136 F Supp 187, DC La 1955, aff'd 234 F 2d 811, CCA 5, 1956.

124. Mayor v. Dowsett, 400 P 2d 234, Ore 1965.

125. Douglas v. Boussabarger, 438 P 2d 829, Wash 1968; Walker v. Distler, 296 P 2d 452, Idaho 1956.

126. Seneris v. Haas, 291 P 2d 915, Cal 1955.

127. Cavero v. Franklin General Benevolent Society, 223 P 2d 471, Cal 1950.

128. Graddy v. New York Medical College, 243 NYS 2d 940, NY 1963; Harris v. Wood, 8 NW 2d 818, Minn 1943; Webb v. Jorns, 488 SW 2d 407, Tex 1972.

129. Brune v. Belinkoff, 235 NE 2d 793, Mass 1968.

130. Spain v. Burch, 154 SW 172, Mo 1913.

131. Yeager v. Dunnavan, 174 P 2d 755, Wash 1946; Biancucci v. Nigro, 141 NE 568, Mass 1923.

132. Sanzari v. Rosenfeld, 167 A 2d 625, NJ 1961.

133. Quintal v. Laurel Grove Hospital, 397 P 2d 161, Cal 1964; Butler v. Layton, 164 NE 920, Mass 1929; Jackson v. Mountain Sanitarium, 67 SE 2d 57, NC 1951.

134. Sawyer v. Jewish Chronic Disease Hospital, 234 NYS 2d 372, NY 1962.

135. Kemalyan v. Henderson, 277 P 2d 372, Wash 1954; Whitfield v. Whittaker Memorial Hospital, 169 SE 2d 563, Va 1969.

136. Hornbeck v. Homeopathic Hospital Association, 197 A 2d 461, Del 1964.

137. Miller v. Raaen, 139 NW 2d 877, Minn 1966.

138. Wolfsmith v. Marsh, 337 P 2d 70, Cal 1959.

139. Raschelbach v. Benincasa, 372 SW 2d 120, Mo. 1963; Bell v. Umstattd, 401 SW 2d 306, Tex 1966.

140. Morwin v. Albany Hospital, 185 NYS 2d 85, NY 1959.

141. "Lost or Broken Teeth," 221 *JAMA* No. 1, page 119, July 3, 1972; Hughes v. Hastings, 469 SW 2d 378, Tenn 1971.

142. Holzberg v. Flower and Fifth Avenue Hospitals, 330 NYS 2d 682, NY 1972.

143. Stephens v. Druid City Hospital Board, 268 So 2d 824, Ala 1972.

144. "Administration of Wrong Drugs," 204 *JAMA* No. 11, page 225, June 10, 1968; Gunning v. Cooley, 281 US 90, 1930; Dean v. Dyer, 149 P 2d 288, Cal 1944; Becker v. Eisenstodt, 158 A 2d 706, NJ 1960.

145. Schulz v. Feigal, 142 NW 2d 84, Minn 1966.

146. Gault v. Poor Sisters of St. Frances, 375 F 2d 539, CCA 6, 1967.

147. Penaloza v. Baptist Memorial Hospital, 304 SW 2d 203, Tex 1957.

148. Larrimore v. Homeopathic Hospital Association, 181 A 2d 573, Del 1962.

149. Troppi v. Scarf, 187 NW 2d 511, Mich 1971.

150. Murray v. Thrifty Drug Store, trial court decision, Sacramento, Cal Super Ct, Docket #209949, 1972.

151. Baldor v. Rogers, 81 So 2d 658, Fla 1955.

152. Rotan v. Greenbaum, 273 F 2d 830, CA DC 1959.

153. Volk v. City of New York, 30 NE 2d 596, NY 1940.

154. Peck v. Towns Hospital, 89 NYS 2d 190, NY 1949.

155. Kaster v. Woodson, 123 SW 2d 981, Tex 1938; Brown v. Shannon West Texas Hospital, 222 SW 2d 248, Tex 1949.

156. Kalmus v. Cedars of Lebanon Hospital, 281 P 2d 872, Cal 1955.

157. Cohran v. Harper, 154 SE 2d 461, Ga 1967.

158. Moore v. Guthrie Hospital, 403 F 2d 366, CCA 4, 1968.

159. Rodiguez v. Columbus Hospital, 326 NYS 2d 439, NY 1971.

160. Barnes v. St. Francis Hospital, 507 P 2d 288, Kans 1973.

161. Norton v. Argonaut Insurance Company, 144 So 2d 249, La 1962.

162. Langford v. Kosterlitz, 290 Pac 80, Cal 1930.

163. Masonic Hospital Association v. Taggart, 43 P 2d 142, Okla 1935.

164. "Tissue Damage from Life-Saving Drug," 202 *JAMA* No. 6, page 317, Nov. 6, 1967.

165. Grantham v. Goetz, 164 A 2d 225, Pa 1960; Sanchez v. Rodriguez, 38 Cal Rptr 110, Cal 1964; Renrick v. City of Newark, 181 A 2d 24, NJ 1962.

166. North Shore Hospital v. Luzi, 194 So 2d 63, Fla 1967.

167. "Paralysis Following Injection," 199 *JAMA* No. 7, page 251, Feb. 13, 1967.

168. "Sciatic Nerve Damage from Injection," 219 *JAMA* No. 6, page 807, Feb. 7, 1972.

169. Bernandi v. Community Hospital Association, 443 P 2d 708, Colo 1968.

170. Johnson v. Phillips, 223 NE 2d 677, Mass 1967; Donahoo v. Lovas, 288 Pac 698, Cal 1930.

171. Bria v. St. Joseph's Hospital, 220 A 2d 29, Conn 1966.

172. Graham v. St. Luke's Hospital, 196 NE 2d 355, Ill 1964; McKinney v. Schaefer, 161 SE 2d 446, Ga 1968.

173. "Patients Who Faint During Office Visits," 195 *JAMA* No. 3, page 261, Jan. 17, 1966.

174. Fontenot v. Aetna Casualty and Surety Company, 166 So 2d 299, La 1964.

175. Carroll v. Richardson, 110 SE 2d 193, Va 1959.

176. Carter v. Metropolitan Dade County, 253 So 2d 920, Fla 1971.

177. Koury v. Follo, 158 SE 2d 548, NC 1968.

178. Tropp v. New York, 290 NYS 2d 612, NY 1968.

179. Neely v. St. Francis Hospital and School of Nursing, 363 P 2d 438, Kans 1961.

180. "Liability for Penicillin Reactions," 212 *JAMA* No. 11, page 2015, June 15, 1970.

181. Yorston v. Pennell, 153 A 2d 255, Pa 1959.

182. Tangora v. Matanky, 42 Cal Rptr 348, Cal 1964.

183. Campos v. Weeks, 53 Cal Rptr 915, Cal 1966.

184. "Tetanus Antitoxin Reactions," 224 *JAMA* No. 4, page 559, April 23, 1973.

185. Gorlin v. Master Contracting Corporation, 180 NYS 2d 84, NY 1958.

186. Reed v. Church, 8 SE 2d 285, Va 1940.

187. Marchese v. Monaco, 145 A 2d 809, NJ 1958.

188. "Physician's Liability for Drug Reactions," 213 *JAMA* No. 12, page 2143, Sept. 21, 1970; "Package Inserts as Evidence," 208 *JAMA* No. 3, page 589, April 21, 1969; "Drug Reactions," 197 *JAMA* No. 8, page 221, August 22, 1966; Barnett, F. J., "Liability for Adverse Drug Reactions," 1 *J Leg Med*, No. 2, page 47, May–June 1973.

189. Henderson v. National Drug Company, 23 A 2d 743, Pa 1942.

190. Agnew v. Larson, 185 P 2d 851, Cal 1947.

191. "Drug Induced Aplastic Anemia," 222 *JAMA* No. 3, page 405, Oct. 16, 1972.

192. Sharpe v. Pugh, 155 SE 2d 108, NC 1967; Mulder v. Parke-Davis & Co., 181 NW 2d 882, Minn 1970.

193. Incollingo v. Ewing, 282 A 2d 206, Pa 1971.

194. Stottlemire v. Cawood, 213 F Supp 897, CA DC 1963; Love v. Wolf, 38 Cal Rptr 183, 58 Cal Rptr 42, Cal 1967.

195. Whitfield v. Daniel Construction Company, 83 SE 2d 460, SC 1954.

196. Kaiser v. Suburban Transportation Company, 398 P 2d 14, Wash 1965.

197. "Civil Liability for Patient's Addiction," 212 *JAMA* No. 9, page 1573, June 1, 1970.

198. King v. Solomon, 81 NE 2d 838, Mass 1948.

199. Los Alamos Medical Center v. Coe, 275 P 2d 175, NM 1954.

200. Woods v. Brumlop, 377 2d 520, NM 1962.

201. Meynier v. DePaul Hospital, 218 So 2d 98, La 1969; Howe v. Citizens Memorial Hospital, 426 SW 2d 882, Tex 1968.

202. Farber v. Olkon, 254 P 2d 520, Cal 1953; O'Rourke v. Halcyon Rest, 117 NE 2d 639, NY 1954; Quinley v. Cocke, 192 SW 2d 992, Tenn 1946.

203. Collins v. Hand, 246 A 2d 398, Pa 1968.

204. Eisele v. Malone, 157 NYS 2d 155, 158 NYS 2d 761, NY 1957.

205. Stone v. Proctor, 131 SE 2d 297, NC 1963.

206. "Psychiatric Procedures and Their Legal Effects," 201 *JAMA* No. 2, page 235, July 10, 1967.

207. Mitchell v. Robinson, 334 SW 2d 11, Mo 1960.

208. "Therapeutic Restraint," 197 *JAMA* No. 1, page 205, July 4, 1966; Powell v. Risser, 99 A 2d 454, Pa 1953.

209. Bellandi v. Park Sanitarium Association, 6 P 2d 508, Cal 1931.

210. Previn v. Tenacre, 70 F 2d 389, CCA 2, 1933; Galesburg Sanitarium v. Jacobson, 103 Ill App 26, Ill 1902.

211. Adams v. Ricks, 86 SE 2d 329, Ga 1955.

212. Brown v. Moore, 247 F 2d 711, CCA 3, 1957.

213. Christy v. Saliterman, 179 NW 2d 288, Minn 1970.

214. "Electroshock Therapy," 210 *JAMA* No. 3, page 631, Oct. 20, 1969; "Legal Risks of Electroshock Therapy," 196 *JAMA* No. 6, page 331, May 9, 1966; Constant v. Howe, 436 SW 2d 115, Tex 1968.

CHAPTER VI

INJURIES

FROM

EQUIPMENT

AND PREMISES

Patients are sometimes injured by falls or other types of accidents in the physician's office or hospital. Other injuries occur as the result of equipment failures or breakdowns. Of course these actions differ from ordinary malpractice suits against the physician or hospital because they generally do not involve negligent treatment and are similar to actions against any home owner if his neighbor trips on his rug or falls down his stairs.

Physician Liability for Equipment Injuries. A patient in a physician's office or hospital occupies the legal status of an "invitee." An invitee, by legal definition is "a person who is invited or permitted to enter or remain on land for the purpose of the occupier." In other words, he is a business visitor. The legal duty of care owed an invitee is "to exercise reasonable care to warn the invitee, or to make the premises safe for him, as to dangerous conditions or activities of which the possessor knows or which he could discover with reasonable care."[1] In short, any occupier of business premises, a physician in his office, the owner of a hospital or clinic, or the owner of a shoe store, is not liable to an invitee for a latent defect of which he is unaware and about which a reasonable man would not have felt the need to investigate.

Some of these cases involve allegations which include not only the claims made in ordinary premises liability suits, but certain aspects of malpractice law as well.

A patient fell from an examining table. There was an allegation of professional negligence, not a claim that the table was defective. The defendant, a dermatologist, was performing a biopsy of a lesion on the patient's back. The patient fainted. The physician gave him a whiff of ammonia and the

175

patient said he felt better. The physician turned away to put the ammonia back in the cabinet and the patient rolled off the table and was injured. The court held the question of negligence should have been submitted to the jury.[2]

Most of these suits, however, do not involve claims of negligence in treatment with the exception of allegations that the physician should have been aware of the defect in the machinery. Several decisions involved patients who were injured when equipment used in a physician's office malfunctioned.

A dentist's Xray machine was attached to the wall by a bolt. He pulled it over a patient's face to Xray her teeth. The machine came off the wall and fell onto her face, injuring her severely. It was determined that the bolt had broken. She was allowed to recover damages. The court held that the dentist should have inspected his machinery.[3]

In cases of this nature involving defective instruments or equipment, the malpractice standard of care has been interpreted to impose liability only if the physician knew or should have known of the defect. This standard of care is normally reduced to the question of fact of whether the defect was apparent to ordinary observation and if it was not, whether it should have been discoverable through reasonable inspection. Negligence liability has been imposed on physicians and hospitals for failure to inspect machinery for obvious defects, but if the latent or unseen defect is not discoverable the owner is generally not held liable for failure to make such tests or inspections.

A patient was injured in a physician's office when an Xray table collapsed under him. The cause of the accident was determined to be a broken pin in a sealed gear box. The court held that while a physician would have a duty to make reasonable checks of equipment for obvious defects, he was not required to investigate the components of the gear box. Since the cause of the accident was a latent defect, the patient could not recover damages.[4]

However, reasonable safety precautions must be used if broken equipment is likely to cause a very serious injury to a patient, even though the statistical possibility of such an accident is small.

A chiropractor used an infrared lamp to treat the plaintiff. The bulb exploded and she was cut. The court held that while the defect in the bulb probably constituted a latent defect, reasonable rules of safety would have required use of a protective screen over all light bulbs used in treatment. The court held that a cause of action existed against the chiropractor.[5]

If the physician or his assistants become aware that something is wrong with equipment, they must stop using it immediately and have it repaired. If they continue to use it, they will be liable if an accident occurs. Courts assume in that situation that the defect has ceased to be latent and has become apparent.

A patient was burned by an electrotherapy machine. The technician who had been using it knew that it was malfunctioning. The court held that her legal liability, and thus that of her employer physician, arose from the fact that she should have shut the machine off and gone for assistance. If that action had been taken, the court held that the problem would have been considered a latent defect, but continued use subjected the clinic to damages.[6]

Therapeutic equipment which breaks down without any connection with treatment and injures a patient may not be covered by the physician's premises liability insurance.

A patient was hurt when an examining table in a physician's office collapsed. He sued the physician and recovered damages. The physician then sued his insurance company because it refused to pay the damages awarded to the patient. The policy was a standard office liability one similar to that taken out by a homeowner. It specifically excluded any claims for malpractice. The court held that because the table was a piece of professional equipment, not a piece of office furniture, it was used in the course of professional services. Since the patient was injured in the course of the physician's practice of medicine, the court held that the accident fell under the malpractice exemption to his policy. Therefore the insurance carrier did not have to pay. Presumably his malpractice carrier would have been liable.[7]

There are surprisingly few recent suits involving injuries from equipment failures in physician's offices. Most physicians prefer to treat patients on an outpatient basis and use a hospital's facilities and equipment instead of investing in their own. However, most of those which do exist involve electrical injuries.

A woman brought her young child to a physician's office. While she was in the waiting room, a nurse asked her if she would assist in holding another child while the girl was being Xrayed and the woman agreed. The patient was lying on the table when the woman entered the room and she was asked to hold her feet. She pointed out to the nurse that the girl's feet were wet, but the nurse told her that it made no difference. The woman assumed the position the nurse asked her to take, and held the child's wet socks. When the nurse turned on the current of the Xray machine, there was an instantaneous flash and sparks. The opinion did not state what happened to the child, but the plaintiff who was holding her was severely burned. The physician was liable. It was not determined if there was a preexisting defect in the Xray or whether the presence of moisture had caused the explosion.[8]

Thus, a physician who owns therapeutic machinery will not be liable for injuries to patients which occur from latent defects in equipment. If the reasonably careful physician or assistant did not realize and should not have realized that the machine was not functioning as usual at the time an accident occurred, he is not liable. The occupier of business premises does not guarantee to keep invitees safe from harm. He merely is held to the standard of protecting them from injuries which they cannot foresee or avoid, but the possibility of which the occupier has noticed. In the use of office equipment, the physician is only liable for injuries which result from those mechanical problems of which he either knew or about which, on the basis of reasonable observation, he should have known.

Hospital Liability for Equipment Injuries.   Courts hold a hospital to a somewhat higher standard of care than they expect from a physician. Obviously, hospitals employ equipment maintenance personnel, whereas physicians generally do not. Therefore, while a hospital is not chargeable with negligence for defective equipment with latent defects, the courts impose a more stringent definition of the term "latent" than they apply to a physician. For example, hospitals are usually required to dismantle and inspect equipment at proper intervals. A hospital also has an obligation, which a physician usually does not, to install equipment safely. For example, it must ground all machinery used in conjunction with explosive anesthetic gases.[9]

It is the clear duty of a hospital to exercise due care to see that its Xray equipment is safe and properly equipped. Furthermore courts hold that hospitals have an obligation to inspect Xray machines at suitable intervals.[10]

A patient was struck on the head by an Xray machine which came loose from the wall. She sued the hospital, which in turn sued the manufacturer. There was no evidence of a defect in manufacture, so the suit brought by the hospital was dismissed. The machine had fallen because a clamp which held it to the wall was missing. The court attributed this to 3 years of normal use and found the hospital negligent for its failure to inspect for such problems.[11]

Other cases involve patients who were shocked when Xray machines short circuited, and again hospitals are usually found liable for negligent maintenance.[12]

Burns are probably the most frequent cause of equipment suits against hospitals.[13] The most common causes of burns are electric lights, electrosurgical instruments, hot water bottles, and heating pads. In protecting a patient from injuries from these sources, the hospital is required to use normal standards of due care. An ambulatory patient is presumed, for example, to be able to turn down a heating pad which is too hot, but when the patient who is burned is senile, unconscious, or a newborn or small child, the hospital is almost invariably found liable, since it has a very high duty of care toward a helpless patient.[14]

A 65-year old man suffered from chronic brain syndrome caused by diabetes. When he was admitted to the hospital his children advised the nurses that he had burned himself repeatedly while smoking. They gave specific instructions that he was not to be left alone with a cigarette. He was tied in a chair, left alone, and found engulfed in flames from a match. He died from his burns. The court held the hospital liable since he had been admitted precisely because this type of accident was likely without close supervision. The risk of fire in view of his childrens' warnings was altogether foreseeable.[15]

Where babies are burned in incubators or small children are burned in treatment, almost invariably the hospital will be found to be negligent.[16]

During open-heart surgery, a small child was burned by a thermal mattress. While there was a claim that a latent defect in the mattress had caused the injury and that the defect could not have been discovered by the use of reasonable care, the court held that in equipment related to surgery, a hospital has a very high duty of careful inspection. It was therefore liable.[15]

Where heating equipment is known to be functioning improperly and hospital personnel continue to use it without having it repaired, the defect has become a patent one and liability for injuries is assured.[18] If the equipment is not defective but is used improperly, of course ordinary principles of negligence law apply.[19] If the attending physician himself positions or directs the placement of a heating device and the patient is burned, the physician, not the hospital, will be found liable in the absence of a defect in the device.[20]

Patients in shock are frequently burned because the heat necessary to treat them is more important than the calculated risk of a burn. Neither the physician nor the hospital will be found liable without clear proof of some specific negligent act.[21] If the illness for which the patient is being treated makes him unusually susceptible to burns the hospital will not be liable if the required standard of due care is used.[22]

Fires are a constant danger in hospitals.[23] Fire control procedures are included as part of accreditation standards and any hospital which does not comply with them and has a fire which injures patients will, without serious question, be liable.

Patients in oxygen tents are occasionally burned by flash fires. If the patient is of reasonably sound mind and intelligence, the hospital is usually not liable if he insists upon smoking, but a senile or disoriented patient must be carefully supervised and smoking materials removed.[24]

A patient died when a flash fire occurred in her oxygen tent. Her executor sued the hospital alleging that she had been allowed to wear a silk nightgown and that the fire had resulted from a spark of static electricity. Testimony from nurses, however, indicated that she was wearing a cotton gown. It was also proved that charred matches had been found inside the tent. Her cigarettes and matches had been removed from her night stand when the oxygen was brought into her room, but she had gotten out of bed and removed them from her purse in the bureau drawer. Since she was alert and in possession of her facilities and had been instructed not to smoke, the hospital was not liable.[25]

Miscellaneous pieces of therapeutic equipment including needles, guide-wires used in venograms, and thermometers have been the subject of other liability suits. In all cases, the hospital is not liable if the defect could not have been discovered by the use of reasonable care. In several recent cases plaintiffs have attempted to apply the same principles of breach of sales warranties as have been successfully used in serum hepatitis actions. These suits allege that when a hospital charges a patient for care which includes the use of equipment, the equipment has been sold to the patient. This is not usually a successful argument.[26]

A patient had a hysterectomy, during which a surgical needle broke. A part of it remained in her body but was not a threat, and the surgeon decided to leave it in place. She sued the hospital, not the surgeon. She alleged that the needle had had an inherent defect and that a hospital which furnished a defective product for patient treatment is liable as the seller of such products and should be subject to the same standards of liability as any other seller. The court, however, rejected this argument. It held that the hospital itself was a purchaser of the needle and therefore would not be liable without proof of negligent use.[27]

In some cases where equipment defects are claimed to have damaged a patient, it may be possible to show that it is at least equally probable that the condition was caused by the patient's illness.

A premature baby was placed in a heated incubator. When she went into convulsions it was found that the incubator was uncomfortably hot. It was eventually discovered that she had severe medical problems, including mental retardation. Her parents sued the hospital and the manufacturer of the incubator. Three physicians testified that her disabilities were the result of the overheated incubator. A pediatric neurologist, however, testified that her problems were congenital. The jury returned a verdict for the hospital and it was upheld on appeal.[28]

Before a patient can recover from injuries caused by defective equipment, he must prove that if the equipment had been working properly his condition would have been improved.

A young man received a brain injury in a wreck. He was taken to the hospital and the attending physician asked for a pulmotor. The first two supplied would not function, and the boy died 2 minutes after the third began to work. His mother sued the hospital and alleged that failure to have a working pulmotor immediately available had caused his death. The court held that it might have been negligence, but that in this case due to the extremely severe nature of his injuries there was no evidence that he might have been saved if the equipment had been available.[29]

In several cases patients alleged that a hospital was negligent in failing to own proper equipment. In general, unless it is clearly demonstrated that a reasonable standard of care would require its availability, courts are reluctant to hold a hospital liable on this ground. A hospital would presumably be considered negligent if it did not have an Xray machine but accepted fracture patients. Failure to have adequate sterilization equipment is demonstrably negligent.[30] Beyond those necessities, however, it is highly unlikely that due care requires any hospital to have all equipment, no matter how expensive, which could be obtained.[31]

A woman had a breast biopsy. The pathologist's immediate report indicated
a malignancy and a mastectomy was performed. The next day examination
of the permanent section indicated that the tissue had not been malignant.
The patient claimed that the freezing microtome which the pathologist had
used and which was the only instrument available in the hospital for the purpose, was obsolete and that the hospital was negligent in having failed to buy
a cryostat. The court dismissed the action.[32]

Where the hospital used makeshift equipment where a proper device is
easily available and not expensive, however, it may be liable if the makeshift damages a patient.

A physician ordered a heat cradle applied to a patient's foot. The hospital
did not have one and used a gooseneck lamp which was placed at the foot of
the bed with its neck inside the sheet. The patient was burned and the
hospital was found liable.[33]

Patients may be injured by furniture which is not directly involved in
treatment.[34]

A patient was seated on a chair in a physician's examining room when it
collapsed. The design of the chair was such that it was quite likely to turn
over. The court held that she had a cause of action against the physician.[35]

Many hospital cases involve injuries from defective or improperly designed beds.[36] In most of these cases, the hospital is found liable.

A patient's fingers were injured when they were caught in a metal V-brace
on the side of the bed. He recovered damages. The court held that the
circumstances of the accident indicated that the bar which fitted into the
groove of the frame at the side of the bed was at least partially concealed
by the mattress.[37]

If a patient is unconscious, sedated, senile, or very young and falls from
an examining table, a stretcher, or bed, the hospital is usually liable.[38]

A woman was brought to a hospital's emergency room. She was disoriented,
hyperventilating, and incoherent. An orderly was called to watch her and
tranquilizers were administered. About an hour later a nurse told the orderly
to leave. When the physician saw her a few minutes later she had improved
and gave coherent statements about her symptoms. He left the room to

order medication. The nurse who came in to administer it found the patient sitting up on the cart staring straight ahead and unresponsive. She went to summon the physician, who was talking on the telephone. Before they returned to the examining room the patient fell off the cart and suffered severe injuries. She sued the hospital, the nurse, and the physician and contended that they had been negligent in leaving her unattended and without restraints. The court held that negligence was probable, but that she would have to prove her case by expert medical testimony to the effect that the standard of care had been violated.[39]

If a patient's condition requires bed rails to prevent him from falling, his physician may be negligent if he fails to order them.[40] If, however, bed rails or other restraints are ordered and hospital personnel neglect to follow the order, a patient who is injured when he falls out of bed has a cause of action against the hospital, not the physician.[41] If a patient is semi-conscious,[42] senile, or extremely young, a hospital may be liable if the nurses do not use bed rails whether or not the physician has ordered them.[43] The determinant is the capacity of the patient to look after himself and the duty of care owed to him is in inverse proportion to his ability to do so.

Wheelchairs are also a source of patient accidents. Some cases have involved defective chairs[44]; others involve negligence in the method of rolling the chair so that the patient is injured or someone is run over.[45]

A woman fractured her right leg. After surgery she was allowed to sit in a wheel chair with the right leg support elevated to a horizontal position. At the time she was injured she was seated in the chair with both legs extended almost horizontally. She raised herself slightly by pressing down on the arms of the chair. As she did so, the right leg support collapsed, causing another fracture and dislocating the surgical nail which had been inserted in her leg. Evidence showed that the leg rest would drop under extremely light pressure. The court held that the hospital was liable because the chair was defective.[46]

A statement in that opinion is a very succinct expression of the rule on a hospital's liability for defective equipment. "As a patient, the plaintiff could rightfully expect from the defendant hospital the exercise of reasonable care in the selection and maintenance of the equipment and facilities furnished for her use. That standard of care in the acquisition of equipment required of the defendant that the wheelchair provided for the patient's use would be in a safe condition both as to structure and maintenance for the use to which it was put in the care of the plaintiff."

Liability of Physicians for Hospital-Owned Equipment. One of the more complicated areas of the law of medical practice involves situations, not infrequently in surgery, where a machine malfunctions and the patient is injured. He usually charges injury by malpractice on the part of the surgeon for having chosen to use the equipment and adds a regular equipment liability suit against the physician, the hospital, and, frequently, the manufacturer.

Where a physician orders tests or procedures such as Xrays or the administration of medication to a hospital patient and these matters take place outside his immediate presence, he is usually not liable for an equipment defect.

Immediately prior to surgery, a newborn baby was placed in an incubator. The nurse placed him too close to an exposed electric light bulb and he was severely burned. His parents sued the surgeon and claimed that he had been negligent in not inspecting the incubator before telling the nurse to put the baby in it. The court held that where the baby was entrusted by the physicain to hospital employees whose regular duty was to prepare patients for surgery, he was entitled to rely on the assumption that the hospital employees would perform their duties properly. He was not required to review their performances.[47]

It should be pointed out that if the physician himself uses hospital equipment, supplies, or machinery or if they are used in his immediate presence, he is obliged to understand and use them according to instructions or to supervise their proper use.[48]

A surgical patient developed an infection in the area of the sutures. The patient sued the surgeon. The court held that there was sufficient evidence to warrant an inference that the surgeon knew that the sutures were contaminated when he used them. He remarked to the patient's husband, "Those damn sutures have caused us so much pain and suffering," and it was proven that he had used sutures from the same supply on an earlier patient who had an infection. The patient recovered damages.[49]

An anesthetized patient was placed on an adjustable operating table. The table was so manipulated that the patient's fingers were caught in the table's openings and crushed when the table was readjusted. The surgeon was found liable. As the court pointed out, he had "full charge and control" of performing the operation and had, in fact, ordered the table moved. He should have noticed where his patient's hands were at the time.[50]

A patient was admitted to the hospital for cosmetic surgery on a forehead scar. After she was anesthetized the plastic surgeon prepared her for the operation by wiping the involved areas with gauze soaked in pure alcohol. He then turned on the current of an electric cautery. As he neared her neck with the cautery, a spark from the needle caused a flash over the entire area, resulting in severe burns on the patient's face. She sued him. The physician testified that the alcohol had started the fire. He said that although he knew it was inflammable, he had used it in over 3000 operations with no untoward results. An expert testifying for him agreed that it was standard operating procedure to use alcohol if at least 10 minutes was allowed for the fumes to evaporate, which he testified that he had done in this case. He could not explain the flash fire in this case if he had waited beyond the prescribed time. The court held that the jury could infer that the surgeon had been negligent as a matter of law. He was in exclusive control of her body using instruments which could cause injury if defective or not properly used and he was, therefore, liable.[51]

Generally speaking, a physician has the right to assume that equipment furnished by the hospital has been inspected and is therefore safe.

A patient was to have a skin graft. The surgeon was chosen by her and was a member of the hospital's staff. After she was anesthetized, he attempted to remove a strip of skin from the donor site using a Dermatome. The skin removed first was too thick and he reset the gauge. The second graft removed was also too thick. The surgeon restitched the patches of skin which he had removed and she had very serious scars. She sued. It was determined that the Dermatome was defective. A spring which determined the thickness of the graft was bent. It was therefore impossible to adjust it correctly. The surgeon testified that he was given the Dermatome, a standard surgical instrument, made a visual inspection, and approved it for the operation. The court held that it is not standard practice for a surgeon performing an operation to take instruments or machines apart to look for latent defects. It is standard practice for a surgeon to accept as suitable for use the surgical instruments which are furnished him by the hospital. Therefore, since there was no evidence that the surgeon had used the Dermatome in a negligent manner, he was not liable for the patient's damage.[52]

The physician also has the right to assume when he goes into the operating room prior to surgery to inspect the equipment that if he leaves, the equipment will not be altered.

Before an operation for treatment of an abscessed lung, the surgeon examined the cauterizing machine, satisfied himself that it was working properly, and went to scrub. In his absence, a hospital employee changed machines. The physical appearances of the two machines were very similar and the surgeon did not notice the substitution. During the operation, the plaintiff received a severe burn on his leg where the electrode had been placed. The second machine was discovered to be faulty. The jury found for the surgeon and the verdict was upheld on appeal.[53]

Most equipment injuries are actually caused, in the last analysis, by negligent use and not defects, and the normal rules of negligence apply. However, when the defect is latent, whether the physician owns the equipment himself or is using that owned by a hospital, he is not liable for injuries.[54] Failure to notice a patent or obvious defect is, of course, negligence.

Manufacturers' Liability.   Primary liability falls on the manufacturer for equipment which is inherently defective because it was made in a negligent manner or because it was improperly designed. Manufacturers are also liable in many cases for side effects or adverse reactions to drugs or other therapeutic substances.

A manufacturer has an obligation to use due care in research and manufacture of any product, regardless of its nature. If a patient is injured by a drug or other product used in treatment he may be able to demonstrate both negligence and breach of contract warranty.[55] Within the past few years, no doubt because of the increasing number of new drugs on the market, there has been a marked increase in the number of suits filed against drug manufacturers.

A contaminated drug, hypodermic needle, or other piece of equipment will, of course, subject the manufacturer to liability. However, the number of "contaminated substances" suits has decreased markedly in the past few years, undoubtedly due to improvements in quality control. If the contaminated substance was sealed by the manufacturer and unsealed for use and no third party could have contributed to the condition, liability is automatic.[56]

A patient died during a tonsillectomy. It was proved that the ether had been contaminated because the seal on the container had been negligently manufactured. Both the surgeon and the manufacturer were liable.[57]

The most usual grounds for suit against drug manufacturers involves damage from side effects. It is absolutely mandatory for a drug company to communicate any adverse effects of which it is aware to the physicians who prescribe the drug.[58] Drug companies which do not exercise due care in discovery of side effects or in bringing them to the attention of physicians will run serious risk of having multimillion dollar verdicts awarded against them on behalf of patients or their estates for death, blindness, or other serious harm.[59] If a manufacturer has given adequate warnings to physicians about side effects of a drug, however, it has no duty to warn a patient who receives a prescription for the substance.[60]

Of course a manufacturer is also governed by applicable sales law, including implied warranties of fitness for use applicable to all sales contracts. A drug manufacturer is held to warrant that the medicine he produces is safe for use with exercise of an ordinary degree of care.[61]

An unstable element in a combination immunization serum caused convulsions and brain damage in several infants. Several courts found that the manufacturer knew that the problem existed but made no effort to identify the cause or warn physicians. The manufacturer was liable both in negligence and for breach of warranty for fitness of use.[62]

Even if printed warnings of known side effects are sent to physicians in sufficient detail so that they might, standing alone, eliminate the manufacturer's liability, if the company's salesmen continue to urge physicians to prescribe the drugs without any mention of these side effects, the company may still be liable.[63]

A drug manufacturer is, of course, only liable for a drug reaction if it knew or should have known that such a reaction was foreseeable.[64] Where a patient's reaction, no matter how severe, is the first one reported and the patient cannot prove that the manufacturer should have discovered the drug's potential for harm during testing, he cannot prove negligence.[65]

Negligent manufacture of medical or surgical equipment will also subject the manufacturer to liability. The old common law rule that only the first purchaser had an action for damages against a manufacturer and that subsequent users did not has long since been abandoned. This rule was predicated on the concept of "privity of contract" and held that, for example, since a patient himself did not deal with or have a contractual relationship with a manufacturer, the manufacturer was not liable to him. This doctrine was discarded many years ago[66] and now there is usually no problem in proving the manufacturer's responsibility for foreseeable damage to the ultimate consumer of any product, including, but not limited to, medical equipment and drugs.[67]

An orthopedic pin bent in the patient's leg causing severe injuries. It was established that the pin had a crack running its entire length, but that the orthopedist who inserted it could not have seen it. The court held the manufacturer liable for breach of warranty of fitness for use even though there was no contract between the patient and the manufacturer.[68]

Medical supplies and drugs are subject to federal statutory regulation such as the Food, Drug and Cosmetic Act,[69] and if the equipment which injures the patient is covered by such a statute there may be an independent action for recovery of damages under the statute as well as a common law action for negligence or breach of warranty.

A nail used in orthopedic surgery was misbranded. It had a larger diameter than was indicated. It therefore could not be withdrawn from the patient's leg after the fracture for which it was inserted had healed. The patient developed serious infections and lost the use of his leg. The manufacturer was liable for negligent misbranding under the Food, Drug and Cosmetic Act.[70]

Negligent design may be the cause of serious injury from medical or surgical equipment.[71] If the design is faulty, even if there is no defect in manufacture, actually, the potential for harm is greater. If negligent manufacture has caused a problem in one of a large number of products, however severe the injuries may be to the one patient who is damaged, that could well be less disastrous than the use of innumerable pieces of the equipment, all of which were made according to careful manufacturing techniques, but all of which are inherently dangerous because of their design.

A wheel fell from a wheelchair as a result of the inadequate design of the rod attaching the wheel to the chair. There was nothing wrong with the particular rod itself. The patient had broken both legs in an accident. When the wheelchair turned over both the patient's legs were refractured. The manufacturer was liable for breach of warranty of fitness for use for defective design even though the patient could not show any negligence in the method of manufacture.[72]

Negligence in manufacture, however, is probably the primary cause of most injuries from equipment. Where this is proved the manufacturer is liable.[73]

A physician in his office was removing moles from the face of a patient. He used an electrocautery which he owned. The cautery, which was made in one piece, broke and the patient's neck was severely burned when the broken piece fell on her. The cause of the breakage was a latent defect which the physician could not have discovered by looking at the cautery. The manufacturer, not the physician, was liable.[74]

A patient was burned when the overhead cable of an Xray machine sparked. The cable was defective. The court held that the manufacturer was liable for negligent failure to discover latent defects.[75]

Polyethylene tubing "kinked" during a heart catherization and could not be removed except by major surgery. While the tubing was not specifically designed for this purpose, it was widely used in that way, to the manufacturer's knowledge. The court found the manufacturer negligent for failing either to correct the defect or to warn surgeons not to use it for that purpose.[76]

Physicians and other medical personnel may themselves be injured by defective equipment which they are using to treat patients. In most cases ordinary rules of negligence apply.[77]

A physician was severely burned while performing surgery under a fluoroscope. He sued the manufacturer. The court held that a cause of action was stated as to any question of negligent design resulting from the failure of the manufacturer to furnish shields and protective filters.[78]

A hospital employee was severely injured when a cylinder of oxygen packed under pressure exploded. A packing nut on the valve had not been tightened. The manufacturer was liable.[79]

Of course, however, a physician or other person who works with medical equipment is assumed to know how to use it carefully. If such persons are injured the manufacturer may have a good defense by proving that it was their own negligence which caused the damage.

Premises Liability. Sometimes patients are injured by falls or other sorts of accidents in a hospital, physician's office, or outside the premises. The usual rules pertaining to invitees apply. The occupier of the premises is not liable for a latent defect of which he is not aware and which a reasonable man would not have felt a need to investigate. Two decisions illustrate the principles applicable in suits brought by patients injured outside medical offices.

A woman took her 5-year old son to the pediatrician's office. She left by the back door stepped in a hole, and hurt her ankle. The hole was in some high grass and neither she nor the pediatrician had noticed it on prior trips to the door. The court found that she was an invitee even though she herself was not a patient. The judgment for the defendant rendered by the trial court was affirmed on appeal because there was no evidence that the physician had known of the hole.[80]

A patient slipped on a stone in the defendant physician's driveway and fell. The court held that the danger was not one which the physician should have anticipated and it was also not one which reasonable care required him to prevent.[81]

In general, a physician is not liable for injuries to patients who slip on snow or ice in his parking lot.

A patient fell in the physician's parking lot after dark following a late afternoon appointment. While she had been in the office, sleet had begun to fall. She slipped as a result of the slush. The court pointed out that snow is so obvious a danger that invitees are presumed to protect themselves from falling while walking in it.[82]

Falls inside the office are governed by the same principles if the patients are healthy individuals who are ordinarily capable of walking properly and observing hazards.

A patient fell on the way from the reception room to the examining room. She claimed that the floor was slippery, but evidence proved that it had last been waxed 11 days before the accident and that there had been no other falls. The court denied recovery of damages. The decision pointed out that at the time of the accident, the woman was wearing high heel shoes and therefore it was quite likely that her fall was due to her own carelessness.[83]

Where a patient is elderly or infirm or unable to see properly, however, a duty of care does arise which does not exist with a normal business visitor.[84]

A elderly woman was at a radiologist's office for a barium enema. After the Xrays were made, the assistant to the radiologist took her to the bathroom and left her. There was a $7\frac{1}{2}$ inch step up to the bathroom from the floor outside and when she came out of the door, she fell down the step and broke her hip. She claimed that she had felt dizzy and had called for help but was not answered. The court found the radiologist liable. The decision pointed out that the duty of care owed to a patient to safeguard her from danger depended on her capacity to care for herself and that the required duty of care might well be higher for an elderly woman than for a younger one.[85]

The same principle has been applied with patients who have been left alone to undress themselves.[86]

A patient was a very elderly woman who walked with a cane. While she was undressing prior to being Xrayed, the defendant's employee removed her cane from the dressing room and then asked her to come out. When she got up to comply with the instructions, she fell. The court held that she had a cause of action against the radiologist.[87]

Landlords of physician's office buildings may also be liable if patients fall and are injured.

A patient had had part of one leg amputated and walked with a crutch. He had been to see his ophthalmologist and had his eyes examined. Drops which had distorted his vision had been used. When he came out of the office into the hall, the janitor was mopping some feet away and had mopped the spot in front of the office a few minutes before. The patient's crutch slipped on a wet spot. He fell and was injured. The court found both the janitorial service and the landlord liable and pointed out that since the mopping was frequently done in the afternoons while patients were still leaving offices, they both had obligations to warn patients in the hall or to wait until people left before making the floor slippery.[88]

Therefore, in cases of falls in physicians' offices, not only does the court consider the conditions of the premises,[89] but also takes into account the abilities of the patients to take ordinary notice of their surroundings and dangers. A patient who is young and agile might well not be able to show negligence for a fall whereas an elderly and somewhat shaky patient might be able to recover considerable damages in the same situation.

Hospitals also are frequent defendants in premises liability suits. The patient accepted by the hospital is an invitee and is therefore entitled to the exercise of reasonable care by the hospital in keeping its premises in reasonably safe condition. The personnel of a hospital are held to assume that people afflicted with all sorts of ailments and personal infirmities will be using their facilities.[90]

A young woman was going to a hospital's emergency entrance for treatment of an injured finger and slipped on ice at the entrance of the emergency room. She admittedly knew of the presence of the ice. The hospital was not liable.[91]

However, where substances such as wax are placed on floors and they become unusually slippery, the hospital may be liable for failure to warn persons walking on them.

A patient left her room to go home from the hospital, slipped, and fell. The floor had just been washed, waxed, and buffed. It was also poorly lighted. She stated a cause of action against the hospital.[92]

Other types of premises liability have been the subject of suits by patients.

A hospital's roof leaked and a patient's bed became wet. Her suit alleged that both the leak and leaving her in the wet bed for 2 hours, which caused pneumonia, were negligence. The court agreed with her.[93]

A hospital patient was standing in her bathroom. A rat ran across her foot. She was frightened, fell into the tub and was injured. The court held that the hospital had the legal duty of exercising due care in respect to the safety of its patients and was therefore liable.[94]

Bathrooms are frequently the scene of patient injuries. Tile floors are usually slippery and where water is spilled on floors, patients frequently fall. If a hospital permits bathroom floors to remain wet without making efforts to have the water mopped up, it is negligent.[95] Bathroom equipment may also injure patients. It is absolutely necessary that hospitals put non-skid mats in the bottoms of all bathtubs and showers. This is a very frequent cause of accidents and in almost all cases where the patient can show that there was not a nonskid substance on the bottom of the shower or tub in which he fell, the hospital will be liable.[96]

Hot water may burn patients who are not aware of the danger. Where a healthy, mentally acute patient turns on hot water and burns himself, the hospital presumably will not be liable. If his condition makes it unlikely that he would be aware of such danger, the hospital is liable if he is burned.[97]

A patient had multiple sclerosis. As a result of this illness, his skin sensitivity was extremely limited. After he was given preoperative sedation, he went to the bathroom. He was found sitting on the toilet with hot water running over his back and shoulders from a bedpan flusher. He was severely burned. The hospital was found liable.[98]

A patient who is subject to weakness or to dizzy spells and who faints and falls in a bathtub or shower when left alone will probably state a cause of action against the hospital. The hospital is presumed to know the patient's condition, predilection to dizzy spells, or weakness and is required to have the patient accompanied by an attendant at any time when he might faint and fall.[99]

If a patient is not able to go to the bathroom alone, it is negligence to leave him for protracted periods without answering his calls for assistance or providing him with a call bell. How much assistance patients must have in moving about depends on their abilities to care for themselves. If a patient is told to stay in bed or not to get up without assistance, the hospital assumes the obligation of providing assistance whenever he requests it. If his calls are not answered within a reasonable time and he tries to assist himself, the hospital is liable even if he without a signaling device, violates instructions.

A patient was left lying on a stretcher in a room distant from the emergency room. After being left unattended for almost 2 hours, he got up to go to the bathroom, fell off the stretcher, and was injured. The hospital was liable.[100]

A 75-year old man had had a cataract operation. He had been told not to get out of bed by himself. He had to go to the bathroom and rang his call bell. He waited for 15 minutes and began ringing his bell continuously for another 15 minutes. After more than half an hour, no one had come to help him. He concluded that the matter was sufficiently urgent to justify disobedience to the instructions, so he got up alone, fell, and broke his hip. The court concluded that if the staff, which was on notice of his helpless condition, had answered his bell within a reasonable time, he would not have gotten up. His getting up was a natural consequence of the hospital's failure to provide him with adequate care.[101]

A hospital visitor is usually held to be a "licensee." A licensee is a person who is privileged to enter upon land by virtue of the consent of the owner, but he does not come for any business purposes. The only duty which the occupier of the premises owes a licensee is to use reasonable care to warn him of any concealed dangerous conditions. Thus the only liability which a hospital owes to a visitor is to keep the premises safe from undisclosed dangers. This standard of care is far lower than that required toward business visitors, including patients. However, if a visitor is injured there may still be grounds for a suit.

A man came to a hospital to identify his deceased son at the morgue. He used the ambulance approach to the morgue instead of the main entrance, slipped, fell in one of the garage stalls, and broke his knee. There was uncontradicted evidence that the hospital employees knew that the public used the ambulance area as an entrance. All the witnesses testified that there had been a large oil slick from an ambulance engine on the concrete and that the man had fallen in the slick. Since the city, which owned the hospital, knew that the public used the ambulance garage area as a walkway, it owed the man the duty to use reasonable care for his safety.[102]

Some courts, in fact, hold that a person who visits a sick friend or relative at the hospital is an invitee and not a licensee.[103]

A hospital visitor tripped on a garden hose which had been laid over the entire width of the steps. She tried to negotiate her way across two or three strands on the steps, reached for the bannister, and tripped. The court held that the hospital was liable.[104]

Since the hospital is obliged to use care in maintenance of such things as steps and hallways for infirm patients, although it may assume that any hospital visitor will not be suffering from any inability to look after himself, courts are very likely to find hospitals negligent for not keeping their premises in good condition.[105]

Hospitals may also be liable if medical personnel are injured on the premises or by its equipment.[106] Most salaried staff members, such as interns, floor nurses, and custodial personnel, recover damages under Workmen's Compensation law.

A patient was being moved from surgery to the intensive care unit. A staff nurse was pulling the front of the bed on which the patient had been placed while two physicians pushed it. Her heel was struck by the lower cross bar to which the wheels were attached. The underside of the bar was very sharp and her tendon was cut. The court held that she stated a cause of action against the manufacturer of the bed but that any claim against the hospital was covered by Workmen's Compensation.[107]

An attending physician, private duty nurse, student, or volunteer worker who is not paid a salary by the hospital may bring an ordinary negligence action if he is injured on the premises. These persons are normally considered to be invitees just as patients are.

The Chief of Surgery at a hospital fell in an elevator. His fall was admittedly the result of equipment malfunction caused by the hospital's negligence. It was held that he could recover damages.[108]

Many cases have involved private duty nurses who have been injured in hospitals. Courts invariably hold that the nurse, paid by the patient, is an invitee, not a hospital employee and the hospital has the duty to make the premises safe for her use.[109] However, a nurse is expected to be aware of ordinary hazardous conditions and to use reasonable care to avoid injury.

A private duty nurse used toilet tissue to clean up a mess on the floor. When she put the tissue in the toilet to flush it away, the toilet backed up. She fell and was hurt while mopping up. The court pointed out that there is no need to warn an invitee of an obvious condition that could cause an injury.[110]

Volunteer workers may also be injured either from premises liability or negligence of medical personnel. Where this is true, they may recover damages.[111]

A 14-year old "candy striper" was asked by a staff nurse to hold a patient while the nurse cleaned him up. The girl became sick to her stomach, fainted, fell against an oxygen cylinder in the room, and broke her nose. The court held that she had a cause of action against the hospital. The nurse should have known not to ask a young girl with no exposure to the more unpleasant aspects of patient care to help with a senile, incontinent patient.[112]

This chapter discussed injuries unrelated to actual treatment which result from physicians' and hospitals' equipment and premises. In general, the patient has the right to assume either in a physician's office or a hospital that the equipment used to treat him is safe for the intended use. Physicians are required to make reasonable inspections of the equipment in their offices, but they are not held liable for defects which could not have been discovered by such reasonable inspections. Hospitals, on the other hand, are assumed to have adequate maintenance personnel and are held to a much more stringent standard of care as to inspection for latent defects. A hospital is therefore much more likely than a physician to be held liable for equipment injuries. The care expected of a hospital in regard to its premises is largely determined by a patient's ability to look after himself.

If he is injured either by lack of restraining equipment such as bed rails or by the defective condition of equipment, in order to avoid liability the hospital must show that he was in a condition where he could have avoided the injury. This defense is not successful in most cases.

In terms of liability for injuries on the premises, both physicians and hospitals are required to make their premises reasonably safe for use. For example, if wax or another substance likely to cause falls is used on floors, patients should be warned and areas should be roped off. On the other hand, if there is no such unusual danger, normally agile patients are presumed to be able to look where they are going. If a patient is elderly, cannot see well, or his condition is such that he is not able to be responsible for his own safety, a hospital is obliged to use extraordinary care in assisting him. Hospitals may also be liable to visitors, medical personnel, or others on the premises. Since the hospital has to be suitable for patients, in general, courts hold that a physician, nurse, or visitor who is injured may also rely on the fact that the premises should have been safe. Therefore it appears that the hospital's duty of keeping its premises safe as to these persons is considerably higher than, for example, that required of a storeowner in keeping his premises safe for his intended visitors.

NOTES

1. "Medical Premises Liability: Part I," 226 *JAMA* No. 5, page 597, Oct. 29, 1973; "Medical Premises Liability: Part II," 226 *JAMA* No. 6, page 717, Nov. 5, 1973.
2. Brawley v. Heymann, 191 SE 2d 366, NC 1972.
3. Bence v. Denbo, 183 NE 326, Ind 1932.
4. Johnston v. Black Company, 91 P 2d 921, Cal 1939.
5. Crow v. McBride, 153 P 2d 727, Cal 1944.
6. Orthopedic Clinic v. Hanson, 415 P 2d 991, Okla 1966.
7. Harris v. Fireman's Fund Indemnity Company, 257 P 2d 221, Wash 1953.
8. Kelly v. Yount, 7 A 2d 582, Pa 1939.
9. Andrepont v. Ochsner, 84 So 2d 63, La 1955; Dierman v. Providence Hospital, 188 P 2d 12, Cal 1948.
10. Tucson General Hospital v. Russell, 437 P 2d 677, Ariz 1968.
11. Nelson v. Swedish Hospital, 64 NW 2d 38, Minn 1954.
12. Taylor v. Beekman Hospital, 62 NYS 2d 637, NY 1946; Rabasco v. New Rochelle Hospital, 44 NYS 2d 293, NY 1943.
13. "Hospital Burns," 214 *JAMA* No. 3, page 653, Oct. 19, 1970.
14. Hand v. Park Community Hospital, 165 NW 2d 673, Mich 1968; Pensacola Sanitarium v. Wilkins, 67 So 124, Fla 1914; Quillen v. Skaggs, 25 SW 2d 33, Ky 1930.
15. Kent v. County of Hudson, 245 A 2d 747, NJ 1968.

16. Danville Community Hospital v. Thompson, 43 SE 2d 882, Va 1947.
17. Weeks v. Latter Day Saints Hospital, 418 F 2d 1035, CCA 10, 1969.
18. Clampett v. Sisters of Charity, 136 P 2d 729, Wash 1943.
19. Swigerd v. Ortonville Hospital, 75 NW 2d 217, Minn 1956.
20. Ware v. Culp, 74 P 2d 283, Cal 1937; Kuglich v. Fowle, 200 NW 648, Wisc 1924.
21. McDermott v. St. Mary's Hospital, 133 A 2d 608, Conn 1957; Wallstedt v. Swedish Hospital, 19 NW 2d 426, Minn 1945.
22. Clovis v. Hartford Accident Company, 223 So 2d 178, La 1969.
23. "Hospital Fires," 223 *JAMA* No. 9, page 1073, Feb. 26, 1973.
24. LeBlanc v. Midland National Insurance Company, 219 So 2d 251, La 1969.
25. Evans v. Newark–Wayne Community Hospital, 316 NYS 2d 447, NY 1970.
26. Hally v. Hospital of St. Raphael, 294 A 2d 305, Conn 1972.
27. Silverhart v. Mount Zion Hospital, 98 Cal Rptr 187, Cal 1971.
28. Horwitz v. Michael Reese Hospital, 284 NE 2d 4, Ill 1970.
29. Huffman v. Lundquist, 234 P 2d 34, Cal 1951.
30. Peck v. Towns Hospital, 89 NYS 2d 190, NY 1949.
31. Winthral v. Callison Memorial Hospital, Cal Super. Ct., San Francisco County, Docket #582565, 1972.
32. Lauro v. The Travelers' Insurance Company, 261 So 2d 261, 262 So 2d 787, La 1972.
33. Medical and Surgical Memorial Hospital v. Cauthorn, 229 SW 2d 932, Tex 1949.
34. Williams v. Orange Memorial Hospital Association, 202 So 2d 859, Fla 1967.
35. Walker v. Rynd, 280 P 2d 259, Wash 1955.
36. St. Luke's Hospital Association v. Long, 240 P 2d 917, Colo 1952.
37. Welsh v. Mercy Hospital, 151 P 2d 17, Cal 1944.
38. Camp v. Booth, 273 A 2d 714, Conn 1970; Bess Ambulance Company Inc. v. Boll, 208 So 2d 308, Fla 1968.
39. Falcher v. St. Luke's Hospital Medical Center, 506 P 2d 287, Ariz 1973.
40. Sivertson v. New York, 252 NYS 2d 623, NY 1964.
41. "Use of Bed Rails, 220 *JAMA* No. 1, page 163, April 3, 1972.
42. Rhodes v. Moore, 398 P 2d 189, Ore 1965; D'Antoni v. Sara Mayo Hospital, 144 So 2d 643, La 1962.
43. Clark v. Piedmont Hospital, 162 2d 468, Ga 1968.
44. Martin v. Aetna Casualty and Surety Company, 387 SW 2d 334, Ark 1965.
45. Morand v. Seaside Memorial Hospital, 264 P 2d 96, Cal 1953; Public Administrator of New York County v. New York, 177 NYS 2d 95, NY 1958; Cleaver v. Dade County, 272 So 2d 559, Fla 1973.
46. Holtfoth v. Rochester General Hospital, 105 NE 2d 610, NY 1952.
47. Porter v. Patterson, 129 SE 2d 70, Ga 1962.
48. "Electrosurgical Instruments," 223 *JAMA* No. 1, page 111, Jan. 1, 1973.
49. Shepherd v. McGinnis, 131 NW 2d 475, Iowa 1964.
50. Peterson v. Richards, 272 Pac 229, Utah 1928.
51. Magner v. Beth Israel Hospital, 295 A 2d 363, NJ 1972.
52. South Highlands Infirmary v. Camp, 180 So 2d 904, Ala 1965.

53. Clary v. Christiansen, 83 NE 2d 644, Ohio 1948.

54. Inouye v. Black, 47 Cal Rptr 313, Cal 1965.

55. "Manufacturer's Liability for Drug Reactions," 213 *JAMA* No. 11, page 1975, Sept. 14, 1970; Edward M. Swartz, "Products Liability: Manufacturer's Responsibility for Defective or Negligently Designed Medical and Surgical Equipment," in *Legal Medicine Annual, 1970* Appleton-Century Crofts, New York, 1970.

56. Abbott Laboratories v. Lapp, 78 F 2d 170, CCA 7, 1935.

57. Moehlenbrock v. Parke Davis and Company, 169 NW 541, Minn 1918.

58. Tuscany v. United States Standard Products Company, 243 SW 2d 207, Tex 1951.

59. Basko v. Sterling Drug Inc., 416 F 2d 417, CCA 2, 1969; Kershaw v. Sterling Drug, Inc., 415 F 2d 1009, CCA 5, 1969; Davis v. Wyeth Laboratories, 399 F 2d 121, CCA 9, 1968.

60. Love v. Wolf, 38 Cal Rptr 183, 58 Cal Rptr 42, Cal 1967; Stottlemire v. Cawood, 213 F. Supp 897, DC DC 1963.

61. Gottsdanker v. Cutter Laboratories, 6 Cal Rptr 320, Cal 1960; Magee v. Wyeth Laboratories, 29 Cal Rptr 322, Cal 1963.

62. Parke, Davis and Company v. Stromstodt, 411 F 2d 1390, CCA 8, 1969; Tinnerholm v. Parke Davis and Company, 411 F 2d 48, CCA 2, 1969.

63. Incollingo v. Ewing, 282 A 2d 206, Pa 1971.

64. "Drug-Induced Aplastic Anemia," 222 *JAMA* No. 3, page 405, Oct. 16, 1972.

65. Johnston v. The Upjohn Company, 442 SW 2d 93, Mo 1969; Cudmore v. Richardson-Merrell, 398 SW 2d 640, Tex 1965.

66. MacPherson v. Buick, 111 NE 1050, NY 1916.

67. Bernstein v. Lily Tulip Cup Corporation, 177 So 2d 362, Fla 1965.

68. Bowles v. Zimmer Manufacturing Company, 277 F 2d 868, CCA 7, 1960.

69. Food, Drug and Cosmetic Act, 21 USCA Sec. 301-392.

70. Orthopedic Equipment Company v. Eutsler, 276 F 2d 455, CCA 4, 1960.

71. Vergott v. Deseret Pharmaceutical Company, 463 F 2d 12, CCA 5, 1972.

72. Putman v. Erie City Manufacturing Company, 338 F 2d 911, CCA 5, 1964.

73. C. R. Bard, Inc. v. Mason, 247 So 2d 471, Fla 1971.

74. Hine v. Fox, 89 So 2d 13, Fla 1956.

75. Sinatra v. National Xray Products Corporation, 141 A 2d 28, NJ 1958.

76. Putensen v. Clay Adams, Inc., 91 Cal Rptr 319, Cal 1970.

77. Thomas v. Pugh, 6 SW 2d 202, Tex 1928.

78. O'Connell v. Westinghouse Xray Company, 41 NE 2d 177, NY 1942.

79. Liberatore v. National Cylinder Gas Company, 193 F 2d 429, CCA 2, 1952.

80. Goldman v. Kossove, 117 SE 2d 35, NC 1960.

81. Butler v. Jones, 68 SE 2d 173, Ga 1951.

82. Jeswald v. Hutt, 239 NE 2d 37, Ohio 1968.

83. Callison v. Red, 149 SW 2d 153, Tex 1941.

84. Cagle v. Bakersfield Medical Group, 241 P 2d 1013, Cal 1952.

85. Urdang v. Mahrer, 158 NE 2d 902, Ohio 1959.

86. Levett v. Etkind, 265 A 2d 70, Conn 1969.

87. French v. Heibert, 262 P 2d 831, Kan 1953.
88. Truxillo v. Gentilly Medical Building, Inc., 225 So 2d 488, La 1969.
89. English v. Sahlender, 47 SW 2d 150, Mo 1932.
90. Norward Clinic v. Spann, 199 So 840, Ala 1941.
91. Gulfway General Hospital v. Pursley, 397 SW 2d 93, Tex 1965.
92. Starr v. Emory University, 93 SE 2d 399, Ga 1956.
93. Tulsa Hospital Association v. Juby, 175 Pac 519, Okla 1918.
94. Hill v. James Walker Memorial Hospital, 407 F 2d 1036, CCA 4, 1969.
95. Crawford Long Memorial Hospital v. Hardeman, 66 SE 2d 63, Ga 1951; Laidlaw v. Andrew Freedman Home, 300 NYS 2d 979, NY 1969.
96. Schuster v. St. Vincent Hospital, 172 NW 2d 421, Wisc 1969.
97. Kopa v. United States, 236 F Supp 189, DC Hawaii 1964.
98. Memorial Hospital of South Bend Inc. v. Scott, 290 NE 2d 80, Ind 1972.
99. Kastler v. Iowa Methodist Hospital, 193 NW 2d 98, Iowa 1971.
100. Cavanaugh v. South Broward Hospital District, 247 So 2d 769, Fla 1971.
101. Jefferson Hospital v. Van Lear, 41 SE 2d 441, Va 1947.
102. Gibo v. City and County of Honolulu, 459 P 2d 198, Hawaii 1969.
103. Lesyk v. Park Avenue Hospital, 289 NYS 2d 873, NY 1968.
104. Sulack v. Miller Hospital, 165 NW 2d 207, Minn 1969.
105. Candler General Hospital v. Purvis, 181 SE 2d 77, Ga 1971.
106. "Hospital Obligation to Nonemployee Personnel," 224 *JAMA* No. 8, page 1329, May 28, 1973.
107. Olsen v. Royal Metals Corporation, 392 F 2d 116, CCA 5, 1968.
108. Lindroth v. Christ Hospital, 123 A 2d 10, NJ 1956.
109. Rose v. Raleigh-Fitkin Memorial Hospital, 57 A 2d 29, NJ 1948; Crockett v. Encino Gardens Care Center Inc., 492 P 2d 1273, NM 1972.
110. Long v. Methodist Home, 187 SE 2d 718, NC 1972.
111. Orphant v. St. Louis State Hospital, 441 SW 2d 355, Mo 1969.
112. Marcus v. Frankford Hospital, 283 A 2d 69, Pa 1971.

CHAPTER VII

VICARIOUS

LIABILITY

The term "vicarious liability" is legal shorthand for a doctrine which involves the responsibility of one person who is not negligent for the wrongful conduct or negligence of another. Thus, the concept of vicarious liability in the context of medical malpractice law involves at least three persons: first, the patient who is injured by negligent treatment; secondly, the person, such as a nurse, who is actually the negligent party; and thirdly, the physician who may or may not be financially responsible for her negligence.

An employer is, with very few exceptions which involve deliberate torts, such as assault and battery, always liable for injuries caused by the negligence of his employees which occur within the scope of their employment. A "servant" in legal terms is a person employed by a "master" to perform any service. The manner in which he performs this service is controlled or is subject to the right of control by the master. Once it is determined that the employee is in fact a servant, the employer is subject to vicarious liability for his negligence.

Without any serious questions, physicians are liable for their office employees' negligence.[1] An office nurse mistakenly gives a patient the wrong medication.[2] An electrical machine in a clinic malfunctions, but the technician who administers treatments with it attempts to fix it herself and the patient is burned.[3] In both cases, the physicians who employ these persons would be liable for the negligence. There are many cases, all to the same end.[4]

An office nurse injected vitamin B complex into a patient's arm in a negligent manner. He developed a wristdrop as a result. The physician was liable for his nurse's negligence.[5]

While a physician was on vacation, an office assistant administered an injection. The needle used in the injection broke off in the patient's arm and the site became infected. The court found the physician liable. The decision pointed out that the nurse did not have any discretion in the matter since the nature of the treatment and the time at which it was to be administered were determined by the physician. He was therefore liable.[6]

With the rise of the new concept of the "paramedical assistant" who will work in a doctor's office and assist him with routine patient care, it should be noticed that the physician will clearly be liable for the negligence of the assistant just as he would be for a nurse or other technician in his employ.[7]

A paramedical assistant working in an orthopedist's office cut a patient while removing a cast. The court held that if the physician delegates such professional responsibilities he is liable if they are performed with less care, skill, and knowledge than would be expected of him if he had removed the cast himself.[8]

A physician who employs another physician for a salary or who reserves the right to control the actions of the second physician regardless of the financial arrangements between them, is liable for the employee-physician's negligence.[9]

A surgeon employed by another surgeon performed an operation to remove an intestinal obstruction. He was assisted by his employer. The woman went into shock and was given Levophed. The drug infiltrated into the tissues of her left hand and she was severely scarred. Both physicians were held negligent. The operating surgeon was negligent because he did not place the woman in the intensive care unit or order someone to stay with her in order to cope with any infiltration situation. The other surgeon was liable as his employer.[10]

It should be noted carefully that employing an unlicensed physician, unless he is educationally qualified and is merely establishing residency to obtain a license, may also result in serious criminal and professional penalties for aiding and abetting the unlawful practice of medicine.[11] Furthermore, if the unlicensed physician is negligent and the employer-physician is sued, a judgment against him may not be covered by his malpractice insurance, since most policies provide coverage only for negligence of "duly qualified" assistants.[12]

A child was seriously ill with osteomyelitis. He was being treated by a physician who was a nationally recognized authority on the subject. The physician went out of town and arranged for an inexperienced general practitioner to care for his patients. The child was injured by the negligence of the general practitioner. The original physician was liable because he had special qualifications and therefore should have provided his patients with a substitute physician of equivalent knowledge.[13]

In general, however, a physician who plans to be away from his practice and recommends to patients that they see another physician or who arranges for a second physician to come in as his substitute ordinarily is not liable for the substitute's negligence if he used due care in choosing him. An employer–employee relationship is usually not created by such actions.[14]

Where physicians volunteer to take each others' calls on occasion, it is quite clear that any negligence by the substitute does not impose liability on the first physician. These physicians are clearly independent practitioners. If a substitute is chosen with due care and is not paid a salary but bills directly for his services, it is unlikely that the first physician will be found liable for his negligence. If, on the other hand, the substitute physician is on salary from the treating physician, the employer is liable for his negligence. A physician must make all reasonable efforts to insure that the substitute is adequately qualified and if he has failed to used due care in the selection process, he may well be liable for the substitute's negligence.[15]

A physician is required to give patients reasonable notice of the fact that a substitute will be caring for them in case the patient does not wish to accept the substitute and prefers to transfer to another physician. If no notice is given, the physician may well be liable for his negligence in failing to notify patients even if he would not otherwise be liable for the substitute's negligence. Of course, the requirement of notice would not apply in an emergency, such as the physician's sudden illness.[16]

An obstetrician went on vacation and provided a substitute. The substitute delivered the plaintiff's child. The baby was healthy and so was the mother, but she sued on the grounds that the defendant, the original obstetrician, had promised to give her a general anesthetic and the substitute refused to do so. She returned to the defendant, however, for postpartum care. Since she had had no notice of any substitution prior to going to the hospital to deliver, the obstetrician was liable.[17]

An intern or resident is not considered an adequate substitute. When a physician hires him to care for his patient and the intern or resident makes a mistake, regardless of the financial arrangements between the two, the patient is usually able to recover damages from the physician.

A patient was brought to the emergency room with a compound fracture. The defendant was the orthopedic specialist on call. He told a resident on the telephone to clean and suture the wound. By the next morning when he saw the patient himself, an infection had set in. The court held that the defendant should have known that the resident could not provide adequate care and should have come to see the patient himself. He was liable for the resident's negligence.[18]

With those exceptions however, a physician is usually not liable for his substitutes.

Where two or more physicians create a partnership for the purpose of practicing medicine, each is liable not only for his own negligence, but also, under general principles of partnership law, for the negligence of any of his partners and for any of the employees of the partnership.[19]

A married woman had an affair with a physician who was a member of a medical partnership. Her husband sued the partnership for alienation of affections. He claimed that the other partners knew of the physician's relationship with his wife and that the partnership consented to and condoned the affair. One of the partners admitted that he was chairman of the staff of the clinic and that the husband had complained to him about the conduct of the other partner, but he did not discuss the matter with the physician. The court held that the partnership failed to prove that it did not consent to the alleged wrongful conduct, particularly because the husband alleged that some of the acts of sexual intercourse took place at the office during office hours. The court ruled that a cause of action was stated by the husband.[20]

Where a partnership exists and is sued, however, assets of the partnership and of the physician who was himself negligent must usually be exhausted before any of the other partners may be asked to contribute from his personal funds to the judgment obtained by the plaintiff. It should be noted that this is standard partnership law and obtains in all cases, including other types of professional partnerships such as that of attorneys and architects.

In the last few years, in order to obtain benefits from federal income tax laws, physicians have formed incorporated "professional associations."[21] This usually has no effect on their individual liability for their own negligence or that of those physicians who formerly would have been considered partners. However, certain aspects of this question are still largely unsettled by the courts of the individual states. Thus any physician who is contemplating forming a professional association which deviates from the standard partnership agreement should inquire of the attorney who draws the corporate charter if the physicians are liable for each others' negligence as if they were partners.

Physicians may share offices without in any way sharing responsibility for each others' patients. In this case, one physician is not usually liable for the other's negligence.[22]

A physician who refers a patient to a specialist and then withdraws from the case is not usually liable for any negligence committed by the specialist unless the patient can show that the specialist was unqualified or incompetent and that the referring physician should have known it.[23]

A patient was treated by a general practitioner who referred him to a specialist for rectal surgery and who thereafter had no contact with the patient. The patient sued both the surgeon and the general practitioner, alleging surgical negligence. The court found that the surgeon had not been negligent, but even if he had been, it held that the general practitioner could not be liable unless there was evidence that he had failed to exercise due care in recommending the surgeon.[24]

A woman broke her leg. A personal friend, who was an internist, engaged an orthopedist whom she did not know for her, at her request. The orthopedist recommended and performed surgery. She sued him for negligence and won. She then sued the internist for having failed to warn her about the dangers of the surgery. The court held that since he had seen the patient only socially and had not rendered professional services in any way after contacting the orthopedist, the internist was not liable for the surgical negligence.[25]

If two physicians treat a patient jointly, each one participating in the decision-making and each one seeing the patient on a continuing basis, both will be liable for any negligence.

An orthopedist and a neurosurgeon were employed jointly to treat the patient's back condition. They made a joint diagnosis, recommending a laminectomy and spinal fusion. Both performed part of the procedure. They also both saw the patient through postoperative treatment. One surgeon had left the operating room before the other closed the wound. When the wound was closed, a sponge was left in the patient. Both physicians were ilable for the negligence.[25a]

Physician Liability for Negligence of Hospital Employees.   In matters involving routine nursing care, a physician is not liable if hospital employee nurses perform his orders negligently.[26]

A surgeon left written orders for administration of an antibiotic to a post-surgical patient. A floor nurse at the hospital injected the drug negligently and the patient's sciatic nerve was damaged causing permanent loss of use of one of his feet. The court held that the doctor was not liable for the nurse's negligence since he did not have sufficient control over her conduct to instruct her on the proper method of giving the injection.[27]

The general rule is that the only time a physician is liable for a hospital nurse's negligence in the course of routine nursing care is when she acts under the direct and personal control of the physician or he knows or should know that she is incompetent.[28]

A senile patient was admitted to the hospital. Her physician ordered use of a hospital heating pad when she complained of being cold. The heating pad burned her. The court held that the physician was not liable. There was no evidence that the physician had any reason to believe that the simple instruction he gave would not be followed properly by trained nurses. Even if they did not do so, the court held that the physician had been entitled to assume that they were able to follow the instructions on the pad, which they had allowed to overheat.[29]

A staff physician's liability for the negligent act of an intern or resident depends on the degree of supervision which the physician should have given to the physician-in-training.[30] The attending physician is not responsible for the negligence of an intern or resident as long as his orders involve treatment which he may reasonably expect the resident to know how to perform, such as administering injections or intravenous solutions.[31] These procedures are normally considered to be routine treatments which the physician or surgeon should have every reason to believe an intern or resident is qualified to perform. Thus they may be delegated to him without resultant liability on the part of the attending physician if negligence occurs.

A cardiologist ordered an aortograph. It was negligently performed by a surgical resident and the patient was paralyzed. The court found that the cardiologist was not liable. It held that since cardiologists do not normally supervise surgery, he was not responsible for the acts performed by the resident.[32]

A supervising surgeon left the operating room while a surgical resident was closing the patient's wound. The resident put phenol instead of alcohol on the patient's skin. The patient was injured and sued the surgeon. The court held that it would be unreasonable to expect the defendant to anticipate that a resident would make such a mistake and pointed out that it was in keeping with ordinary medical practice for the surgeon to leave the room at that point. Thus the surgeon was not liable.[33]

Obstetrical cases present another situation. If a physician has been caring for a patient during the prenatal period and allows an intern or resident to deliver the baby, he may not be liable for any negligence committed by the resident. He will, however, probably be liable for breaching the contract he made with the patient for his personal care.[34]

An attending physican has an obligation to visit his patient regularly. If he leaves orders for treatment to be administered by either an intern or a resident, he may be liable if negligence is committed which he should have, by the reasonable frequency of his visits, seen and corrected.

A 5-year old boy broke his right leg. He was taken to a hospital for indigents, given treatment in the emergency room by a surgical resident, and admitted to the hospital. The Chief of Orthopedics who supervised the resident saw the child the next day and 6 or 7 times within the next 3 weeks. At that time, the services changed and a new resident assumed care of the patient. The staff orthopedist did not see the patient for an additional 10 days. The cast on his leg had caused a severe pressure sore and the child was permanently damaged. The court held that attending staff physicians have final responsibility for the care of patients and the responsibility of supervising activities of the residents and that they are liable, therefore, for their residents' negligence.[35]

It should be noted that the same rule would apply if a private patient were treated by a resident under orders of his attending physician.[36]

Where the physician is himself in attendance, he is liable for negligence committed by interns and residents in his presence.[37] The general law of liability for the negligence of an intern or resident is well stated in one case.

The defendant surgeon inserted a drainage tube and left orders that it be irrigated, the usual procedure. He eventually asked a resident to remove the tubes and the patient's lung collapsed in the process. The court found the attending surgeon was not liable and said, "A surgeon rendering post-operative care to a patient is not liable for the negligence of a hospital employee when the orders given are not potentially dangerous to the patient and fall within the ambit of the resident's training and qualification and are the accepted medical practice. As long as tasks are assigned in keeping with the training of the physician who is to carry out the orders or are not so dangerous that extra supervision is required and the attending physician or surgeon sees his patient frequently enough so that if there is continuing negligence he may attempt to correct it, he is not liable for the errors of the intern or resident."[38]

Vicarious Liability in the Operating Room. Most states hold a surgeon responsible for all negligence which occurs in the operating room at the time he is performing surgery on a patient. While the negligent persons technically may be employees of the hospital, most courts hold that they are, for the purposes of performing surgical procedures, "borrowed servants" and are under the total supervision and control of the operating surgeon. Many cases illustrate this point, but a few examples will serve.

A defendant surgeon had delivered a baby by Cesarian section. The mother began to hemorrhage very badly. While he was attending to her immediate needs, he asked an intern to apply drops to the baby's eyes. The intern used the wrong solution. The baby's eyes were damaged, and the parents sued. The surgeon was liable for the intern's negligence because, although he was busy with the mother at the time he asked the intern to do it, the intern was under his direct supervision and control. He had the responsibility of telling the intern what solution to use.[39]

An orderly was preparing to strap an unconscious patient to the operating table. The strap did not work and the orderly took his hands off the patient to find another strap. The plaintiff fell off the operating table. The surgeon was liable for the orderly's negligence because he had told the orderly to place the patient on the table and instructed him in the manner in which he wished the patient to be strapped down.[40]

Although most hospitals have administrative regulations covering such things as sponge counts and the methods nurses must follow in performing them, and the surgeon usually cannot direct the nurse to vary this routine, he is invariably liable if there is a mistake made in the sponge count.[41]

A baby was operated on and a sponge was left. As a double check, the sponge count was supposed to be made by two nurses. However, the circulating nurse was out of the room at the time and the scrub nurse's count was relied upon. The scrub nurse had made a mistake. The surgeon and the hospital were jointly liable.[42]

The same rule would hold for any other form of negligence caused by an operating room nurse in the normal course of surgical procedures. Use of the wrong preoperative sterilizing agent with the result that the patient is burned[43] or improper positioning by a nurse of a patient on the operating table so that some part of his body is injured are two types of situations where the surgeon would be found liable.

A patient was admitted to the hospital for an operation on her neck. She suffered burns on her legs during the surgery. She sued the hospital. The court held that the surgeon, not the hospital, was liable for the nurse's negligence in spilling hot water on the patient.[44]

However, where the surgeon is not present in the operating room and preliminary routine acts are performed to prepare the patient, the hospital, not the surgeon, may be negligent.

After administration of a spinal anesthesia, a nurse applied zephiran solution to the operative area. After she completed this procedure, she made no inspection to see if the bed linen was soaked. About 15 minutes later when the surgeon began using a cautery, the drapes around the patient caught fire from the combination of the zephiran and the electric cautery. The court found that the surgeon was not liable because he could not be expected to supervise anything so elementary as the application of a solution.[45]

With the increasing complexity of surgical machinery, there are a few cases which indicate that if a nurse is in charge of a very highly specialized machine belonging to the hospital which the surgeon himself does not know how to operate, if it is negligently used, the hospital and not the surgeon will be liable.

A cautery which had malfunctioned during an earlier operation was used during a hemorrhoidectomy. The patient was burned on the chest where the electrode had been placed. In finding that the surgeon was not negligent, the court pointed out that the hospital owned the machine and that the operating room nurses, not the surgeons, were trained to operate it. In this case it was held that when technical equipment and personnel to man it which are furnished by a hospital cause injuries from malfunction, the hospital will be solely liable. The doctrine that the surgeon is captain of the ship does not apply.[46]

However, when the physician is an active participant in directing the use of the machine or positioning the patient on the table, he may be liable for his own negligence.

A patient received severe leg burns from the contact plate on an electro-surgical machine. The hospital was liable for the improper placement of the plate by the nurse, but she had asked the surgeon to check the placement and he had done so. The patient therefore also stated a cause of action against him.[47]

Therefore, the general rule as to negligence in the performance of an operation is that barring some exceptionally complex procedure which hospital personnel are trained to do, the surgeon is liable for all negligence of his assistants in the operating room.[48]

He is also responsible for care of the patient immediately following surgery in most cases while the patient is in the recovery room.

Where anesthesia is given by a nurse, in most, but not all cases, the surgeon is liable for her negligence because the surgeon usually directs what type and method of anesthesia will be given.[49]

An 8-year old boy died during a tonsillectomy. The anesthetic had been given by a nurse and the cause of death was an overdose of ether. The court held the surgeon liable for the nurse anesthetist's negligence because he had the power of immediate control and direction over her actions.[50]

However, in some cases nurse anesthetists who prepare a patient while the surgeon is absent from the room and are negligent in doing so are considered employees of the hospital and not of the physician.

A nurse started anesthetic procedures on a patient while the surgeon went to scrub. The surgeon did not supervise the procedure in any way. When he returned a few minutes later, he sat on a stool about 8 feet away from the operating table until the nurse told him the patient was properly anes-thetized. When he commenced surgery, the nurse said that the presence of reflexes in the throat indicated that the patient needed more anesthetic. The surgeon sat down again while the nurse adjusted the ether machine. After about a minute, the nurse noticed the patient's abdomen was distending and called this to the doctor's attention. She immediately turned off the machine. The patient recovered from the effects of gas in the abdomen but sued the surgeon and the hospital. This court concluded that the nurse was not an agent of the surgeon because he had not directed her in any way.[51]

These cases are, however, extremely rare and the general rule certainly is that physicians are liable for the negligence of nurse anesthetists.

Anesthesiologists, however, are themselves considered to be "captains of the ship" in their sphere of activity.[52]

A patient had spinal anesthesia for an appendectomy. He was partially paralyzed. Evidence held that the anesthesia had been negligently administered. The court found the anesthesiologist negligent, but not the surgeon. He had no control or influence over the anesthesiologist's decision-making as he would have had over a nurse.[53]

The leading case on the subject of surgeon's liability for anesthesiologists' errors is *Thompson v. Lillehei*.[54]

A team of physicians from a medical school attempted to perform cross-circulation heart surgery on an 8-year old girl with a congenital heart defect. It was only the seventeenth operation of its kind that had ever been attempted. The child's mother was to serve as the donor after cross-circulation was established. It was planned that the donor's heart and lungs would be used to pump and purify the patient's blood. Two surgeons and an anesthesiologist worked with the child. Two additional surgeons made the cutdown on the donor and another anesthesiologist was part of the team attending the donor. A third anesthesiologist was to operate certain machines after cross-circulation had been established. The mother had been in the operating room for about an hour, but the circulation hook-up had not been completed when her pulse dropped. It was reestablished quickly, but she was paralyzed by organic brain damage. The cause was an air embolism, caused by the negligence of one of the anesthesiologists who permitted a glucose and water container to become empty. The court said that the surgeon heading the entire team was not responsible for the negligence of the anesthesiologist.

A patient died the day after he had a cardiac arrest during surgery. The surgeon had requested an anesthesiologist from a partnership. An anesthesiologist arrived and the surgeon told him he wanted him to use an epidural block. After the anesthesiologist began the anesthesia, the surgeon went to scrub. While he was absent from the operating room, the patient went into cardiac arrest. The anesthesiologist called the surgeon who took the proper steps to revive the patient. He died the next day. The anesthesiologist settled the case and the surgeon refused to do so. The patient's surviving spouse alleged that since the surgeon had selected both the anesthesiologist and the type of anesthesia, he should be liable for the anesthesiologist's negligence. However, the court rejected this plea. There was no evidence to show that the surgeon had the right to control the anesthesiologist in his specialty. There was evidence that the anesthesiologist was in full control of the administration of the anesthesia after being instructed by the surgeon as to the nature and purpose of the anesthesia desired.[55]

Thus an anesthesiologist or the physician who is administering the anesthetic is usually considerd to be an independent agent rather than an assistant to the surgeon, since he and not the surgeon makes the decision about the type and methods of administering the anesthesia.[56] There are some exceptions to this rule,[57] but, in general, a surgeon is not liable for an anesthesiologist's negligence.

It should be noted, however, that a resident in anesthesiology, because he is presumably subject to more control by the operating surgeon than is a fully qualified anesthesiologist, may impose liability on a surgeon if he is negligent.[58]

It should be pointed out that an anesthesiologist is usually not liable for surgical negligence.[59]

Hospital Liability. Hospitals are liable for negligence of their employees who cause injuries in the course of their duties. The definition of employment, however, is not a simple one. Interns, residents, and staff nurses who are paid salaries by the hospital are invariably considered to be employees. So are other paramedical personnel and people such as janitors, maids, and elevator operators. Therefore, unless one of these employees is, during the time of negligence, a "borrowed servant" of a physician, the hospital will be liable for negligence.

A patient complained of severe head pains so a friend took him to the emergency room. A resident there took his blood pressure, but made no further examination and told him to go home. He died in the car before he got there. The cause of death was a cerebral hemorrhage. The heirs sued the hospital. The neurosurgeon who testified for the plaintiff stated that there were enough objective symptoms presented by the patient to have alerted any reasonably careful physician that a very serious problem existed. The verdict for the plaintiff was upheld on appeal.[60]

A service man was hospitalized in a military hospital with chest pains. No diagnosis had been made, but the possibility of heart trouble had not been ruled out. Three days after his discharge, he went back to the emergency room, again with severe chest pains. The resident on call was a first year resident who had had very limited experience in reading electrocardiograms. He made an electrocardiogram but misread it and thus he did not realize that the man was having an acute heart problem. He urged the man to be admitted to the hospital, but told him that he did not think he was having a heart attack, so the patient went home and died. The court held that the hospital was liable for having allowed an inexperienced physician to read electrocardiograms without supervision and was therefore liable for his negligence.[61]

Private duty nurses, however, are generally considered to be employees of the patient even when they are hired through the hospital's registry and, therefore, if a private duty nurse is negligent, the hospital is not liable.[62]

A hospital is also liable in its own right if it uses negligence in the employment and retention of unqualified or incompetent personnel.

A student nurse who was passing but at the bottom of her class was assigned to work under a registered nurse. She administered cleaning fluid to a patient instead of a laxative. The court held that she was not, as a matter of law, unqualified to have administered the medication. If she had been, however, the hospital would have been liable for her negligence.[63]

The head nurse on a surgical patient's floor gave him an injection. The needle broke off in his buttock. The nurse did not report the incident to anyone or tell the patient. The embedded needle caused a severe infection and was very difficult to remove. The court found that such conduct by the nurse in failing to report the incident was so far below the standard of care required of a head floor nurse that a cause of action had been stated against the hospital. The patient was held to have presented sufficient evidence to go to the jury on whether the hospital had been negligent in putting the nurse in her supervisory position.[64]

The question of a hospital's liability for a professional tenant is a very complex one. Pathologists, anesthesiologists, and radiologists often practice within the hospital and use the hospital's facilities under various arrangements. Where the physician is employed on a fixed salary, there is no problem in establishing that he is the hospital's employee and that the hospital is liable for his negligence.

A pathologist misread a frozen section and told the surgeon that a patient had cervical cancer. A hysterectomy was performed. It was later proven that the patient had never had a malignancy. Since the pathologist was on a straight salary from the hospital, the hospital was liable for his negligence.[65]

A patient was admitted to the hospital complaining of chest and stomach pains. A gastric cytology test was ordered. A laboratory technician in the pathology department used sodium hydroxide instead of sodium chloride and the jury returned a $162,000 verdict against the hospital for the patient's injuries. The hospital's insurance company filed a suit against the director of the pathology department. They alleged that the director of the pathology department was an independent contractor and the technician was his borrowed servant and therefore he, and not the hospital, was liable for the technician's negligence. The appellate court found that both the pathologist and the technician were employees of the hospital.[66]

Even if a physician bills patients directly and not through the hospital, he may still be held to be an agent of the hospital. If the hospital has the right to control the method of practice or restrict his practice to its patients, he may, even though he bills separately, subject the hospital to liability.[67] Hospitals are frequently liable for negligence of pathologists, anesthesiologists, and radiologists, or at least the question is sufficiently cloudy so that in most cases the trial judge will order the jury to make the determination of whether or not the physician is an independent contractor or an employee.[68]

As emergency room medicine is becoming a discrete specialty, an increasing number of hospitals are being confronted with the question of liability for contract physicians. Most decisions so far hold that contract partnerships which take care of emergency patients at a hospital do not impose liability on the hospital for negligence, but the deciding factor is usually the contractual arrangement between the hospital and the physicians.

A partnership ran the emergency service in the defendant hospital. A patient died after treatment, allegedly as the result of physician negligence. The court examined the contract between the group and the hospital and noted that it specifically provided that the physicians would be considered independent contractors and not employees. The decision indicated that a hospital is not liable for the negligence of a physician employed by it if the negligence relates to medical judgment, since the hospital does not and cannot exercise control over that judgment.[69]

A patient had been injured in a wreck. He was examined by a physician on contract to the emergency room. The physician did not diagnose fractured dislocations of the fifth and sixth cervical vertebrae. The case against the hospital was dismissed. The court found that the physician was an independent contractor by terms of the agreement with the hospital and not an employee and, even if he had been negligent, the hospital would not be liable.[70]

More and more states, however, are beginning to realize that contract physicians for emergency rooms are, in the public mind, employees of the hospitals. New questions are at least being raised about these emergency room partnerships.

A hospital's emergency room was covered by a partnership on contract to the hospital. A 9-year old girl cut her knee and was taken to the emergency room where she was seen by a member of the partnership. He sewed up the cut and advised her parents to take her to her family doctor 5 days later to have the sutures removed. Prior to that time, on Sunday afternoon when her family physician could not be located, she was brought back to the hospital in great pain. Another partner saw her and realized that the leg was infected. All he did in the way of treatment was to tell the parents to soak the wound. She died of the infection. The trial court held that the physicians were independent contractors and not employees. However, on appeal, the appellate court questioned the automatic finding that independent contractors impose no liability on the hospital for their negligence. The decision pointed out that a private hospital has no obligation to maintain an emergency room at all, but if it does, it must use due care in providing services. If the public assumes that physicians who treat patients in emergency rooms are employees of the hospital and that the hospital might be responsible, the court found that the hospital might be liable. In this particular case, however, the record was incomplete on any details of the contractual arrangement and therefore the case was remanded to a lower court for further determination of the matter.[71]

The most frequent cause of suits against a hospital for nonemployee physician liability is one in which a staff physician who is taking his turn on call in the emergency room is negligent. If he is assigned to the patient by a rotating system and the patient has no choice in his selection, the question of whether or not the hospital is liable is a major issue in medical law at the present time.[72]

Prior to 1965 a physician on call in the emergency room was considered an independent contractor and in no state was a hospital liable for any malpractice in his treatment of a patient. However, in that year, the Supreme Court of Illinois decided the very famous case of *Darling v. Charleston Community Hospital*.[73]

An 18-year old college student was preparing for a career as a coach. He was injured while playing in a football game out of town. He was rushed to the emergency room of a small, but accredited, community hospital. The only physician on call that day was a 58-year old general practitioner who had not treated a fracture for 3 years. The physician examined the student, had Xrays made, and determined that both bones in the right leg were broken. Without the assistance of any other physicians, he reduced the fracture and applied a plaster cast. The student complained continually of pain and the following Tuesday the physician split the cast. He did not call in any specialist for consultation and after 2 weeks the student was transferred to a larger hospital and put under the care of an orthopedist. Interference with blood circulation caused by the tight cast made it necessary to amputate the leg, which in turn eliminated the student's hopes of being a coach. The hospital was found liable in this case. The court held that the hospital was negligent because the floor nurses did not recognize the deteriorating condition of his leg. The court also held that the hospital was negligent for failing to require the general practitioner to consult with orthopedists who were available on the hospital staff.

Thus, at least in Illinois, a physician in private practice who is on call in the emergency room may render the hospital liable for his negligence. Only one other case, however, has followed this precedent.

A boy suffered a fractured jaw in an automobile accident. The physician on call who saw him in the emergency room arranged for a dentist to perform oral surgery. The anesthesia was administered by a nurse. While under the anesthetic, the boy had a convulsion and a cardiac arrest. The physician had left and no other physician was present in the operating room or available in the hospital at the time the incident occurred. No physician could be found to examine the boy for an hour and a half. Hospital regulations required that patients who required dental service must be coadmitted by a member of the medical staff and that no oral surgery could be performed unless there was a physician as well as a dentist in the operating room. The hospital was liable for the physician's negligence in leaving the hospital.[74]

Those two cases are the only ones in which liability had been imposed to date. In most states, courts have held that the on-call physician does not subject the hospital to liability.

A man went to the hospital with symptoms of a heart attack. The nurse on duty called his family physician at the wife's request. The physician left his office to come to see him, but stopped by a drugstore where he engaged in an hour's casual conversation. By the time the physician got to the hospital, the man was dying. The court held that the hospital was not liable for the physician's negligent delay.[75]

A 16-year old boy was hit by a truck while riding his bicycle. When he complained of a headache and began to vomit, his mother took him to the emergency room where he was seen by an on-call staff physician. Xray films were taken by the physician, but no skull fracture was revealed. The physician did not check any of the boy's vital signs nor examine the back of his head, which was the area of the injury. The boy was sent home and died during the night. The cause of death was a basal skull fracture. There was no evidence that his life could have been saved if he had received proper care, but the court held that even if the physician had been provably negligent, he was an independent contractor and the hospital would not be liable for his negligence.[76]

If a physician indicates that he is acting as an employee of the hospital, the hospital may be liable. The difference between an independent contractor and an employee of the hospital is usually considered to be a question of fact to be considered by a jury.

A 16-year old girl twisted her ankle. Her mother could not find their family physician, so she took the girl to the emergency room and asked the nurse in the emergency room to locate a physician. The physician who responded on call put a cast on her leg. The cast was too tight and injury resulted. The patient sued the hospital as well as the physician. The trial court found that the physician was not an agent of the hospital since he was not paid a salary. However, on appeal, the case was ordered sent back to a lower court for a jury determination of the physician's employment status. The court held that it was the prerogative of the jury to decide if the hospital had referred the girl to the physician in his private capacity or whether he had been acting as a physician for and on behalf of the hospital. The hospital argued that since it did not pay the physician for his service in the emergency room, he could not possibly be considered an employee. The court held that that fact might be relevant, but was not conclusive.[77]

Thus, in most states, an on-call physician who is negligent does not impose liability upon the hospital. It is likely, however, in the future that more and more courts will arrive at the conclusion that in the minds of the public who come to the emergency room, the physician is a representative or agent of the hospital even though he receives no salary for his duties, and the hospital may very well be liable.

In all these cases, courts make it quite clear that where a hospital knows or should know that a physician is professionally incompetent, they will in all cases be liable for his negligence.[78]

If a patient can show that he has been injured by an emergency room physician who was serving his term on call, but who was known by the hospital to be incompetent, he may recover damages even if the physician is an independent contractor.

A patient's wife took him to the hospital because of severe chest pains. The staff physician in the emergency room gave him a prescription and sent him home. His condition worsened and he died of a heart attack on the way back to the hospital. The court found that the widow stated a good cause of action against the hospital and found that the hospital authority would be liable if its staff members were negligent in approving new members of the staff. The opinion pointed out that a hospital must act in good faith and use reasonable care in selection of its staff physicians and that mere possession of a license to practice does not guarantee competence.[79]

Thus a hospital which continues to allow a known incompetent to be a member of its active staff and treat patients, either privately or through the emergency room, may be liable if his privileges are not revoked.

A seaman employed by a tanker company injured his eye while welding. He was taken to the United States Public Health Service Hospital and a diagnosis of glaucoma was made. The surgeon who operated on him had been admitted a few months before to a psychiatric facility for treatment of acute alcoholism and other mental problems. He was released, but was still in therapy and making no progress. The psychiatrist had advised the medical director of the hospital that the surgeon might benefit from extremely limited duty, but it was made quite clear on more than one occasion that he was not discharged from treatment and under no circumstances whatever was he competent to perform surgery. Although the hospital knew all this information, he went back on full duty immediately. He performed the operation on the seaman's eye most negligently and postoperative treatment was also negligent. As a result, the man lost his eye and committed suicide. The court held that the government had been negligent in allowing an incompetent surgeon to operate and was therefore liable.[80]

Thus, if a patient can show negligent selection of staff, he may be able to recover damages from the hospital even though the physician is an independent contractor.[81]

This may in fact mean, in addition to possible liability from assignments in the emergency room, that a hospital may have an obligation to revoke staff privileges of physicians who become incompetent in reference to treatment of private patients.

A surgeon was sued for negligent performance of an intestinal operation on one of his private patients. Evidence showed that he had been negligent in his use of the same procedure on two prior patients. The hospital was sued for allowing an incompetent surgeon to remain on its staff without restriction of privileges. The jury's award to the patient against both the hospital and the surgeon was upheld on appeal.[82]

A qualified orthopedic surgeon was on the staff of a hospital. One of his private patients was a teenage boy on whom he attempted to perform an experimental back operation. He had not told the boy's parents that the operation was experimental. The boy died. The court held him negligent for failing to have gotten their informed consent, as well as for negligence in the performance of the surgery, but the hospital was not liable because they had no reason to suspect that the surgeon was incompetent, and in fact he was clearly not basically incompetent.[83]

This decision stated the rule very succinctly: "Where treatment is provided by an individual physician, a hospital serves the function of a specialized service. A hospital will not be held liable for an act of malpractice performed by an independently retained physician unless it had reason to know that the act of malpractice would take place." Most decisions follow the same rule involving both emergency and elective patients.[84] It is therefore unlikely that a hospital will be liable for negligence by members of its attending staff unless the patient can prove negligence in selection. However, as to interns, residents, and contract physicians in the emergency room, the hospital is clearly liable for the negligence of its interns and residents and its liability for the negligence of the contract physicians is largely determined by the contract between the physician and the hospital.

Industrial Physicians. An employer is not generally liable for the negligence of an employee physician to another employee. At common law, an employer's responsibility to his workman was limited to discovering which prospective fellow servants were incompetent, but the master was not a guarantor of competence and was liable only for a lack of proper care in selecting an employee. If he took all reasonable precautions and the servant later proved to be negligent or incompetent, there was no liability on the part of the employer.[85]

If a company physician misdiagnoses or negligently mistreats an employee of a corporation, the company is usually not liable.[86] Since one employee could not at common law sue another employee or the employer for injuries, negligence by an industrial physician tends to be compensable only under Workmen's Compensation, and payments tend to be much lower than damages awarded in an ordinary negligence action.

A worker injured her right index finger by impaling it with a rivet. The medical director of the plant treated it and she claimed negligence. The court held that both physician and patient were employees of the same employer, and Workmen's Compensation was the plaintiff's exclusive remedy. She could neither sue the company for damages nor sue the physician personally.[87]

A patient hurt his back while working on a General Motors assembly line. The defendant, a staff physician, saw him, treated him for a minor injury and sent him back to work. He became paralyzed a few hours later and it was eventually discovered that his original injury had been quite serious and had been aggravated by further labor. It was held that neither the company nor the physician was liable in damages other than through Workmen's Compensation.[88]

A company physician failed to recognize the fact that an employee had tuberculosis. Delayed diagnosis caused severe injury to the workman. The court held that neither the employer nor the physician was liable except in Workmen's Compensation. The physician was acting within the scope of his employment and therefore would not be personally liable unless he was acting willfully or recklessly or was intoxicated when he treated the patient.[89]

In Missouri, courts have ruled that a fellow employee may sue a company physician personally. He may not, however, sue the company.[90]

Where a company gratuitously supplies medical assistance, it is generally not liable for the physician's malpractice.[91] The physician is invariably held to be an independent contractor because the company does not have the right to control him professionally or tell him how to treat patients. However, again, if an employer does not use due care in selection of a physician and the physician is demonstrably incompetent, the corporation may be liable for his negligence.[92]

A mine employee sustained a leg fracture in the course of his employment. He was hospitalized. He was treated by a physician in private practice in the community on contract to treat the employer's workmen. The physician was paid on a fee basis for services rendered. The court found that he was not an employee, but an independent contractor. The court ruled that there was no evidence that the company had the right to control the manner in which the physician performed his duties other than to refer surgical problems to other physicians and an employer—employee relationship did not exist; therefore the physician was personally liable.[93]

An employee who is hurt at work and who is collecting Workmen's Compensation from the employer is not barred from bringing an action in malpractice against a private physician who treats his injuries as long as the physician is neither an agent nor an employee of the workman's employer. Ordinary rules of negligence apply and there is no bar to a regular negligence suit against the physician.[94]

As was pointed out in Chapter I, a company physician who performs preemployment physical examinations is not generally considered to have a duty of care to the person examined because no physician–patient relationship is established by performance of the examination for the employer and not for the applicant.[95]

However, a few recent decisions indicate that an employer–physician is obliged to perform preemployment physicals with due care.

A man applied for a position as a pilot with an aircraft manufacturer. He was required to undergo a physical examination at the corporation's clinic. The routine examinations included, among other things, a blood test. Blood was sent to a private laboratory and the blood test indicated the strong probability of a malignancy, but a secretary filed the report in the man's folder and did not report it to the physician. He was hired and several months later his malignancy was discovered. The court agreed with the corporation's position that it had not breached the duty to disclose known results since the results were unknown, but held that when it undertook to examine the man, it did have an obligation to examine him with due care. Even if the physician who carried out the examination was not negligent, the secretary who was also an employee of the corporation was negligent and therefore the corporation was liable for her negligence.[96]

A shipowner is not generally liable for injuries to the passengers by negligence in treatment by a ship's surgeon, but under the Jones Act of 1920[97] by statutory enactment, a shipowner is liable for negligence by a ship's surgeon to seamen.[98]

A passenger who knew he had a serious heart condition returned from Israel in the defendant's cruise ship. At no time did he notify anyone connected with the vessel of his problem. However, during the cruise, he had a heart attack and alleged negligent treatment by the ship's physician. The court held that the shipping company was not the physician's master. The court stated that the carrier was not in the business of carrying patients and provided the physician solely out of consideration for the passengers. The physician was considered to be an independent practitioner and the passengers who were his patients dealt with him and not the company.[99]

Statutes also regulate liability of railroads for medical malpractice. Because of the Federal Employers Liability Act,[100] railroads are usually held responsible for negligent treatment of employees by company physicians who work for the railroad on a part-time basis.[101]

This chapter has examined the myriad possibilities of liability of a hospital or a physician for someone else's negligence. In summary, the financial relationship between the hospital or the physician and the person who is in fact negligent determines whether or not the patient can sue the "employer." In general, most nurses, paramedical personnel, and salaried physicians are considered employees. Nonsalaried physicians, though they may use the hospital's facilities exclusively to practice are in most, but not all, cases considered independent contractors, not employees, and the general rule is that there is no liability for the negligence of an independent contractor.

NOTES

1. "Negligence of Office Assistants," 204 *JAMA* No. 2, page 257, April 8, 1968; Delaney v. Rosenthall, 196 NE 2d 878, Mass 1964.
2. Schulz v. Feigal, 142 NW 2d 84, Minn 1966.
3. Orthopedic Clinic v. Hanson, 415 P 2d 991, Okla 1966.
4. "Injections by Office Assistants," 204 *JAMA* No. 4, page 193, April 22, 1968.
5. Bauer v. Otis, 284 P 2d 133, Cal 1955.
6. Mullins v. DuVall, 104 SE 513, Ga 1920.
7. "Irregular Assistants and Legal Risks," 207 *JAMA* No. 6, page 1231, Feb. 10, 1969; "Use of Irregular Paramedical Personnel," 207 *JAMA* No. 5, page 1027, Feb. 3, 1969
8. Thompson v. Brent, 245 So 2d 751, La 1971.
9. Donald v. Swann, 137 So 178, Ala 1931; Heimlich v. Harvey, 39 NW 2d 394, Wisc 1949.
10. Carpenter v. Campbell, 271 NE 2d 163, Ind 1971.
11. O'Reilly v. Board of Medical Examiners, 58 Cal Rptr 7, Cal 1967; "Physicians Employed by Physicians," 204 *JAMA* No. 1, page 257, April 1, 1968; "Unlicensed Treatment," 214 *JAMA* No. 1, page 209, Oct. 5, 1970.
12. Glesby v. Hartford Accident and Indemnity Company, 44 P 2d 365, Cal 1935.
13. Stohlman v. Davis, 220 NW 247, Neb 1928.

14. Wilson v. Martin Memorial Hospital, 61 SE 2d 102, NC 1950.

15. Beauchamp v. Davis, 217 SW 2d 822, Ky 1948; Myers v. Holborn, 33 Atl 389, NJ 1895.

16. Dashiell v. Griffith, 35 Atl 1094, Md 1896.

17. Miller v. Dore, 148 A 2d 692, Maine 1959.

18. United States v. Morin, 229 F 2d 824, CCA 9, 1956.

19. Hess v. Lowery, 23 NE 156, Ind 1890; Wolfsmith v. Marsh, 337 P 2d 70, Cal 1959.

20. Maclay v. Kelsey-Seybold Clinic, 456 SW 2d 229, 466 SW 2d 716, Tex 1971.

21. "Professional Corporations," 207 *JAMA* No. 10, page 1983, March 10, 1969.

22. Graddy v. New York Medical College, 243 NYS 2d 940, NY 1963.

23. "Liability of Referring Physician," 204 *JAMA* No. 3 page 273, April 15, 1968; Floyd v. Michie, 11 SW 2d 657, Tex 1928; Tramutola v. Bortone, 304 A 2d 197, NJ 1973; Smith v. Beard, 110 P 2d 260, Wyo 1941.

24. Ross v. Sher, 483 SW 2d 297, Tex 1972.

25. Harwick v. Harris, 166 So 2d 912, Fla 1964.

25a. Crump v. Piper, 425 SW 2d 924, Mo 1968.

26. "Physician's Liability for Acts of Hospital Nurses," 209 *JAMA* No. 11, page 1791, Sept 15, 1969.

27. Bernardi v. Community Hospital Association, 443 P 2d 708, Colo 1968.

28. Burns v. Owens, 459 SW 2d 303, Mo 1970.

29. Burke v. Pearson, 191 SE 2d 721, SC 1972.

30. "Liability for Resident's Negligence, 213 *JAMA* No. 1, page 181, July 6, 1970.

31. Barrette v. Hight, 230 NE 2d 808, Mass 1967; Baidach v. Togut, 190 NYS 2d 120 NY 1959.

32. Salgo v. Stanford University, 317 P 2d 170, Cal 1957.

33. Richardson v. Denneen, 82 NYS 2d 623, NY 1947.

34. Alexandridis v. Jewett, 388 F 2d 829, CCA 1, 1968.

35. Moeller v. Hauser, 54 NW 2d 639, Minn 1952.

36. Capps v. Valk, 369 P 2d 238, Kans 1962.

37. Yorston v. Pennell, 153 A 2d 255, Pa 1959.

38. Stumper v. Kimel, 260 A 2d 526, NJ 1970.

39. McConnell v. Williams, 65 A 2d 243, Pa 1949.

40. Beadles v. Metayka, 311 P 2d 711, Colo 1957.

41. Martin v. Perth Amboy General Hospital, 250 A 2d 40, NJ 1969; Grant v. Touro Infirmary, 223 So 2d 148, La 1969; Burke v. Washington Hospital Center, 475 F 2d 364, CA DC 1973.

42. French v. Fischer, 362 SW 2d 926, Tenn 1962.

43. Nichter v. Edmiston, 407 P 2d 721, Nev 1965.

44. Aderhold v. Bishop, 221 Pac 752, Okla 1923.

45. Bing v. Thunig, 143 NE 2d 3, NY 1957.

46. May v. Broun, 492 P 2d 776, Ore 1972.

47. Monk v. Doctors' Hospital, 403 F 2d 580, CA DC 1968.

48. Thomas v. Hutchinson, 275 A 2d 23, Pa 1971; Tonsic v. Wagner, 289 A 2d 138, Pa 1972.

49. "Nurse Anesthetists," 211 *JAMA* No. 9, page 1591, March 2, 1970; McKinney v. Tromly, 386 SW 2d 564, Tex 1965.

50. Jackson v. Joyner, 72 SE 2d 589, NC 1952.

51. Kemalyan v. Henderson, 277 P 2d 372, Wash 1954.

52. "Surgeons and Anesthesiologists," 211 *JAMA* No. 10, page 1753, March 9, 1970.

53. Huber v. Protestant Deaconess Hospital Association of Evansville, 133 NE 2d 864, Ind 1956.

54. Thompson v. Lillehei, 273 F 2d 376, CCA 8, 1959.

55. Kennedy v. Gaskell, 78 Cal Rptr 753, Cal 1969.

56. Marvulli v. Elshire, 103 Cal Rptr 461, Cal 1972; Dohr v. Smith, 104 So 2d 29, Fla 1958.

57. Rockwell v. Stone, 173 A 2d 48, Pa 1961.

58. Voss v. Bridwell, 364 P 2d 955, Kans 1961.

59. Morey v. Thybo, 199 Fed 760, CCA 7, 1912.

60. Reeves v. North Broward Hospital, 191 So 2d 307, Fla 1966.

61. McBride v. United States, 462 F 2d 72, CCA 9, 1972.

62. Ware v. Culp, 74 P 2d 283, Cal 1937.

63. Habuda v. Trustees of Rex Hospital, Inc., 164 SE 2d 17, NC 1968.

64. Helms v. Williams, 166 SE 2d 852, NC 1969.

65. Lundberg v. Bay View Hospital, 191 NE 2d 821, Ohio 1963.

66. Insurance Company of North America v. Prieto, 442 F 2d 1033, CCA 6, 1971.

67. Kober v. Stewart, 417 P 2d 476, Mont 1966.

68. James v. Holder, 309 NYS 2d 385, NY 1970.

69. Pogue v. Hospital Authority of DeKalb County, 170 SE 2d 53, Ga 1969.

70. Dickinson v. Mailliard, 175 NW 2d 588, Iowa 1970.

71. Schagrin v. Wilmington Medical Center, 304 A 2d 61, Del 1973.

72. "Who Should Provide Emergency Care?" 210 *JAMA* No. 4, page 775, Oct. 27, 1969; "Professional Negligence in Hospital Emergency Rooms," 208 *JAMA* No. 1, page 231, April 7, 1969; "Hospital Emergency Room Liability," 208 *JAMA* No. 2, page 761, April 14, 1969; "Emergency Room Liability," 220 *JAMA* No. 5, page 761, May 1, 1972.

73. Darling v. Charleston Community Hospital, 200 NE 2d 145, 1964, 211 NE 2d 253, Ill 1965; "The Darling Case," 206 *JAMA* No. 7, page 1665, Nov. 11, 1968; "The Darling Case Revisited," 206 *JAMA* No. 8, page 1875, Nov. 18, 1968.

74. Pederson v. Dumouchel, 431 P 2d 973, Wash 1967.

75. Bulloch County Hospital Association v. Fowler, 183 SE 2d 586, Ga 1971.

76. Cooper v. Sisters of Charity of Cincinnati, 272 NE 2d 97, Ohio 1971.

77. Vanaman v. Milford Memorial Hospital, 272 A 2d 718, Del 1970.

78. "Negligent Selection of Hospital Staff," 223 *JAMA* No. 7, page 833, Feb. 12, 1973.

79. Joiner v. Mitchell County Hospital Authority, 186 SE 2d 307, Ga 1972.

80. Penn Tanker Company v. United States, 310 F Supp 613, DC Tex 1970.

81. "Hospital Liability for Physician Negligence," 214 *JAMA* No. 9, page 1755, Nov. 30, 1970.

82. Purcell v. Zimbelman, 500 P 2d 335, Ariz 1972.

83. Fiorentino v. Wenger, 272 NYS 2d 557, 280 NYS 2d 373, rev'd on other grounds 227 NE 2d 296, NY 1967.

84. Clary v. Hospital Authority of the City of Marietta, 126 SE 2d 470, Ga 1962; Hundt v. Proctor Community Hospital, 284 NE 2d 676, Ill 1972.

85. "The Physician As a Fellow Servant," 223 *JAMA* No. 10, page 1203, March 5, 1973.

86. Jines v. General Electric Corporation, 303 F 2d 76, CCA 9, 1962.

87. Bergen v. Miller, 250 A 2d 49, NJ 1969.

88. Jones v. Bouza, 160 NW 2d 881, Mich 1968.

89. Wickham v. North American Rockwell Corporation, 87 Cal Rptr 563, Cal 1970.

90. Wilson v. Hungate, 434 SW 2d 580, Mo 1968.

91. Metzger v. Western Maryland Railway Company, 30 F 2d 50, CCA 4, 1929.

92. Bowman v. Southern Pacific Corporation, 204 Pac 403, Cal 1921; Crawford v. Davis, 134 SE 247, SC 1926.

93. Lemonovich v. Klimoski, 315 F Supp 1288, DC Pa 1970.

94. Jones v. Laird Foundation, Inc., 195 SE 2d 821, W Va 1973.

95. Battistella v. Society of the New York Hospital, 191 NYS 2d 626, NY 1959.

96. Coffee v. McDonnell-Douglas Corporation, 503 P 2d 1366, Cal 1972.

97. Jones Act of 1920, 46 USC Section 688.

98. DeZon v. American President Lines, 318 US 660, 1943.

99. Amdur v. Zim Israel Navigation Company, 310 F Supp 1033, DC NY 1969; "Liability of Company for Ship's Surgeon," 215 *JAMA* No. 8, page 1381, Feb. 22, 1971.

100. Federal Employer's Liability Act, 45 USC Section 51.

101. Mangrum v. Union Pacific Railroad Company, 41 Cal Rptr 536, Cal 1964.

CHAPTER VIII

CONSENT

TO

TREATMENT

It is a fundamental principle of our legal system that all persons have the right to make major decisions involving their bodies. The doctrine that a patient who is subject to medical treatment without his consent has a cause of action against the physician or surgeon comes from two principles basic to our belief in the inalienable rights of man.[1]

The relationship between patient and physician is one known to the law as a "fiduciary relationship." Any person such as a physician, attorney, priest or other who enters into a relationship of trust and confidence wtih another has a positive obligation to disclose all relevant facts. If an individual wishes to buy a pig from a farmer, the farmer is not obliged to point out defects of the pig. If specifically questioned, the farmer commits fraud if he answers dishonestly, but he is not obliged to volunteer information which may be detrimental to the sale. However, since the essence of a professional relationship is that the professional knows more about his subject than the person who seeks his help, the normal rules of buyer and seller do not apply. In these fiduciary relationships, including that existing between a physician and his patient, an affirmative duty of disclosure has always existed.

The other principle involved in the doctrine of the right to consent to medical treatment is that a person of sound mind has the right to make his own decisions about what becomes of his body.[2] Neither the state nor another individual has the right to compel him to accept treatment he does not want.[3]

In the first case on this subject, Justice Cardozo, then on the Supreme Court of New York, wrote: "Every human being of adult years and sound mind has the right to determine what shall be done with his own body and a surgeon who performs an operation without his patient's consent commits an assault for which he is liable in damages."[4]

A patient had a malignancy. Following surgery, her surgeon referred her to a radiologist, the defendant. He administered cobalt radiation treatments and she was very seriously burned. She had not been told anything about the risks of this treatment and the court held that the radiologist had been obligated not only to refrain from misleading her as to the dangers of treatment, but that he had a positive duty to disclose the risks as a matter of law. The court held further that if she had taken the cobalt treatments after he had warned her that there was great risk of bodily injury or death, she could not have recovered damages. However, evidence clearly showed that if she had been properly informed, she would not have undergone treatment. In that decision, the court said: "A man is the master of his own body and he may expressly prohibit the performance of life-saving surgery or other medical treatment. A doctor may well believe that an operation or other form of treatment is desirable and necessary, but the law does not permit him to substitute his own judgment for that of the patient by any form of artifice or deception."[5]

The doctrine of informed consent therefore may be defined as the duty to warn a patient of the hazards, possible complications, and expected and unexpected results of standard treatment.[6] In particular, when therapy is new, experimental, or unusual, there is a particular duty to warn the patient that all the effects of the treatment may not be completely known.[7] As the probability or severity of risk to the patient increases, the duty to inform him of it increases. In short, the patient has a right to know what he is "getting into," and he must understand the inherent risks of the proposed procedure as well as its general nature. If the patient does not understand this, any consent that he does give will, in all probability, be held to be legally invalid.

A physician gave a patient a local anesthetic to remove what he had diagnosed as a minor cyst on her neck. The cyst was deeper than he thought, but he did not tell the patient, who was completely conscious, that he would have to undertake a more drastic procedure. A facial nerve was damaged. The court found him negligent in failing to tell the patient what the situation was and asking her if she wanted him to continue.[8]

If an untoward result occurs, the patient can show that he had no warning that it was possible, and medical testimony shows that a duly careful physician or surgeon would have told him, he has a cause of action against the physician for failure to obtain a valid consent even though no negligence is shown.[9] The basis of the complaint is not that the procedure had been performed negligently, but rather that it had been performed at all.[10]

A patient had an angiogram and sustained permanent paralysis from the waist down as the result of the injection of Urokon. Neither the patient nor his wife had been informed of any risks even though the procedure was very new at that time. Negligence was found in the failure to furnish any information. The court said: "A physician violates his duty to his patient and subjects himself to liability if he withholds any facts which are necessary to form the basis of an intelligent consent by the patient to the proposed treatment. Likewise, the physician may not minimize the known dangers of a procedure or operation in order to induce his patient's consent."[11]

How the physician chooses to discharge this obligation to inform his patient is a matter of medical judgment as long as the method used is sufficient to insure genuine understanding. In short, the doctrine of informed consent requires that the physician explain to the patient at least what normally happens in a case such as his and some of the more serious complications which might occur even though the physician does not think that they are likely. If the patient tells the physician that he does not want to know about possible risks, however, the physician is not obligated to pursue the subject further.[12]

Naturally the doctrine of informed consent does not apply in a genuine emergency. When a patient is unconscious or sufficiently ill to be unable to comprehend what is being said to him, the physician has the right to render necessary treatment without attempting to explain or inform the patient of any risks.[13]

A patient was bitten by a rattlesnake. He developed gangrene after injections of antivenom. He proved that his physician had not discussed the dangers of antivenom with him in any great detail. The court held that there was a valid consent because there had been no time or duty to discuss in full the various risks in such an acute emergency.[14]

If other members of the patient's family are available, the procedure which is to be undertaken should be explained to them if the patient himself is in no condition to understand. If the patient's condition would be adversely affected by the necessity of full disclosure, the physician may discuss the risk instead with another adult who is a close family member.[15]

Where the patient is unduly apprehensive of the surgery or treatment and the physician feels that explaining all the risks will induce him to refuse the necessary treatment, it is clear that the physician does not have to offer explanations beyond that which he thinks it is safe for the patient to know. This is particularly true when the risks are highly improbable.[16] If a reasonably careful physician would consider it detrimental to the patient's best interests to make a full disclosure, he may justify his failure to do so on the grounds that good medical judgment required him to withhold the information.[17]

As a general rule of thumb, if the risk of untoward result is statistically high, the patient should be informed regardless of the effect of his morale. If the risk is statistically low, but the consequence of the rare occurrence may be extremely severe, the patient should likewise be informed. On the other hand, if the statistical risk is low and its severity is not great, the physician may safely tailor his warnings so as not to excite the patient.[18]

There are some situations in which courts have held that full risks must be disclosed. For example, most courts hold that it is absolutely mandatory to disclose the risks of electroshock therapy to a mentally competent patient even if he is extremely emotionally disturbed.[19] In all cases where there are potentially dangerous diagnostic surgical procedures, such as angiograms and arteriograms, the patient must be informed of the risk in the absence of an acute situation in which his condition would be seriously jeopardized.[20] Warnings must always be given of any serious side effects of drugs.[21] The dangers of burns or other complications of radiation therapy must be disclosed.[22] On the other hand, less serious risks do not have to be disclosed, such as the danger of the effects of German measles during pregnancy,[23] any remote danger of minor surgery, or the danger of peritonitis.[24]

A physician did not warn a patient of the risks of using wire to repair a shoulder separation. The wire broke and the patient was injured. However, there was no expert testimony to indicate that the complication was sufficiently likely so that the patient should have been warned about it.[25]

There are two different legal theories to support actions by plaintiffs alleging lack of consent. The original theory on which this cause of action was predicated was that treatment to which the patient had not knowingly consented was a classic example of the tort of "assault and battery."[26] This is still the case where the patient is in total ignorance of what is to be done.

A physician told a patient that he was going to perform a biopsy on her breast and flatly denied that he was going to perform a mastectomy. When she awoke from surgery, she discovered that he had done so. The defendant had performed a completely unauthorized operation.[27]

A man was admitted to the hospital for treatment of a foot injury. A scalene node biopsy was performed, apparently by mistake. The court held since he had not consented to any operation at all, the surgeon was liable for assault and battery.[28]

The other approach to this problem is to treat it as negligence and allege that a physician's failure to explain the consequences of treatment to which the patient has consented without understanding is negligence per se and a violation of the requisite standards of due care.[29] In most cases in which the doctrine of informed consent arises, the patient is aware of the nature of the procedure which he is to undergo and has in fact signed a consent for it. What he does not understand is that there are some risks of permanent damage inherent in the procedure. Failure to have told him this means that the action is one in negligence.[30]

The practical difference between the two theories is that if assault and battery is alleged, no expert testimony is required to prove it. Lay witnesses are sufficient. On the other hand, in most, but not all, states, before a claim of medical negligence can go to the jury for determination, expert testimony to the fact that the reasonably careful physician would have explained the given risk is required.

In determining whether or not disclosures are sufficient and constitute duly careful treatment of the patient, most courts have established the standard of the "reasonably careful medical practitioner in the same or similar community, in the same or similar circumstances." Whether the physician has the duty to disclose facts, and, if so, what facts he is obliged to reveal largely depends on the normal practice in his community.[31] In other words, the physician is not usually required to inform his patient of risks which other physicians in his community would not think were necessary to disclose.[32]

A patient underwent a thyroidectomy. The method chosen by the physician damaged one of her laryngeal nerves. She claimed that she had not been told that this was a possibility. However, the defendant presented expert testimony that none of the physicians in the community discussed these dangers with their patients. The physician was therefore not liable for failure to inform the patient.[33]

A patient developed serum hepatitis after a blood transfusion. She sued the physician for having failed to tell her before the transfusion that this was a possibility. Expert evidence for him indicated that in the community it was not standard practice where a blood transfusion was necessary to warn the patient of the possibility of hepatitis. The physician in charge of the case testified that such a warning might have unduly alarmed the patient and caused adverse medical effects.[34]

However, this rule is not accepted in some states.[35] In these, courts hold that the scope of disclosure that a physician must make to his patient is not to be determined by what the reasonable physician would disclose under similar circumstances. It is to be determined by laymen.

A 19-year old man was paralyzed after a laminectomy. The court rejected the defendant's claim that there was no practice to disclose the risk and upheld the plaintiff's cause of action. The court stated that the patient's right of self-determination shapes the boundaries of the physician's duty to disclose all material risks, all serious inherent and potential hazards, alternative methods of treatment, and the likely results of nontreatment.[36]

A patient was admitted to a hospital for surgical treatment of a duodenal ulcer. He was informed of the nature of the operation and the risks of the operation. Shortly after his discharge from the hospital, emergency surgery was required because of a severed artery near the spleen and the spleen was removed. He later developed a gastric ulcer and 50% of his stomach had to be removed. In a suit against the surgeon and the hospital the patient claimed that the operation was negligently performed and his informed consent had not been obtained. The evidence indicated that injuries of this nature occurred in approximately 5% of these operations. The jury returned a verdict in his favor. The surgeon appealed. The Supreme Court of California ruled that there was no evidence of negligence. However, the court noted that a physician has a duty to disclose whatever is determined by the patient's need and that need is whatever information is material to the patient's decision. The decision went on to say that the patient need not be given a "mini-course in medical science." However, if a procedure inherently involves a known risk of death or serious bodily harm, the patient must be informed of such a risk. In case of complicated procedures, the court said that the physician must explain in lay terms any complications that might occur.[37]

A patient was misdiagnosed as having a malignancy. Radiation burns were so severe that eight operations were required to correct them. The court rejected the concept that the physician had no duty to disclose risks unless there was a community practice to do so. It held that the patient has the right to decide whether or not he has treatment in the light of knowledge of all material risk. A "material risk" was defined as one a reasonable person would consider significant.[38]

Before a patient is allowed to recover damages, he must present evidence that he would not have had the operation or allowed the procedure if he had known what the foreseeable consequences would be.[39] If he admits he would have gone ahead anyway, he cannot recover.[40]

A woman had a corneal disease in both eyes. She was told before she consented to surgery both by her ophthalmologist and by the surgeon who performed an operation on one eye that there was no possibility of blindness. She was blind thereafter in that eye. She testified that no explanation of risk had been given to her and in fact alleged that misleading statements had been made. However, because there was no evidence to show that she would not have agreed to take the risk and go ahead with the operation if she had known that there was a possibility she would lose the sight in that eye she could not recover damages.[41]

A patient does not usually have to undergo any treatment at all if he does not choose to do so. In particular, a terminally ill patient has the right to decide to "die with dignity" and to refuse expensive or painful treatment which will save his life.[42]

When a physician wishes to treat a patient's complaint by a method which entails certain risks and he knows that an alternative treatment exists, he is obliged to advise the patient to that effect. The patient has the right to decide for himself which course of action, if either, he prefers. He may choose not to have any treatment at all. Failure to explain an alternative, if one exists, may be construed as negligence.[43]

A patient with a prostate disorder was admitted to the hospital for surgery. The surgeon did not advise him that the operation planned would inevitably sterilize him. He also did not advise him that an alternative surgical method was available which carried with it a higher risk of infection. The patient underwent the operation which sterilized him. He sued the physician when he discovered later that he was sterile. The court upheld the jury's award of damages to the patient. The court held that in the absence of an emergency, the patient should have been advised of all available alternatives and that he had a right to make up his own mind as to the alternative he preferred.[44]

A patient had oral surgery after a fracture of the left condyle. The surgeon did not tell her that he preferred to use a method involving surgery on both sides instead of one and that other surgeons used a method involving only one. After surgery her teeth were so far apart she could not chew. The court said that she stated a cause of action against the surgeon for failing to tell her that an alternate procedure was possible.[45]

It should be noted that a patient is never held to consent to the risks of negligent treatment. Thus the fact that the patient was advised of all the risks of proper treatment is no defense for a physician or surgeon who has been negligent.[46]

A 6-year old boy suffered severe visual impairment after a tonsillectomy. The cause was the injection of three drugs prior to surgery. In holding that the surgeon had no obligation to warn his mother of this possible complication, the court said "The informed consent doctrine only applies where there are inherent and probable substantial risks." The decision went on to state that the doctrine of informed consent does not require the physician to disclose the risks of improper performance of the appropriate procedure.[47]

The only hazards which the physician is ever expected to explain to the patient are those which he has reasonably foreseen. He is not liable for failure to forewarn the patient of unexpected aftereffects or unexplained events during surgery. For example, it is unnecessary to explain that infections have been known to occur in the postoperative period. Those risks which are not in fact inherent in the procedure are beyond the scope of the requirements of informed consent.[48]

A physician who has been sued for treating a patient without informed consent cannot complain that he told the patient what he was going to do, as long as he knew or should have known when he told the patient that it was "over his head." Since each patient is different, it is the physician's duty to pursue the requisite explanation until he knows that the patient or his family understand it.[49]

A patient consented to a laminectomy. The court found as a fact that the patient did not understand what was involved in the procedure because he did not understand what the word "laminectomy" meant. Since he did not understand the technical meaning of the term and since there was no evidence that the defendant gave him any specific warnings, the court found that there was no informed consent. When the patient was paralyzed after the operation the surgeon was liable.[50]

One obvious problem included in the concept of informed consent is the surgeon's dilemma when he discovers after commencing an operation that the patient suffers from a condition different from that which he expected at the time he talked with the patient and obtained his consent. Whether or not a surgeon may extend the surgery beyond that to which the patient has consented largely depends upon the facts of the case. If an emergency arises during surgery authorized by the patient, a physician may always deal with that.[51] In most states a surgeon may extend the operation if any abnormal condition is discovered during surgery, if it is reasonably advisable for the welfare of the patient.

A patient was diagnosed as having an ectopic pregnancy. When surgery was begun, the surgeon discovered that she had a normal pregnancy but acute appendicitis and removed her appendix. The patient sued him for taking out her appendix without her consent. The court held that he was entirely justified and pointed out that if her appendix had been allowed to remain, she and the unborn child could have been seriously jeopardized.[52]

During an appendectomy the surgeon discovered that his patient had several large ovarian cysts, which he punctured. The patient sued him for assault and battery but did not allege negligence. The court dismissed the action and stated that it was "unreasonable to hold a physician to the exact operation that the preliminary examination indicates is necessary. A complete diagnosis may not be possible until the incision is made. The surgeon may extend the operation to remedy any abnormal or diseased condition in the area of the original incision whenever he, in the exercise of sound professional judgment, determines that correct surgical procedure demands it."[53]

Where there is no emergency condition, before the surgeon proceeds to extend surgery he should attempt to get the consent of someone in the patient's family. If this is not possible, he should probably decide not to extend the scope of the surgery unduly. An extension of a minor operation into a major one is usually considered assault and battery in the absence of an emergency.[54]

A patient had frequent miscarriages. The family physician had told her that her uterus was lacerated when she consulted him because she could not get pregnant. He referred her to a surgeon whom she told that she wished to be "fixed up" so she could get pregnant. When he operated, he found that her fallopian tubes were full of pus and performed a hysterectomy. The court found him liable. The operation was not an emergency one. Treatment for the condition could have been attempted by nonsurgical means and he was well aware of the fact that the patient very much wanted to get pregnant.[55]

A 20-year old girl was operated on for appendicitis. During the operation the surgeon concluded that her fallopian tubes were so bady infected that he should remove them. He did so without consulting her stepmother whom he knew to be in the hospital during the operation. Since there was no emergency and the consequences of such a procedure were very serious in terms of the girl's future, he was found liable for assault and battery.[56]

Thus, in the absence of any indication from the patient that an extension of surgery is absolutely prohibited and if extension involves such things as removal of an appendix or some other minor procedure which will not leave the patient permanently disabled, the physician can undoubtedly go ahead as long as the surgery is within the operative field and is justified by prevailing medical opinion.[57] However, where there is any possibility that the patient will have permanent ill-effects, every effort should be made to obtain consent either from the patient or from a family member.

Some medical procedures raise unusual questions involving consent by the patient or his next of kin.

Autopsies.   Unless there is some statutory justification for an autopsy without the consent of the next of kin of the deceased, a cause of action exists against the coroner and the physician who performs one without it.[58] A suit on this ground is the one exception to the general rule that mental anguish damages may not be collected without proof of physical harm to the plaintiff. In this case courts are willing to assume that actual suffering is inflicted upon a widow or a child by an unauthorized autopsy on a husband or father.[59]

The next of kin under our law and under the early common law of England has a right of possession of any corpse in order to afford it decent burial.[60] Any interference of this right is therefore also an interference with a property right.[61] The proper party to complain is the next of kin, not the executor of the decedent's estate.[62] If there is a surviving spouse he or she is normally the one who is entitled to bring an action and is the person to be asked for consent to an autopsy.[63] Parents, of course, must consent to an autopsy of their child. Where the adult decedent is survived by neither spouse nor children, siblings or parents have the authority to consent.[64] When the next of kin gives permission for an autopsy he has the right to make any limitations on its extent which he wishes.

A widow had specifically stated that the autopsy on her deceased husband's body was to be performed in a "decent manner." It was carried out in broad daylight in a cemetery in full view of the residents of the whole neighborhood. The court agreed that she was entitled to damages.[65]

Permission to perform an autopsy on only one portion of the body is upheld as long as the restriction is reasonable in terms of the medical study required.[66] Permanent retention of organs after the autopsy is not usually contemplated by the permission granted by the next of kin. A cause of action will lie if all the organs are not returned in due course.[67]

Of course, in all states autopsies are allowed without the consent and even over the objection of the next of kin where there is a suspicion that the deceased came to his death through any criminal means. Some states also permit autopsies if the cause of death is unexplained. Where circumstances of the death come within operation of the applicable statute no permission is required and in fact autopsies may be performed over the family's objections. Numerous cases have held that in most states if a death occurs shortly after admission to the hospital and without any diagnosis having been made, authority for the autopsy from the family is usually unnecessary.[68] If the body is found on a street, in a car, or in some similar place, courts usually hold that the circumstances warrant an autopsy without permission.[69]

A 16-year old boy suffered from Marfan's Syndrome. He died in his sleep at boarding school. There was no external indication of the cause of death, so the medical examiner performed an autopsy. The cause of death was determined to be the effects of this condition. His mother sued for performance of an unauthorized autopsy. Since state law provided for an autopsy "when the cause of death is obscure" her action was dismissed.[70]

On the other hand, those states which permit autopsies only where foul play is suspected severely restrict the right to perform an autopsy when no suspicion exists of criminal means. In those cases, both the coroner and the physician may be liable in damages for an unauthorized autopsy.

A child was found dead in a dry swimming pool. There was no evidence of criminal activity. The coroner performed an autopsy without parental consent and was liable. Under the statute of the state involved, he had no authority to act in the absence of reasonable suspicion of a felony.[71]

An 82-year old patient died in a hospital after surgery. The next of kin twice refused autopsy permission, but the medical examiner performed one. The family sued and recovered damages. Under the state statute the medical examiner was required to obtain permission from the family or an order from the prosecutor. Since no criminal act was suspected he had no right to perform an autopsy without permission of the next of kin.[72]

In all states when an autopsy is ordered by a coroner or other public official, the burden of proving it unjustified is on the plaintiff. A public official is always presumed to act in good faith, and without proof of bad faith, the coroner's authority cannot be attacked.[73] Where a good faith mistake has been made by a pathologist who incorrectly thinks that permission has been granted by the family, he is usually not liable.

A widow sued a pathologist for performing an unauthorized autopsy on her husband's body. The evidence showed that he and the other man in his hospital room had died within 5 minutes of each other and the other family had given autopsy permission. The nurse in charge put the tag for autopsy on the wrong body. The court decided that the pathologist had acted in accord with normal procedure and had every reason to believe that permission had been granted. He was not liable.[74]

Generally speaking, the law does not recognize the right of a private economic interest, such as that of an insurance carrier which wishes to investigate the death of its insured, to override the rights of the next of kin. Courts have held in numerous cases that insurance companies have no right to an autopsy if a widow refuses to allow one.[75]

An insured man drowned in a swimming pool. Ten weeks after he was buried his life insurance carrier asked his widow for permission to exhume his body and have an autopsy. She refused. The carrier asked for a court order for exhumation, but the case was dismissed on the grounds that the widow's right to refuse was absolute in the absence of reasonable cause to suspect that a crime had been committed.[76]

Therefore, unless there is reasonable cause to believe that a crime has been committed, in the absence of specific consent by the next of kin, no autopsy should be performed without a coroner's order. Interference with a corpse in a way which does not cause mutilation is usually not considered sufficient to give rise to a suit for mental anguish.

A man was killed in an automobile accident. Because there was reasonable cause to believe that he had been driving while intoxicated the policeman in charge of the investigation asked the embalmer to draw a blood sample prior to embalming the body. The embalmer complied with the request. There was a very high alcohol level in the blood. The test result was admitted in evidence in suits brought by others injured in the accident against the driver's estate and they were awarded very substantial damages. The widow sued the embalmer for mental anguish for his disturbance of her husband's body.

The court dismissed her complaint, holding that removal of blood did not disfigure the corpse, thus she had no cause of action.[77]

Consent to Transplant or Donation of Body.   There is a recognized right in a competent adult to make a testamentary disposition of all or part of his body for transplant or research purposes.[78]

Grace Metalious, author of **Peyton Place,** left instructions in her Will that she did not want any form of funeral service and that she wanted her body donated to either Dartmouth or Harvard Medical Schools. Her widower and children sought to have those portions of the will invalidated. Both medical schools voluntarily declined to accept her body in view of the family's objections, so the suit was brought by the widower against the executor of her estate to force him to have a funeral. The court held that the instructions in the Will should be carried out in preference to the opposing wishes of the survivors.[79]

The Uniform Anatomical Gift Act now adopted in almost all states also empowers a person to execute a written instrument which is legally binding on the next of kin at death. There is a uniform donation card which has been prepared by the American Medical Association and which is available to physicians for distribution to those of their patients who may wish to make use of them, indicating the desire for the person's body or as much of it as he wishes to be used for transplantation or research. However, in any area of this country in which such legislation has not been enacted, no such gift may be made. Without the enabling statute or a testamentary disposition, only the next of kin has the right to make such a gift since he has the sole property right in the body.

A man arranged to donate his body to a medical school. His mother employed a funeral home to transport it by ambulance to the school and wished to ride there with the body. The funeral home made a mistake and the body was shipped by train. When the mother arrived to go with the body it had already left. The railroad lost it and it took 3 days to trace it. She sued the funeral home for damages for mental anguish. The court dismissed the action, holding that in view of her son's donation she had no property right in the body.[80]

If there has been no statement by the patient before death, the next of kin has the right to release or refuse to release part of the body for transplant or dissection purposes.

UNIFORM DONOR CARD

OF _____

Print or Type name of donor

In the hope that I may help others, I hereby make this anatomical gift, if medically acceptable, to take effect upon my death. The words and marks below indicate my desires.

I give: (a)_____any needed organs or parts

       (b)_____only the following organs or parts

_____

Specify the organ(s) or part(s)

for the purposes of transplantation, therapy, medical research or education;

       (c)_____my body for anatomical study if needed.

Limitations or

special wishes, if any: _____

Signed by the donor and the following two witnesses in the presence of each other:

_____	_____
Signature of Donor	Date of Birth of Donor
_____	_____
Date Signed	City & State
_____	_____
Witness	Witness

This is a legal document under the Uniform Anatomical Gift Act or similar laws.

For further information consult your physician or

American Medical Association
535 N. Dearborn, Chicago, Ill. 60610

Where organs are transplanted from living persons, the normal rule is that an adult patient has the right to consent to donation of a part of his body for transplant purposes.[81] One very interesting decision, however, indicates that there is no constitutional right to donate.

A man was a prisoner under sentence of death in Florida. He sought to be taken to Denver to be tested for his suitability as a kidney donor for a small boy to whom he was no relation. The court denied his plea and pointed out that transporting the prisoner to Colorado for testing and then back for surgery would require the expensive services of many guards and other personnel and that moving a prisoner under the death sentence would be extremely dangerous for the public. He was not allowed to donate.[82]

Two unreported decisions have dealt with the donation of an organ by a child who is a twin of the patient.[83] In these cases the physicians had refused to allow the child to be a donor even with parental consent without an order from the appropriate court. In both cases, in view of both clergy and psychiatric testimony that the risk to the donor child was less serious than the emotional trauma he would suffer from the death of his twin, the courts decided that it was in the best interest of the children to be allowed to donate. However, this should never be assumed to be the law. A recent Louisiana intermediate appellate decision, for example, held that a retarded 17-year old boy could not donate a kidney to his 22-year old sister. The court found that such a donation would not protect or promote the minor's best interests.[84]

No physician should ever use a child or incompetent person as a donor, even with parental consent, without a written court order. If one has not been obtained, when the donor child reaches majority, a suit for removal of an organ without informed consent could and would lie against the physician.

In another recent case, an incompetent adult was allowed to donate a kidney.

A mentally incompetent adult was allowed by court order to donate a kidney to his brother because there was sufficient medical evidence that no other donor was available. There was psychiatric testimony to the effect that the link between the brothers was so strong that the death of one would impair the welfare of the other.[85]

No assumption should ever be made that such a consent would be automatically forthcoming from a court which is asked to rule on this question, and thus a physician is extremely unwise to use any donor who is not a competent adult without an order from the appropriate court.[86]

Involuntary Hospitalization. The rights of a prisoner or other person who has been involuntarily committed to a mental institution has been the subject of innumerable court decisions, as was seen when the subject of unjustified commitment was discussed in the chapter on errors in malpractice in diagnosis, and the refusal to release a patient whose condition no longer warrants confinement was discussed in the chapter on negligence in treatment.

A prisoner or other person who is to be confined against his will in a mental institution has a constitutional and legal right to due process of law 'prior to commitment and adequate psychiatric treatment after his admission.[87]

A 16-year old college freshman was very unhappy and wanted to quit school. She went home to talk things over with her parents and they convinced her to go back with the proviso that she could leave if she was still unhappy after a given period of time. At the end of that period she decided to leave and notified the Dean of Women. When the Dean and the college physician could not talk her out of her decision they called the police and had her admitted to a mental hospital. She persuaded a hospital social worker to call a friend, who called her father. He had her released immediately. The student sued and recovered damages from the school, the Dean, and the physician.[88]

He must, for example, have the right to counsel at the commitment hearing.[89] He may no longer be indefinitely committed.[90]

A man had been arrested for a misdemeanor, the sentence for which would have been 1 year. He was, however, involuntarily committed to a mental institution instead of being tried and had been in the hospital for 4 years at the time the decision was rendered. He sought a writ of habeas corpus for release. The court upheld his constitutional right to release with the following statement: "The purpose of involuntary hospitalization is treatment, not punishment. Absent treatment, the hospital is transformed into a penitentiary where one could be held indefinitely for no convicted offense." The court further held that indefinite confinement without treatment violates constitutional guarantees against cruel and unusual punishment found in the Eighth Amendment. Further, where the person is confined longer than the maximum sentence he would have served in jail, the court held that he has also been denied his right to due process of law. The court thus concluded that continuing failure to provide adequate treatment could not be justified by claims of lack of either staff or facilities.[91]

Another accused person was sent to a mental institution before trial. He sought release on the grounds that he was receiving no treatment. The court found that the hospital was so understaffed that the man was in fact not being treated, but was receiving only custodial care and it was clear from expert testimony that he had an excellent chance of recovery if he were adequately treated. The court found that failure by the state to have placed him in an institution where he could be treated denied him equal protection of the laws in comparison with patients in less understaffed institutions.[92]

A patient admitted for observation and diagnosis also has a right to adequate care in those areas.[93] One federal district court judge has issued an injunction against the state of Alabama giving it 6 months from the date of the decision to produce a treatment plan for all patients which would meet the requirements of accredited institutions and indicated that if one were not forthcoming, the court would appoint experts to devise one.[94] A patient who has been involuntarily committed to a mental hospital has a constitutional right at least to periodic examinations.[95] It is extremely likely that other actions of this type will be filed in the very near future in most of the states where inadequate treatment programs now exist.

A patient must also be protected from mistreatment or beatings by hospital attendants and other patients and failure to do so violates his constitutional rights and also gives rise to a negligence action against the hospital.[96] However, because the Federal Tort Claims Act exempts the government from liability for deliberate torts, such as assault and battery committed by employees, only the assailant is liable if a patient is attacked in a federal hospital.[97]

In terms of consent to either medical or psychiatric treatment, the mentally ill person presents peculiar problems. Where a physician is asked to treat a noninstitutionalized mentally incompetent patient for a medical problem, if a guardian has been judicially appointed, consent must be obtained from the guardian. Where there has been no judicial proceeding the consent of any competent adult in the patient's family, particularly one with whom the incompetent resides, is sufficient. The American Bar Foundation study, *The Mentally Disabled and the Law*[98] stands as the preeminent work in this field. For any person particularly interested in the rights of the mentally disabled person to refuse or to receive treatment, this book is a monumental examination of the subject.

The rights of the mentally ill also received study by the Senate Committee on the Judiciary in 1970.[99] The Committee proposed as legislation various guarantees to protect the rights of persons in mental institutions. Some of these proposals are necessarily technical, but, in general, they serve as outstanding guidelines to the best available opinions on the subject.

Section 21-561 of the Committee's bill deals with the right of the mental patient to communicate. It felt that a person hospitalized in a public or private hospital ought to be allowed to correspond by sealed mail with an

individual or official agency in or out of the hospital and to receive un-
censored mail from his attorney and from his personal physician. The
Committee accepted the fact that there may be medically justifiable reasons
for reading incoming mail before it is delivered to the patient except for
mail from his attorney or physician. There should be no constitutional or
medical justification whatever for denying any person, no matter how disturbed he may be, communication with his attorney.

In several cases it was obvious to the courts that mail restrictions were
used to prevent patients from notifying their attorneys that they were being
improperly held. In two New York cases, a hospital's failure to forward
letters to attorneys was held to constitute an unreasonable restraint on the
patient's freedom.[100]

A woman told her husband that she wanted a divorce. The next day a
psychiatrist whom she had never met appeared at her house, but he did not
tell her that he was there for an examination. Several days later the psychiatrist and another physician signed commitment papers and she was forcibly
removed from her home and taken to the psychiatrist's hospital. She refused
food and medication for 6 days and the psychiatrist later admitted that he
refused to allow her to mail letters or use the telephone or communicate with
her attorney. On one occasion a nurse and three orderlies held her down and
gave her an injection of tranquilizers. She finally found a telephone and contacted relatives who had her released immediately by court order. She sued
and recovered $40,000.00 from the psychiatrist. The court found him liable for
assault and battery, for false imprisonment, and for refusing to allow her to
communicate with her attorney, in clear contravention of her constitutional
rights.[101]

All letters censored for medical reasons or not given to the patients
should, of course, be returned to the writer. Although some mental patients
may write threatening or offensive letters or their communications may be
libelous, there are serious doubts as to whether any patient's mail can
constitutionally be restricted. The best approach is probably to allow the
mail to go out unread, but to stamp the envelope with a notice that the
patient is confined to a mental hospital and that the letter should be interpreted accordingly.

Little or no consideration has been given by courts to whether a mental
hospital can give dangerous treatments without the patient's consent. Normally, of course, as was discussed earlier in this chapter, a physician may
not treat a patient without his consent except in an emergency. Many mental patients are simply incompetent, however, to make valid determinations

and their consent might be considered legally ineffective if they gave it. Many patients do not have close family members who can be consulted, and even if the patient is considered mentally competent there would be a serious question as to whether he would feel free to withhold his consent if he felt that his release was contingent upon his acceptance. If a guardian has been appointed for the patient, the guardian must always be informed. If there is no guardian, however, it is possible that even psychosurgery and other extremely dangerous treatments may be performed on duly committed mental patients without their consent.[102] It is likely, however, that a competent mental patient, no matter how disturbed, may not be given treatment if it violates his religious convictions and those convictions predate the onset of illness.[103]

The right to refuse electroshock treatment is covered only by California statutes which give the patient an unqualified right to refuse it at will.[104] It is obvious that legislation is advisable in all states to determine the question of the right of a legally incompetent patient to refuse treatment. It is perfectly obvious that current statutes do not adequately protect their rights in many cases and state legislatures should take steps to do so. In the meantime, a physician who does not obtain the incompetent patient's consent for reasonable and accepted treatment which is theoretically beneficial to him probably will not be guilty of either assault and battery or negligence for failure to do so.

Involuntary Sterilization. The question of involuntary sterilization of mental patients or of those who are considered to be mentally deficient was ignored in this country for many years until quite recently. Eugenic sterilization is based on the theory, which has enjoyed far less psychiatric, sociological, and psychological support in recent years, that a mentally retarded or disturbed person would probably give birth to a child who is himself mentally deficient and that even if the child has an adequate intelligence at birth the person could not serve as an adequate parent. In 1927 the United States Supreme Court upheld as constitutional state statutes which provided for compulsory sterilization of retarded persons. The decision included the famous sentence "Three generations of imbeciles is enough."[105] There has been no consideration of the constitutionality of compulsory sterilization by the Supreme Court since that time and therefore most states which have compulsory sterilization statutes take the position that they are constitutional.[106] There are very few current decisions on the subject.

A retarded woman had eight children. She was confined to a state institution for the mentally retarded. Sterilization was made a prerequisite of her release.

The constitutional attack on the statute failed when the state supreme court upheld it as a valid exercise of the state's police power. The court pointed out that while there is a natural right to have children, no individual's right to do so is superior to the common good. The court also held that the state did not have to demonstrate that any children the woman might have would inherit her retardation.[107]

In 1972 another state supreme court upheld the sterilization of a 13-year old retarded girl.[108]

Most states' statutes provide that compulsory sterilization cannot be performed on a person who is not a resident of an institution for the retarded. Where there is no statute allowing compulsory sterilization, the state has no power to order it. In fact, since the would-be patient is legally incompetent to consent, if she wishes to do so, the procedure is probably not permissible at all.[109] In those states with involuntary sterilization statutes, before it can be performed, constitutional guarantees of due process of law mandate that the would-be patient be given notice, a guardian be appointed, and a hearing be held.[110] Presumably the right to counsel must be given at these hearings as well. In the light of the abortion decisions' conclusion that a woman has the constitutional right not to bear a child, the same reasoning would logically apply conversely and make it quite likely that in a future case contesting sterilization for economic or genetic reasons, those statutes will also be declared unconstitutional. It is altogether probable that in the future the Supreme Court will rule that if a woman who wants an abortion has the right not to bear a child, then the woman who might be compulsorily sterilized is equally able to have as many children as she wants.

In any situation involving involuntary sterilization under court order a physician is well advised both in terms of possible professional disciplinary action and civil suits by patients to consult local counsel and to make certain that all the patient's legal rights have been protected. It is absolutely mandatory that a judicial hearing be held and that counsel and a guardian be appointed to represent the incompetent patient's viewpoint if the reason for the sterilization is that the patient is incompetent. Punitive sterilization for purposes of dealing with criminal offenders has long been declared unconstitutional.[111] Sterilization as an alternative to imprisonment for those accused of a sex crime is totally unconstitutional and no physician should perform one even under court order.

Artificial Insemination.   The question of consent, of course, may be relevant in cases of artificial donor insemination.[112] There is no legal prohibition on artificial insemination in this country. Several states have enacted statutes regularizing the rights of the child as if he were the product of normal marital sexual relations. A child who is born after artificial insemination in a state where there is no statute is also invariably held to be legitimate as long as the husband consented to the procedure. If the couple later separates, the husband is responsible for child support to the same extent as he would be if the child had been conceived normally during the marriage.[113] A woman may not, during a divorce proceeding, attempt to defeat her husband's rights to custody or visitation by alleging that since the child was the product of artificial insemination he has no legal rights toward the child.[114] If, however, he was not consulted and did not consent prior to the insemination he is not liable for support of the child in case of a later divorce.[115]

Under no circumstances should a married woman be artificially inseminated without her husband's full knowledge and consent. The physician would be extremely ill-advised to allow her to take the consent form home for his signature and thus fail to discuss the situation in person with her husband. The possibility of a suit alleging that the physician engaged in sexual relations with his patient and that the pregnancy resulted from such contact should never be discounted. While it is unusual, some unmarried women have requested artificial insemination. Although the decision to comply with her request is entirely a matter of medical judgment, the ethical physician must be very sure that she understands the legal, sociological, and psychological problems for her and for her child which flow from illegitimacy.

In the absence of a state statute declaring that a child who is the product of artificial insemination inherits as if he were the natural product of the marital relationship, a physician should advise a couple considering this course of action to consult an attorney for a complete discussion of the child's rights of inheritance from them and from relatives such as grandparents.

There are virtually no cases on the subject of artificial insemination except those involving child support liability in a subsequent divorce and therefore many obvious questions have no definitive answers. For example, since the identity of the donor is and should be kept secret from the recipient and her husband, if the child is born with an inherited defect, the physician who should have known or should have tested the donor for the defect might well be liable in negligence for failure to use due care in the selection process.

Child Abuse. Child abuse is another problem which presents peculiar questions of consent and responsibility for the physician.[116] The problem in this country has grown markedly in terms of awareness, if not in incidence, in the last few years and the "battered baby" problem is a serious one in every part of the nation. In addition to proceedings which declare the child to be neglected and dependent for the purpose of removing him from the custody of the parent and placing him in a foster home, the parent may also be charged with a violation of the criminal law. If the child recovers from the injury, the usual charge, in the absence of a specific statute providing penalties for child abuse in the state, is assault and battery. If the child dies, most prosecutions are for manslaughter as opposed to intentional homicide. Jail sentences in these cases are by no means uncommon although most courts now try to provide supportive psychological counseling for the parents.

The county welfare department had placed two children in a foster home. One, a 4-year old, was brought to the hospital dead. The examining physician testified that she had died of beatings and that there was medical evidence of other assaults. The other, younger child also gave physical indications of being beaten. At the trial witnesses testified that they had seen the foster parents beating both children with a stick while they were all working in the berry field. The jury found both foster parents guilty of manslaughter and convictions were upheld upon appeal. No discussion was given to the possible civil liability of the agency or their employees who placed the children in their untenable positions and in that unacceptable situation. At least hypothetically any agency would be liable in negligence.[117]

Almost all states provide that the physician who in good faith reports a suspected case of child abuse to the proper authorities would be immune from any suit for negligence or defamation if he turns out to be mistaken. He is protected for a good faith error without any question, even in the absence of such a statute, as long as the reasonably prudent physician would have thought the child's injuries indicated some form of abuse.[118] If the physician does not accept the responsibility to intervene in this matter even over the objections of the parents, he must live with the knowledge that the child might very well be killed in the next beating. The extreme youth of most of these children and their corresponding defenselessness increases responsibilities, both moral and legal, that any physician encountering one of these cases must ethically accept.

In terms of legal responsibility he has none whatsoever to an abusive parent. The child, not the parent, is his patient and even if he has been treating the parent, all courts hold that no physician–patient privilege exists in a child abuse case.[119] Therefore, if he telephones the police or the juvenile court and makes a report, he is not in any way violating a confidential relationship between the parent and himself. Thus it is not only permissible, it is ethically mandatory, and is required by statute in most states for a physician to report child abuse to the proper authorities for further steps to be taken.

Custody and Adoption. Physicians are frequently involved in adoption cases.[120] Child welfare agencies of course rely on the physician's examination for evaluation of the child's condition. Some physicians and attorneys place children in private adoptions.

If a physician is negligent in examining a newborn or older child and assures adoptive parents and the agency that the child is healthy when in fact the child has some congenital disease, he may be liable for negligence if the conditions could have been diagnosed with the use of normal care.[121]

It would appear to be fraud as a matter of law for a physician or adoption agency not to reveal a child's known medical problems to prospective parents, but most cases involve conditions, physical or mental, which are not discoverable at birth in spite of utmost care. With retardation that carries physical symptoms, such as hydrocephalus, a physician who did not examine the child carefully enough to discover it would presumably be guilty of negligence. Retardation without physical manifestation might well not become apparent for many months or years, however, and in that case it is highly unlikely that any agency or physician would be subject to a suit for fraud, breach of warranty, or negligence.

In some states, a surrender for adoption by the natural mother or by both parents if the child is legitimate, is irrevocable only after it is given to a licensed child placement agency. If the child is placed through a private adoption, the parent may revoke up to the minute that the adoption decree is granted. Adoption is solely a statutory procedure. In all states therefore, statutes regulate surrender rights in either agency or private placements. While private, nonagency adoptions can be criticized, most of them are done for altruistic reasons. If a physician does help to arrange a private adoption it is absolutely incumbent upon him for the sake of all parties concerned to inquire from his attorney what his state's requirements are for execution of a valid surrender and to comply with them exactly and precisely.

A physician arranged an adoption. The natural mother gave the baby to him and gave him her consent in a letter. He placed the child with a couple who instituted appropriate adoption proceedings. The natural mother revoked her consent the day before the adoption hearing. The court held that she was entitled to regain custody of her child because the statute in that state made consent binding before a decree only when given to a licensed agency.[122]

In some cases judges may appoint a physician or psychiatrist to examine prospective adoptive parents or the opposing parties in a child custody case. In both cases, no physician–patient privilege exists and the parties examined may not object to admission of the psychiatrist's testimony evaluating their mental health.[123]

Where a physician or psychiatrist has been treating a party to a custody suit, most states hold that he may be compelled to testify as to his patient's condition. While most legal actions do not constitute a sufficiently urgent reason for compelling disruption of the confidentiality of the physician–patient relationship, the best interests of children who are the subject of custody suits are the paramount concern of all courts, and parental rights, including this one, must give way to the need of the court to have as much information as possible for the best determination of custody.[124]

Mental illness, of course, may well constitute sufficient grounds for removal of a child from the control of his parent.[125] A person who is adjudicated mentally incompetent and whose prospects of recovery are remote may not give valid consent to the release of his children for adoption under the common law rule that an incompetent has no capacity to consent.[126] However, most states now provide statutory authority for appointment of a guardian for an incompetent parent and release for adoption of the children by the guardian if there is substantial medical evidence that the parent will not recover.[127]

A mother had been diagnosed schizophrenic and committed four times to a state mental hospital. Her illegitimate child had been placed in a foster home by the Welfare Department and she only visited the child once during her period of release. She was committed a fifth time suffering from constant delusions. The court allowed release of the child for adoption. It held that his right to be removed from "the limbo of foster homes" was more important than the mother's right to custody. The decision states the rule, accepted in all jurisdictions, that in order to terminate parental rights it must be shown that the parent is presently unable to meet the physical and emotional needs of the child and that the condition will continue for a period of time sufficient to render unlikely the successful integration of the child into a family.[128]

Mental retardation may also constitute adequate cause for termination of parental rights. The test is the ability of the parent to meet the child's needs.[129] Considerable retardation must, therefore, be shown.

An unmarried mother's tested IQ was 45. She and eight relatives, all of whom were equally or more retarded, lived together in abject poverty. No one in the house was capable of employment. The court held that the best interests of her newborn child would require that he be placed in the custody of the Welfare Department, which was empowered to release him for adoption.[130]

Allegations of mental illness, sometimes totally unjustified, frequently arise in custody disputes during divorce proceedings. While an active psychotic or person who is in a mental hospital at the time the question is adjudicated will not usually receive custody, the fact that a parent has been hospitalized at some time in the past certainly does not preclude an award of custody.[131] If the nature of the emotional problem is such that it will affect the welfare of the child, a minor illness may be sufficient to award custody to the opposing party, whereas a more serious illness not involving the child would not. A mother whose neurotic fear of germs was so strong she would not let her children play outside although she was perfectly normal in all other respects, was denied custody in one case.[132] Alcoholism is usually considered sufficient to preclude a custody award,[133] and narcotic addiction would undoubtedly preclude custody as well. On the other hand, behavior such as extreme sexual promiscuity is usually insufficient to deprive a parent of custody as long as sufficient discretion is used to insure that the children are not aware of or harmed by it.[134]

Unlike other decrees, child custody awards are never final. Changes in circumstances or the mental health of the parent are grounds for change of custody.[135] The sole interest of the court is the welfare of the child, and the rights of all adult parties, including physicians who may be directly or indirectly involved in the case, are subordinated to that consideration.

Experimentation. Informed consent is the primary consideration in situations in which medical experimentation takes place. The three situations in which innovative deviation from standard medical or surgical practice may occur are: (1) a subject, usually a person free from illness, is used for research for the exclusive benefit of the investigator and not for any purpose medically beneficial to the subject; (2) a patient is treated by an innovative method when standard remedies have not been applied before the innovation is attempted; and (3) a seriously ill patient is treated innovatively after standard remedies have failed.

In the first situation it is absolutely clear that ethical and moral as well as legal considerations demand that the consent of the subject be free and voluntary.[136] Not only must the risk of the experiment be made clear, but it must be equally certain that the consent must not have been induced or given under any form of duress. While there are as yet no decisions on the point, prisoners are a fertile source for testing new medications. If a prisoner is expressly or by implication given any remission of sentence or special privileges for participation in an experimental program, even if he has been informed of all possible risks, any court in the country might be inclined to hold that his agreement to participate was not genuinely free and voluntary.

A mental patient was charged with murder and rape of a nurse at the hospital in which he was an involuntary patient. He was transferred to a maximum security hospital without trial. Seventeen years later he was taken to a research institute for use as a subject in a study of the effects of psychosurgery on aggression. He was told that the surgery was completely experimental and signed a consent. The consent was approved by two committees of physicians at the institute. Newspaper publicity resulted in a suit for his release and an injunction against the surgery brought by a mental health group. The court held that psychosurgery could not constitutionally be performed on involuntarily confined persons since their capacity to consent would inevitably be affected by their incarceration in an inherently coercive atmosphere. Furthermore, the court found that the particular patient involved was not capable of comprehending the risks even when they were fully explained to him. Thus it was held that the patient was unconstitutionally detained for medical experimentation to which he did not have the capacity for voluntary consent.[136a]

Should a person who is incompetent to assent, such as a child or a person who is mentally retarded, be used as an experimental subject, his guardian or next of kin must be fully informed both of the nature of the experiment and of all risks.[137]

The federal Food, Drug and Cosmetic Act[138] requires the Secretary of Health, Education and Welfare to enforce very strict regulations[139] in all clinical trials of drugs. These regulations require full and free consent of all persons used as clinical subjects or of their guardians or personal representatives. Since these regulations appear to be the minimum standards required by law, they are reprinted in full.

FDA, POLICY STATEMENT ON CONSENT
IN CLINICAL INVESTIGATION

Section 130.37. Consent for use of investigational new drugs on humans; statement of policy.

(*a*) Section 505(i) of the act provides that regulations on use of investigational new drugs on human beings shall impose the condition that investigators "obtain the consent of such human beings or their representatives, except where they deem it not feasible or, in their professional judgment, contrary to the best interest of such human beings."

(*b*) This means that the consent of such human beings (or the consent of their representatives) to whom investigational drugs are administered primarily for the accumulation of scientific knowledge, for such purposes as studying drug behavior, body processes, or the course of a disease, must be obtained in all cases and, in all but exceptional cases, the consent of patients under treatment with investigational drugs must be obtained.

(*c*) "Under treatment" applies when the administration of the investigational drug for either diagnostic or therapeutic purposes constitutes responsible medical judgment taking into account the availability of other remedies or drugs and the individual circumstances pertaining to the person to whom the investigational drug is to be administered.

(*d*) "Exceptional cases," as used in paragraph (*b*) of this section, which exceptions are to be strictly applied, are cases where it is not feasible to obtain the patient's consent or the consent of his representative, or where, as a matter of professional judgment exercised in the best interest of a particular patient under the investigator's care, it would be contrary to that patient's welfare to obtain his consent.

(*e*) "Patient" means a person under treatment.

(*f*) "Not feasible" is limited to cases where the investigator is not capable of obtaining consent because of inability to communciate with the patient or his representative; for example, where the patient is in a coma or is otherwise incapable of giving informed consent, his representative cannot be reached, and it is imperative to administer the drug without delay.

(*g*) "Contrary to the best interests of such human beings" applies when the communication of information to obtain consent would seriously affect the patient's disease status and the physician has exercised a professional judgment that under the particular circumstances of this patient's case, the patient's best interests would suffer if consent were sought.

(*h*) "Consent" or "informed consent" means that the person involved has legal capacity to give consent, is so situated as to be able to exercise free power of choice, and is provided with a fair explanation of all material information concerning the administration of the investigational drug, or his possible use as a control, as to enable him to make an understanding decision as to his willingness to receive said investigational drug. This latter element requires that before the acceptance of an affirmative decision by such person the investigator should make known to him the nature, duration, and purpose of the administration of said investigational drug; the method and means by which it is to be administered; all inconveniences and hazards reasonably to be expected, including the fact, where applicable, that the person may be used as a control; the existence of alternative forms of therapy, if any; and the effects upon his health or person that may possibly come from the administration of the investigational drugs. Said patient's consent shall be obtained in writing by the investigator.[140]

Failure to comply with this standard of informed and free consent will not only subject the experimenter to a damage suit, but will also be quite likely to result in a disciplinary proceeding.

A physician injected cancer cells into chronically ill patients. None of the patients were told that the cells were malignant. The hospital administrator sued to compel the physician to turn over all records to him for use in disciplinary proceedings. The administrator won the right to possession of the records. The physician's license was revoked for a year, but sentence was suspended and he was allowed to practice on probation.[141]

Recent disclosures indicate that for decades men who had syphilis and were supposedly treated at a public health facility received no treatment at all, even after the discovery of penicillin. They were never told that their conditions would have been alleviated by medication. The researchers were simply interested in observing the effects of untreated syphilis. Suits for both medical malpractice and a violation of the patients' constitutional rights will presumably be successful.[142]

The Nuremburg Tribunals accepted the proper use of human testing, but laid down very strict guidelines for consent of the subject in writing its code.[143] The principles of ethics of the American Medical Association[144] also provide for full and voluntary consent of the subject, a requirement of animal experimentation prior to human trials of the medication or procedure, and proper medical supervision of the experiment. Thus, it is obvious that a clinical investigator who proceeds to use a human subject in an experiment without a full disclosure of all the risks involved and the nature and purpose of the investigation, especially in a situation in which consent may be obtained by duress, express or implied, may be in serious legal and disciplinary difficulties.

If a patient whose condition would respond to approved methods is treated by an innovative procedure or course of therapy, he or his guardian must be explicitly informed that the procedure is experimental and the risks and alternative course of action must be explained in full.[145] This is particularly important if no emergency is present.

A 14-year old boy had a curvature of the spine. The defendant performed an operative procedure which he had invented. He had used it in 35 previous cases. He was the only surgeon who performed it anywhere in the world. Nothing was said to the boy's mother about the experimental nature of the method to be used or that conservative treatment might correct the problem. The boy died 2 weeks later of a hemorrhage. The surgeon was liable for his failure to obtain an informed consent from the child's parent even though no negligence in his use of the surgical method was demonstrated.[146]

A patient whose condition justifies a departure from standard methods is also required to give his informed consent, but a physician may certainly innovate if it is obvious that accepted modes of treatment are not benefiting his condition.[147]

A cancer patient was treated without success with a drug developed by his physician. He sued the physician for failing to treat him by more conventional methods. The court held that in view of the fact that there was no cure for the disease, the defendant was not liable for the use of the innovation.[148]

In the only decision in this country involving heart transplants, for example, the court found that both the patient and his wife had been fully and completely informed of the experimental nature of the surgery. They had consented when the patient's condition deteriorated to the point that standard treatments were unavailing and death was imminent. The surgeon was found not liable for the patient's death.[149]

Obvious special moral and ethical as well as legal issues are present in any experimental situation not designed to benefit the subject. Thus all possible risks must be explained. However, where the experiment is designed to alleviate the patient's illness, normal rules of informed consent apply.

This chapter has attempted to explain the basic principles involved in the concept of informed consent to medical treatment. The patient, not the physician, has the right to decide if he wishes to be treated and which, if any, risks he is willing to assume. Some medical or surgical procedures present special problems in obtaining a genuinely informed consent; some patients present special problems regardless of the nature of the treatment. With the exception of a very few situations in which compulsory treatment may be administered within very strict limitations, a free human in a free nation has a constitutional and legal right to make the decision as to what, if anything, is to be done to either his mind or his body.

NOTES

1. "Informed Consent, Parts I, II and III," Vol. 214 *JAMA* No. 6, page 1181, Nov. 9, 1970; 214 *JAMA* No. 7, page 1383, Nov. 16, 1970; 214 *JAMA* No. 8, page 1611, Nov. 23, 1970.
2. "Medical Treatment Without Consent," 200 *JAMA* No. 5, page 229, May 1, 1967.
3. Pratt v. Davis, 79 NE 562, Ill 1906.
4. Schloendorff v. Society of New York Hospital, 105 NE 92, NY 1914.
5. Natanson v. Kline, 350 P 2d 1093, 354 P 2d 670, Kans 1960.
6. Mitchell v. Robinson, 334 SW 2d 11, Mo 1960.
7. Karp v. Cooley, 349 F Supp 827, DC Tex 1972; Fiorentino v. Wenger, 272 NYS 2d 557, rev'd on other grounds, 227 NE 2d 296, NY 1967.
8. Wall v. Brim, 138 F 2d 478, CCA 5, 1943.
9. "Liability for Unauthorized Treatment," 196 *JAMA* No. 10, page 293, June 6, 1966.
10. Darrah v. Kite, 301 NYS 2d 286, NY 1969.
11. Salgo v. Leland Stanford Board of Trustees, 317 P 2d 170, Cal 1957.
12. Putensen v. Clay Adams, Inc., 91 Cal Rptr 319, Cal 1970.
13. Luka v. Lowrie, 136 NW 1106, Mich 1912.
14. Crouch v. Most, 432 P 2d 250, NM 1967.
15. Lester v. Aetna Casualty and Surety Co., 240 F 2d 676, CCA 5, 1957.
16. Roberts v. Wood, 206 F Supp 579, DC Ala 1962; Weiser v. Hampton, 445 SW 2d 224, Tex 1969.
17. Nishi v. Hartwell, 473 P 2d 116, Hawaii 1970; Dunham v. Wright, 423 F 2d 940, CCA 3, 1970.
18. Louisell and Williams, *Medical Malpractice*, New York, Matthew Bender and Co., 1960 and annual revisions, Section 22.02.
19. Mitchell v. Robinson, 334 SW 2d 11, Mo 1960; Woods v. Brumlop, 377 P 2d 520, NM 1962.
20. Berkey v. Anderson, 82 Cal Rptr 67, Cal 1969.

21. Sharpe v. Pugh, 155 SE 2d 108, NC 1967; Koury v. Follo, 158 SE 2d 548, NC 1968.

22. Belcher v. Carter, 234 NE 2d 311, Ohio 1967; Zebarth v. Swedish Hospital Medical Center, 499 P 2d 1, Wash 1972; Natanson v. Kline, 350 P 2d 1093, 354 P 2d 670, Kans 1960; "Radiation Therapy," 220 *JAMA* No. 13, page 1807, June 26, 1972.

23. Stewart v. Long Island College Hospital, 296 NYS 2d 41, NY 1968.

24. Grosjean v. Spencer, 140 NW 2d 139, Iowa 1966.

25. Getchell v. Mansfield, 489 P 2d 953, Ore 1971.

26. "Surgical Assault and Battery," 198 *JAMA* No. 11, page 299, Dec. 12, 1966.

27. Corn v. French, 289 P 2d 173, Nev 1955.

28. Bryson v. Stone, 190 NW 2d 336, Mich 1971.

29. "Liability for Unauthorized Treatment," 196 *JAMA* No. 10, page 293, June 6, 1966.

30. Belcher v. Carter, 234 NE 2d 311, Ohio 1967; Sisler v. Jackson 460 P 2d 903, Okla 1969.

31. Scott v. Wilson, 396 SW 2d 532, Tex 1965; Govin v. Hunter, 374 P 2d 421, Wyo 1962; Petterson v. Lynch, 299 NYS 2d 244, NY 1969; Miles v. Van Gelder, 137 NW 2d 292, Mich 1965.

32. Dietze v. King, 184 F Supp 944, DC Va 1960; Williams v. Menehan, 379 P 2d 292, Kans 1963; Ditlow v. Kaplan, 181 So 2d 226, Fla 1965; Ross v. Hodges, 234 So 2d 905, Miss 1970.

33. Di Fillipo v. Preston, 173 A 2d 333, Del 1961.

34. Fischer v. Wilmington General Hospital, 149 A 2d 749, Del 1959.

35. "More About Informed Consent," Part I and Part II, 224 *JAMA* No. 13, page 1831, June 25, 1973, 225 *JAMA* No. 1, page 95, July 2, 1973, Hunter v. Brown, 484 P 2d 1162, Wash 1971; Cooper v. Roberts, 286 A 2d 647, Pa 1971.

36. Canterbury v. Spence, 464 F 2d 772, CA DC 1972.

37. Cobbs v. Grant, 502 P 2d 1, Cal 1972.

38. Wilkinson v. Vesey, 295 A 2d 676, RI 1972.

39. Haven v. Randolph, 342 F Supp 538, DC DC 1972.

40. Shetter v. Rochelle, 409 P 2d 74, Ariz 1965.

41. McDermott v. Manhattan Eye, Ear, Nose and Throat Hospital, 228 NYS 2d 143, 203 NE 2d 469, NY 1964.

42. "The Right to Refuse Necessary Treatment," 221 *JAMA* No. 3, page 335, July 17, 1972; Palm Springs General Hospital v. Martinez, Fla Cir Ct, Dade Co., Docket #71-12687, 1971; In re Appointment of a Guardian of the Person of Maida Yetter, Docket #1973-533 (Pa Ct Common Pleas) Northampton Co., 1973.

43. Dunham v. Wright, 423 F 2d 940, CCA 3, 1970.

44. Bang v. Charles T. Miller Hospital, 88 NW 2d 186, Minn 1958.

45. Campbell v. Oliva, 424 F 2d 1244, CCA 6, 1970.

46. Mull v. Emory University, 150 SE 2d 276, Ga 1966; Block v. McVay, 126 NW 2d 808, SD 1964.

47. Mallett v. Pirkey, 466 P 2d 466, Colo 1970.

48. Yeates v. Harms, 401 P 2d 659, Kans 1965.

49. Pedesky v. Bleiberg, 59 Cal Rptr 294, Cal 1967.

50. Gray v. Grunnagle, 223 A 2d 663, Pa 1966.

51. Jackovach v. Yocom, 237 NW 444, Iowa 1931; Wheeler v. Barker, 208 P 2d 68, Cal 1949; Robinson v. Wirts, 127 A 2d 706, Pa 1956.

52. Barnett v. Bachrach, 34 A 2d 626, DC 1943.

53. Kennedy v. Parrott, 90 SE 2d 754, NC 1956.

54. Valdez v. Percy, 217 P 2d 422, Cal 1950; Perry v. Hodgson, 148 SE 659, Ga 1929; Mohr v. Williams, 104 NW 12, Minn 1905; Hundley v. St. Frances Hospital, 327 P 2d 131, Cal 1958; Beringer v. Lackner, 73 NE 2d 620, Ill 1947.

55. King v. Carney, 204 Pac 270, Okla 1922.

56. Tabor v. Scobee, 254 SW 2d 474, Ky 1952.

57. Russell v. Jackson, 221 P 2d 516, Wash 1950.

58. "Authorization for Autopsies," 203 *JAMA* No. 5, page 199, Jan. 29, 1968; "Unauthorized Autopsies," 214 *JAMA* No. 5, page 967, Nov. 2, 1970.

59. Huntly v. Zurich Accident Ins. Co., 280 Pac 183, Cal 1929; Chaparro v. Jackson & Perkins Co., 346 F 2d 677, CCA 2, 1965.

60. Gelfand, Leo, "Modern Concepts of Property in a Dead Body," in *Legal Medicine Annual: 1971*, page 229, Cyril H. Wecht, Ed., New York, Appleton-Century-Crofts, 1971.

61. Larson v. Chase, 50 NW 238, Minn 1891; Jackson v. Rupp, 228 So 2d 916, Fla 1969.

62. In re Estate of Mgurdichian, 291 NYS 2d 453, NY 1968.

63. McPosey v. Sisters of the Sorrowful Mother, 57 P 2d 617, Okla 1936.

64. Love v. Aetna Casualty & Surety Co., 99 SW 2d 646, Tex 1936.

65. Hill v. Travelers' Insurance Co., 294 SW 1097, Tenn 1927.

66. Terrill v. Harbin, 376 SW 2d 945, Tex 1964.

67. Hendriksen v. Roosevelt Hospital, 297 F Supp 1142, DC NY 1969.

68. Cremonese v. City of New York, 215 NE 2d 157, NY 1966; Gahn v. Leary, 61 NE 2d 844, Mass 1945.

69. Hirko v. Reese, 40 A 2d 408, Pa 1945; Brown v. Broome County, 170 NE 2d 666, NY 1960.

70. Donnelly v. Guion, 467 F 2d 290, CCA 2, 1972.

71. Gurganious v. Simpson, 197 SE 163, NC 1938.

72. Jackson v. Rupp, 228 So 2d 916, Fla 1970.

73. Kingsley v. Forsyth, 257 NW 95, Minn 1934; Frick v. McClelland, 122 A 2d 43, Pa 1956.

74. Schwalb v. Connely, 179 P 2d 667, Colo 1947.

75. Louisville and Nashville Railroad Co. v. Blackmon, 59 SE 341, Ga 1907.

76. Equitable Life Assurance Society v. Young & Revel, Inc., 250 A 2d 509, Del 1969.

77. Hazelwood v. Stokes, 483 SW 2d 576, Ky 1972.

78. O'Donnell v. Slack, 55 Pac 906, Cal 1899.

79. Holland v. Metalious, 198 A 2d 654, NH 1964.

80. Rauhe v. Langeland Memorial Chapel, Inc., 205 NW 2d 313, Mich 1973.

81. "Transplant Problems," 223 *JAMA* No. 11, page 1315, March 12, 1973; Sadler and Sadler, "Recent Developments in the Law Relating to Transplantation," in *Legal Medicine Annual: 1971*, Cyril H. Wecht, Ed., New York, Appleton-Century-Crofts, 1971, page 245.

82. Campbell v. Wainwright, 416 F 2d 949, CCA 5, 1969.

83. Wasmuth, Carl E., "Organ Transplantation," in *Legal Medicine Annual: 1969*, page 391, Cyril H. Wecht, Ed.; New York, Appleton-Centruy-Crofts, 1969; Wasmuth and Wasmuth, *Law and the Surgical Team*, Baltimore, Williams and Wilkins Co., 1969, Chapter 8, pages 342–344.

84. In re Richardson, 284 So 2d 185, La 1973.

85. Strunk v. Strunk, 445 SW 2d 145, Ky 1969.

86. "Organ Donation by Incompetent," 213 *JAMA* No. 3, page 513, July 20, 1970.

87. "The Right to Treatment," 220 *JAMA* No. 8, page 1165, May 22, 1972.

88. Maniaci v. Marquette University, 184 NW 2d 168, Wisc 1971.

89. Heryford v. Parker, 396 F 2d 393, CCA 10, 1968.

90. Petition of Rohrer, 230 NE 2d 915, Mass 1967.

91. Rouse v. Cameron, 373 F 2d 451, DC CA 1966.

92. Nason v. Superintendent of Bridgewater State Hospital, 233 NE 2d 908, Mass 1968.

93. In re Curry, 452 F 2d 1360, CA DC 1971.

94. Wyatt v. Stickney, 325 F Supp 781, DC Ala 1971.

95. Dixon v. Jacobs, 427 F 2d 589, CA DC 1970.

96. Bennett v. New York, 299 NYS 2d 288, NY 1969; Davis v. New York, 322 NYS 2d 569, NY 1972.

97. Cotter v. United States, 279 F Supp 847, DC NY 1968.

98. Brakel and Rock, Eds., *The Mentally Disabled and the Law*, Rev. ed. University of Chicago Press, Chicago 1971.

99. *Constitutional Rights of the Mentally Ill*, Hearings before the U.S. Senate Committee on the Judiciary, 91st Congress 1969–70, Washington, DC, U.S. Printing Office.

100. Hoff v. New York, 18 NE 2d 671, NY 1939; People ex rel Jacobs v. Worthing, 4 NYS 2d 630, NY 1938.

101. Stowers v. Wolodzko, 191 NW 2d 355, Mich 1971.

102. *The Mentally Disabled and the Law*, *op. cit. supra* at 98, pages 161–162.

103. Winters v. Miller, 446 F 2d 65, CCA 2, 1971.

104. Cal Welfare and Institutions Code, Section 5325, 1968.

105. Buck v. Bell, 274 U.S. 200, 1927.

106. "Compulsory Sterilization," 221 *JAMA* No. 2, page 229, July 10, 1972.

107. In re Cavitt, 157 NW 2d 171, Neb 1968.

108. Cook v. Oregon, 495 P 2d 768, Ore 1972.

109. Holmes v. Powers, 439 SW 2d 579, Ky 1969; Frazier v. Levi, 440 SW 2d 393, Tex 1969; Wade v. Bethesda Hospital, 337 F Supp 671, DC Ohio 1971.

110. State ex rel Smith v. Schaffer, 270 Pac 604, Kans 1928; In re Hendrickson, 123 P 2d 322, Wash 1942; Brewer v. Valk, 167 SE 638, NC 1933.

111. Skinner v. Oklahoma, 316 US 535, 1942.

112. Dienes, C. Thomas, "Artificial Donor Insemination: Perspectives on Legal and Social Change," 54 *Iowa Law Rev* 253, October 1958; Guttmacher, Alan F., "Artificial Insemination," 18 *DePaul Law Rev* 566, Summer 1969; Smith, George, "Through a Test-Tube Darkly: Artificial Insemination and the Law," 67 *Mich Law Rev* 127,

November 1968; Wadlington, Walter, "Artificial Insemination: The Dangers of a Poorly Kept Secret," 64 *Northwestern Law Rev* 777, Jan.–Feb. 1970.

113. People v. Sorensen, 66 Cal Rptr 7, Cal 1968; Anonymous v. Anonymous, 246 NYS 2d 835, NY 1964.

114. New York ex rel Abajian v. Dennett, 184 NYS 2d 178, NY 1958; Strnad v. Strnad, 78 NYS 2d 390, NY 1948; In re adoption of Anonymous, 345 NYS 2d 430, NY 1973.

115. Gursky v. Gursky, 242 NYS 2d 406, NY 1963.

116. "Child Abuse and the Physician," 222 *JAMA* No. 4, page 517, Oct. 23, 1972.

117. State v. Parmenter, 444 P 2d 680, Wash 1968.

118. Haewsky v. St. John Hospital, Mich. Cir Ct., Wayne Co. Docket 136-064, June 10, 1970.

119. In re John Children, 306 NYS 2d 797, NY 1969.

120. "The Physician and Adoption," 223 *JAMA* No. 8, page 953, Feb. 19, 1973.

121. Chappell v. Masten, 255 So 2d 546, Fla 1971.

122. Sampson v. Holton, 185 NW 2d 216, Iowa 1971.

123. In re adoption of Schroetter, 67 Cal Rptr 819, Cal 1968.

124. Usen v. Usen, 269 NE 2d 442, Mass 1971.

125. "Mental Illness and Parental Rights," 216 *JAMA* No. 3, page 575, April 19, 1971.

126. Pitzenberger v. Schnack, 245 Iowa 745, 1932.

127. People ex rel Nabstedt v. Barger, 121 NE 2d 781, Ill 1954; People ex rel Strohsahl v. Strohsahl, 222 NYS 319, NY 1927.

128. State v. Blum, 463 P 2d 367, Ore 1970.

129. In re Rathburn, 266 A 2d 423, Vt 1970.

130. State ex rel Paul v. Department of Public Welfare, 170 So 2d 549, La 1965.

131. Willey v. Willey, 115 NW 2d 833, Iowa 1962; Nichols v. Nichols, 247 SW 2d 143, Tex 1952; Combs v. Combs, 327 P 2d 164, Cal 1958.

132. Ericson v. Ericson, 195 Pac 234, Wash 1921.

133. Hardman v. Hardman, 214 SW 2d 391, Ky 1948.

134. West v. West, 170 So 2d 160, La 1964; Wendland v. Wendland, 138 NW 2d 185, Wisc 1965.

135. Pfeifer v. Pfeifer, 280 P 2d 54, Cal 1955.

136. "Healthy Subjects In Clinical Investigation," 203 *JAMA* No. 9, page 369, Feb. 26, 1968.

136a. Kaimowitz v. Department of Mental Health, Civil Action #73-19434-AW (Mich., Wayne Co Cir Ct, 1973).

137. "Common Law and Clinical Investigation," 203 *JAMA* No. 6, page 231, Feb. 5, 1968; "Consent in Clinical Investigation," 203 *JAMA* No. 7, page 281, Feb. 12, 1968.

138. Food, Drug and Cosmetic Act, 21 USC Section 355, 1964.

139. Food and Drug Administrative Regulations 21 C.F.R. Section 130.37.

140. 31 Fed. Reg. 11415 (1966).

141. Hyman v. Jewish Chronic Disease Hospital, 206 NE 2d 338, NY 1965; 151 *Science* 663–666, 1963.

142. "Report of Ad Hoc Committee," *New York Times*, June 13, 1973, page 21, Column 3.

143. 2 The Medical Case, 181–183, U.S. Printing Office 1947.

144. *Principles of Medical Ethics*, American Medical Association, 1960, page 14.

145. Fortner v. Koch, 261 NW 762, Mich 1935; Brown v. Hughes, 30 P 2d 259, Colo 1934.

146. Fiorentino v. Wenger, 227 NE 2d 296, NY 1967.

147. "Critical Areas in Clinical Investigation," 203 *JAMA* No. 8, page 241, Feb. 19, 1968; "Alternative Medical Procedures," 212 *JAMA* No. 2, page 385, April 13, 1970; McHugh v. Audet, 72 F Supp 394, DC Pa 1947.

148. Baldor v. Rogers, 81 So 2d 658, Fla 1955.

149. Karp v. Cooley, 349 F Supp 827, DC Tex 1972.

CHAPTER IX

INTENTIONAL

TORTS

Although all but a few suits by patients involve allegations of negligence on the part of a physician, failure in some way to use due care in diagnosis or treatment, there are a few in which patients have sued for redress of legal wrongs involving deliberate, intentional acts by physicians against them. While situations discussed in this chapter are rare, they do occur. All physicians should be aware that standard medical malpractice insurance policies do not usually cover deliberate torts. The physician is protected only from accidents and good faith mistakes and errors of judgment. He is not protected against deliberate actions which harm his patients for the very simple reason that he could have avoided them.

Assault and Battery.   Assault and battery is wrongful, harmful, or offensive contact with another's body or putting the other person in fear of such an attack; in other words, a deliberate attack of some type upon the patient.

Most cases in which physicians are charged with assault and battery involve good faith errors of treatment involving a failure to obtain the patient's informed consent. These are generally dealt with as ordinary negligence cases and are, of course, covered by malpractice insurance.[1] However, a suit is occasionally brought by a patient against a physician for deliberate physical attack or sexual assault. These are incidents totally outside the scope of any legitimate medical treatment. A civil suit in this area is invariably successful if the patient can prove the attack occurred. Furthermore, it should also be noted that assault and battery is a crime as well as a tort, and particularly in cases in which physicians have had illicit sexual intercourse with patients, whether or not force was used, heavy criminal penalties have been assessed. It should also be noted that assault on a patient either sexually or in anger is amply sufficient to constitute grounds for revocation of a physician's license.

A physician was charged by the Board of Medical Examiners with sexual assault on two patients, as well as illegal prescription of narcotics, but it appears that no criminal charges were filed. The court held that the State Board of Medical Examiners was justified in revoking his license.[2]

Some assault and battery cases do involve treatment situations. For example, a patient was strapped to a mechanical table and given stretching treatments in spite of his vehement objections. The physician was held liable for assault and battery.[3]

If a mentally competent patient refuses to take medication for religious or other reasons, it is generally considered assault and battery to force it upon him.

A woman was taken to a mental hospital by a policeman when she refused to move to a different room in the hotel where she lived. She was apparently quite dirty, disheveled, and unresponsive to questions. She was involuntarily committed to a mental hospital under an order allowing her to be confined for 60 days. She had been a practicing Christian Scientist for 10 years and on admission she refused to allow the physician to take her blood pressure, giving her religion as her reason. Over her continued objections she was given medication, mostly tranquilizers, both orally and by injection for 6 weeks while in the hospital. She sued. The court allowed recovery. She had never been found mentally ill or mentally incompetent and the court pointed out that an ordinary patient suffering from a physical ailment would have been able to reject the medication. The court held that the only circumstance under which compulsory medication may be given over the religious objection of the patient is if the patient has been harmful to himself or others and found that in this case she was not. Therefore, a cause of action for assault and battery against the physicians and the hospital was stated.[4]

A few cases involve physical attacks on patients with no "medical" justification whatever. When this occurs, it is not only a criminal offense, but is clear proof of malpractice.[5]

A 4-year old child had cut her toe. The toe was sutured by the defendant who instructed her mother to bring her back some days later for removal of the sutures. At the time the sutures were to be removed the defendant suggested that the child should lie on the examining table and the mother was instructed to help hold her down. The little girl began to cry and tried to sit up, all of which made the physician's task somewhat difficult. He spanked her quite hard, and the bruises admittedly remained visible on the child's buttocks for a period of 3 weeks. Her mother removed her from the physician's office and another physician removed the sutures without incident. She then sued the physician for assault and battery and the jury returned a verdict in her favor. The physician appealed. The court held that the damages awarded had been excessive in view of the fact that there was no continuing pain to the child and the injury had not been severe. However, on principle the court held that assault and battery had been committed.[6]

A patient came to a private mental hospital as a voluntary patient. He decided he wished to leave and when he attempted to do so, a physician and members of the hospital staff forcibly administered ether and placed a tourniquet around his neck. Both of these activities took place while he was held down on the floor by a physician and six nurses. He died from either an overdose of ether or the tourniquet around his neck and the physician was properly held liable for wrongful death.[7]

A child bit a medical student's finger to the bone as he was trying to treat her lacerated tongue. When all other methods of removing his finger from her mouth failed, he slapped her on the cheek to force her to open her mouth and release it. The procedure was successful. The child's parents sued him for assault and battery, but the court held that the circumstances indicated the physician's absence of malice and in view of the lack of injury to the child, the parents could not recover damages.[8]

Mental hospitals are a frequent source of successful actions for assault and battery against attendants. In most situations if an attendant beats a patient, the hospital is liable for his assault.[9]

A 15-year old boy had been in a state mental hospital for 3 years. His father received a telegram that he was dead. At a hearing to determine the cause of death, three patients and a hospital employee testified as to the beating that hospital employees had given the boy. According to the testimony two attendants hit him in the pit of the stomach and he was bleeding from the mouth and nose. The autopsy report listed the cause of death as traumatic rupture of the duodenum. The father was allowed to recover substantial damages.[10]

However, under the Federal Tort Claims Act the federal government assumes liability only for torts involving negligence committed by its employees. Deliberate torts, such as assault and battery, defamation of character, and false imprisonment are excluded from the list of torts for which the government will assume liability. Therefore, in a federal hospital if a patient is beaten either by an attendant or a physician, only the federal employee himself is liable for his actions. The government is not.

A patient was confined to the "disturbed ward" of a VA hospital. He became overactive while being taken to the dining hall. The attendant who was accom-

panying him pushed him against the wall and he slumped to the floor unconscious. The hospital admitted that he suffered multiple fractures of the ribs
and head injuries. He died about 2 weeks later of bronchopneumonia. The
court held that the government was not liable for an assault on a patient
committed by an employee or by another inmate.[11]

One very famous case involving a patient in a psychiatric hospital resulted not only in civil liability, but in criminal liability as well. The employee was found guilty of manslaughter.

A 71-year old patient in a state hospital required help with eating. The defendant, a practical nurse, fed her 3 tablespoons of cubed potatoes. She held
the patient's head back by grasping her hair with one hand and feeding her
with the other. At intervals during the feeding, the defendant covered the
patient's mouth and nose with a towel. Another attendant held the patient's
arms and a patient sat on her lap. After the third spoon of food was put in
her mouth the patient collapsed and died. The cause of death was asphyxia
from the aspiration of stomach contents. The manslaughter prosecution
against the employee was upheld on appeal and the state was liable for civil
damages.[12]

Sexual intercourse with a patient during medical treatment is not only
unethical, it also constitutes criminal assault and battery or rape if the
patient's consent is not entirely free. Physicians who sexually assault
patients, particularly if they have administered some form of sleep-inducing
medication prior to intercourse generally receive extremely lengthy jail
sentences.

A 20-year old single girl consulted the defendant for a physical examination.
After part of the examination was completed he suggested stopping by her
apartment to finish it. He suggested that she be in bed and have her nightgown on when he came by to finish the examination, which she did. During
the course of the examination in her apartment, which took place several
hours after her office appointment, he asked her if she had trouble sleeping
and she answered in the affirmative. He gave her an injection and she lost
consciousness. She awakened while he was sexually molesting her, but pre-
tended to remain unconscious for fear that he might seriously harm her if he
knew that she was awake. The phone rang at that point and when she sat up,
the physician told her that she "had had a bad dream" and left her apartment. She called the police who instructed her to keep her next appointment
with him and advise them of future developments. The physician again sug-

gested stopping by the patient's apartment for "medical treatment" and she reported this to the police. They arranged to have a closed circuit television camera concealed in a shoe box in her apartment. When the physician arrived two policemen, a policewoman, an assistant county medical examiner, and a neighbor watched the television monitor from a neighboring apartment. The physician again asked her how she was sleeping and gave her an injection. She lost consciousness almost immediately and the physician proceeded to remove her clothing from the waist down. At this point the policemen entered the apartment and found her unconscious on her back on the couch with the physician on top of her. They arrested the physician. He was charged with attempted rape, assault with intent to rape, assault and battery, and assault. He was convicted of assault and battery and was sentenced to 5 years imprisonment. The state supreme court upheld his conviction on the grounds that there was no evidence that he was acting in good faith. His conduct at that time was completely unrelated to any physician—patient relationship and therefore the conviction would be upheld.[13]

Even though no force is used if a physician tells a woman that sexual intercourse is necessary to treatment or if he in some way makes her unaware of what he is doing and proceeds to have intercourse with her, "rape by fraud" is a crime, and the penalties in most states are the same as forcible rape.[14] In some states, however, physical force is absolutely necessary to constitute rape.[15] Even in those jurisdictions, however, if the woman is rendered unconscious by medication it is then considered to be forcible rape.[16] Moreover if the statutory crime of rape is not proven because the woman consented under the impression that she was consenting to medical or psychiatric treatment, it is ample grounds for revocation of the physician's license and award of substantial civil damages.[17]

Whether or not a charge by a patient of sexual molestation is justified there is absolutely nothing more harmful to a physician's reputation. Therefore, male physicians should be very careful to comply with standard procedures to have nurses in the examining room while they examine female patients.

There is no excuse for the use of force on a patient of any age. Courts recognize the fact that it is very difficult to plead truthfully in defense to a charge of beating or molesting a patient in any way that it was undertaken within the scope of "medical treatment." Therefore, of course, a patient does not have to present expert medical testimony to the effect that slapping, beating, or choking is a failure of due care. Thus, the physician is not protected by most of the procedural benefits which accrue to him in an ordinary negligence case.

Defamation of Character.   Defamation of character is a communication by one person about a second person to a third person in such terms as to diminish the reputation of the person about whom the discussion was held. Written or broadcast defamation is "libel," while oral defamation is "slander." Both are torts and grounds for award of civil damages. Suits against physicians for defamation of character are closely intertwined with those charging invasion of the patient's right of privacy or disclosure of confidential information. However, in some instances an action has been brought exclusively on a complaint of libel or slander.

A 13-year old girl developed a foot infection. She was taken to the family physician for treatment and he advised her parents that she should stay at home in bed and that they should ask the school for a home teacher. The form signed by the physician which was sent to the superintendent of schools incorrectly stated that the girl was pregnant. Her parents tried repeatedly to obtain the report or to have him correct it and he told them that he had checked his files and found nothing that would indicate that he had made such a report. He also said that if they would bring it to his office he would do what he could to correct any error if he had made one, but the school would not release the report. The parents called the physician several times to no avail and finally his office nurse told the parents to stop bothering him about it and that he would not call the school. The father brought a libel suit on behalf of his daughter. A jury awarded $7000.00 in damages and the award was affirmed on appeal. If the physician had made the error in good faith, which was undoubtedly true, but had moved to retract it immediately, he undoubtedly would have been exonerated. His persistent refusal to correct or retract the false report was sufficient to induce the jury to return substantial damages.[18]

A young man had seen a psychiatrist during a considerable period. He was engaged to be married and the girl's parents asked their family physician to find out anything he could about the boy. The physician asked the psychiatrist to write and give him "your impression" of the young man. The psychiatrist answered this request in writing and said that his diagnosis was manic depression and psychopathic personality. The psychiatrist also told the physician in the letter that the boy's father had committed suicide as well as giving other information about his relatives of an extremely distressing nature. The letter was given by the family physician to the girl's parents. They gave it to the girl. The couple was married over her parents' objections and she was disinherited. The patient sued the psychiatrist for libel. The court said that although ordinarily the truth is a defense to a charge of libel, a physician is not free to disclose all the information he knows about a patient just because it is true. The court recognized that in some cases the physician has a qualified duty to disclose information if there is a compelling reason to furnish it, but in this case the court held that the young man stated a cause of action against the psychiatrist.[19]

If a patient asks a physician to make partial disclosure of information to a third party, the physician may be obligated to report all the facts as long as he does it fairly.

A patient consulted a psychiatrist for alcoholism. On a number of occasions the patient requested and the psychiatrist supplied incomplete medical statements to explain his absence from work. While the patient suffered from various physical ailments, all of them were the result of his alcoholism and the psychiatrist entered the physical ailments only on the absence certificates. The Air Force, of which the patient was a civilian employee, sent the psychiatrist a letter requesting that he explain the "underlying cause" of the patient's illnesses. He told the patient this and then complied and informed the Air Force that the patient was an alcoholic. The patient lost his job and sued the psychiatrist. The court dismissed the action. It held that in view of the fact that the patient had initiated the request for the prior incomplete certificates, the physician had the right, if not the duty, to make full disclosure of the facts. Since the patient placed the doctor in the position of telling "part of the truth" he was precluded from preventing the psychiatrist from divulging the remainder.[20]

These cases actually involve more of an invasion of privacy than defamation because the facts are true and the physician–patient relationship extends for a period of time sufficient to allow the physician to know whereof he speaks. A hasty diagnosis of a patient which turns out to be wrong and which results in difficulties for the patient may very well constitute libel.

A government physician saw a patient only once, when he performed a preemployment examination for the Post Office. After the examination, he issued a report describing the patient as "having many of the outward appearances of a heavy user of alcoholic beverages." The patient did not drink. He sued the physician for defamation of character when the medical report was given as the reason why the man was not employed. The court held that the patient had a cause of action against either the government or the physician personally for slander.[21]

A surgeon for a railway company wrote to the president of the railroad and told him that an employee had refused to pay a bill for professional services. Since the action was barred by the statute of limitations at the time the surgeon sued the patient, the letter included a statement that the patient "having no other defense, cowardly slinks behind the defense of statutory limitation." The court held that the patient had a cause of action for libel against the surgeon.[22]

Most statements made in court or to attorneys representing patients involved in pending litigation of any kind, true, untrue, malicious, or not malicious, have absolute privilege if they are relevant to the case under consideration. Thus no action for defamation will lie.[23] However, in most cases involving civil litigation a physician does have an obligation not to aid the party in adverse interest to his patient.

A treating physician gave a report on his patient's condition as the result of an automobile accident to the physician employed by the adverse party in litigation arising out of the accident. The court held that he was liable for breach of confidentiality.[24]

The same rule of privilege applies to a publc official who makes a statement in the course of his duties.[25] Most of these cases involve official reports placed in a patient's hospital record and not divulged to outside parties.

Where a communication is made by one physician to another physician it is also usually held to be privileged.

A family physician referred a patient to a specialist for diagnosis. The specialist reported to the family physician that the plaintiff had a bad case of syphilis. This diagnosis was incorrect. The patient sued the specialist for libel. The court held that the information was privileged since it was the defendant's duty to communicate his diagnosis to the family physician. A cause of action for negligent diagnosis might be upheld, but not one for libel.[26]

A physician's office nurse was a defendant in a slander suit. A woman who worked as a caterer had a condition which raised false positive reports on Wasserman tests, but she did not and had never had syphilis and her physician knew it. At a social occasion which she catered the nurse told the hostess that the woman was being treated by her employer for syphilis. Naturally, this information destroyed her business. The court held that she had a good cause of action for slander against the nurse.[27]

Disclosure of Confidential Information.   It should be noted that libel and slander involve allegations of publication of untrue defamatory material about a plaintiff. Truth is a defense to the ordinary defamation suit. However, a physician, because of the fiduciary nature of his relationship with the patient, may be liable for disclosure of confidential information about a patient even if it is true.

Since the time of Hippocrates medical ethics, if not law, have obliged physicians to refrain from discussions of their patients' business.[28] Even if information related about a patient by a physician is true, the patient may still have a cause of action. Normally, discussing the patient's problem with a third party is unlawful disclosure, and breach of confidence is a well recognized cause of action against a physician.[29] Social conversation involving a patient is invariably sufficient to give rise to a successful suit against a physician. This is so intertwined with the practice of medicine that in most states, courts have held that disclosure of confidential information does constitute malpractice for purposes of determining coverage by the physician's malpractice insurance, although the terms of many policies exclude it and where this is true, those terms control. In some states, however, courts have held that tortious disclosure does not constitute malpractice for purposes of insurance coverage.[30]

Because of the extreme importance of the confidential relationship between a physician and his patient, there are statutes in some states which provide that a physician may lose his license for unjustified dissemination of confidential information. It is also a criminal offense in at least one state.[31]

Release of information about a patient as a matter of gossip is always unjustified, but the physician is protected if the disclosures which he made are required by law. For example, statutes which require reporting of cases of venereal disease, other contagious diseases, or child abuse make it incumbent on the physician to do so. In these cases he not only has the right to disclose the information to the proper authorities, he has the duty. Also, the physician may have the right to disclose information to a third party for the protection of that person or for the protection of his patient. In this case an action for wrongful disclosure will not succeed.

A physician diagnosed a patient's case as syphilis, but told him that he could not be sure without further tests. The patient lived in a hotel and the physician told him to move out until a definite diagnosis was made to prevent spreading of the disease. The next day the physician discovered that the patient was still in residence and telephoned the hotel proprietor and told him that he thought the patient had a "contagious disease." The proprietor forced the patient to move. The Wasserman test was negative. The patient sued the physician. The court held that under these circumstances the physician had a duty to disclose this information.[32]

In a recent case involving a very tragic set of circumstances, however, it was held by one court that the physician is under no legal obligation to make such disclosures.

A university student in voluntary psychotherapy at the student health center told the psychologist who was treating him that he was going to kill a girl, also a student, who had jilted him. The psychologist told two physicians what the boy had said. The three called the campus police who picked up the student. The head of the department of psychiatry ordered him released. The boy killed the girl 2 months later. Her parents sued the university and the psychiatrist for failing to warn her or them of the threat. The court held that no duty to give such a warning was imposed because no physician—patient relationship existed between any of the medical personnel involved and either the girl or her parents.[33]

A college physician in most states, however, would be held to have a special obligation to report his estimation of a student's condition either to the administration or to the student's parents. This is obviously justified in case of a disease which could spread to other students or in circumstances in which it is reasonable to believe that the student may harm himself or others. In either case most courts would hold that the physician would be remiss if he failed to notify the appropriate persons so that further treatment of the student could be undertaken and other students would be protected. Except in those two circumstances, however, a student has the same right of confidentiality when he sees a school physician as any other patient has with a physician.[34]

In any situation in which a patient is reasonably believed to have a communicable disease, the physician is not liable if he advises those who are in close contact with the patient. In fact, there have been several decisions in recent years holding that a physician has a duty to warn either the patient or his family if there is a possibility that those living in the house with the patient might contract the disease.[35]

A man was examined and treated for about 2 years before a diagnosis of tuberculosis was made. His 2-year old daughter contracted tuberculosis of the spine and both father and child required extensive treatment. The father sued the physician for the injuries sustained by the child. The court held that once the existence of the disease was known the physician had a duty to inform the patient of its nature and any precautionary steps to be taken to prevent other members of the patient's family from contracting it.[36]

A woman was employed as a clerk in a store. She became ill at work and consulted the store nurse, who diagnosed her problem as venereal disease and reported this to the woman's supervisor. The woman was fired. It was established without any question that the diagnosis was in error. The court held that the woman could not recover damages because the nurse had made a good faith mistake and that she had had a legal duty to report the diagnosis to the store.[37]

Of course, if the patient and not the physician spreads the news that a communicable disease exists, the physician is not liable under any circumstances.

A physician wrote a patient a letter telling her that she had a venereal disease. She showed the letter to two or three other women. When the physician came to her home to talk to her about it, a friend was visiting her. The patient discussed the diagnosis with the physician in the presence of her friend. She sued the physician for breach of confidentiality. No recovery was allowed.[38]

Reporting to one spouse information concerning the condition of the other is not usually considered a breach of confidence, even if the physician has reason to believe that the information will be used against his patient in a future action to dissolve the marriage. In one case the couple had separated, to the physician's knowledge, but was not divorced. The wife sued the physician for divulging information to the husband, but the court held that the husband had the right to know.[39] In another, the physician knew that information he gave her husband would be used against his patient in a pending divorce action, but the court held that the patient's rights had not been violated.[40]

Once a divorce has been granted, disclosure to a former spouse would be judged by principles involving disclosure to any third party except in extremely rare situations where the health and safety of children in the custody of the patient absolutely demanded it. Other communications would be considered a violation of the patient's rights. For example, if a gynecologist told a physician who was a close friend that the physician's former wife had come to him for contraceptive pills and had divulged that she was having an affair it is highly probable that the patient could recover substantial damages.

Medical reports written in good faith to agencies which have a legitimate interest in dealing with the patient do not violate confidentiality requirements.[41]

A university health center's psychiatrist saw a student and wrote a report on his emotional problems which was placed in the permanent university file. The report was such that if it had been transferred to a prospective employer, the student would undoubtedly not have been hired. The student sued the psychiatrist. The court held that no malice or intent to injure the student had been demonstrated and no recovery would be allowed.[42]

Whether or not a physician is justified in cooperating without the patient's consent with an insurance carrier investigating the patient's condition depends on the circumstances of the case. If an intentionally false report is filed with an insurance company, this will be held in all circumstances to give rise to a damage suit.[43] It is clear that a carrier may also be liable for inducing a breach of confidence from a physician if results adverse to the patient occur.[44]

A pediatrician did not tell the parents of a newborn baby that the child had a heart defect and the father proceeded to purchase a life insurance policy on the baby. When the baby died a few months later the pediatrician told the insurance investigator that the heart condition had existed from birth. The carrier refused to pay and the father sued the pediatrician. The court held that even though there was no concept of physician–patient privilege at common law, any patient has the right to object to any disclosure unless his interest or the public interest demands it. The court held that an insurance case constituted "public interest" and therefore the disclosure was not a violation of the father's rights.[45]

There are no reported decisions in which a physician has been sued for disclosing information given to him by a patient in confidence about another person, but in an appropriate case it is very clear that both the patient and the person involved would have a good cause of action. For example, in one situation a woman consulted a psychiatrist about her marital problems and told him that her husband was having an affair with another woman, whom she named. The psychiatrist reported this to the husband's employer who was, to the psychiatrist's knowledge, but not to the patient's, a relative of the "other woman" and a personal friend of the psychiatrist's, although the psychiatrist did not reveal the source of the information or indicate that it had come from a patient. The husband lost his job. Both the husband and the wife would undoubtedly have had a cause of action against the psychiatrist if they had chosen to sue. In these situations the hearsay information may or may not be true and, in any case, a patient has the right to assume that information he reveals about others as well as himself to any physician and especially to a psychiatrist will not be revealed even though the psychiatrist does not name the patient as the source of the information.

Thus, barring statutory obligation to disclose information in the case of communicable disease or in a situation in which the welfare of the patient or others demands it, a physician commits a tort when he discusses his patients' business with third parties. A patient has the absolute right to assume that information he has give his physician will not be transmitted without his knowledge.

Invasion of Privacy.   A patient has the right to privacy in the course of medical treatment. Most states have established such a right either by court decision or statute and the Supreme Court has recognized it as a constitutional right.[46] The existence of this right was first argued in an 1890 article in the *Harvard Law Review*[47] written by Louis D. Brandeis prior to his appointment to the Supreme Court and has been used for many years to protect persons from unwarranted commercial exploitation, such as unauthorized use of their photographs in advertisements. There are several decisions in which this right has been applied to the physician–patient relationship.

A physician went to a patient's home to deliver her baby. He took a friend who was not a physician with him and the friend was present throughout the delivery. The court held that the woman had had a legal right to privacy at the time her child was born and the physician was liable in damages for having violated it.[48]

It is quite clear that the admission of nonessential persons during treatment without the specific consent of the patient constitutes a violation of his right of privacy.

Allowing a layman to perform medical treatment may not only result in an action for negligence, but may involve an action for invasion of privacy.

A representative of a company which sold a cauterization machine was trying to persuade the physician to buy it. A patient came into the office with a growth on her uterus which required cauterization. In order to find out how well the machine worked, the physician allowed the salesman to perform the procedure. Disastrous effects occurred and the woman sued not only for negligence in allowing a layman to perform the procedure, but invasion of privacy. She collected damages.[49]

Publication of pictures or discussion of a patient without his consent if he is or can be identified by name or appearance may lead to a successful suit for invasion of privacy even if the pictures or information are published in a medical journal for legitimate scientific purposes.

Two surgeons performed plastic surgery on a patient's nose. They took two photographs before and two after the operation. The four photographs were published without the patient's knowledge or consent in a medical journal as part of an article bearing the title "The Saddlenose." The patient sued the two surgeons claiming that the use of the pictures were for advertising purposes prohibited by a statute forbidding invasion of privacy for financial gain. The court allowed recovery and said that it cannot be concluded that the article was written solely for scientific purposes. The decision pointed out that an article, even in a scientific publication, may be nothing more than someone's "advertisement in disguise," and allowed recovery.[50]

A patient may very well give consent to taking photographs to be used in medical journals.[51] However, if the scope of use of films to which the patient has consented is violated he may have a cause of action.

A patient agreed before undergoing a Cesarean to allow the surgeon to take a motion picture for use at a medical society meeting. The physician and the motion picture producer who made the film exhibited it publicly in two theaters in New York City as a motion picture entitled "Birth." The exhibition was clearly for the purposes of trade. The court held that she had a cause of action.[52]

Even if the patient consents to the use of photographs or information, the physician is obliged to protect his privacy as much as possible. For example, common consideration requires that if facial photographs are used in professional journals, the patient's eyes should be blacked out unless they are relevant to the disease about which the photograph is an illustration. In all cases reasonable effort must be taken to disguise the identity of the patient. The name, for example, should never be published. This may be particularly true where the patient is a prominent, newsworthy person whom the physician is treating. In most cases he should never issue news statements without the consent of the patient or his immediate family.

While there are a few persons, such as the President of the United States, whose medical conditions are a matter of genuine news value and about whose illnesses the public has a definite right to know, the physician should be most careful in giving statements about less obviously prominent persons to any news media. In cases where statements should be issued, as for example, about a President's illness, the press secretary presumably has the right to consent to the statements.

Hospitals may also be liable for invasion of privacy.

A newborn baby's heart was outside its body, and the family physician referred the child to the defendant hospital for surgery. The child died before the operation was performed. The hospital permitted a photographer to take pictures of the baby after he died. The pictures were sold to the newspapers. The hospital was liable for invasion of the parents' privacy.[53]

Although it may be permissible to use photographs or information about a patient's case for legitimate scientific purposes in medical journals, it is never permissible to publish information about a patient in the popular press, unless the patient has given his explicit consent in full understanding that that is where the information is to be published.

A patient sued a newspaper. She had consulted two surgeons who discovered that she had a hemostat in her abdomen left from a prior operation, which they removed. The gave the Xrays to a reporter. The reporter, in turn, gave the Xray to a newspaper which printed it. The reporter knew that the patient had not consented to have an article written about her case. She sued the newspaper and recovered damages.[54]

Publication of a story released by the physician in a daily newspaper about a patient's unique ailment which caused her to eat as much as 10 normal people and which included her name and picture was also held to be a violation of the patient's right to privacy.[55]

A psychoanalyst wrote a book which was in effect a case history of a patient and her family. The manuscript contained lengthy verbatim statements by the patient which had been taken from the psychiatrist's file. The book was intended for both lay and professional readers and was advertised in daily newspapers and sold in ordinary bookstores. The court held that even though the psychiatrist had made some effort to disguise the patient's identity, the patient had the right to an injunction to prevent further sale of the book to protect her rights to privacy and the confidentiality of the physician–patient relationship.[56]

Even where the patient consents to discussion in scientific journals, all efforts should be made to protect his identity and under no circumstances should the patient's condition be discussed even in a scientific journal without his knowledge and written consent.[57]

A producer made a film in an institution for the criminally insane. The filming was done originally with the consent of the officials of the institution and the purpose was to produce a film documenting the inadequate treatment the inmates received. No scenes were staged and the film merely recorded routine activities. After the film was made, it was released to the general public for an admission charge, although the stipulation to which the officials had consented indicated that it would be exhibited for educational purposes only. The attendants in the ward brought suit for invasion of privacy. The court held that the conduct of the employees, the plaintiffs in the action, toward the patients and the type of treatment administered to those patients were matters of legitimate public interest since a state hospital was involved. The constitutional guarantee of free speech and freedom of the press prevented the court from issuing an injunction against the producer unless the employees could show that the movie was a false report. They had admitted that the conditions as shown were actual. In some cases the patients were shown in complete nudity and the court held that while some or all of them might have had a right to sue for invasion of privacy, their custodians clearly did not.[58]

Another case involved an injunction action brought against movie producers for violation of patients' rights of privacy. In January 1966 a superintendent of an institution for the criminally insane granted a film-maker permission to make a movie subject to the condition that a valid release would be obtained from each patient in the film. The filming continued for 3 months, and the crew was given access to all departments except the treatment center for the sexually dangerous patients. The superintendent saw the motion picture when it was completed and objected to the showing of nude inmates. The state attorney general advised the producer that in his opinion the privacy of the inmates had been violated and that they were not competent to sign releases. The film was shown to the public for profit. The trial judge held that it was an unwarranted invasion of the inmates' privacy and degraded them. He enjoined showing the film to a commercial audience and the producer appealed. The appellate court held that the trial judge was justified in holding that most of the inmates were not competent to understand the releases which they signed and pointed out that the movie contained closeups, so some of the patients were identifiable. Therefore, the court banned further exhibition of the movie to the general public. However, since it did give a striking picture

of the problems of treating the emotionally disturbed, the court did not enjoin showing it to legislators, judges, attorneys, sociologists and social
workers.[59]

Duress.   Duress by legal definition is "unlawful constraint exercised upon
a person whereby he is forced to do some act which he otherwise would
not have done." It may consist of any means coercing or actually inducing
a person to perform an act contrary to his free will. While there are no
reported appellate decisions on the subject of duress between a physician
and a patient, there have been innumerable reports in the press recently of
patients who were forced by threats to submit to sterilizations which they
did not want.

It should be noted that duress will completely vitiate consent to any
procedure and thus, in addition to a civil action for duress as a separate
tort, the patient would presumably have a cause of action for assault and
battery and performance of the procedure without a genuine consent. If
the duress is applied to a patient by a physician who is employed by, affiliated with, or receives a payment from any agent or agency of the federal
or state government it is perfectly obvious that any duress perpetuated
upon the patient has violated his constitutional rights.

An 18-year old girl, one of 10 children whose mother was on welfare, was
allegedly told by a county social worker that if she refused to be sterilized
her mother would lose her welfare income. Although the state in question had
an involuntary sterilization statute for mental defectives resident in state institutions, no allegation was ever made that the girl in question was mentally
retarded or incompetent. She was never tested to determine her intelligence.
No court order was obtained. She submitted to the procedure. Upon reaching
legal age and after her mother's death, she, by that time employed as a
licensed practical nurse at a hospital in New York City, filed suit against the
social worker who had required her to be sterilized, the county welfare department, the physician who performed the sterilization, and the hospital in
which the operation was performed. Although at this time her suit has not
come to trial, if she can prove her allegations she will undoubtedly have a
good cause of action for treatment without consent, for duress against the
social worker and the county, and for violation of her constitutional rights. In
a situation of this nature if the physician can show that he did not know that
such duress had been applied, presumably he would not be liable.[60]

It is absolutely obvious as a matter of law without any reported decisions that duress applied to a patient constitutes an actionable tort. Where

treatment is medically indicated a physician is never justified in telling a patient that it will not be given or that he will be committed to a mental institution or in using any other threats or pressures to compel him to submit to unrelated medical treatment.

An obstetrician was the only physician in an isolated, rural county who would give prenatal care to Medicaid patients. State Medicaid regulations prohibited patients from consulting out-of-state physicians and the nearest physicians other than the obstetrician practiced across the state line. He told women who were Medicaid patients pregnant with their third babies that he would not deliver them unless they consented to sterilization at the time of delivery because he disapproved of welfare mothers. At least 16 women signed consents in less than 1 year and the procedures were performed. One woman, however, refused and went to the local newspaper.[61]

Where medical treatment is given, as the physician in the above case admitted in the press, because he "disapproved as a matter of social policy of welfare mothers having more children" and where there is no medical justification for it, it is perfectly obvious that suits would undoubtedly be successful. The statement of the American Medical Association's Committee on Ethics in this case was as follows:

> The American Medical Association's stated policy is that a physician may choose whom he will serve but that he should respond to any request in an emergency or whenever temperate public opinion expects such service. It would seem that a physician could not properly impose some personal social philosophy on a patient if, by doing so, he prevented his patient from getting needed medical care. The woman has to be delivered. She does not have to be sterilized. If the doctor precludes her from being delivered by imposing sterilization as a condition, this action would seem to be contrary to the accepted practice of the medical profession.[62]

Fraud. The legal definition of fraud is an "intentional perversion of truth for the purpose of inducing another, in reliance upon it, to part with some valuable thing belonging to him or to surrender a legal right; a false representation of a matter of fact, whether by words or by conduct, by false or misleading allegations, or by concealment of that which should have been revealed which deceives and is intended to deceive another so that he shall act upon it to his legal injury." Where the ordinary relationship of buyer and seller exist, a seller generally has no particular duty to make unfavorable statements about the merchandise to the buyer. However, in any fiduciary relationship such as that between a physician and a patient, or an attorney and a client, silence under circumstances in which the patient or client obviously believes "X" to be the case when "Y" is actually true and the physician or the attorney is aware of that impression, obliges the physician or attorney to make full disclosure of the truth to the person relying on him.

There are several decisions in which physicians have been sued by patients for fraud.[63] Assuring a patient that no risk is involved when he knows that proposed treatment carries a potential of serious harm may make the physician liable for fraud, as well as for any problems arising from the foreseeable consequence of the therapy.[64]

Most cases involving fraud allege misrepresentations to a patient that a certain operation or medical treatment had been given as planned. If a physician knows, for example, that he has left a foreign object in the patient's body, but remains silent or tells the patient that "everything is fine," he will probably be liable for fraud.[65] If he misrepresents the nature of the procedure which has been performed to the patient, he is equally subject to a fraud action.[66]

Fraud also occurs when a physician knows that surgery or other medical treatment would have no reasonable medical justification, but tells the patient that it is necessary for the surgeon's economic advantage.[67] In order to prove fraud, as opposed to an honest mistake in diagnosis which leads to a recommendation of surgery which is later proved to be unnecessary, the patient must prove that the physician or surgeon knew at the time he advised him of the treatment that it was unnecessary. This is, of course, extremely difficult and, therefore, there are very few cases on the subject.

A pregnant woman who had had several miscarriages and no living children was told by her physician that she had appendicitis. She refused to consent to an appendectomy because she was very concerned that she would have another miscarriage. She told the physician that under no circumstances would she do anything which might cause her to lose her baby and he assured her that the appendectomy could not possibly result in a miscarriage. She therefore consented to surgery. Several days later she did have a miscarriage and by that time it was also evident that she had not had appendicitis. As the result of the miscarriage, she became mentally ill and was hospitalized for a considerable period of time. She then sued the physician for fraud, on both counts for having told her that she had had appendicitis and that it would not disturb her pregnancy to have her appendix removed. The court found that the diagnosis had been made in good faith and thus dismissed the fraud count as to that allegation. However, in the face of testimony from several expert witnesses for the patient that the risk of harm to an unborn child was very great, the court did find that she did have a good claim against the physician on the second allegation.[68]

A woman had severe stomach pains. She was examined by a surgeon and claimed that he told her and her husband, who corroborated her testimony, that her spleen was "hanging by a thread." Both of them also testified that he told her that her spleen was hanging from her collar bone. She consented to surgery which he explained to her and to her husband was "designed to build up ligaments" in her spleen. After the operation he told the husband that it had been necessary to remove the spleen. The pathology report indicated that there was no evidence of any disease at all and that her spleen had been perfectly healthy. The woman and her husband brought an action for fraud. The jury returned a verdict in their favor. The surgeon appealed the jury verdict on the grounds that the patient had presented no expert testimony in support of her claims. However, the court dismissed his appeal. It held that obviously neither the woman nor her husband had ever consented in any way to the removal of the spleen and that a lay jury was competent without expert testimony to determine the factual issue of consent and what statements had been made to induce that consent. Either the surgeon had made the statements to which she testified about the nature of her illness and the procedure he intended to perform to alleviate it or he did not, as he claimed. Since the jury believed her the court did not disturb the verdict.[69]

If a postoperative patient reports pain or difficulty and the physician, knowing that the patient's condition will not improve, assures him that all will be well, where the physician knows he had given negligent treatment, he will be liable for fraud.[70]

A patient who happened to be a lawyer had a cataract operation. He was virtually blind in the eye on which surgery had been performed. The ophthalmologist kept assuring him that the eye was normal, "everything was fine," and his vision would improve. After considerable time the patient went to New York City and consulted another ophthalmologist who told him that half the iris in his eye had been removed. He sued the surgeon for both negligence in performing the surgery and the deceit. The court upheld both claims. As to the charge of deceit the court found that the physician had not merely maintained silence about his mistake, but he also made positive assertions which he knew to be untrue when he made them.[71]

In December 1961, a patient consulted a physician about a lump in her breast. He arranged for another physician to perform surgery and a radical mastectomy was performed. The surgeon recommended radiation therapy and the original physician referred the patient to a radiologist who administered treatments. The woman received severe burns and was in intense and constant pain. She was hospitalized 15 times under the care of the original physician and his two associates. Several years later, she brought suit. She charged the radiologist and the original physician with giving intentionally false reassurances and wilfully concealing the fact that the radiologist had been negligent. The physicians denied having intentionally misinformed the patient. At the time of the burns the original physician had been asked by the woman's husband if malpractice on the part of the radiologist could have occurred and the physician told him emphatically that it had not, and that the woman's reaction to the Xrays was due entirely to hypersensitivity on her part and had occurred without negligence on the radiologist's part. While in the hospital for surgery on the area of her burns, the woman overheard a physician discussing her case with some medical students. The physician commented that this was "the sort of thing which happened when the radiologist puts a patient on the table and goes out and has a cup of coffee." At that point the woman began to have serious doubts about the care which she had been receiving and consulted another physician. The appellate court held that the trial judge had made an error when he dismissed the action against the physicians. The patient should have had an opportunity for a jury determination of both the alleged negligence by the radiologist and the alleged fraud and conspiracy among all physicians involved. The court said that a physician has the duty to disclose to his patient the facts of the case and silence is sufficient to constitute fraud.[72]

It should be noted that any physician who is tempted to keep his patient from finding out that a mistake has been made is very ill-advised to conceal the facts. If he admits to the patient that malpractice has occurred and makes an effort to alleviate the condition himself or sends the patient to someone else for treatment, at worst he is guilty of ordinary negligence. If, however, he conceals the situation, the probability of eventual discovery by the patient is fairly high and at that point the physician will be liable not only for the original negligence, but for fraud as well.

Misrepresentations of the physical, mental, or social condition of a child who is being placed for adoption may also constitute fraud.[73] In most states, however, while the couple may recover damages they cannot annul the adoption.[74]

A couple applied to a county welfare department for a child, and a girl apparently about 6-years old was placed with them. They were assured that she was healthy, intellectually normal, and of an acceptable family background. In fact, the agency's records indicated that the child had been diagnosed as retarded, the father was in the penitentiary for incest with his oldest daughter, and the mother's sexual history was bizarre in the extreme. All the child's older siblings were retarded and several were in institutions for delinquents. The court awarded damages for fraud and, in a most unusual decree, annulled the adoption.[75]

Inducing a patient to enter into treatment by misrepresentation of fact by any party in a position of authority over him is fraud and if the physician knows that fraud has been committed by another, but goes ahead and treats the patient, he, too, will be liable.

An illiterate mother whose young daughters aged 12 and 14 were receiving contraceptive shots at the local OEO-Sponsored Family Planning Clinic was given "a paper to sign." She made her X on the paper. The girls were taken to the hospital and sterilized. The father of the children who was literate and far more intelligent than the mother was not contacted by the clinic personnel and his consent to the surgery was not obtained. After he discovered that his children had been sterilized he contacted a lawyer who contacted the press and the matter received wide publicity. The mother swore in preliminary legal proceedings that the nurse for the clinic had told her that she needed her signature on the document in order to give the girls some immunizations and that the immunizations were all the mother thought were involved. Suit was filed on behalf of the girls by their father against the nurse from the clinic, the physician who performed the sterilizations, the Department of Health, Education and Welfare as sponsor of the Family Planning Clinic, and the hospital in which the sterilizations were performed. While the suit was withdrawn with leave to refile later and has not at this date been tried, at least as to the nurse, if the fact that she misrepresented the nature of the treatment which the girls were to receive is proven, damages for fraud will clearly lie against her and her employers.[76] The immediate result of the publicity from this incident was an announcement by the Department of Health, Education and Welfare that all federally funded sterilizations of either minors, with or without parental consent, or mentally incompetent persons, would be halted until further investigations could be made.[77]

Thus, any medical practitioner has an absolute obligation to tell a patient the truth and not misrepresent the patient's condition either before or after the procedure or misrepresent in any way what is to be done to the patient. Furthermore, in the relationship between a physician and a patient or a nurse and a patient, silence alone may be sufficient to constitute actionable fraud.

Undue Influence.   Undue influence is defined as "any improper or wrongful constraint or machination whereby the will of any person is overpowered and he is induced to do or forebear to do an act which he would not do or would do if left to act freely. It is influence which deprives the person influenced of a free agency or the freedom of his will. It may consist of a use by one in which a confidence is posed of a confidence or authority for the purposes of obtaining an unfair advantage over him."

While cases alleging undue influence do not normally involve patients' medical conditions, if a patient makes a will during a terminal illness for which a physician is treating him which leaves to the physician a large amount of money, or if the patient at any time sells the physician valuable goods or property at far less than they would have been worth to any other purchaser, the law presumes that the physician has taken advantage of his relationship with the patient in order to induce the patient to favor him with the legacy or sale.

If these situations do occur, the physician and not the patient or his heirs has the burden of proof that undue influence was not present, particularly if the patient is senile or his mental competency during his illness is subject to some question, even though he may be mentally normal when he is well.[78]

A patient was 76-years old and had been treated by the physician for a number of years. He was an alcoholic of long standing, was infirm of mind and body, and had numerous chronic illnesses, although he was not legally declared to be mentally incompetent. The patient owned very valuable real estate, but had financial problems, one of which was a large federal income tax lien. He had authorized his son-in-law to negotiate with a developer for the sale of the land to obtain funds with which to settle the tax lien. The developer had offered $1000.00 an acre, but the son-in-law had refused that offer because he thought the land more valuable. The son-in-law and the developer were renegotiating the contract. The patient signed a contract at the physician's office after a week in which he had been in great pain and had been treated by the physician at least once a day. The physician, under the contract, had the right to buy twenty acres of this choice tract for

$361.00 an acre. The consideration under the contract was $4000.00 and a new Cadillac. On the date of the contract when the physician had the right to buy the land for $361.00 an acre, the land had a market value of $1200.00 an acre. Shortly after the contract was signed the son-in-law, who knew nothing about it, sold the developer 66 acres of the 125-acre tract at $1500.00 an acre. The physician then brought a suit to enforce the contract with the patient and gain possession of 20 acres, which were also covered by the contract with the developer. The court refused to allow the physician to do it. It said that the gross inadequacy of the purchase price of the land and the confidential physician—patient relationship between the two resulting from the patient's infirmities gave rise to a presumption that the physician had taken advantage of his patient. The physician had the burden of overcoming that presumption by affirmative proof of the fairness of the transaction and he was also required to prove that the patient fully understood the contract's terms and that the patient's agreement to the contract was a deliberate exercise of his own judgment uninfluenced in any way by the physician. The court found that there was no evidence suggesting a reason other than undue influence for the patient's agreement to a bargain so disadvantageous to him, not only because of the low purchase price, but also because it interfered with the son-in-law's negotiation for sale of the entire tract. The physician further had not transferred the Cadillac to the patient, but the court found that including the new car as a part of the price was calculated to cloud the patient's judgment and was an unfair inducement. The contract was avoided.[79]

If a physician wishes to do business with a patient who is young, healthy, and unquestionably of sound mind concerning property which the patient owns, it is highly unlikely that a valid attack on the sale could be made on the grounds that the physician exercised undue influence. However, if the patient's intelligence or mental competency is in the least questionable and if under any circumstances the price for which the patient is willing to sell the property to him is substantially less than the market value, under no circumstances should the physician proceed to consummate the purchase without informing his attorney that the seller is in fact one of his patients. This is particularly true in all circumstances regardless of the patient's age where there is a close and continuing relationship between the patient and physician as in a situation, for example, in which a psychiatrist wished to buy property from a patient.

In all these cases it should be pointed out that the physician has the burden of proving in any challenge to the transaction by either the patient or his family that undue influence was not applied.[80] If the patient is elderly or there is even a remote possibility of senility the physician under no circumstances should do business without advice of counsel. Under any such circumstances he should inform the patient's family of the proposed transaction and allow them to object. If they do he should have no further part of the transaction.

If a patient leaves money to his physician in a will which is intended to compensate the physician for services which were rendered, but for which there was no payment prior to the patient's death, that provision in the will would probably be enforceable and the physician would probably be allowed to accept the inheritance.[81] On the other hand, a legacy far in excess of the value of any services rendered by the physician would undoubtedly be met with suspicion by the probate court and the patient's family.[82] If a physician knows that a patient whose mental competency is questionable is preparing to draw a will in which he will be left a legacy, he should contact his attorney immediately for advice on this situation. Although the physician may not know that the patient intends to leave him a legacy until after the patient has died and the will is probated, he should be prepared for severe criticism by the heirs in the case where there is a substantial amount of money involved and he wishes to accept it. Again, the burden of proof is on him to show that the bequest was in fact voluntary and he did not induce it. This is very hard to do when the will is made during the illness for which the physician is treating the patient and when the patient dies while in the care of the physician, and in some states, by statute, a physician who attends a patient during his last illness cannot take property under a will signed during that illness.[83]

Under no circumstances is a physician entitled to witness a will in which he is a beneficiary. If any beneficiary under a will is a witness, the validity of the will is destroyed and in most states would mean that the patient dies intestate.

This is a most delicate situation and a physician may well not realize that an elderly patient is so grateful for his services that he intends to leave him a rather large bequest. Where it occurs, the physician should immediately obtain advice of the counsel to avoid even the accusation of undue influence.

If a physician uses his relationship with a patient to induce her to have sexual intercourse with him or to give him money during the social relationship, he is also liable for malpractice and for undue influence.[84] A sexual relationship with at married patient may also induce an action for alienation of affection and undue influence by the patient's spouse.[85]

False Imprisonment. While the subject of false imprisonment, which usually involves patients involuntarily committed to mental hospitals, as opposed to medical or surgical patients, has been discussed in the chapter on negligence in treatment, and although it generally occurs along with a good faith misdiagnosis of the patient's condition, in some situations it is perfectly obviously intentional and in these cases damages are invariably extremely high.

Where a commitment to a mental institution can be proved to be the result of malice and personal spite on the part of the physician, an action for false imprisonment and abuse of process is generally the legal recourse of the patient, not an action for malpractice.

Two physicians set up a corporation which operated a hospital. They were the principal stockholders. After several years of operation, disputes arose between them and at a meeting of stockholders each physician sought to oust the other from the Board of Directors. Later that day the medical staff at the hospital withdrew one of the physician's staff privileges. Ten days later he obtained a court order restraining those connected with the hospital from interfering with his access to patients. Later the same day, the hospital executive secretary and the other physician filed a sworn lunacy complaint against him. He was arrested, given a mental examination, and released after 3 hours. There was no substantial evidence at any time that the physician was mentally ill. There was no testimony by the physician who had signed the arrest warrant that he actually believed that the other physician was mentally ill. The evidence showed that he was angry with the second physician and wanted him out of the hospital, that no one else had ever considered this physician to be of unsound mind, and that the lunacy complaint had been filed the same day that the second physician obtained the restraining order. The great weight of the evidence indicated that the first physician had had a spiteful motive in filing the lunacy complaint. He was liable for false imprisonment.[86]

A woman who was married to a physician's brother filed suit for divorce. Two days later the physician signed a certificate saying that she was psychotic and in need of psychiatric treatment and on the basis of his statements in the certificate the court committed her to a mental hospital. She was released 24 hours later on a writ of habeas corpus. She claimed that she was sane and competent at all times and the physician wilfully and maliciously signed a certificate which he knew to be false at the time he signed it, and that he did so in conspiracy with his brother to hinder the divorce proceedings. She sued the physician for $150,000.00. The court held that she stated a cause of action and submitted the case for a hearing by a jury.[87]

Although most actions for false imprisonment involve psychiatric patients, in some cases medical or surgical patients who are refused permission to leave a hospital or are physically restrained from doing so are complainants.

A patient who had been in an automobile accident was admitted to a hospital for treatment of a fracture of his right clavicle. A staff physician ordered that the patient remain flat on his back with his arm immobilized by a sling. Four days after admission to the hospital, he kicked a nurse's aide when she brought his lunch tray. The aide then threw something at him. The patient denied kicking the aide and said she threw a pot of tea at him first. That evening his daughter visited him and another altercation occurred. His version and the physician's version of what occurred at that time were conflicting. The patient claimed that the physician told his daughter that she would have to get him out of the hospital in 5 minutes and find another physician to take over the case. The patient also testified that his daughter told him that the physician was going to send him to a psychiatric hospital because he had kicked the nurse's aide. While the daughter was trying to contact another physician, the patient partially dressed and started downstairs to leave the hospital. The patient claimed that the physician held him by the shoulder and told him that he had called the police. The policeman who arrived on the scene testified that the physician asked him to take the patient to the psychiatric ward of the county hospital, but that he refused to do so because the patient appeared to be quite reasonable. Another physician, whom the daughter had contacted, called and spoke to both the patient and the staff physician. The second physician obtained a bed at a private mental sanitarium for the patient and he went there. The patient was released from the sanitarium a few days later. The patient charged the first physician with assault and false imprisonment for preventing him from leaving the hospital. The physician contended that medical discretion was an absolute defense to the charge of restraining the patient's liberty and in view of the nature of his serious injuries, he was obliged to do so. The court upheld the physician.[88]

Failure to make a reasonable examination may subject a psychiatrist to damages for false imprisonment. While a psychiatrist who makes an honest error of judgment in committing patients may be liable for negligence, he is usually not liable for false imprisonment unless such gross negligence or maliciousness and failure to comply with statutory procedures is shown so that the "examination" is actually nonexistent.

A woman told her husband that she intended to file for divorce. Several days later a psychiatrist appeared at their home. There was confusion as to whether or not he told her he was a psychiatrist and he admitted that he did not tell her that he was there to examine her. Several days later, the psychiatrist and another physician who had never seen her, at the request of her husband and without the authorization or knowledge of the woman, signed a statement that they had examined her and found her to be mentally ill. She was forcibly taken by ambulance to a mental hospital owned by the psychiatrist. She was prevented from using the telephone or writing letters. She was placed in a security room, bare except for a bed, for 6 days and she refused to eat for 5 of those days and refused medication at all times. She could not receive or place telephone calls, receive visitors, or write letters. She was particularly prevented from using the telephone to call her brother. Her young children were allowed to visit her, but when she told one to call her brother, the child's uncle, the psychiatrist told her that if "she ever tried that again" she would never see her children. The psychiatrist also refused her permission to call her attorney. At one time she was held by three nurses and attendants and given an injection. She eventually found an unlocked telephone and called her brother and by the next day she had been released by court order. The jury returned a verdict against the psychiatrist of $40,000.00 and the appellate court upheld it on appeal. The court held that there was no question that she was mentally competent and therefore her original commitment stated a cause of action for false arrest. Furthermore, denial of her rights to communicate with her relatives or her attorney after her admission further constituted a continuing tort of false imprisonment.[89]

Generally speaking simple medical negligence in diagnosis with the result that a patient is involuntarily hospitalized does not support an action for false imprisonment.[90] However, if a psychiatrist or other physician certifies that he has examined a patient for commitment when he has not, a civil action for false imprisonment will lie and criminal penalties may also result.[91] With an increasing frequency, however, decisions do seem reflect a determination to ground an action for erroneous commitment in false imprisonment, not in negligence, thus eliminating the necessity of expert testimony on behalf of the patient. In all cases where a patient can show a malicious conspiracy between the physician and other persons, usually the patient's relatives, a cause of action on this ground does exist.[92] However, even without proof of malice, violation of statutory provisions providing for proper commitment of mental patients may also be enough to make a case of false imprisonment.

A patient's husband, clearly, it was later proved, in bad faith, told a psychiatrist that she was in need of commitment. When the patient talked to the defendant he gave her a "knock-out" injection and she work up in his mental hospital. She was given electroshock treatments over her objection. At the trial expert testimony was introduced to the effect that she had never been mentally ill. While the court held that the physician was not responsible for investigating her husband's motive, involuntary hospitalization without any regard whatever to required legal procedures was sufficient to constitute false imprisonment.[93]

A student came to the President of his university and made wild accusations. He was referred to the Dean of Men, who saw him in the presence of the student health service physician. The men concluded that the boy was hallucinating and tricked him into being taken to the hospital by the campus police. They told him that they were taking him to report his views to law enforcement authorities. No judicial commitment was ever attempted. The court held that a cause of action for false imprisonment existed against the physician.[94]

Damages for false imprisonment can be very considerable. In one case a plaintiff collected $300,000.00 in damages from the State of New York. Because proper records were not kept on him, he was incarcerated in a mental hospital for 14 years, 3 months, and 20 days longer than he should have been. He also proved his allegations of medical and psychiatric neglect and physical brutality by hospital personnel, all of which had been attributed to "paranoia." No one had ever investigated his claims that he should be released and his statements were dismissed as a "persecution complex."[95]

In all the decisions in which damages were awarded for false imprisonment, the physicians involved made absolutely no effort to comply with statutory requirements for commitment of the patient. Had they done so, thus indicating that they acted in good faith, all decisions indicate that they may have been found liable for negligence for improper commitment, but certainly not for false imprisonment.[96] In order to recover damages for false imprisonment, it is not enough for a patient to show that he was not mentally ill at the time of the commitment and that the physician's diagnosis was incorrect. He is also obliged to show both the lack of good faith and probable cause for believing that malice was present.[97] Failure to comply with statutory commitment procedures is generally construed as sufficient evidence to be indicative of wrongful commitment far exceeding the bounds of simple negligence. Under no circumstances, not even in an emergency, should a physician have anything to do with commitment of a patient in violation of statutory provisions. The physician is held to know the statutory provisions in his state regarding the involuntary hospitalization of mental patients. If he does not know them, he is certainly obliged to contact his attorney and find out what they are before he signs commitment orders on any patient. No court would uphold as a "good faith error of judgment" a written statement by a physician that he has examined a patient and found him to be in need of care and attention in a mental hospital when he has not seen the patient. Mere violation of a statutory provision in that regard is enough to guarantee a successful action for false imprisonment and an award of very substantial damages in the patient's favor. Even if statutory requirements are met, thus eliminating grounds for a suit for false imprisonment, an unjustified commitment may be sufficient to sustain a claim for damages for abuse of process.

A 16-year old girl, a freshman at a university, became very dissatisfied with college life. On a visit home, she complained to her parents and they convinced her that she should go back to school and try again, but told her that she had their permission to leave if she still was not happy. A few days after she returned to school, she decided to leave. She withdrew her money from the bank and a representative of the bank notified the Dean of Women that the student said she was leaving. Various school officials tried to persuade her to stay, but she insisted that she was going to leave and gave a number of reasons why she disliked the school. She did not, however, tell them that she had her father's permission, because none of the officials who spoke to her asked her if she had discussed it with her parents. The Dean of Women finally called the physician in charge of the school infirmary. He and a nurse talked to the girl for about 2 hours and when they were unable to contact the student's father, the physician in the infirmary suggested to the Dean that the student be put in a mental hospital. The police were called and brought temporary emergency commitment papers. The application for temporary commitment was filled out by the physician and signed by him, the Dean of Women, and an infirmary nurse. They stated in the application that the student was believed to be mentally ill for the reason that she wanted to leave the university and go home. The application indicated that they believed that the student was irresponsible and should be confined. It requested immediate detention not exceeding 5 days and also requested a judicial inquiry to determine her mental condition. She was taken by the police to the hospital where she was confined in a locked ward. Her clothes were removed and she was given a bath. She was given a uniform housecoat to wear and locked in a room with several other female patients, some of whom were engaged in sexual conduct which she found shocking. The student persuaded a social worker at the hospital to call an adult friend of her family and tell him where she was. The friend was permitted to talk to her only after she told the nurse that she was engaged to him. He notified her father, who contacted the physician and insisted that his daughter be released immediately. By this time, which was late at night, the physician told her father that he could not have her released, but he did have her transferred to a private room, where she was also locked in. She was released early the next morning, was taken by her parents to the dormitory, removed her belongings, and went home. The student and her parents brought action against the university to recover damages for false imprisonment. They received $35,000.00 in damages from the university, damages of $2000.00 from the physician and $5000.00 from the Dean of Women, but the court reduced the damages to $12,000.00 from the university and $1000.00 from the Dean of Women. The state supreme court found that there was no cause of action against the university under any theory of false imprisonment, which it defined as unlawful restraint. Since she had been hospitalized in compliance with legal procedures there was no unlawful restraint of her freedom even though it was entirely medically unjustified. However, the court found that her complaint supported a cause of action for "abuse of process," which by definition is the use of a legal process against another to accomplish a purpose for which it is not designed. The court held that the physician's use in this case of the statute providing for temporary detention of a mentally ill person was a perversion of the purpose of the statute and thus constituted abuse of process.[98]

The torts discussed in this chapter are all unrelated to good faith medical errors, the type of negligence which has otherwise been discussed throughout this book. All of these torts are deliberate, willful violations of patients' legal rights. It is, for example, impossible for a psychiatrist to beat a patient by mistake or because he is not paying attention to what he is doing. A beating is a deliberate act. Libel is a deliberate act. Signing a commitment on a patient one has never seen is a deliberate act. An illicit sexual relationship with a patient is a deliberate act. In all these cases, it goes without saying that these situations can be avoided by the use of common sense, and no expert knowledge of law is required to understand that basic human ethics and common decency to patients require better treatment than that used in some of the cases discussed in this chapter. Honest mistakes in diagnosis or treatment are one thing, the actions discussed in this chapter are quite another. They are usually not covered by malpractice insurance for that reason. A malpractice carrier insures a physician for a mistake, not a premeditated and deliberate wrongful act, because the physician in many cases may not be able to prevent an untoward result of medical treatment and insures against that eventuality. He can, of course, prevent any of the deliberate torts discussed in this chapter.

NOTES

1. "Surgical Assault and Battery," 198 *JAMA* No. 11, page 299, Dec. 12, 1966.
2. Martinez v. Texas State Board of Medical Examiners, 476 SW 2d 400, Tex 1972.
3. Caldwell v. Knight, 89 SE 2d 900, Ga 1955.
4. Winters v. Miller, 446 F 2d 65, CCA 2, 1971.
5. Hammer v. Rosen, 165 NE 2d 756, NY 1960; Morgan v. New York, 319 NYS 2d 151, NY 1970.
6. Burton v. Leftwich, 123 So 2d 766, La 1960.
7. Bellandi v. Park Sanitarium Association, 6 P 2d 508, Cal 1931.
8. Mattocks v. Bell, 194 A 2d 307, DC DC 1963.
9. St. Pierre v. New York, 48 NYS 2d 613, NY 1944; Temple v. New York, 65 NYS 2d 50, NY 1946; Galesburg Sanitarium v. Jacobson, 193 Ill App 26, 1902; Previn v. Tenacre, 70 F 2d 389, CCA 3, 1933; "Therapeutic Restraint," 197 *JAMA* No. 1, page 205, July 4, 1966.
10. Davis v. New York, 332 NYS 2d 569, NY 1972.
11. Cotter v. United States, 279 F Supp 847, DC NY 1968.
12. People v. McCaughan, 317 P 2d 974, Cal 1957.
13. Avery v. Maryland, 292 A 2d 728, Mary 1972.
14. State v. Atkins, 292 SW 422, Mo 1926; Commonwealth v. Goldenberg, 155 NE 2d 187, Mass 1959.
15. State v. Lung, 28 Pac 235, Nev 1891.
16. State v. Still, 202 NW 479, SD 1925.
17. Zipkin v. Freeman, 436 SW 2d 753, Mo 1968.
18. Vigil v. Rice, 397 P 2d 719, NM 1964.
19. Berry v. Moench, 331 P 2d 814, Utah 1958.
20. Clark v. Geraci, 208 NYS 2d 564, NY 1960.
21. Smith v. DiCara, 329 F Supp 439, DC NY 1971.
22. Hollenbeck v. Ristine, 86 NW 377, Iowa 1901.
23. Mickens v. Davis, 294 Pac 896, Kans 1931; Hager v. Major, 186 SW 2d 564, Mo 1945.
24. Alexander v. Knight, 177 A 2d 142, Pa 1962.
25. Glenn v. Kerlin, 248 So 2d 834, La 1971; Taylor v. Glotfelty, 201 F 2d 51, CCA 6, 1952; Schwartz v. Thiele, 51 Cal Rptr 767, Cal 1966.
26. Thornburg v. Long, 101 SE 99, NC 1919.
27. Schessler v. Keck, 271 P 2d 588, Cal 1954.
28. "Disclosure of Confidential Information," 216 *JAMA* No. 2, page 385, April 12, 1971; "Liability Insurance for Slander and Libel," 206 *JAMA* No. 13, page 2985, Dec. 23, 1968.
29. Boyd v. Wynn, 150 SW 2d 648, Ky 1941; New York v. Leyra, 98 NE 2d 553, *rev'd* 347 U.S. 556, 1951; "Keeping the Patients' Secrets," 195 *JAMA* No. 5, page 227, Jan. 31, 1966; "Physician's Liability for Improper Disclosure," 198 *JAMA* No. 7, page 331, Nov. 14, 1966.

30. Hammer v. Polsky, 233 NYS 2d 110, NY 1962.
31. Michigan Stats Ann., Section 14.533.
32. Simonsen v. Swenson, 177 NW 831, Neb 1920.
33. Tarasoff v. Regents of the University of California, 108 Cal Rptr 878, Cal 1973.
34. Maniaci v. Marquette University, 184 NW 2d 168, Wisc 1971.
35. Golia v. Greater New York Health Insurance Plan, 166 NYS 2d 889, NY 1957.
36. Hofmann v. Blackmon, 241 So 2d 752, Fla 1970.
37. Cochran v. Sears Roebuck & Co., 34 SE 2d 296, Ga 1945.
38. Shoemaker v. Friedberg, 183 P 2d 318, Cal 1947.
39. Pennison v. Provident Life Insurance Co., 154 So 2d 617, La 1963.
40. Curry v. Corn, 277 NYS 2d 470, NY 1966.
41. Iverson v. Frandsen, 237 F 2d 898, CCA 10, 1956.
42. Morris v. Rousos, 397 SW 2d 504, Tex 1965.
43. Felis v. Greenberg, 273 NYS 2d 288, NY 1966.
44. Hammonds v. Aetna Casualty & Surety Co., 237 F Supp 96, DC Ohio 1965; Panko v. Consolidated Mutual Insurance Co., 423 F 2d 41, CCA 3, 1970.
45. Hague v. Williams, 181 A 2d 345, NJ 1962.
46. Griswold v. Connecticut, 381 US 479, 1965.
47. *Harvard Law Rev.* 4 (1890): 193.
48. DeMay v. Roberts, 9 NW 146, Mich 1881.
49. Carr v. Shifflette, 82 F 2d 874, CA DC 1936.
50. Griffin v. Medical Society of the State of New York, 11 NYS 2d 109, NY 1939.
51. "Legal Implications of Photographing Surgical Operations," 198 *JAMA* No. 13, page 221, Dec. 26, 1966.
52. Feeney v. Young, 181 NYS 481, NY 1920.
53. Bazemore v. Savannah Hospital, 155 SE 194, Ga 1930.
54. Banks v. King Features Syndicate, Inc., 30 F Supp 352, DC NY 1939.
55. Barber v. Time, Inc., 159 SW 2d 291, Mo 1942.
56. Doe v. Roe, 345 NYS 2d 560, NY 1973.
57. Bachrach v. Farbenfabriken Bayer AG, 344 NYS 2d 286, NY 1973.
58. Cullen v. Grove Press, Inc., 276 F Supp 727, DC NY 1967.
59. Commonwealth of Massachusetts v. Wiseman, 249 NE 2d 610, Mass 1969.
60. *New York Times*, July 13, 1973, page 43, Col. 4.
61. *New York Times*, July 22, 1973, page 30, Col. 4; August 1, 1973, page 27, Col. 1.
62. *The Charlotte Observer*, July 17, 1973, page 4A.
63. "Fraud and Duress," (in press).
64. Woods v. Brumlop, 377 P 2d 520, NM 1962; Bowers v. Talmage, 159 So 2d 888, Fla 1963.
65. Hinkle v. Hargens, 81 NW 2d 888, SD 1957.
66. Allison v. Blewett, 348 SW 2d 182, Tex 1961.
67. Latson v. Zeiler, 58 Cal Rptr 436, Cal 1967.
68. Fausette v. Grim, 186 SW 1177, Mo 1916.

69. Nolan v. Kechijian, 64 A 2d 866, RI 1949.

70. Birnbaum v. Seigler, 76 NYS 2d 173, NY 1948; Keen v. Coleman, 20 SE 2d 175, Ga 1942; Haskins v. Howard, 16 SW 2d 20, Tenn 1929; Garlock v. Cole, 18 Cal Rptr 393, Cal 1962; Baum v. Turel, 206 F Supp 490, DC NY 1962.

71. Hundley v. Martinez, 158 SE 2d 159, W Va 1967.

72. Lopez v. Swyer, 300 A 2d 563, NJ 1973.

73. Chappell v. Masten, 255 So 2d 546, Fla 1971.

74. Allen v. Allen, 330 P 2d 151, Ore 1958; "The Physician and Adoption," 223 *JAMA* No. 8. page 953, Feb. 19, 1973.

75. County Department of Public Welfare v. Morningstar, 151 NE 2d 150, Ind 1958.

76. *New York Times*, June 27, 1973, page 44, Col. 3; June 28, 1973, page 14, June 29, 1973, page 28; July 2, 1973, p. 10.

77. *New York Times*, July 8, 1973, Sec. 4, page. 4, Col. 4.

78. Kopprasch v. Stone, 65 NW 2d 852, Mich 1954.

79. Hodge v. Shea, 168 SE 2d 82, SC 1969.

80. Clinton v. Miller, 186 Pac 932, Okla 1919.

81. Zeigler v. Illinois Trust & Savings Bank, 91 NE 1041, Ill 1910.

82. Foster v. Brady, 86 P 2d 760, Wash 1939.

83. *Louisiana Civil Code*, Art. 1489.

84. Zipkin v. Freeman, 436 SW 2d 753, Mo 1968.

85. Maclay v. Kelsey-Seybold Clinic, 456 SW 2d 229, 466 SW 2d 716, Tex 1971.

86. Pendleton v. Burkhalter, 432 SW 2d 724, Tex 1968.

87. Chudy v. Chudy, 420 SW 2d 401, Ark 1967.

88. Felton v. Coyle, 238 NE 2d 191, Ill 1968.

89. Stowers v. Wolodzko, 191 NW 2d 355, Mich 1971.

90. "Erroneous Commitment," 219 *JAMA* No. 10, page 1389, March 6, 1972.

91. Karjavinen v. Buswell, 194 NE 295, Mass 1935; Dunbar v. Greenlaw, 128 A 2d 218, Maine 1956.

92. Lowen v. Hilton, 351 P 2d 881, Colo 1960.

93. Maben v. Rankin, 358 P 2d 681, Cal 1961.

94. Meier v. Combs, 263 NE 2d 194, Ind 1970.

95. Whitree v. New York, 290 NYS 2d 486, NY 1968.

96. Beaumont v. Morgan, 427 F 2d 667, CCA 1, 1970; Olepa v. Mapletoff, 141 NW 2d 350, Mich 1966.

97. Application of Howe, 295 NYS 2d 883, NY 1968.

98. Maniaci v. Marquette University, 184 NW 2d 168, Wisc 1971.

CHAPTER X

DEFENSES

TO

MALPRACTICE

ACTIONS

The first and most obvious defense to any allegation of professional negligence is the denial of liability. If the physician can prove that he followed due care in diagnosis and treatment of the patient's complaint, the patient obviously cannot prove, regardless of the gravity of the untoward result, that the physician was negligent. The vast majority of malpractice cases are tried with the physician defending on the simple factual issue that he was not negligent.

It should be remembered that the patient has the burden of proving negligence beyond "reasonable probability." While he does not have to prove beyond a "shadow of a doubt" that negligence has occurred, the burden of proof in a civil action is satisfied if the patient proves that the injury is the result more probably than not of negligence and other causes are excluded to the same degree. Therefore, the plaintiff is required to prove that the physician was negligent; in most cases the physician is not expected to prove that he was not negligent, although there are some unusual factual situations which are so obviously not likely to occur in the absence of negligence, such as leaving a sponge in a patient's body, that courts hold that these do raise an inference of negligence. Once the patient proves that such an act occurred, it is incumbent on the physician to rebut that presumption by a defense of his own. These situations, while they are increasing in number in most jurisdictions, are, however, still a small minority of the subjects about which most malpractice actions are brought.

The physician's medical records on the patient's case may be of critical importance in proving that no negligence occurred or in refuting the patient's factual allegations of improper diagnosis or treatment.[1] While proper completion of all records on each patient is obviously time consuming and probably an active nuisance, a physician who is sued by a patient some considerable time after treatment terminated will be in a much more favorable position when his records indicate clearly to the court that proper treatment had been given. On the other hand, records which disclose negligent treatment will materially benefit the patient's case. Records which have been altered for any reason, even the most innocent, should always include notations of the date and reason for change. If a negligence suit is filed subsequent to alteration of a record, and that alteration is apparent, it will undoubtedly be construed as a dishonest attempt to avoid liability.

Simple passage of time, in fact, may make a physician totally forget a patient. If he is confronted with a suit one, two, or more years after he had last seen the patient, he may simply not remember anything about the case. If his records can disclose facts to refresh his recollection and on which he may establish his defense, he can refute the patient's case. If he cannot remember the patient and there are no adequate records, he may, through no fault of his own, be found liable.

A patient had a thyroidectomy. After the operation she had very pronounced voice impairment. It was established that her recurrent laryngeal nerve had been severed. She claimed that this was the result of surgical negligence. The surgeon defended the case on the grounds that this had been an unavoidable inherent risk and did not indicate that he had failed to use due care in surgery. Expert testimony indicated that this result may occur in from 1 to 5% of cases without any negligence. The court held, however, that the surgeon bore the burden of proof of refuting a case of negligence on these facts. The patient's hospital records contained very few operative notes and none of them indicated any unusual problems during surgery. The surgeon admitted quite frankly to the court that he had no independent recollection of the operation at all, and that his records did not aid his memory. The court found that a surgeon has a legal obligation to describe accurately and fully in his postoperative reports everything of any consequence which occurs during surgery. Since he could not remember, although the pathologist's report stated that the woman's thyroid had been three times normal size, which the court assumed meant some problem had existed, the fact that he did not prepare a detailed report could not be used as a good defense to the charge of negligence. Thus, he was liable simply because he could not remember facts to refute the inference of negligence in this case.[2]

Properly kept records usually are sufficient to enable physicians to show that they used due care in a given case. In particular, if a patient sues on the grounds that he did not give an informed consent to treatment, copies of a detailed and explicit form signed by the patient would prove beyond any doubt that the necessary disclosures had been made.

A patient was in critical condition as a result of heart disease, but was of perfectly sound mind and understanding. He was admitted to a hospital as a possible recipient of a heart transplant. The surgeon advised him of the development of a mechanical heart and told him that it had never before been used on a human patient. He further told the patient that if death appeared imminent the mechanical device would be used until a donor could be found. The consents for both procedures were extremely detailed and specific. In particular the consent relating to the use of the mechanical heart included a statement that it had never before been used on a human and that the patient had been advised to that effect. The patient's condition became suddenly worse, the mechanical device was used, and several days later a transplant was performed. The patient died and his widow sued on the grounds that there had been no informed consent. The court dismissed the action solely on the basis of the consent forms submitted by the defendant. Since they were extremely explicit, the court found that the patient had had full understanding of the procedure.[3]

Of course, office or hospital records may also indicate a deviation from the standard of care, and if so, negligence is likely to be found,[4] particularly if the records are incomplete.

A patient had poliomyelitis and was in a general hospital for several months where his primary physician was a resident in medicine. He was transferred to a rehabilitation hospital and it was there discovered that he had empyema. There were indications on his chart from the general hospital that he had complained of symptoms which allegedly should have indicated that a lung problem existed, but no attention was paid to the matter and no diagnosis had ever been made. At the time that he was given a physical examination prior to transfer to the rehabilitation hospital, the resident noted "negative for heart, chest, and lungs" on the transfer document. The court held that the records proved that resident had been negligent in failing to discover the empyema.[5]

A woman was admitted to a hospital in labor and died of a streptococcus infection 31 hours later. An intern took no history on admission and simply noted that she was about to deliver, made no record indicating that she had a bad cold, and did not call her obstetrician when her condition worsened after the baby was born and her obstetrician had left. The obstetrician testified that if her records had indicated in any way that she had a cold he would have given her antibiotics. The court was not at all reluctant to find the hospital liable for the intern's negligence in failure to record her condition.[6]

Any medical records which are altered without explicit, good faith reason with both the date and reason for the alteration written onto the record itself may be and usually are construed in a malpractice case as a deliberate attempt to avoid liability. It should also be pointed out that attempting to alter the outcome of a case, civil or criminal, by such methods as altering records under subpoena or which are likely to be subject to subpoena is a criminal offense, although there are no cases indicating that a physician has even been criminally prosecuted. It is considered an attempt to obstruct justice in most cases where charges are filed.

A woman was being treated for a stopped tear duct. An instrument used in the treatment brushed her cornea and abrasions resulted. After the incident, her daughter, who happened to be a nurse, asked to inspect her mother's records at the physician's office. After her inspection, suit was filed. At the trial the daughter testified that her mother's records which she had seen in the physician's office had been materially altered by the time they were admitted into evidence. It was also established that one visit that the patient made after the accident was not recorded at all. The court held that the altered records created a presumption of negligence.[7]

A patient had mumps. Her physician gave her a penicillin injection and she died of anaphylactic shock. Her mother filed suit. There was no claim in the suit that the physician had negligently caused the reaction, but the mother's theory was that it was negligent to have used penicillin for mumps at all. This position was supported by several experts who testified on her behalf. The records submitted by the physician to the court showed that some time after he had written in "mumps" on her record under "diagnosis" the phrase "and pharyngitis" had been added above the line and with a different pen. Since it was unarguable that if the patient had in fact had pharyngitis the physician would have been correct in administering penicillin, the court held that whether the records had been materially altered should have been submitted to the jury as a question of fact.[8]

Thus, any physician should keep very complete records on all patients both in his office and on hospital charts. Such a record is very frequently the best and only proof of nonnegligent diagnosis or treatment. Under no circumstances should the records be altered to defeat liability claims. Whatever difficulties the physician may incur as a result of the fact that his records reflect inadequate treatment, he is far better off in that position and offering a settlement of the claim than he is if he goes to trial and submits records to the court which have been altered without a clear reason for the alteration.

In addition to a denial-defense there are several affirmative defenses commonly used in malpractice cases. Instead of merely denying that the patient's condition is the result of any lack of due care, the physician proceeds with an affirmative defense to show that some cause other than his professional conduct was responsible for the patient's condition or the poor result of treatment.

Contributory Negligence.   One of the standard defenses in any form of negligence action, including a malpractice suit against a physician, is "contributory negligence." Contributory negligence is defined as "conduct on the part of a plaintiff, contributing as a legal cause to the harm he has suffered, which falls below the standard to which he is required to conform for his own protection."[9] In short, where contributory negligence applies, the patient charges the physician with negligence in either diagnosis or treatment. The defendant replies "your injury is your own fault."

In most states which adhere to this doctrine, even if the physician was probably negligent, if he can show contributory negligence on the part of the patient, the patient cannot recover any damages at all. However, an increasing number of states have abandoned this principle in favor of a doctrine known as "comparative negligence" in which damages are apportioned on the basis of the percentage of negligent participation by both parties. Generally a defense on the grounds that the patient was contributorily negligent is not terribly successful because the physician is responsible for the treatment process.

The rule of contributory negligence requires that the patient's negligence must be concurrent with that of the physician. If it occurs after the physician's negligence and merely adds to the effects, as opposed to being the cause of the patient's problem it will not relieve the physician from liability; it will merely serve to "mitigate" or lessen the amount of damages awarded to the patient.[10]

In those rare cases in which a patient can be considered negligent at the time treatment is being administered he generally cannot recover any damages.

A patient, who was to be under a local anesthetic, was told by the surgeon prior to an esophagoscopy that under no circumstances could he move. However, he did move without warning and died as a result of a punctured esophagus. The court held that this was contributory negligence which would constitute a complete defense to the action against the surgeon.[11]

A physician was grossly and obviously intoxicated at the time he was preparing to give a patient an injection. In spite of the fact that the patient knew the physician was drunk, he allowed him to continue and was injured. The court denied recovery of damages on the grounds that a reasonably prudent man would have refused to allow a drunken physician to administer an injection in the absence of any emergency. Both patient and physician, as can be seen, were negligent at the same time and thus the patient could not recover.[12]

Negligence concurrent with medical treatment is extremely unusual, because the patient is usually inactive at that time. The most usual allegation made in a defense of contributory negligence is that the patient refused to comply with the physician's instructions or refused to submit to proper treatment. In some cases the doctrine is successfully pleaded as a complete defense to an action for malpractice. The physician can prove that his treatment was proper and the fact that the patient did not cooperate was the sole cause of his failure to recover from his illness or injury. Where there is evidence that the physician was negligent, but that the patient's later refusal to follow instructions compounded the difficulty, there is no defense to the physician on the issue of negligence and the amount of the patient's damages is simply lessened.[13]

A patient had been in an automobile accident and his leg had been fractured. The defendant put it in a cast. While the patient was in the hospital he disobeyed all instructions about leaving the cast alone. He pushed a traction weight down with his leg until it became useless. He attempted to remove the plaster cast with a table knife which he had stolen from his dinner plate and the result was that his leg was permanently disabled. The court held that he could not recover for his damages.[14]

A woman had an operation for tic douloureux. The surgeon told her that following the operation she would have a temporary corneal anesthesia and facial paralysis. He also told her that during that period she could not feel any foreign object in her eye and therefore infection would be highly likely unless she followed instructions exactly. She did develop conjunctivitis and a corneal infection which required surgery. The final result was that she lost the sight of her eye. The physician contended that he had not performed the surgery negligently. He argued that the patient was the sole cause of her own damage because she failed to follow his instructions to keep her eye clean with a saline solution and, further, she did not obtain immediate medical attention when her eye became obviously infected. There was evidence showing that the patient had been instructed by the surgeon to keep her eye clean by using saline solution, but that she had never used it after her discharge from the hospital. There was also evidence that the patient told the physician during a postoperative examination that she was using eye drops recommended by another physician and the drops were helping her eye. The drops were actually some which had been prescribed for her husband. There was also proof that she did not seek medical attention when she developed pus in her eye to such an extent as to make the fact that it was infected obvious to the most casual observer. The court held that the issues of contributory negligence should have been submitted to the jury.[15]

A patient had been severely beaten and was hospitalized. Against his physician's advice, he left the hospital the next day. In addition to leaving the hospital prematurely he had been told to eat nothing but baby food, but ate a normal diet and drank alcoholic beverages. He died a day later of fecal peritonitis. His widow sued the physician for negligent treatment of his condition. The jury found that the patient's death was entirely the result of his own willful failure to follow instructions and he was solely responsible for his own death. No recovery was allowed.[16]

Following an abdominal operation a patient was instructed not to get out of bed to go to the bathroom, but to ring for a bedpan. He did not follow this instruction, went to the bathroom, and was found eviscerated on the toilet. It was held that his failure to comply with instructions was a complete defense to the action his widow brought against the surgeon.[17]

A farmer broke his arm and the defendant set it, instructing him not to use it for picking up any heavy objects. He attempted to pick up a heavy sack of fertilizer and the arm failed to heal. The court held that he could not recover damages for negligent treatment.[18]

As the court has said in one case: "It is the duty of the patient to follow the reasonable instructions and submit to reasonable treatment prescribed by his physician."[19] However, if the patient knows that the original treatment was negligent, he does not have to continue it under any circumstances. He is perfectly free to terminate the professional relationship at any time and see another physician, even though the physician who was negligent probably would have discovered that the treatment was improper and taken steps to correct it.[20] It is perfectly obvious that a physician whose negligence requires major corrective surgery has no complaint if the patient refuses to allow him to perform it. The patient is clearly not contributorily negligent if he removes himself from further contact with the would-be surgeon.[21]

A woman slipped, fell, and cut her right hand on a broken jar, injuring the ulnar nerve. She was taken to the emergency room where she requested the services of a specific surgeon. Since he was not available, she was treated by an osteopath who was on call. After he had cleaned the wound, the osteopath told the patient to come to his office several days later. Instead of seeing him, however, she saw the surgeon. The patient brought an action against the osteopath for negligence and improper treatment of the injury to her ulnar nerve. He had never performed surgery on an ulnar nerve and did not know that the nerve was damaged. The surgeon treated her six times and eventually performed surgery to repair the nerve. He stated that repair within 6 hours after the injury would have given better results than a later repair. The court found that the woman was not contributorily negligent in failing to go back to the osteopath, since he had been negligent in his treatment and she had the right to consult a physician of her choice.[22]

However, the patient is not usually required to submit to major corrective surgery in order to recover damages.[23]

A patient had surgery on a nerve in his hand. The surgeon knew that he had made an error, but did not tell the patient that he knew why he was in intense pain. The surgeon advised him to go to another hospital, but the patient refused. The court in holding that he did not have to seek further medical care said: "The plaintiff, in failing to avail himself of further treatment violated the standard of ordinary care incumbent upon him." However, the court pointed out that as a layman with a disastrous experience with hospitalization, it was equally reasonable for him to fear further treatment and therefore he could recover damages from the surgeon.[24]

It may be contributorily negligent to fail to consult another physician immediately even if the treating physician has been negligent. The patient has the perfect right to cease to consult the negligent physician, but in reasonable care for his own safety, he may be obliged to seek medical attention elsewhere. If he does not, he may not be able to sue the original physician for negligence.

A patient got cement particles in his eye. A physician removed some, but not all, of them. The man did not feel that he had been properly treated, so he simply ceased to keep appointments. He also did not see another physician for over 3 months. The court held that while he had a right to change physicians, he was contributorily negligent in failing to seek any medical treatment at all. Thus he could not recover damages from the physician for failure to discover the remaining particles which eventually caused an infection.[25]

In 1952 a patient had a routine chest Xray at work which showed signs of tuberculosis. He was referred to his family physician. A sputum analysis test was negative, but the physician instructed him to return for chest Xrays at frequent intervals, which he did not do. He also had "a tired feeling" as well as "coughs and colds" most of the time. In 1956 it was discovered that he had severe and active tuberculosis. The court held that he had been contributorily negligent in failing to seek medical advice when told it was necessary and therefore could not recover damages.[26]

Failure to abide by physician's instructions to take proper medication is also usually a good defense to an action for negligence.

A man was cut in an accident. A physician sutured the wound and gave him a prescription for tetanus antitoxin since he had none at his office. He instructed the patient to go immediately to the drug store, have the prescription filled, and bring it back to his office for an injection. The patient took the prescription, but went home instead of going to the drug store. The physician did not know where the patient lived or where to find him. Several days later the physician was summoned to the patient's home because the man had developed tetanus. At that time he administered the vaccine, but the patient died. It was held that the patient's contributory negligence precluded any recovery against the physician.[27]

Violation of instructions to exercise or undergo other forms of rehabilitation therapy may also raise a claim of contributory negligence.[28]

A patient injured his hand in an industrial accident. He was allegedly negligently treated by a general practitioner. A week later the general practitioner referred him to an orthopedic surgeon, who amputated three of the patient's fingers. The patient sued the general practitioner, who claimed that the patient had failed to exercise his hand as per instructions. The court held that recovery would not be precluded since his failure to exercise did not occur until after he had been discharged by the defendant. It would, however, mitigate damages.[29]

Failure to comply with instructions pertaining to one's activities in the hospital may also constitute contributory negligence in a suit against the physician.[30] Failure of a patient to follow instructions may also be a good defense if a hospital is charged with negligent care of a patient.

A patient died of burns when a flash fire occurred in her oxygen tent. Her daughter, who filed the suit, alleged that the patient had been allowed to wear silk nightgowns in the tent and the fire was the result of a spark caused by static electricity. Testimony from the staff nurses who cared for her, however, indicated that the patient had been wearing a cotton hospital gown when the fire occurred. It was also proved that a book of matches was found inside the oxygen tent after the fire. The patients had been alert and in possession of her faculties. Her cigarettes and matches had been removed from her night stand when the oxygen was brought into the room. She was given explicit instructions not to smoke. There were some cigarettes in her purse in the bureau across the room and evidence showed that she must have gotten out of bed to get them. The court held that she had been solely responsible for her own injuries and the hospital had a good defense to the action.[31]

A hospital patient is also required to use reasonable care for his own safety even without explicit instructions. The hospital is not liable for failure to protect him from dangers which he should reasonably have foreseen himself.

A hospital patient was to be discharged. On his last day there, by which time he was fully ambulatory, he took two showers. He had one in the morning without incident. In the evening he fell while covered with soap and hurt his knee. He sued the hospital for negligently providing a slippery shower floor. The court pointed out that the patient took two showers while completely aware that the curved surfaces of the shower-tub could be potentially hazardous and that no bath mat had been provided. He did not ask for a nonskid mat after the first shower, nor did he use the towel as a substitute. Although he argued that the hospital had been negligent in not installing bars at a height convenient for one taking a shower, the court held that the patient was fully ambulatory and of sound mind and should have been able to take care of his own safety. The verdict in favor of the hospital was affirmed.[32]

The definition of contributory negligence implicitly includes the requirement that the patient must be capable of reasonably apprehending instructions and of looking out for his own safety. His physical and mental condition is the most relevant factor in determining whether or not a patient can be considered contributorily negligent.

A mentally ill patient verbally abused an attendant in a state mental institution. The attendant hit him and broke his jaw. When the patient sued the hospital, the defense was contributory negligence. In addition to holding that verbal abuse cannot under any circumstances constitute negligence, the court's opinion indicated that a mentally ill patient was not to be held to the same standards of self protection as would be applied to others.[33]

Unconscious patients obviously cannot be guilty of contributing to their own injuries.[34]

An unconscious patient was brought into the hospital emergency room. She was left unattended on the ambulance stretcher in a room near the emergency room, rolled off the stretcher, and broke her hip. The court rejected any defense based on contributory negligence, holding that the only way that contributory negligence could have occurred would have been if she had regained consciousness, unfastened her straps, and tried to stand up. Since she was admittedly unconscious at the time she fell, the ambulance company was liable.[35]

An elderly, senile patient who is confused or disoriented and cannot follow instructions also cannot be contributorily negligent.

A 65-year old patient suffered from chronic brain syndrome, diabetes, and arthritis. He could not care for his physical functions, he had dizzy spells, and he fell frequently. When he was admitted to the hospital's geriatrics section for long-term nursing-home care, the nurses in charge were told by his children that he had had previous cigarette fires because of his senility and they were asked to control his smoking and to stay with him while he smoked. The nurse in charge of the unit took his cigarettes, locked them in the medication chest, and issued instructions that the patient was not allowed to smoke unless an attendant stayed with him. Four months later a nurse's aide heard screams coming from a solarium on the floor. She entered and found the patient on fire and tied to a chair by a leather belt. He died of his burns. The court held that the patient had not been contributorily negligent in violating instructions about smoking. There was no evidence from which it could be inferred that he voluntarily did anything that contributed to the accident. Even if there were evidence that he had caused the fire himself, because of his mental condition he could not be contributorily negligent. The hospital knew the risk which his smoking caused and assumed that risk when they admitted him. The age of the patient and his mental condition precluded the finding that smoking on his part absolved the hospital of the effects of negligence in failure to watch him. The hospital was negligent because its employees failed to comply with instructions given to it at the time he was admitted.[36]

A 73-year old hospitalized woman was told not to get out of bed. Her physician ordered a vaporizer to be placed in her room and hospital personnel put it immediately next to her bed. She got out of bed contrary to instructions and burned herself. The court held that considering her age and infirmities, there could be no contributory negligence. The opinion stated: "A hospital's duty of care extends to safeguarding a patient from any known or reasonably apprehended danger from himself which may be due to his mental capacity."[37]

If the patient is rational, however, disobedience of instructions to stay in bed generally constitutes contributory negligence.[38]

Whether or not a child can be capable of contributory negligence depends on the age and intellectual development of the child. A small child, of course, is not capable of looking after himself, although an older child might be.

An 8-year old girl broke her arm. The defendant set it improperly and an infection resulted. She was given corrective orthopedic exercises, but failed to do them. Her arm was permanently crippled. The defense to the suit brought by her parents against the physician was contributory negligence. The court held that in the first place if she were capable of contributory negligence, which it did not determine, it would only mitigate the damages which she could recover and would not preclude her suit. Her capacity for negligence was held to be a jury question and the jury found that she had not had that capacity.[39]

It is highly unlikely in a medical malpractice suit that any jury in this country would hold that a child's injuries from treatment were the child's own fault even if the child were in his early teens.

A parent's contributory negligence in following a physician's instructions on how to care for a sick child may, however, constitute a defense to an action against the physician.[40]

A $2\frac{1}{2}$-year old girl had a boil on her back. The physician gave her mother instructions on its care, including the use of hot packs. When her condition grew worse, the physician injected a local anesthetic prior to lancing the boil and the child died of anaphylactic shock. The defense was that the mother had not followed instructions and also failed to bring the child to the physician soon enough. It was held that there was enough proof of contributory negligence to submit the question to the jury. The verdict for the defendant was upheld.[41]

A 6-year old child had a tube inserted in her side for the relief of pleurisy. The tube disappeared and was eventually located in the child's body. The mother sued the physician who implanted it. The evidence showed the court that the mother herself had caused the problem by manipulating the tube contrary to instructions from the physician. Recovery of damages was denied.[42]

A physician has a good defense to an action if he can show that the patient's conduct or that of the person in charge of his care, such as a parent, was solely responsible for the injuries suffered.[43] If the patient is negligent at the time he is treated, the physician may have a good defense to all allegations of negligence. That is, however, extremely unlikely because of the passive nature of the patient's role in medical treatment. However, damages will only be lessened and the physician will not be found blameless where the negligence of the patient follows negligent treatment and merely serves to aggravate his injuries.

It should be noted that the capacity for self-help is contingent on the patient's age and mental and physical condition. It is perfectly obvious that even persons of normal intelligence in times of sickness or great pain may not be relied upon to exercise the same discretion or judgment as they do when they are well.[44]

Assumption of Risk.   The doctrine of "assumption of risk" means that the patient understands the possibility of all risks of untoward, unpreventable results of treatment and knowingly consents to that treatment. Where it applies, this is usually a good defense to an action for negligence on the part of the physician. It should be noted that this doctrine is, of course, related to the doctrine of informed consent. If all risks which in fact occur have not been carefully explained to the patient, as a matter of law the doctrine of assumption of risk cannot apply. For example, a patient does not assume the risk of becoming a narcotics addict as a result of drugs prescribed for medical treatment unless he is told that addiction is possible and no other drugs are available which are as effective in treating his problem.[45] Since most patients' knowledge of medicine does not permit them to understand these risks, without clear proof of totally informed consent, the defense of assumption of risk is not successful.

Under no circumstances does any patient ever assume the risk of negligent medical treatment. For example, radiation burns may occur without any negligence at all. If the patient has been told that this may occur and is given a choice of acception or rejection of radiation therapy and is then burned in the absence of negligent application of radiation therapy, he is held to assume the risk of the burns.[46] On the other hand, he does not assume the risk of burns resulting from negligent overexposure.[47]

A diabetic patient was warned in advance of surgery that his condition might result in an unavoidable infection. He told the physician that he wished to proceed. His leg had to be amputated as a result of postoperative infection. It was held that he had assumed the risk.[48]

If there are special risks in any treatment, the physician who is reasonably aware of the necessity of protecting his own interests should invariably have a written consent form signed by the patient which lists those risks which have been explained to him.

A man fractured his arm and the defendant set it. Some weeks later it was apparent that the bones were slightly out of alignment. There was no clear indication whether the original setting of the fracture had been negligent or whether the bones had been displaced through no fault of the surgeon. The patient asked the defendant to operate on the arm, break it, and reset it. The defendant opposed the suggestion because he thought this would be bad medical practice, but he eventually agreed. The outcome of the second operation was far worse than the original misalignment. The court held in favor of the surgeon and said that if a physician tells a patient that an operation is improper and advises against it and the patient still insists upon it, the patient assumes the risk because he relies upon his own judgment and not that of the surgeon.[49]

An adult patient had had his ears washed out on several occasions because they became plugged with wax. He came to the office of his physician without an appointment and told a nurse that he wanted his ears washed out. He was told that both physicians who practiced in the office were at the hospital and that his ears could not be treated until one of the physicians could examine him and order such a procedure. He insisted that the nurse do it without requiring him to wait for the physician's return and she finally agreed to do so. During the washing process, both his eardrums were ruptured. The court held that the fact that the patient came to the office without an appointment and persuaded the nurse against her better judgment to perform the procedure without waiting for an examination by a physician was sufficient to support a finding that he had assumed the risk.[50]

This defense is usually, except under exceptional circumstances such as these examples, not a viable one. A physician is not liable in any case for any untoward result as long as his diagnosis or treatment did not fall below the expected standard of due care. As long as the patient understands the unavoidable risks, the physician is not liable and the patient cannot recover damages even without a specific defense of assumption of risk. Under no circumstances, however, does this defense apply to a negligence case. If the physician advises the patient of the risks of proper care and then provides improper care, he cannot defend himself on the ground that the patient has assumed any risks.[51]

A hospital patient also may be held to assume the risk of failure to take reasonable care of himself. For example, a patient of sound mind who crawls over the foot of a bed with siderails generally is held to assume the risk of a fall.[52]

A patient was in a hospital for treatment but was about to be discharged as cured. There was no question of her mental capabilities. As she was packing to leave, she fell over a TV antenna cord which was placed about a foot above the floor in her room. Since the risk was an obvious one and was known to the patient, who in fact had complained that it was dangerous, the court held that she voluntarily assumed the risk involved in stepping over the cord.[53]

Even though a hospital has a duty of care to a patient to protect him from harm caused by his condition, that duty extends only to risks which are reasonably foreseeable.

A stroke patient was placed in a semiprivate room and was given medication to prevent or control seizures. The four siderails on the side of her bed were raised. There were no rails at the foot of the bed. The patient was found on the floor at the foot of her bed with blood on her face, hands, and gown from a facial cut. The patient told the nurse who found her that she was going to the bathroom when she fell. Although there was a call light in the room, the patient had not used it. The woman and her husband brought suit against the hospital. The court held that if the patient was able to tell the nurse what she was doing and where she was going, she could not have been in such a mental state that her efforts to climb over the foot of the bed were involuntary. It was the hospital's duty to give the patient reasonable care and to see that she had such attention as her condition made necessary. It had done so by placing the rails on the bed. It had had no obligation to guard the patient against an unanticipated danger of this nature.[54]

Emergency. Since the standard of care required of physicians and surgeons is that of the duly careful practitioner under the circumstances involved in the case, the fact that treatment was given during a life and death emergency may be a good defense to a suit alleging that the treatment was negligent. If the patient's condition is such that death is imminent and it is absolutely necessary to provide treatment as speedily as possible, it may very well be a good defense to prove that it was given during an emergency.

After a normal delivery a woman had a sudden, massive hemorrhage. She went into shock, and packing her uterus with gauze proved to be ineffective. The physician administered a blood transfusion through a vein in her ankle. The blood infiltrated and it became necessary to amputate her leg. The court held that the physician's testimony indicated that he had had to make the choice of saving the women's leg or her life and, therefore, the circumstances which necessitated the speedy action absolved him from any liability for any negligence which might have been proven in a less urgent case.[55]

The defense of emergency is the usual plea where a patient has been damaged after a cardiac arrest.

A cardiac arrest occurred during delivery. The obstetrician had the patient's chest opened and was massaging her heart within 1 minute after the arrest occurred. The court held that since there was no evidence that he had been responsible for the arrest and since he acted with instant attention when it occurred, he was not liable for her brain damage.[56]

A child had a cardiac arrest during a tonsillectomy. The anethesiologist was found not liable on the grounds that he had moved quickly and dealt properly with the situation. The appellate court approved the trial judge's charge to the jury that although due care must be used in emergency, not as much time is available for thought and contemplation as to alternatives which exists in nonemergency situations. Whether or not an emergency in fact existed is a question of fact which is properly decided by the jury.[57]

For example, if during a surgical emergency it is perfectly obvious that surgery must be terminated at once to save the patient's life, the physician is not usually liable if a foreign object is left in the body.[58]

A child severed an artery in his foot and emergency surgery was necessary. During the operation the surgeon broke two needles in the foot. While he was attempting to locate them, the child stopped breathing. The surgery was terminated as quickly as possible with the needles left in place. The needles eventually emerged without medical intervention. The court held that the surgeon had not, under the circumstances, been negligent in leaving them behind.[59]

If an emergency during a surgical or medical procedure is caused by the physician's negligence he cannot then use it as a defense.[60] Whether or not care given to a patient whose condition constitutes an emergency at the time treatment is instituted can be successfully explained as a justified departure from the standard of due care depends upon the circumstances. For example, several decisions have involved patients who had been brought into emergency rooms with critical head injuries received in automobile accidents. Proper treatment was instituted for the head injuries, but there was a failure to discover such other injuries as fractured arms and legs.

A patient sustained severe head injuries and a fractured hip in an automobile accident. The hip injury was not diagnosed for a period of a month, during which time he recovered without difficulty from his head injury. The court held that the question of whether or not the physician who was intent on treating the head injury in the emergency room should have found the hip injury was one which was properly submitted to the jury. Its verdict for the patient was sustained by the appellate court.[61]

A 16-month old child cut her hand very severely. An intern treated her under extremely difficult conditions in the emergency room, including the necessity of forcibly restraining her while the hand was sutured. He failed to discover that she had severed a tendon in her finger. He was found not liable because the child had offered all resistance possible. The court held that the emergency and other circumstances were such that the treatment was within the standard of care which could be expected under those circumstances.[62]

A man was bitten by a rattlesnake and went to the emergency room in very serious condition. The physician administered antivenom for the bite and the patient developed gangrene from the injection. He sued on the grounds that the injection had been given without his informed consent. The court held that due to the extremely serious nature of the emergency and the necessity for as much haste as possible, the physician was not negligent in failing to sit down and discuss the "pros and cons" of relative types of treatment with the patient prior to administering the injection.[63]

A physician who offers a defense of emergency when faced with a malpractice action, particularly if the emergency is one which occurred during a surgical or medical procedure, must bear the burden of proving to the jury that the emergency in fact existed and also that it was not occasioned by any fault of his.

In addition to these factual defenses, there are also various technical legal defenses which may be of assistance to the physician.

Release of Tortfeasor.   If a patient is brought to a physician for treatment as the result of an accident caused by another individual and suit is later filed against the other, release of the original wrongdoer, known as a "tort-feasor" will, in most states, release the physician from any claim for malpractice. The standard example, of which there are literally hundreds, is the case of a patient injured in an automobile accident caused by the fault of another driver, who is then brought to the emergency room and treated by a physician. He later sues the other driver for negligence, settles the case, and signs a release in favor of the other driver. He then sues the physician for malpractice in the treatment of the injuries caused by the original tortfeasor. In general, the original tortfeasor is responsible for any subsequent malpractice in the care of the original injury as long as the injured party exercises reasonable care in the selection of a physician.[64] The legal theory for this rule is that only one injury, that caused by the original tortfeasor has occurred and that the medical malpractice which then takes place simply continues the chain of proximate causation of that injury.[65]

A child was hit by a taxicab and was negligently treated by a physician for her injuries. Her parents moved her to another hospital and she was placed under the care of another physician, but she died a few days later. A release was given to the owner of the taxicab. The court held that that release ended the physician's liability for negligent treatment. As long as he was selected with due care, the taxicab owner was responsible for all injuries which flowed directly from his negligence.[66]

However, if the release is explicitly not intended to cover the physician's negligence it may not serve to release him.[67] Where there are joint suits against a hospital and the treating physician for negligence, release of one may release the other from any liability, but this is not always the case.

A patient had a cause of action against both a hospital and a surgeon. He settled the case against the hospital for $60,000.00 and then went to trial against the surgeon. The court held that the surgeon could not deduct the $60,000.00 from the verdict against him when the hospital had not been made a party to the action and there had been no judgment of joint negligence against it.[68]

The rule that the original tortfeasor is generally legally liable for the subsequent malpractice of a physician who treats the injuries caused in an accident is accepted in most states.[69] The significant point is that the release given by the patient to the original tortfeasor is held sufficient to bar an action against the doctor unless the wording of the release expressly reserves the right on the part of the patient to pursue another action against the physician.[70] Moreover, his entire claim is always considered to be satisfied if the settlement with the tortfeasor specifically includes full compensation for the injuries caused by the treating physician.

A young man was riding a motorcycle and collided with an automobile driven by a physician. The physician undertook to treat his injuries at the scene but did so negligently. He also treated the accident victim at the hospital. Suit was brought against him for causing the original motorcycle accident and the motorcyclist won the case. Thereafter the plaintiff brought another suit against the physician for malpractice. The court held that since two separate wrongs had been involved, those arising out of the automobile accident and those arising out of the negligent treatment, the plaintiff had the right to sue "each wrongdoer" even though they were the same person.[71]

If the injured person is negligent in his selection of a physician the original wrongdoer is not liable for aggravation of the injury by the physician's negligence and therefore a release of the original wrongdoer does not release the physician.[72] The physician is also not released in the case of his own gross negligence.[73]

If the negligence of the physician causes an injury unrelated to the injury from the accident, the original wrongdoer is also not liable for the physician's negligence and the physician is consequently not absolved by a release given to the original tortfeasor.[74]

A man was in an accident. He was taken to the hospital where a surgeon mistook him for another patient and operated on the wrong part of his body. The court held that the person who had caused the accident was not liable for the surgeon's negligence.[75]

After an automobile accident a man was taken to the hospital. A physician administered a preliminary sensitivity test for tetanus antitoxin. The results clearly indicated an allergy. However, the physician administered the injection and the patient was severely damaged. The court held that the release of the driver did not affect the physician or make him immune from suit.[76]

A man was injured in an automobile accident and received $2300.00 in damages from the other driver in settlement. He signed a general release discharging the other party from any further claims arising out of the accident. He did not then know that the accident had caused a ruptured intervertebral disc. Several months later he selected an orthopedic surgeon to treat him, and surgery was performed. During the procedure a sponge was left in his body, and a second operation was necessary. The man sued the surgeon for negligence. The surgeon claimed that release of the other driver "for all injuries resulting from the automobile accident" had released the man's claim against him. The court however, dismissed the surgeon's argument. The release, of course, had been executed before the injury was discovered. The patient said that he had not intended to release the surgeon for liability for any subsequent wrongdoing and the amount received in the settlement was not adequate to cover his later injuries. The court found that his position was correct. Since the surgeon was not named in the release and had not made payment toward satisfaction of any liability, the burden of proof was on him to show that the release was intended to include him. Since he had not seen the patient at the time the release was executed, the court held that he was not entitled to rely upon it.[77]

A patient suffered a back injury as the result of an automobile accident and was admitted to a hospital. She sued the hospital for damages for an abdominal burn which occurred while she was under anesthesia. The court held that this was an "original injury," was not related to the automobile accident itself, and therefore release of the other driver did not release the physician.[78]

At the time the patient settles with the original wrongdoer he may be unaware that medical negligence in the treatment of his injuries has already occurred. In this situation courts in most states allow a later suit against the physician, holding that the action is not affected by the release of the original tortfeasor.[79]

A woman was knocked down by a taxi and broke her leg. She settled with the cab company, relying on her physician's statements that the fracture had healed properly. She subsequently discovered that his examination had been negligent and that she would have permanent disabilities. The court allowed her to sue the physician.[80]

If, however, the patient knows, in spite of the physician's reassurances, that he has sustained permanent damages, the release bars action against the physician.[81]

A general release executed by an injured person which contains no reservation of rights to proceed against other parties was once held in most states to bar an action for malpractice for negligent treatment as long as all the elements of damage, including the medical aggravation of the initial injury, were fully known at the time of the settlement against the original tortfeasor.[82] Even where this rule is still applied, however, if the release explicitly indicates either that the victim intended to discharge only the original wrongdoer or contains an express reservation of rights against other parties, of course it will not bar a subsequent action against the physician.[83]

However, since 1955 many states have enacted statutes allowing separate recovery from the physician unless he has been specifically named in the release. In these jurisdictions physicians may be subject to later suit even if the patient has signed a release absolving the driver "and all other persons" from liability.[84]

A woman was hospitalized for emergency treatment after an automobile accident. A tracheostomy was performed. She was later transferred to another hospital where she was treated by two physicians. She and her husband settled their claims against the other driver and signed a release. They then sued the physicians at the second hospital, claiming that negligent treatment had resulted in permanent damage to her larynx. The court held that they had a right to sue because the physicians had not been named in the original release. However, it was also stipulated that in no event could she recover more than the amount required for full satisfaction of the damages.[85]

A young boy sustained serious and permanent injuries in a wreck and was treated by a neurosurgeon. His parents executed a release in favor of the driver and "all other persons" for $10,500.00. The neurosurgeon was not named in the release. They later sued him contending that he had been negligent in failing to diagnose and remove a subdural hematoma which caused further damage to their son's brain. The court pointed out that the neurosurgeon and the driver did not act in concert to produce a single injury, rather the surgeon's injury to the child was subsequent to the automobile accident and created a separate cause of action. Taken at face value the court conceded that the release would appear to free the neurosurgeon from liability. However, he was not a party to the agreement between the parties involved in the accident, contributed nothing to the settlement, and was not named in the release. Thus, the court saw no reason why he should share in the benefits conferred by the release unless he could prove that such was the intention of the parties. Since he could not do so, the parents had the right to sue him.[86]

Courts in most jurisdictions which adopt this rule hold that these statutes apply both to actions for personal injury brought by the accident victim himself and those brought for his wrongful death from either the accident or the subsequent malpractice.[87] Others, however, do hold that a wrongful death settlement bars a subsequent action against the physician.[88] In states where these statutes exist, a party who wishes to show that he should be absolved from liability under a release given to the original tortfeasor must prove that the amount of compensation is sufficient to allow the injured party to receive complete financial satisfaction of all aspects of the injuries and that the parties intended the release to satisfy all aspects of the claim.[89]

A third group of states have always held, even without such statutes, that a person not a party to a release is not released by it unless he is specifically named therein.[90]

A 12-year old boy was given an injection by a physician and a nurse, both of whom were salaried employees of a hospital. As the result of the physician's negligence in administering the hypodermic, the boy's sciatic nerve was damaged and he received permanent injuries. He settled the case against the physician for $25,000.00 and an agreement not to sue him for further damages. The covenant provided that the acceptance of payment would not be construed as a release of any other persons. The court held that the hospital was not covered by the release and therefore the boy had the right to sue the hospital.[91]

If a hospital and a physician are sued together and either one pays the full judgment entered, another suit then cannot thereafter be brought against the remaining party.

Suit was filed against an obstetrician and a hospital for the wrongful death of a woman and her newborn baby. The jury returned a verdict of $60,000.00 against both the physician and the hospital. The trial judge granted a motion for a new trial and, thereafter, prior to the second trial a settlement figure of $31,803.00 was agreed upon. The physician paid the amount of the judgment. The widower of the dead woman brought another suit against the hospital, but the court dismissed it.[92]

Of course a patient who sues a physician for malpractice unrelated to any other accident or injury may settle his claim and sign a release specifically in favor the physician. In most cases he is bound by the release and cannot later sue the physician. However, if the physician fraudulently tells the patient that he has recovered from his injury or conceals any aspect of negligence from the patient, the patient has the right to initiate another suit.

A patient was burned during surgery. He sued the surgeon and settled the case. He later claimed that he signed the release because the surgeon told him that he would completely recover from his injuries, which was, to the surgeon's knowledge at the time, not the case. The court held that the release was invalid and that he had the right to sue the surgeon for the additional damages.[94]

Any failure to disclose fully to the patient any injuries suffered or negligent conduct on the part of the physician constitutes fraudulent misrepresentation which will invalidate any release.[95]

If a physician employed by the person who has caused the original injury to examine the accident victim prior to trial misrepresents his condition to the victim and therefore induces him to settle the case against the original tortfeasor, the release is also invalid on the grounds of fraud even though the physician never treated the patient.[96]

A patient may not be asked to sign a release against negligence as a condition of admission to a hospital or treatment by a physician. The general rule is that the person supplying the medical service may not contract against the effect of his own negligence and therefore any contract to this effect is null and void.[97]

A man was admitted to a research hospital. Upon his entry he signed a document setting forth certain "conditions of admission," among which was a clause that he would not sue the hospital or its employees for any negligence which occurred during the course of his treatment. He was injured by negligence of two physicians on the staff of the hospital. The court allowed him to sue and recover damages in spite of the release which he had signed on admission. The court found that such a contract was invalid as against the public interest because requiring a contract in advance which excuses the physician or hospital from negligence is tantamount to a license to fail to use due care.[98]

Other cases have indicated that a physician also cannot require an office patient to sign a contract that he will not sue if he is injured during treatment.[99]

Even where these agreements are not absolutely invalid, they are always construed strictly against the physician or hospital and in favor of the patient.

A patient died in a private sanitarium. He and his wife had signed a "release" which gave the sanitarium permission to administer any form of recognized medical treatment including electroshock and included a release of the sanitarium and its employees from any negligence in the course of the procedure. After an electroshock treatment the deceased was permitted to walk around and he fell down a flight of stairs. He died of his injuries. The court held that the release was insufficient to relieve the defendant of liability for the negligent medical treatment of the deceased after the fall.[100]

A release signed by a patient in advance of an operation which purported to relieve the surgeon from "any and all liability or complication" was held void as against public policy. The court held that a patient did not assume the risk of subjecting himself to carelessness on the part of the surgeon when he had no alternative but to seek medical care. The court noted that in the "bargaining" process prior to the patient's signing the release, the surgeon exercised a decisive advantage since the patient was in absolute need of the surgery.[101]

In most states a person who sustains injuries is entitled to recover only an amount which would compensate him fully for his total injury. Thus, in these cases in which malpractice follows an accident caused by another person, money recovered in settlement with the original tortfeasor must be considered a "set off" in a subsequent malpractice action and the amount of the settlement is deducted from the amount of the judgment received.

A release by a patient will thus constitute a good defense for a physician in most states only if he can show (1) that he was a named party to it or (2) that the wording of the release in favor of the original tortfeasor was such as to include him in unmistakable terms. For example, the release might state specifically that it covers all damages "including those caused by malpractice." A physician who is sued under these circumstances has the right to enter into evidence copies of any agreements between the patient and the original tortfeasor.[102] If a settlement of a malpractice case is made by the defendant doctor or by his insurer, that settlement generally under all circumstances except fraud bars another action brought against the physician.

Res Judicata. Once a claim has been litigated to completion it cannot be retried between the same parties. This is known as the doctrine of *"res*

judicata," "the thing has been decided." A judgment in favor of a physician
in a malpractice suit is a bar, for example, to a separate contract suit for
breach of warranty arising out of the same transaction.[103]

If a physician sues for an unpaid bill and the patient who knows at that
time that malpractice has occurred does not dispute the claim on the
grounds that he did not pay his bill because treatment given was negligent,
some states hold that the patient cannot later sue the physician for
negligence.[104]

In most states, however, a judgment in favor of the physician for his fee
does not bar a subsequent negligence action unless the patient pleaded malpractice as a defense to the action at the trial of the physician's claim.[105]
If the patient defaults in an action by a physician for an unpaid bill, meaning that he does not answer the complaint and does not present a defense
at the trial, he is not held to have waived his right to sue the physician for
negligence at a later time.[106]

A patient brought a malpractice action. The physicians then sued him in
another court to recover the value of their professional services. The patient
defaulted and the physicians obtained a judgment for the full amount
claimed. The court held that they could not use this judgment as a **res
judicata** defense against the patient in his malpractice case.[107]

In a suit by a physician for his fee, professional negligence is considered to be a good defense on the part of the patient. If, however, the
patient has filed a malpractice suit prior to the time the physician sues and
has lost the case, he cannot allege the same negligence as a defense to a
subsequent suit brought by the physician.[108]

Res judicata may also apply against the physician. If the patient sues
the physician for malpractice and the physician does not, in defending the
suit, plead that the patient has not paid the bill, when the physician wins
the malpractice case he cannot later sue the patient for compensation for
his professional services. The courts generally hold that if he wishes to receive compensation from the patient, he should counterclaim for that
amount in the patient's original suit.[109]

There is no uniform rule on the effect of the doctrine of *res judicata* on
Workmen's Compensation cases. In most states an employee who is receiving Workmen's Compensation awards for injuries which originated during
his employment and which were aggravated by medical malpractice cannot maintain an action against the physician.[110] In some jurisdictions, however, medical negligence is not included in Workmen's Compensation payments. Therefore, the worker may sue the physician and *res judicata* is
not a good defense.[111]

A company physician prescribed pain pills for an employee involved in an on-the-job injury. On the way home from work the patient went to sleep at the wheel of his car as the result of the side effects of the medication. He caused an accident. The court held that the Workmen's Compensation claim against the employer did not bar a later malpractice suit against the physician.[112]

If in a suit against an original wrongdoer, evidence of medical malpractice is submitted by the plaintiff in an attempt to recover full compensation both for the original injury and the negligent medical treatment and that defendant pays the judgment, the physician has a claim of *res judicata* in any subsequent malpractice action against him alone.[113]

It should be noted that *res judicata* does not apply unless the parties and issues in the first action are identical to those in the second. The usual rule is that if the evidence necessary to support the claim is the same in both actions, the second is barred. Thus, if the parties are not the same or if the facts are not the same *res judicata* is not applicable.

It should always be remembered that a patient who is sued for a fee where circumstances indicate the possibility of negligent treatment is much more likely to counterclaim for damages for professional negligence or to be tempted to bring a malpractice suit than he would have been if the physician had just ignored the bill. A patient who is dissatisfied with treatment and who does not pay his bill for that reason is the patient most likely to become more litigation-minded because he has been sued for failure to pay his medical bills. Except in extremely rare cases where the physician is absolutely certain beyond any possible doubt that a patient's dissatisfactions are entirely unjustified, he should not take the risk of precipitating a malpractice action by filing a suit for his fee.

Statutes of Limitation.   All states have statutes requiring a plaintiff to file any legal action in which money damages are sought within a certain period of time. If a negligence action is filed 15 or 20 years after an accident occurred, it may be impossible to prove the case either for the plaintiff or the defendant because witnesses have died or become difficult to locate or documentary evidence may have been destroyed or lost. The statute of limitations as applied to a medical malpractice case requires the patient to file his suit within a given time from the date on which the medical negligence occurred. All states have statutes of limitation, but they vary tremendously. Some states may have a period of 1 year during which a negligence action of any type may be brought; other states' period of limitation may be as long as 6 years. Some states may have special statutes involving only malpractice actions. Furthermore, there are at least three different means of determining the onset of the period of time which is covered by the statute. The old rule still accepted in most states was that the statute begins to run from the time negligence occurs. If the patient has not discovered within that prescribed time that medical negligence has occurred, he may not sue when he discovers it later.[114] A second group of states has evolved the "last treatment" rule. On the theory that as long as the physician is treating the patient, the negligence is a continuing process, the statutory period does not begin until the course of treatment has ended. A third group of states, one which is increasing in number, has adopted the "discovery" rule, which is much more favorable to the patient than the other two. In these states, the period allowed by the statute of limitations does not begin until the patient knew or should have known that negligence has been committed.

In the states which compute the beginning date of the statutory period from the time the negligence occurs whether or not the patient knows what has happened, there may still be exceptions to the strict application of the time period, but these are extremely rare.

A patient sued a physician and alleged that a mastectomy had been both unnecessary and negligently performed. She did not discover that the diagnosed malignancy had not existed until several years after the operation. Suit was not filed until after the applicable period had elapsed. The court dismissed her action.[115]

A patient had a gall bladder operation in 1954. In 1971 another operation revealed that a piece of gauze had been left in his abdomen. The court dismissed the suit, holding that the action accrued at the time of the injury. It had long since been barred by the statute of limitations.[116]

Most states make a specific exception to the time-of-negligence rule for cases filed as the result of foreign objects which have been left in patients' bodies. These may be extremely difficult to detect and there are cases on record where a sponge or clamp was not discovered for 20 years or more. The patient is allowed to sue at the time the object is discovered since the evidence, the object itself, is available and the inference of negligence so clear that it is not usually necessary to produce out-of-date records or actual witnesses to the procedure.[117] All jurisdictions, however, do not follow this rule and in some states even though the claim involves a foreign object the period begins on the date of the surgery.[118]

A patient had an operation in 1958. In 1968 further surgery revealed that a pair of forceps had been left in his abdomen. The court allowed his suit even though the statutory period had long expired and held that in that state the limitation period for foreign object cases did not begin to apply until discovery.[119]

In some states the statute begins to run on the date of the last treatment by the physician for the injury or disease involved in the claim. This is usually simple to compute, but in some cases it may be more complicated.

A patient took a drug for a skin infection and went blind. She sued the drug manufacturer, the physician who had prescribed it, and an ophthalmologist whom she had seen when her vision first began to fail. The ophthalmologist had not realized the cause of her problem because she had not told him she was taking the medication. As to both physicians, the court held that the last treatment rule applied. Since she had continued to take the medication on her own initiative for years after the last time she had seen the physician who prescribed it, any action against him was barred.[120]

Where the patient knows that the physician has been negligent as soon as the event has occurred, the last treatment rule does not apply.[121]

A patient was operated on by a member of a multispeciality clinic. The surgeon told her after the operation that he had removed a nerve because he thought it was a tumor. She continued to be treated by other physicians on the staff of the same clinic for several years thereafter. Eight years after the operation she sued the surgeon. She claimed that the statute did not begin to run until she was no longer a patient of any of the physicians at the clinic. The court rejected this argument and held that in case of provable knowledge of negligence, the statutory period runs from the date of that knowledge.[122]

If a patient realizes that something is wrong, but continues to consult the same physician without making any effort to discover the cause of his problem, the last treatment rule also does not apply.

Immediately after a kidney operation a patient had severe pains in her leg and knew for several years that she had phlebitis. At the end of this period she discovered from another surgeon that a vein in her leg had been severed at the time of the first operation. The court held that since she knew from pain and other symptoms that something was wrong, she should have pursued the matter immediately. Her failure to do so beyond the statutory period eliminated her right to sue.[123]

An increasing number of states have adopted the rule that the statutory limitation period in a professional liability suit does not begin to run until the patient knows or should have known of the negligence.[124]

A woman filed suit against the estate of a deceased surgeon 23 years after she had had a hysterectomy. She claimed that she had had considerable abdominal difficulties during all the years following surgery. Exploratory surgery revealed a surgical sponge. The court allowed her to sue.[125]

Lumps on a patient's nose and cheeks were treated by radiation therapy in 1957. In 1962 and 1963 the same physician cauterized the area. In 1967 the patient discovered that she had had a malignancy and sued. The court allowed the action.[126]

Some states have established the discovery rule by court decisions. Others, however, have rejected it.[127] Several state legislatures, including those of Illinois,[128] Alabama,[129] and Connecticult,[130] have enacted statutes providing that the limitation period in medical malpractice cases does not begin to run until the patient has discovered the injuries. However, adoption of this theory does not necessarily result in an increased number of successful suits against physicians. Even if a patient is successful in demonstrating that the statute of limitation should not apply in a case where the inquiry was not discovered for some time, he still must prove that the physician was negligent. The same passage of time which makes it difficult for a physicain to prove he was not negligent, of course, means that the patient will have a very difficult time establishing negligence by any reasonable evidence.

One major problem involving the discovery rule is the difficulty of determination of the date of "discovery." All states which have adopted this rule define it as the date on which a reasonable person should have discovered the negligence had occurred. This is not necessarily the date on which the patient actually discovered the negligence.

A patient's wife got pregnant twice after he had a vasectomy. After the first pregnancy was discovered the physician told him he was sterile. He therefore did not sue until after the second pregnancy was discovered. The court held, however, that a reasonable man should have known that he was not in fact sterile as of the date of the diagnosis of the first pregnancy and dismissed the suit.[131]

A woman was given a transfusion of the wrong type of blood in 1962. In 1966 she had a stillborn child. In 1969 she had another stillborn child. After the second pregnancy ended she underwent exhaustive tests which revealed the problem. She then filed suit against the hospital in which the transfusion had been given. The court held that she had been on notice that investigation of the problem should be made at the time her first child was stillborn and she was not allowed to recover.[132]

A woman had a mastectomy followed by radiation treatments. She was badly burned by the Xrays and had to be hospitalized 15 times for treatment. The burns occurred in 1962. Five years later while she was in the hospital, she heard a physician tell another physician that the radiologist had been negligent. As soon as she was released from the hospital, she went to a lawyer and filed a suit. The period of limitations in that state was 2 years. The court held that while she obviously knew she had been burned, the question of whether or not she knew that the burns were the result of negligence or whether, as she claimed, she had believed that the burns were an unavoidable result of the radiation therapy, was a question of law which should have been determined by the trial judge. She was allowed to bring suit.[133]

Regardless of the applicable theory for determining the limitation period, if a physician knows that he had been negligent and conceals the facts from the patient in no state does the limitation period begin to run until the patient has discovered the truth.[134]

A young man had a myelogram. The pantopaque dye could not be removed after the procedure was completed. The physician who had left it told the patient, although he knew it was not true, that it was normal practice to leave the dye and that his body would absorb it. The government physician knew the name and address of the patient's family physician, but had not advised him of the fact that the dye had been left. A day or two after the patient was released from the hospital, he was injured in an automobile accident. The family physician thought that the patient's discomfort was the result of the automobile accident and therefore did not investigate the possibility of any negligence in performance of the myelogram. He assumed that the government physician would have told him if there had been any problems. When the facts were eventually discovered, the patient sued. The court held that there was no reason either the patient or his family physician should have known about the dye and that the statute of limitations did not bar his right to sue.[135]

A patient had a thyroidectomy. Her recurrent laryngeal nerve was damaged and the surgeon knew it, as operative notes indicated. She repeatedly discussed her voice problems with him and he assured her that she would be "all right in time" and actively discouraged her from consulting any other physician. When she eventually discovered what had happened, the limitation period had elapsed, but the court allowed her to sue. It held that the physician's conduct had amounted to concealment. Thus he could not take advantage of the fact that she had not known what was wrong.[136]

A lawyer had a cataract operation. To the surgeon's knowledge, his eye was damaged during the procedure. The surgeon repeatedly assured him that it would be "all right in time" and he continued to be treated by the same surgeon for a considerable period of time. He finally went to a major medical center and consulted another ophthalmologist. The ophthalmologist advised him of the permanent damage to his eye. The court said that the physician had concealed the true facts of the case and therefore the patient could sue in spite of the fact that the limitation period had expired.[137]

Fraudulent concealment sufficient to eliminate the defense of the statute of limitations, however, is very difficult to prove. Before a patient may use it as a justification for filing an action after the period has elapsed, he must be able to show that the physician knew what was wrong and deliberately did not tell him. This is obviously very difficult to prove. If the physician makes an honest mistake and does not realize what is wrong with the patient, the statutory period applies in all states.[138]

A woman had an abdominal operation many years before subsequent surgery revealed that her vagus nerve had been severed. She sued and the surgeon pleaded the statute of limitations. The court upheld his defense since, although the plaintiff alleged fraudulent concealment, she submitted no evidence that he had been aware of the fact that the nerve had been severed.[139]

Some states have special statutes allowing shorter times for filing suits which apply only to medical malpractice cases. These statutes are based on the theory that proof of professional liability claims against physicians is so much more complex than that in other tort claims that simple justice requires them to be brought as soon as possible.[140] The permissible period for suit under these statutes is usually 1 or 2 years if the general negligence statute is 3 years or more.

Where these statutes apply they have been upheld as constitutional, but in most cases they apply only to the actions brought against physicians. Unless there is a specific provision in the statute which makes it applicable to hospitals, the ordinary limitations period will apply to them.[141] Even those states' statutes which apply the shorter statutory period to hospitals do not include nursing homes.[142]

In order for the period specified by any statute of limitation to apply the patient must be legally competent to bring a suit.[143] A patient who cannot for some reason bring a legal action is not bound by limitation provisions. The period begins to run only at the time his disability no longer exists. A minor may always bring a suit within a specified period after reaching the age of majority, regardless of his age at the time the act of negligence occurred.[144]

Patients who are mentally incompetent are also not bound by the statutory limitation, particularly if the hospital in which they have been confined is the defendant in the suit, even though they have not been adjudicated mentally incompetent.

A patient had been involuntarily committed to a mental hospital and kept there for several years. When she was finally released, she sued the hospital for false imprisonment. The court found that the date of the false imprisonment was the date of admission. That was the date on which the tort would actually have occurred. The action would normally have been barred by the statute of limitations. However, the court refused to dismiss her case. The state claimed in defense that she had been mentally incompetent at the time she was admitted and therefore the "imprisonment" was justified. The hospital could not at the same time maintain that position and state in the same case that she had been sufficiently competent to bring a suit on that date.[145]

A woman in a mental hospital was given a very heavy dose of sedation. While under its influence she set herself on fire with a match. She and her husband brought separate suits against the hospital several years after the fire, by which time under normal circumstances the statutory period would have expired. The court held that since her husband had suffered from no legal disability, his suit had been properly dismissed, but that hers would be allowed. The period began to run as of the date on which she had been released from the hospital.[146]

The usual statutory period of limitation on a contract suit is considerably longer than that allowed in a negligence action. For that reason if a patient can bring a suit for breach of contract as opposed to negligence in a case in which he alleges medical malpractice, he may have an excellent chance of recovery even though the suit would have been barred under the negligence statute.[147] For example, contract actions are usually allowed within 6 years after the date of the breach. Negligence actions, on the other hand, may have a permissible period as short as 1 or 2 years. However, where the major thrust of the action is one in negligence the court will apply that limitation period even though the patient alleges breach of contract.[148]

A postsurgical patient developed a staphylococcus infection. The limitation period for negligence in that state was 2 years, for contracts, 6 years. Four years after the operation she sued the hospital for breach of contract. She alleged that its acceptance of her as a patient constituted a contract with a warranty that she would be properly protected from harm. The court held that the hospital could not be sued because the period of limitation for negligence had run. Even though the patient called her action "breach of contract," it actually stated a complaint in negligence.[149]

If the patient can prove a specific warranty or agreement to cure his complaint and a subsequent breach of that guarantee he may, however, have a right to sue in contract even if the negligence period has expired.[150] Where assault and battery is charged, which is common in cases where the patient claims treatment was instituted in the absence of informed consent, the statute covering assault and battery, not the statute covering negligence, applies.

Charitable and Governmental Immunity. Many states allow immunity from suit for hospitals which are privately owned but charitably incorporated, by definition those in which no profit accrues to any of the stockholders.[151] The earliest case involving charitable immunity in the United States was a Massachusetts decision in 1876.[152] The theory behind charitable immunity was either that funds donated to a private charitable institution should not be diverted to payments of damage judgments or that since the owners of the charitable hospital derive no financial benefit from it they should not be liable for any negligence. In no state has there ever been immunity for a profit-making hospital.[153]

In our common law heritage from England, the rule was that "the king can do no wrong." Thus at common law no entity of the federal, state, or local government was subject to suit without its consent. At the present time, unless this immunity has been waived by statute, hospitals owned by any level of government are still immune from liability for negligence. The Federal Tort Claims Act enacted in 1946[154] allows negligence suits by non-military patients in hospitals owned by the federal government.[155] The legal status of hospitals owned by state or local governments varies widely from states in which they are not granted any type of immunity to those which absolutely forbid any suit against them.

Some states differentiate as to immunity between suits brought by paying and by nonpaying patients. A hospital may be completely immune from a suit brought by a charity patient who has paid none of his hospital expenses, but subject to suit by a paying patient.[156] In other states, however, no distinction is made between the two types of patients.[157] With the increasing number of patients who are covered by private insurance, Medicare, or Medicaid, it is obvious that where this distinction still exists very few persons are now legally "charity" patients. In still other states there is no absolute prohibition against suit, but damages may not be awarded in excess of the amount of liability insurance carried by the hospital and, therefore, if the hospital carries no insurance it is not amenable to suit.

In most states a person who is not a patient, such as a patient's visitor who trips and falls on a wet spot on a hospital floor, is not barred from suit by either governmental or charitable immunity.[158] Charitable hospitals are also liable under Workmen's Compensation statutes to employees injured on the premises without regard to any immunity which might be present in a suit brought by a patient.[159]

Immunity operates only in favor of a hospital. If such a defense is available to the institution it will not be liable for the negligence of a staff physician or nurse. It should be noted that the individual is not personally immune from suit. The problem which arises when the negligent party is an intern, staff nurse, or other salaried employee is that most do not carry large amounts of malpractice insurance coverage and, therefore, it is not usually worthwhile to file a suit. However, the legal principle is clear—the employee of the immune hospital is himself liable for his own negligence.

If the hospital is subject to suit, in most states there is a corresponding statutory provision which absolves its employees from personal liability. So the patient must sue either the hospital where it is not immune or the employee personally in states where the hospital is immune. For example, under the Federal Tort Claims Act, negligence by medical personnel is compensable only by the government as the employer. The physician is not personally liable. However, there is an exception in the Tort Claims Act for "deliberate torts," such as assault and battery, for which the government is not liable. In that case the physician or employee himself would be the only party subject to suit.

A patient in a VA hospital was brutally beaten by an orderly who was assigned to walk with him to the dining room. He died of his injuries. The heirs of the decedent sued the government. The court held that under the exemption in the Federal Tort Claims Act applicable to deliberate torts the government was not liable for the orderly's action. However, the orderly himself could be sued.[160]

Even where charitable or governmental immunity exists, hospitals are liable if they have used negligence in selection of their employees and in some cases in selection of their medical staff.[161]

A 9-year old girl who was a patient in a hospital was sexually molested by an orderly. The orderly had been convicted of sex crimes, including being a "peeping tom," prior to being hired at the hospital. The hospital had made no investigation of his background before they hired him. The court held that the allegation that the hospital was negligent in hiring him stated a good cause of action even though the rule in the state was that a charitable or governmental hospital would normally be immune to suit.[162]

The same result may be reached as to a hospital's liability for negligent acts committed by nurses or professional medical personnel whose credentials are not investigated before they are added to the hospital staff.[163]

A patient with severe chest pains went to the hospital. The staff physician in the emergency room gave him a prescription for indigestion and sent him home. His condition worsened and he died of a heart attack on the way back to the hospital. The court held that the hospital authority would be liable if its staff members had been negligent in selecting new staff. The opinion pointed out that even though a hospital would ordinarily be protected by charitable or governmental immunity, it must act in good faith and with reasonable care in selection of its staff physicians. Simply because a physician had a license to practice in the state did not guarantee that he was in fact a competent physician. The court held that the widow had a right to allow the jury to decide if the hospital, which would ordinarily be immune from suit, had been negligent in its selection of the physician who had examined her husband.[164]

There is a definite trend toward abolition of both charitable and governmental immunity both by judicial decision and statutory enactment.[165] It is highly unlikely that any form of immunity will be accepted in most states within a few more years.[166] It is obviously unfair for a patient to be subjected to careless treatment in a hospital without allowing him the right to compensation simply because the hospital is owned by a governmental or charitable agency. In some cases immunity might be construed as a license on the part of the hospital or its employees to tolerate carelessness without regard for the quality of the attention given to the patient. The anomalies of the immunity doctrine were well pointed out in one decision:

It is a strange distinction between a charitable institution and a charitable individual, relieving the one and holding the other for like service and like lapse in circumstances. The hospital may maim or kill a charity patient by negligence, yet the members of its medical staff attending without pay or thought of recompense dare not lapse in a tired or hurried movement.[167]

This chapter has dealt with some of the more obvious affirmative defenses which a physician may be able to raise if he is sued for malpractice. Some of them revolve around the facts of the situation, such as assumption of risk by the patient. Others involve legal points such as the statute of limitations. It should be noted that while most states adopt similar rules for application of the factual defenses, there is a wide variation among states as to the legal defenses.

NOTES

1. "The Importance of Medical Records," 228 *JAMA* No. 1, page 118, April 1, 1974.
2. Patrick v. Sedwick, 391 P 2d 453, 413 P 2d 169, Alaska 1964.
3. Karp v. Cooley, 349 F Supp 827, DC Tex 1972.
4. "Failure to Take Medical History," 226 *JAMA* No. 4, page 509, Oct. 22, 1973.
5. Alden v. Providence Hospital, 382 F 2d 163, CA DC 1967.
6. Foley v. Bishop Clarkson Memorial Hospital, 173 NW 2d 881, Neb 1970.
7. James v. Spear, 338 P 2d 22, Cal 1959.
8. Rotan v. Greenbaum, 273 F 2d 830, CA DC 1959.
9. American Law Institute, *Restatement of the Law of Torts*, Section 463.
10. Morse v. Rapkin, 263 NYS 2d 428, NY 1965; "Contributory Negligence: Part 1," 218 *JAMA* No. 5, page 785, Nov. 1, 1971.
11. Page v. Brodoff, 169 A 2d 901, Conn 1961.
12. Champs v. Stone, 58 NE 2d 803, Ohio 1944.
13. "Negligence of Patient Subsequent to That of Physician," 205 *JAMA* No. 2, page 161, July 8, 1968.
14. Stacy v. Williams, 69 SW 2d 697, Ky 1934.
15. Ernst v. Schwartz, 445 SW 2d 377, Mo 1969.
16. Musachia v. Rosman, 190 So 2d 47, Fla 1966.
17. General Hospital of Greater Miami, Inc. v. Gager, 160 So 2d 749, Fla 1964.
18. Schirey v. Schlemmer, 223 NE 2d 759, Ind 1967.
19. Merrill v. Odiorne, 94 Atl 753, Me 1915.
20. Williams v. Wurdemann, 128 Pac 639, Wash 1912.
21. Thackery v. Helfrich, 175 NE 449, Ohio 1931.
22. Bird v. Pritchard, 291 NE 2d 769, Ohio 1973.

23. Updegraff v. City of Ottumwa, 226 NW 928, Iowa 1929.

24. Johnson v. United States, 271 F Supp 205, DC Ark 1967.

25. Hanley v. Spencer, 115 P 2d 399, Colo 1941.

26. Somma v. United States, 180 F Supp 519, DC Pa 1960.

27. Gerber v. Day, 6 P 2d 535, Cal 1931.

28. Paull v. Zions First National Bank, 417 P 2d 759, Utah 1966; "Contributory Negligence: Part II," 218 *JAMA* No. 6, page 933, Nov. 8, 1971.

29. Blair v. Eblen, 461 SW 2d 370, Ky 1970.

30. Memorial Hospital of South Bend, Inc. v. Scott, 290 NE 2d 80, Ind 1972.

31. Evans v. Newark–Wayne Community Hospital, 316 NYS 2d 447, NY 1970.

32. Schuster v. St. Vincent Hospital, 172 NW 2d 421, Wisc 1969.

33. Bennett v. New York, 299 NYS 2d 288, NY 1969.

34. Steele v. Woods, 327 SW 2d 187, Mo 1959.

35. Bess Ambulance Co., Inc. v. Boll, 208 So 2d 308, Fla 1968.

36. Kent v. County of Hudson, 245 A 2d 747, NJ 1968.

37. Clark v. Piedmont Hospital, 162 SE 2d 468, Ga 1968.

38. Our Lady of Mercy Hospital v. McIntosh, 461 SW 2d 377, Ky 1970.

39. Flynn v. Stearns, 145 A 2d 33, NJ 1958.

40. "Contributory Negligence: Part III," 218 *JAMA* No. 7, page 1109, Nov. 15, 1971.

41. Puffinbarger v. Day, 24 Cal Rptr 533, Cal 1962.

42. Cyr v. Landry, 95 Atl 883, Me 1915.

43. Robinson v. Campbell, 97 SE 2d 544, Ga 1957.

44. Williams v. Marini, 162 Atl 796, Vt 1932; "Contributory Negligence in Malpractice," 12 *Cleveland-Marshall Law Rev* 455, 1963; "Contributory Negligence in Medical Malpractice," 21 *Cleveland State Law Rev* 58, Jan. 1972.

45 King v. Solomon, 81 NE 2d 838, Mass 1948; Los Alamos Medical Center v. Coe, 275 P 2d 175, NM 1954.

46. Facer v. Lewis, 40 NW 2d 457, Mich 1950.

47. Natanson v. Kline, 350 P 2d 1093, 354 P 2d 670, Kans 1960.

48. Mainfort v. Giannestras, 111 NE 2d 692, Ohio 1951.

49. Gramm v. Boener, 56 Ind 497, 1877.

50. Brockman v. Harpole, 444 P 2d 25, Ore 1968.

51. Valdez v. Percy, 217 P 2d 422, Cal 1950.

52. Munson v. Bishop Clarkson Memorial Hospital, 186 NW 2d 492, Neb 1971.

53. Charrin v. Methodist Hospital, 432 SW 2d 572, Tex 1968.

54. Dollins v. Hartford Accident and Indemnity Co., 477 SW 2d 179, Ark 1972.

55. Chapman v. Carlson, 240 So 2d 263, Miss 1970.

56. Dunlap v. Marine, 51 Cal Rptr 158, Cal 1966.

57. Linhares v. Hall, 257 NE 2d 429, Mass 1970.

58. Swanson v. Hill, 166 F Supp 296, DC ND 1958; Dietze v. King, 184 F Supp 944, DC Va 1960.

59. Steinmetz v. Humphrey, 160 SW 2d 6, Ky 1942.

60. Piper v. Halford, 25 So 2d 264, Ala 1946; Long v. Sledge, 209 So 2d 814, Miss 1968.
61. Weintraub v. Rosen, 93 F 2d 544, CCA 7, 1937.
62. Christian v. Wilmington General Hospital Association, 135 A 2d 727, Del 1957.
63. Crouch v. Most, 432 P 2d 250, NM 1967.
64. Phillips v. Werndorff, 243 NW 525, Iowa 1932.
65. Sams v. Curfman, 137 P 2d 1017, Colo 1943; Thompson v. Fox, 192 Atl 107, Pa 1937; Borden v. Sneed, 291 SW 2d 485, Tex 1956; Tanner v. Espey, 190 NE 229, Ohio 1934; Mier v. Yoho, 171 SE 535; W Va 1933; Poltera v. Garlington, 489 P 2d 334, Colo 1971; "Release of Original Wrongdoer," 196 *JAMA* No. 12, page 217, June 20, 1966.
66. Cannon v. Pearson, 383 SW 2d 565, Tex 1964.
67. Leech v. Bralliar, 275 F Supp 897, DC Ariz 1967.
68. Mazer v. Lipshutz, 360 F 2d 275, CCA 3, 1966.
69. Muse v. DeVito, 137 NE 730, Mass 1923; Martin v. Cunningham, 161 Pac 355, Wash 1916.
70. Hartley v. St. Francis Hospital, 129 NW 2d 235, Wisc 1964.
71. Parkell v. Fitzporter, 256 SW 239, Mo 1923.
72. Retelle v. Sullivan, 211 NW 756, Wisc 1927; Keown v. Young, 283 Pac 511, Kans 1930.
73. Fletcher v. Hand, 358 F 2d 549, CA DC 1966.
74. Piedmont Hospital v. Truitt, 172 SE 237, Ga 1933; Corbett v. Clarke, 46 SE 2d 327, Va 1948.
75. Purchase v. Seelye, 121 NE 413, Mass 1918.
76. Anderson v. Martzke, 266 NE 2d 137, Ill 1970.
77. Feiser v. St. Francis Hospital and School of Nursing Inc., 510 P 2d 145, Kans 1973.
78. Frost v. Des Moines Still College, 79 NW 2d 306, Iowa 1956.
79. DiNike v. Mowery, 418 P 2d 1010, Wash 1966; Kropp v. DeAngelis, 138 NYS 2d 188, NY 1955; Guth v. Vaughn, 231 Ill App 143, 1923; Martin v. Cunningham, 161 Pac 355, Wash 1916.
80. Derby v. Prewitt, 187 NE 2d 556, NY 1962.
81. Wellander v. Brooklyn Hospital, 174 NYS 2d 107, NY 1958.
82. Malvica v. Blumenfield, 310 NYS 2d 329, NY 1970.
83. Staehlin v. Hockdoerfer, 235 SW 106, Mo 1921; Sobotta v. Vogel, 194 NW 2d 564, Mich 1971; Miller, Frank R., "Does Release of the Original Tortfeasor Release the Subsequently Negligent Physician?," 36 *Insurance Counsel Journal*, No. 3, page 360, July 1969.
84. Von Blumenthal v. Cassola, 3 NYS 2d 246, 6 NYS 2d 342, NY 1938; Galloway v. Lawrence, 145 SE 2d 861, NC 1966.
85. McMillen v. Klingensmith, 467 SW 2d 193, Tex 1971.
86. Knight v. Lowery, 185 SE 2d 915, Ga 1971.
87. Simmons v. Wilder, 169 SE 2d 480, NC 1969; Amrieri v. St. Joseph's Hospital, 228 NYS 483, NY 1936.
88. Almquist v. Wilcox, 131 NW 796, Minn 1911.
89. Wecker v. Kilmer, 294 NE 2d 132, Ind 1973.

90. Ash v. Mortensen, 150 P 2d 876, Cal 1944; Couillard v. Charles T. Miller Hospital, 92 NW 2d 96, Minn 1958; Daily v. Somberg, 146 A 2d 676, NJ 1958.

91. Edgar County Bank & Trust Co. of Paris v. Paris Hospital, Inc., 294 NE 2d 319, Ill 1973.

92. Grantham v. Board of County Commissioners for Prince George's County, 246 A 2d 548, Md 1968.

93. Hospital Authority of Emanuel County v. Gray, 181 SE 2d 299, Ga 1971.

94. Estes v. Magee, 109 P 2d 631, Idaho 1940.

95. Beatty v. Armstrong, 73 NW 2d 719, Iowa 1955.

96. Matthews v. Atchison, Topeka & Santa Fe Railway Co., 129 P 2d 435, Cal 1942.

97. Meimen v. Rehabilitation Center, Inc., 444 SW 2d 78, Ky 1969.

98. Tunkl v. Regents of the University of California, 383 P 2d 441, Cal 1963.

99. Kozan v. Comstock, 270 F 2d 839, CCA 5, 1959.

100. Brown v. Moore, 247 F 2d 711, CCA 3, 1957.

101. Belshaw v. Feinstein, 65 Cal Rptr 788, Cal 1968.

102. Dorsey, J. S., "Release of Tortfeasor, Release of Physician," 15 *NC Law Rev*. 293, 1937; "Effect of Release Given Tortfeasor Causing Initial Injury on Later Action for Malpractice Against Treating Physician," 40 *NC Law Rev*. 88, 1961.

103. Forman v. Wolfson, 98 NE 2d 615, Mass 1951.

104. Lawson v. Conaway, 16 SE 564, W Va 1892; Gates v. Preston, 41 NY 113, 1869; Blair v. Bartlett, 75 NY 150, 1878.

105. House v. Hanson, 72 NW 2d 874, Minn 1955.

106. Gwynn v. Wilhelm, 360 P 2d 312, Ore 1961; Barton v. Southwick, 101 NE 928, Ill 1913.

107. Jordhal v. Berry, 75 NW 10, Minn 1898.

108. Haynes v. Ordway, 58 NH 167, 1877.

109. Black v. Dillon, 28 Cal Rptr 678, Cal 1963.

110. Duvardo v. Moore, 98 NE 2d 855, Ill 1951; Paine v. Wyatt, 251 NW 78, Iowa 1933; Lotspeich v. Chance Vought Aircraft Co., 369 SW 2d 705, Tex 1963.

111. White v. Matthews, 223 NYS 415, NY 1927; Wimer v. Miller, 383 P 2d 1005, Ore 1963; Gay v. Greene, 84 SE 2d 847, Ga 1954.

112. Wilson v. Hungate, 434 SW 2d 580, Mo 1968.

113. Powell v. Troland, 183 SE 2d 184, Va 1971.

114. "Surgical Infections from the Standpoint of Statute of Limitations," 197 *JAMA* No. 5, page 221, Aug 1, 1966.

115. Mantz v. Follingstad, 505 P 2d 68, NM 1972.

116. Peterson v. Roloff, 203 NW 2d 699, Wisc 1973.

117. Parker v. Vaughn, 183 SE 2d 605, Ga 1971; Axcell v. Phillips, 473 SW 2d 554, Tex 1971.

118. Sellers v. Edwards, 265 So 2d 438, Ala 1972.

119. Melnyk v. The Cleveland Clinic, 290 NE 2d 916, Ohio 1972.

120. Johnson v. Sterling Drug Co., 190 NW 2d 77, Minn 1971.

121. Ciccarone v. United States, 350 F Supp 554, DC Pa 1972.

122. Koenig v. Group Health Cooperative, 491 P 2d 702, Wash 1971.

123. Crawford v. McDonald, 187 SE 2d 542, Ga 1972.

124. Nitka v. Bell, 487 P 2d 379, Colo 1971; Hecht v. First National Bank and Trust Co., 490 P 2d 649, Kans 1971; "Expanding Statutes of Limitations," 210 *JAMA* No. 13, page 2467, Dec. 29, 1969; "Statutes of Limitations: Discovery Rule," 210 *JAMA* No. 10, page 1983, Dec. 8, 1969.

125. Ruth v. Dight, 453 P 2d 631, Wash 1969.

126. Acker v. Sorensen, 165 NW 2d 74, Neb 1969.

127. Rothman v. Silber, 216 A 2d 18, NJ 1966.

128. Illinois Rev. Stat., C. 83, Section 22.1.

129. Ala Code, Title 7, Section 25(1).

130. Conn Gen Stat Section 52-584.

131. Hays v. Hall, 477 SW 2d 402, Tex 1972.

132. Olson v. St. Croix Valley Memorial Hospital, 201 NW 2d 63, Wisc 1972.

133. Lopez v. Swyer, 300 A 2d 563, NJ 1973.

134. Acton v. Morrison, 155 P 2d 782, Ariz 1945; Nutt v. Carson, 340 P 2d 260, Okla 1959.

135. Toal v. United States, 438 F 2d 222, CCA 2, 1971.

136. Swope v. Printz, 468 SW 2d 34, Mo 1971.

137. Hundley v. Martinez, 158 SE 2d 159, W Va 1967.

138. Ray v. Scheibert, 484 SW 2d 63, Tenn 1972.

139. Nichols v. Smith, 489 SW 2d 719, Tex 1973.

140. "Recent Decisions on Statutes of Limitations; Part II," 227 *JAMA* No. 12, page 1500, March 25, 1974.

141. Kambas v. St. Joseph's Hospital, 189 NW 2d 879, Mich 1971; Dyke v. Richard, 198 NW 2d 797, Mich 1972.

142. Morris v. Monterey-Yorkshire Nursing Inn, 278 NE 2d 686, Ohio 1971.

143. "Recent Decisions on Statutes of Limitations: Part I," 227 *JAMA* No. 11, page 1336 March 18, 1974.

144. Lametta v. Connecticut Light & Power Co., 92 A 2d 731, Conn 1952; Nigro v. Flinn, 192 Atl 685, Del 1937; Colley v. Canal Bank and Trust Co., 159 F 2d 153, CCA 5, 1947; Fay v. Mundy, 54 Cal Rptr 591, Cal 1966.

145. Boland v. New York, 333 NYS 2d 410, NY 1972.

146. Jaime v. Neurological Hospital Association, 488 SW 2d 641, Mo 1973.

147. Wolfe v. Virusky, 306 F Supp 519, DC Ga 1969.

148. Billings v. Sisters of Mercy of Idaho, 389 P 2d 224, Idaho 1964.

149. Adams v. Poudre Valley Hospital District, 502 P 2d 1127, Colo 1972.

150. McCoy v. Wesley Hospital and Nurse Training School, 362 P 2d 841, Kans 1961; Doerr v. Villate, 220 NE 2d 767, Ill 1966; Seanor v. Browne, 7 P 2d 627, Okla 1932; Frankel v. Wolper, 169 NYS 15, NY 1918; Creighton v. Karlin, 225 So 2d 288, La 1969.

151. "Charitable Immunity," 197 *JAMA* No. 9, page 201, Aug. 29, 1966.

152. McDonald v. Massachusetts General Hospital, 120 Mass 432, 1876.

153. Hedlund v. Sutter Medical Service Co., 124 P 2d 878, Cal 1942; Jefferson Hospital Inc. v. Van Lear, 41 SE 2d 441, Va 1947.

154. Federal Tort Claims Act, 28 USCA, Section 1346 et seq.

155. "Government Liability for Negligent Treatment: Parts I, II and III," 224 *JAMA* No. 1, page 163, April 2, 1973, 224 *JAMA* No. 2, page 279, April 9, 1973, 224 *JAMA* No. 3, page 433, April 16, 1973.

156. Vanderbilt University v. Henderson, 127 SW 2d 284, Tenn 1938; Morton v. Savannah Hospital, 96 SE 887, Ga 1918; Mississippi Baptist Hospital v. Holmes, 55 So 2d 142, Miss 1951; Arkansas Midland Railroad Co. v. Pearson, 135 SW 917, Ark 1911.

157. Durney v. St. Francis Hospital, 83 A 2d 753, Del 1951.

158. Candler General Hospital v. Purvis, 181 SE 2d 77, Ga 1971.

159. Mulliner v. Evangelischer Diakonniessenverein of Minnesota District of German Evangelical Synod of North America, 175 NW 699, Minn 1920.

160. Cotter v. United States, 279 F Supp 847, DC NY 1968.

161. Darling v. Charleston Community Hospital, 200 NE 2d 149, 211 NE 2d 253, Ill 1965; McDermott v. St. Mary's Hospital, 133 A 2d 608, Conn 1957; St. Vincent Hospital v. Stine, 144 NE 537, Ind 1924.

162. Hipp v. Hospital Authority of the City of Marietta, 121 SE 2d 273, Ga 1961.

163. "Negligent Selection of Hospital Staff," 223 *JAMA* No. 7, page 833, Feb. 12, 1973.

164. Mitchell County Hospital v. Joiner, 189 SE 2d 412, Ga 1972.

165. Collopy v. Newark Eye and Ear Infirmary, 141 A 2d 276, NJ 1958.

166. Rabon v. Rowan Memorial Hospital, 152 SE 2d 485, NC 1967; Frye, Robert, M. D., "The Demise of Charitable Immunity," in *Legal Medicine Annual: 1970*, at page 115, Cyril H. Wecht, Ed., Appleton-Century-Crofts, New York 1970.

167. President and Directors of Georgetown College v. Hughes, 130 F 2d 810, DC DC 1942.

CHAPTER XI

MALPRACTICE

AND

DISCIPLINARY

ACTIONS

It is quite certain that each state has the right to make reasonable restrictions on the conduct of a professional person. All states have statutory grounds for revocation of a physician's license although most proscribed conduct does not involve malpractice, and in most states malpractice is not, in fact, grounds for revocation of a license. Under the constitutional authority of inherent "police power," it is a clear right of a state to revoke a physician's license for any of the causes specified in that state's statute. State statutes as to grounds for license revocation vary widely, but as long as the restrictions are reasonable, the revocation authority is clear.[1]

In the early years of this century, a physician placed an ad in a newspaper stating that she could cure cancer. Her license to practice was revoked for "unprofessional conduct" on the grounds that she had advertised for business. She attacked the constitutional right of the state to revoke her license. The court upheld the revocation and said: "Legislation of the character embraced within the general scope of the act in question insofar as it provides for the revocation of the certificate of a physician . . . is sustained upon the ground that the legislature has authority under its general police power to provide all reasonable regulations that may be necessary affecting the public health, safety, or morals, with this object in view to provide for the dismissal from the medical profession of all persons whose principles, practice or character render them unfit to remain in it."[2]

Most of the constitutional questions of the authority of states to take such action were settled many years ago.[3] Most recent cases have involved specific factual denials of the substance of the offense charged or claims that the offense with which the doctor was charged was not "reasonable ground" for revocation of his license or claims that he was denied some constitutionally mandated procedural right.

Only in very rare instances will federal courts enjoin boards of medical examiners from holding disciplinary hearings. Several physicians who have been charged by boards with offenses against state criminal statutes have recently asked federal courts to intervene. In all cases, as long as the physician has been given proper notice of hearing and cannot give proof that the hearing at which he is to defend himself will not be fair, the courts will not intervene.[4]

A physician was convicted of carrying an unregistered firearm. He was given notice of a hearing at which time he was to show cause why his license should not be revoked for conviction of a felony. He asked the federal district court to enjoin the hearing, pointing out that the state statue specifying grounds for revocation of a physician's license included "any felony," whereas the statutes concerning dentists involved only felonies involving "moral turpitude." This, he argued, constituted an unconstitutional discrimination against physicians. The court refused to intervene.[5]

It is quite clear that acquittal of a criminal offense followed by proceedings to revoke a physician's license does not violate the physician's right against double jeopardy guaranteed in the Fifth and Fourteenth Amendments.

A physician was charged with committing an illegal abortion. He denied that he had done it and was acquitted by the jury. The Board of Medical Examiners served notice of charges and set a hearing to revoke his license. He claimed that any such procedures would constitute double jeopardy. The court dismissed his claim. It held that the procedure to revoke a license to practice medicine is an administrative procedure, not a criminal action, and that constitutional provisions against double jeopardy did not apply. Further, the court held that double jeopardy may, under all circumstances, only be pleaded in criminal actions and since the purpose of revocation of a professional license is not a penal one, but one designed to protect the public, it was completely inapplicable.[6]

Due Process of Law.   Courts have long required administrative procedures of any type to conform to constitutional requirements of due process of law and elementary fairness.[7] Notice of hearing, the right to appear and submit evidence on one's behalf, and presumably, although there are no specific cases on the point, the right to be represented by counsel are all included in the concept of "due process of law" in a disciplinary hearing. The hearing must be conducted in a fair and impartial manner. The specific misconduct which constitutes the grounds of the hearing must be presented to the physician in a written complaint with factual allegations indicating the reasons the Board of Medical Examiners has for believing that the conduct is improper.[8] The obvious purpose in requiring specification of the facts involved in the case is to clarify the issues. Elemental fairness, as well as constitutional guarantees of due process, mandate that the accused physician be aware of all aspects of the charge in order to prepare his defense. If notice of the charges is inadequate, a new hearing will be ordered.

A physician was convicted of counterfeiting and sent to prison. While he was there, his attorney died. Notice of a hearing by the Board of Medical Examiners for the purpose of revoking the prisoner's license was sent to the lawyer's office after his death and no notice was sent to the physician. Upon his release, he discovered that the hearing had been held and that his license had been permanently revoked without his knowledge. He petitioned for a new hearing and it was granted. The court found that he was entitled to adequate notice, which he had not received through neither his fault nor the Board's since it did not know of his attorney's death.[9]

Specific facts must be charged. Courts usually hold that simply charging the physician with "gross immorality" or "unprofessional conduct" without further clarification is insufficient notice.[10]

Of course the physician is entitled to be given full particulars of the date, time, and place of the hearing and he is entitled to receive the complaint sufficiently in advance to allow him adequate time to prepare and present a defense. He has the right to a full, fair, and impartial hearing. He must, for example, have the right to offer witnesses on his own behalf, if he wishes to do so.[11] If a physician is being held in jail at the time of his license revocation hearing, he has been denied due process if he is not allowed to appear. Arrangement should be made either with the warden to transfer him to the hearing or the hearing should be postponed until his release from prison.[12]

Evidence must be taken in the presence of the physician and his counsel to protect the right of the physician to cross-examine all witnesses who testify against him. Hearsay evidence may not be received, but judicial restrictions on the other types of evidence admissible in a disciplinary hearing are much less strict than those applied in court.[13]

A physician was charged with referring a woman to another physician for a criminal abortion. The woman who had had the abortion testified at the hearing that the man who had impregnated her took her to the defendant physician's office, but that the physician told her that he did not perform abortions. The man and the physician then had a conversation in a language which she did not understand. The man told her later that the physician had suggested another physician who performed the abortion a few days later. The accused physician denied that he had referred them to anyone. Neither the physician who allegedly performed the abortion or the woman's friend who arranged it were present to testify. The court held that the accused had not been given a fair hearing with the admission of such hearsay evidence.[14]

Constitutional guarantees of due process have been interpreted to require that a charge considered by an administrative body of any type must be supported by "substantial evidence" for a finding of guilt. The proof must satisfy the proposition that the physician is more likely to be guilty than that he is not, and evidence on each charge of which he is convicted must be proved to that extent.[15] However, the facts do not have to be proved "beyond the reasonable doubt" which would be required in a criminal proceeding.[16] Far less proof is required to revoke the license of a physician already placed on probation or whose license has been suspended in a prior proceeding before the same board than is required to suspend or revoke it on the initial charge.[17] In some states, in fact, no hearing is required to revoke the license of a physician who is on probation and who commits another offense. However, in view of the fact that the Supreme Court of the United States has recently ruled that a criminal probation cannot be revoked and the probationer sent to jail without a full-scale hearing, a test case of the point might well result in à finding that a physician, too, is entitled to a full hearing in this circumstance.

The burden of proof, of course, is on the body which wishes to revoke the license. However, if the physician's license has been suspended and he wishes to petition for restoration on the grounds that he has been rehabilitated, he bears the burden of proving that he has made such progress.[18]

Courts do have the right to review decisions of boards revoking physicians' licenses.[19] Judicial review in these cases is generally quite limited in scope, since courts assume that physicians on a board of medical examiners are far more knowledgeable than judges would be to determine whether or not a given activity constitutes "unprofessional conduct." Judicial intervention is therefore restricted to investigations of "elemental fairness," which usually involves only a determination that the verdict is "supported by substantial evidence,"[20] and the physician bears the burden of proving that it was not.

A physician was charged with failure to keep adequate records of dispensing narcotics. He demonstrated that during an illness he had taken Demerol himself and had given some to his wife and their children. In all four cases, the court found that there was ample medical justification for his giving the medication. He had been in traction following an orthopedic procedure and had given his wife the narcotic after she had had a hysterectomy. The children also had legitimate medical complaints which also made it necessary to give it to them. In all four cases, the physicians who were primary physicians for the family knew and approved of what he had done. The court reversed the Board of Medical Examiners' findings that the physician was guilty of unprofessional conduct and held that the evidence presented was inadequate in every particular to support the charges since there was undisputed evidence presented by the physician that the medication was used legitimately.[21]

A physician's license in one state had been revoked after he had been committed to a mental hospital as an alcoholic. He had been certified by the FAA to perform physical examinations on persons wishing to qualify for pilots' licenses and at the time of the commitment, that certificate had been cancelled. However, he was also licensed to practice in another state and continued to perform FAA examinations in that state after having been notified to cease doing so. As a result, his license was revoked for unprofessional conduct in the second state. In discussing the scope of judicial review, the court pointed out that the only questions which would be examined on an appeal from an administrative hearing would be questions of constitutionality, actions which allegedly exceeded the authority of the board under the statute which establishes it, the use of unlawful procedures, the allegation that the result was unsupported by substantial evidence, and the allegation that the board acted arbitrarily or capriciously. The revocation was upheld.[22]

"Arbitrary and capricious" decisions generally are construed to mean those which evidence indicates were not made on the basis of fairness, but were made for malicious or personal reasons by members of the board. In recent years there have been no decisions in which any courts found that an action of a board of medical examiners was arbitrary and capricious.[23]

A physician who is convicted of a crime but appeals his conviction may in some circumstances have his license revoked before the appeal is decided. This does not deny him due process of law.

A physician was convicted of driving under the influence of alcohol and put on probation for 5 years. During that period he was charged with attempting to commit an abortion and his probation was revoked by the court. At that time he filed an appeal on the probation revocation, but before it was heard, the Board of Medical Examiners filed notice of charges to revoke his license.

The court held that failure to wait until the criminal appeal was decided did not under the circumstances deny him due process.[24]

In each state the applicable statute confers authority and jurisdiction on the boards of medical examiners in regard to disciplinary cases and these boards may not exceed such authority as is granted in the enabling legislation. If a board does not wish to take action against a physician however, it may not be judicially compelled to do so.[25]

A patient was attended by an obstetrician and an anesthesiologist during childbirth. She suffered severe brain damage as a result of clearly improper administration of anesthesia. Guardians were appointed to represent her interests and brought a malpractice action against the physicians, who settled the case. Thereafter her father who was, with her husband, one of her guardians, wrote to the state Board of Medical Examiners setting forth complaints against the physicians and enclosing a transcript of the malpractice trial. He demanded that the Board conduct hearings to revoke their licenses and stated that he would produce witnesses to testify as to their professional incompetence. The Board advised him that it would conduct is own investigation and 3 months later notified him that it had decided not to file charges. The father sued to compel the Board to file disciplinary charges and to hold hearings. The Board moved to dismiss the suit on the grounds that it could not be compelled to act and the court affirmed its position. The decision pointed out that the Board has the right in its own discretion to determine whether or not disciplinary action would be taken. The Board was responsible for making that decision and the court would not substitute its own judgment.[26]

Grounds for Revocation of License.   States vary widely in their statutory grounds for revocation of a physician's license, but the broad categories include conviction of a criminal offense or those related to the ethics of professional activities. Most states provide for revocation of a license on the grounds of unprofessional or infamous conduct. Only a few provide for revocation on the grounds of "manifest incapacity and gross carelessness." Most statutes also include lists of various types of conduct which are specifically prohibited.

Until the Supreme Court decisions of 1973 indicating that a woman has a right to an abortion and thus that it cannot be a criminal offense to perform one, abortion was in almost all states grounds for revocation of a physician's license.[27] In most states a physician who was charged with performance of a criminal abortion but pleaded guilty to a lesser charge, such as assault, could also have his license revoked.[28] It is highly unlikely that a physician's license may now be revoked on an abortion charge even if a state board of medical examiners should take the position that abortion is "immoral" and attempts to revoke his license for "unprofessional conduct" on that ground. It is quite clear that specific statutes which provide for license revocation for abortions are now unconstitutional in view of those decisions.[29] Those physicians whose licenses were revoked when the anti-abortion statutes were valid presumably do not have a cause of action to have them restored, however, since the abortions were in violation of the criminal law at the time of the revocation.

Advertising for example, in a newspaper, that a physician can cure ailments, specific or otherwise, is in contravention of ethics and under most state statutes is specific grounds for revocation of a license.[30]

Criminal Offenses. Conviction of a crime is the most usual ground for revocation of physicians' licenses.[31] It is quite clear that the crime charged does not necessarily have to involve the practice of medicine. For example, there are probably more license revocation proceedings after physicians have been convicted of violation of income tax laws than on any other grounds.[32] Other physicians have recently had their licenses revoked after convictions for counterfeiting[33] and carrying an unregistered firearm.[34] In short, conviction of any felony is generally considered sufficient to revoke a medical license even if the physician is convicted on a charge which is not a crime in the state of license.[35] After revocation or suspension of a license, if a physician continues to treat patients he is also guilty of the criminal offense of practicing medicine without a license. This is, of course, the same statutory authority with which the state may forbid laymen to treat medical problems.[36] Further, however, the physician may find himself in criminal contempt for practicing in contravention of the order of a board of medical examiners or a court and contempt penalties in most states are more severe than those provided by the medical practice statutes.[37]

A physician who has a valid license in one state, however, is not subject to prosecution for practicing without a license or to disciplinary action if he treats an emergency patient in another state.[38] A physician, for example, who is on vacation in a state where he is not licensed and who is summoned to help a person who has had a heart attack or who delivers a baby on an airliner is not subject to any form of penalty.

Physicians who are properly establishing residencies for purpose of obtaining licenses, interns or residents, and physicians attached to armed forces hospitals or other federal facilities are also not subject to criminal or disciplinary sanction for failure to have valid state licenses.[39] Moreover, in these cases an otherwise qualified physician without a valid license is not considered negligent per se and a patient who wishes to sue him cannot use his failure to have a license as relevant evidence to show a failure to use due care in diagnosis or treatment.[40]

Physicians who have been charged with violation of the alcohol and narcotics laws involving their own use of the substances frequently suffer the losses of their licenses.[41] Alcohol problems particularly, with or without criminal prosecution, have been involved in many disciplinary decisions.[42]

A physician's license was suspended and he was placed on probation for the use of narcotics, public drunkenness, of which he was convicted, and a charge of receiving stolen goods which had been dismissed by the court on the grounds of insufficient evidence. At the time he was put on probation he voluntarily surrendered his license to prescribe narcotics. While on probation, the physician, his minor son, and a teenage friend of the son were arrested in his car driven by the teenager after a police chase at 110 miles per hour. They were all arrested and spent the night in jail. At the time the three were arrested the police found an open bottle of whiskey and a large quantity of phenobarbital in the physician's car. The Board of Medical Examiners found that he had violated the terms of his probation and revoked his license. He appealed, but the appellate court upheld his revocation. The decision pointed out that there was substantial evidence that he had violated the terms of his probation even though the evidence produced from that episode alone probably would not have been sufficient to revoke his license if he had not been in previous difficulties.[43]

A physician was twice arrested for driving while intoxicated. On the first occasion he pleaded no contest, but the plea was later changed to not guilty and the charges were dropped. He was convicted on the second charge. At the disciplinary hearing a psychiatrist who was treating him testified that the physician was an alcoholic. The court upheld the Board's claims that he should be put on probation. While the court pointed out that a physician's private life is usually not the concern of a disciplinary body, where excessive use of alcohol or drugs is proven, a question of adequacy of professional judgment was raised and therefore the court found his probation to be reasonable.[44]

Violation of narcotics laws by prescribing drugs to addicts without medical justification is, of course, specifically prohibited by the criminal law and is sufficient grounds for revocation of a physician's license.[45] Even acts which are not prohibited by narcotics laws may be considered by a board of medical examiners as "unprofessional conduct" if such acts are proved by adequate, competent evidence. Therefore, a physician who is not charged with criminal violation of narcotics laws may still have his license revoked for misuse of prescription drugs.[46]

Some states provide in their disciplinary statutes that the offense for which a license may be revoked must be a felony. Other states simply specify that the physician must have been "convicted of a crime," which would apparently include misdemeanors. However, there are no cases in which a physician's license was in fact revoked after conviction of a misdemeanor. It is highly unlikely that a court would uphold revocation of a physician's license on the grounds that he had received a speeding ticket or was guilty of some other form of misdemeanor as long as there was no danger to human life or moral turpitude involved in the offense.

In several cases physicians pleaded "no contest," known as a plea of *nolo contendere,* to criminal charges. It is very clear that the effect of a plea of no contest is for these purposes the equivalent of a plea of guilty and therefore may be used as the basis of a license revocation.[47]

Fraud. Fraud is also sufficient grounds for revocation of a physician's license. A license which has been issued as the result of a fraudulent application is considered invalid from the date of issue and therefore can be annulled.[48]

The physician must, however, be proved to have committed some willful or intentional act which actively induced the issuance of his license. In order to revoke a license on the grounds that it was granted by fraud the board must find that false answers were made to material questions affecting the physician's qualifications to practice medicine.[49] For example, a license to practice obtained by presentation of a diploma from a fraudulent medical school is always subject to revocation.[50]

Proof of fraud in filing claims for payment from companies or governmental bodies such as welfare departments for services which were stated as rendered but were not in fact given is also sufficient to revoke a license whether or not criminal proceedings result.[51] The preparation of a false medical report or bill in any context, including those to be used as evidence in a personal injury law suit, is sufficient.[52]

A physician's license was suspended for 6 months. He was charged with making fraudulent claims that he had performed office surgery on four Medicaid patients, but three of the four patients testified that they had had no such operations. He claimed that the bills were sent to the Welfare Department as an innocent error made by his secretary and that no intent to defraud was present. His suspension was upheld.[53]

A patient consulted a physician about some spots on his face and scalp which the physician told him were caused by syphilis. The physician then falsified a laboratory report recording the patient's blood tests as positive for syphilis in order to keep the patient from discovering that he had made a diagnostic error. The court upheld the board's revocation of the physician's license on the ground that he had made a fraudulent diagnosis.[54]

Even in the absence of a specific statute allowing revocation of a license on grounds of fraud, it is clearly "unprofessional conduct," but because the definition of fraud necessarily includes an intent to deceive, an innocent mistake or misrepresentation of fact on a claim form or medical report does not constitute fraud.[55]

A fraudulent assurance given to a patient in the course of treatment is also sufficient to revoke a license.[56] For example, assuring a patient that an incurable disease can be cured by that particular physician is considered fraud for the purposes of revoking a license.[57] Any advertisement or statement to a patient that the physician has a "secret cure" is sufficient fraud to support revocation of a license. While this falls into the category of fraud in those states where the statutes provide for revocation on those grounds, it is also considered unprofessional conduct in those states which do not.[58]

A doctor with an active license described his diagnostic tool as a piece of wood pulp paper moistened by the patient's own saliva which was placed on a selected spot on the patient's abdomen. Different drugs were then placed in the patient's hand. The left hand was used for females and the right hand was used for males. If the drug or medicine which the patient held would cure him, a reaction allegedly apparent to the physician occurred on the paper. In this manner, the physician claimed to be able to determine the proper medication for any ailment. He further testified that his method of diagnosis was quite dependable without his seeing or examining a patient. All he needed was a prepared test paper which was moistened by the patient's tongue. This paper would be mailed to him, and placed on another person's abdomen. Different drugs were placed in the substitute patient's hands and the diagnosis would be made. These patients received expensive "medications" containing nothing but table sugar and milk. The physician claimed that these pills received therapeutic potency from "energy" with which he charged them from an electric machine of his own invention. The court said that the physician's diagnostic methods were so clearly "bald quackery" that his license could be revoked for fraud.[59]

Honest and legitimate innovative use of medication is, of course, not sufficient to sustain a loss of license on the grounds of fraud as long as a physician treats patients in good faith and in keeping with accepted medical standards.

A physician treated obesity with a special diet and drugs which he had himself developed. Careful physical examinations were made prior to administration of medication and a diet was recommended. The court held that although there were a great many physicians who would disagree with his theories on diet, if use of new methods of treatment paved the way for charges of fraud and deceit against physicians, medical research would be terminated.[60]

Since fraud implies a willful mistatement of facts, as long as the physician does not make outlandish claims for his diagnoses or treatments or his own qualifications, he cannot be convicted of fraud.

Sexual Misbehavior. Sexual misbehavior with a patient of either sex is amply sufficient to revoke a physician's license for unprofessional conduct even if the activity does not constitute a criminal offense. Furthermore, sex crimes involving nonpatients may also provide grounds for revocation.

A resident in pediatrics pleaded no contest to a charge of child molestation. The girl was 11 years old and his patient in the hospital at the time the epi-side took place. His license was revoked.[61]

A teenage girl engaged in innumerable and totally promiscuous acts of sexual intercourse. She was sent to a psychiatrist for treatment. His treatment consisted of having sexual relations with her. He was convicted of statutory rape. The Board of Medical Examiners revoked his license to practice medicine for unprofessional conduct on the grounds of having been convicted of a crime involving moral turpitude. He claimed that statutory rape did not necessarily involve moral turpitude. The court said that while that position might be correct in some situations, it would uphold the revocation in this case, noting particularly that he had violated the position of trust in which he had placed himself.[62]

Furthermore, sexual acts performed under the guise of medical treatment may very well constitute fraud[63] as well as a criminal act. Sexual acts with patients which are improper, but which do not constitute either fraud or violations of criminal statutes may also support revocation of a license.[64]

It is highly probable that a physician who was convicted of rape, sexual assault, homosexual activities, or similar felonies, even if the victim was not a patient, would find that his license could be revoked.[65] One of the more bizarre cases in recent years involved an attorney, but given equivalent or similar facts, presumably a physician's license would also be revoked. The man had had sexual intercourse with his step-daughter for years. She finally got pregnant in her late teens, but had passed the age of consent. He was therefore not guilty of statutory rape. At that point, the attorney divorced his wife, the girl's mother, and married the girl with her mother's consent. He, both wives, the baby, the children of the attorney and his first wife, other children by the first wife's previous marriage, and various other relations all lived in the same house, apparently on a basis satisfactory to all. However, he was disbarred for "gross immorality" and the disbarment was upheld. The court pointed out that while technically speaking he had not committed a crime and that while a man's personal life usually was not relevant to his professional ability or ethics, this case was so extreme that it went far beyond "the acceptable limits of peccadillos" and constituted outright moral depravity, even if it were not a criminal offense.[66]

Another case which probably would not now be considered to constitute sufficient "general depravity" was decided by the Supreme Court of the United States in 1903.

A committee of three was appointed by a town meeting of citizens of Emporia, Kansas to present charges to the Board of Medical Examiners against a physician who had had a series of sexual affairs, none of which involved patients, but some of which apparently involved wives of other physicians in the community. The charge contained a copy of a resolution adopted by the School Board dismissing one of its female teachers for associating with the physician. It also contained the statement that the physician was a "man notorious in the community for his immorality." Attached to the charge was a request signed by 18 practicing physicians stating, "We have grounds to believe that he is grossly immoral and we know he is guilty of other unprofessional conduct of such a degree that we will not meet him in consultation or recognize him as a member of the medical profession." Pastors of 9 churches and 38 business men signed a petition stating that the physician was "grossly immoral" and asked that his license be revoked. His defense was that his license could not be revoked for offenses other than those which grew out of the manner in which he conducted his practice. The United States Supreme Court upheld the decision in which the Supreme Court of Kansas rejected this argument and said: "The law is not that Board must find that such a person has been grossly immoral with his patients but that he is grossly immoral in his general habits. The object sought is the protection of the home of the sick and distressed from the intrusion therein, in professional character, of vicious and unprincipled men wholly destitute of all moral sensibilities."[67]

Conviction of a homosexual offense even though the other participant is not a patient is also sufficient to justify loss of a license to practice.[68] Even if the other party to a homosexual act is a consenting adult and has no professional relationship with the physician the courts are apparently likely to feel that although the crime is totally unrelated to the practice of medicine and is not a felony, it is a sufficient indictment of moral character to result in the loss of a license.

Moral Turpitude Offenses. If a physician is convicted of any crime involving moral turpitude, even though it is not related to the practice of medicine, he may very well lose his license.

A physician was convicted of having furnished an alcoholic beverage to a person under 21. The Board of Medical Examiners brought charges against him for "unprofessional conduct by virtue of having committed a crime involving moral turpitude." On appeal, the California Supreme Court held that the offense of which the doctor had been convicted had not involved moral turpitude and declared that "Moral turpitude is not inherent in a crime itself unless a conviction in every case would evidence bad moral character. Only if the minimum elements for convictions necessarily involve moral turpitude can be conviction be held to be 'an offense involving moral turpitude'. We conclude that the offense of giving an alcoholic beverage to a person under the age of twenty-one years does not in every case evidence a bad moral character." The court went on to observe that the Board could have proceeded validly against the physician on the basis of immoral conduct rather than on the basis of his conviction.[69]

Criminal violations of narcotic laws are automatically considered crimes involving moral turpitude.[70] Income tax invasion and counterfeiting have also been considered crimes involving moral turpitude. However, a conviction of disturbing the peace was considered not to be an "immoral activity" sufficient to support revocation of license.[71]

Unprofessional Conduct. Unprofessional conduct is generally considered to cover a wide variety of other noncriminal activities. It includes a very broad range of behavior and whether or not a given activity falls within a state's statute depends on the attitude adopted by its courts.

Unprofessional conduct by legal definition is considered to be "conduct of such a character that would in the common judgment be deemed dishonorable or unprofessional"[72] or otherwise defined as "failing to observe the standards of professional conduct which are accepted by the physicians in the community."[73] These definitions have been upheld as legally sufficient to overcome objections on the constitutional grounds of vagueness.[74]

A physician's license was revoked on the grounds of "unprofessional and dishonest conduct," but he was not charged with any of the specific acts which were enumerated in the statute defining these grounds. The court examined the statute and held that although the legislature had chosen to list some types of conduct, it did not intend thereby to exclude all other acts or conduct affecting the practice of medicine. The court found that it would not be practical to specify every act or course of conduct which would constitute unprofessional behavior because any conduct which by "common opinion and fair judgment is found by the Board of Medical Examiners in its sound discretion to be by its very nature unprofessional and dishonest conduct is adequate grounds for revocation of license."[75]

Unprofessional conduct can sometimes take very bizarre forms. Malicious betrayal of a professional secret may be conduct sufficient for revocation of a license on the grounds of unprofessional conduct.[76] Selling examination questions prior to a state board examination is also sufficient grounds for revocation on this ground.[77] Fee-splitting is clearly unprofessional conduct.[78] Commitment as an alcoholic even without criminal charges may be sufficient.[79] Making disparaging remarks regarding other physicians may in some cases constitute unprofessional conduct.

A physician had referred to another physician as "the city drunk." He called a second doctor in the same community "a lousy old midwife who had probably killed more persons than she ever helped." A third physician was charged with being incompetent. The Board of Medical Examiners maintained that the physician's acts amounted to "unprofessional conduct." However, the court concluded that the petitioner's conduct was no threat to the protection of the public health, safety, and welfare and therefore overruled the Board of Medical Examiners.[80]

A physician was disciplined by his county medical society for three separate incidents which his fellow physicians considered unethical. Two of them were upheld by the appellate court as valid causes of disciplinary action; the third was not. In the first case he said to a hospital nurse that a patient's physician had no justification for performing a Cesarian on her just as the patient was being wheeled into surgery. She overheard the remarks, which were made in a loud voice, and her husband, who was standing beside her, heard them also. In the second, he said to either a woman or her brother that the woman should not have had an operation which had already been performed by another surgeon, who had consulted two other surgeons prior to the surgery. In the third, he made disparaging comments about the ability of a pathologist to an attorney who was preparing to file a suit involving a death which had been investigated by the pathologist. The court held that any communication involving a judicial proceeding would be considered privileged information and expressing his honest opinion to the attorney could not be considered unethical behavior. The other two instances, however, were held to justify the action taken.[81]

A physician's license was revoked because of unprofessional conduct in (1) failing to make tests to corroborate a diagnosis on an elderly woman; (2) as to the same patient, signing her death certificate before she died; and (3) attempting to deliver her body to a medical school contrary to her express desires.[82]

Aiding and abetting an unlicensed person in the practice of medicine is also considered unprofessional conduct.[83]

A physician permitted a bookkeeper employed by him to engage in the practice of medicine in his office under his direction. The bookkeeper received and examined patients, made diagnoses, dispensed treatment, and accepted fees which he turned over to the physician. The physician's loss of license for unprofessional conduct was upheld by state courts.[84]

If a physician employs another qualified physician to work in his office while the employee is establishing residence for the purpose of obtaining a state license, he is not violating these statutes as long as he exercises reasonable supervision over the physician.[85] It is clear that statutes under which licenses have been revoked for allowing unlicensed persons to practice medicine have been designed to stop physicians who allow untrained laymen to treat patients because of the obvious dangers to the patient. However, the same problem does not occur with a qualified physician who simply does not have a state license because he has not yet met residency requirements to obtain it.

It would appear that any behavior which is a serious breach of ethics or morality, even though not a criminal offense, will sustain a license revocation on the grounds of unprofessional conduct. Most, if not all, of the cases involving charges of unprofessional conduct have involved the practice of medicine or such matters as alcohol or drug abuse by the physician himself which in turn might reasonably be expected to impair his medical judgment. Except in extremely rare cases involving bizarre forms of eccentricities, other aspects of a physician's life apparently do not justify a disciplinary proceeding on this ground. For example, a physician who engages in legal, but unpopular, political activity could not be disciplined for unprofessional conduct. Fraud in the submission of a bill for patient care is undoubtedly unprofessional conduct but a physician who defrauds the purchaser of his house probably is not subject to disciplinary action.

Professional Incompetence.   Professional or personal incapacity is another basis for revocation of license. A physician who has been declared mentally incompetent, but is later restored to legal competency may still lose his license on the grounds that he is no longer capable of practicing medicine, even in the absence of actual professional negligence.[86]

In a few states, the licensing statutes specify incompetence, negligence, and/or malpractice as grounds for revocation of a license, but in most, the statutes do not.[87] According to the Report of the Commission on Malpractice established by the Secretary of Health, Education and Welfare, only 15 states permit a license to be revoked on these grounds and the Commission recommended that such statutes be enacted in all states.[88]

In one very famous case, a physician had his license revoked on the grounds of professional incompetence. He had received A.B. and M.D. degrees from Harvard Medical School, was certified by the American Board of Surgery, and was a Fellow of the American College of Surgeons. Around 15 years after he was Board certified, he began practice in a small town and applied for membership as a surgeon at the local hospital. The hospital rejected his application, whereupon he sued to compel admission to the staff and won his case. The hospital then admitted the physician and allowed him to perform surgery while it appealed the decision. On appeal, the hospital won; he was dismissed from the staff and revocation proceedings were begun. An informal complaint was made to the State Board of Medical Examiners and a Board member investigated the charge. A few months later a formal complaint was filed by the Board charging that he had been guilty of unprofessional conduct in the handling of certain surgical cases. A lengthy and thorough hearing was held and the Board of Medical Examiners revoked his license. He appealed the decision to a trial judge, who found that he was not professionally incompetent and that the record did not support the Board's findings. The State Supreme Court reversed the judge's decision and the license was revoked. Eleven surgical cases were the subject of the investigation and two physicians from other states where he had practiced testified as to his incompetence there. The physician defended his procedures against allegations of incompetence, but admitted certain deficiencies. The applicable state statute provided for revocation on the grounds of "unprofessional, improper, unauthorized and unqualified practice of the Healing Arts," and the court noted that the whole purpose of the Medicine Licensing Act was the protection of the public from improper treatment and that the goal of the statute was to secure for the public the services of competent physicians. Therefore it was necessary to exclude incompetents from the practice of medicine.[89]

A few other cases have also held that physicians found incompetent may lose their licenses.[90]

A physician told a patient that he had a rectal fissure and advised an operation for its removal. The patient consented and was charged $150.00. After the operation, the patient, suffering from acute constipation, contacted another physician who examined him and told him that he still had the fissure. The second surgeon then removed it for $50.00. License revocation proceedings were brought on the grounds that the first physician had treated the patient in a "fraudulent, dishonorable, unprofessional, and incompetent" manner. The treatment was fraudulent because he implied to the patient that he had corrected the diseased condition when he had not done so and knew it. His behavior was dishonorable because the fee he charged was exhorbitant and it was unprofessional because he had behaved in a manner not compatible with established standards of medical conduct. He was found to be incompetent because, although he claimed to be a proctologist, his background and experience did not justify this statement; he did not precede the treatment with an enema and he neglected to sterilize the instruments he used. The court upheld his revocation.[91]

Another physician was brought before a license revocations proceeding for "ignorant malpractice." The basis of the charge was that the amounts of narcotics he prescribed were larger than those which would be prescribed by any normal physician in good faith in like circumstances. The court held that if expert testimony was given as to the dosages commonly used, revocation would be upheld.[92]

"Gross carelessness and manifest incapacity" has also been upheld as a statutory ground for revocation of a license against a charge that it was unconstitutional. One court held that the term "gross carelessness" had been interpreted quite clearly by courts to mean "that entire want of care which would raise the presumption of conscious indifference to consequences; an entire want of care, or such a slight degree of care as to raise the presumption of an entire disregard for or indifference to, the safety and welfare of others; the want of even slight care and diligence." The term "manifest incapacity" was also defined in the same case as "the lack of power to comprehend or to act, such lack being so obvious that no proof is necessary to establish it other than proof of the act itself."[93]

The verdict of a jury finding a physician negligent in an ordinary malpractice case does not constitute professional incompetence for license revocation purposes. Unless a physician treated a patient while he was drunk or on narcotics or deliberately disregarded the patient's welfare, it is highly unlikely that disciplinary proceedings would follow one mistake. In all these decisions involving incompetence as a ground for revocation, a pattern of gross negligence had been established by the evidence.

Incompetence may, of course, result in disciplinary actions short of revocation of a license. For example, in most states, negligent selection of hospital staff members renders a hospital liable for their negligence even where the hospital is protected from suit for negligent actions committed by a qualified physician who is a member of its staff. Thus incompetence known to the hospital is sufficient grounds for denial or revocation of hospital privileges.[94]

Disciplinary Actions and Medical Societies. A medical society or other professional organization is usually "a voluntary association." Courts in recent years have held that if its members receive either economic or professional benefits as a result of membership, which is, after all, the purpose of the association, qualified applicants may not be denied admission for arbitrary reasons.[95] In cases involving voluntary associations of any type, if an applicant cannot demonstrate an economic benefit such as, in cases involving physicians, a right to belong to a hospital staff or increased professional status, courts will not compel a professional society to accept him as a member.[96] In late years, however, courts have been inclined to find that applicants to any type of professional society are damaged by denial of right to membership in those societies. Therefore, an applicant who has been denied membership or a member who has been expelled may well have a right to sue the society. A medical society or bar association is, after all, quite different from a country club and denial of membership can result in serious, professionally damaging, consequences.

A voluntary association usually has a constitution and bylaws. If it is incorporated, as an increasing number of professional associations are, it must have such documents in order to qualify for a corporate charter. If members disobey written rules and regulations, which they are presumed to know by virtue of the fact that such regulations were in effect at the time they joined the association, courts hold that they may be disciplined or expelled for violation of those bylaws.[97] However, there is a judicial requirement that disciplinary or exclusionary actions by professional associations be fundamentally fair both in terms of substantive grounds and in procedures followed in regard to both applicants and members.[98]

Before a medical society can expel a member, he has a right to a hearing, but if he is given adequate notice, he may be expelled by default.

A member of a medical society routinely threw his mail from the organization in the trash without reading it. Therefore he did not receive notice that a hearing was being held to expel him. His expulsion was upheld on the grounds that it was his own fault that he did not receive notice of the hearing.[99]

Whatever provisions for procedural due process are included in a society's bylaws must be followed at the hearing, and reasonable procedural fairness is required even without a specific provision establishing it.[100] Before an expelled member of a medical society may go to court for an order of reinstatement, he must demonstrate that he has already exhausted whatever appeals are provided by the administrative structure.[101] For example, in a medical society, the usual appeal route is to the county committee from a city association and from the county committee to the state committee. Only when the petitioner has carried out these appeals may he request judicial relief.[102]

Even though the society's bylaws may not specifically allow it, it is entirely probable that courts would hold that a physician is entitled to be represented by counsel at a disciplinary hearing.

All the grounds for revocation of a medical license of course apply to expulsions from medical societies. A physician who has engaged in conduct which would justify revocation of his license may, of course, be subjected to the lesser penalty of expulsion from a society. However, there are other grounds which would not constitute grounds for revocation of a license to practice, but do constitute a valid reason for expulsion from a medical society. Grounds for expulsion must be reasonable and not whimsical. A physician, for example, could not be expelled from a medical society for getting a divorce or for engaging in legal, but unpopular, political activities. A female member could not be expelled for wearing a pantsuit to meetings.

Since criminal behavior is sufficient grounds for revocation of a license,

it is also grounds for expulsion from a medical society. Prior to the
Supreme Court decisions, many physicians, for example, who were not
criminally charged with violation of abortion laws were expelled from
medical societies and hospital staffs for performing them.[103] It is also clear
that a physician who has been acquitted of criminal charges may be disciplined by his professional peers on the grounds of unprofessional conduct
and even if the state board of medical examiners does not wish to revoke
his license, he may be expelled from his county's medical society.[104] Any
crime which does not involve moral turpitude and is not grounds for revocation of a license is, however, probably insufficient to justify expulsion
from a medical society.[105] Such behavior as "using loud and profane language" and serving alcoholic beverages to a minor, for example, have been
considered criminal offenses which do not constitute moral turpitude.[106]
On the other hand, income tax evasion and similar crimes, even if they do
not result in license revocation proceedings, would suffice to expel a member from a medical society. Therefore, while expulsion and revocation proceedings may exist independently of each other, at least where criminal
conduct is charged, the grounds must be equally legally sufficient in both
cases. Any other action which is considered sufficient for a revocation of
license may also result in expulsion from a medical society without license
revocation proceedings being commenced.[107]

Even though the facts of sexual misbehavior with patients or others do
not justify license revocation or criminal prosecution, such conduct may
provide grounds for expulsion from a medical society.[108]

The same rules apply to memberships in other types of medical organizations.

A surgeon was charged with grossly incompetent treatment of a patient.
The hospital suspended his surgical privileges pending an investigation by
the American College of Surgeons to which he belonged. The College concluded that he had been extremely negligent and gave him his choice of
resignation or expulsion from the College. He sued and the court held that
he had no vested right to belong to the organization.[109]

Hospital Staff Privileges.   Since a hospital may be liable for a staff physician's malpractice, all courts hold that an incompetent physician may be
removed from its staff or denied the right to privileges. The hospital would
be remiss in its duty to provide medical care for its patients if it allowed incompetent physicians to practice as members of its staff.[110] It would appear
clear that if a physician does not have appropriate credentials, but is admitted to a hospital staff, the institution may be liable for his negligence if

he is allowed to treat patients.[111] If, for example, a hospital knows that a surgeon is under treatment for alcoholism and continues to allow him to operate, it might very well be liable for his mistakes. If, however, there is no knowledge or suspicion that anything is wrong, usually the hospital would not be liable. If a surgeon or physician makes repeated mistakes or frequently performs surgery which pathology reports indicate is unnecessary, it would appear that the hospital is obliged to take steps to restrict or remove his privileges to protect its own legal position, but it is highly unlikely that one negligent act would be sufficient to make a hospital liable for a physician's negligence as long as he is properly qualified. Incompetent treatment without some obvious cause such as alcoholism presents a more difficult question, but repeated mistakes in diagnosis or treatment which are severe enough to be known by other members of a hospital staff ought to put the hospital on notice that serious legal questions might be raised.

Since a substantial part of most physicians' practice takes place in hospitals, failure to allow them staff privileges has severe economic consequences. The basic question in determining the existence of any right to staff privileges in the absence of proof of incompetence is the determination of whether the hospital is a public or private institution.[112]

A public hospital is one which is established by public funds and created or controlled by some governmental entity. While it is perfectly clear that hospital privileges may be restricted on the grounds of incompetence[113] and that a physician does not have any constitutional right to automatic privileges in any given hospital,[114] he may have a right to staff privileges in a public hospital as long as he abides by legal and professional standards. Both public and private hospitals may adopt and enforce reasonable regulations as to the physicians who wish to be admitted to membership on their staff as long as those restrictions deal with the professional qualifications of the physicians, but where restrictions are based on race, sex, or "personality," denying or terminating his privileges at a public hospital may violate the physician's constitutional rights.

In general, a private hospital has the right to establish any regulations it wishes as to staff and these are not usually subject to judicial review.[115]

A physician's staff privileges at a Roman Catholic hospital were revoked the day after his wife obtained a divorce decree. No hearing was held on his right to maintain his staff privileges. The courts upheld the action of the hospital.[116]

A physician does not have the vested constitutional right to be admitted to practice in a private hospital. Denying him membership on the staff of a private hospital does not usually constitute a legal wrong to him.[117] Courts in some states, however, have ruled that even private hospitals may not arbitrarily refuse admission to a qualified physician.[118]

A private hospital was the best one in terms of equipment and other criteria within a six-county area. It received federal construction funds. The hospital bylaws provided that only those physicians whose offices were located within the same county were eligible for staff admission. The court held that this was unconstitutional discrimination against physicians who were located nearby but in a different county, and therefore they could not be excluded from the staff.[119]

A neurosurgeon with impeccable credentials applied for staff membership at a private hospital. He was refused admission on the ground that he was "temperamentally difficult." The reason for this conclusion was that he had testified for several plaintiffs in malpractice suits. The hospital claimed that it had an absolute right as a private hospital to exclude any physician it chose without regard to his professional competence or educational achievement. The court refused to accept this and ordered the physician admitted to the staff.[120]

A private hospital also has the right to make reasonable limits on the number of physicians admitted to the staff in any one specialty.[121]

Whether it is public or private, in no case may a hospital or other instituion which receives any form of governmental funds exclude either physicians or patients on the basis of race or segregate them once they are admitted.[122] Physicians may also not be deprived of the right to privileges at public hospitals on any other class-discrimination grounds.

A physician was an osteopath with an unrestricted license to practice medicine. He applied for membership on the staff of the only hospital in his small town in which he was incidentally the only physician. The hospital had been closed before he came to the community. The hospital had been built by public subscription and it received tax funds for the care of indigents. The bylaws involving staff appointments provided that a physician applying for privileges must be a graduate of an AMA approved medical school. The court held the bylaw unreasonable and required the physician to be admitted in the absence of any evidence of professional incompetence.[123]

A public hospital is subject to federal constitutional restrictions and therefore must abide by strict standards of due process if it wishes to exclude or restrict a physician from practicing therein and the only reasons for restriction or denial of privileges are those germaine to professional qualifications.[124]

Hospitals may validly require certain educational and professional qualifications prior to allowing a physician to joint its staff as a surgeon.[125] In general, however, any physician who meets fair and reasonable educational and professional requirements has a vested legal right to staff membership at a public hospital and his patient has the right to be admitted there to be treated by him.

Most courts hold that a public hospital may not require membership in the local medical society before a physician may be admitted to the staff if he is otherwise qualified.[126] In many cases in which physicians were arbitrarily excluded from county or state medical societies for racial reasons and were thereafter denied staff memberships in public hospitals, courts held that their constitutional rights had been violated.

A hospital could not discriminate indirectly by making medical society membership a prerequisite for staff admission when its trustees knew that black physicians could not comply with the requirements of recommendations from two active members to be admitted to the medical association.[127]

Prior unprofessional conduct is considered ample grounds for refusal to admit a physician to a public hospital staff, but "temperamental unsuitability" is not.

A physician was denied admission to the staff of a public hospital. The hospital took the position that he had argued with other staff members at hospitals where he had practiced. The court pointed out that the evidence showed that in most of the arguments specified, all of which had dealt with patient care, the physician had been right and that harmony was less important than adequate care of patients and held that his inability to get along with other physicians was irrelevant to his fitness to be admitted to the staff of a public hospital.[128]

Genuine evidence of unprofessional conduct is, however, quite sufficient to uphold a public hospital's refusal to admit a physician.

A physician was denied staff privileges at a public hospital. He was proved to have previously denied care to obstetrical patients who could not pay his bills and had gone into "rages" at patients. Moreover, he had pleaded guilty to two felony charges and his licenses in two other states had been suspended.

The court held that on the face of the record, the reasons for denying privileges were reasonable.[129]

A plaintiff was an osteopath. The public hospital at which he applied for membership had a requirement for graduation from an AMA approved school, but by the time the litigation involved in this case had come to the trial stage that requirement had been dropped and other osteopaths had been admitted. The hospital had claimed that the plaintiff was "personally unstable," as evidenced by protracted litigation with former associates and that he had engaged in "mass production practice" in order to extricate himself from serious financial problems. The court held that the decision of the hospital would be upheld.[130]

Public hospitals may also not make other unnecessary requirements for staff membership, such as a stipulation of the amount of medical malpractice insurance a staff member must carry.[131] On the other hand, however, either a public hospital or a private one may require its staff members to abide by reasonable bylaws, such as the requirement that they serve their turn in the emergency room.[132] Once a physician has been admitted to a hospital staff, public and private hospitals are entirely justified in reducing or revoking his privileges in the face of a number of factors.

A physician moved to a community and was given temporary privileges at the community's only hospital. These privileges were later revoked. The court accepted the hospital's claim that incomplete and misleading answers had been given on his application for privileges. He had indicated one narcotics charge, but not that he had served a prison sentence for it. He had misstated the situation surrounding his suspension from the staff of another hospital and the status of his licenses. Furthermore, while on the staff in his temporary status, he had usurped the function of another physician on call in the emergency room and refused to post times when he planned to perform surgery. The court held that the hospital was justified in refusing to allow him to continue on the staff once they had begun investigation into the statements he had made on his application. There is no absolute right to practice even in a public hospital.[133]

If a physician's staff privileges at a public hospital are to be revoked or suspended, he is entitled to due process of law.[134] The basic constitutional right to procedural due process and a fair hearing require that the physician has the right to adequate notice,[135] specific statements as to the charges against him, a fair and impartial hearing, an opportunity to testify in his own behalf, and the right to present such evidence as he wishes.[136]

In a public hospital, this invariably applies where the violations charged involve failure to comply with hospital regulations which are reasonable but do not involve patient welfare.[137]

A physician refused to take his turn in the emergency room as required by a hospital bylaw. The court held that he could not be dismissed from the hospital prior to a hearing.[138]

Another physician yelled obscenities at a nurse, made extremely unprofessional remarks about other staff members, and failed to keep adequate records. The court held that she was also entitled to a hearing before she was removed from the hospital staff.[139]

If suspension or restrictions on a physician's staff membership are grounded on professional incompetency, his privileges may be revoked prior to a hearing if it may reasonably be considered imminently necessary for the medical welfare of his patients.[140]

A chief of surgery suspended a surgeon's right to perform gastrectomies pending a hearing. The staff member had performed a gastrectomy on a patient who died after removal to another hospital and a second operation. The Chief of Surgery was present at the second operation and observed the results of the surgeon's work and as a result of what he saw, suspended the surgeon's privileges for this type of surgery immediately. A hearing followed within a short time. The court upheld the action on the grounds that a hospital's first duty was to the welfare of its patients.[141]

A surgeon was charged with the removal of a healthy appendix. The court sustained the right of the hospital staff to suspend him prior to a hearing even though it was a public hospital.[142]

These due process requirements may not, however, be necessary to expel a physician from the staff of a private hospital in some cases.[143] A physician, for example, may be told by a private hospital that he will not be reappointed at the end of a term. In most cases a private hospital has the right to do this on the theory that a physician does not have a vested right to privileges and thus courts hold this to be within the discretion of the hospital board. Generally speaking, if a private hospital's bylaws do not require a hearing before privileges are terminated, courts will not impose such a requirement.[144] If, however, the bylaws do provide for a hearing the hospital must conform strictly to those provisions.[145]

Bylaws of a hospital specified that any physician was entitled to notice of charges brought against him. No specification as to charges was given to a physician before the hearing on his privileges. The hospital's dismissal of the physician's privileges was reversed and he was ordered reinstated.[146]

An increasing number of states, however, require the same standards of due process in a private hospital as they demand in a public one.[147] While some states require only that a private hospital afford a fair hearing to a physician,[148] other states require a private hospital to give all the evidence of notice, specification of charges, a fair hearing, and a right of cross-examination as are applicable to all public hospitals.[149]

Most courts do seem to take the position that a private hospital has the right summarily to revoke, suspend, and reduce the physician's privileges or fail to reappoint him for any reasons satisfactory to the hospital board unless a hearing is required by the hospital bylaws.

A plaintiff was denied the right to perform major surgery at a private hospital although he was allowed to continue his medical practice there. He was a general practitioner and had been elected president of the medical staff and occupied that position at the time of the reduction of privileges. In an effort to upgrade the hospital so it could be accredited, the medical staff agreed to conform to standards requiring all surgeons to meet the requirements of a surgical residency. The plaintiff objected most strenuously to this during his participation at all the meetings which the staff had on the subject. When he was notified that he could no longer perform major surgery, he sued on the grounds that he had not been given a hearing. However, since he was quite familiar with the proceedings the court did not accept this argument.[150]

Therefore, a private hospital has a far broader right to terminate a physician's staff membership than does a public hospital,[151] but in all states incompetence and unprofessional conduct are amply sufficient to revoke privileges even in a public hospital.[152]

A physician was charged with exhibiting gross professional incompetence in the handling of one patient's case. There was an immediate decision that he could not use narcotic drugs with any patient for more than 48 hours without the approval of the department chief. The court held that the staff of the public hospital was required as a matter of due process of law to use reasonable standards in reducing privileges. Since the bylaw on which the action was based contained no requirement as to skill or conduct, it granted the decision-making authority the right to act in an arbitrary manner. Thus, without making a judgment that the cause of action was necessarily insufficient to justify the reduction of privileges, the court held that procedural fairness had not been granted in view of the fact that the physician did have the right to practice in a public hospital if he had a valid license.[153]

Courts will not substitute their judgments for those rendered by physicians on a board at any hospital on what in fact constitutes incompetence.

A physician admitted that he had committed those acts which were the basis of the finding of incompetence for which he had been removed from the hospital staff. However, he wished to call other members of the surgical staff of the hospital to demonstrate by their testimony under cross-examination that they had made as many mistakes as he had in order to demonstrate that the action taken against him was discriminatory. In refusing to allow a rehearing, the court held that medical standards were to be determined by physicians and even at a public hospital no court had the right to substitute its substantive judgment on the subject.[154]

Incompetence does not have to be spelled out in hospital bylaws to constitute a grounds for revocation of privileges.

A physician was charged with 12 separate acts of incompetence. Among other things, he was charged with unsterile administration of spinal anesthesia and appearing in an operating room to perform surgery when "he was in no physical or mental condition to do so." He cancelled that operation when two physicians who saw him go into the operating room advised him to do so. He had been present with his counsel at the hearing and he did not object to any procedural rules or charge unfairness. The sole basis on which he attempted to reverse the ruling dismissing him from the staff was that incompetence was not prohibited by the hospital bylaws. The court found that although there is a right to practice in a public hospital, that right is not absolute and that patient welfare overrides it. The ruling of the Board was held in keeping with the hospital's responsibility to its patients and no indication of arbitrary action was found. The United States Supreme Court refused to review the decision of the state supreme court.[155]

Thus it would appear that a public hospital may not revoke privileges for matters which are irrelevant to patient care. It is, however, perfectly obvious that incompetence or unprofessional conduct and fraud are very acceptable reasons which are legally sufficient to support revocation of privileges in either public or private hospitals.

Generally, courts take a very restricted view of the areas of their right of review of the actions of private hospital boards.[156] In most cases the rule in cases involving private hospitals is that the entire scope of a court's determination is one of determining whether or not the bylaws have been observed. Arbitrary, capricious, or discriminatory action in determination of the issue of the hearing is of course always subject to judicial review. If a physician can prove that he did not receive impartial treatment, no matter how exactly his procedural rights were respected he may obtain relief and reinstatement to the staff.[157] The important point, however, is that courts do not substitute their own judgment for that of physicians who have presided at the hearing on matters of professional judgment. If acts are proved which are in the decision of the medical members of the board sufficient to constitute professional incompetence, a court will not disturb their professional findings as long as those findings were fair. In other words, courts sit on questions of law, but judges are not physicians and will not presume to override a decision involving professional medical judgment.

Criminal Prosecution for Patient's Death. Criminal prosecutions of physicians for negligent treatment of a patient are so rare as to be virtually nonexistent.[158] Obviously the most skilled physician will lose some patients unless he practices in a specialty in which death is virtually unknown. Failure to adhere to the proper standards of due care, skill, and knowledge and thus becoming liable in civil damages is by no means sufficient to impose criminal liability on a physician.

Where a physician performs an illegal procedure and the patient dies, he does run a substantial risk of being indicted for murder and there were several cases prior to the Supreme Court's abortion decisions in which a physician who performed an illegal abortion was tried and convicted of either first degree murder or manslaughter.[159] However, in some of the cases where the women died during criminal abortions, the physicians were not guilty of murder, but only for the offense of abortion. In one such case, the appellate court said:

> Where death results from the consequence of negligence, it would seem that to create criminal responsibility, the degree of negligence must be so gross as to amount to recklessness. Mere inadvertence while it might create civil liability would not suffice to create criminal liability.[160]

In very rare cases, negligence has been so reckless as to result in criminal prosecution, but even in those situations in which juries convicted physicians, appellate courts have been inclined to reverse their verdicts.

The pelvic examination of a woman suffering from cancer of the uterus sup-posedly killed her when her physician allegedly broke the wall of her uterus. The jury convicted the physician of manslaughter but the appellate court re-versed. Medical experts testified at the trial that the results charged in the indictment simply could not have occurred. The appellate court found that the physician had not been negligent, much less had he been so grossly negligent as to incur criminal liability.[161]

Criminal negligence, where it occurs, is a matter of degree.

A physician was charged with manslaughter for "culpable negligence, gross ignorance and lack of ordinary knowledge." During an operation he had per-formed on a patient, he made large rents in her uterus and pulled her intes-tines through them. With a great deal of medical testimony in support of the prosecution's case, the conviction was upheld. The court found that although a physician may use his best skill and judgment in an honest effort to cure the patient, he may be so grossly ignorant of the facts of surgery as to render him criminally responsible for the results of his ignorance.[162] It should be noted however that this case was decided in 1905 and there has not been another case of successful criminal prosecution for good-faith medical treat-ment since.

A patient died of burns from overexposure to Xrays administered by the de-fendant, who was indicted for manslaughter. The standard of criminal liability was very succinctly stated in that opinion: "Not every careless act is crim-inal. Only when a physician exhibits a gross lack of competency or inattention or wanton indifference to a patient's safety which may arise from gross igno-rance or gross negligence does criminal liability attach. Where the patient's death results from an error of judgment or an accident there is no criminal liability."[163]

Of course, assault and battery is a crime, and if the patient has not con-sented at all to the procedure performed upon him and he dies during or as a result of the operation, the question of manslaughter may be raised.[164] Of course, before any person can be convicted of causing the death of another, the prosecution must demonstrate that the act did in fact cause the death.

A nurse was convicted of manslaughter but the appellate court reversed. She was in charge of a state institution for the retarded and as such she ordered medication given to the patients under the general direction of a physician not located at the hospital. When a patient became unruly she ordered that paraldehyde be given to her. Unknown to the defendant, the solution was contaminated and four times as strong as it was supposed to be. The patient died of pneumonia. The defendant's conviction of involuntary manslaughter followed. Medical testimony indicated that if the overdose had been the real reason for the cause of death, the woman would have died within 4 to 6 hours, not 5 days later. Without more evidence as to the exact cause of death, the conviction was not sustained.[165]

While conviction of certain felonies is usually sufficient to justify revocation of a physician's license, at least one decision indicates that an indictment, as opposed to a conviction, for manslaughter is not sufficient to justify a temporary suspension until time of trial.

An osteopath was indicted for manslaughter. Fifteen of his patients had died from hepatitis following injections he had administered to them. The appropriate state agency ordered him not to administer any more drugs until the trial verdict was reached. His license to practice was also suspended pending a verdict by the jury. He appealed. The court agreed that "manslaughter could be deduced from criminal negligence through gross ignorance," but held that a license to practice could not be suspended until he was convicted and that an indictment was not sufficient evidence of criminal conduct. However, the order forbidding him to administer drugs until after a verdict was upheld as reasonable.[166]

Under old Greek law, a physician whose patient died would be put to death himself, but that is not a common practice in our modern society. As long as the treatment given any patient is one that is approved by at least a respectable minority of the medical profession and is in itself legal, no criminal liability will attach if a patient dies unless there is clear evidence of total and wanton disregard for the welfare of the sick person. If a surgeon, for example, performed a nonemergency operation while drunk or under the influence of narcotics to the degree that he became totally reckless and the patient died, he might be subject to criminal prosecution, but anything less than that, including gross stupidity, will presumably not constitute sufficient negligence to support a criminal charge. All the decisions in which physicians were convicted of criminal ignorance to the point to sustain criminal charges are more than half a century old and the standards of medical education as they exist today make it highly unlikely that such physicians even exist at present.

However, nonphysicians who undertake to practice medicine are in a very precarious legal position if their patients die. Nonphysicians who take it upon themselves to "play doctor" are also, of course, guilty of the crime of practicing medicine without a license. While it is relatively uncommon for nonphysicians to be prosecuted for the deaths of their patients, it does happen from time to time, although most prosecutions are for manslaughter not for homicide, since the latter requires proof of intent to kill.[167]

A naturopath ordered that his patient be kept in flannels saturated with kerosene. Unsurprisingly she died in 3 days. His conviction for manslaughter was upheld. The appellate court said that "one who prescribes with foolhardy presumption and gross recklessness a course of treatment that causes the death of his patient is guilty of manslaughter even without intent to kill."[168]

A person who attempts to treat the sick with nothing more substantial than good intentions may indeed run afoul of the criminal law.[169] Ignorance, like good intention, is no excuse for causing the death of another person.

A defendant held himself out to be a physician although he was not and had never attended medical school. His patient was a diabetic taking insulin which had been prescribed by his family physician. The defendant gave him drugs made from herbs and took him off of insulin. The man died and the pseudo-doctor was convicted of manslaughter. The appellate court upheld his conviction and said: "Criminal negligence occurs when a physician or person acting as such exhibits gross lack of competence and this may arise from the gross ignorance of the effects of his action."[170]

Several chiropractors have been convicted of manslaughter while "practicing medicine," for example, taking a diabetic off insulin[171] and telling a paralyzed patient to fast, which he did for 35 days until he starved to death.[172] Another chiropractor who performed surgery from which the patient died was also convicted of manslaughter.[173] The court held that he acted with a "shocking degree of unskillfulness, evincing an almost incredible ignorance of surgery and anatomy and utterly wanting in skill." It is, however, absolutely necessary that the defendant's actions contribute at least in some material degree to the death of a sick person.

A man held himself out to be a physician although he was not. He attempted to cure a woman who was sick with pneumonia by the laying on of hands and the administration of a brew of hog hooves. The court upheld his conviction of manslaughter.[174]

A patient had tuberculosis for which his family doctor had strenuously advised protracted hospitalization, but he consulted two chiropractors who put him on a vegetarian diet with 14-day periods of complete fasting. He died of starvation and the effects of the disease. The appellate court found that the jury was justified in finding that the method of treatment amounted to culpable negligence and that the requisite causal connection had been demonstrated.[175]

If there is no evidence that the patient could have been saved by proper medical treatment, there is serious doubt that a manslaughter conviction against a charlatan can be sustained.[176]

If a chiropractor or other nonphysician knows that standard medical treatment should be obtained for a patient and refuses to tell the patient or his family, he may very well be convicted of manslaughter.

An 11-year old girl had cancer of her left eye. Her parents consulted physicians and consented to the surgical removal of the eye. However, shortly before the operation was to be performed, they took her to a chiropractor who promised to cure the child without surgery, so the parents refused to proceed with the operation. He gave the child 100 pills a day, enemas, foot massage, iodine water, and food supplements and told her mother that the condition was connected with the nerves in her foot. She died and he was convicted of second degree murder. Medical evidence proved that the treatment had hastened her death. The Dean of a chiropractic school also testified that the treatment was not even approved by their standards of practice. The verdict of guilty was upheld on appeal.[177]

This chapter has discussed some of the consequences other than a civil action brought by the patient, his heirs, or his guardian of professional negligence. In no case does "ordinary, reasonable negligence" result in the loss of a license to practice, it usually does not result in dismissal from a hospital staff, and it certainly will not result in criminal prosecution. All physicians at some time in their career inevitably make errors in judgment. If a physcian misdiagnoses a patient's condition or prescribes improper treatment even though the treatment may constitute civil negligence, as long as he was in good faith, was not under the influence of any substance such as drugs or alcohol, and followed a course of treatment accepted by a respectable minority of the medical profession, even if the patient dies there is absolutely no remote possibility that any of these proceedings will be instituted against him. Where disciplinary actions have been taken or hospital privileges have been revoked on grounds of incompetence, there is invariably a long history of inadequate patient care. Only one or two good-faith errors of judgment is not sufficient to terminate a physician's right to practice.

NOTES

1. Barsky v. Board of Regents, 347 US 422, 1954.
2. Hewitt v. Board of Medical Examiners, 84 Pac 39, Cal 1906.
3. Seidenberg v. New Mexico Board of Medical Examiners, 452 P 2d 469, NM 1969; *Disciplinary Digest*, Law Division, American Medical Association, Chicago, 1967.
4. Geiger v. Jenkins, 316 F Supp 370, DC Ga 1970; "Disciplinary Proceedings, Part I," (in press).
5. Prosch v. Baxley, 345 F Supp 1063, DC Ala 1972.
6. Younge v. State Board of Registration, 451 SW 2d 346, Mo 1969.
7. "Disciplinary Proceedings, Part II," (in press).
8. "Due Process in the Disciplinary Hearing," 208 *JAMA* No. 11, page 2229, June 16, 1969.
9. Bruni v. Department of Registration, 290 NE 2d 295, Ill 1972.
10. Munk v. Frink, 116 NW 525, Neb 1908; State ex rel Kerr v. Landwehr, 32 SW 2d 83, Mo 1930.
11. D'Alois v. Allen, 297 NYS 2d 826, NY 1969.
12. State ex rel Weathers v. Davis, 196 So 187, Fla 1940; Schireson v. State Board of Medical Examiners of New Jersey, 28 A 2d 879, NJ 1942; State v. Hanson, 207 NW 769, Iowa 1926.
13. State ex rel Sorensen v. Lake, 236 NW 762, Neb 1931.
14. Sos v. Board of Regents, 281 NYS 2d 831, NY 1967.
15. Chew v. State Board of Medical Examiners, 265 So 2d 542, Fla 1972.
16. Arkansas State Medical Board v. Grimmett, 463 SW 2d 662, Ark 1971.
17. State Board of Medical Examiners v. Gandy, 188 SE 2d 846, SC 1972.
18. Margoles v. Wisconsin State Board of Medical Examiners, 177 NW 2d 353, Wisc 1970; Reddick v. Board of Regents, 297 NYS 2d 339, NY 1969.
19. "Disciplinary Proceedings, Part VI," (in press).
20. Texas State Board of Medical Examiners v. Scott, 377 SW 2d 104, Tex 1964; Dugdale v. Board of Registration in Medicine, 169 NE 547, Mass 1930; Schyman v. Department of Registration, 133 NE 2d 551, Ill 1956.
21. Korndorffer v. Texas State Board of Medical Examiners, 460 SW 2d 879, Tex 1970.
22. Strance v. New Mexico Board of Medical Examiners, 487 P 2d 1085, NM 1971.
23. Cadilla v. Board of Medical Examiners, 103 Cal Rptr 455, Cal 1972.
24. Cooper v. Texas State Board of Medical Examiners, 489 SW 2d 129, Tex 1972.
25. "Discretion in Disciplinary Hearings," 209 *JAMA* No. 4, page 611, July 28, 1969.
26. Berman v. Board of Registration, 244 NE 2d 553, Mass 1969.
27. Minaker v. Adams, 203 Pac 806, Cal 1921; Sherman v. McEntire, 179 P 2d 797, Utah 1947; Munk v. Frink, 116 NW 525, Neb 1908; Stuck v. Board of Medical Examiners,

211 P 2d 389, Cal 1949; Kudish v. Board of Registration in Medicine, 248 NE 2d 264, Mass 1969.

28. Mascitelli v. Board of Regents, 299 NYS 2d 1002, NY 1969; Younge v. State Board of Registration, 451 SW 2d 346, Mo 1969.

29. Minnesota v. Hodgson, 204 NW 2d 199, Minn 1973; New Mexico v. Strance, 506 P 2d 1217, NM 1973; Illinois v. Frey, 294 NE 2d 257, Ill 1973; Vuitch v. Hardy, 473 F 2d 1370, CCA 4, 1973; Thompson v. Texas, 493 SW 2d 913, Tex 1973.

30. Doran v. State Board of Medical Examiners, 240 Pac 335, Colo 1925; Choate v. Oklahoma, 232 P 2d 634, Okla 1951; Weiss v. Board of Regents, 265 NYS 2d 314, NY 1965.

31. *Report of the Secretary's Commission on Medical Malpractice*, DHEW Publication No. (05) 73-88, 1973, page 52.

32. Margoles v. Wisconsin State Board of Medical Examiners, 177 NW 2d 353, Wisc 1970; Weiner v. Board of Regents, 158 NYS 2d 730, NY 1956; Furnish v. Board of Medical Examiners, 308 P 2d 924, Cal 1957; In re Kindschi, 319 P 2d 824, Wash 1958; Morris v. Board of Medical Examiners, 41 Cal Rptr 351, Cal 1964.

33. State Medical Board v. Rodgers, 79 SW 2d 83, Ark, 1935; Bruni v. Department of Registration, 290 NE 2d 295, Ill 1972.

34. Prosch v. Baxley, 345 F Supp 1063, DC Ala 1972.

35. Reddick v. Board of Regents, 297 NYS 2d 339, NY 1969.

36. Michigan v. Bricker, 208 NW 2d 172, Mich 1973; Reams v. Florida 279 So 2d 839, Fla 1973; California v. Eckley, 108 Cal Rptr 52, Cal 1973.

37. Louisiana State Board of Medical Examiners v. Heiman, 230 So 2d 405, La 1970.

38. "Unlicensed Treatment," 214 *JAMA* No. 1, page 209, Oct. 5, 1970; Chayet, Neil L., *Legal Implications of Emergency Care*, New York, Appleton-Century-Crofts, 1969, pages 171–173.

39. Lindsey v. Michigan Mutual Liability Insurance Co., 156 So 2d 313, La 1963; Meiman v. Rehabilitation Center, Inc., 444 SW 2d 78, Ky 1969.

40. Martin v. Carbide and Carbon Chemical Co., 197 SW 2d 798, Tenn 1946.

41. DuVall v. Board of Medical Examiners, 66 P 2d 1026, Ariz 1937; Fort v. City of Brinkley, 112 SW 1084, Ark 1908; Board of Medical Registration and Education of Indiana v. Armington, 178 NE 2d 741, Ind 1961; Glenn v. Colorado State Board of Medical Examiners, 284 P 2d 230, Colo 1955;Texas State Board of Medical Examiners v. McClellan, 307 SW 2d 317, Tex 1957; Knoop v. State Board of Health, 103 Atl 904, RI 1918; Fick v. Board of Medical Examiners for the State of California, 107 Cal Rptr 260, Cal 1973.

42. Cooper v. Texas State Board of Medical Examiners, 489 SW 2d 129, Tex 1972.

43. State Board of Medical Examiners v. Gandy, 188 SE 2d 846, SC 1972.

44. Grannis v. Board of Medical Examiners, 96 Cal Rptr 863, Cal 1971.

45. Tompkins v. Board of Regents, 87 NE 2d 517, NY 1949; Bernanke v. Board of Regents, 264 NYS 2d 399, NY 1965; Geiger v. Jenkins, 316 F Supp 370, DC Ga 1970; Louisiana State Board of Medical Examiners v. Heiman, 230 So 2d 405, La 1970; Collins v. Board of Medical Examiners, 105 Cal Rptr 634, Cal 1972.

46. McKay v. State Board of Medical Examiners, 86 P 2d 232, Colo 1938.

47. Collins v. Board of Medical Examiners, 105 Cal Rptr 634, Cal 1972; Schireson v. State Board of Medical Examiners of New Jersey, 28 A 2d 879, NJ 1942.

48. State Board of Medical Examiners v. Morlan, 3 So 2d 402, Fla 1941.

49. Schireson v. Walsh, 187 NE 921, Ill 1933; Board of Examiners in Medicine v. Jacobson, 42 A 2d 887, RI 1945.

50. Rinaldo v. Board of Medical Examiners, 42 P 2d 724, Cal 1935; Pennsylvania State Board v. Schireson, 61 A 2d 343, Pa 1948.

51. In re Hawkins, 194 SE 2d 540, NC 1973; Kansas State Board v. Seasholtz, 504 P 2d 576, Kans 1972; Seidenberg v. New Mexico Board of Medical Examiners, 452 P 2d 469, NM 1969.

52. Wassermann v. Board of Regents, 182 NE 2d 264, NY 1962; Application of Shaw, 212 NYS 2d 701, NY 1961; Frank v. Board of Regents, 264 NYS 2d 413, NY 1965; Burns v. Board of Regents, 233 NYS 2d 927, NY 1962; In re Mandel, 264 NYS 2d 867, NY 1964.

53. D'Alois v. Allen, 297 NYS 2d 826, NY 1969.

54. Brown v. Hassig, 15 P 2d 401, Kans 1932.

55. "Disciplinary Proceedings: Part V," (in press).

56. Chew v. State Board of Medical Examiners, 265 So 2d 542, Fla 1972; Jaffe v. State Department of Health, 64 A 2d 330, Conn 1949.

57. Graeb v. State Board of Medical Examiners, 139 Pac 1099, Colo 1913.

58. Stammer v. Board of Regents, 39 NE 2d 913, NY 1942; Brinkley v. Hassig, 83 F 2d 351, CCA 10, 1936; Board of Medical Registration v. Kaadt, 76 NE 2d 669, Ind 1948.

59. Minnesota State Board of Medical Examiners v. Schmidt, 292 NW 255, Minn 1940.

60. Sherman v. Board of Regents, 266 NYS 2d 39, NY 1966.

61. Cadilla v. Board of Medical Examiners, 103 Cal Rptr 455, Cal 1972.

62. Bernstein v. Board of Medical Examiners, 22 Cal Rptr 419, Cal 1962.

63. Texas State Board of Medical Examiners v. Koepsel, 322 SW 2d 609, Tex 1959; Texas State Board of Medical Examiners v. Haynes, 388 SW 2d 258, Tex 1965.

64. Martinez v. Texas State Board of Medical Examiners, 476 SW 2d 400, Tex 1972.

65. "Personal Character and Licensure," 207 *JAMA* No. 13, page 2517, March 31, 1969.

66. The Florida Bar v. Hefty, 213 So 2d 422, Fla 1968.

67. Meffert v. State Board of Medical Registration, 72 Pac 247, 195 US 625, 1903.

68. Florida Bar Association v. Kay, 232 So 2d 378, Fla 1970.

69. Lorenz v. Board of Medical Examiners, 298 P 2d 537, Cal 1956.

70. White v. Andrew, 197 Pac 564, Colo 1921; DuVall v. Board of Medical Examiners of Arizona, 66 P 2d 1026, Ariz 1937.

71. Wyatt v. Cerf, 149 P 2d 309, Cal 1944.

72. People to Use of State Board of Health v. McCoy, 17 NE 786, Ill 1888.

73. Board of Medical Examiners of the State of Oregon v. Mintz, 378 P 2d 945, Ore 1963; Sapero v. State Board of Medical Examiners, 11 P 2d 555, Colo 1932.

74. "Licensure and Unprofessional Conduct," 205 *JAMA* No. 7, page 191, Aug. 12, 1968; Czarra v. Board of Medical Supervisors, 25 App DC 433, DC 1925; State Board of Medical Examiners v. Macy, 159 Pac 801, Wash 1916; Forman v. State Board of Health, 162 SW 796, Ky 1914.

75. State ex rel Lentine v. State Board of Health, 65 SW 2d 943, Mo 1933.

76. McPheeters v. Board of Medical Examiners, 284 Pac 938, Cal 1930.

77. Pepe v. Board of Regents, 295 NYS 209, NY 1968.

78. "Analysis of Fee-Splitting Statutes," 208 *JAMA* No. 6, page 1083, May 12, 1969; "The Courts and Fee-Splitting," 208 *JAMA* No. 7, page 1241, May 19, 1969; Forziati v. Board of Registration in Medicine, 128 NE 2d 789, Mass 1955.

79. Strance v. New Mexico Board of Medical Examiners, 487 P 2d 1085, NM 1971.

80. Boswell v. Board of Medical Examiners, 293 P 2d 424, Nev 1956.

81. Bernstein v. Alameda-Contra-Costa Medical Association, 293 P 2d 862, Cal 1956.

82. Gibson v. Connecticut Medical Examining Board, 104 A 2d 890, Conn 1954.

83. State Board of Medical Education v. Ferry, 94 A 2d 121, Pa 1953; O'Neill v. Board of Regents, 74 NYS 2d 762, NY 1947; Rockett v. Texas State Board of Medical Examiners, 287 SW 2d 190, Tex 1956.

84. Hughes v. State Board of Health, 159 SW 2d 277, Mo 1942.

85. Magit v. Board of Medical Examiners, 366 P 2d 816, Cal 1961; Rilcoff v. State Board of Medical Examiners, 203 P 2d 844, Cal 1949.

86. Hake v. Arkansas State Medical Board, 374 SW 2d 173, Ark 1964; Hubbard v. Washington State Medical Disciplinary Board, 348 P 2d 981, Wash 1960.

87. "Licensure and Unprofessional Conduct," 205 *JAMA* No. 7, page 191, Aug. 12, 1968.

88. *Report of the Secretary's Commission on Medical Malpractice, op cit supra* at 31, page 52.

89. The Kansas State Board of Healing Arts v. Foote, 436 P 2d 828, Kans 1968; "Revocation of License for Professional Incompetence," 208 *JAMA* No. 4, page 751, April 28, 1969.

90. "Incompetence as Unprofessional Conduct," 208 *JAMA* No. 5, page 927, May 5, 1969; Traer v. State Board of Medical Examiners, 76 NW 833, Iowa 1898; Sage-Allen Co., Inc. v. Wheeler, 179 Atl 195, Conn 1935.

91. Jaffee v. State Department of Health, 64 A 2d 330, Conn 1949.

92. McKay v. State Board of Medical Examiners, 86 P 2d 232, Colo 1938.

93. Yoshizawa v. Hewitt, 52 F 2d 411, CCA 9, 1931.

94. "Negligent Selection of Hospital Staff," 223 *JAMA* No. 7, page 833, Feb. 12, 1973.

95. Pinsker v. Pacific Coast Society of Orthodontists, 81 Cal Rptr 623, Cal 1969; Maricopa County Medical Society v. Blende, 448 P 2d 68, Ariz 1968; Falcone v. Middlesex County Medical Society, 170 A 2d 791, NJ 1961; 75 *Harvard Law Rev* 1142, 1962.

96. Schooler v. Tarrant County Medical Society, 457 SW 2d 644, Tex 1970.

97. Bryant v. District of Columbia Dental Society, 26 App DC 461, DC 1906.

98. "Expulsion from Medical Society, Part I," 229 *JAMA* No. 11, page 1502, Sept. 9, 1974.

99. Arizona Osteopathic Medical Association v. Fridena, 457 P 2d 945, Ariz 1969.

100. Smith v. Kern County Medical Association, 120 P 2d 874, Cal 1942.

101. Irwin v. Lorio, 126 So 669, La 1930.

102. Brown v. Harris County Medical Society, 194 SW 1179, Tex 1917.

103. Zimmerman v. Board of Regents, 294 NYS 2d 435, NY 1968.

104. Miller v. Hennepin County Medical Society, 144 NW 1091, Minn 1914.

105. "Expulsion from Medical Society, Part II," 229 *JAMA* No. 12, page 1656, Sept. 16, 1974.

106. Wyatt v. Cerf, 149 P 2d 309, Cal 1944; Lorenz v. Board of Medical Examiners, 298 P 2d 537, Cal 1956.

107. People ex rel Bartlett v. Medical Society, 32 NY 185, NY 1865; State ex rel Mayfield v. St. Louis Medical Society, 91 Mo App 76, Mo 1901.

108. Jacobi v. Board of Medical Examiners, 308 SW 2d 261, Tex 1957.

109. Duby v. American College of Surgeons, 468 F 2d 364, CCA 7, 1972.

110. "Hospital Liability for Physician Negligence," 214 *JAMA* No. 9, page 1755, Nov. 30, 1970; "Negligent Selection of Hospital Staff," 223 *JAMA* No. 7, page 833, Feb. 12, 1973; "Hospital Liability for Staff Negligence," 224 *JAMA* No. 8, page 1225, May 21, 1973.

111. Penn Tanker Co. v. United States, 310 F Supp 613, DC Tex 1970; Mitchell County Hospital v. Joiner, 189 SE 2d 412, Ga 1972.

112. "Hospital Staff Privileges," 213 *JAMA* No. 7, page 1233, Aug. 17, 1970.

113. "Restriction of Hospital Privileges," 215 *JAMA* No. 9, page 1547, March 1, 1971.

114. Hayman v. City of Galveston, 273 US 414, 1927.

115. Moore v. Andalusia Hospital, Inc., 224 So 2d 617, Ala 1969; Hughes v. Good Samaritan Hospital, 158 SW 2d 159, Ky 1942.

116. Natale v. Sisters of Mercy of Council Bluffs, 52 NW 2d 701, Iowa 1952.

117. Leider v. Beth Israel Hospital, 182 NE 2d 393, NY 1962; Henderson v. City of Knoxville, 9 SW 2d 697, Tenn 1928; West Coast Hospital Association v. Hoare, 64 So 2d 293, Fla 1953.

118. "Hospital Staff Privileges, Part II," (in press), Burkhart v. Community Medical Center, 432 SW 2d 433, Ky 1968.

119. Sams v. Ohio Valley General Hospital Association, 413 F 2d 826, CCA 4, 1969.

120. Sussman v. Overlook Hospital, 231 A 2d 389, NJ 1967.

121. Davis v. Morristown Memorial Hospital, 254 A 2d 125, NJ 1969.

122. Simpkins v. Moses H. Cone Memorial Hospital, 323 F 2d 959, CCA 4, 1963.

123. Greisman v. Newcomb Hospital, 192 A 2d 817, NJ 1963.

124. Findlay v. Board of Supervisors, 230 P 2d 526, Ariz 1951; State ex rel Bronaugh v. City of Parkersburg, 136 SE 2d 783, W Va 1964.

125. Edson v. Griffin Hospital, 144 A 2d 341, Conn 1958; Porter Memorial Hospital v. Harvey, 279 NE 2d 583, Ind 1972.

126. Hamilton County Hospital v. Andrews, 84 NE 2d 469, 85 NE 2d 365, Ind 1949.

127. Foster v. Mobile County Hospital Board, 398 F 2d 227, CCA 5, 1968; "Hospital Staff Privileges: Part III," (in press).

128. Rosner v. Eden Township Hospital District, 375 P 2d 431, Cal 1962.

129. Sosa v. Board of Managers of Val Verde Memorial Hospital, 437 F 2d 173, CCA 5, 1971.

130. Don v. Okmulgee Memorial Hospital, 443 F 2d 234, CCA 10, 1971.

131. Rosner v. Peninsula Hospital District, 36 Cal Rptr 332, Cal 1964.

132. Yeargin v. Hamilton Memorial Hospital, 195 SE 2d 8, Ga 1972.

133. Dunbar v. Hospital Authority of Gwinnett County, 182 SE 2d 89, Ga 1971

134. Silver v. Castleman Memorial Hospital, 497 P 2d 564, Hawaii 1972.

135. Johnson v. City of Ripon, 47 NW 2d 328, Wisc 1951.

136. Milford v. People's Community Hospital Authority, 155 NW 2d 835, Mich 1968.

137. Chiaffitelli v. Dettmer Hospital, 437 F 2d 429, CCA 6, 1971; Hoffman v. Wilkins, 270 NE 2d 594, Ill 1971.

138. Meredith v. Allen County War Memorial Hospital Commission, 397 F 2d 33, CCA 6, 1968.

139. Anderson v. Board of Trustees of Caro Hospital, 159 NW 2d 347, Mich 1968.

140. "Hospital Staff Privileges: Part VI," (in press).

141. Chitta v. Delaware Valley Hospital, 313 F Supp 301, DC Pa 1970.

142. Mizell v. North Broward Hospital District, 175 So 2d 583, Fla 1965.

143. Khoury v. Community Memorial Hospital, 123 SE 2d 533, Va 1962; Anderson v. Board of Trustees of Caro Hospital, 159 NW 2d 347, Mich 1968.

144. Shiffman v. Manhattan Eye, Ear and Throat Hospital, 314 NYS 2d 823, NY 1970; Levin v. Sinai Hospital, 46 A 2d 298, Md 1936; Woodward v. Porter Hospital, 217 A 2d 37, Vt 1966; Mulvihill v. Butterfield Memorial Hospital, 329 F. Supp 1020, DC NY 1971; Weary v. Baylor University Hospital, 360 SW 2d 895, Tex 1963.

145. Shulman v. Washington Hospital Center, 222 F Supp 59, DC DC 1963.

146. Stevens v. Emergency Hospital, 121 Atl 475, Md 1923.

147. Burkhart v. Community Medical Center, 432 SW 2d 433, Ky 1968.

148. Woodbury v. McKinnon, 447 F 2d 839, CCA 5, 1971.

149. Silver v. Castle Memorial Hospital, 497 P 2d 564, Hawaii 1972.

150. Edson v. Griffin Hospital, 144 A 2d 341, Conn 1958.

151. Bricker v. Sceva Speare Memorial Hospital, 181 A 2d 589, NH 1971.

152. Johnson v. City of Ripon, 47 NW 2d 328, Wisc 1951; Meredith v. Allen County War Memorial Hospital Commission, 397 F 2d 33, CCA 6, 1968.

153. Milford v. People's Community Hospital Authority, 155 NW 2d 835, Mich 1968.

154. Woodbury v. McKinnon, 447 F 2d 839, CCA 5, 1971.

155. Moore v. The Board of Trustees of Carson-Tahoe Hospital, 495 P 2d 605, Nev 1972.

156. Levin v. Sinai Hospital, 46 A 2d 298, Md 1946; "Hospital Staff Privileges: Part VI," (in press).

157. Woodward v. Porter Hospital, 217 A 2d 37, Vt 1966.

158. "Criminal Prosecution for Patient's Death," 222 *JAMA* No. 10, page 1341, Dec 4, 1972.

159. People v. Long, 96 P 2d 354, Cal 1939.

160. State v. McMahan, 65 P 2d 156, Idaho 1937.

161. Gorden v. State, 90 SW 636, Tex 1904.

162. Hampton v. State, 39 So 421, Fla 1905.

163. State v. Lester, 149 NW 297, Minn 1914.

164. Washington v. Gile, 35 Pac 417, Wash 1894.

165. State v. Comstock, 70 SE 2d 648, W Va 1952.

166. State Board of Medical Examiners v. Weiner, 172 A 2d 661, NJ 1961.

167. "Cultist Threapy As Criminal Negligence," 196 *JAMA* No. 13, page 249, June 27, 1966.

168. Commonwealth v. Pierce, 138 Mass 165, 1885.

169. "Homicide by Quackery," 222 *JAMA* No. 9, page 1219, Nov. 27, 1972.

170. State v. Karsunky, 84 P 2d 390, Wash 1938.

171. State v. Heines, 197 So 787, Fla 1940.

172. Feige v. State, 194 SW 865, Ark 1917.

173. People v. Hunt, 147 Pac 476, Cal 1915.

174. Barrow v. Oklahoma, 188 Pac 351, Okla 1920.

175. Gian-Cursio v. State, 180 So 2d 396, Fla 1965.

176. State v. McFadden, 93 Pac 414, Wash 1908; Craig v. State, 155 A 2d 684, Md 1959.

177. People v. Phillips, 75 Cal Rptr 720, Cal 1969, appealed to Federal Court as Phillips v. Pitchess, 451 F 2d 913, CCA 9, 1971.

CHAPTER XII

TERMINATION

OF THE

PHYSICIAN–PATIENT

RELATIONSHIP

The physician–patient relationship is properly terminated in a variety of ways. The most usual, of course, is the recovery of the patient from the condition for which he was receiving medical or surgical treatment, thus rendering continuation of the relationship unnecessary.[1]

Secondly, the patient may wish to terminate the relationship. He is, of course free to discharge the physician and end the contractual relationship at any time.[2] The physician undoubtedly has a duty to warn him in this situation of the necessity of obtaining further medical care and to provide the successor physician with sufficient information to permit continuation of treatment without delay, and if those conditions are met the physician has no further obligation to the patient. The physician should, however, write the patient a letter confirming that the patient has discharged him and reiterating the need for continuing treatment. If possible the physician should obtain a signed statement of the facts from the patient, but a very disgruntled patient may refuse to comply with such a request. Written proof that the patient, not the physician, terminated the relationship is very important because these patients are the ones who, justifiably or not, are most likely to pursue legal action against the physician.[3]

The physician is also free to withdraw from a case for any reason satisfactory to himself, including, but not limited to, failure of the patient to pay his bill or to follow proper medical instructions.

A physician whose patient is uncooperative and refuses to follow instructions generally is not liable for abandonment if he removes himself from the case as long as a reasonable patient would have followed the instructions and the physician gives reasonable notice of an intent to withdraw. This was decided as early as 1896.

> If an office patient fails to come to the office for further treatment from the physician or surgeon whom he employs and

from whom he has received careful and skillful treatment, against instructions and in consequence of this error suffers injury, he is not entitled to maintain an action against the physician because it is his own default and misfeasance.[4]

In one case, at least, it was pointed out that the physician cannot always expect a patient to abide by instructions because of the emotional factors inherent in the patient's condition and in that case the physician may not withdraw.

A woman had been in labor for a prolonged time. The physician who was attempting to deliver the baby decided that a forceps delivery was necessary and went and got the proper instrument. When she saw it the woman screamed, jumped, and shrank back and he had to let go of the forceps. The same thing happened again. The third time that she became upset, he told her to be quiet and then he told her that "if she did not quit acting like that he would quit." He abruptly left the house without a word of explanation to anyone. The woman's husband followed him into the street begging him to return and the physician refused to do so. More than an hour later, during which time the patient had no physician at all, another physician was brought in and delivered the baby. The court held that the physician was entirely unjustified in abandoning his patient under those circumstances and stated that "such conduct is evidence of wanton disregard not only of professional ethics but of the terms of his actual contract."[5]

The physician may not withdraw in a preremptory manner from the treatment relationship and leave the patient stranded without medical attention.[6] He must give the patient reasonable notice which, again for the physician's own protection, should be in writing and preferably sent "return receipt requested."[7] He must give the patient sufficient time to locate another physician who is willing to accept the case; thus a period of at least a week from the date of mailing such a notice should be allowed before the first physician actually ceases to see the patient.

A small boy had two skin grafts, one of which did not "take." The surgeon instructed the child's father that he had to be "built up" before more grafting could be done and told the man that he should take the child home. He instructed the father on how to change the dressings and care for the child. It was held that adequate notice of discharge had been given.[8]

Even if the physician is the party who withdraws from the relationship, he is obligated to provide sufficiently adequate records and information to his successor to insure proper continuing care. This, of course, assumes that there is a successor physician available. If a physician is, as is true in many communities in this country, the only one in town, it would appear that regardless of provocation he must continue to see the patient.

Failure to provide adequate notice may make the physician liable in damages for abandonment. Abandonment has been defined as "the unilateral severance by the physician of the professional relationship between himself and a patient without reasonable notice, at a time when there is still the necessity of continuing medical attention.[9]

Abandonment, of course, in its classical sense, involves an intent on the part of the physician to terminate improperly the contractual relationship.[10] However, closely related to it is the situation in which there is no such intention by the physician, but he is so dilatory in his obligation that he does not see the patient as often as due care in treatment would demand and the patient is in effect denied the benefit of the physician–patient relationship without a deliberate intent on the part of the physician to do so. To further differentiate, classical abandonment gives rise not only to an action for negligence, but one for breach of contract.[11] Malpractice involving treatment which results either from failure to see the patient sufficiently often or from an incorrect conclusion that the patient's condition is such that no further treatment is necessary involves an action in negligence alone.[12]

The practical impact of the difference between the two is that in a case alleging negligent and inadequate treatment the patient must present expert medical testimony, as is true in all but a few types of medical malpractice suits. Juries are not, however, required to hear expert testimony for the plaintiff before declaring that the physician has abandoned his patient in an action for breach of contract.[13]

If a physician explicitly tells a patient who is still in need of his care that he is removing himself from the case, then the patient will surely recover damages. The only genuine question is the amount which will be awarded.

A patient had a hernia operation and complained vigorously of intense postoperative pain. The surgeon told him that he was "sick in the head" and that he was withdrawing from the case. Another surgeon eventually discovered that the operation had been incorrectly performed and it was with very ample reason that the patient had complained. The man was awarded damages both for negligent performance of the surgery and for the abandonment.[14]

The same type of abandonment may occur when a physician does not visit a patient in the hospital.

A patient had a varicose vein operation and gangrene set in. The surgeon told the patient that amputation of his foot was immediately required and the patient consented. The surgeon left the room and the patient thought the operation would be performed at once. Four days later when the surgeon had not returned or communicated with the patient in any way, the man insisted on being transferred to another hospital and another surgeon performed the amputation. The court held that abandonment had occurred.[15]

In addition to the requirements of the normal physician–patient relationship, courts very frequently hold that an obstetrics patient has a particular right to be delivered by the same obstetrician whom she has consulted for prenatal care and therefore they are, for psychological and emotional reasons, quite likely to award higher damages for a patient who has been deserted in this situation by her own physician and delivered by an unknown obstetrician than they are in cases in which a physician has refused to see other types of patients. This duty toward an obstetrical patient is considered absolute even if the physician's excuse is that he was with another patient who was also delivering.[16]

A woman went into labor several weeks before the date on which her baby was due and her husband called her physician, who told him she could not possibly be in labor. Her pains continued and the physician saw her the next day and assured her again that she was not in labor. Her pains continued. The husband called the physician twice more and on the second occasion the physician told them that he was withdrawing from the case. While the husband went to look for another doctor the woman delivered her child alone. The court held that abandonment had occurred and pointed out that negligent failure to treat a patient at all is as much of a failure of due care as is the administration of negligent treatment.[17]

A physician was giving prenatal care to a patient. She went into labor at home and he gave her medication at 8:00 p.m. to induce delivery. He told the patient's husband that it would probably be midnight before he would be needed, so he was going back to his office. By 11:00 p.m. the woman's pains were very intense. A call to his office met with no response and he could not be located. Shortly after 1:00 a.m. another physician delivered the child, who died a few minutes after birth. The first physician had gone to attend another patient who was also delivering and did not get to the home of the patient until about 3:00 a.m. Finding the other physician there, he did not enter. The court held that since he had given the woman medication to accelerate her labor, it was his absolute duty to remain where he could be reached when needed or to provide a competent substitute. The fact that he was called to attend another patient was not an excuse.[18]

A child had been in an automobile accident and had received severe injuries to his mouth and a badly fractured jaw. A dentist was called in to perform oral surgery. Hospital regulations provided that a surgeon was required to remain in the operating room at all times when a dentist was operating, but the surgeon left and went home. The anesthetic was given by a nurse who had been both a narcotics addict and an alcoholic and had a history of incredible professional irresponsibility. Cardiac arrest occurred and the child was severely injured because the dentist had had no training in emergency procedures in a cardiac arrest case or even in the use of general anesthesia. The court found the surgeon liable for abandonment.[19]

An express declaration by the physician that he will not further attend the patient is, of course, the clearest form of abandonment and thus the easiest to prove.

A surgeon removed a woman's appendix and continued to treat her for 12 months without any sign of the incision healing. When eventually the patient remarked that there must have been something wrong with the operation, the surgeon became furious and said that "if that was the way she felt about it she could get right out of his office," he "would not do any more for her" and he threatened her by telling her that if she did not leave his office he would call the sheriff to eject her. Subsequently the woman went to another surgeon and another operation revealed a gauze sponge in her incision. In finding the surgeon liable the court said that he had owed her an obligation to continue to administer her needs until all the effects of the operation had subsided and that therefore abandonment had occurred.[20]

If, however, there is no causal connection between the withdrawal and injury to the patient, it is highly unlikely that substantial damages will be awarded.[21] In other words, if a patient proceeds immediately to another doctor so that necessary treatment is not delayed or denied, while abandonment has occurred, generally substantial damages are not usually awarded.[22]

Refusal to attend to the patient's needs even though the physician may not have made any express declaration to the effect that he does not intend to see the patient further may also be considered abandonment even if the lack of attention is due to the physician's preoccupation with another patient.[23] This type of abandonment may be found as a fact if the physician fails to see to the patient at intervals necessary for the proper treatment of whatever condition the patient has.[24] Frequency of attendance is usually considered by courts to be as much a part of careful treatment as any other aspect, such as prescription of proper therapeutic drugs.[25]

The principle involved is that the patient has the right to expect that his doctor will keep himself informed as to the patient's condition, which he cannot do if he removes himself from the case without notice or does not visit the patient frequently enough to be aware of what is happening.[26]

A physician was caring for a pregnant woman and was expected to deliver her child. He told her the last time he saw her that he would come on a certain day, but prior to that date, in spite of the fact that her family called him on numerous occasions to tell him that she was in labor, he refused to come and see her. Six days later another physician surgically removed the dead baby, but in the meantime she had suffered from an acute infection and was permanently paralyzed. The appellate court upheld the verdict in her favor and held that "when engaging a physician to treat his case a patient implicitly engages him to attend throughout the illness or until his services are dispensed with. Part of the correct treatment of the case is the careful and proper determination by the physician of the moment when that relationship will end. When the relationship is prematurely terminated, abandonment has occurred."[27]

A patient had a continuing heart condition for which his physician had treated him on prior occasions. When he became ill again, his wife called the physician, who ordered him admitted to the hospital. After the man was admitted to the hospital, the physician did not see him for several days or write any orders for treatment, although he was in the hospital daily to see other patients. When he finally saw the man, he realized that he was critically ill and ordered oxygen to be given immediately, but the patient died a few minutes later. The court held that abandonment had occurred.[28]

A patient was brought in to the hospital late at night with a gunshot wound and was examined by the defendant, a surgeon. The surgeon did not order a tracheotomy or a transfusion, although expert testimony later clearly indicated that both were absolutely necessary. Although the patient was having great difficulty breathing, the defendant went home without leaving explicit instruction for care. There was clear testimony that the surgeon had been drinking, but there was considerable disagreement among witnesses as to the degree of influence under which he was functioning. When the patient's condition became critical a nurse called the surgeon and asked if he would return or if another physician could see the man. The surgeon hung up the telephone on her. By the time a second surgeon also called the surgeon, argued with him for a considerable time, finally got him to release the patient, and finally got the patient to the operating room, the man had died. The court held that abandonment had occurred.[29]

Therefore the simple failure to see a patient when necessary may, in the first place constitute abandonment, and in the second it may be negligence in terms of the standard of care of both diagnosis and treatment owed to the patient in the sense that if the physician had been properly attentive he might well have known what was wrong with the patient and treated it properly.[30] Thus, even if a physician comes back to see the patient, if he has unreasonably refused to come at the time when the patient needs him, he may well have been so negligent as to be held to have abandoned his patient. The longer the delay, of course, the more likely that a court will find abandonment.

A physician gave a patient repeated injections of a drug whose elements contained arsenic. The patient became violently ill and the physician refused to come to see him. Other physicians called by the patient's family refused to come as long as the original physician considered the man to be his patient. The patient died of arsenic poisoning. The court held that the physician was liable both for abandonment and for negligent treatment.[31]

A child had his tonsils removed and was taken home almost immediately after the operation. In the middle of the night his father notified the two surgeons who had operated that the child was vomiting blood and getting weaker and he asked one of them to come and stop the bleeding. The surgeon did not come until the next morning but the father had located another surgeon who came in the night and treated the child. The child died from his blood loss. The court found that in the first place the tonsillectomy had been negligently performed and secondly that the operating surgeons had abandoned their patient.[32]

A man sustained a fracture of his arm. The defendant placed it in a cast and injected tetanus antitoxin. The patient called the physician again the next evening, the physician refused to come, and he stated that he did not wish to be troubled again with telephone calls until the following Monday when the patient was to present himself at the office. The man developed a severe infection and died from gas gangrene prior to the day of the appointment. Expert testimony indicated that proper medical practice would have been to inspect the arm every 2 or 3 hours for several days after the injury and to give other needed treatment and therefore the physician was held to have abandoned the patient.[33]

In particular, a physician who undertakes the responsibility of prenatal care and agrees to deliver a baby must be there or arrange for a reasonable substitute or, in all cases with or without any express declaration on his part that he does not wish to continue to be the patient's physician, the courts will hold that abandonment has occurred. The abandonment situation is, in fact, most frequently alleged in obstetrics cases since the arrival of the baby cannot be predicted with any real accuracy.[34]

A woman called her obstetrician to tell him that she was in labor. He told his nurse to call his partner to meet the woman at the hospital. The partner did not arrive on time and injury resulted when the episiotomy was performed by a first-year obstetrics resident. The court held that the obstetricians were liable for abandonment and for breach of contract because they had impliedly promised by accepting her as an obstetrical patient to be available at the time the woman went into labor.[35]

Physicians who withdraw from cases in which patients still require medical treatment on the grounds that the patient has not paid a past due bill do not have a good defense in an abandonment case. The financial question is absolutely irrelevant to the question of a patient's care.

A charity patient had a miscarriage and was treated by a physician that day and for 2 days thereafter. He refused to see her again, even though he knew she had retained the placenta, because she could not pay him. The court held that the physician was guilty of abandonment.[86]

A patient had an infected hand on which a surgeon had operated. He was discharged from the hospital, which was owned by the surgeon, but complications set in a few days later and he returned for further treatment. He was being prepared for a second operation when the surgeon refused to allow him to remain or to receive any treatment because he had not paid his bill for the first hospital stay. He was obliged to walk in a pouring rainstorm to another hospital several blocks away to have the second operation. The court held that abandonment had occurred.[37]

If, however, other provisions are made for a patient who cannot pay his bill abandonment may not be found to have occurred.

A surgeon lanced and drained a patient's infected thumb. When the man's wife called and reported complications, the physician established that the patient was unemployed and refused to see him. However, he told the woman to take her husband to the county hospital immediately and evidence showed that another physician was in charge of the case and had administered proper treatment within half an hour of the wife's telephone call. The court conceded that the patient had probably been abandoned, but declined to allow any recovery of damages because there was no proof that the delay had caused any injury.[38]

Physicians are not usually required to sit by their patients' bedsides either at home or at the hospital and may, of course, see the patient and leave orders for others to administer.[39]

An obstetrician did not stay with his patients continuously during labor. In one case he had left the hospital with strict instructions to the labor room attendants to telephone him at once if the woman appeared to be about to deliver. They did not call him soon enough and he did not get there to deliver the baby. The court held, however, that there was no proof that the woman's urinary difficulties which appeared several months after childbirth were attributable to the delayed arrival of the obstetrician.[40]

Where reasonable care would demand seeing a patient very frequently, however, then the physician may be liable even if he sees the patient at 24-hour intervals.

A little girl fell off a swing and broke her arm on a Wednesday afternoon. She was rushed to the hospital where a physician treated her, but he did not examine her arm again until Friday. In the meantime the child had developed gas gangrene. Her arm was amputated. Expert testimony indicated that the infection would have been discovered if the patient had been examined every 8 to 10 hours as reasonable medical practice would have demanded.[41]

A 2-year old boy ate a dozen aspirins and his parents immediately took him to a clinic, arriving about 10:00 p.m. The nurse informed the physician on call of their arrival and followed his orders which were to put the child to bed and tell the parents that he would be "right on down," but he did not arrive until 9:00 a.m. the next morning. The child died and the court held that the parents stated a cause of action against the physician.[42]

A physician who is employed either to assist or consult with another physician but who does not assume responsibility as the primary physician is not guilty of abandonment if he does not perform services which were not part of his original agreement.[43]

A man had a dislocated shoulder. His family physician agreed to set it, but said that it would be necessary to have another physician assist him and engaged the services of another surgeon. When the patient began to have complications he called the first surgeon on the telephone but could not locate him. The second refused to come. The court held that the second physician had not abandoned the patient. There was no reasonable expectation by the patient at the time the second physician appeared on the scene that he would do anything but assist at the procedure and thus he had a right to refuse to be employed further.[44]

A consultant was called in to examine a patient's diseased arm and he did so properly. None of the arrangements between the parties indicated that the specialist expected to be called again or that the patient was in any doubt that the primary physician was again assuming responsibility for the case. The consultant was not liable for his failure to come when the patient called him.[45]

Many older cases involved surgeons who "rode circuit." They would come into town and perform surgery which was too complicated for the local physicians to undertake and then leave immediately with the patient left in the care of his primary physician for postsurgical treatment. Under such an agreement, the surgeon was not liable for abandonment if he did not supervise postsurgical care as long as the patient was aware that this situation obtained and the surgeon indicated directly to the patient that he did not plan to supervise the postoperative care and the patient concurred.[46]

In most teaching hospitals the attending surgeon supervises the surgery, which is actually performed by an intern or resident, and the attending surgeon generally is not held to assume responsibility for following the patient's progress during the postsurgical period. Where this is the standard practice in the hospital, the attending surgeon is not liable for abandonment if he does not continue to care for or assume responsibility for observation of the patient after the operation is concluded.

A chief of surgery at a hospital was asked by an intern to assist him in amputation of the plaintiff's toe. The surgeon was not the patient's private physician. The surgery itself was uneventful, but negligence allegedly occurred in the recovery room. The patient had been transferred to the care of those physicians who were routinely assigned to supervise postoperative treatment and sued the attending surgeon for abandonment. The court held that since the usual hospital system had been followed there was no abandonment.[47]

If a physician talks to a patient by telephone either to receive reports as to his condition or to give instructions, he may have a justification for failure to attend the patient personally. If he elects to make a diagnosis on the telephone, however, it may very well be later proven to be incorrect, although if a reasonable physician would conclude that he could make an adequate diagnosis in the case on the basis of a telephone conversation, the patient probably does not have an action for abandonment.

A woman called her physician in the middle of the night and complained of a stomachache. There was an epidemic of "intestinal flu" in town and the physician assumed that that is what she had and prescribed accordingly. It eventually transpired that the woman had a ruptured appendix. The court held that expert testimony would be required to prove that a duly careful physician would have seen the patient on the basis of the symptoms related to the physician in view of the number of cases of a very common ailment in the community on that date.[48]

A child left the hospital the morning after an operation for appendicitis. That afternoon his mother called the surgeon and described his symptoms and the surgeon told the mother that it was not necessary for him to come and see the child. He told her to come and pick up some medication at his office, which she did. The following day, the boy's father called the surgeon and described more symptoms and was told to come and get more medication, which he did. The court held that the defendant did not act improperly in failing to see the patient personally since he had enough information on which to make an accurate estimation of the child's condition.[49]

If a patient understands that the physician does not intend to come unless called, no abandonment occurs if the physician is not called. "Call me if you need me" is a very common instruction to patients and is clearly understandable to most persons. In this situation a physician is not obliged to initiate further visits in the absence of a summons as long as that instruction has been made clear.[50]

Failure to return when told to do so by the physician is, of course, under most circumstances considered to be contributory negligence; therefore, the the physician whose patient does not follow instructions to report for further treatment is not generally considered guilty of abandonment.[51]

A 6-year old boy broke his arm. The defendant surgeon set it and urged the father in the strongest possible terms to hospitalize the child. The father was from a neighboring community and said that because he could not get into town to visit the child very often, he would refuse to leave the child and took him home. Complications set in and the arm was eventually amputated. The father sued the physician for abandonment. Since the father refused to do what the physician strenuously and repeatedly advised, the court held that he and not the physician had deprived the child of the necessary attention and that no abandonment had occurred.[52]

If the physician does not, however, give adequate instructions or those which are understood by the patient to mean that there is a need for further treatment he may be held to be guilty of abandonment for that failure to instruct.[53]

A piece of steel was imbedded in a man's eye as the result of an accident. He was examined but he did not return to the physician for several days, during which time an infection had developed. The physician testified that he had told the patient to return promptly the next day for further examinations, but the patient denied that he was told to do so. The court held that the conflict should properly have been decided by the jury and if they believed the patient they were entitled to hold that abandonment had occurred. However, there was expert testimony that the delay in treatment did not worsen the condition of the patient's eye, which undoubtedly would have been lost in any case as the result of the trauma sustained, and therefore the court held that even if the patient had been abandoned as a matter of law, the delay was not the cause of the infection and resultant loss of sight and thus no damages would be awarded.[54]

While negligent failure to admit a patient to a hospital in an emergency or to see him after admission is not technically abandonment, since no actual physician–patient relationship has been created, in terms of liability, however, the two situations are similar.[55]

A pedestrian who had been struck by an automobile was taken to the hospital. A nurse in the emergency room telephoned the physician on call and reported his condition. The physician did not come to see him but ordered him admitted to the hospital as an in-patient. The patient went into shock, but the staff nurse in charge of his floor did not telephone the physician for a considerable time and by the time the physician arrived, the man was dying. The court held that the hospital was liable for the nurse's negligence in failing to report the changed condition of the patient to the physician more promptly and that the physician was negligent in failing to realize that a pedestrian who has been hit by a car is very likely to be severely injured even if there are no overt symptoms immediately.[56]

A patient was shot and left in a hospital's emergency room without attention for 2 hours. He was noticed by nurses and the physician on call, whose sole treatment was the summoning of an ambulance to take him to another hospital. The physician knew that the patient was in shock by the time the ambulance arrived, but did absolutely nothing about it, including failing to administer rudimentary first aid. The patient died in the ambulance before reaching the other hospital. The court held that his death was attributable to the abandonment. Although the hospital had not been obliged to receive him, once they did so, they were required to care for him.[57]

Discharging a patient from the hospital prior to the time when his condition justifies it is abandonment, whether the discharge is because the patient cannot pay his bill or results from an honest mistake as to his condition and need for further medical care.

After an appendectomy, a man had obvious symptoms of an intestinal obstruction, but the surgeon who had removed his appendix discharged him from the hospital without investigating his complaints. The court said that the patient stated a good cause of action for abandonment and the appellate court decided that the jury had been justified in finding that the defendant was guilty of negligence in not realizing what was wrong with the patient.[58]

A hysterectomy patient discovered 6 weeks after surgery that her vagina was completely closed. The gynecologist who had performed the operation had not examined her from the time of surgery until this discovery was made at the time she first tried to have intercourse with her husband. The court held that the gynecologist had abandoned her because postoperative care and treatment is as much a part of a surgical case as is the care and skill with which the operation is performed and that lack of due care in such matters constitutes both abandonment and negligence.[59]

A small boy suffered from osteomyelitis. After a lengthy stay in the hospital he was discharged because his father could not pay the bill. The surgeon who owned the hospital assured the father that the child would be seen at home, but his substitute, who saw the child thereafter, knew nothing about the disease. The surgeon never came himself to see the child, who was permanently crippled as a result of inadequate treatment. The court held that the premature discharge without regard to his condition constituted willful abandonment. The court also held that the surgeon had been negligent in failing to tell the father how serious the disease was or that he should have contacted another physician.[60]

A woman had surgery for a strangulated hernia. After making an unskillful opening into the patient's abdomen and without attempting to do anything to correct the condition, the surgeon sewed up the wound and told the patient that she was going to die and that he could do nothing more for her. The same afternoon he sent her home from the hospital in a hearse, a macabre touch which did not escape the notice or wrath of the court. He did not call upon her after the operation, making the excuse that he was too busy. The surgeon did, however, make arrangements for a visiting nurse to come to the woman's house and attend changing the surgical dressings. The court held that he had been guilty of abandonment, as well as negligent performance of the operation. The court found that it was the duty of the surgeon "to require his patient to remain in the hospital after surgery as long as her condition required it and thereby avoid the risk to her life which may be incident to any removal to another place." The fact that the nurse came to assist the patient did not relieve the surgeon from his liability for failure to have kept her in the hospital for the necessary length of time.[61]

A postsurgical patient began to manifest symptoms of psychosis. The surgeon immediately sent word to her family to come and get her, but did not tell them what was wrong. When they arrived the surgeon insisted that she be removed from the hospital immediately although her pulse and temperature showed clearly that she was in no condition to make the long train trip to reach her home. The combined effects of her mental condition and the surgery caused her to become violently insane and she was in a state mental hospital for several years. The court found that the jury was justified in finding the physician guilty of abandonment.[62]

Thus the only legitimate criteria for discharge of a patient from a hospital is that good medical judgment would indicate that he no longer needs to be there.[63]

In summary, once a physician has undertaken to treat a patient without any specific limitation as to the time, place, and nature of the treatment, the courts still adopt the rule which was enunciated by the court in an 1891 decision, which is the earliest one on abandonment which can be located, agreeing that a physician "cannot cease his visits except, first with the consent of the patient, or secondly upon giving the patient time and notice so that he may employ another doctor or thirdly when the condition of the patient is such that medical treatment is no longer required and of that condition the physician must judge at his peril."[64]

Physicians are, of course, entitled to reasonable time away from their practices either for vacations and other activities or to attend professional meetings as long as arrangements are made for a competent, qualified substitute and notice of the impending substitution is given to the physician's patients.[65] If a substitute employed by the physician is adequately qualified, the general rule in most states is that the physician is not liable for the substitute's negligence as long as due care was used in his selection.

A patient broke his leg. The physician who set it left the city for several days to attend a medical meeting but had made arrangements with an experienced and qualified physician who attended and cared for the man during his absence. The court held that his absence did not constitute any negligence. The court held that it was a matter of common knowledge that a broken leg, after it is set, does not require the continuous presence of a physician if the patient abides by his instructions.[66]

If the substitute is an "employee" of the physician, however, standard rules of vicarious liability apply. If he is not carefully chosen and is incompetent or unqualified the physician may also be liable for his negligence. In these cases, notice of the substitution must be given to the patient because the patient may prefer to consult another doctor whom he knows instead of being treated by the unknown substitute. If the notice of the substitution is not given and the physician's absence causes an adverse effect on the patient's condition the physician may well be held to have abandoned his patient.[67]

A physician administered a tonic containing arsenic, and the treatment made the patient very ill as well as causing a rash. At her last visit to the physician he told her that if she did not feel better to return the following morning to his office and he would give her other medication. The patient did return the next day, but the defendant was not at his office. She searched for him for several days and eventually consulted another physician. Some 5 days after he left, she discovered that the defendant had asked another physician to look after his patients if any of them went to him, but he had not given the other physician any information whatever about her case. The court held that she stated a cause of action for abandonment against the physician since this arrangement did not satisfy the defendant's obligation to provide the woman with a physician in his place.[68]

The same rule would not, of course, apply if the physician himself became suddenly ill or had to leave town for the illness of a member of his family without notice, although if the illness from which the physician suffered was not an emergency it would seem likely that he would have to make reasonable efforts to find a substitute while he was away from his practice.[69]

A 6-year old boy had peritonitis and it was discovered that his appendix had already ruptured. A surgeon performed an emergency operation. The child was in critical condition, but his condition was not deteriorating and the defendant visited him every morning until about a week after the operation, when the surgeon went to another city to a meeting, intending to return the same evening. However, he had an automobile accident and stayed overnight, arriving at home the next morning. When the surgeon had realized that he would not be able to see the child that night, he called his wife and told her to call another surgeon and have him see the patient. However, during his absence the patient died. The court found that he was not guilty of negligence since he had attempted to provide a substitute.[70]

Several cases indicate that failure to provide an adequate and qualified substitute may be seriously harmful to a patient.[71]

A patient's arm was set by a surgeon. She complained from the outset that the cast was too tight but he did not examine it or split the cast. He went on vacation for two weeks and did not designate a substitute. She went to the hospital, which was, incidentally, owned by the surgeon, almost daily to complain, but no other physician saw her, although nurses applied heat treatments. When the cast was removed, it was discovered that a piece of plaster about the size of a cigarette was imbedded in her arm and she was permanently disabled. She recovered damages for abandonment.[72]

A teenage boy was in the hospital after fracturing his leg. The defendant set it. His father called the defendant for 2 days without persuading him to see the boy and explained both times that the boy was running considerable fever and exhibiting other symptoms of infection, as well as being in severe pain. On the third day the defendant left town on a vacation without arranging for a substitute and without seeing the boy. When he returned from his trip he ordered the boy discharged from the hospital, again without seeing him in spite of the fact that the nurse in charge of that floor told him that the boy had a high fever. The boy's leg eventually had to be amputated and the court found that the defendant had abandoned him.[73]

A child had osteomyelitis and was being treated by a physician who was considered the most eminent expert on the subject in the geographical area in which the child lived. The physician became ill with a nonemergency condition and decided to go to Arizona for a protracted period of recuperation. In preparation for his absence he hired a substitute who was in fact his own son, with only 4 years of experience in practice. The substitute's treatment of the child was later proved to be negligent. The court held that the physician had abandoned the patient because he should have given the boy's family notice of the substitute's lesser qualifications and thus given them the option of electing to continue to have the child treated by the substitute or turning the problem over to another physician.[74]

The question of substitutes usually revolves around whether or not the physician used reasonable care in selecting him. If the physician has done what the reasonable physician would do to insure that his patients are left in the care of a qualified person, he usually is not liable for either abandonment or for the substitute's negligence.[75] The question of substitution in obstetrical cases is particularly vexing, but reasonable substitutes are usually allowed.

Before a woman delivered, her obstetrician went out of town and provided a substitute to care for her. The baby was perfectly healthy and so was the mother, but she complained that she had agreed with the defendant that he would give her a general anesthetic and that the substitute had refused to do so. She returned to the original obstetrician for postpartum care. The court held that there was no proof of any agreement about the anesthesia which was binding on the substitute. Because the patient had had no notice of any substitution prior to going to the hospital to deliver and fully anticipated seeing her regular doctor at the time she was admitted, however, the opinion stated the general rule applicable in all jurisdictions and held that she had been abandoned. When a physician wishes to have a substitute care for his patients, except in an emergency such as his own acute illness, he must give his patient adequate and timely notice of the impending substitution.[76]

If physicians who practice together see each other's patients on a rotating basis, none of them can be held to have abandoned a patient if another member of the group or partnership has been to see him.

Two obstetricians practiced in partnership. One of them exclusively cared for the plaintiff during her pregnancy, but prior to the time her baby was due, he closed his practice and moved away. His former partner assumed responsibility for the care of all his patients and delivered the plaintiff's baby. The woman had a hemorrhage and sued her original physician for abandonment. The court held that since she had had reasonable notice of the withdrawal of

her physician from practice, and since the partner possessed the same qualifications as the original physician, no abandonment had occurred.[77]

The question of the equal qualifications of the substitute is generally held
to be for the determination of the jury.[78] The operative question is, of
course, whether the lesser qualification of the substitute contributed to the
untoward result of which the patient complains or whether it would have
been unpreventable even if the original physician had been present. Interns
or residents are usually not considered adequate substitutes.

An 8-inch drainage tube was left in a surgical incision. The surgeon who had
performed the operation administered most of the postoperative care himself,
but instructed a resident to remove the tube. Instead of removing it, the resident cut the tube off at skin level and sutured the incision, leaving a long
portion of the tube in the patient's body. The surgeon was liable for abandonment because he should have supervised the resident.[79]

A child had had her fractured leg set by an orthopedic surgeon and was in
traction. The cast was too tight and she was injured. The attending physician
did not see her after he set the leg because he had told an orthopedic resident at the hospital to assume responsibility for her care. The court held that
the physician had not provided an adequate substitute and had had an obligation to visit the patient himself and was therefore liable for damages.[80]

A patient was brought to the emergency room with a compound fracture.
The attending orthopedist on call told a resident who called him on the telephone and asked the orthopedist to come see the patient, to clean and suture
the wound. By the next night when the orthopedist saw the patient himself, a
severe infection had set in. The court held that from the facts of the accident,
which had taken place at a farm, the orthopedist should have known that an
infection was quite likely to occur. He was required by reasonable standards
of due care to have come to the hospital to see the patient himself and was
negligent in delegating so much decision-making power to a resident.[81]

Where a physician refers a patient to a second physician the first physician obviously cannot be held liable for abandonment.[82] He is also not
liable for any negligence committed by the physician to whom he referred
the patient as long as he used due care in selecting him.

A physician may not, however, avoid liability by withdrawing after joint
negligence has occurred and then claiming that the other physician was a
duly qualified substitute.

A woman fell and broke her hip. She sent for the defendant, a surgeon, who immediately called in her own son-in-law, who was also a surgeon, and together they made a diagnosis and treated the woman. After a few visits, the defendant ceased all connections with the case without notifying the plaintiff and allowed her son-in-law alone to assume responsibility for the patient's treatment, although she continued to consult with and advise her son-in-law about the case and the bill was sent to the patient in both names. There was allegedly negligence in the son-in-law's treatment of the patient. The court held that both physicians were liable if either one of them had been negligent, since the evidence justified the conclusion that the employment was joint and their services were jointly performed in spite of the first physician's claim that she had terminated her connection with the case and therefore her liability when her son-in-law began treating the patient alone.[83]

A physician, of course, has the right to make reasonable limitations on his practice.[84] He is under no legal obligation whatever to treat any patient who wishes him to exceed the stated limitations of that practice. A physician whose policy is not to make house calls is not obliged to do so and is perfectly justified in telling the patient to come to the office or to see him at the hospital.[85]

A patient had an operation which caused an abortion. When she was dismissed from the hospital, the surgeon had told her that "if things did not go just right" she should come back to see him at his office for further treatment within the next 2 or 3 days. She called him and he refused to visit her at her home, which was at another city. The court held that the failure of the surgeon to go to her residence did not constitue negligence because, by the terms of his contract, he did not undertake to treat the case except to give service at his office. He was not, therefore, liable for abandoning her.[86]

A physician has also the right to limit the scope of his practice. An internist, for example, who refuses to perform a surgical operation is not abandoning his patient when he refers him to a surgeon.[87]

A woman was injured in an automobile accident and an orthopedic surgeon set her leg. After the procedure he told her not to bear any weight on the leg and gave her other quite proper instructions. While she was still in the hospital under his care she developed a traumatic psychosis and was referred to a mental hospital. All her records, orthopedic and medical, were sent with her. While in the mental hospital, she claimed she was forced to walk on her injured leg and she sued the orthopedist for abandonment. He had resumed care of the patient when she was released from the mental hospital and returned to the scene of her first hospitalization. The court held that he did not have an obligation to follow his patient to the mental hospital and, in fact, could not have done so since he was not a member of its staff. He had made all records and instructions available to the physicians at the mental hospital and was not liable for their failure to follow them.[88]

A physician may, without being accused of abandonment, also refuse to deliver babies or treat patients in any location other than in a hospital.[89]

A patient had a boil on his finger. He appeared at his physician's office on a Sunday morning and the physician refused to lance it except during regular office hours which he conducted at one hospital in the community. The patient wished to be seen either in the physician's office or a second hospital, both of which the physician refused to do. The patient went to another physician and sued the first physician for abandonment. The court held that he had no right to insist on being treated at a certain place.[90]

The physician also does not have to go to another community to treat a patient.[91]

A physician made a contract whereby he agreed to treat an elderly woman "at any time or place during any spell of indisposition," for the remainder of her life, in return for a fixed compensation to be paid by her executor after her death. This contract was held not to require the physician to accompany her to any place she might see fit to go, but only to bind him to treat her at her permanent abode. The court therefore held that the physician had not breached the contract when he refused to accompany the patient, who was a resident of Chicago, to California for a year.[92]

Abandonment, then, can occur either by express withdrawal by the physician from a case or by his failure to continue to treat the patient without any express statement. It should be noted that if abandonment occurs, the patient must still show that the delay or failure of treatment resulted in some damage to him. If he was able to contact another physician before any harm was done, he cannot recover damages even if the abandonment was both legally and ethically unjustified. Thus dismissal by the patient, a discharge of the patient as cured by the physician, withdrawal by the physician after due notice, provision of a substitute physician for the patient, and abandonment are the usual means by which the physician–patient relationship is terminated.

Medical Records.   One very important aspect of the physician–patient relationship which usually does not arise until after treatment has been concluded is the ownership of medical records and what rights, if any, the patient has in those records. Very few cases can be found which center on the question of whether the physician or patient owns such records.

The plaintiff was a physician who treated a workman for a work-related injury and his bill was to have been paid by the company for which the man worked, but the company would not pay because the physician refused to turn over the Xray films which he had made of the workman's injuries to them. The court held that since the Xray films belonged to the physician and not to either the patient or his employer, such a refusal did not affect the obligation to pay for the physician's services.[93]

Xray films are usually held to belong to the radiologist, not to the referring physician who may receive the radiologist's report or to the patient, unless the films are delivered to the patient who takes them to his physician for interpretation and the radiologist tells the patient that he does not expect them to be returned. With that exception, most cases indicate that the radiologist retains ownership of his films.[94]

A physician is generally held to have ownership of his office records subject to his ethical obligation to furnish them to another physician who assumes responsibility for care of the patient. The question of what to do with these records when the physician dies is the one which is the subject of more actual litigation than any other aspect of this problem.

A physician died and left instructions in his will that all his professional records should be burned by his executor. A number of patients sued to have the provision invalidated. The court found that the records did belong to the estate, not to the patients. However, it very carefully reviewed the rules of professional conduct of the American Medical Association's Judicial Council and recognized that a physician is ethically obligated to cooperate with and transfer records to the physician who succeeds him in caring for the patient. On that basis, the court held that, although the records were the property of the physician and therefore of his estate, it would strike out that provision of the will. However, the court took pains to explain that the records were to be turned over to the patients' current physicians and not given to the patients themselves.[95]

The American College of Radiology issued a statement in which they declared that while Xrays are the legal property of the radiologist or the hospital by which they were made, the radiologist is obliged to loan the Xray films to the referring physician and if the patient no longer consults the referring physician, but sees a second physician, those films should be turned over to the second physician even if the first physician objects. The College indicates, however, that the radiologist has a right to refuse to release films for use as evidence in court except under subpoena.[96]

The rule that records should be supplied to a successor physician, however, does not apply to a physician who is asked to turn over records to an unqualified practitioner, such as a chiropractor, whom the patient may be consulting. Since chiropractors do not have licenses to practice medicine, if the patient has a medical or surgical problem the chiropractor will presumably be practicing medicine if he treats it. A physician might, in fact, be conceivably criminally liable as an accessory before the fact if he places medical records in a chiropractor's hands and allows the chiropractor to treat the patient and the patient is harmed as a result of the chiropractor's criminal negligence.[97] Most courts would hold at least that the physician would be guilty of aiding and abetting the unlawful practice of medicine.

Hospital records are normally considered the property of the hospital.[98] However, a patient, his guardian, or his attorney, with written permission from the patient, has the right to inspect and to copy any of these records if they are relevant to any legal proceedings.[99]

A guardian of an incompetent minor who was a patient in the state institution for the retarded went to inspect the child's records. The hospital refused on the grounds that they were covered by physician–patient privilege. The purpose of the inspection was to gather information for a possible lawsuit on whether or not the child had been neglected while at the institution. The appellate court held that since the privilege of the confidential relationship belongs to the patient and not the physician, the competent patient can waive that privilege. In this case the court concluded that the guardian who stood in the place of his ward could exercise that right and he was therefore allowed to inspect the records. It should be noted, however, that in this case the guardian had the right to inspect the records at the hospital and he had not even requested the right to remove them or transfer them to another location.[100]

A former hospital patient asked for a court order directing the hospital to deliver certain Xray films to the patient's succeeding physician. The court refused to order delivery of the films, but did direct the hospital to afford access to them on the hospital premises under proper viewing conditions as often, within reason, as the successor physician asked to see them.[101]

Any information in hospital records which applies solely to the patient who requests the information or on whose behalf the information is requested must be made available to the patient or to his attorney. In some states the patient does not have the right to read his records himself, but his attorney in all states does have that right as long as he has the written permission of his client.[102]

Hospital records which refer to more than one patient, such as a surgical logbook, probably are not subject in their entirety to either subpoena or inspection by a patient, although the patient or his representative does have the right to be furnished with a copy of that portion of the logbook or record which refers to his own case.[103] In some states "incident reports" made for internal hospital records and for the hospital's insurance carrier describing the circumstances of an accident to a patient are not subject to inspection or subpoena.[104] In other states, however, they are admissible in evidence in a suit against the hospital or its employees.[105]

Some states have statutes which remove the transcripts of deliberations of hospital tissue committees from those papers which may be subpoenaed in malpractice cases in order to protect the privacy of the members of the committee. The same privilege, however, usually does not apply to a statement made by a physician about his treatment of a patient to a staff committee inquiry into possible negligence [106]

The rule that office records are the physician's property does not apply if the physician has agreed with the patient that he will turn the records over to the patient at the end of the treatment or if the physician is an employee of another person or an institution such as a hospital. In those cases the hospital or other employer is generally considered the owner of the records.

A physician had been employed by a clinic as a doctor for $4\frac{1}{2}$ years. The clinic's owner died and a dispute arose between his widow, who was the executrix of his estate, and the physician. The physician received a court order evicting him from the premises, but when he left, he took with him the records of about 100 patients. The executrix sued to get the records back. Of those 100 patients, 86 signed statements that they considered themselves patients of the physician and that they did not wish to have their records returned to the clinic. They wished him to retain them since they intended to consult him in the future. The court ruled that the physician should be permitted to retain those 86 records, but he was required to return the records of the other patients to the executrix. He was, after all, the "successor" physician for the 86 patients even though he had seen them first in his capacity as an employee and "succeeded" as an independent contractor in his own office.[107]

If a patient's attorney is investigating records to discover if medical negligence has occurred and the physician or hospital unjustifiably refuses to allow him access to those records, courts may very well hold that such a refusal is "fraudulent concealment" of a sufficient degree to toll the statute of limitations; thus the patient's right to sue extends from the time the records are made available to the attorney or the patient's representative.[108]

Hospital records are much more likely to be concerned with hearsay statements in some cases than physicians' records. Most courts hold that even though physicians' office records may be full of third party statements known as hearsay which would otherwise not be admissible in court, the records themselves can be admitted even with the inclusion of the statements under the general rule that business records may be admitted even if they include hearsay. In most states the Uniform Business Records as Evidence Act has made admissible all hospital records specifically involving the injury which is the subject of any litigation. These records are of two classes. First, there may be notes made by the person who actually knew of treatment given, such as a nurse's indication on a chart that she had administered an injection ordered by the physician. Secondly, there may be entries in which a hospital employee or physician has recorded information supplied by the patient which includes such things as how the automobile accident which resulted in his injuries occurred. Generally only those portions of the record which can be attributed directly to the knowledge of the person who made the entry can be admitted in evidence and then only when the entry involves such medical matters as the extent of the patient's injuries and the treatment he received.[109] Psychiatrist's records, for obvious reasons, present a very peculiar legal situation. In most courts it is held that a psychiatrist's records are admissible only to prove or disprove any allegation by the patient of negligent psychiatric treatment. They are never admissible under any circumstances to prove the truth or falsity of any factual statement made to the psychiatrist. If a hospital record includes a narrative statement by a patient as to the manner in which an accident happened or some other event took place or any description of how he was injured, some states admit such a statement in evidence in a later trial against the person who allegedly caused the injury if the record indicates that it was made to the physician or nurse who entered it into the patient's record and it was written exactly as it came from the patient, not from a third party. To be admissible as evidence, the statement must be a word-for-word transcription of what the patient said; it cannot be the writer's interpretation of the patient's statement.[110]

Even when the statement is a verbatim account of what the patient said about the cause of the accident, most states do not allow such a statement to be used in evidence.[111] In all states any statement by a patient as to criminal activities of another, such as the patient's identification of a rapist or assailant are not admissible evidence in a criminal trial.[112] These statements are considered too remote from the purpose of the record to guarantee accuracy of identification. However, where the defense in a criminal trial is that the "victim" was not injured, as in a case in which the defense to a charge of rape is that the victim consented to intercourse and force was not applied, hospital records of the extent of her injuries and the treatment given are admissible by the prosecution.[113]

Hospital records as to the condition of the patient himself, such as the state of his mental competency if he makes a will while he is a patient, are usually considered sufficiently related to the diagnostic and treatment process to be admissible.[114] States vary in their admission in evidence of records which indicate that a patient was under the influence of narcotics or alcohol at the time he was brought to the hospital. If the patient files suit against the other driver after an automobile accident, all states allow admission of records tending to show that he himself was drunk at the time of the accident because the patient was the party who raised the issue and brought his physical condition into court.[115] These records, however, are usually not admissible against the patient in a criminal trial such as that on a charge of driving while intoxicated.[116]

Office records of the physician of course are subject to subpoena if a patient sues him if they can be identified as that patient's records.[117] Thus physicians and hospitals are the owners of their Xray films, photographs, and all other records, with the provision that reasonable inspection must be allowed to persons with a legitimate interest in seeing the records. In most cases, records should not be released to government agencies, social welfare departments, or similar investigatory agencies without the explicit consent of the patient. In most situations the government has no more right to inspect medical records without a court order than does the patient's next door neighbor. This, of course, was the reason for the burglary of Daniel Ellsberg's psychiatrist's office. A court would have subpoenaed any records in which the government could show that it had a legitimate interest, but the organizers of the burglary were at least sufficiently competent attorneys to know that no such showing could be made, regardless of what must be concluded about their ethics.

The length of time after the patient is discharged from treatment for which records should be kept varies from jurisdiction to jurisdiction, but all records should be kept for at least the number of years included in the statute of limitations in the state after the last contact with the patient. If the patient is a minor his records should be kept until he reaches the age of majority plus the period of time allowed in that state for a suit to be brought by a minor for injuries he sustained during his minority. In most states, that period is usually 1 year, and therefore a minor's records should be kept at least until his twenty-second birthday.

NOTES

1. Engle v. Clarke, 346 SW 2d 13, Ky 1961.
2. Miles v. Harris, 194 SW 839, Tex 1917.
3. Pearson v. Norman, 106 P 2d 361, Colo 1940; Duke Sanitarium v. Hearn, 13 P 2d 183, Okla 1932.
4. Dashiell v. Griffith, 35 Atl 1094, Md 1896.
5. Lathrope v. Flood, 63 Pac 1007, Cal 1901.
6. Capps v. Valk, 369 P 2d 238, Kans 1962.
7. Lee v. Dewbre, 362 SW 2d 900, Tex 1962; Burnett v. Layman, 181 SW 157, Tenn 1915.
8. McManus v. Donlin, 127 NW 2d 22, Wisc 1964.
9. Stohlman v. Davis, 220 NW 247, Neb 1928; Mucci v. Houghton, 57 NW 305, Iowa 1894; Groce v. Myers, 29 SE 2d 553, NC 1944; McIntire, Leon L., "The Action of Abandonment in Medical Malpractice Litigation," 36 *Tulane Law Rev* 834, 1962.
10. "Abandonment of Patient," 198 *JAMA* No. 9, page 247, Nov. 28, 1966.
11. Chase v. Clinton County, 217 NW 565, Mich 1928; Alexandridis v. Jewett, 388 F 2d 829, CCA 1, 1968.
12. Thomas v. Corso, 288 A 2d 379, Md 1972.
13. "Abandonment: Part I," 225 *JAMA* No. 9, page 1157, Aug. 27, 1973.
14. Collins v. Meeker, 424 P 2d 488, Kans 1967.
15. McGulpin v. Bessmer, 43 NW 2d 121, Iowa 1950.
16. Hood v. Moffett, 69 So 664, Miss 1915; Singer v. Bossingham, 188 NW 155, Minn 1922.
17. Norton v. Hamilton, 89 SE 2d 809, Ga 1955.
18. Young v. Jordan, 145 SE 41, W Va 1928.
19. Pederson v. Dumouchel, 431 P 2d 976, Wash 1967.
20. Gillette v. Tucker, 65 NE 865, Ohio 1902.
21. Childers v. Frye, 158 SE 744, NC 1931.
22. Skodje v. Hardy, 288 P 2d 771, Wash 1955; Carroll v. Griffin, 101 SE 2d 764, Ga 1958.
23. Sinclair v. Brunson, 180 NW 358, Mich 1920.
24. "Abandonment: Part II," 225 *JAMA* No. 10, page 1285, Sept. 3, 1973.
25. Boyd v. Andrae, 44 SW 2d 891, Mo 1932.
26. Tadlock v. Lloyd, 173 Pac 200, Colo 1918.
27. Cazzell v. Schofield, 8 SW 2d 580, Mo 1928.
28. Levy v. Kirk, 187 So 2d 401, Fla 1966.
29. Johnson v. Vaughn, 370 SW 2d 591, Ky 1963.
30. Baird v. National Health Foundation, 144 SW 2d 850, Mo 1940.

31. Thaggard v. Vafes, 119 So 647, Ala 1928.

32. Flentie v. Townsend, 30 P 2d 132, Kans 1934.

33. Gamradt v. DuBois, 230 NW 774, Minn 1930.

34. Mehigan v. Sheehan, 51 A 2d 632, NH 1947; Young v. Jordan, 145 SE 41, W Va 1928.

35. Alexandridis v. Jewett, 388 F 2d 829, CCA 1, 1968.

36. Becker v. Janinski, 15 NYS 675, NY 1891.

37. Ricks v. Budge, 64 P 2d 208, Utah 1937.

38. Gray v. Davidson, 130 P 2d 341, Wash 1942.

39. Smith v. Wharton, 154 SE 12, NC 1930.

40. Bonner v. Conklin, 62 F 2d 875, CA DC 1932.

41. Jackson v. Burton, 147 So 414, Ala 1933.

42. Gray v. Weinstein, 42 SE 2d 616, NC 1947.

43. Shannon v. Ramsey, 193 NE 235, Mass 1934.

44. Tomer v. Aiken, 101 NW 769, Iowa 1904.

45. Nelson v. Farrish, 173 NW 715, Minn 1919.

46. Harris v. Fall, 177 Fed 79, CCA 7, 1910; McLendon v. Daniel, 141 SE 77, Ga 1927.

47. Sheridan v. Quarrier, 16 A 2d 479, Conn 1940.

48. Bailey v. Williams, 203 NW 2d 454, Neb 1973.

49. Riggs v. Christie, 173 NE 2d 610, Mass 1961.

50. Van Skike v. Potter, 73 NW 295, Neb 1897; Miller v. Blackburn, 185 SW 864, Ky 1916.

51. Roberts v. Wood, 206 F Supp 579, DC Ala 1962; Fleishmann v. Richardson-Merrell, Inc., 226 A 2d 843, NJ 1967.

52. Brown v. Dark, 119 SW 2d 529, Ark 1938.

53. Doan v. Griffith, 402 SW 2d 855, Ky 1966; Christy v. Saliterman, 179 NW 2d 288, Minn 1970; Welch v. Frisbie Memorial Hospital, 9 A 2d 761, NH 1939.

54. Barnes v. Bovenmyer, 122 NW 2d 312, Iowa 1963.

55. Barcia v. Society of the New York Hospital, 241 NYS 2d 373, NY 1963; Ruvio v. North Broward Hospital District, 186 So 2d 45, Fla 1966; Andrews v. Lofton, 57 SE 2d 338, Ga 1950.

56. Thomas v. Corso, 288 A 2d 379, Md 1972.

57. New Biloxi Hospital, Inc. v. Frazier, 146 So 2d 882, Miss 1962.

58. Reed v. Laughlin, 58 SW 2d 440, Mo 1933.

59. Wooten v. Curry, 362 SW 2d 820, Tenn 1961.

60. Meiselman v. Crown Heights Hospital, 34 NE 2d 367, NY 1941.

61. Morrell v. Lalonde, 120 Atl 435, RI 1923.

62. Fausette v. Grim, 186 SW 1177, Mo 1916.

63. Gross v. Partlow, 68 P 2d 1034, Wash 1937.

64. Becker v. Janinski, 15 NYS 675, NY 1891.

65. "Abondonment; Part III," 225 *JAMA* No. 11, page 1429, Sept. 10, 1973; Browning v. Hoffman, 111 SE 492, W Va 1922.

66. Stacy v. Williams, 69 SW 2d 697, Ky 1934.

67. Gerken v. Plimpton, 70 NYS 793, NY 1901.
68. Howell v. Biggart, 152 SE 323, W Va 1930.
69. Dashiell v. Griffith, 35 Atl 1094, Md 1896; Warwick v. Bliss, 195 NW 501, SD 1923.
70. Bartolas v. Coleman, 161 NE 20, Ohio 1927.
71. Nash v. Royster, 127 SE 356, NC 1925.
72. Livingston v. Portland General Hospital Association, 357 P 2d 543, Ore 1960.
73. Vann v. Harden, 47 SE 2d 314, Va 1948.
74. Stohlman v. Davis, 220 NW 247, Neb 1928.
75. "Abandonment: Part III," 225 *JAMA* No. 11, page 1429, Sept. 10, 1973.
76. Miller v. Dore, 148 A 2d 692, Maine 1959.
77. Lee v. Dewbre, 362 SW 2d 900, Tex 1962.
78. Wilson v. Martin Memorial Hospital, 61 SE 2d 102, NC 1950.
79. Capps v. Valk, 369 P 2d 238, Kans 1962.
80. Moeller v. Hauser, 54 NW 2d 639, Minn 1952.
81. United States v. Morin, 229 F 2d 824, CCA 9, 1956.
82. Engle v. Clarke, 346 SW 2d 13, Ky 1961; Clark v. Wichman, 179 A 2d 38, NJ 1962.
83. Bolles v. Kinton, 263 Pac 26, Colo 1928.
84. "Abandonment, Part IV," 225 *JAMA* No. 12, page 1571, Sept. 17, 1973.
85. Rogers v. Lawson, 170 F 2d 157, DC CA 1948; Urritia v. Patino, 297 SW 512, Tex 1928.
86. Nash v. Meyer, 31 P 2d 273, Idaho 1934.
87. Skodje v. Hardy, 288 P 2d 771, Wash 1955.
88. Clark v. Wichman, 179 A 2d 38, NJ 1962.
89. Vidrine v. Mayes, 127 So 2d 809, La 1961.
90. Dabney v. Briggs, 121 So 394, Ala 1929.
91. McNamara v. Emmons, 97 P 2d 503, Cal 1939.
92. Zeigler v. Illinois Trust and Savings Bank, 91 NE 1041, Ill 1910.
93. McGarry v. J. A. Mercier Co., 262 NW 296, Mich 1935.
94. Hayt, Emanuel and Hayt, Jonathan, *Legal Aspects of Medical Records*, Physicians' Record Co., Berwyn, Illinois, 1964, pages 58–62.
95. In re Culbertson's Will, 292 NYS 2d 806, NY 1968.
96. Hayt and Hayt, *op cit supra* at 94, pages 60–62.
97. "Physician's Records and the Chiropractor," 224 *JAMA* No. 7, page 1071, May 14, 1973.
98. Helfman, Dennis, Jarrett, Glenn, Lutzker, Susan, Schneider, Karen and Stein, Peter, "Access to Medical Records," *Appendix to the Report of the Secretary's Commission on Medical Malpractice*, DHEW Publication (os) 74-89, 1973, pages 177–213.
99. Wallace v. University Hospitals of Cleveland, 164 NE 2d 917, Ohio 1959.
100. Gaertner v. Michigan, 187 NW 2d 429, Mich 1971.
101. Falum v. Medical Arts Center Hospital, 160 New York Law Journal 2, 1968.
102. Bush v. Kallen, 302 A 2d 142, NJ 1973.
103. Unick v. Kessler Memorial Hospital, 257 A 2d 134, NJ 1969.

104. Sligar v. Tucker, 267 So 2d 54, Fla 1972.

105. Bernandi v. Community Hospital Association, 443 P 2d 708, Colo 1968.

106. Pindar v. Parke Davis and Co., 337 NYS 2d 452, NY 1972.

107. Jones v. Fakehany, 67 Cal Rptr 810, Cal 1968.

108. Emmett v. Eastern Dispensary and Casualty Hospital, 396 F 2d 931, CA DC 1967.

109. Poweshiek County National Bank v. Nationwide Mutual Insurance Co., 156 NW 2d 671, Iowa 1968; Tryon v. Casey, 416 SW 2d 252, Mo 1967.

110. Cox v. New York, 171 NYS 2d 818, NY 1958.

111. Kelly v. Sheehan, 259 A 2d 605, Conn 1969; Dorsten v. Lawrence, 253 NE 2d 804, Ohio 1969.

112. Washington v. White, 433 P 2d 682, Wash 1967; Ohio v. Tims, 224 NE 2d 348, Ohio 1967.

113. Massachusetts v. Concepcion, 290 NE 2d 514, Mass 1972.

114. In re Estate of Searchill, 157 NW 2d 788, Mich 1968; In re Estate of Bernatzki, 460 P 2d 527, Kans 1969.

115. Wilder v. Edwards, 173 SE 2d 72, NC 1970; Rivers v. Union Carbide Corporation, 426 F 2d 633, CCA 3, 1970.

116. Koump v. Smith, 250 NE 2d 857, NY 1969.

117. Benjamin v. Havens, Inc., 373 P 2d 109, Wash 1962.

CHAPTER XIII

THE

MALPRACTICE

CASE

IN THE LEGAL

PROCESS

The incidence of malpractice cases filed each year in this country is apparently rising steadily. The concern of physicians, hospitals, insurance companies, and, of course, patients with the phenomenon has led to several studies of the problem by the federal government, which are, together with an American Medical Association survey, the only reliable statistical indices of the problem.

In 1969 the Sub-Committee on Executive Reorganization of the Committee on Government Operations of the United States Senate, chaired by Senator Abraham Ribicoff of Connecticut, undertook a study of the apparent increase in medical malpractice litigation to determine what role, if any, the federal government should play in solutions of the problem.[1] In 1971 President Nixon ordered the Secretary of Health, Education and Welfare to appoint a commission to study the problem of medical malpractice and the increase in suits and to make recommendations for amelioration of the "negative health systems consequences" to prevent any further rise in the amount of litigation.[2] The Malpractice Commission included members of the public, most of whom were consumer advocates for health maintenance organizations, attorneys, physicians, hospital administrators, social workers, and representatives of malpractice insurance companies. The report was completed on December 31, 1972 and issued by the Department of Health, Education and Welfare on January 16, 1973.[3] With these reports one can make certain reasonable estimates of the statistical magnitude of the problem of malpractice cases in this country.

The American Medical Association made a small survey of such cases as well.[4] The AMA Legal Department examined all medical malpractice cases which had reached appellate courts within the period of a year.

There were 107 reported decisions in which negligence in provision of patient care was claimed against either physicians or hospitals. It should be remembered that the proportion of cases which ever reach the appellate level and therefore have reported decisions is miniscule in comparison to the number of claims brought, cases filed, cases settled, and cases terminated at the trial court level, at which most judges do not write opinions. This figure, therefore, cannot be used as an accurate guide to the incidence of malpractice claims. However, the AMA study did indicate the same results as the later and more comprehensive findings by the Commission: that some geographical areas and some types of specialists far exceed others in numbers of cases filed. Of the 107 cases analyzed by the AMA, orthopedics was the most frequently involved specialty, accounting for 22 cases. Claims against general surgeons were involved in 19 decisions. Internal medicine was the subject of another 19. Of the cases in that category, 4 involved misdiagnoses, 6 suits involved adverse drug reactions, 3 resulted from nerve injuries caused by injections, and 5 were on miscellaneous subjects. In 15 decisions obstetricians and gynecologists were defendants. Neurosurgery was the subject of 7 cases, most of which involved questions of informed consent for procedures such as angiography. Pathologists were sued in 4 decisions and cardiologists in 3. Four cases dealt with radiology and 3 with urology. One or 2 cases apiece were reported in the fields of ophthalmology, otolaryngology, pediatrics, anesthesiology, and plastic and thoracic surgery. All decisions reported against psychiatrists dealt with claims for allegedly wrongful commitments or false imprisonments.

The AMA Legal Department also analyzed the 125 defendants in these 107 cases by training and other criteria.[5] Ninety-seven defendants were in private practice, the others were full-time hospital staff, residents, administrators, or teachers. Thirteen of the 125 were either deceased or retired from active practice by the time the survey was made. Twenty-three defendants were general practitioners, the other 72 were specialists, certified by 15 different specialty boards. The AMA survey concluded that the biographical profiles of these defendants indicated no significant variation from the profiles of the total physician population.

The Malpractice Commission made a much more comprehensive study, including a survey of all the medical malpractice claim files which were closed by the 26 major malpractice insurance companies in 1970. Of course not all of these files involve complaints by patients. Most malpractice insurance policies require a physician involved in an incident which he thinks may involve a later claim to report it to his insurer and, therefore, this "file" criteria includes those incidents physicians reported themselves even though no claim was ever filed by the patient.

The malpractice insurance companies reported 14,500 claim-producing incidents occurring in 1970, 70%, or about 12,600, of which represented claims asserted by patients and the remaining 30% of which were those arising from reports from the physician or hospital involved.[7] Since the average physician treated 3396 patients in the same year, the Commission concluded that there is less than 1 chance in 100,000 of an incident occurring which will give rise to a medical malpractice suit each time a physician treats a patient.[8] The Commission studies concluded that different states vary enormously in the number of malpractice claims filed which may be largely attributable to two factors, although there were no explanations offered by the Commission. First, where medicine is still largely practiced on a "small-town" basis there is a much more personal relationship between the physician and his patient. Secondly, there is a much more personal relationship in a small city between the physicians and the attorneys in the community and therefore attorneys may well be much more reluctant to bring a suit against a friend, however unjust this may be to a patient with a legitimate case. Highly urbanized states do, without regard to cause, have a higher rate of malpractice claims filed than the more rural areas. The states with the highest rate of suits per physician-population are New Jersey, California, Montana, Arizona, Washington and Nevada with the West on the whole having the largest number of suits. The East has slightly fewer and the South has the least. Alaska had the lowest number of claims closed per 100 practicing physicians and Nevada had the highest in the survey.[9]

The Commission's results corroborated the AMA's survey findings that the risk of being sued is not shared equally among all practitioners. Orthopedists and anesthesiologists were subject to more claims than any other specialists.[10] This does not, of course, indicate that orthopedic surgeons and anesthesiologists are likely to be more inept than other types of medical practitioners; it is an inescapable result of the fact that the activities which are an integral part of their professional practice are those procedures which carry the highest amount of inherent risks and untoward results.

One most interesting factor for which the Commission offered no explanation is that women physicians are sued far less frequently than their proportionate number would indicate probable.[11] While some may argue that discrimination against women in admissions to medical schools meant that those few who survived and went into practice became unusually competent physicians, a more likely cause is that for reasons of personal preference or discrimination in allocation of specialty residencies, women have simply not entered high-risk fields such as orthopedics and neurosurgery. The Commission's studies did not, unfortunately, correlate incidence of claims by sex of defendant in the same fields, i.e., female anesthesiologists compared to male anesthesiologists.

Of the claims surveyed by the Commission staff, of the ones it considered "justified" 19% caused permanent adverse effects to the patient and in another 18% the patient died as the result of the negligence. "Psychological harm" only was involved in 12% of the claims. Two-thirds of the injuries involved damage from which the patient eventually made a total recovery. Improper treatment was involved in 86%; only 1 in 7 claims involved misdiagnosis. Nonemergency treatment was involved in 66% of the claims. Of the claims which arose while the patient was in the hospital, 57.2% were surgical; the rest were nonsurgical or involved injuries unrelated to treatment, such as falls from bed.[12]

While physicians assume apparently, that plaintiffs collect large judgments in all malpractice cases this does not prove to be the case. In 1970 the major malpractice insurance carriers closed 16,000 claim files, some of which had been open for as long as 9 years and some of which had been open for less than a year. Of these files 50% were closed without a suit. In half of that 50%, in other words, in 25% of the total claims, the claimant and his legal representative received some payment. The other 25% were abandoned or were settled without any payment. The other half of the files closed in 1970 involved suits. Of these 80% were settled and never went to trial. In 60% of the settled cases the claimant received some payment. The remaining 20% of the suits were resolved by trial. Of the cases which went to trial the verdict was in favor of the plaintiff only 20% of the time. Thus the Commission found that there was payment in approximately 45% of all claims, with or without a suit, but in those which proceeded to trial, only 20% resulted in a verdict in favor of the patient. Furthermore, the average claimant paid received less than $3000.00, with 49.4% receiving less than $2000.00, and only 3% receiving $100,000.00 or more.[13]

The Commission found that a medical malpractice case is still a relatively rare event. In 1970 a malpractice incident was reported for 1 out of 158,000 patient-visits to doctors and a claim was asserted for 1 out of every 226,000 patient visits to doctors, and fewer than 1 trial was held for every 10 claims closed. In another survey from 1960 to 1970 of 2045 physicians in Maryland, 84% of the physicians had not been sued, 14% had been sued once, and only 2% were sued more than once. The Commission placed the matter in prospective with the following statement: "If the average person lives 70 years he will have, based on 1970 data, approximately 400 contacts as a patient with doctors and dentists. The chances that he will assert a medical malpractice claim are 1 in 39,500."[14]

The Commission also analyzed the underlying causes of malpractice suits. It recognized, of course, that modern medical treatment carries certain risks which will result in some injuries no matter how much skill and judgment is applied.[15] No surgery, for example, is absolutely safe. Any drug of real value has some potential for danger and the ultimate question is one of balancing the advantage of a cure against the risk. The Commission pointed out that many patients do not understand this, sit home, watch Marcus Welby on television, assume that to be the norm of medical care, and therefore expect their own physicians to be equally understanding, kind, considerate, patient, and infallible.[16] The same phenomenon, incidentally, has been noticed by many lawyers who have the feeling that their clients assume that they will win every case "just like Perry Mason does."

One reason the incidence of suits has risen is the development of new procedures which save lives daily. Forty years ago a physician's only treatment of a patient's illness might be to sit at the side of the bed and comfort his patient and the family while the patient died. The same patient today may be treated by very complex methods, such as open heart surgery, from which he is more likely than not to recover, but in which the incidence of untoward result is high. The patient forgets that 40 years ago he would have died without medical intervention and now he expects perfection from the surgeon and files suit for the untoward result.

It is very clear, according to all sources, that one of the great problems leading to the filing of malpractice suits is a breakdown in communication and rapport between the physician and the patient. Most patient's problems which actually result in lawsuits arise from a combination of two important factors. One is a bad result, which may or may not be attributable to negligence, and the other is bad public relations by the physician. If the physician has not sat down with the patient and talked to him honestly about his problems, has offended him by ignoring his legitimate complaints, or has simply behaved in a way which indicates to the patient that the physician "couldn't care less" whether he recovers or not, that patient is quite likely to be completely uninhibited about consulting a lawyer and filing a suit. As one expert in the field of medical malpractice defense law, R. Crawford Morris, has pointed out, "When the physician–patient rapport remains at a high level of trust and confidence, most patients will ride out a bad result, but when that rapport is inadequate in the beginning or is permitted to deteriorate in route, a suit is likely to follow."[17] Regardless of the reasons for the shortage of physicians or what steps should be taken to eliminate it, the fact is that a shortage of physicians, particularly in some areas of the country, does exist at the present time. Thus, the individual physician has inadequate time to spend with the individual patient which increases the problem of maintaining rapport.

It should be noted that an incredible number of malpractice cases are triggered by a physician's filing suit or making a claim through a collection agency for his fee. If a patient has the resources to pay a physician's bill and does not do so, it may very well be because he is dissatisfied with the treatment he has received. If he is let alone, nothing may happen, but if he gets an insulting letter from a bill collection agency, his next step will probably be to consult a lawyer about his "malpractice claim." Thus, lawyers representing physicians are unanimous in advising them that attempting to collect bills by any procedure more strenuous than notes from the physician himself requesting payment is absolutely the wrong policy.[18] It is almost always better to lose a fee than to run the risk that a patient who is already dissatisfied with the quality of care, whether justified or not, will become so incensed by being approached by a bill collection agency that he proceeds to file a suit.

There is a growing trend toward litigation of all types in this country. All professions note an increase in the number of malpractices cases filed against their numbers, although lawyers, architects, and engineers are being caught in a far less rapid rate of increase than physicians. The consequences of professional negligence in other areas presumably are not as severe. After all, a lawyer who is negligent and loses a case for a client may have cost him considerable money, but a physician who is negligent in treating a patient may have killed him.

A further cause of the rise in the incidence of malpractice litigation is that the legal rules discussed in this text mean that a physician involved in a malpractice suit operates under a disadvantage which other tort defendants, such as drivers charged with negligent operation of a motor vehicle, do not have. The doctrine of *res ipsa loquitur,* for example, is used very frequently in malpractice cases in some states. In cases of rare medical accidents some courts are willing to assume that negligence has occurred simply because the event happened. This is virtually unknown in other types of tort litigation. The number of cases involving informed consent, a doctrine also inapplicable in other situations, is also rising steadily. The fact that statutes of limitations in medical malpractice cases may begin to run from the date of discovery instead of the date of the event has also precipitated more suits during a far longer time span than those filed against other tort defendants. However, of course, if one is injured in an automobile accident one presumably knows that the incident has occurred, whereas, if a sponge is left in one's abdomen one may not be aware of it for some considerable time thereafter. There may be, therefore, reasons essential to the administration of justice for differentiations in legal doctrines between malpractice suits and other types of tort litigation, but the Malpractice Commission advised that legal rules should be applied in malpractice suits in the same manner as they apply to all classes of tort defendants.[19]

Another possible cause of the high number of medical malpractice cases is the system of contingent legal fees. A prospective plaintiff's lawyer agrees to take the case for a percent of recovery. If the patient wins the case the attorney may receive as his fee anywhere from 20 to 50% of the amount of the award. If, however, he loses, the attorney recovers nothing. There is considerable question in the minds of most physicians and some attorneys of the ethics of the contingent fee system. It does have two statistically provable effects. The Commission found that meritorious small claims are usually rejected by most contingent fee attorneys.[20] A patient may have a very good claim of medical negligence, but if the recovery is expected to be small compared to the number of hours necessarily spent in preparation of the case, a plaintiff's attorney will refuse to take it. It does in some circumstances give patients with no financial resources of their own a chance to obtain necessary legal representation.

The Commission found that on the basis of hours worked per fee there does not appear to be any real discrepancy between the lawyer's hourly charge for defending a malpractice suit and the contingent fee system for the plaintiff.[21] The Commission also found that since a plaintiff's counsel does not recover anything on a contingent fee basis if he loses the case, the system did tend to be an effective screening device against unfounded claims. The Commission recommended that all states enact legislation requiring a uniform scale of contingent fees in which the fee rate decreases in inverse proportion to the amount of damages recovered.[22] The problem for those who cannot afford to pay legal fees could of course be solved if public legal assistance mechanisms provided adequate representation to genuinely injured patients without regard to the expected amount of financial recovery.[23] Most Legal Aid Offices are not allowed to bring any legal action which could engender money judgments. The organized Bar objects to removing this type of client from the private practice sector, for obvious reasons.

The problems of lack of rapport, frustrating hospital regulations not necessary to the care of the patient, but instituted for the convenience of employees, and a medical practice on a schedule for the convenience of the physician should be the subject of much study by the medical profession. The patient's dignity is very precious to him. If it is abused the situation may well end in a law suit.[24]

The physician is also required to cope with the fact that the patient today may have greatly exaggerated ideas concerning the technical capabilities of medicine, caused in large measure by news magazines and other media. While the Commission did not discuss this problem, some physicians writing for the popular press give grossly distorted views of certain procedures. For example, one very distinguished surgeon recently wrote an article on breast cancer in a nationally circulated women's magazine and stated flatly: "Refuse to submit to a radical mastectomy. Lesser procedures are just as effective."[25] No indication either from the author or in the form of editorial comment indicated that while less than a radical mastectomy may be appropriate in some cases, at present these research results have not been definitively established and there is at least a considerable body of surgical thought to the contrary. That article, read by a woman who is suffering from the unavoidable psychological effects of removal of a breast, would be amply sufficient to provoke an unjustified malpractice case against her surgeon who had sincerely believed that a radical was necessary. Physicians who write for the popular press should be very cautious about engaging in hyperbole and should try as best they can to present a balanced report on the subjects on which they write.

The Legal Process in a Medical Malpractice Case.   Numerous supporting studies were published as supplements to the Commission's report. One of these is a survey of attorneys who devote considerable time to medical malpractice cases. The survey indicated that 96% of the lawyers, whether or not they represented plaintiffs or defendants, regarded medical malpractice cases as the most complex and time-consuming type of law suit.[26] The reasons for this are perfectly obvious. The other large class of personal injury suits is automobile accidents. If a given client fractures his leg in an intersectional collision in which the other driver allegedly ran a red light, the "fault" is not difficult to determine. Either the client or the other party ran the red light; there is no other possibility, and determination of the facts of the problem is not particularly difficult. However, let us assume that the same client has fallen out of bed in a hospital and receives an identical injury, a fractured leg. The complexities of determining whether or not the hospital had used due care in having failed to provide bed rails, whether the hospital in fact provided a bed rail but it broke or if, perhaps, the patient crawled over the foot of the bed, and whether a reasonable careful physician should have had the patient placed in restraints present incredibly difficult problems to solve without regard to the amount of the claim in dispute. Most lawyers who handle medical malpractice cases, either for plaintiffs or defendants, have physicians whom they consult either informally or on a formal fee basis on each case brought to them. This is unknown and unnecessary in the vast majority of other tort suits. Furthermore, the trial of the suit is enormously more difficult. Expert witnesses for the plaintiff usually have to be located which is at least time consuming, although the old concept of the "conspiracy of silence"[27] which made it allegedly impossible for plaintiff's attorneys to find expert witnesses to testify for their clients seems to be diminishing. It does not, by contrast, require an expert witness to tell a jury that it is negligent to run a red light. Any medical malpractice case is thus more likely to require an extreme investment of time, effort, and energy by the attorneys for both sides than is true in other types of personal injury cases. The Commission staff concluded that : (1) The vast majority of malpractice claims are rejected by the lawyers consulted by prospective plaintiffs. About 12% of the cases were accepted.[28] (2) All lawyers involved estimated that approximately four times as much work is required in a malpractice suit than in any other type of personal injury case. (3) Case delays as the result of crowded court dockets vary from 15 to 28 months and up to 5 years in some urban areas. Dispositions of cases among the lawyers surveyed show that 64% were settled, 29% were tried, 5% were abandoned, and there were other dispositions of 2%. Most cases were settled either before suit was filed or before the trial.[29]

Lawyers in this field of practice usually are no more satisfied with the current system as it applies to medical malpractice cases than are physicians. However, it may be that the current system of treating a medical malpractice case as an ordinary tort and applying the ordinary procedures in the legal process to it may be the best alternative. It may be a situation similar to the statement Winston Churchill made about democracy: "It is a terrible system, the only thing worse is any other system of government which has ever been tried." While there are new approaches to the resolution of medical malpractice problems which will be discussed later in this chapter, all of them have serious disadvantages, as of course does the current method of procedure.

Once a lawyer has been retained by the patient, the basic outline, much oversimplified, of an ordinary malpractice suit runs as follows:

(1) The plaintiff files a complaint, which in some states is known as a petition. This document sets forth the facts of the problem which he alleges results from the defendant physician's negligence and asks that he be awarded monetary damages.

(2) The defendant may file a motion called a "demurrer" to have the case dismissed on the grounds that the complaint does not state a cause of action. For example, if a patient files a petition in which he alleges medical negligence, but does not indicate that he has been caused any damage or

does not indicate that the medical negligence was the proximate cause of this damage, the defendant may be able to have the case dismissed.

(3) At the same time, or in some cases, after any preliminary motions are argued and denied by the trial judge, the defendant files his answer. In the answer he specifically admits, denies, or presents other factual information as to each of the patient's claims in the order in which they are submitted in the petition. Any affirmative defense such as contributory negligence or statutes of limitations will also be set forth in the answer.

(4) In some, but not all states, the plaintiff is then permitted to file a reply to any affirmative defenses. Since there is a specified statutory period in all states given to the opposing party to answer each of these documents this process will usually take several months. At the time the complaint, answer, and reply, if any, have been filed with the court "issues are drawn." This means that only those issues outlined in these documents may be argued at the trial unless the pleadings are amended, which in most states is an extremely complicated procedure.

(5) In most states before the trial each party has the right to elicit certain information from the other. Either one may submit to the adverse party written interrogatories, a list of questions to be answered under oath, or require sworn oral depositions, narrative statements, under subpoena. These are questions and answers similar to actual testimony at trial. However, the use of a sworn statement as evidence is extremely restricted in some states since the jury may have the right to hear the witness himself and not simply to have his deposition read to them.

(6) In a malpractice suit in many states the physician has the right to ask the court to appoint an independent medical expert to examine the patient and corroborate or deny the existence of the injuries claimed by the patient. In other states the defendant may require the patient to be examined by a physician of the physician's choice.

(7) After all these matters have been resolved, in most jurisdictions the judge will call a pretrial conference in an attempt to settle the matter. The judge and both attorneys attend the conference; the parties may attend but are not usually required to come.

Only at this point, which may be as much as a year after the suit was filed, which in turn may be two, three, or more years after the incident occurred, is the case called for trial.

(8) Once the case is called the jury is selected. Juries are usually chosen at random from voter lists.

(9) Each side then presents its opening statement, a narrative account of what each side expects its evidence to establish.

(10) The plaintiff then presents his evidence. He calls his witnesses and

questions them; this is known as direct examination. The defendant's attorney then cross-examines the plaintiff's witness to try to discredit his testimony or to confuse it.

(11) After the plaintiff has finished presenting all his evidence the defendant can move for a direct verdict. This means that the judge, assuming all evidence as factually true which has been presented by the plaintiff, is asked to rule that the plaintiff has no case. If the motion is granted the case is dismissed.

(12) If the motion is denied, the defendant then presents his case and calls his witnesses, who are in turn cross-examined by the plaintiff's attorney.

(13) The plaintiff has an opportunity to present other evidence to rebut that given by the defendant.

(14) Again the defendant may move for a directed verdict at the close of the evidence and if that motion is denied, closing arguments to the jury are presented.

(15) The judge instructs the jury on the law. This is called a "charge" to the jury and is given in both civil and criminal cases. He also explains how they determine a damage figure if they find in favor of the patient. The judge in most states does not have the right to comment on the facts.

(16) The jury then deliberates and returns a verdict. Most states require unanimous verdicts in civil cases, but a few do not. If the necessary number of votes cannot be obtained there is a "hung jury" and a new trial will be ordered.

(17) After a verdict the losing side may decide to appeal. If so, both sides prepare written briefs, lengthy statements and arguments of points of law, and present oral arguments at a hearing before the appellate court. The parties rarely, if ever, attend the appellate hearing.

Most appellate courts in this country do not review factual issues. Their jurisdiction involves only questions of law. If, for example, a plaintiff sues a surgeon for leaving a foreign object in his body and the jury finds in favor of the plaintiff, that is a conclusive factual determination that the foreign object was left in the patient. A question of law, which is the only type argued on appeal in most states, is whether or not, for example, expert testimony should have been presented in favor of the plaintiff to prove that leaving the object in the plaintiff was negligent as a matter of the applicable standard of due care.

As can be seen these procedures are extremely time consuming. The physician-defendant and the patient-plaintiff must be present throughout the trial. It takes a great deal of time, effort and energy to resolve these cases. The same procedures are followed in any other type of personal injury case, such as a fall down a neighbor's front steps or an automobile accident, but the complexity of the issues involved in most medical malpractice cases requires more time to produce the same results than is necessary in the other types of claims.

There are other economic and medical impacts of the malpractice problem. According to the Malpractice Commission Report, physicians, dentists, hospitals, and allied health personnel paid between $200,000,000.00 and $350,000,000.00 for professional liability insurance coverage in 1970.[30] Obviously the cost of patient care was increased by that amount. The cost of the physician's insurance is necessarily passed on through his fees and is therefore paid by the patient or his own health insurance premiums. Numerous complaints in the popular press about the rising cost of medical care frequently ignore this problem.

Defensive Medical Practice.   Probably the most serious effect of an increased likelihood of malpractice suits is the practice of what is known as "defensive medicine," including unnecessary tests, some of which may in themselves carry a certain amount of risk, which certainly add to the cost of medical treatment and which are not medically justified, but are carried out primarily because a physician is afraid that if he does not order the test, he may be charged with negligence. "Negative defensive medical practice" occurs when a physican does not perform a procedure or conduct a test which he regards as medically justified because of his fear that he will be sued for an untoward result occurring during the test.[31] In any event the quality of patient care is obviously being affected by the number of law suits being brought and most defense attorneys naturally feel that it has a harmful effect.[32] The Malpractice Commission agreed with this supposition, but felt that the only solution was "moral suasion" by medical organizations and peer-review boards to monitor hospital care.[33]

Plaintiffs' attorneys frequently claim that the threat of malpractice suits has forced the medical profession to improve its standards.[34] This is true only if one assumes that physicians as a class are not dedicated people who care about their patients. Most physicians, for reasons of their own ethics and self-respect obviously do not want a patient to be needlessly injured. Threats of malpractice suits therefore do nothing to improve the physician's attitude and, in fact, may have an adverse effect. As an article written for the Office of the General Counsel of the American Medical Association has pointed out, there is no proof that persons drive cars more carefully because they know they can be sued for an accident or drive more negligently when they are covered by higher levels of insurance. Nobody wants to have an automobile accident and no physician wants to mangle a patient. There may be a few situations, such as drug reaction cases, where commonly accepted practices have caused avoidable accidents and the number of incidents was not known until several cases arose on the same point and it does appear that one effect of increased litigation has been ultraconservative medical treatment in these areas.[35]

Medical malpractice cases have a tremendous impact on the legal system. Courts in this country would still be overcrowded by all the remaining types of cases if all malpractice suits vanished immediately, and since medical malpractice cases take two to three times as long to try than do other personal injury cases as a result of their evidentiary complexities, they have a tremendous impact on court case loads out of proportion to their numbers.[36]

There is a very basic question as to the capabilities of lay juries to make findings of fact based upon complex medical evidence. It is statistically demonstrable that juries tend to be much more swayed by emotional argument than are judges when they try the same types of cases without juries. Very large jury verdicts in cases where negligence is questionable but the effects are horrendous, such as a cardiac arrest, are increasing daily. While these emotional factors, of course, are very difficult to document they do have an effect and the simple question of whether justice is being done in jury-tried medical malpractice cases is being seriously debated by many people.

The medical malpractice problem has an unhappy impact on both physicians and patients. The present system works to the serious disadvantage of an impecunious patient who is injured due to negligence, but whose claim is of small monetary value. As the Commission points out, a $1000.00 award might be extremely important to a patient, but the one-third fee collected by his attorney on a contingent basis will not adequately recompense the lawyer for his time, since the amount of time expended on a medical malpractice case for either the plaintiff or defendant is not related to the amount sought. The simplest malpractice case where damages would be quite low at best takes as much time to prepare or to defend as the most complex. The impact on physicians is incredible. Physicians do appear, justified or not, to practice in daily fear of law suits. It is altogether one thing to tell a physician that the statistical likelihood of his being sued is really quite small and another to convince him of it. The author, for example, has been called by physician friends and asked for her advice and specific guidance on what to tell a patient about the risks of treatment. It is a far cry from the old fashioned physician–patient relationship when a doctor feels a real need to consult his lawyer about treatment of a patient before he is willing to undertake it. Therefore, the current legal system creates enormous problems for the fair resolution of disputes between physicians and patients involving allegedly negligent injuries.

Alternatives to the Litigation Process.   In an attempt to find alternatives to the process which inevitably perpetuates these problems, other types of conflict-resolution systems are being used in some areas of the United States and in other countries.

Screening Panels.   In an effort to diminish the number of malpractice suits filed without cause and to provide expert testimony without undue difficulty for those patients who do have legitimate claims, malpractice "screening panels" have been established in various areas of this country.[37] While these vary in structure and function the object is to make available a forum outside the courtroom in which the problem may be solved without the expense, publicity, and difficulty of court proceedings. In all states except New Hampshire and New Jersey, these panels issue only advisory opinions and in no case may a patient be compelled to submit his claim to a panel instead of going to court.

In some states the medical society itself has what is known as a "physician review panel."[38] When an action is filed the physician notifies his insurance carrier and the committee, which has been appointed by the medical society. At a hearing the physician and his lawyer present his side of the problem and the committee of physicians advises him whether he should settle or defend the claim. These panels are not designed as a solution to the medical malpractice problem or to assist a patient by making a determination of the merits or justice of his claim, they are merely to advise the physician and his insurer.[39] These panels exist in Idaho, Maine, Maryland, New Hampshire, Oregon, and Rhode Island. In Honolulu, Hawaii, the physician panel includes an attorney who is a nonvoting member and who acts only to give the panel legal advice, as well as a clergyman who represents the public and does have the right to vote. In King County, Washington, the county medical society and the Seattle-King County Bar Association have established an all-physician panel, but it also includes an advisory member of the local bar association.[40]

Joint screening panels composed of both physicians and lawyers exist in many areas of the country. In one state the panel has been established by statute and two have established panels under Supreme Court rule. Those established by agreement of medical societies and bar associations include panels in Alaska; Pima County, Arizona; Maricopa County, Arizona; Colorado; Delaware; Hillsborough County, Florida; South Central Idaho; Scott County, Iowa; Cumberland County, Maine; Androscoggin County, Maine; Montana; Nevada; New Mexico; Nassau County, New York; Suffolk County, New York; Columbus and Franklin Counties, Ohio; Montgomery County, Ohio; Burkes County, Pennsylvania; Philadelphia County, Pennsylvania; Virginia; Pierce County, Washington; Spokane County,

Washington; and Milwaukee County, Wisconsin.[41] All these panels have joint representation by both physicians and lawyers and both groups are voting members. The number of members of the panel varies from two physicians, two attorneys, and a chairman in some areas to ten persons from each group in others.

The usual procedure to initiate a panel hearing is for the claimant and his attorney to file a written, signed request for the panel to consider the claim. Some panels require both the claimant and the physician to consent to panel action. The claimant must agree to give written authorization to the panel for access to all his medical and hospital records. Some allow the physician to require the claimant to be examined by a disinterested physician. All screening panels emphasize the confidentiality of the proceedings. Except in Hawaii, where the findings of the panel without names of the parties are circulated among physicians for "quality-control" purposes, no transcripts are made at most hearings and the majority of agreements establishing medical society–bar association screening panels provide that nothing said before the panel may be used as evidence in any future litigation. The reason for this provision is obvious. Few physicians or attorneys would agree to serve on panels if they thought they could be subjected to a subpoena in every case which came before them. In one case appealed from a panel decision, however, the court held that statements made by the parties to the dispute at the panel hearing might be used to impeach testimony they gave at a later trial of the same issues.

A surgical patient was burned when too much antiseptic was applied to her skin and ignited on contact with an electric cautery. She sued the surgeon after the matter had been submitted to a joint screening panel. The agreement she signed prior to the panel hearing included the provision that "discussions of any member of the panel are privileged . . . and no panel member will be asked to testify. . . ." She claimed at the trial that the surgeon had made statements at the hearing indicating negligence which conflicted with his testimony in court. The court held that only statements by panel members were exempt from use as evidence and that the physician could be cross-examined about his statement before the panel.[42]

Another decision indicates, however, that where physician review panels are established to aid in defense of the claim, the patient does not have the right to know the names of the physicians who are on the panel.[43]

The plaintiff is assured by the same agreement that if the panel finds that negligence has occurred, he will be provided with names of expert witnesses who will testify on his behalf. However, as a matter of practice if these panels find negligence, immediate settlement is the normal outcome.

One problem with screening panels is that most of them have jurisdiction only over a member of the medical society which has established the panel. A few, but not many, permit review of medical malpractice cases arising out'of their areas, but which must involve physicians who are nonresident members of their medical society. Generally, the claimant must also be from the county in which the panel sits. This can create obvious complications in counties where many patients are from outside the state and come for specialized treatment at medical centers.[44]

Furthermore, where a drug manufacturer or hospital has been sued jointly with the physician the panel has no right to make any determination of the presence or absence of negligence on the part of such parties. Almost half of the cases analyzed by the Malpractice Commission involved such multiple defendants.[45]

All panel hearing procedures are by comparison to the legal system very informal. Although rules of evidence vary, all seem to be highly informal as well. Most of the screening panels permit any of the parties or the panel itself to call witnesses. The claimant may present expert testimony, but the reason most claimants come before these panels is that they are unable to obtain the services of experts and therefore have none to offer at that stage.

The finding of a screening panel is simply that in the panel's opinion there was or was not malpractice. If they do find negligence, except in the case of the New Hampshire panel, which is established by state law, the panel does not make any finding of fact as to the amount of damages. They merely advise the physician and the claimant that a case exists or that it does not. Decisions of panels are usually by majority, not unanimous vote and virtually all allow dissenters from the decision to submit written statements.

Results of panel decisions on the parties are many and varied. The inducement to claimants to submit their cases to the panel is the guarantee that if they prevail they will receive the names of experts who will cooperate in advising and testifying on their behalf. None of the screening panels can legally bar litigation even if the panel finds against the patient, but the Arizona and New Mexico plans, to which attorneys also belong through their bar associations, prohibits the claimant's lawyer from filing a court action based on the case "unless personally satified that strong and overriding reasons compel such action." In other words, bar pressure on the attorney will prevent his filing a suit without good reason if his client has lost before the panel. In 1969, in New Mexico of eight cases in which the panel found no evidence of negligence, three later went to court.[46]

It is of course greatly in the interest of both the medical and legal professions to establish these screening panels. It makes the justified claim much easier to process and insulates the physician from those "nuisance suits" which are unjustified. However, the researchers for the Malpractice Commission reported that[47] "The panels are also dangerous to the consumer and public at large in allowing a close-knit group of attorneys and physicians to determine the merits of claims without full adversary proceeding." Assuming, which it is preferable to do if one is sick or in need of legal assistance, that all physicians and all attorneys are not inherently corrupted by their social or economic prejudices, it is difficult to see this as a major problem. If attorneys are so friendly with physicians that they will not bring claims to screening panels, it is highly likely that they would even less often consider filing ordinary suits with the obviously greater adverse publicity for the physician. Statistics indicate no such delicate sensibilities exist among plaintiffs' counsel.

The screening panel is very inexpensive and therefore a desirable means of sorting out claims. While the physician-only panel does, by design, support the physician's viewpoint,[48] many studies indicate that plaintiffs' counsel feel that panels which consist of both attorneys and physicians do arrive at results which are fair to both parties.[49] For example, in one study, the decisions of the Pima County Screening Panel were analyzed and results were compared with a similar county which had no screening panel. In the county which used it, panel verdicts tended to be almost identical to those in similar cases tried by juries in the other county.[50]

Where attorneys are on the panel the plaintiff's lawyer is far less likely to bring a "nuisance" action since his professional brethren are there to scrutinize the claim. On the other hand, the physician whose lawyer advises him that he has no reasonable defense may well decide to settle before his case is presented to his peers. In the first 5 years of the New Mexico plan, none of the 43 physicians the panel found nonnegligent were later sued. Virtually all cases in which the panel did find negligence were settled without a suit. Thus, formal legal process with all its inherent difficulties does seem to be avoided without sacrificing a reasonably just determination of fault when joint screening panels are used. A 1973 report states that not a single malpractice case had been filed against any member of the New Mexico Medical Association in 2 years because all disputes were dismissed or settled on the basis of panel decisions.[51]

In no case can a screening panel deprive the patient-claimant of his right to a day in court if he does not wish to waive that right. One problem of substitution of nonjudicial alternative plans to settle legal disputes is the right to access to our legal system as guaranteed under the Constitution. Thus, any plan which provided that no plaintiff could proceed from a panel to court or which required the plaintiff to go to the panel at all would never be upheld as constitutional. It would undoubtedly violate both due process rights and rights to equal protection of the laws to establish a compulsory procedure in malpractice cases which would not apply equally to all forms of personal injury litigation. Further, within the system of federal courts and in most states as well, the plaintiff has a constitutional guarantee to the right of trial by jury in civil cases.

In two counties in New York and in New Jersey, courts have established screening panels. The New York City Medical Malpractice Mediation Panel, the use of which is mandatory to assist in settlements of malpractice cases, began operations in September 1971.[52] It was created as the result of a backlog of approximately 50 malpractice cases on court dockets in the city with docket delays in all of them of from 3 to 4 years, not an uncommon period of time in major cities. The Medical Society of the County of New York has provided a panel of approximately 200 specialists and the Bar Association of the City of New York provided a similar list of attorneys. One member of each group, the physician member always a specialist in the field of the patient's complaint, plus an appellate judge constitute the panel in each case. At the mediation hearing only the attorneys are present, but the parties are brought in to hear the panel's decision. The panel has three decision alternatives. It may decide that there is no evidence of negligence, that there is some evidence of negligence, but that the plaintiff's claim is for an excessive amount of damages and that there should be settlement for a small amount, or that there is evidence of negligence and of resultant severe injury and that the case should be settled for a substantial amount. Between the beginning date of the experiment and April 21, 1972, the panels considered 232 cases, of which 29 were open as of the latter date, 2 were discontinued, 56 were settled, and 143 were docketed for trial. The unusually large number of unsettled cases did not result from any defect in the mediation system, but rather from the fact that it was discovered that no employee in the bureaucracy of the New York City Municipal Government had the legal authority to approve settlements of suits against city-owned hospitals or their employees for whose negligence the municipality was liable. When that administrative difficulty was resolved the number of settlements increased greatly. Approximately half the cases are now settled as the result of the mediation attempts and the 50% which are not are placed on an expedited docket and guaranteed early trial.[53]

In New Jersey the plan operates on a state-wide basis with panels consisting of two physicians, two attorneys, and a judge who acts as chairman. Members are appointed by the Administrative Director of the Courts from lists furnished by the Supreme Court for attorneys and the New Jersey Medical Society for physicians.[54]

The sole reason for establishing these three plans was to try to reduce court backlogs in very densely populated urban areas. In New Jersey there is some degree of judicial control in the operation of the plan on the parties. The patient may, but is not required to, agree prior to the panel hearing that if he is not supported by the panel's findings he will not institute any legal proceedings and that if he has already begun a suit he must agree to dismiss it in case of an adverse decision. In return for his agreement, if the panel upholds his claim of negligence he will receive the names of three expert witnesses who will assist him in a suit. If he does not sign the agreement experts will not be arranged for him even if the panel finds in his favor. The findings of the panel bind the lawyer, not the claimant, however. In case of an adverse decision the patient may proceed to trial, but he may not be represented by the same counsel who appeared before the panel and disciplinary action may be taken against any attorney who violates this provision. Two decisions have been rendered on this "binding option."

A patient signed an agreement to abide by the panel's decision. After signing it, but before the date set for the hearing, he changed lawyers. The second lawyer obtained an expert witness who was willing to testify for the patient, and the patient then withdrew his agreement to go to the panel. Since the court found the decision to appear before the panel could not be made involuntary, the patient was allowed to change his mind.[55]

Another patient appeared before the panel, which rendered a decision of nonnegligence. He thereafter wished to sue the physician and be represented by the same counsel who had appeared before the panel. He claimed that the only reason that he had signed the binding option at all was that the physician had refused to appear before the panel if he did not do so and that he had thus been subjected to duress. The court dismissed the complaint and indicated that since the patient had known what he signed he would be bound by its terms.[56]

In New Hampshire a screening panel was established by a statute which went into effect on January 1, 1972.[57] Under the statutory procedure, claims against doctors, dentists, and lawyers are heard by three-member panels which are composed of one state court judge, one member representing the public, and one member of the profession of the person against whom the claim is filed. It alone of all the panels may determine both the issues of fault and also ascertain the amount of damages to be awarded. However, the damage award is only advisory. The parties are free to accept or reject the finding of the panel and sue or settle. This should, of course, provide a much more rational basis for settlement and lead to an increase in the number of cases settled. However, there are very few malpractice cases in New Hampshire anyway, and it may be several years before the effects of this new panel can be evaluated. The New Hampshire plan is the only one requiring the administration of oaths before presentation of evidence to the panel. The rules of panel procedure under that plan are also apparently more formal than most others, but not nearly as formal as those required in court.

The Commission's conclusion on panels was that "it recognized the value of local efforts to mediate medical malpractice disputes by screening panels" and recommended continued experimentation with voluntary mediation devices. The Commission also recommended that persons other than attorneys and physicians be included as public members of any panel. In most cases, as is now done in the Hawaii plan, the public member would be a person such as a clergyman who would be considered to be sufficiently well educated to understand the complexities of the medical testimony, which is one major problem with cases presented to lay juries, but who on the other hand would be sympathetic to the patient's viewpoint.[58]

Arbitration.   The second method of resolving malpractice disputes is arbitration. Arbitration is a nonjudicial, but final and binding, settlement of disputes between private parties. Unlike the joint screening panel, which does not restrict the right to sue except by agreement of the claimant and which never has been proposed as the exclusive remedy for a patient, who is free to ignore the panel altogether and proceed directly to court, arbitration is designed as a complete substitute for court proceedings.[59] Ordinarily, the arbitration procedure is called into action only by the voluntary agreement of all parties to the dispute. Where this is true arbitration is undeniably a viable solution to the problem. In two general situations involving any type of claim, agreements to arbitrate may arise. First, where a dispute has already arisen, the parties may agree to binding settlement by arbitration. Secondly, agreements may be made to arbitrate any dispute which arises in the future. The latter agreement is enforceable only if specifically authorized by statute. Arbitration is most commonly used in settling labor disputes, but under statutes in most states there is no prohibition on arbitration for other sorts of cases.

The American Arbitration Association, founded in 1926, has developed rules of procedure for arbitration, maintains panels of arbitrators with expertise in various fields including malpractice, and works with various organizations to establish arbitration procedures and programs. The Association has been actively engaged in arbitration of medical legal problems in several areas of the country.

Arbitration does appear to offer very great advantages over court proceedings. For one thing, much time is saved. An arbitration hearing can usually be held within a few months of submission and court dockets are longer. Arbitration is also cheaper, and it provides for greater privacy for the parties. Arbitration eliminates the jury and therefore materially decreases the emotional element in jury verdicts and in most cases the rules of evidence in arbitration are much less strict than in court.

As a result of these factors, arbitration has been suggested very seriously as the best possible solution for the resolution of malpractice problems.[60]

A medical group in California, known as the Ross-Loos Group, which furnishes prepaid health care to approximately 90,000 subscribers has since 1930 required as a term of acceptance for participation an agreement by the subscriber that in the event of any controversy between him or his dependent and the group involving a claim of negligent care, the conflict would be settled by arbitration. Very few claims against the group, which includes about 160 physicians and 400 other personnel, have gone to full arbitration and most are settled prior to that point at an average annual cost of about $30,000.00.[61]

One child who had allegedly been injured by negligence of a member of the group brought a law suit. Her father first submitted the claim to arbitration, but changed his mind and prior to the arbitrator's decision he filed a suit. The child claimed that since she had not been a party signatory to it, she could not be bound by the agreement to arbitrate. The trial court held that the child was bound by the contract and the California Supreme Court held that the father did have the authority as her natural guardian to enter into a contract for her medical care which would bind her to arbitration. The court further held that the provision for arbitration was not an unreasonable restriction on the minor's rights.[62]

In some places, including Philadelphia and Alleghany County, Pennsylvania courts, by rule, have initiated a requirement for arbitration of all tort disputes involving less than $10,000.00.[63] However, upon completion of arbitration either party may demand a court trial, although the loser who does so is subject to certain penalties such as payment of all court costs if he loses at trial. This type of arbitration with an appeal to the court has a great deal to recommend it in the field of medical malpractice and the Commission thoroughly approves, as long as the right to a jury trial subsequent to arbitration is preserved.[64] Further, the Commission requested that detailed results of all arbitration actions in the malpractice field be made available for study in the hope of improving the quality of medical practice, without sacrificing the privacy of the innocent individuals involved.

The Commission report concluded that the widespread use of the arbitration process to resolve medical malpractice suits would have a far greater impact on the litigation case load than any other plan studied. A great advantage of arbitration from the physician's viewpoint is that it would tend to make money damage awards much more uniform, since the arbitrators are generally more experienced and sophisticated and thus less likely to be swayed by sympathy than a lay jury.

Arbitration panels are generally selected in one of two ways. In the first each party selects a partisan arbitrator and then the two partisans agree on a neutral arbitrator. The second method utilizes the administrative assistance of the Board of the American Arbitration Association. The Board provides identical lists of potential arbitrators to all parties to the dispute who then have a week to number the list in order of preference and to object to anyone on it. The numbered lists are then matched to select arbitrators who are agreeable to all parties and sides. If no matching is possible, a new list is submitted. Jurisdiction in arbitration tends to be much broader than that of screening plans. Arbitration can include both contract and tort claims, while screening panels do not consider breach of contract suits. Under most plans, arbitrators determine both the presence or absence of legal liability and amount of damages, if any, to which the claimant is entitled, unlike screening panels which do not rule on damages, with the exception of the New Hampshire panel. The basic legal difference between arbitration and screening panels, however, is that arbitration findings in 40 states are binding and enforceable by the courts. Arbitration awards, in labor and other types of disputes where they have been common for years, are filed with the court for entry of judgment as if they had been rendered in a law suit, and if the judgment is not voluntarily paid, the plaintiff may proceed with execution and levy on the property of the defendant as if it were a judgment of the court.

There are serious constitutional questions involved in any compulsory process which will remove any type of case from the general jurisdiction of the courts.[65] It is now generally recognized that the role of arbitration boards is supplementary to that of courts. As long as there is a right of appeal from the decision of an arbitration panel to the courts, in most cases mandatory arbitration plans have been upheld as constitutional, but any arrangement which would deny the right of appeal would undoubtedly be unconstitutional. Due process objections which have been raised against arbitration procedures in other types of cases have led to decisions requiring hearings, the right to appearance by the claimants, the right to present evidence and to cross-examine witnesses, and the right to counsel. As long as these rights are observed, however, it is highly unlikely that any due process challenge to arbitration would be successful. The Fourteenth Amendment to the Constitution provides that no states shall deny to any person equal protection of the laws. In most cases involving a statutory requirement of arbitration instead of litigation of small claims, all claims below a certain amount are subject to the same restriction. As long as all cases of a given amount or less regardless of origin, are subject to arbitration, courts will presumably not hold that the claimant's equal protection guarantees have been violated. However, if arbitration should ever be required only for certain types of malpractice cases of any amount, serious issues of equal protection will be raised. In Illinois, for example, the no-fault automobile insurance statute imposed a ceiling on the dollar amount of arbitrators' awards with respect only to claims arising from collisions involving private vehicles. The statute was struck down as unconstitutional on the grounds that this was an unreasonable classification within the general category of automobile accidents.[66]

Authorities on the subject indicate that the constitutional implications for the initiation of medical malpractice arbitration might take the following form: A statute would undoubtedly be upheld which provided, for example, that all claims for personal injury damages, regardless of cause, which involve less than $10,000 must be arbitrated. Most feel that an arbitration statute concerning only malpractice claims which involve less than $10,000.00 would probably be upheld. However, any statute requiring arbitration in malpractice cases arising out of one particular procedure, such as heart surgery, would clearly violate equal protection guarantees. There is, of course, a basic constitutional problem on the question of whether or not a claimant who has fractured his leg as the result of a hospital accident may be forced to arbitrate, while a claimant with the same injury who fractured his leg in an automobile accident might not. However, it is at least arguable that the differential would be a reasonable classification and therefore acceptable under the Fourteenth Amendment equal protection guarantees because of the unique complexities of malpractice litigation.[67]

The right to a jury trial in civil cases is set forth in the Seventh Amendment as it concerns the federal courts. The right to jury trial in civil matters is granted as well by 48 of the 50 state constitutions. Therefore, the basic constitutional question in arbitration is whether or not a person may be required to waive this right. Particularly in malpractice cases where jury verdicts do tend to be higher in most cases than those decided by arbitration involving the same type of injury, this may be the most important question. Most constitutional authorities feel that in order to circumvent this constitutional objection to arbitration there must be provision for a right of appeal to a trial court for retrial by a jury *de novo* ("from the beginning"), not simply a right to a hearing by an appellate court. In the cases of no-fault automobile insurance, for example, the Illinois Supreme Court did hold that the compulsory arbitration provisions created an unconstitutional denial of the right to jury trials.

In addition to the general constitutional considerations which apply to all compulsory arbitration statutes involving any type of dispute, there are unique legal and constitutional problems inherent in agreements to arbitrate future medical malpractice claims.[68]

An enforceable contract to arbitrate a dispute which may arise in the future between two equal parties is one thing, a requirement by a physician that a patient agree to arbitrate future professional negligence is quite another. A labor union negotiating an arbitration agreement with a corporation is one thing and a sick person who is told by a physician or a hospital that unless he waives his right to go to court he will not be treated is quite another. Any contract on any subject is nullified by mistake, fraud, or duress, and duress is, of course, the issue in physician–patient arbitration contracts. Under the doctrine of "adhesion," contracts may be invalidated if one party, who is in an inferior bargaining position, is required to sign a contract to waive his legal rights in order to obtain an urgently needed service from the party in the superior bargaining position.[69]

Virtually the only case in this area would indicate the likelihood that a court would arrive at the decision that such an agreement was unconscionable.

A teaching hospital required all patients to sign a statement as a condition of admission that the patient would not sue the hospital or hold it or any of its employees liable for any negligence which might arise during treatment. This provision was held to be unconstitutional. The court held that the contract between the hospital and the patient was void and against the public interest and the opinion included the following statement: "In insisting that the patient accept the provision of waiver in the contract, the hospital certainly exercises the decisive advantage in bargaining. The would-be patient is in no position to reject the proffered agreement, to bargain with the hospital, or, in lieu of the agreement, to find another hospital. The admissions room of a hospital contains no bargaining table where, as in a private business transaction the parties can debate the terms of their contract. As a result we cannot but conclude that the instant agreement manifested the characteristics of the so-called adhesion contract. Finally, when the patient signed the contract he completely placed himself in the control of the hospital and sub-jected himself to the risk of its carelessness."[70]

Even if the problem of possible duress were solved, the obvious problem which is overlooked by all experts who have written on the subject, including those who wrote analyses for the Malpractice Commission, is the problem of the patient's informed consent to arbitration. Given the number of decisions discussed in this text as well as hundreds more already in court involving claims by patients that they did not understand the medical procedures to be performed upon them, any attempt to require patients to sign arbitration agreements would inevitably result in another deluge of cases alleging that they did not give an informed consent to the arbitration clause on the hospital admissions form or the one which they had to sign in order to receive treatment from a physician. Therefore, what may well result from any attempt to institute compulsory arbitration agreements before the injury occurs is that the physician will be sued and have to go through litigation on the subject of the patient's informed consent to the arbitration clause. The physician is probably better served in the long run by the present system, which at worst involves the adequacy of his explanation to the patient about medical matters, which presumably he himself understands.

It is perfectly ludicrous to assume that the average patient who signs an arbitration agreement on admission to a hospital understands its implications. There are too many decisions in which patients have recovered large amounts of damages because they signed surgical consents to "mastectomy" or "laminectomy" without understanding what those words meant to make any inference that the same patients would understand the word "arbitration." Furthermore, it is the author's firm conviction that very few physicians have any real grasp of all the legal implications of these clauses and any discussion between physician and patient on the subject could easily degenerate into the classic case of "the blind leading the blind."

The American Arbitration Association administers an experimental program involving nine participating Los Angeles hospitals under the sponsorship of the California Medical Association and the California Hospital Association.[71] Admissions documents include an agreement to arbitrate any future claims of negligence, but the problems inherent in the adhesion contract are allegedly overcome by placing on the same form a space in which the patient may indicate that he will not accept the provision and by providing a period of 30 days after discharge from the hospital during which the patient may revoke his consent to arbitrate. However, most patients who eventually file suits do not retain counsel within a month after a medical injury and in numerous cases do not even discover that they have been injured within so short a time. Thus, whether these arrangements provide for a genuinely informed consent to the arbitration provision or whether they are merely window-dressing on a basically inequitable mechanism will inevitably be determined in court eventually. No information can be located on whether or not oral explanations of the legal implications of the agreement are given the patient in addition to the statements on the form, but even if they are, since an explanation of surgical risk given to a patient by an admissions clerk would hardly be legally sufficient to relieve a surgeon of his obligation to explain those risks to the patient himself, it is equally unlikely that the same secretary's explanation of a waiver of legal rights would be held sufficient by any court. The only guaranteed method of insuring that an arbitration agreement signed on admission to a hospital is signed with full and informed consent is to install a lawyer in the admitting office to advise the patient of his rights and explain the implications if he waives them. It is highly unlikely that most hospitals would choose to do this.

A discussion of the California experiment[72] states that during one period under survey, 400,000 patients in the 9 participating hospitals signed arbitration clauses on the admissions form and only 200–300 refused to do so. The author states that the ones who refused "were lawyers, lawyers' wives, and legal secretaries." It is quite likely that this group was the only one which operated with any genuine understanding of the implications of the clause. Before statutory attempts to still the raging tide of malpractice litigation by compulsory arbitration agreements entered into prior to treatment are enacted in any state and open a legal Pandora's box of cases involving informed consent to these clauses, it probably would be edifying to the proponents of any such plan to interview a random sample of the 400,000 patients in the same survey and find out if they were even aware that they had signed such a clause in the first place and if so if they could verbalize some rudimentary understanding of what is meant. The author of the study concludes that there was "overwhelming public acceptance" of the arbitration agreement; the author of this text is convinced that the real answer is overwhelming public ignorance.

By contrast, a perfectly constitutional and legally acceptable plan combining the best features of screening panels and the arbitration process is in effect in Franklin County (Dayton) and Columbus, Ohio. Under the Franklin County plan, either a patient or a physician may request arbitration of a dispute. If the patient requests the procedure the physician or hospital is required to proceed; if the physician requests it, participation by the patient is not mandatory. Three physicians, three attorneys, and a chairman, an attorney or retired judge, are selected as panel members from lists acceptable to all parties which have been prepared by the American Arbitration Association.

The panel determines only whether or not negligence has occurred and if it has, whether or not the patient has sustained injury as a result. No finding of the amount of damages to be awarded is made by the panel in case a finding of negligence is made. If the panel finds in favor of the physician, the claimant is bound by the finding and may not proceed to litigation. If the panel finds in favor of the patient, a recommendation that the matter be settled is made to the physician and if he refuses to accept that determination the names of two expert witnesses who will testify on his behalf are given to the patient. This plan alone among all the various experimental methods studied requires also that if any claimant is a minor or an incompetent, he must be represented before the panel by a legal guardian appointed in the same manner as guardians are appointed to bring lawsuits. Further, any commitment by the guardian to abide by an adverse ruling of the panel must be approved by the Probate Court which has jurisdiction over these persons' special needs. This guardianship mechanism is strangely absent from all other plans because it would be legally mandatory in all jurisdictions before any agreement would be binding on these patients.

In the *Doyle* case, discussed above. the court upheld the binding nature of an arbitration agreement entered into by a parent on behalf of a child prior to treatment, but the suit to disavow it was brought by the child's father as her guardian prior to the time she came of age. There have been no cases in which a patient himself, upon reaching the age of majority, sought to dissaffirm an arbitration clause which had been agreed to on his behalf while he was still a minor. Under normal contract law it is quite likely that he could do so, since minors upon coming of age usually have the right to disaffirm contracts which operate to their disadvantage.

The legal differences between these two arbitration plans are obvious. In the California experimental program a patient who is in the admissions office of a hospital and therefore may be presumed to be both sick and frightened is handed a document which binds him to waiver of legal rights unless he understands enough of its terms to make a positive effort to disavow it or unless he takes such steps within 30 days of his release from the hospital, by which time it is unlikely that he has obtained legal advice. On the other hand, in the Franklin County plan, the agreement to arbitrate arises after the patient is aware that he has been injured and has consulted an attorney, who presumably may be sued for malpractice himself if he does not obtain from his client or the client's guardian a genuinely informed consent to waiver of any legal rights.

The California plan and those of a similar nature are subject to serious objections, both legal and moral. There is, however, no question that arbitration agreements made after a dispute has arisen and with full knowledge by the parties of all the legal consequences are perfectly acceptable. It is the author's opinion that plans similar to the one in Franklin County are, overall, probably the fairest and most feasible solution to the massive problems of resolution of malpractice disputes in this country.

The most valuable aspect of arbitration may well be in the adjudication of small claims.[73] As has already been indicated, these cases may not receive any attention under the present system because an attorney cannot afford, even on a contingent fee basis, to invest the necessary time in a case where recovery will be low. In less formal arbitration proceedings where the matter can be resolved quickly and less expensively, the problem is much more easily settled, and quite possibly a system similar to a small-claims court could be established in which a patient could proceed without legal representation.[74]

The Malpractice Commission recommended that arbitration procedures be established in all states with a maximum claims figure as part of the establishment of jurisdiction and that those claims which exceed the ceiling amount, probably $10,000.00, would be submitted to the standard legal process. Claims for smaller amounts would be submitted to arbitration by statute, not by agreements of the parties.[75] Since all states have small claims courts which exist outside the regular judicial hierarchy, an arbitration system for medical malpractice claims which was fixed at the same ceiling amount which already applies to those courts would undoubtedly not be subject to any constitutional objections violating patients' guarantees to equal protection of the laws.

The Malpractice Commission explicitly recommends that except for agreements involving prepaid comprehensive health care services in which an arbitration agreement may be part of the overall contract for future care, no patient should ever be required to sign an agreement to arbitrate future negligence disputes as a condition for receiving care.[76] Several proposals for federally financed health care programs contain provisions which would require health maintenance organizations to offer binding arbitration agreements to their patients and this would be a condition for receiving federal financial assistance for the HMO.[77] The Commission believed and most constitutional lawyers would undoubtedly agree, that the same principle that invalidates individual arbitration agreements made under duress would also apply to required coercion of arbitration agreements by health care providers as a condition for receiving federal funds. The Commission announced that it was opposed in principle to "any form of governmental activity which would induce or compel a physician or a patient to agree to arbitrate disputes prior to the event that gives rise to the dispute."[78] In addition to the Commission's opinion, any court in the United States would probably find this requirement unconstitutional as soon as it was enacted.

"No-Fault" Insurance. The most far-reaching approach to resolution of the medical malpractice problem is the concept of no-fault malpractice insurance. A system recently begun in New Zealand, for example, aims at the idea that every accidentally injured worker, whether he is injured on the job, in the course of medical treatment, or from any other cause is entitled to full compensation from the government including economic reparation.[79] The typical no-fault system proposal would be similar to the Workmen's Compensation system, in which an injured person is compensated automatically without regard to fault. In return, as is true in Workmen's Compensation situations, the person is denied the right to sue for negligence.[80] The system of no-fault automobile insurance is apparently working reasonably well in the states which have adopted it, although it was declared unconstitutional in Illinois and has not been tested in some of the other states in which it has been introduced.

There are, however, as the Commission pointed out radical differences between an automobile accident and an injury from medical treatment.[81] For one thing there is very little dispute as to the meaning of the term "automobile accident." It is also not particularly difficult to determine the injuries which are suffered in an automobile accident or to differentiate them from preexisting conditions from which the injured party suffered. The attempt to define a "medical injury" is, on the other hand, fraught with horrendous possibilities. The recommended definition of "medical injury" submitted to the Commission was "a compensable injury is defined as any physical harm, bodily impairment, disfigurement or delay in recovery which (1) is more probably associated in whole or in part with medical intervention rather than the condition for which such intervention occurred and (2) is not consistent with or reasonably to be expected as the consequence of any such intervention or (3) is the result of medical intervention to which the patient has not given his informed consent." "Physical harm" was stated as including pain and suffering; "delay in recovery" was defined as "any undue or additional time spent under care and not substantially attributable to the condition for which medical intervention occurred" and the most important definition, that of "medical intervention," was given as "the rendering, as well as the omission, of any care, treatment or services provided within the course of treatment administered by or under the control of a health care provider or within a health care institution."[82] The obvious problem with that definition of intervention is that it apparently does *not* include cases where the patient's problem is the result of the fact that he was not treated at all. As in the cases discussed earlier in this text if a patient goes to the hospital emergency room with chest pains, the intern tells him that there is nothing wrong with him and orders him to go home and the patient goes home and drops dead of a heart attack, under this definition, since no treatment was ever given, the patient's injuries would not be compensable.[83]

Beyond that, however, most people who die have been treated by hospitals and medical personnel for the injury or illness which led to death. This being the case, the obvious question is whether all unexpected deaths will be "compensable incidents." While physicians can treat many conditions, some persons just require a longer time than the average to recover. Some patients simply die for no particularly understandable reason in spite of excellent medical care. Should these be considered compensable incidents? The Commission did not believe that the nation should leap headlong into an untested no-fault system. It found that further study is warranted of the no-fault principle and urged that one or more state governments study, investigate, and perhaps establish a pilot program of no-fault malpractice insurance, but did not recommend it in either theory or practice.[84] Included within the definitions were all medical injury situations currently compensated within the tort liability system and, as well, all injuries resulting from unavoidable accidents and known risks of treatments.[85] The malpractice system as it now exists is incredibly expensive and a new system of compensation including persons now excluded would be astronomical in cost. The advocates of such a system would provide for a system similar to that of Workmen's Compensation in which an actuarial board would be set up to determine the amount of payments which would be made on a standard scale. For example, loss of a hand would pay certain preestablished benefits and lost earnings would be compensated at a certain rate. The obvious difficulty with that approach is that patients are not standardized. Suppose, as the result of negligent administration of Levophed, two patients lose the use of their right arms. One is a poverty-level-income ditchdigger who is thereafter unemployable. The other is a Supreme Court Justice who is an avid amateur violinist, but whose actual earning potential is not affected by the injury. Should the two receive the same payment? If not, which should receive more?

Studies of the Workmen's Compensation program indicate, as is true of arbitration, that smaller and less serious injuries are compensated at least as well or better than they would be under the conventional court system because of the extreme reluctance of attorneys to involve themselves in cases where the amount of recovery is very limited. On the other hand Workmen's Compensation payments for wrongful death and for serious permanent injuries, such as loss of an arm or leg or brain damage, are generally far below those awarded by most juries. No-fault automobile insurance invariably provides that claims over a certain amount must be processed in regular court proceedings. Furthermore, no-fault automobile insurance only covers actual damage such as hospital bills and lost income, and does not provide damages for pain and suffering, and mental anguish. It would be absolutely impossible to compensate a patient by a preexisting scale for such intangibles under no-fault insurance.

Thus, of the different plans for dealing with the increasing problem of medical malpractice claims in this country, each has its merits and demerits. Arbitration and screening panels are much less expensive, experts are generally not required, and the entire process is much more expeditious than court proceedings. There are, however, advantages both to claimant and to physicians in ordinary jury trial litigation. The purpose of this discussion has not been to advocate the adoption of one over another, but to indicate some of the advantages and disadvantages of each. Our current legal process may creak and groan, but the constitutional guarantees of trial by jury which were first established by the Magna Carta in 1215 have served this nation's people well. Any system which is designed to replace it as opposed to a system designed to supplement it should be instituted with extreme care.

The Malpractice Commission also made recommendations aside from solutions involving changes in the legal process or the direct administration of treatment for the prevention of those situations likely to ripen into malpractice cases. The Commission pointed out the obvious fact that the human element in medical care may well determine the patient's reaction to an untoward event. The Commission recommended quite strongly that all health-care personnel, particularly nursing, dental, and medical students, but including all levels of hospital employees, such as nurses' aides and orderlies, be required to take appropriate courses in psychology and interpersonal aspects of patient care.[86] It further recommended establishment, as a precondition for the receipt of any federal funds, of patient grievance procedures in all hospitals.[87] Personnel in the grievance office would listen to and attempt to resolve patient complaints before they escalate into full-blown conflicts. These persons, of course, would have no authority to intervene in the treatment process, but they might serve a most useful purpose in explaining the necessity of certain procedures to a dissatisfied patient. Their primary service to the patient would be to intervene in nontreatment problems and sources of discontent such as a tactless, insulting, or unnecessarily unpleasant remark made by a hospital employee to the patient. Personnel with more professional training, probably lawyers, would be able to assist in settlement of actual claims filed.[88] How many malpractice cases have been triggered when a patient rang his bell for an hour without response in an attempt to get a bedpan no one will ever know, but the Commission concluded, and virtually everyone who has ever been subjected to hospital care would undoubtedly agree, that this type of total disregard for the patient and the absence of simple human concern is the root cause of a large number of legal actions. One recent article half-seriously suggested during a very scholarly discourse on the sources of discontents of hospital patients that all medical students, interns, and residents should be required to spend a week as a bed-fast hospital patient and be subjected to all the procedures such as barium enemas, hourly arterial blood samples, and hours on a stretcher outside an Xray department, clad only in a hospital gown, which physicians consider "routine" before being allowed to order them for patients, in an attempt to make the physician aware of the discomforts and humiliations he may unwittingly inflict.[89] These unnecessary indignities perpetrated on patients who are viewed by hospital personnel or physicians as either nuisances or teaching vehicles, but certainly not as human beings, are, in the last analysis, the cause of a large number of legal actions against both the physician and the hospital.

NOTES

1. *Medical Malpractice: The Patient versus the Physician*, Subcommittee on Executive Reorganization. Committee on Government Operations, United States Senate, 91st Congress, 1st Session, Released November 20, 1969, U.S. Government Printing Office, Washington, D.C.

2. Presidential Health Message, February 18, 1971.

3. *Medical Malpractice: Report of the Secretary's Commission on Medical Malpractice*, Department of Health, Education and Welfare, Washington, D.C. (DHEW Publication No. (OS) 73-88) (referred to hereafter as "Malpractice Commission Report").

4. "Twelve Months of Medicine in Court," 217 *JAMA* No. 9, page 1287, Aug. 30, 1971.

5. "Profiles of Medical Defendants," 219 *JAMA* No. 12, page 1687, March 20, 1972; "Classification of Medical Defendants," 219 *JAMA* No. 13, page 1833, March 27, 1972.

6. Malpractice Commission Report, Chapter 2, "Magnitude and Impact of the Medical Malpractice Problem."

7. *Ibid.*, page 6.

8. *Ibid.*, pp 5–6.

9. *Ibid.*, page 8.

10. *Ibid.*, page 8.

11. Mirabella, Myers and Rudov, "Medical Malpractice Insurance Claims Files Closed 1970" pp. 1–25, *Appendix to the Report of the Secretary's Commission on Medical Malpractice* (hereafter referred to as "Appendix") at page 17.

12. Malpractice Commission Report, pages 9–11.

13. *Ibid.,*, page 10.

14. *Ibid.*, page 12.

15. *Ibid.*, page 24.

16. Byrnes, Michael, "The Media and Medical Malpractice," Appendix, pages 653–657 at page 657; Commission Report, page 70.

17. "The Rise of Medical Liability Suits," 215 *JAMA* No. 5, page 843, Feb. 1, 1971.

18. "How to Avoid Malpractice Claims," 211 *JAMA* No. 13, page 2233, March 30, 1970.

19. Malpractice Commission Report, page 31.

20. *Ibid.*, page 32.

21. *Ibid.*, page 33.

22. *Ibid.*, pages 34–35.

23. *Ibid.*, page 35.

24. *Ibid.*, Chapter 6, "The Human Dimension."

25. Crile, George, M.D., "Breast Cancer: A Patient's Bill of Rights," *Ms* Sept. 1973, page 66, at page 94.

26. Dietz, Stephen, Baird, C. Bruce and Berul, Lawrence, "The Medical Malpractice Legal System," Appendix, pp 87–167 at page 101.

27. Agnew v. Parks, 343 P 2d 118, Cal 1959.

28. Dietz, Baird and Berul, *op. cit. supra* at note 26, page 97.

29. *Ibid.*, pages 103–104.

30. Malpractice Commission Report, page 12.

31. Hershey, Nathan, "The Defensive Practice of Medicine—Myth or Reality?" *Milbank Memorial Fund Quarterly*, January 1972, pages 69–97; "The Malpractice Threat," A Study of Defensive Medicine," *Duke Law Journal*, December 1971, pages 939–993; Bernzweig, Eli P., "Defensive Medicine," Appendix pages 38–40.

32. "Lawsuits and Quality of Patient Care," 215 *JAMA* No. 7, page 1211, Feb. 15, 1971.

33. Malpractice Commission Report, page 15.

34. *Proceedings of the Conference on Malpractice*, Center For the Study of Democratic Institutions, Santa Barbara 1971; *Newsweek*, December 24, 1973, pages 104–105 at page 105.

35. "Effects of Increased Litigation," 215 *JAMA* No. 6, page 1043, Feb. 18, 1971; "Problems of Malpractice Insurance," 215 *JAMA* No. 3, page 529, Jan. 18, 1971.

36. Malpractice Commission Report, page 18.

37. "Joint Screening Panels," 215 *JAMA* No. 10, page 1715, March 8, 1971.

38. Baird, C. Bruce, Munsterman, G. Thomas and Stevens, Julian P., "Alternatives to Litigation, I: Technical Analysis," Appendix pages 214–314, at page 224.

39. "For the Defense," Defense Research Institute *Newsletter*, March 1967, pages 1 and 2; "A Physician's Defense Panel is a Must," *Medical Economics*, March 1, 1971, page 103.

40. *The Bulletin*, King County Medical Society, February 1969, page 45.

41. Baird, Munsterman and Stevens, *op. cit. supra* at 38, pages 280–281.

42. Nichter v. Edminston, 407 P 2d 721, Nev 1965.

43. Brown v. Superior Court, 32 Cal Rptr 527, Cal 1963.

44. Baird, Munsterman and Stevens, *op. cit., supra* at 38, page 218.

45. Malpractice Commission Report, page 91.

46. Report, Medical–Legal Committee, Annual Meeting, House of Delegates, New Mexico Medical Association, May 1970.

47. Baird, Munsterman and Stevens, *op. cit. supra* at 38, page 297.

48. "Are Malpractice Screening Panels the Answer?"; *Med Econ*, March 1, 1971, page 112.

49. Louisell and Williams, *Medical Malpractice*, Matthew Bender Co., New York, 1960 and Annual Supplements, pages 162, 166; Baird, Munsterman and Stevens, *op. cit. supra* at 38, pages 263–269.

50. Baird, Munsterman and Stevens, *op. cit. supra* at 38, page 248–254.

51. Busek, Linda C., "Where Malpractice Suits Have Been Cut to Zero," *Medical Economics*, April 2, 1973, page 91; *The Albuquerque Journal*, December 7, 1969.

52. *New York Times*, page 30, Col. 1, June 25, 1972, "Mediation of Liability Claims," 222 *JAMA* No. 2, page 241, Oct. 9, 1972.

53. Gibbs, Richard F., M.D., "Malpractice Screening Panels and Arbitration in Medical Liability Disputes," *J Legal Med*, May/June 1973, page 30.

54. New Jersey Supreme Court Rule 4:25 B, adopted February 21, 1966; Karcher, Joseph T., "Malpractice Claims Against Doctors: New Jersey's Screening Procedure," 53 *American Bar Association Journal* page 328, April 1967.

55. Marsello v. Barnett, 236 A 2d 869, NJ 1967.

56. Grove v. Seltzer, 266 A 2d 301, NJ 1970.

57. New Hampshire Revised Statutes Annotated, Section 519-A:1-519-A:10, 1971.

58. Malpractice Commission Report, page 91.

59. "Arbitration of Medical Liability," 211 *JAMA* No. 1, page 175, Jan. 5, 1970.

60. "Medical Arbitration Experiments," 211 *JAMA* No. 2, page 351, Jan. 12, 1970.

61. Rubsamen, David, "The Experience of Binding Arbitration in the Ross-Loos Medical Group," Appendix, pages 424–449.

62. Doyle v. Giuliucci, 401 P 2d 1, Cal 1965.

63. Malpractice Commission Report, page 92; 74 *Harvard Law Rev* 448, 1961.

64. *Ibid.*, page 93.

65. Adams, Charles C., Jr. and Bell, Alexander, "Alternatives to Litigation, II: Constitutionality of Arbitration Statutes," Appendix, pages 315–325.

66. Grace v. Howlett, 283 NE 2d 474, Ill 1972.

67. Adams and Bell, *op. cit. supra* at 65, page 318.

68. Henderson, Stanley D., "Alternatives to Litigation, III: Contractual Problems in the Enforcement of Agreements to Arbitrate Medical Malpractice," Appendix, pages 326–345.

69. Louisell and Williams, *Medical Malpractice, op. cit. supra* at 49, Section 1.11 (pages 12.6–12.7); 43 *Colorado Law Review* 629, 1943; Henderson, *ibid.*, pages 334–337.

70. Tunkel v. Regents of the University of California, 383 P 2d 441, Cal 1963.

71. Gibbs, Richard F., *op. cit. supra* at 53, page 35.

72. *Ibid.*, pages 35–36.

73. Zimmerly, James G., M.D., "Is Arbitration the Answer?" *J. Legal Med.*, March/April 1973, page 48.

74. Rubsamen, David S., "The Experience of Binding Arbitration in the Ross-Loos Medical Group," Appendix, pages 424–449.

75. Malpractice Commission Report, page 93.

76. *Ibid.*, page 96.

77. *e.g.*, Health Maintenance Organization and Resources Development Act of 1972, S. 3327, 92nd Congress, 2nd Session, 1972.

78. Malpractice Commission Report, pages 96–97.

79. Bernstein, Arthur H., "No-Fault Compensation for Personal Injury in New Zealand," Appendix, pages 836–848.

80. Dornette, William H. L., M.D., "Medical Injury Insurance—A Possible Remedy for the Malpractice Problem, *J Legal Med*, March/April 1973, page 28; "Malpractice Suits: Is the End in Sight?," *Med. Econ.*, June 7, 1971, page 27.

81. Malpractice Commission Report, pages 100–102.

82. Roth, Edwin and Rosenthal, Paul, "Non-Fault Based Medical Injury Compensation Systems," Appendix, pages 450–493, page 460.

83. *e.g.*, O'Neill v. Montefiore Hospital, 202 NYS 2d 436, NY 1960.

84. Malpractice Commission Report, pages 101–102.

85. Roth and Rosenthal, *op cit supra* at 82 at page 460.

86. Malpractice Commission Report, page 69.

87. *Ibid.*, at pages 83–84.

88. Thompson, Fango, Lupton, Andrew and Feldesman, James, "Patient Grievance Mechanisms In Health Care Institutions," Appendix, pages 758–835.

89. Welch, William J., "Pity the Poor Devils with Pains," *Prism*, November 1973, page 22.

SELECTED BIBLIOGRAPHY

General Works. The following survey works deal extensively or exclusively with the broad range of legal problems in the field of medical malpractice law. While some are written primarily for physicians and others for attorneys, all should be of interest to members of either profession. Notations are given, however, of those works the authors suggest are aimed at physician-readers even though most of them include comprehensive legal citations of interest to attorneys. Also noted are those books including, but not limited to, technical discussions of legal matters designed to be of use to practicing attorneys. Those without notations are written for both groups of readers.

1. Bear, Larry A., Ed. *Law, Medicine, Science and Justice,* C.C. Thomas Co., Springfield, Illinois, 1964.
2. Brown, Kent L., *Medical Problems and the Law,* C.C. Thomas Co, Springfield, Illinois, 1971. (Physicians.)
3. Curran, William J. and Shapiro, E. Donald, *Law, Medicine and Forensic Sciences,* 2nd ed., Little, Brown and Co., Boston, 1970.
4. Harney, David M., *Medical Malpractice,* Allen Smith Co., Indianapolis, Indiana, 1973. (Attorneys.)
5. Harolds, Louis R. and Block, Melvin, Eds., *Medical Malpractice—The American Trial Lawyers' Seminar,* Lawyers Co-Operative Publishing Co., Rochester, New York, 1966. (Attorneys.)
6. Long, Rowland H., *The Physician and the Law,* 3rd ed. Appleton-Century-Crofts, New York, 1968. (Physicians.)
7. Louisell, David W. and Williams, Harold, *Medical Malpractice,* 2 vols, Matthew Bender and Co., New York. Originally published 1960, annual supplements. (Primarily for attorneys, but the most comprehensive reference work in the field).
8. Moritz, Alan R. and Morris, R. Crawford, *Handbook of Legal Medicine,* 3rd ed., C.V. Mosby Co., Saint Louis, Missouri, 1970.
9. Morris R. Crawford and Moritz, Alan R., *Doctor and Patient and the Law,* 5th ed., C.V. Mosby Co. Saint Louis, 1971.
10. Polsky, Samuel L., ed., *The Medico-Legal Reader.* Oceana Publications, Dobbs Ferry, New York, 1956.
11. Practicing Law Institute, *Medical Malpractice* (Proceedings of the 15th Annual Advocacy Institute), Practicing Law Institute, New York, 1969.
12. Practicing Law Institute, *Modern Hospital Liability—Law and Tactics,* Practicing Law Institute, New York, 1969.
13. Roady, Thomas G. and Anderson, William R., Eds., *Professional Negligence,* Vanderbilt University Press, Nashville, 1960 (Attorneys. Comprehensive discussion of malpractice law involving attorneys, architects, and other professional groups as well as physicians.)

14. Sharpe, David J. and Head, Murdock, *Problems in Forensic Medicine*, 2nd ed., Andromeda Books, Washington, D.C., 1970.
15. Shindell, Sidney, *The Law in Medical Practice*, University of Pittsburgh Press, Pittsburgh, 1966. (Physicians.)
16. Shartel, Burke and Plant, Marcus L., *The Law of Medical Practice*, C.C. Thomas Co., Springfield, Illinois, 1959.
17. Waltz, Jon R., and Inbau, Fred E., *Medical Jurisprudence*, MacMillan Co., New York, 1971.
18. Wasmuth, Carl E., *Law for the Physician*, Lea and Febiger, Philadelphia, 1966. (Physicians.)
19. Werne, Benjamin, *Law for Doctors*, Practicing Law Institute, New York, 1969. (Physicians.)

Specialized References.   Most of the following works discuss the medio-legal problems of particular medical specialties. Some are exclusively devoted to consideration of the malpractice problems in relation to the particular field, others include a much broader range of legal subjects related to the area. A third group of works deals with in-depth studies of selected topics in medical law which cut across specialty lines.

1. Allen, Richard C., Ferster, Elyce Z., and Rubin, Jesse G., Eds., *Readings in Law and Psychiatry*, Johns Hopkins Press, Baltimore, 1968.
2. Brackel, Samuel J. and Rock, Ronald S., Eds., *The Mentally Disabled and the Law*, Rev. ed., University of Chicago Press, Chicago, 1971.
3. Chayet, Neil L., *Legal Implications of Emergency Care*, Appleton-Century-Crofts, New York. 1969.
4. Dornette, W.H.L., Ed., *Legal Aspects of Anesthesia*, F.A. Davis Co., Philadelphia, 1972.
5. Eisele, C. Wesley, *The Medical Staff in the Modern Hospital*, McGraw-Hill, New York, 1967.
6. Havinghurst, Clark C., Ed., *Medical Progress and the Law*, Oceana Publications, Dobbs Ferry, New York, 1969.
7. Hayt, Emanuel and Hayt, Jonathan, *Legal Aspects of Medical Records*, Physicians' Record Company, Berwyn, Illinois, 1964.
8. McNiece, Harold F., *Heart Disease and the Law*, Prentice-Hall Co., Englewood Cliffs, N.J., 1961.
9. Sagall, Elliott L., and Reed, Barry C., *The Heart and the Law*, MacMillan Co., New York, 1968.
10. Sagall, Elliott L. and Reed, Barry C., *The Law and Clinical Medicine*, J.B. Lippincott Co., Philadelphia 1970.
11. Wasmuth, Carl E., *Anesthesia and the Law*, C.C. Thomas Co., Springfield, Illinois, 1961.
12. Wasmuth, Carl E. and Wasmuth, Carl E., Jr., *Law and the Surgical Team*, Williams and Wilkins, Baltimore, 1969.

13. Wecht, Cyril H., Ed., *Exploring the Medical Malpractice Dilemma* (Proceedings of the National Medical Malpractice Seminar), Futura Publishing Company, Mt. Kisco, New York, 1972.
14. Wecht, Cyril H., Ed., *Legal Medicine Annuals,* (1969, 1970, 1971) Appleton-Century-Crofts, New York, 1969, 1970, 1971.

Periodicals of Interest.   Both the *Journal of the American Medical Association* and the *New England Journal of Medicine* have articles on selected subjects in the field of medical malpractice law in each issue. The articles from the *Journal of the American Medical Association* have been collected in *The Best of Law and Medicine '66–68, The Best of Law and Medicine '68–70* and *The Best of Law and Medicine '70–73* available from the American Medical Association, 535 North Dearborn Street, Chicago, Illinois 60610. Presumably, further collections will be published at regular intervals.

The *Journal of Legal Medicine,* published four times a year by the American College of Legal Medicine, is exclusively devoted to various aspects of the stated field, and the majority of articles in each issue concern malpractice problems. (GMT Medical Information Systems, Inc. 777 Third Avenue, New York, New York, 10017.)

Legal References.   A.   The following continuing legal reference works published in-depth analyses of selected topics in malpractice law.

1. *American Law Reports,* 1st, 2nd, and 3rd, Bancroft-Whitney and Lawyers Cooperative Publishing Company, San Francisco and Rochester, N.Y.
2. *Proof of Facts,* Bancroft Whitney Company, San Francisco.

B.   The following legal references supplemented at least annually deal in exhaustive detail with medicolegal problems encountered in all aspects of personal injury law, including but not limited to malpractice cases.

1. Gray, Rosco N., *Attorneys' Textbook of Medicine,* Matthew Bender Co., (10 vols).
2. Grankel, Charles J., Ed., *Attorney's Medical Cyclopedia,* The Allen Smith Company, Indianapolis, 1958 (9 vols.).

CASES

New York Ex rel Abajian v. Dennett, 184 NYS 2d 178, NY 1958. Ch 8, n 114.

Abbott Laboratories v. Lapp, 78 F 2d 170, CCA 7, 1935, Ch 6, n 56.

Acker v. Sorensen, 165 NW 2d 74, Neb 1969. Ch 10, n 126.

Acton v. Morrison, 155 P 2d 782, Ariz 1945. Ch 10, n 134.

Adams v. Poudre Valley Hospital District, 502 P 2d 1127, Colo 1972. Ch 10, n 149.

Adams v. Ricks, 86 SE 2d 329, Ga 1955. Ch 5, n 211.

Adams v. State, 429 P 2d 109, Wash 1967. Ch 4, n 104.

Adams v. State of Indiana, 299 NE 2d 834, Ind 1973. Ch 1, n 92a.

Aderhold v. Bishop, 221 Pac 752, Okla 1923. Ch 7, n 44.

Adkins v. Ropp, 14 NE 2d 727, Ind 1938. Ch 2, n 6; Ch 4, n 1.

In re adoption of Anonymous, 345 NYS 2d 430, NY 1973. Ch 8, n 114.

Agnew v. Larson, 185 P 2d 851, Cal 1947. Ch 3, n. 10; Ch 5, n 190.

Agnew v. Parks, 343 P 2d 118, Cal 1959. Ch 1, n 23.

Akins v. Novinger, 322 F Supp 1205, DC Tenn 1970. Ch 2, n 24.

Albright v. Powell, 147 SE 2d 848, Ga 1966. Ch 3, n 84.

Albritton v. Bossier City Hospital, 271 So 2d 353, La 1972, Ch 5, n 110.

Alden v. Providence Hospital, 382 F 2d 163, CA DC 1967, Ch 3, n 1; Ch 10, n 5.

Ales v. Ryan, 64 P 2d 409, Cal 1936. Ch 5, n 4.

Alexander v. Knight, 177 A 2d 142, Pa 1962, Ch 9, n 24.

Alexandridis v. Jewett, 388 F 2d 829, CCA 1, 1968. Ch 7, n 34; Ch 12, n 11; Ch 12, n. 35.

Allen v. Allen, 330 P 2d 151, Ore 1958. Ch 9, n 74.

Allen v. Voje, 89 NW 924, Wisc 1902. Ch 4, n 28.

Allison v. Blewett, 348 SW 2d 182, Tex 1961. Ch 9, n 66.

Almquist v. Wilcox, 131 NW 796, Minn 1911. Ch 10, n 88.

Amdur v. Zim Israel Navigation Company, 310 F Supp 1033, DC NY 1969. Ch 7, n 99.

Amrieri v. St. Joseph's Hospital, 228 NYS 483, NY 1936. Ch 10, n 87.

Anderson v. Board of Trustees of Caro Hospital, 159 NW 2d 347, Mich 1968. Ch 11, n 193; Ch 11, n. 143.

Anderson v. Martzke, 266 NE 2d 137, Ill 1970. Ch 10, n 76.

Anderson v. Nixon, 139 P 2d 216, Utah 1943. Ch 3, n 29.

Andrepont v. Ochsner, 84 So 2d 63, La 1955. Ch 5, n 118; Ch 6, n 9.

Andrews v. Lofton, 57 SE 2d 338, Ga 1950. Ch 12, n 55.

Anonymous v. Anonymous, 246 NYS 2d 835, NY 1964. Ch 8, n 113.

Antowill v. Friedmann, 188 NYS 777, NY 1921. Ch 5, n 94.

Application of Howe, 295 NYS 2d 883, NY 1968. Ch 9, n 97.

Application of President and Directors of Georgetown College, Inc., 331 F 2d 1000, CA DC 1964. Ch 1, n 65.

Application of Shaw, 212 NYS 2d 701, NY 1961. Ch 11, n 52.

441

Arizona v. Marcus, 450 P 2d 689, Ariz 1969. Ch 1, n 176.

Azirona Osteopathic Medical Association v. Fridena, 457 P 2d 945, Ariz 1969. Ch 11, n 99.

Arkansas Midland Railroad Co. v. Pearson, 135 SW 917, Ark 1911. Ch 10, n 156.

Arkansas State Medical Board v. Grimmett, 463 SW 2d 662, Ark 1971. Ch 11, n 16.

Armstrong v. Svoboda, 49 Cal Rptr 701, Cal 1966. Ch 2, n 7; Ch 4, n 99.

Armstrong v. Wallace, 47 P 2d 740, Cal 1935. Ch 5, n 4.

Arshanasky v. Royal Concourse Co., 283 NYS 2d 646, NY 1967. Ch 2, n 36.

Ash v. Mortensen, 150 P 2d 876, Cal 1944. Ch 10, n 90.

Atkins v. Humes, 107 So 2d 253, Fla 1958. Ch 4, n 73.

Aurelio v. Laird, 223 NE 2d 531, Mass 1967. Ch 4, n 33.

Austin v. Sisters of Charity of Providence, 470 P 2d 939, Ore 1970. Ch 5, n 109.

Avery v. Maryland, 292 A 2d 728, Md 1972. Ch 9, n 13.

Axcell v. Phillips, 473 SW 2d 554, Tex 1971. Ch 10, n 117.

Ayers v. Parry, 192 F 2d 181, CCA 3, 1951. Ch 5, n 123.

B. v. S., 335 NYS 2d 131, NY 1972. Ch 1, n 139.

Bach v. Long Island Jewish Hospital, 267 NYS 2d 289, NY 1966. Ch 1, n 116.

Bachrach v. Farbenfabriken Bayer AG, 344 NYS 2d 286, NY 1973. Ch 9, n. 57.

Baidach v. Togut, 190 NYS 2d 120, NY 1959. Ch 7, n 31.

Bailey v. Williams, 203 NW 2d 454, Neb 1973. Ch 12, n 48.

Baird v. National Health Foundation, 144 SW 2d 850, Mo 1940. Ch 12, n 30.

New York ex rel Baker v. Narcotics Addiction Control Commission, 297 NYS 2d 1018, NY 1968. Ch 1, n 52.

Bakker v. Welsh, 108 NW 94, Mich 1906. Ch 1, n 120.

Baldor v. Rogers, 81 So 2d 658, Fla 1955. Ch 2, n 15; Ch 4, n 9; Ch 5, n 151; Ch 8, n 148.

Ball v. Mallinkrodt Chemical Works, 381 SW 2d 563, Tenn 1964. Ch 4, n 26.

Ball Memorial Hospital v. Freeman, 196 NE 2d 274, Ind. 1964. Ch 5, n 121.

Ballance v. Dunnington, 217 NW 329, Mich 1928. Ch 4, n 20; Ch 5, n 94.

Ballard v. Anderson, 484 P 2d 1345, Cal 1971. Ch 1, n 134.

Bang v. Charles T. Miller Hospital, 88 NW 2d 186, Minn 1958. Ch 8, n 44.

Banks v. King Features Syndicate Inc., 30 F Supp 352, DC NY 1939. Ch 9, n 54.

Baptisa v. St. Barnabas Medical Center, 262 A 2d 902, 270 A 2d 409, NJ 1970. Ch 5, n 75.

Barber v. Time, Inc. 159 SW 2d 291, Mo 1942. Ch 9, n 55.

Barcia v. Society of the New York Hospital, 241 NYS 2d 373, NY 1963. Ch 1, n 27; Ch 12, n 55.

Barham v. Widing, 291 Pac 173, Cal 1930. Ch 2, n 93.

Barnes v. Bovenmyer, 122 NW 2d 312, Iowa 1963. Ch 2, n 75; Ch 4, n 136; Ch 12, n 54.

Barnett v. Bachrach, 34 A 2d 626, CA DC 1943. Ch 2, n 62; Ch 3, n 38; Ch 3, n 43; Ch 8, n 52.

Barker v. Heaney, 82 SW 2d 417, Tex 1935. Ch 1, n 137.

Barnes v. Gardner, 9 NYS 2d 785, NY 1939. Ch 1, n 7.

Barnes v. St. Francis Hospital, 507 P 2d 288, Kans 1973. Ch 5, n 160.

Barrette v. Hight, 230 NE 2d 808, Mass 1967. Ch 7, n 31.

Barrow v. Oklahoma, 188 Pac 351, Okla 1920. Ch 11, n 174.

Barsky v. Board of Regents, 347 US 442, 1954. Ch 11, n 1.

People ex rel Bartlett v. Medical Society, 32 NY 185, NY 1865. Ch 11, n 107.

Bartolas v. Coleman, 161 NE 20, Ohio 1927. Ch 12, n 70.

Barton v. Southwick, 101 NE 928, Ill 1913. Ch 10, n 106.

Basko v. Sterling Drug Inc., 416 F 2d 417, CCA 2, 1969. Ch 6, n 59.

Battistella v. Society of the New York Hospital, 191 NYS 2d 626, NY 1959. Ch 1, n 80; Ch 7, n 95.

Bauer v. Otis, 284 P 2d 133, Cal 1955. Ch 7, n 5.

Baum v. Turel, 206 F Supp 490, DC NY 1962. Ch 9, n 70.

Bazemore v. Savannah Hospital, 155 SE 194; Ga 1930. Ch 9, n 53.

Beadles v. Metayka, 311 P 2d 711, Colo 1957. Ch 7, n 40.

Beadling v. Sirotta, 176 A 2d 546, NJ 1961. Ch 1, n 82; Ch 3, n 108.

Beatty v. Armstrong, 73 NW 2d 719, Iowa 1955. Ch 10, n 95.

Beauchamp v. Davis, 217 SW 2d 822, Ky 1948. Ch 7, n 15.

Beaudoin v. Watertown Memorial Hospital, 145 NW 2d 166, Wisc 1966. Ch 4, n 66.

Beaumont v. Morgan, 427 F 2d 667, CCA 1, 1970. Ch 9, n 96.

Beck v. The German Klinik, 43 NW 617, Iowa 1889. Ch 2, n 46; Ch 4, n 137.

Becker v. Eisenstodt, 158 A 2d 706, NJ 1960. Ch 5, n 144.

Becker v. Janinski, 15 NYS 675, NY 1891. Ch 12, n 36; Ch 12, n 64.

Beeck v. Tucson General Hospital, 500 P 2d 1153, Ariz 1972. Ch 5, n 111.

Belcher v. Carter, 234 NE 2d 311, Ohio 1967. Ch 8, n 22; Ch 8, n 30.

Belk v. Schweizer, 149 SE 2d 565, NC 1966. Ch 2, n 74.

Bell v. Umstattd, 401 SW 2d 306, Tex 1966. Ch 5, n 139.

Bellandi v. Park Sanitarium Association, 6 P 2d 508, Cal 1931. Ch 5, n 209; Ch 9, n 7.

Belshaw v. Feinstein, 65 Cal Rptr 788, Cal 1968. Ch 10, n 101.

Bence v. Denbo, 183 NE 326, Ind 1932. Ch 6, n 3.

Benjamin v. Havens, Inc., 373 P 2d 109, Wash 1962. Ch 12, n 117.

Bennett v. Los Angeles Tumor Institutes, 227 P 2d 473, Cal 1951. Ch 5, n 102.

Bennett v. Murdy, 249 NW 805, SD 1933. Ch 5, n 22.

Bennett v. New York, 299 NYS 2d 288, NY 1969. Ch 8, n 96; Ch 10, n 33.

Benson v. Dean, 133 NE 125, NY 1921. Ch 2, n 27; Ch 4, n 8; Ch 5, n 25; Ch 5, n 50.

Benzmiller v. Swanson, 117 NW 2d 281, ND 1962. Ch 4, n 127.

Berg v. New York Society for the Relief of the Ruptured and Crippled, 136 NE 2d 523, NY 1956. Ch 5, n 73.

Bergen v. Miller, 250 A 2d 49, NJ 1969. Ch 7, n 87.

Beringer v. Lackner, 73 NE 2d 620, Ill 1947. Ch 8, n 54.

Berkey v. Anderson, 82 Cal Rptr 67, Cal 1969. Ch 8, n 20.

Berman v. Board of Registration, 244 NE 2d 553, Mass 1969. Ch 11, n 26.

Bernandi v. Community Hospital Association, 443 P 2d 708, Colo 1968. Ch 5, n 169; Ch 8, n 274; Ch 12, n 105.

Bernanke v. Board of Regents, 264 NYS 2d 399, NY 1965. Ch 11, n 45.

Bernsden v. Johnson, 255 P 2d 1033, Kans 1953. Ch 5, n 51.

Bernstein v. Alameda-Contra-Costa Medical Association, 293 P 2d 862, Cal 1956. Ch 11, n 81.

Bernstein v. Board of Medical Examiners, 22 Cal Rptr 419, Cal 1962, Ch 11, n 62.

Bernstein v. Lily Tulip Cup Corporation, 177 So 2d 362, Fla 1965. Ch 6, n 67.

Berry v. Moench, 331 P 2d 814, Utah 1958. Ch 9, n 19.

Bess Ambulance Company, Inc. v. Boll, 208 So 2d 308, Fla 1968. Ch 6, n 38; Ch 10, n 35.

Biancucci v. Nigro, 141 NE 568, Mass 1923. Ch 5, n 131.

Billings v. Sister of Mercy of Idaho, 389 P 2d 224, Idaho 1964. Ch 10, n 148.

Bing v. Thunig, 143 NE 2d 3, NY 1957. Ch 7, n 45.

Bird v. Pritchard, 291 NE 2d 769, Ohio 1973. Ch 10, n 22.

Birnbaum v. Seigler, 76 NYS 2d 173, NY 1948. Ch 9, n 70.

Bishop v. Cox, 320 F Supp 1031, DC Va 1970. Ch 1, n 55.

Bishop v. Shurly, 211 NW 75, Mich 1926. Ch 1, n 120.

Black v. Caruso, 9 Cal Rptr 634, Cal 1960. Ch 2, n 86.

Black v. Dillon, 28 Cal Rptr 678, Cal 1963. Ch 10, n 109.

Blair v. Bartlett, 75 NY 150, 1878. Ch 10, n 104.

Blair v. Eblen, 461 SW 2d 370, Ky 1970. Ch 2, n 67; Ch 10, n 29.

Blankenship v. Baptist Memorial Hospital, 168 SW 2d 491, Tenn 1942. Ch 2, n 14; Ch 2, n 60; Ch 5, n 92.

Blinder v. California, 101 Cal Rptr 635, Cal 1972. Ch 1, n 78.

Block v. McVay, 126 NW 2d 808, SD 1964. Ch 8, n 46.

Board of Examiners in Medicine v. Jacobson, 42 A 2d 887, RI 1945. Ch 11, n 49.

Board of Medical Examiners of the State of Oregon v. Mintz, 378 P 2d 945, Ore 1963. Ch 11, n 73.

Board of Medical Registration and Education of Indiana v. Armington, 178 NE 2d 741, Ind 1961. Ch 11, n 41.

Board of Medical Registration v. Kaadt, 76 NE 2d 669, Ind 1948, Ch 11, n 58.

In re Boe, 322 F Supp 872, DC DC 1971. Ch 1, n 133.

Boland v. New York, 333 NYS 2d 410, NY 1972. Ch 10, n 145.

Boll v. Sharpe and Dohme, Inc., 120 NE 2d 836, NY 1954. Ch 5, n 88.

Bolles v. Kinton, 263 Pac 26, Colo 1928. Ch 12, n 83.

Bonner v. Conklin, 62 F 2d 875, CA DC 1932. Ch 12, n 40.

Bonner v. Moran, 126 F 2d 121, CA DC 1941. Ch 1, n 115.

Booth v. United States, 155 F Supp 235 (Ct Cl 1957) Ch 3, n 1.

Borden v. Sneed, 291 SW 2d 485, Tex 1956. Ch 10, n 65.

Boswell v. Board of Medical Examiners, 293 P 2d 424, Nev 1956. Ch 11, n 80.

Bourgeois v. Dade County, 99 So 2d 575, Fla 1957. Ch 3, n 54.

Bowers v. Olch, 260 P 2d 997, Cal 1953. Ch 5, n 5.

Bowers v. Talmadge, 159 So 2d 888, Fla 1963. Ch 4, n 53; Ch 9, n 64.

Bowles v. Zimmer Manufacturing Company, 277 F 2d 868, CCA 7, 1960. Ch 6, n 68.

Bowman v. American National Red Cross, 241 NYS 2d 971, NY 1963. Ch 5, n 89.

Bowman v. Southern Pacific Corporation, 204 Pac 403, Cal 1921. Ch 7, n 92.

Boyd v. Andrae, 44 SW 2d 891, Mo 1932. Ch 12, n 25.

Boyd v. Coca Cola Bottling Works, 177 SW 80, Tenn 1915. Ch 2, n 3.

Boyd v. Wynn, 150 SW 2d 648, Ky 1941. Ch 9, n 29.

Bradshaw v. Blaine, 134 NW 2d 386, Mich 1965. Ch 4, n 40.

Bradshaw v. Wilson, 94 NE 2d 706, Ohio 1950. Ch 4, n 78.

Brawley v. Heymann, 191 SE 2d 366, NC 1972. Ch 6, n 2.

Brewer v. Valk, 167 SE 638, NC 1933. Ch 8, n 110.

Bria v. St. Joseph's Hospital, 220 A 2d 29, Conn 1966, Ch 5, n 171.

Bricker v. Sceva Speare Memorial Hospital, 281 A 2d 589, NH 1971. Ch 11, n 151.

Brinkley v. Hassig, 83 F 2d 351, CCA 10, 1936. Ch 11, n 58.

Brockman v. Harpole, 444 P 2d 25, Ore 1968. Ch 10, n 50.

Brody v. Overlook Hospital, 296 A 2d 668, NJ 1972. Ch 5, n 65.

State Ex rel Bronaugh v. City of Parkersburg, 136 SE 2d 783, W Va 1964. Ch 11, n 124.

Brooks v. Serrano, 209 So 2d 279, Fla 1968. Ch 4, n 59.

In re Brooks' Estate, 205 NE 2d 435, Ill 1965, Ch 1, n 68.

Brown v. Broome County, 170 NE 2d 666, NY 1960. Ch 8, n 69.

Brown v. Dark, 119 SW 2d 529, Ark 1938. Ch 12, n 52.

Brown v. Harris County Medical Society, 194 SW 1179, Tex 1917. Ch 11, n 102.

Brown v. Hassig, 15 P 2d 401, Kans 1932. Ch 11, n 54.

Brown v. Hughes, 30 P 2d 259, Colo 1934. Ch 2, n 93; Ch 8, n 145.

Brown v. Moore, 247 F 2d 711, CCA 3, 1957. Ch 5, n 212; Ch 10, n 100.

Brown v. Scullin Steel Company, 260 SW 2d 513, Mo 1953. Ch 3, n 79.

Brown v. Shannon West Texas Hospital, 222 SW 2d 248, Tex 1949. Ch 5, n 87; Ch 5, n 155.

Brown v. Superior Court, 32 Cal Rptr 527, Cal 1963. Ch 13, n 43.

Browning v. Hoffman, 111 SE 492, W Va 1922. Ch 12, n 65.

Bruce v. United States, 167 F Supp 579, DC Cal 1958. Ch 2, n 14; Ch 4, n 25.

Brune v. Belinkoff, 235 NE 2d 793, Mass 1968. Ch 2, n 80; Ch 5, n 115; Ch 5, n 129.

Bruni v. Department of Registration, 290 NE 2d 295, Ill 1972. Ch 11, n 9; Ch 11, n 33.

Bryant v. District of Columbia Dental Society, 26 App DC 461, DC 1906. Ch 11, n 97.

Bryson v. Stone, 190 NW 2d 336, Mich 1971. Ch 3, n 110; Ch 8, n 28.

Capps v. Valk, 369 P 2d 238, Kans 1962. Ch 5, n 14; Ch 7, n 36; Ch 12, n 6; Ch 12, n 79.

Capuano v. Jacobs, 305 NYS 2d 837, NY 1969. Ch 1, n 22; Ch 3, n 89.

Carbone v. Warburton, 91 A 2d 518, 94 A 2d 680, NJ 1953. Ch 2, n 75.

Carpenter v. Blake, 60 Barbour 488, NY 1871. Ch 4, n 22.

Carpenter v. Campbell, 271 NE 2d 163, Ind 1971. Ch 7, n 10.

Carr v. Shifflette, 82 F 2d 874, CA DC 1936. Ch 9, n 49.

Carrigan v. Roman Catholic Bishop, 178 A 2d 502, NH 1962. Ch 2, n 88; Ch 3, n 45.

Carroll v. Griffin, 101 SE 2d 764, Ga 1958. Ch 12, n 22.

Carroll v. Richardson, 110 SE 2d 193, Va 1959. Ch 5, n 175.

Carruthers v. Phillips, 131 P 2d 193, Ore 1942. Ch 2, n 99.

Carter v. Metropolitan Dade County, 253 So 2d 920, Fla 1971. Ch 5, n 176.

Carter v. Ries, 378 SW 2d 487, Mo 1964. Ch 3, n 95.

Carter v. Taylor Diving and Salvage Co., 341 F Supp 628, DC La 1972. Ch 1, n 37.

Cartwright v. Bartholomew, 64 SE 2d 323, Ga 1951. Ch 1, n 2.

Cates v. Ciccone, 422 F 2d 926, CCA 8, 1970. Ch 1, n 59.

Cavenaugh v. South Broward Hospital District, 247 So 2d 769, Fla 1971. Ch 6, n 100.

Cavero v. Franklin General Benevolent Society, 223 P 2d 471, Cal 1950. Ch 5, n 127.

In re Cavitt, 157 NW 2d 171, Neb 1968. Ch 8, n 107.

Cawthon v. Coffer, 264 So 2d 873, Fla 1972. Ch 1, n 94.

Caylor v. Virden, 217 F 2d 739, CCA 8, 1955. Ch 5, n 113.

Cazzell v. Schofield, 8 SW 2d 580, Mo 1928. Ch 12, n 27.

Champion v. Bennetts, 236 P 2d 155, Cal 1951. Ch 5, n 13.

Champs v. Stone, 58 NE 2d 803, Ohio 1944. Ch 10, n 12.

Chaparro v. Jackson & Perkins Co., 346 F 2d 677, CCA 2, 1965. Ch 8, n 59.

Chapman v. Carlson, 240 So 2d 263, Miss 1970. Ch 5, n 86; Ch 10, n 55.

Chappell v. Masten, 255 So 2d 546, Fla 1971. Ch 8, n 121; Ch 9, n 73.

Charrin v. Methodist Hospital, 432 SW 2d 572, Tex 1968. Ch 10, n 53.

Chasco v. Providence Memorial Hospital, 476 SW 2d 385, Tex 1972. Ch 2, n 54.

Chase v. Clinton County, 217 NW 565, Mich 1928. Ch 12, n 11.

Chesley v. Durant, 137 NE 301, Mass 1922. Ch 5, n 13.

Chew v. State Board of Medical Examiners, 265 So 2d 542, Fla 1972. Ch 11, n 15; Ch 11, n 56.

Chiaffitelli v. Dettmer Hospital, 437 F 2d 429, CCA 6, 1971. Ch 11, n 137.

Childers v. Frye, 158 SE 744, NC 1931. Ch 1, n 3; Ch 12, n 21.

Chitta v. Delaware Valley Hospital, 313 F Supp 301, DC Pa 1970. Ch 11, n 141.

Choate v. Oklahoma, 232 P 2d 634, Okla 1951. Ch 11, n 30.

Christian v. Wilmington General Hospital Association, 135 A 2d 727, Del 1957. Ch 10, n 62.

Christy v. Saliterman, 179 NW 2d 288, Minn 1970. Ch 2, n 81; Ch 4, n 140; Ch 5, n 213; Ch 12, n 53.

Chudy v. Chudy, 420 SW 2d 401, Ark 1967. Ch 9, n 87.

Church v. Hegstrom, 416 F 2d 449, CCA 2, 1969. Ch 1, n 53.

Ciccarone v. United States, 350 F Supp 554, DC Pa 1972. Ch 10, n 121.

Clampett v. Sisters of Charity, 136 P 2d 729, Wash 1943. Ch 6, n 18.

In re Clark, 185 NE 2d 128, Ohio 1962. Ch 1, n 69.

Clark v. United States, 402 F 2d 950, CCA 4, 1968. Ch 3, n 31.

Clark v. Geraci, 208 NYS 2d 564, NY 1960. Ch 9, n 20.

Clark v. Piedmont Hospital, 162 SE 2d 468, Ga 1968. Ch 4, n 145; Ch 6, n 43; Ch 10, n 37.

Clark v. Wichman, 179 A 2d 38, NJ 1962. Ch 4, n 76; Ch 12, n 82; Ch 12, n 88.

Clary v. Christiansen, 83 NE 2d 644, Ohio 1948. Ch 6, n 53.

Clary v. Hospital Authority of the City of Marietta, 126 SE 2d 470, Ga 1962. Ch 7, n 84.

Cleaver v. Dade County, 272 So 2d 559, Fla 1973. Ch 6, n 45.

Clinton v. Miller, 186 Pac 932, Okla 1919. Ch 9, n 80.

Clovis v. Hartford Accident Company, 223 So 2d 178, La 1969. Ch 6, n 22.

Cobbs v. Grant, 502 P 2d 1, Cal 1972. Ch 8, n 37.

Cochran v. Sears Roebuck & Co., 34 SE 2d 296, Ga 1945. Ch 9, n 37.

Coe v. Gerstein, Case No. 72-1842- Civ JE (DC Fla, Aug. 14, 1973) cert. den. 1974 Ch 1, n 141.

Coffee v. McDonnell—Douglas Corporation, 503 P 2d 1366, Cal 1972. Ch 7, n 96.

Cohran v. Harper, 154 SE 2d 461, Ga 1967. Ch 5, n 157.

Coleman v. California Friends Church, 81 P 2d 469, 470, Cal 1938. Ch 2, n 1.

Coleman v. Johnston, 247 F 2d 273, CCA 7, 1957. Ch 1, n 49.

Colley v. Canal Bank and Trust Co., 159 F 2d 153, CCA 5, 1947. Ch 10, n 144.

Collins v. Board of Medical Examiners, 105 Cal Rptr 634, Cal 1972. Ch 11, n 45; Ch 11, n 47.

Collins v. Davis, 254 NYS 2d 666, NY 1964. Ch 1, n 66.

Collins v. Hand, 246 A 2d 398, Pa 1968. Ch 5, n 203.

Collins v. Meeker, 424 P 2d 488, Kans 1967. Ch 3, n 13; Ch 12, n 14.

Collopy v. Newark Eye and Ear Infirmary, 141 A 2d 276, NJ 1958. Ch 10, n 165.

Combs v. Combs, 327 P 2d 164, Cal 1958. Ch 8, n 131.

Commonwealth v. Goldenberg, 155 NE 2d 187, Mass 1959. Ch 9, n 14.

Commonwealth v. Pierce, 138 Mass 165, 1885. Ch 11, n 168.

Commonwealth of Massachusetts v. Wiseman, 249 NE 2d 610, Mass 1969. Ch 9, n 59.

Conrad v. Lakewood General Hospital, 410 P 2d 785, Wash 1966. Ch 5, n 12.

Constant v. Howe, 436 SW 2d 115, Tex 1968. Ch 5, n 214.

Cook v. Oregon, 495 P 2d 768, Ore 1972. Ch 8, n 108.

Coolahan v. Maryland, 270 A 2d 669, Md 1970. Ch 1, n 76.

Cooper v. Roberts, 286 A 647, Pa 1971. Ch 8, n 35.

Cooper v. Sisters of Charity of Cincinnati, 272 NE 2d 97, Ohio 1971. Ch 1, n 45; Ch 3, n 53; Ch 7, n 76.

Cooper v. Texas State Board of Medical Examiners, 489 SW 2d 129, Tex 1972. Ch 11, n 24; Ch 11, n 42.

Copeland v. Robertson, 112 So 2d 236, Miss 1959. Ch 3, n 112.

Corbett v. Clarke, 46 SE 2d 327, Va 1948. Ch 10, n 74.

Corn v. French, 289 P 2d 173, Nev 1955. Ch 8, n 27.

Correia v. United States, 339 F 2d 596, CCA 1, 1964. Ch 2, n 65.

Corson v. United States, 304 F Supp 155, DC Pa 1969. Ch 5, n 37.

Costa v. Regents of the University of California, 254 P 2d 85, Cal 1953. Ch 5, n 96.

Cotter v. United States, 279 F Supp 847, DC NY 1968. Ch 8, n 97; Ch 9, n 11; Ch 10, n 160.

Couch v. Rice, 261 NE 2d 187, Ohio 1970. Ch 1, n 100; Ch 1, n 105.

Couillard v. Charles T. Miller Hospital, 92 NE 2d 96, Minn 1958. Ch 10, n 90.

County Department of Public Welfare v. Morningstar, 151 NE 2d 150, Ind 1958. Ch 9, n 75.

Cox v. New York, 171 NYS 2d 818, NY 1958. Ch 12, n 110.

Craig v. State, 155 A 2d 684, Md 1959. Ch 1, n 73; Ch 11, n 176.

Crawford v. Davis, 134 SE 247, SC 1926. Ch 7, n 92.

Crawford v. McDonald, 187 SE 2d 542, Ga 1972. Ch 10, n 123.

Crawford Long Memorial Hospital v. Hardeman, 66 SE 2d 63, Ga 1951. Ch 6, n 95.

Creamer v. Georgia, 192 SE 2d 350, Ga 1972. Ch 1, n 92.

Creighton v. Karlin, 225 So 2d 88, La 1969. Ch 10, n 150.

Cremonese v. City of New York, 215 NE 2d 157, NY 1966. Ch 8, n 68.

Crockett v. Encino Gardens Care Center Inc., 492 P 2d 1273, NM 1972. Ch 6, n 109.

Crouch v. Most, 432 P 2d 250, NM 1967. Ch 8, n 14; Ch 10, n 63.

Crovella v. Cochrane, 102 So 2d 307, Fla 1958. Ch 2, n 78; Ch 3, n 34.

Crowe v. McBride, 152 P 2d 727, Cal 1944. Ch 6, n 5.

Crump v. Piper, 425 SW 2d 924, Mo 1969. Ch 7, n 25.

Cudmore v. Richardson-Merrell, 398 SW 2d 640, Tex 1965. Ch 6, n 65.

In re Culbertson's Will, 292 NYS 2d 806, NY 1968. Ch 12, n 95.

Cullen v. Grove Press, Inc., 276 F Supp 727, DC NY 1967. Ch 9, n 58.

Cullum v. Seifer, 81 Cal Rptr 381, Cal 1969. Ch 3, n 64.

Cunningham v. MacNeal Memorial Hospital, 266 NE 2d 897, Ill 1970. Ch 5, n 64.

Curley v. McDonald, 160 NE 796, Mass 1928. Ch 5, n 112.

In re Curry, 452 F 2d 1360, CA DC 1971. Ch 8, n 93.

Curry v. Corn, 277 NYS 2d 470, NY 1966. Ch 9, n 40.

Custodio v. Bauer, 59 Cal Rptr 463, Cal 1967. Ch 1, n 152; Ch 4, n 6.

Cyr v. Landry, 95 Atl 883, Maine 1915. Ch 5, n 15; Ch 10, n 42.

Czarra v. Board of Medical Supervisors, 25 App DC 433, DC 1925. Ch 11, n 74.

Dabney v. Briggs, 121 So 394, Ala 1929. Ch 1, n 160; Ch 12, n 90.

Dahl v. Wagner, 151 Pac 1079, Wash 1915. Ch 2, n 11.

Daily v. Somberg, 146 A 2d 676, NJ 1958. Ch 10, n 90.

D'Alois v. Allen, 297 NYC 2d 826, NY 1969. Ch 11, n 11; Ch 11, n 53.

D'Antoni v. Sara Mayo Hospital, 144 So 2d 643, La 1962. Ch 6, n 42.

Danville Community Hospital v. Thompson, 43 SE 2d 882, Va 1947. Ch 6, n 16.

Darling v. Charleston Community Memorial Hospital, 211 NE 2d 253, Ill 1965, 200 NE 2d 149, Ill 1964. Ch 1, n 43; Ch 2, n 39; Ch 7, n 73; Ch 10, n 161.

Darrah v. Kite, 301 NYS 2d 286, NY 1969. Ch 8, n 10.

Dashiell v. Griffith, 35 Atl 1094, Md 1896. Ch 7, n 16; Ch 12, n 4; Ch 12, n 69.

Davie v. Lenox Hill Hospital, 81 NYS 2d 583, NY 1948. Ch 4, n 31.

Davis v. Morristown Memorial Hospital, 254 A 2d 125, NJ 1969. Ch 11, n 121.

Davis v. New York, 315 NYS 82, NY 1970. Ch 4, n 27.

Davis v. New York, 322 NYS 2d 569, NY 1972. Ch 8, n 96; Ch 9, n 10.

Davis v. Wilmerding, 24 SE 2d 337, NC 1943. Ch 2, n 18.

Davis v. Wilson, 143 SE 2d 107, NC 1965. Ch 5, n 69.

Davis v. Wyeth Laboratories, 399 F 2d 121, CCA 9, 1968. Ch 6, n 59.

Dean v. Dyer, 149 P 2d 288, Cal 1944. Ch 5, n 144.

Deckard v. Sorenson, 2 Cal Rptr 121, Cal 1960. Ch 2, n 91.

Dees v. Pace, 257 P 2d 756, Cal 1953. Ch 4, n 36.

Delaney v. Rosenthall, 196 NE 2d 878, Mass 1964. Ch 7, n 1.

DeMartini v. Alexandria Sanitarium, 13 Cal Rptr 564, Cal 1961. Ch 4, n 105.

DeMay v. Roberts, 9 NW 146, Mich 1881. Ch 9, n 48.

Demchuck v. Bralow, 170 A 2d 868, Pa 1961. Ch 4, n 50.

Derby v. Prewitt, 187 NE 2d 556, NY 1962. Ch 10, n 80.

Derr v. Bonney, 231 P 2d 637, Wash 1951. Ch 4, n 2.

DeZon v. American President Lines, 318 US 660, 1943. Ch 1, n 90; Ch 7, n 98.

Dibblee v. Groves Latter Day Saints Hospital, 364 P 2d 1085, Utah 1961. Ch 5, n 75.

Dickerson v. St. Peter's Hospital, 432 P 2d 293, Wash 1967. Ch 5, n 36.

Dickinson v. Mailliard, 175 NW 2d 588, Iowa 1970. Ch 7, n 70.

Dierman v. Providence Hospital, 188 P 2d 12, Cal 1948. Ch 5, n 117; Ch 6, n 9.

Dietze v. King, 184 F Supp 944, DC Va 1960. Ch 2, n 90; Ch 3, n 48; Ch 5, n 25; Ch 5, n 52; Ch 8, n 32; Ch 10, n 58.

DiFillipo v. Preston, 173 A 2d 333, Del 1961. Ch 2, 13; Ch 4, n 87; Ch 8, n 33.

DiGiovanni v. Pessel, 250 A 2d 756, NY 1969. Ch 1, n 154; Ch 3, n 24.

DiNike v. Mowery, 418 P 2d 1010, Wash 1966. Ch 10, n 79.

Dinner v. Thorp, 338 P 2d 137, Wash 1959. Ch 2, n 73; Ch 3, n 73.

Ditlow v. Kaplan, 181 So 2d 226, Fla 1965. Ch 8, n 32.

Dixon v. Jacobs, 427 F 2d 589, CA DC 1970. Ch 4, n 114; Ch 8, n 95.

Doan v. Griffith, 402 SW 2d 855, Ky 1966. Ch 2, n 31; Ch 4, n 135; Ch 12, n 53.

Doe v. Bolton, 410 US 179, 1973, Ch. 1 n. 133.

Doe v. General Hospital of the District of Columbia, 434 F 2d 423, CA DC 1970. Ch 1, n 142; Ch 1, n 145.

Doe v. Roe, 345 NYS 2d 560, NY 1973. Ch 9, n 56.

Doerr v. Movius, 463 P 2d 477, Mont 1970. Ch 3, n 107.

Doerr v. Villate, 220 NE 2d 767, Ill 1966. Ch 1, n 11; Ch 1, n 152; Ch 4, n 6; Ch 10, n 150.

Dohr v. Smith, 104 So 2d 29, Fla 1958. Ch 5, n 19; Ch 7, n 56.

Dollins v. Hartford Accident and Indemnity Co., 477 SW 2d 179, Ark 1972. Ch 10, n 54.

Domina v. Pratt, 13 A 2d 198, Vt 1940. Ch 1, n 108; Ch 3, n 19.

Don v. Okmulgee Memorial Hospital, 443 F 2d 234, CCA 10, 1971. Ch 11, n 130.

Donahoo v. Lovas, 288 P 698, Cal 1930. Ch 5, n 170.

Donald v. Swann, 137 So 178, Ala 1931. Ch 7, n 9.

Donnelly v. Guion, 467 F 2d 290, CCA 2, 1972. Ch 8, n 70.

Doran v. State Board of Medical Examiners, 240 Pac 335, Colo 1925, Ch 11, n 30.

Dorsten v. Lawrence, 253 NE 2d 804, Ohio 1969. Ch 12, n 111.

Douglas v. Bussabarger, 438 P 2d 829, Wash 1968. Ch 2, n 70; Ch 5, n 125.

Doyle v. Giuliucci, 401 P 2d 1, Cal 1965. Ch 13, n 62.

Duby v. American College of Surgeons, 468 F 2d 364, CCA 7, 1972. Ch 11, n 109.

Dugdale v. Board of Registration in Medicine, 169 NE 547, Mass 1930. Ch 11, n 20.

Duke Sanitarium v. Hearn, 13 P 2d 183, Okla 1932. Ch 12, n 3.

Dunbar v. Greenlaw, 128 A 2d 218, Maine 1956. Ch 1, n 154; Ch 9, n 91.

Dunbar v. Hospital Authority of Gwinnett County, 182 SE 2d 89, Ga 1971, Ch 11, n 133.

Dunham v. Wright, 423 F 2d 940, CCA 3, 1970. Ch 8, n 17; Ch 8, n 43.

Dunlap v. Marine, 51 Cal Rptr 158, Cal 1966. Ch 4, n 41; Ch 10, n 56.

Dunn v. Campbell, 166 So 2d 217, Fla 1964. Ch 4, n 68.

Dunn v. New York, 312 NYS 2d 61, NY 1970. Ch 4, n 112.

Durfee v. Durfee, 87 NYS 2d 275, NY 1949. Ch 1, n 110.

Durney v. St. Francis Hospital, 83 A 2d 753, Del 1951. Ch 10, n 157.

DuVall v. Board of Medical Examiners of Arizona, 66 P 2d 1026, Ariz 1937. Ch 11, n 41; Ch 11, n 70.

Duvardo v. Moore, 98 NE 2d 855, Ill 1951. Ch 10, n 110.

Dyke v. Richard, 198 NW 2d 797, Mich 1972. Ch 10, n 141.

Eaglen v. State, 231 NE 2d 147, Ind 1967. Ch 1, n 73.

Eckleberry v. Kaiser Foundation Northern Hospitals, 359 P 2d 1090, Ore 1961. Ch 2, n 59.

Edgar County Bank & Trust Co. of Paris v. Paris Hospital, Inc., 294 NE 2d 319, Ill 1973. Ch. 10, n 91.

Edson v. Griffin Hospital, 144 A 2d 341, Conn 1958. Ch 11, n 125; Ch 11, n 150.

Edwards v. Duncan, 355 F 2d 993, CCA 4, 1966. Ch 1, n 48.

Eisele v. Malone, 157 NYS 2d 155, 158 NYS 2d 761, NY 1957. Ch 5, n 204.

Eisenstadt v. Baird, 405 US 438, 1972. Ch 1, n 129; Ch 1, n 146.

Emery v. Fisher, 148 Atl 677, Maine 1930, Ch 5, n 33.

Emmett v. Eastern Dispensary and Casualty Hospital, 396 F 2d 931, CA DC 1967. Ch 12, n 108.

Emrie v. Tice, 258 P 2d 332, Kans 1953. Ch 5, n 105.

Engle v. Clarke, 346 SW 2d 13, Ky 1961. Ch 1, n 162; Ch 4, n 95; Ch 12, n 1; Ch 12, n 82.

English v. Sahlender, 47 SW 2d 150, Mo 1932, Ch 6, n 89.

Equitable Life Assurance Society v. Young & Revel, Inc., 250 A 2d 509, Del 1969. Ch 8, n 76.

Erickson v. Dilgard, 252 NYS 2d 705, NY 1962. Ch 1, n 68.

Ericson v. Ericson, 195 Pac 234, Wash 1921. Ch 8, n 132.

Ernen v. Crofwell, 172 NE 73, Mass 1930. Ch 5, n 29.

Ernst v. Schwartz, 445 SW 2d 377, Mo 1969. Ch 10, n 15.

Estes v. Magee, 109 P 2d 631, Idaho 1940. Ch 10, n 94.

Evans v. Clapp, 231 SW 79, Mo 1921. Ch 5, n 102.

Evans v. Newark–Wayne Community Hospital, 316 NYS 2d 447, NY 1970. Ch 6, n 25; Ch 10, n 31.

Facer v. Lewis, 40 NW 2d 457, Mich 1950. Ch 10, n 46.

Falcher v. St. Luke's Hospital Medical Center, 506 P 2d 287, Ariz 1973. Ch 6, n. 39.

Falcone v. Middlesex County Medical Society, 170 A 2d 791, NJ 1961; 75 *Harvard Law Review* 1142, 1963. Ch 11, n 95.

Fallis v. Department of Motor Vehicles, 70 Cal Rptr 595, Cal 1968. Ch 1, n 101.

Falum v. Medical Arts Center Hospital, 160 *New York Law Journal* 2, 1968. Ch 12, n 101.

Farber v. Olkon, 254 P 2d 520, Cal 1953. Ch 5, n 202.

Fausette v. Grim, 186 SW 1177, Mo 1916. Ch 9, n 68; Ch 12, n 62.

Favalora v. Aetna Casualty Co., 144 So 2d 544, La 1962. Ch 2, n 44.

Fay v. Mundy, 54 Cal Rptr 591, Cal 1966. Ch 10, n 144.

Feeney v. Young, 181 NYS 481, NY 1920. Ch 9, n 52.

Feige v. State, 194 SW 865, Ark 1917. Ch 11, n 172.

Feiser v. St. Francis Hospital and School of Nursing, Inc., 510 P 2d 145, Kans 1973. Ch 10, n 77.

Felber v. Foote, 321 F Supp 85, DC Conn 1970. Ch 1, n 79.

Felis v. Greenberg, 273 NYS 2d 288, NY 1966. Ch 9, n 43.

Felton v. Coyle, 238 NE 2d 191, Ill 1968. Ch 9, n 88.

Fernandez v. Baruch, 244 A 2d 109, NJ 1968. Ch 4, n 109.

Ferrara v. Galluchio, 152 NE 2d 249, NY 1958. Ch 3, n 119.

Fick v. Board of Medical Examiners for the State of California, 107 Cal Rptr 260, Cal 1973. Ch 11, n 41.

Findlay v. Board of Supervisors, 230 P 2d 526, Ariz 1951. Ch 1, n 23; Ch 11, n 124.

Fiorentino v. Wenger, 272 NYS 2d 557, NY 1966, rev'd on other grounds, 227 NE 2d 296, NY 1967. Ch 2, n 17; Ch 7, n 83; Ch 8, n 7; Ch 8, n 146.

Fischer v. Wilmington General Hospital, 149 A 2d 749, Del 1959. Ch 8, n 34.

Flagler Hospital v. Hayling, 344 F 2d 950, CCA 5, 1965. Ch 1, n 41.

Fleishmann v. Richardson Merrell, Inc., 226 A 2d 843, NJ 1967. Ch 12, n 51.

Flentie v. Townsend, 30 P 2d 132, Kans 1934. Ch 12, n 32.

Fletcher v. Hand, 358 F 2d 549, DC CA 1966. Ch 10, n 73.

The Florida Bar v. Hefty, 213 So 2d 422, Fla 1968. Ch 11, n 66.

Florida Bar Association v. Kay, 232 So 2d 378, Fla 1970. Ch 11, n 68.

Floyd v. Michie, 11 SW 2d 657, Tex 1928. Ch 2, n 37; Ch 7, n 23.

Flynn v. Stearns, 145 A 2d 33, NJ 1958. Ch 10, n 39.

Foley v. Bishop Clarkson Memorial Hospital, 173 NW 2d 881, Neb 1970. Ch 10, n 6.

Fontenot v. Aetna Casualty and Surety Company, 166 So 2d 299, La 1964. Ch 5, n 174.

Forman v. State Board of Health, 162 SW 796, Ky 1914. Ch 11, n 74.

Forman v. Wolfson, 98 NE 2d 615, Mass 1951. Ch 10, n 103.

Fort v. City of Brinkley, 112 SW 1084, Ark 1908. Ch 11, n 41.

Fortner v. Koch, 261 NW 762, Mich 1935. Ch 3, n 81; Ch 4. n 29; Ch 8, n 145.

Forziati v. Board of Registration in Medicine, 128 NE 2d 789, Mass 1955. Ch 11, n 78.

Foster v. Brady, 86 P 2d 760, Wash 1939. Ch 9, n 82.

Foster v. Mobile County Hospital Board, 398 F 2d 227, CCA 5, 1968. Ch 11, n 127.

Foxluger v. New York, 203 NYS 2d 985, NY 1960. Ch 2, n 12.

Frank v. Board of Regents, 264 NYS 2d 413, NY 1965. Ch 11, n 52.

Frankel v. Wolper, 169 NYS 15, NY 1918. Ch 10, n 150.

Fraser v. Sprague, 76 Cal Rptr 37, Cal 1969. Ch 4, n 88.

Frazier v. Levi, 440 SW 2d 393, Tex 1969. Ch 8, n 109.

Frederic v. United States, 246 F Supp 368, DC La 1965. Ch 4, n 106.

French v. Fischer, 362 SW 2d 926, Tenn 1962. Ch 5, n 5; Ch 7, n 42.

French v. Heibert, 262 P 2d 831, Kan 1953. Ch 6, n 87.

Frick v. McClelland, 122 A 2d 43, Pa 1956. Ch 8, n 73.

Frost v. Des Moines Still College, 79 NW 2d 306, Iowa 1956. Ch 10, n 78.

Funk v. Bonham, 183 NE 312, Ind 1932. Ch 5, n 8.

Furnish v. Board of Medical Examiners, 308 P 2d 924, Cal 1957. Ch 11, n 32.

Furr v. Herzmark, 206 F 2d 468, CA DC 1953. Ch 5, n 40; Ch 5, n 54.

Gaertner v. Michigan, 187 NW 2d 429, Mich 1971. Ch 12, n 100.

Gahn v. Leary, 61 NE 2d 844, Mass 1945. Ch 8, n 68.

Galesburg Sanitarium v. Jacobson, 103 Ill App 26, Ill 1902. Ch 5, n 210; Ch 9, n 9.

Galloway v. Lawrence, 145 SE 2d 861, NC 1966. Ch 4, n 70; Ch 10, n 84.

Gamradt v. DuBois, 230 NW 774, Minn 1930. Ch 12, n 33.

Garlock v. Cole, 18 Cal Rptr 393, Cal 1962. Ch 9, n 70.

Gates v. Preston, 41 NY 113, 1869. Ch 10, n 104.

Gault v. Poor Sisters of St. Frances, 375 F 2d 539, CCA 6, 1967. Ch 4, n 146.

Gay v. Greene, 84 SE 2d 847, Ga 1954. Ch 10, n 111.

Gebhardt v. McQuillen, 297 NW 301, Iowa 1941. Ch 4, n 75.

Geddes v. Daughters of Charity, 348 F 2d 144, CCA 5, 1965. Ch 4, n 113.

Geiger v. Jenkins, 316 F Supp 370, DC Ga 1970. Ch 11, n 4; Ch 11, n 45:

General Hospital of Greater Miami, Inc. v. Gager, 160 So 2d 749, Fla 1964. Ch 10, n 17.

Gerber v. Day, 6 P 2d 535, Cal 1931. Ch 10, n 27.

Gerhardt v. Fresno Medical Group, 31 Cal Rptr 633, Cal 1963. Ch 4, n 84.

Gerken v. Plimpton, 70 NYS 793, NY 1901. Ch 12, n 67.

Getchell v. Mansfield, 489 P 2d 953, Ore 1971. Ch 8, n 25.

Giambozi v. Peters, 16 A 2d 833, Conn 1940. Ch 5, n 67.

Gian-Cursio v. State, 180 So 2d 396, Fla 1965. Ch 11, n 175.

Gibo v. City and County of Honolulu, 459 P 2d 198, Hawaii 1969. Ch 6, n 102.

Gibson v. Connecticut Medical Examining Board, 104 A 2d 890, Conn 1954. Ch 11, n 82.

Gielskie v. New York, 200 NYS 2d 691, NY 1960. Ch 2, n 10.

Gile v. Kennewick Public Hospital District, 296 P 2d 662, Wash 1956. Ch 5, n 75.

Gillette v. Tucker, 65 NE 865, Ohio 1902. Ch 12, n 20.

Gist v. French, 288 P 2d 1003, Cal 1955. Ch 3, n 69; Ch 4, n 97.

United States ex rel Gittlemacker v. County of Philadephia, 413 F 2d 84, CCA 3, 1969. Ch 1, n 55.

Glenn v. Colorado State Board of Medical Examiners, 284 P 2d 230, Colo 1955. Ch 11, n 41.

Glenn v. Kerlin, 248 So 2d 834, La 1971. Ch 9, n 25.

Glesby v. Hartford Accident and Indemnity Company, 44 P 2d 365, Cal 1935. Ch 7, n 12.

Gluckstein v. Lipsett, 209 P 2d 98, Cal 1949. Ch 1, n 10; Ch 4, n 91.

Goldman v. Kossove, 117 SE 2d 35, NC 1960. Ch 6, n 80.

Goedecke v. Price, 506 P 2d 1105, Ariz 1973. Ch 3, n 97.

Goelz v. Wadley Institute, 350 SW 2d 573, Tex 1961. Ch 5, n 75.

Golia v. Health Insurance Plan of Greater New York, 166 NYS 2d 889, NY 1957. Ch 4, n 121; Ch 9, n 35.

Gonzales v. Peterson, 359 P 2d 307, Wash 1961. Ch 3, n 49; Ch 4, n 13.

Gorden v. State, 90 SW 636, Tex 1904. Ch 11, n 161.

Gore v. Brockman, 119 SW 1082, Mo 1909. Ch 5, n 90.

Gorlin v. Master Contracting Corporation, 180 NYS 2d 84, NY 1958. Ch 5, n 185.

Gorman v. St. Francis Hospital, 208 NE 2d 653, Ill 1965. Ch 5, n 99.

Gottsdanker v. Cutter Laboratories, 6 Cal Rptr 320, Cal 1960. Ch 6, n 61.

Govin v. Hunter, 374 P 2d 421, Wyo 1962. Ch 8, n 31.

Grace v. Howlett, 283 NE 2d 474, Ill 1972. Ch 13, n 66.

Graddy v. New York Medical College, 243 NYS 2d 940, NY 1963. Ch 5, n 128; Ch 7, n 22.

Graeb v. State Board of Medical Examiners, 139 Pac 1099, Colo 1913. Ch 11, n 57.

Graham v. Sisco, 449 SW 2d 949, Ark 1970. Ch 4, n 61.

Graham v. St. Luke's Hospital, 196 NE 2d 355, Ill 1964. Ch 5, n 172.

Gramm v. Boener, 56 Ind 497, 1877. Ch 10, n 49.

Grannis v. Board of Medical Examiners, 96 Cal Rptr 868, Cal 1971. Ch 11, n 44.

Grant v. Touro Infirmary, 223 So 2d 148, La 1969. Ch 5, n 8; Ch 7, n 41.

Grantham v. Board of County Commissioners for Prince George's County, 246 A 2d 548, Md 1968. Ch 10, n 92.

Grantham v. Goetz, 164 A 2d 225, Pa 1960. Ch 5, n 165.

Gravis v. Physicians' and Surgeons' Hospital, 415 SW 2d 674, Tex 1967. Ch 5, n 123.

Gray v. Davidson, 130 P 2d 341, Wash 1942. Ch 12, n 38.

Gray v. Grunnagle, 223 A 2d 663, Pa 1966. Ch 2, n 97; Ch 8, n 50.

Gray v. Weinstein, 42 SE 2d 616, NC 1947. Ch 12, n 42.

Green v. Hussey, 262 NE 2d 156, Ill 1970. Ch 5, n 107.

Greenwood v. Harris, 362 P 2d 85, Okla 1961. Ch 3, n 35.

Greisman v. Newcomb Hospital, 192 A 2d 817, NJ 1963. Ch 11, n 123.

Gresham v. Ford, 241 SW 2d 408, Tenn 1951. Ch 2, n 41.

Griffin v. Medical Society of the State of New York, 11 NYS 2d 109, NY 1939. Ch 9, n 50.

Griswold v. Connecticut, 381 US 479, 1965. Ch 1, n 128; Ch 1, n 146; Ch 9, n 46.

Groce v. Myers, 29 SE 2d 553, NC 1944. Ch 12, n 9.

Grosjean v. Spencer, 140 NW 2d 139, Iowa 1966. Ch 8, n 24.

Gross v. Partlow, 68 P 2d 1034, Wash 1937. Ch 1, n 13; Ch 12, n 63.

Gross v. Robinson, 218 SW 924, Mo 1920. Ch 5, n 106.

Grove v. Seltzer, 266 A 2d 301, NJ 1970. Ch 13, n 56.

Guillen v. Martin, 333 P 2d 266, Cal 1958. Ch 4, n 82.

Gulf and Ship Island RR Co v. Sullivan, 119 So 501, Miss 1928. Ch 1, n 120.

Gulfway General Hospital v. Pursley, 397 SW 2d 93, Tex 1965. Ch 6, n 91.

Gunning v. Cooley, 281 US 90, 1930. Ch 5, n 144.

Gurganious v. Simpson, 197 SE 163, NC 1938. Ch 8, n 71.

Gursky v. Gursky, 242 NYS 2d 406, NY 1963. Ch 8, n 115.

Guth v. Vaughn, 231 Ill App 143, 1923. Ch 10, n 79.

Gwynn v. Wilhelm, 360 P 2d 312, Ore 1961. Ch 10, n 106.

Haase v. Garfinkel, 418 SW 2d 108, Mo 1967. Ch 4, n 100.

Habuda v. Trustees of Rex Hospital, Inc., 164 SE 2d 17, NC 1968. Ch 7, n 63.

Hachat v. Hachat, 71 NE 2d 927, Ind 1947. Ch 1, n 112.

Haewsky v. St. John Hospital, Mich Cir Ct, Wayne Co. Docket 136-064, June 10, 1970. Ch 8, n 118.

Hager v. Major, 186 SW 2d 564, Mo 1945. Ch 9, n 23.

Hague v. Williams, 181 A 2d 345, NJ 1962. Ch 9, n 45.

Haines v. Ebert, 187 NE 2d 522, Ohio 1961. Ch 4, n 85.

Hake v. Arkansas State Medical Board, 374 SW 2d 173, Ark 1964. Ch 11, n 86.

Hales v. Raines, 141 SW 917, Mo 1911. Ch 4, n 20; Ch 5, n 106.

Hall v. Bacon, 453 P 2d 816, Idaho 1969. Ch 3, n 99.

Hall v. Delvat, 389 P 2d 692, Ariz 1964. Ch 5, n 20.

Hall v. Ferry, 235 F Supp 821, DC Va 1964. Ch 3, n 47.

Hall v. United States, 136 F Supp 187, DC La 1955. aff'd 234 F 2d 811, CCA 5, 1956. Ch 5, n 123.

Hally v. Hospital of St. Raphael, 294 A 2d 305, Conn 1972. Ch 6, n 26.

Ham v. Holy Rosary Hospital, Docket No. 14910 Mont Dist Ct. Custer County, Feb. 13, 1973. Ch 1, n 150.

Hamilton County Hospital v. Andrews, 84 NE 2d 469, 85 NE 2d 365, Ind 1949. Ch 11, n 126.

Hammer v. Polsky, 233 NYS 2d 110, NY 1962. Ch 9, n 30.

Hammer v. Rosen, 165 NE 2d 756, NY 1960. Ch 9, n 5.

Hammonds v. Aetna Casualty & Surety Co., 237 F Supp 96, DC Ohio 1965. Ch 4, n 44.

Hampton v. State, 39 So 421, Fla 1905. Ch 11, n 162.

Hand v. Park Community Hospital, 165 NW 2d 673, Mich 1968. Ch 6, n 14.

Hanley v. Spencer, 115 P 2d 399, Colo 1941. Ch 10, n 25.

Hanson v. Thelan, 173 NW 457, ND 1919. Ch 4, n 70.

Hardman v. Hardman, 214 SW 2d 391, Ky 1948. Ch 8, n 133.

Harley v. St. Francis Hospital, 129 NW 2d 235, Wisc 1964. Ch 10, n 70.

Harris v. Fall, 177 Fed 79, CCA 7, 1910. Ch 12, n 46.

Harris v. Fireman's Fund Indemnity Co., 257 P 2d 221, Wash 1953. Ch 1, n 6; Ch 6, n 7.

Harris v. Wood, 8 NW 2d 818, Minn 1943. Ch 5, n 128.

Harrison v. Wilkerson, 405 SW 2d 649, Tenn 1966. Ch 5, n 25.

Hart v. Van Zandt, 399 SW 2d 791, Tex 1965. Ch 2, n 53.

Harvey v. Silber, 2 NW 2d 483, Mich 1942. Ch 1, n 20.

Harwick v. Harris, 166 So 2d 912, Fla 1964. Ch 2, n 35; Ch 7, n 25.

Haskins v. Howard, 16 SW 2d 20, Tenn 1929. Ch 9, n 70.

Hathaway v. Worcester City Hospital, 475 F 2d 701, CCA 1, 1973. Ch 1, n 148.

Haven v. Randolph, 342 F Supp 538, DC DC 1972. Ch 8, n 39.

In re Hawkins, 194 SE 2d 540, NC 1973. Ch 11, n 51.

Hawkins v. McCain, 79 SE 2d 493, NC 1954. Ch 1, n 9.

Hawkins v. McGee, 146 Atl 641, NH 1929. Ch 4, n 5.

Hayman v. City of Galveston, 273 US 414, 1927. Ch 11, n 114.

Haynes v. Ordway, 58 NH 167, 1877. Ch 10, n 108.

Hays v. Hall, 477 SW 2d 402, Tex 1972. Ch 10, n 131.

Hazelwood v Stokes, 483 SW 2d 576, Ky 1972. Ch 8, n 77.

Hecht v. First National Bank & Trust Co., 490 P 2d 649, Kans 1971. Ch 10, n 124.

Hedlund v. Suttter Medical Service Co., 124 P 2d 878, Cal 1942. Ch 10, n 153.

Heimlich v. Harvey, 39 NW 2d 394, Wisc 1949. Ch 7, n 9.

Helms v. Williams, 166 SE 2d 852, NC 1969. Ch 7, n 64.

Henderson v. City of Knoxville, 9 SW 2d 697, Tenn 1928. Ch 11, n 117.

Henderson v. National Drug Company, 23 A 2d 743, Pa 1942. Ch 5, n 189.

Hendricksen v. Roosevelt Hospital, 297 F Supp 1142, DC NY 1969. Ch 8, n 67.

In re Hendrickson, 123 P 2d 322, Wash 1942. Ch 8, n 110.

Henslin v. Wheaton, 97 NW 882, Minn 1904. Ch 5, n 94.

Heryford v. Parker, 396 F 2d 393, CCA 10, 1968. Ch 8, n 89.

Hess v. Lowery, 23 NE 156, Ind 1890. Ch 7, n 19.

Hess v. Rouse, 22 SW 2d 1077, Tex 1929. Ch 5, n 91.

Hester v. Ford, 130 So 203, Ala 1930. Ch 1, n 4.

Hewitt v. Board of Medical Examiners, 84 Pac 39, Cal 1906. Ch 11, n 2.

Hicks v. United States, 368 F 2d 626, CCA 4, 1966. Ch 3, n 20.

Higgins v. New York, 265 NYS 2d 254, NY 1965. Ch 4, n 110.

Hill v. James Walker Memorial Hospital, 407 F 2d 1036, CCA 4, 1969. Ch 6, n 94.

Hill v. Stewart, 209 So 2d 809, Miss 1968. Ch 3, n 83.

Hill v. Travelers' Insurance Co., 294 SW 1097, Tenn 1927. Ch 8, n 65.

Hine v. Fox, 89 So 2d 13, Fla 1956. Ch 6, n 74.

Hinkle v. Hargens, 81 NW 2d 888, SD 1957. Ch 9, n 65.

Hipp v. Hospital Authority of the City of Marietta, 121 SE 2d 273, Ga 1961. Ch 10, n 162.

Hirko v. Reese, 40 A 2d 408, Pa 1945. Ch 8, n 69.

Hirons v. Patuxent Institution, 351 F 2d 613, CCA 4, 1965. Ch 1, n 48.

Hoder v. Sayet, 196 So 2d 205, Fla 1967. Ch 5, n 57.

Hodge v. Shea, 168 SE 82, SC 1969. Ch 9, n 79.

Hoener v. Bertinato, 171 A 2d 140, NY 1961. Ch 1, n 69.

Hoff v. New York, 18 NE 2d 671, NY 1939. Ch 8, n 100.

Hoffman v. Misericordia Hospital, 267 A 2d 867, Pa 1970. Ch 5, n 66.

Hoffman v. Rogers, 99 Cal Rptr 455, Cal 1972. Ch 1, n 88.

Hoffman v. Wilkins, 270 NE 2d 594, Ill 1971. Ch 11, n 137.

Hofman v. Blackmon, 241 So 2d 752, Fla 1970. Ch 4, n 121; Ch 9, n 36.

Hoglin v. Brown, 481 P 2d 458, Wash 1971. Ch 2, n 61; Ch 3, n 36.

Hohenthal v. Smith, 114 F 2d 494, CA DC 1940. Ch 5, n 48.

Holland v. Metalious, 198 A 2d 654, NH 1964. Ch 8, n 79.

Hollenbeck v. Ristine, 86 NW 377, Iowa 1901. Ch 9, n 22.

Holmes v. Powers, 439 SW 2d 579, Ky 1969. Ch 8, n 109.

Holtfoth v. Rochester General Hospital, 105 NE 2d 610, NY 1952. Ch 6, n 46.

Holzberg v. Flower and Fifth Avenue Hospitals, 330 NYS 2d 682, NY 1972. Ch 5, n 142.

Hood v. Moffett, 69 So 664, Miss 1915. Ch 12, n 16.

Horace v. Weyrauch, 324 P 2d 666, Cal 1958. Ch 4, n 54.

Hornbeck v. Homeopathic Hospital Association, 197 A 2d 461, Del 1964. **Ch 5,** n 136.

Jackson v. Burton, 147 So 414, Ala 1933. Ch 12, n 41.

Jackson v. Indiana, 406 US 715, 1972. Ch 4, n 118.

Jackson v. Joyner, 72 SE 2d 589, NC 1952. Ch 7, n 50.

Jackson v. Mountain Sanitarium, 67 SE 2d 57, NC 1951. Ch 5, n 133.

Jackson v. Muhlenberg Hospital, 249 A 2d 65, NJ 1969. Ch 5, n 62.

Jackson v. Rupp, 228 So 2d 916, Fla 1969. Ch 8, n 61; Ch 8, n 72.

Jackson v. United States, 182 F Supp 907, DC Md 1960. Ch 5, n 44.

Jacobi v. Board of Medical Examiners, 308 SW 2d 261, Tex 1957. Ch 11, n 108.

Jacobs v. Grigsby, 205 NW 394, Wisc 1925. Ch 5, n 23.

People ex rel Jacobs v. Worthing, 4 NYS 2d 630, NY 1938. Ch 8, n 100.

Jaeger v. Stratton, 176 NW 61, Wis 1920. Ch 3, n 117.

Jaffe v. State Department of Health, 64 A 2d 330, Conn 1949. Ch 9, n 91; Ch 11, n 56.

Jaime v. Neurological Hospital Association, 488 SW 2d 641, Mo 1973. Ch 10, n 146.

James v. Holder, 309 NYS 2d 385, NY 1970. Ch 5, n 82; Ch 7, n 68.

James v. Spear, 338 P 2d 22, Cal 1959. Ch 10, n 7.

Jarboe v. Harting, 397 SW 2d 775, Ky 1965. Ch 2, n 63; Ch 3, n 33.

Jeanes v. Milner, 428 F 2d 598, CCA 8, 1970. Ch 3, n 91.

Jefferson Hospital v. Van Lear, 41 SE 2d 441, Va 1947. Ch 6, n 101; Ch 10, n 153.

Jefferson v. United States, 77 F Supp 706, 1948; 340 US 135, 1950. Ch 5, n 2.

Jessin v. County of Shasta, 79 Cal Rptr 359, Cal 1969. Ch 1, n 144.

Jeswald v. Hutt, 239 NE 2d 37, Ohio 1968. Ch 6, n 82.

Jines v. General Electric Corporation, 303 F 2d 76, CCA 9, 1962. Ch 1, n 80; Ch 7, n 86.

In re John Children, 306 NYS 2d 797, NY 1969. Ch 8, n 119.

In re Johnson's Estate, 16 NW 2d 504, Neb 1944. Ch 3, n 15; Ch 3, n 41.

Johnson v. Borland, 26 NW 2d 755, Mich 1947. Ch 3, n 27.

Johnson v. City of Ripon, 47 NW 2d 328, Wisc 1951. Ch 11, n 135; Ch 11, n 152.

Johnson v. Ely, 205 SW 2d 759, Tenn 1947. Ch 5, n 18.

Johnson v. Phillips, 223 NE 2d 677, Mass 1967. Ch 5, n 170.

Johnson v. St. Paul Mercury Insurance Company, 219 So 2d 524, La 1969. Ch 3, n 4.

Johnson v. Sterling Drug Co., 190 NW 2d 77, Minn 1971. Ch 10, n 120.

Johnson v. United States, 271 F Supp 205, DC Ark 1967. Ch 10, n 24.

Johnson v. Vaughn, 370 SW 2d 591, Ky 1963. Ch 4, n 15; Ch 4, n 129; Ch 12, n 29.

Johnston v. Black Company, 91 P 2d 921, Cal 1939. Ch 6, n 4.

Johnston v. The Upjohn Company, 442 SW 2d 93, Mo 1969. Ch 6, n 65.

Joiner v. Mitchell County Hospital Authority, 186 SE 2d 307, 189 SE 2d 412, Ga 1972. Ch 7, n 79; Ch 10, n 164; Ch 11, n 111.

Jones v. Bouza, 160 NW 2d 881, Mich 1968. Ch 1, n 86; Ch 7, n 88.

Jones v. Fakehany, 67 Cal Rptr 810, Cal 1968. Ch 12, n 107.

Jones v. Laird Foundation, Inc., 195 SE 2d 821, W Va 1973. Ch 7, n 94.

Jones v. Smith, 278 So 2d 339, Fla 1973. Ch 1, n 138.

Jones v. Stanko, 160 NE 456, Ohio 1928. Ch 4, n 123.

Jordahl v. Berry, 75 NW 10, Minn 1898. Ch 10, n 107.

Joseph v. Groves Latter Day Saints Hospital, 348 P 2d 935, Utah 1960. Ch 5, n 72.

Joyner v. Alton Ochsner Medical Foundation, 230 So 2d 913, La 1970. Ch 1, n 46.

Just v. Littlefield, 151 Pac 780, Wash 1915. Ch 3, n 14.

Kaimowitz v. Department of Mental Health, Civil Action #73-19434-AW Mich, Wayne Co Cir Ct 1973, Ch 8, n 136-A.

Kaiser v. Suburban Transportation System, 398 P 2d 14, Wash 1965. Ch 2, n 51; Ch 4, n 141; Ch 5, n 196.

Kalmus v. Cedars of Lebanon Hospital, 281 P 2d 872, Cal 1955. Ch 5, n 156.

Kambas v. St. Joseph's' Hospital, 189 NW 2d 879, Mich 1971. Ch 10, n 141.

Kansas State Board v. Seasholtz, 504 P 2d 576, Kans 1972. Ch 11, n 51.

The Kansas State Board of Healing Arts v. Foote, 436 P 2d 828, Kans 1968. Ch 11, n 89.

Kaplan v. New York, 100 NYS 2d 693, NY 1950. Ch 5, n 41; Ch 5, n 47.

Karjavinen v. Buswell, 194 NE 295, Mass 1935. Ch 1, n 154; Ch 9, n 91.

Karp v. Cooley, 349 F Supp 827, DC Tex 1972. Ch 4, n 23; Ch 8, n 7; Ch 8, n 149; Ch 10, n 3.

In re Karwath, 199 NW 2d 147, Iowa 1972. Ch 1, n 71.

Kaster v. Woodson, 123 SW 2d 981, Tex 1938. Ch 5, n 155.

Kastler v. Iowa Methodist Hospital, 193 NW 2d 98, Iowa 1971. Ch 6, n 99.

Keen v. Coleman, 20 SE 2d 175, Ga 1942. Ch 9, n 70.

Keene v. Methodist Hospital, 324 F Supp 233, ND Ind 1971. Ch 1, n 20.

Kelly v. Carroll, 219 P 2d 79, Wash 1950. Ch 2, n 9.

Kelly v. Hollingsworth, 181 NW 959, SD 1921. Ch 3, n 106.

Kelly v. Sheehan, 259 A 2d 605, Conn 1969. Ch 12, n 111.

Kelly v. Stern, 132 Atl 234, NJ 1926. Ch 5, n 30.

Kelly v. Yount, 7 A 2d 582, Pa 1939. Ch 6, n 8.

Kemalyan v. Henderson, 277 P 2d 372, Wash 1954. Ch 5, n 135; Ch 7, n 51.

Kennedy v. Gaskell, 78 Cal Rptr 753, Cal 1969. Ch 6, n 55.

Kennedy v. Parrott, 90 SE 2d 754, NC 1956. Ch 8, n 53.

Kennedy Hospital v. Heston, 279 A 2d 670, NJ 1971. Ch 1, n 67.

Kent v. County of Hudson, 245 A 2d 747, NJ 1968. Ch 6, n 15; Ch 10, n 36.

Keown v. Young, 283 Pac 511, Kans 1930. Ch 10, n 72.

Kern v. Kogan, 226 A 2d 186, NJ 1967. Ch 3, n 85.

State ex re Kerr v. Landwehr, 32 SW 2d 83, Mo 1930. Ch 11, n 10.

Kershaw v. Sterling Drug Inc., 415 F 2d 1009, CCA 5, 1969. Ch 6, n 59.

Key v. Caldwell, 104 P 2d 87, Cal 1940. Ch 5, n 7.

Khoury v. Community Memorial Hospital, 123 SE 2d 533, Va 1962. Ch 11, n 143.

In re Kindschi, 319 P 2d 824, Wash 1958. Ch 11, n 32.

King v. Carney, 204 Pac 270, Okla 1922. Ch 8, n 55.

King v. Solomon, 81 NE 2d 838, Mass 1948. Ch 5, n 198; Ch 10, n 45.

Kingsley v. Forsyth, 257 NW 95, Minn 1934. Ch 8, n 73.

Kirschner v. Equitable Life Assurance Society, 284 NYS 506, NY 1935. Ch 1, n 4.

Kleber v. Stevens, 241 NYS 2d 497, NY 1963. Ch 1, n 154.

Kleinman v. Armour, 470 P 2d 703, Ariz 1970. Ch 3, n 40.

Knight v. Lowery, 185 SE 2d 915, Ga 1971. Ch 10, n 86.

Knoop v. State Board of Health, 103 Atl 904, RI 1918. Ch 11, n 41.

Kober v. Stewart, 417 P 2d 476, Mont 1966. Ch 7, n 67.

Koenig v. Group Health Cooperative, 491 P 2d 702, Wash 1971. Ch 10, n 122.

Kopa v. United States, 236 F Supp 189, DC Hawaii 1964. Ch 6, n 97.

Kopprasch v. Stone, 65 NW 2d 852, Mich 1954. Ch 9, n 78.

Korman v. Hagen, 206 NW 650, Minn 1925. Ch 4, n 59.

Korndorffer v. Texas State Board of Medical Examiners, 460 SW 2d 879, Tex 1970. Ch 11, n 21.

Kosak v. Boyce, 201 NW 757, Wisc 1925. Ch 3, n 57.

Koump v. Smith, 250 NE 2d 857, NY 1969. Ch 12, n 116.

Koury v. Follo, 158 SE 2d 548, NC 1968. Ch 1, n 108; Ch 5, n 177; Ch 8, n 21.

Kozan v. Comstock, 270 F 2d 839, CCA 5, 1959. Ch 10, n 99.

Kraus v. Spielberg, 236 NYS 2d 143, NY 1962. Ch 3, n 121.

Kritzer v. Citron, 224 P 2d 808, Cal 1950. Ch 1, n 137.

Kropp v. DeAngelis, 138 NYS 2d 188, NY 1955. Ch 10, n 79.

Krusilla v. United States, 287 F 2d 34, CCA 2, 1961. Ch 2, n 49; Ch 4, n 143.

Kudish v. Board of Registration in Medicine, 248 NE 2d 264, Mass 1969. Ch 11, n 27.

Kuglich v. Fowle, 200 NW 648, Wisc 1924. Ch 6, n 20.

Kuhn v. Banker, 13 NE 2d 242, Ohio 1938. Ch 2, n 88.

Lacey v. Laird, 139 NE 2d 25, Ohio 1956. Ch 1, n 120; Ch 1, n 122.

Laidlaw v. Andrew Freedman Home, 300 NYS 2d 979, NY 1969. Ch 6, n 95.

Lametta v. Connecticut Light & Power Co., 92 A 2d 731, Conn 1952. Ch 10, n 144.

Landon v. Kansas City Gas Co., 10 F 2d 263, CCA 8, 1926. Ch 1, n 12.

Landsberg v. Kolodny, 302 P 2d 86, Cal 1956. Ch 5, n 6.

Landsdown v. Worthey, 448 F 2d 485, CCA 8, 1972. Ch 1, n 54.

Lane v. Calvert, 138 A 2d 902, Maryland 1958. Ch 2, n 57; Ch 4, n 3.

Lane v. Cohen, 201 So 2d 804, Fla 1967. Ch 1, n 153.

Lane v. United States, 225 F Supp 850, DC Va 1964. Ch 4, n 46.

Lange v. United States, 179 F Supp 777, DC NY 1960. Ch 4, n 102.

Langford v. Kosterlitz, 290 Pac 80, Cal 1930. Ch 2, n 22; Ch 5, n 162.

Lanier v. Trammell, 180 SW 2d 818, Ark 1944. Ch 4, n 32.

Largess v. Tatem, 291 A 2d 398, Vt 1972. Ch 2, n 21.

Larrabee v. United States, 254 F Supp 613, DC Cal 1966. Ch 4, n 62.

Larrimore v. Homeopathic Hospital Association, 181 A 2d 573, Del 1962. Ch 5, n 148.

Larson v. Chase, 50 NW 238, Minn 1891. Ch 8, n 61.

Lathrope v. Flood, 63 Pac 1007, Cal 1901. Ch 12, n 5.

Latson v. Zeiler, 58 Cal Rptr 436, Cal 1967. Ch 9, n 67.

Lauro v. The Travelers' Insurance Company 261 So 2d 261, 262 So 2d 787, La 1972. Ch 6, n 32.

Lawson v. Conaway, 16 SE 564, W Va 1892. Ch 10, n 104.

LeBlanc v. Midland National Insurance Company, 219 So 2d 251, La 1969. Ch 6, n 24.

Lee v. Dewbre, 362 SW 2d 900, Tex 1962. Ch 12, n 7; Ch 12, n 77.

Leech v. Bralliar, 273 F Supp 897, DC Ariz 1967. Ch 10, n 67.

Leider v. Beth Israel Hospital, 182 NE 2d 393, NY 1962. Ch 11, n 117.

Leighton v. Sargent, 27 NH 460, 1853. Ch 2, n 59.

Lemon v. Kessel, 209 NW 393, Iowa 1926. Ch 4, n 142.

Lemonovich v. Klimoski, 315 F Supp 1288, DC Pa 1970. Ch 7, n 93.

State ex rel Lentine v. State Board of Health, 65 SW 2d 943, Mo 1933. Ch 11, n 75.

LePrince v. McLeod, 171 So 2d 189, Fla 1965. Ch 2, n 92.

Lester v. Aetna Casualty and Surety Co., 240 F 2d 676, CCA 5, 1957. Ch 8, n 15.

Lesyk v. Park Avenue Hospital, 289 NYS 2d 873, NY 1968. Ch 6, n 103.

Leverman v. Cartall, 393 SW 2d 931, Tex 1965. Ch 3, n 101.

Levett v. Etkind, 265 A 2d 70, Conn 1969. Ch 6, n 86.

Levin v. Sinai Hospital, 46 A 2d 298, Md 1946. Ch 11, n 144; Ch 11, n 156.

Levy v. Kirk, 187 So 2d 401, Fla 1966. Ch 4, n 17; Ch 12, n 28.

Lewis v. Casenburg, 7 SW 2d 808, Tenn 1928. Ch 5, n 98.

Lewis v. Reed, 193 A 2d 255, NJ 1963. Ch 2, n 73.

Levin v. Sinai Hospital, 46 A 2d 298, Md 1946. Ch 11, n 144; Ch 11, n 156.

Liberatore v. National Cylinder Gas Company, 193 F 2d 429, CCA 2, 1952. Ch 6, n 79.

Lindroth v. Christ Hospital, 123 A 2d 10 , NJ 1956. Ch 6, n 108.

Lindsey v. Michigan Mutual Liability Insurance Co., 156 So 2d 313, La 1963. Ch 11, n 39.

Linhares v. Hall, 257 NE 2d 429, Mass 1970. Ch 4, n 42; Ch 10, n 57.

Lippard v. Johnson, 1 SE 2d 889, NC 1939. Ch 5, n 121.

Lipsey v. Michael Reese Hospital, 262 NE 2d 450, Ill 1970. Ch 3, n 66.

Livingston v. Portland General Hospital Association, 357 P 2d 543, Ore 1960. Ch 4, n 14; Ch 12, n 72.

Lockart v. Maclean, 361 P 2d 670, Nev 1961. Ch 2, n 65.

Logan v. Field, 75 Mo App 594, Mo 1898. Ch 2, n 27.

Long v. Methodist Home, 187 SE 2d 718, NC 1972. Ch 6, n 110.

Long v. Sledge, 209 So 2nd 814, Miss 1968. Ch 5, n 11; Ch 10, n 60.

Lopez v. Swyer, 300 A 2d 563, NJ 1973. Ch 9, n 72; Ch 10, n 133.

Lorenz v. Board of Medical Examiners, 298 P 2d 537, Cal 1956. Ch 11, n 69; Ch 11, n 106.

Los Alamos Medical Center v. Coe, 275 P 2d 175, NM 1954. Ch 5, n 199; Ch 10, n 45.

Lotspeich v. Chance Vought Aircraft Corporation, 369 SW 2d 705, Tex 1963. Ch 1, n 81; Ch 10, n 110.

Louisiana State Board of Medical Examiners v. Heiman, 230 So 2d 405, La 1970. Ch 11, n 37; Ch 11, n 45.

Louisville and Nashville Railroad Co. v. Blackmon, 59 SE 341, Ga 1907. Ch 8, n 75.

Love v. Aetna Casualty & Surety Co., 99 SW 2d 646, Tex 1936. Ch 8, n 64.

Love v. Wolf, 38 Cal Rptr 183, 58 Cal Rptr 42, Cal 1967. Ch 5, n 194; Ch 6, n 60.

Loveland v. Nelson, 209 NW 835, Mich 1926. Ch 5, n 121.

Lovett v. Emory University, 156 SE 2d 923, Ga 1967. Ch 5, n 63.

Lowen v. Hilton, 351 P 2d 881, Colo 1960. Ch 9, n 92.

Luka v. Lowrie, 136 NW 1106, Mich 1912. Ch 1, n 113; Ch 8, n 13.

Lundahl v. Rockford Memorial Hospital Association, 235 NE 2d 671, Ill 1968, Ch 2 n 42.

Lundberg v. Bay View Hospital, 191 NE 2d 821, Ohio 1963. Ch 1, n 21; Ch 3, n 87; Ch 7, n 65.

Maben v. Rankin, 358 P 2d 681, Cal 1961. Ch 3, n 22; Ch 9, n 93.

Maclay v. Kelsey–Seybold Clinic, 456 SW 2d 229, 466 SW 2d 716, Tex 1971. Ch 7, n 20; Ch 9, n 85.

MacPherson v. Buick, 111 NE 1050, NY 1916. Ch 6, n 66.

Maercklein v. Smith, 266 P 2d 1095, Colo 1954. Ch 3, n 15; Ch 4, n 47.

Maertins v. Kaiser Foundation Hospital, 328 P 2d 494, Cal 1958. Ch 3, n 61.

Magee v. Wyeth Laboratories, 29 Cal Rptr 322, Cal 1963. Ch 6, n 61.

Magit v. Board of Medical Examiners, 366 P 2d 816, Cal 1961. Ch 11, n 85.

Magner v. Beth Israel Hospital, 295 A 2d 363, NJ 1972. Ch 6, n 51.

Mainfort v. Giannestras, 111 NE 2d 692, Ohio 1951. Ch 4, n 21; Ch 10, n 48.

Mallett v. Pirkey, 466 P 2d 466, Colo 1970. Ch 8, n 47.

Malvica v. Blumenfield, 310 NYS 329, NY 1970. Ch 10. n 82.

In re Mandel, 264 NYS 2d 867, NY 1964. Ch 11, n 52.

Mandelbaum v. Weil, 203 NYS 289, NY 1924. Ch 5, n 46.

Mangrum v. Union Pacific Railroad Company, 41 Cal Rptr 536, Cal 1964. Ch 7, n 101.

Maniaci v. Marquette University, 184 NW 2d 168, Wisc 1971. Ch 8, n 88; Ch 9, n 34; Ch 9, n 98.

Manion v. Tweedy, 100 NW 2d 124, Minn 1959. Ch 2, n 24; Ch 2, n 29.

Manlove v. Wilmington General Hospital, 169 A 2d 18, 174 A 2d 135, Del 1961. Ch 1, n 40.

Mantz v. Follingstad, 505 P 2d 68, NM 1972. Ch 10, n 115.

Marchese v. Monaco, 145 A 2d 809, NJ 1958. Ch 5, n 187.

Marchlewski v. Casella, 106 A 2d 466, Conn 1954. Ch 2, n 64.

Marcus v. Frankford Hospital, 283 A 2d 69, Pa 1971. Ch 6, n 112.

Margoles v. Wisconsin State Board of Medical Examiners, 177 NW 2d 353, Wisc 1970. Ch 11, n 18; Ch 11, n 32.

Maricopa County Medical Society v. Blende, 448 P 2d 68, Ariz 1968. Ch 11, n 95.

Marsello v. Barnett, 236 A 2d 869, NJ 1967. Ch 13, n 55.

Martin v. Aetna Casualty and Surety Company, 387 SW 2d 334, Ark 1965. Ch 6, n 44.

Martin v. Carbide and Carbon Chemical Co., 197 SW 2d 798, Tenn 1946. Ch 11, n 40.

Martin v. Cunningham, 161 Pac 355, Wash 1916. Ch 10, n 69; Ch 10, n 79.

Martin v. Eschelman, 33 SW 2d 827, Tex 1930. Ch 5, n 104.

Martin v. Parks, 165 So 2d 220, Fla 1964. Ch 3, n 105.

Martin v. Perth Amboy General Hospital, 250 A 2d 40, NJ 1969. Ch 5, n 9; Ch 7, n 41.

Martinez v. Mancusi, 443 F 2d 921, CCA 2, 1970. Ch 1, n 50.

Martinez v. Texas State Board of Medical Examiners, 476 SW 2d 400, Tex 1972. Ch 9, n 2; Ch 11, n 64.

Martisek v. Ainsworth, 459 SW 2d 679, Tex 1970. Ch 4, n 138.

Marvin v. Talbott, 30 Cal Rptr 893, Cal 1963. Ch 1, n 9.

Marvulli v. Elshire, 103 Cal Rptr 461, Cal 1972. Ch 7, n 56.

Mascitelli v. Board of Regents, 299 NYS 2d 1002, NY 1969. Ch 11, n 28.

Masonic Hospital Association v. Taggart, 43 P 2d 142, Okla 1935. Ch 5, n 163.

Massachusetts v. Concepcion, 290 NE 2d 514, Mass 1972. Ch 12, n 113.

Massachusetts v. Miller, 282 NE 2d 394, Mass 1972. Ch 1, n 76.

Massey v. State, 177 SE 2d 79, Ga 1970. Ch 1, n 93.

Matthews v. Atchison, Topeka & Santa Fe Railway Co., 129 P 2d 435, Cal 1942. Ch 10, n 96.

Mattocks v. Bell, 194 A 2d 307, DC DC 1963. Ch 9, n 8.

May v. Broun, 492 P 2d 776, Ore 1972. Ch 7, n 46.

Mayers v. Litow, 316 P 2d 351, Cal 1957. Ch 4, n 86.

State ex rel Mayfield v. St. Louis Medical Society, 91 Mo App 76, Mo 1901. Ch 11, n 107.

Mayo v. McClung, 64 SE 2d 330, Ga 1951. Ch 2, n 88.

Mayor v. Dowsett, 400 P 2d 234, Ore 1965. Ch 5, n 124.

Mazer v. Lipschutz, 327 F 2d 42, 360 F 2d 275, CCA 3, 1966. Ch 5, n 77; Ch 10, n 68.

McBride v. Roy, 58 P 2d 886, Okla 1936. Ch 3, n 96.

McBride v. Saylin, 56 P 2d 941, Cal 1936. Ch 3, n 58.

McBride v. United States, 462 F 2d 72, CCA 9, 1972. Ch 7, n 61.

McCandless v. McWha, 22 Pa 261, Pa 1853. Ch 4, n 35.

McCarthy v. Boston City Hospital, 266 NE 2d 292, Mass 1971. Ch 5, n 100.

McCartney v. Austin, 298 NYS 2d 26, NY 1969. Ch 1, n 70.

McCollum v. Mayfield, 130 F Supp 112, DC Cal 1955. Ch 1, n 48.

McConnell v. Williams, 65 A 2d 243, Pa 1949. Ch 7, n 39.

McCoy v. Wesley Hospital and Nurse Training School, 362 P 2d 841, Kans 1961. Ch 10, n 150.

McDermott v. Manhattan Eye, Ear and Throat Hospital, 228 NYS 2d 143, 203 NE 2d 469, NY 1964. Ch 4, n 90; Ch 8, n 41.

McDermott v. St. Mary's Hospital, 133 A 2d 608, Conn 1957. Ch 6, n 21; Ch 10, n 161.

McDonald v. Massachusetts General Hospital, 120 Mass 432, 1876. Ch 10, n 152.

McGarry v. J. A. Mercier Co., 262 NW 296, Mich 1935. Ch 12, n 93.

McGulpin v. Bessmer, 43 NW 2d 121, Iowa 1950. Ch 1, n 14; Ch 2, n 67; Ch 10, n 15.

McHugh v. Audet, 72 F Supp 394, DC Pa 1947. Ch 2, n 11; Ch 3, n 6; Ch 8, n 147.

McKay v. State Board of Medical Examiners, 86 P 2d 232, Colo 1938. Ch 11, n 46; Ch 11, n 92.

McKinney v. Schaefer, 161 SE 2d 446, Ga 1968. Ch 5, n 172.

McKinney v. Tromly, 386 SW 2d 564, Tex 1964. Ch 5, n 120; Ch 7, n 49.

McLendon v. Daniel, 141 SE 77, Ga 1927. Ch 12, n 46.

McLennan v. Holder, 36 P 2d 448, Cal 1934. Ch 5, n 9.

McManus v. Donlin, 127 NW 2d 22, Wisc 1964. Ch 12, n 8.

McMillen v. Klingensmith, 467 SW 2d 193, Tex 1971. Ch 10, n 85.

McNamara v. Emmons, 97 P 2d 503, Cal 1939. Ch 1, n 157; Ch 12, n 91.

McNevins v. Lowe, 40 Ill 209, Ill 1866, Ch 1, n 7.

McPheeters v. Board of Medical Examiners, 284 Pac 938, Cal 1930. Ch 11, n 76.

McPosey v. Sisters of the Sorrowful Mother, 57 P 2d 617, Okla 1936. Ch 8, n 63.

McQuinn v. St. Lawrence County Laboratory, 283 NYS 2d 747, NY 1967. Ch 3, n 68.

Meador v. Arnold, 94 SW 2d 626, Ky 1936. Ch 4, n 75.

Medical and Surgical Memorial Hospital v. Cauthorn, 229 SW 2d 932, Tex 1949. Ch 6, n 33.

Meffert v. State Board of Medical Registration, 72 Pac 247, Kans, 195 US 625, 1903. Ch 11, n 67.

Mehigan v. Sheehan, 51 A 2d 632, NH 1947. Ch 12, n 34.

Meier v. Combs, 263 NE 2d 194, Ind 1970. Ch 9, n 94.

Meier v. Ross General Hospital, 67 Cal Rptr 471, Cal 1968. Ch 4, n 103.

Meimen v. Rehabilitation Center, Inc., 444 SW 2d 78, Ky 1969. Ch 10, n 97; Ch 11, n 39.

Meiselman v. Crown Heights Hospital, 34 NE 2d 367, NY 1941. Ch 12, n 60.

Melnyk v. The Cleveland Clinic, 290 NE 2d 916, Ohio 1972. Ch 10, n 119.

Memorial Hospital of South Bend, Inc. v. Scott, 290 NE 2d 80, Ind 1972. Ch 6, n 98; Ch 10, n 30.

Merchants National Bank v. United States, 272 F Supp 409, DC ND 1967. Ch 2, n 56; Ch 3, n 28; Ch 4, n 111.

Meredith v. Allen County War Memorial Hospital Commission, 397 F 2d 33, CCA 6, 1968. Ch 11, n 138; Ch 11, n 152.

Merker v. Wood, 210 SW 2d 946, Ky 1948. Ch 4, n 12.

Merrill v. Odiorne, 94 Atl 753, Maine 1915. Ch 2, n 52; Ch 10, n 19.

Methodist Hospital v. Ball, 362 SW 2d 475, Tenn 1961. Ch 1, n 44.

Metropolitan Life Insurance Co. v. Evans, 184 So 426, Miss 1938. Ch 1, n 80.

Metzger v. Western Maryland Railway Company, 30 F 2d 50, CCA 4, 1929. Ch 7, n 91.

Meynier v. DePaul Hospital, 218 So 2d 98, La 1969. Ch 5, n 201.

In re Estate of Mgurdichian, 291 NYS 2d 453, NY 1968. Ch 8, n 62.

Michael v. Roberts, 23 A 2d 361, NH 1941. Ch 4, n 98.

Michigan v. Bricker, 208 NW 2d 172, Mich 1973. Ch 11, n 36.

Mickens v. Davis, 294 Pac 896, Kans 1931. Ch 9, n 23.

Mier v. Yoho, 171 SE 535, W Va 1933. Ch 10, n 65.

Miles v. Harris, 194 SW 839, Tex 1917. Ch 12, n 2.

Miles v. Hoffman, 221 Pac 316, Wash 1923. Ch 2, n 46; Ch 4, n 131.

Miles v. Van Gelder, 137 NW 2d 292, Mich 1965. Ch 8, n 31.

Milford v. People's Community Hospital Authority, 155 NW 2d 835, Mich 1968. Ch 11, n 136; Ch 11, n 153.

Miller v. Blackburn, 185 SW 864, Ky 1916. Ch 12, n 50.

Miller v. Dore, 148 A 2d 692, Maine 1959. Ch 7, n 17; Ch 12, n 76.

Miller v. Hennepin County Medical Society, 144 NW 1091, Minn 1914. Ch 11, n 104.

Miller v. Raaen, 139 NW 2d 877, Minn 1966. Ch 5, n 137.

Miller v. Toles, 150 NW 118, Mich 1914. Ch 2, n 19; Ch 4, n 28.

Minaker v. Adams, 203 Pac 806, Cal 1921. Ch 11, n 27.

Minnesota v. Hodgson, 204 NW 2d 199, Minn 1973. Ch 11, n 29.

Minnesota State Board of Medical Examiners v. Schmidt, 292 NW 255, Minn 1940. Ch 11, n 59.

Mississippi Baptist Hospital v. Holmes, 55 So 2d 142, Miss 1951. Ch 5, n 70; Ch 10, n 156.

Mitchell v. Robinson, 334 SW 2d 11, Mo 1960. Ch 5, n 207; Ch 8, n 6; Ch 8, n 19.

Mizell v. North Broward Hospital District, 175 So 2d 583, Fla 1965. Ch 11, n 142.

Modrzynski v. Lust, 88 NE 2d 76, Ohio 1949. Ch 4, n 37.

Moehlenbrock v. Parke Davis and Company, 169 NW 541, Minn 1918. Ch 6, n 57.

Moeller v. Hauser, 54 NW 2d 639, Minn 1952. Ch 4, n 130; Ch 7, n 35; Ch 12, n 80.

Mohr v. Williams, 104 NW 12, Minn 1905. Ch 8, n 54.

Mondot v. Vallejo General Hospital, 313 P 2d 78, Cal 1957. Ch 2, n 95; Ch 5, n 20.

Monk v. Doctor's Hospital, 403 F 2d 580, CA DC 1968. Ch 7, n 47.

Moore v. Andalusia Hospital, Inc., 224 So 2d 617, Ala 1969. Ch 11, n 115.

Moore v. Belt, 212 P 2d 509, Cal 1949. Ch 4, n 55.

Moore v. The Board of Trustees of Carson–Tahoe Hospital, 495 P 2d 605, Nev 1972. Ch 11, n 155.

Moore v. Guthrie Hospital, 403 F 2d 366, CCA 4, 1968. Ch 5, n 158.

Moore v. Steen, 283 Pac 833, Cal 1929. Ch 5, n 103.

Moore v. Tremelling, 78 F 2d 821, CCA 9, 1935. Ch 2, n 88.

Morand v. Seaside Memorial Hospital, 264 P 2d 96, Cal 1953. Ch 6, n 45.

Morey v. Thybo, 199 Fed 760, CCA 7, 1912. Ch 7, n 59.

Morgan v. Aetna Casualty Company, 185 F Supp 20, DC La 1960. Ch 3, n 122.

Morgan v. Engles, 127 NW 2d 382, Mich 1964. Ch 2, n 31.

Morgan v. New York, 319 NY 2d 151, NY 1970. Ch 9, n 5.

Morgan v. Sheppard, 188 NE 2d 808, Ohio 1963. Ch 2, n 43.

Morrell v. Lalonde, 120 Atl 435, RI 1923. Ch 12, n 61.

Morris v. Board of Medical Examiners, 41 Cal Rptr 351, Cal 1964. Ch 11, n 32.

Morris v. Monterey–Yorkshire Nursing Inn, 278 NE 2d 686, Ohio 1971. Ch 10, n 142.

Morris v. Rousos, 397 SW 2d 504, Tex 1965. Ch 9, n 42.

Morse v. Moretti, 403 F 2d 564, CA DC 1968. Ch 2, n 84.

Morse v. Rapkin, 263 NYS 2d 428, NY 1965. Ch 10, n 10.

Morton v. Savannah Hospital, 96 SE 887, Ga 1918. Ch 10, n 156.

Morwin v. Albany Hospital, 185 NYS 2d 85, NY 1959. Ch 5, n 140.

Mucci v. Houghton, 57 NW 305, Iowa 1894. Ch 12, n 9.

Mulder v. Parke Davis & Co., 181 NW 2d 882, Minn 1970. Ch 5, n 192.

Mull v. Emory University, 150 SE 2d 276, Ga 1966. Ch 8, n 46.

Mulligan v. Wetchler, 332 NYS 2d 68, NY 1972. Ch 3, n 7.

Mulliner v. Evangelischer Diakonniessenverein of Minnesota District of German Evangelical Synod of North America, 175 NW 699, Minn 1920. Ch 10, n 159.

Mullins v. DuVall, 104 SE 513, Ga 1920. Ch 7, n 6.
n 144.

Mulvihill v. Butterfield Memorial Hospital, 329 F Supp 1020, DC NY 1971. Ch 11, n 144.

Munk v. Frink, 116 NW 525, Neb 1908. Ch 11, n 10; Ch 11, n 27.

Munson v. Bishop Clarkson Memorial Hospital, 186 NW 2d 492, Neb 1971, Ch 10, n 52.

Murphy v. Little, 145 SE 2d 760, Ga 1965. Ch 2, n 71.

Murray v. Thrifty Drug Store, trial court decision, Sacramento Cal Super Ct. Docket #209949, 1972. Ch 5, n 150.

Murray v. United States, 329 F 2d 270, CCA 4, 1964. Ch 1, n 30.

Musachia v. Rosman, 190 So 2d 47, Fla 1966. Ch 10, n 16.

Muse v. DeVito, 137 NE 730, Mass 1923. Ch 10, n 69.

Myers v. Holborn, 33 Atl 389, NJ 1895. Ch 7, n 15.

People ex rel Nabstedt v. Barger, 121 NE 2d 781, Ill 1954. Ch 8, n 127.

Naccarato v. Grob, 180 NW 2d 788, Mich 1970. Ch 2, n 82; Ch 3, n 80.

Nance v. Hitch, 76 SE 2d 461, NC 1953, Ch 5, n 93.

Nash v. Meyer, 31 P 2d 273, Idaho 1934. Ch 1, n 158; Ch 12, n 86.

Nash v. Royster, 127 SE 356, NC 1925. Ch 12, n 71.

Nason v. Superintendent of Bridgewater State Hospital, 233 NE 2d 908, Mass 1968. Ch 8, n 92.

Natale v. Sisters of Mercy of Council Bluffs, 52 NW 2d 701, Iowa 1952. Ch 11, n 116.

Natanson v. Kline, 354 P 2d 670, 350 P 2d 1093, Kans 1960. Ch 4, n 19; Ch 5, n 107; Ch 8, n 5; Ch 8, n 22; Ch 10, n 47.

National Homeopathic Hospital v. Phillips, 181 F 2d 293, CA DC 1950. Ch 5, n 68.

Necolayff v. Genesee Hospital, 73 NE 2d 117, NY 1947. Ch 5, n 80.

Neely v. St. Francis Hospital and School of Nursing, 363 P 2d 438, Kans 1961. Ch 5, n 179.

Nelson v. Farrish, 173 NW 715, Minn 1919. Ch 12, n 45.

Nelson v. Swedish Hospital, 64 NW 2d 38, Minn 1954. Ch 6, n 11.

New Biloxi Hospital v. Frazier, 146 So 2d 882, Miss 1962. Ch 1, n 28; Ch 12, n 57.

Newman v. Anderson, 217 NW 306, Wisc 1928. Ch 4, n 139.

Newman v. Spellberg, 234 NE 2d 152, Ill 1968. Ch 4, n 51.

New Mexico v. Strance, 506 P 2d 1217, NM 1973. Ch 11, n 29.

New York v. Leyra, 98 NE 2d 553, *rev'd* 347 US 556, 1951. Ch 9, n 29.

New York v. Seaman, 315 NYS 2d 743, NY 1970. Ch 1, n 100.

Nichols v. Nichols, 247 SW 2d 143, Tex 1952. Ch 8, n 131.

Nichols v. Smith, 489 SW 2d 719, Tex 1973. Ch 10, n 139.

Nichter v. Edminston, 407 P 2d 721, Nev 1965. Ch 7, n 43; Ch 13, n 42.

Nigro v. Flinn, 192 Atl 685, Del 1937. Ch 10, n 144.

Nishi v. Hartwell, 473 P 2d 116, Hawaii 1970. Ch 1, n 137; Ch 8, n 17.

Nitka v. Bell, 487 P 2d 379, Colo 1971. Ch 10, n 124.

Nolan v. Kechijian, 64 A 2d 866, RI 1949. Ch 9, n 69.

North Shore Hospital v. Luzi, 194 So 2d 63, Fla 1967. Ch 5, n 166.

Norton v. Argonaut Insurance Company, 144 So 2d 249, La 1962. Ch 5, n 161.

Norton v. Hamilton, 89 SE 2d 809, Ga 1955. Ch 12, n 17.

Norwood Clinic v. Spann, 199 So 840, Ala 1941. Ch 6, n 90.

Nutt v. Carson, 340 P 2d 260, Okla 1959. Ch 10, n 134.

O'Beirne v. Superior Court of Santa Clara County, Sup. Ct. Cal, December 7, 1967. Ch 1, n 140.

Oberlin v. Friedman, 213 NE 2d 168, Ohio 1965. Ch 5, n 122.

O'Brien v. Stover, 443 F 2d 1013, CCA 8, 1971. Ch 3, n 63.

O'Connell v. Westinghouse Xray Company, 41 NE 2d 177, NY 1942. Ch 6, n 78.

O'Donnell v. Slack, 55 Pac 906, Cal 1899. Ch 8, n 78.

O'Grady v. Wickman, 213 So 2d 321, Fla 1968. Ch 4, n 45.

Ohio v. Tims, 224 NE 2d 348, Ohio 1967. Ch 12, n 112.

Oleksiw v. Weidener, 207 NE 2d 375, Ohio 1964. Ch 5, n 32; Ch 5, n 47.

Olepa v. Mapletoff, 141 NW 2d 350, Mich 1966. Ch 9, n 96.

Olsen v. Royal Metals Corporation, 392 F 2d 116, CCA 5, 1968. Ch 6, n 107.

Olson v. St. Croix Valley Memorial Hospital, 201 NW 2d 63, Wisc 1972. Ch 5, n 74; Ch 10, n 132.

Olson v. Weitz, 221 P 2d 537, Wash 1950. Ch 4, n 74.

O'Neil v. New York, 323 NYS 2d 56, NY 1971. Ch 2, n 55; Ch 3, n 13.

O'Neill v. Board of Regents, 74 NYS 2d 762, NY 1947. Ch 11, n 83.

O'Neill v. Montefiore Hospital, 202 NYS 2d 436, NY 1960. Ch 1, n 15; Ch 13, n 83.

O'Reilly v. Board of Medical Examiners, 58 Cal Rptr 7, Cal 1967. Ch 7, n 11.

Orendino v. Clarke, 402 P 2d 527, Ore 1965. Ch 4, n 146.

O'Rourke v. Halcyon Rest, 117 NE 2d 639, NY 1954. Ch 5, n 202.

Orphant v. St. Louis State Hospital, 441 SW 2d 355, Mo 1969. Ch 6, n 111.

Orthopedic Clinic v. Hanson, 415 P 2d 991, Okla 1966. Ch 6, n 6; Ch 7, n 3.

Orthopedic Equipment Company v. Eutster, 276 F 2d 544, CCA 4, 1960. Ch 6, n 70.

Osborne v. Frazor, 425 SW 2d 768, Tenn 1968. Ch 2, n 25.

Our Lady of Mercy Hospital v. McIntosh, 461 SW 2d 377, Ky 1970. Ch 10, n 38.

Page v. Brodoff, 169 A 2d 901, Conn 1961. Ch 10, n 11.

Paine v. Wyatt, 251 NW 78, Iowa 1933. Ch 10, n 110.

Palm Springs General Hospital v. Martinez, Fla Cir Ct, Dade Co., Docket #71-12687, 1971. Ch 1, n 63; Ch 8, n 42.

Panko v. Consolidated Mutual Insurance Co., 423 F 2d 41, CCA 3, 1970. Ch 9, n 44.

Parke Davis and Company v. Stromstadt, 411 F 2d 1390, CCA 8, 1969. Ch 6, n 62.

Parkell v. Fitzporter, 256 SW 239, Mo 1923. Ch 10, n 71.

Parker v. Port Huron Hospital, 105 NW 2d 1, Mich 1960. Ch 5, n 71; Ch 5, n 76.

Parker v. Vaughan, 183 SE 2d 605, Ga 1971. Ch 10, n 117.

Pasquale v. Chandler, 215 NE 2d 319, Mass 1966. Ch 5, n 52.

Passey v. Budge, 38 P 2d 712, Utah 1934. Ch 5, n 35.

Patrick v. Sedwick, 391 P 2d 453, 413 P 2d 169, Alaska 1964. Ch 4, n 86; Ch 10, n 2.

Patterson v. Marcus, 265 Pac 222, Cal 1928. Ch 3, n 40.

State ex rel Paul v. Department of Public Welfare, 170 So 2d 549, La 1965. Ch 8, n 130.

Paull v. Zions First Natoinal Bank, 417 P 2d 759, Utah 1966. Ch 10, n 28.

Paulson v. Stocker, 4 NE 2d 609, Ohio 1935. Ch 3, n 42.

Pearce v. United States, 236 F Supp 431, DC Okla 1964. Ch 3, n 1.

Pearson v. Norman, 106 P 2d 361, Colo 1940. Ch 12, n 3.

Peck v. Towns Hospital, 89 NYS 2d 190, NY 1949. Ch 5, n 154; Ch 6, n 30.

Peddicord v. Lieser, 105 P 2d 5, Wash 1940. Ch 2, n 10.

Pederson v. Dumouchel, 431 P 2d 976, Wash 1967. Ch 1, n 43; Ch 2, n 68; Ch 7, n 74; Ch 12, n 19.

Pedesky v. Bleiberg, 59 Cal Rptr 294, Cal 1967. Ch 8, n 49.

Penaloza v. Baptist Memorial Hospital, 304 SW 2d 203, Tex 1957. Ch 5, n 147.

Pendergraft v. Royster, 166 SE 285, NC 1932. Ch 2, n 98; Ch 5, n 16.

Pendleton v. Burkhalter, 432 SW 2d 724, Tex 1968. Ch 9, n 86.

Pennison v. Provident Life Insurance Co., 154 So 2d 617, La 1963. Ch 9, n 39.

Pennsylvania State Board v. Schireson, 61 A 2d 343, Pa 1948. Ch 11, n 50.

Penn Tanker Company v. United States, 310 F Supp 613, DC Tex 1970. Ch 7, n 80; Ch 11, n 111.

Pensacola Sanitarium v. Wilkins, 67 So 124, Fla 1914. Ch 6, n 14.

People v. Edwards, 249 NYS 2d 325, NY 1964. Ch 1, n 73.

People v. Hunt, 147 Pac 476, Cal 1915. Ch 11, n 173.

People v. Long, 96 P 2d 354, Cal 1939. Ch 11, n 159.

People v. Lowe, 248 NE 2d 530, Ill 1969. Ch 1, n 93.

People v. McCaughan, 317 P 2d 974, Cal 1957. Ch 9, n 12.

People v. Phillips, 75 Cal Rptr 720, Cal 1969. Appealed to Federal Court as Phillips v. Pitchess, 451 F 2d 913, CCA 9, 1971. Ch 11, n 177.

People v. Pierson, 68 NE 243, NY 1903. Ch 1, n 73.

People v. Sorensen, 66 Cal Rptr 7, Cal 1968. Ch 8, n 113.

People to use of State Board of Health v. McCoy, 17 NE 786, Ill 1888. Ch 11, n 72.

Pepe v. Board of Regents, 295 NYS 2d 209, NY 1968. Ch 11, n 77.

Percifield v. Foutz, 285 P 2d 130, Nev 1955. Ch 5, n 43.

Perlmutter v. Beth David Hospital, 123 NE 2d 792, NY 1954. Ch 5, n 60.

Perry v. Hodgson, 148 SE 659, Ga 1929. Ch 8, n 54.

Peterson v. Hunt, 84 P 2d 999, Wash 1938. Ch 3, n 40.

Peterson v. Richards, 272 Pac 229, Utah 1928. Ch 6, n 50.

Peterson v. Roloff, 203 NW 2d 699, Wisc 1973. Ch 10, n 116.

Petterson v. Lynch, 299 NYS 2d 244, NY 1969. Ch 8, n 31.

Pfeifer v. Pfeifer, 280 P 2d 54, Cal 1955. Ch 8, n 135.

Phillips v. Wendorff, 243 NW 525, Iowa 1932. Ch 10, n 64.

Piedmont Hospital v. Truitt, 172 SE 237, Ga 1933. Ch 10, n 74.

Pike v. Honsinger, 49 NE 760, NY 1898. Ch 2, n 5; Ch 4, n 137.

Pindar v. Parke Davis and Co., 337 NYS 2d 452, NY 1972. Ch 12, n 106.

Pinsker v. Pacific Coast Society of Orthodontists, 81 Cal Rptr 623, Cal 1969. Ch 11, n 85.

Piper v. Halford, 25 So 2d 264, Ala 1946. Ch 10, n 60.

Piper v. Menifee, 51 Ky 465, 1851. Ch 4, n 125.

Pitzenberger v. Schnack, 245 Iowa 745, 1932. Ch 8, n 126.

Podvin v. Eickhorst, 128 NW 2d 523, Mich 1964. Ch 1, n 161.

Pogue v. Hospital Authority of DeKalb County, 170 SE 2d 53, Ga 1969. Ch 7, n 69.

Poltera v. Garlington, 489 P 2d 334, Colo 1971. Ch 10, n 65.

Poor Sisters of St. Francis v. Long, 230 SW 2d 659, Tenn 1950. Ch 4, n 63.

Porter Memorial Hospital v. Harvey, 279 NE 2d 583, Ind 1972. Ch 11, n 125.

Porter v. Patterson, 129 SE 2d 70, Ga 1962. Ch 6, n 47.

Porter v. Powell, 44 NW 295, Iowa 1890. Ch 1, n 112.

Poudre Valley Hospital District v. Heckart, 491 P 2d 984, Colo 1971. Ch 1, n 123.

Powell v. Fidelity Casualty Company, 185 So 2d 324, La 1966. Ch 5, n 85.

Powell v. Risser, 99 A 2d 454, Pa 1953. Ch 4, n 34; Ch 5, n 208.

Powell v. Troland, 183 SE 2d 184, Va 1971. Ch 10, n 113.

Poweshiek County National Bank v. Nationwide Mutual Insurance Co., 156 NW 2d 671, Iowa 1968. Ch 12, n 109.

Pratt v. Davis, 79 NE 562, Ill 1906. Ch 8, n 3.

President and Directors of Georgetown College v. Hughes, 130 F 2d 810, DC DC 1942. Ch 10, n 167.

Previn v. Tenacre, 70 F 2d 389, CCA 3, 1933. Ch 9, n 9.

Prewett v. Philpot, 107 So 880, Miss 1926. Ch 5, n 17.

Price v. Neyland, 320 F 2d 674, CA DC 1963. Ch 2, n 78; Ch 3, n 86; Ch 5, n 81.

Prosch v. Baxley, 345 F Supp 1063, DC Ala 1972. Ch 11, n 5; Ch 11, n 34.

Public Administrator of New York County v. New York, 177 NY 2d 95, NY 1958. Ch 6, n 45.

Puffinbarger v. Day, 24 Cal Rptr 533, Cal 1962. Ch 4, n 147; Ch 10, n 4.

Pugh v. Swiontek, 253 NE 2d 3, Ill 1969. Ch 2, n 63; Ch 3, n 33.

Purcell v. Zimbelman, 500 P 2d 335, Ariz 1972. Ch 7, n 82.

Purchase v. Seelye, 121 NE 413, Mass 1918. Ch 10, n 75.

Putensen v. Clay Adams, Inc., 91 Cal Rptr 319, Cal 1970. Ch 6, n 76; Ch 8, n 12.

Putnam v. Erie City Manufacturing Company, 338 F 2d 911, CCA 5, 1964. Ch 6, n 72.

Quillen v. Skaggs, 25 SW 2d 33, Ky 1930. Ch 6, n 14.

Quinley v. Cocke, 192 SW 2d 992, Tenn 1946. Ch 5, n 202.

Quintal v. Laurel Grove Hospital, 397 P 2d 161, Cal 1964. Ch 4, n 43; Ch 5, n 133.

Rabasco v. New Rochelle Hospital, 44 NYS 2d 293, NY 1943. Ch 6, n 12.

Rabon v. Rowan Memorial Hospital, 152 SE 2d 485, NC 1967. Ch 10, n 166.

Ragin v. Zimmerman, 276 Pac 107, Cal 1929. Ch 5, n 101.

Ragsdale v. Arkansas, 432 SW 2d 11, Ark 1968. Ch 1, n 105.

Rahn v. United States, 222 F Supp 775, DC Ga 1963. Ch 2, n 31.

Rainer v. Grossman, 107 Cal Rptr 469, Cal 1973. Ch 1, n 17.

Raleigh–Fitkin Memorial Hospital v. Anderson, 201 A 2d 537, NJ 1964. Ch 1, n 64.

Ramberg v. Morgan, 218 NW 492, Iowa 1928. Ch 2, n 28.

Ramsey v. Ciccone, 310 F Supp 600, DC Mo 1970. Ch 1, n 47; Ch 1, n 56.

Rannard v. Lockhead Aircraft 157 P 2d 1, Cal 1945. Ch 1, n 83.

Raschelbach v. Benincasa, 372 SW 2d 120, Mo 1963. Ch 5, n 139.

In re Rathburn, 266 A 2d 423, Vt 1970. Ch 8, n 129.

Rauhe v. Langeland Memorial Chapel, Inc. 205 NW 2d 313, Mich 1973. Ch 8, n 80.

Ray v. Scheibert, 484 SW 2d 63, Tenn 1972. Ch 10, n 138.

Ray v. Wagner, 176 NW 2d 101, Minn 1970. Ch 4, n 134.

Reams v. Florida, 279 So 2d 839, Fla 1973. Ch 11, n 36.

Reddick v. Board of Regents, 297 NYS 2d 339, NY 1969. Ch 11, n 18; Ch 11, n 35.

Redding v. United States, 196 F Supp 871, DC Ark 1961. Ch 5, n 68.

Reder v. Hanson, 338 F 2d 244, CCA 8, 1964. Ch 2, n 85.

Reed v. Church, 8 SE 2d 285, Va 1940. Ch 2, n 40; Ch 4, n 34; Ch 5, n 186.

Reed v. Laughlin, 58 SW 2d 440, Mo 1933. Ch 12, n 58.

Reeves v. North Broward Hospital, 191 So 2d 307, Fla 1966. Ch 1, n 29; Ch 3, n 26; Ch 7, n 60.

Reis v. Reinard, 117 P 2d 386, Cal 1941. Ch 2, n 52.

Renrick v. City of Newark, 181 A 2d 24, NJ 1962. Ch 5, n 165.

Retelle v. Sullivan, 211 NW 756, Wisc 1927. Ch 10, n 72.

Rewis v. United States, 369 F 2d 595, CCA 5, 1966. Ch 3, n 5.

Rhodes v. United States, 369 F 2d 595, CCA 5, 1966. Ch 3, n 5.

Rhodes v. Lamar, 292 Pac 335, Okla 1930. Ch 5, n 21.

Rhodes v. Moore, 398 P 2d 189, Ore 1965. Ch 6, n 42.

Rice v. Rinaldo, 119 NE 2d 657, Ohio 1951. Ch 1, n 23.

In re Richardson, 284 So 2d 185, La 1973. Ch 8, n 84.

Richardson v. Denneen, 82 NYS 2d 623, NY 1947. Ch 7, n 33.

Ricks v. Budge, 64 P 2d 208, Utah 1937. Ch 12, n 37.

Riggs v. Christie, 173 NE 2d 610, Mass 1961. Ch 3, n 94; Ch 12, n 49.

Rilcoff v. State Board of Medical Examiners, 203 P 2d 844, Cal 1949. Ch 1, n 34; Ch 11, n 85.

Rinaldo v. Board of Medical Examiners, 42 P 2d 724, Cal 1935. Ch 11, n 50.

Riste v. General Electric Corporation, 289 P 2d 338, Wash 1955. Ch 1, n 80.

Ritchey v. West, 23 Ill 329, Ill 1860. Ch 1, n 7.

Rivers v. Union Carbide Corporation, 426 F 2d 633, CCA 3, 1970. Ch 12, n 115.

Roberts v. Wood, 206 F Supp 579, DC Ala 1962. Ch 8, n 16; Ch 12, n 51.

Robins v. Finestone, 127 NE 2d 330, NY 1955.

Robinson v. Campbell, 97 SE 2d 544, Ga 1957. Ch 10, n 43.

Robinson v. Gatti, 184 NE 2d 509, Ohio 1961. Ch 3, n 46.

Robinson v. Wirts, 127 A 2d 706, Pa 1956. Ch 8, n 51.

Rockett v. Texas State Board of Medical Examiners, 287 SW 2d 190, Tex 1956. Ch 11, n 83.

Rockhill v. Pollard, 485 P 2d 28, Ore 1971. Ch 1, n 33.

Rockwell v. Stone, 173 A 2d 48, Pa 1961. Ch 7, n 57.

Rodriguez v. Columbus Hospital, 326 NYS 2d 439, NY 1971. Ch 5, n 159.

Roe v. Wade, 410 US 113, 1973. Ch 1, n 132.

Rogers v. Lawson, 170 F 2d 157, DC CA 1948. Ch 1, n 159; Ch 12, n 85.

Rogers v. United States, 216 F Supp 1, DC Ohio 1963. Ch 3, n 116.

Petition of Rohrer, 230 NE 2d 915, Mass 1967. Ch 8, n 90.

Rose v. Friddell, 423 SW 2d 658, Tex 1967. Ch 4, n 72 .

Rose v. Raleigh–Fitkin Memorial Hospital, 57 A 2d 29, NJ 1948. Ch 6, n 109.

Rosenberg v. Feigin, 260 P 2d 143, Cal 1953. Ch 1, n 137.

Rosner v. Eden Township Hospital District, 375 P 2d 431, Cal 1962. Ch 11, n 128.

Rosner v. Peninsula Hospital District, 36 Rptr 332, Cal 1964. Ch 11, n 131.

Ross v. Hodges, 234 So 2d 905, Miss 1970. Ch 8, n 32.

Ross v. Sher, 483 SW 2d 297, Tex 1972. Ch 7, n 24.

Rostron v. Klein, 178 NW 2d 675, Mich 1970. Ch 3, n 55.

Rotan v. Greenbaum, 273 F 2d 830, CA DC 1959. Ch 4, n 10; Ch 5, n 152; Ch 10, n 8.

Rothman v. Silber, 216 A 2d 18, NJ 1966. Ch 10, n 127.

Rouse v. Cameron, 373 F 2d 451, CA DC 1966. Ch 4, n 115; Ch 8, n 91.

Routen v. McGehee, 186 SW 2d 779, Ark 1945. Ch 5, n 99.

Rudick v. Prineville Memorial Hospital, 319 F 2d 764, CCA 9, 1963. Ch 2, n 89.

Rule v. Cheeseman, 317 P 2d 472, Kans 1957, Ch 1, n 8; Ch 2, n 73.

Runyan v. Goodrum, 228 SW 397, Ark 1921. Ch 5, n 95.

Rural Educational Association v. Busch, 298 SW 2d 761, Tenn 1956. Ch 5, n 9.

Russell v. Community Blood Bank, 185 So 2d 749, Fla 1966. Ch 5, n 61.

Russell v. Jackson, 221 P 2d 516, Wash 1950. Ch 8, n 57.

Ruth v. Dight, 453 P 2d 631, Wash 1969. Ch 10, n 125.

Ruvio v. North Broward Hospital District, 186 So 2d 45, Fla 1966. Ch 12, n 55.

Rytkonen v. Lojacono, 257 NW 703, Mich 1934. Ch 1, n 137.

Safian v. Aetna Life Inc. Co., 24 NYS 2d 92, NY 1940. Ch 1, n 10.

Sage-Allen Co., Inc. v. Wheeler, 179 Atl 195, Conn 1935. Ch 11, n 90.

St. Luke's Hospital Association v. Long, 240 P 2d 917, Colo 1952. Ch 6, n 36.

St. Pierre v. New York, 48 NYS 2d 613, NY 1944. Ch 9, n 9.

St. Vincent Hospital v. Stine, 144 NE 537, Ind 1924. Ch 10, n 161.

Salgo v. Leland Stanford Board of Trustees, 317 P 2d 170, Cal 1957. Ch 4, n 53; Ch 7, n 32; Ch 8, n 11.

In re Sampson, 317 NYS 2d 641, NY 1970. Ch 1, n 72.

Sampson v. Holton, 185 NW 2d 216, Iowa 1971. Ch 8, n 122.

Sams v. Curfman, 137 P 2d 1017, Colo 1943. Ch 10, n 65.

Sams v. Ohio Valley General Hospital Association, 413 F 2d 826, CCA 4, 1969. Ch 11, n 119.

Sanchez v. Rodriguez, 38 Cal Rptr 110, Cal 1964. Ch 4, n 83; Ch 5, n 165.

Sanzari v. Rosenfeld, 167 A 2d 625, NJ 1961. Ch 5, n 132.

Sapero v. State Board of Medical Examiners, 11 P 2d 555, Colo 1932. Ch 11, n 73.

Sas v. Maryland, 334 F 2d 506, CCA 4, 1964. Ch 4, n 120.

Saunders v. Lischkoff, 188 So 815, Fla 1939. Ch 1, n 158; Ch 3, n 18.

Sawyer v. Jewish Chronic Disease Hospital, 234 NYS 2d 372, NY 1962. Ch 5, n 134.

Sawyer v. Sigler, 445 F 2d 818, CCA 8, 1971. Ch 1, n 50.

Scardina v. Colleti, 211 NE 2d 762, Ill 1965. Ch 4, n 96.

Schagrin v. Wilmington Medical Center, 304 A 2d 61, Del 1973. Ch 7, n 71.

Schessler v. Keck, 271 P 2d 588, Cal 1954. Ch 9, n 27.

Schireson v. State Board of Medical Examiners of New Jersey, 28 A 2d 879, NJ 1942. Ch 11, n 12; Ch 11, n 47.

Schireson v. Walsh, 187 NE 921, Ill 1933. Ch 11, n 49.

Schirey v. Schlemmer, 223 NE 2d 759, Ind 1967. Ch 10, n 18.

Schloendorff v. Society of New York Hospital, 105 NE 92, NY 1914. Ch 8, n 4.

Schmerber v. California, 384 U.S. 757, 1966, Ch 1, n 96.

Schneider v. Little Co., 151 NW 587, 588, Mich 1915. Ch 2, n 2.

Schooler v. Tarrant County Medical Society, 457 SW 2d 644, Tex 1970. Ch 11, n 96.

In re adoption of Schroetter, 67 Cal Rptr 819, Cal 1968. Ch 8, n 123.

Schulman v. Washington Hospital Center, 222 F Supp 59, DC DC 1963. Ch 11,
    n 145.

Schulz v. Feigal, 142 NW 2d 84, Minn 1966. Ch 5, n 145; Ch 7, n 2.

Schuster v. St. Vincent Hospital, 172 NW 2d 421, Wisc 1969. Ch 6, n 96; Ch 10,
    n 32.

Schwalb v. Connely, 179 P 2d 667, Colo 1947. Ch 8, n 74.

Schwartz v. Thiele, 51 Cal Rptr 767, Cal 1966. Ch 9, n 25.

Schwartz v. United States, 226 F Supp 84 DC DC 1964. Ch 4, n 106.

Schwartz v. United States, 230 F Supp 536, DC Pa 1964. Ch 3, n 13; Ch 4, n 11.

Schyman v. Department of Registration, 133 NE 2d 551, Ill 1956. Ch 11, n 20.

Scott v. McPheeters, 92 P 2d 678, Cal 1939. Ch 4, n 58.

Scott v. Salem County Memorial Hospital, 280 A 2d 843, NJ 1971. Ch 4, n 80.

Scott v. Wilson, 396 SW 2d 532, Tex 1965. Ch 8, n 31.

Seanor v. Browne, 7 P 2d 627, Okla 1932. Ch 10, n 150.

In re Estate of Searchill, 157 NW 2d 788, Mich 1968. Ch 12, n 114.

Seidenberg v. New Mexico Board of Medical Examiners, 452 P 2d 469, NM 1969.
    Ch 11, n 3; Ch 11, n 51.

Sellers v. Edwards, 265 So 2d 438, Ala 1972. Ch 10, n 118.

Seneris v. Haas, 291 P 2d 915, Cal 1955. Ch 2, n 96; Ch 5, n 126.

Shaffer v. Jennings, 314 F Supp 588, DC Pa 1970. Ch 1, n 51.

Shannon v. Ramsey, 193 NE 235, Mass 1934. Ch 12, n 43.

Sharpe v. Pugh, 155 SE 2d 108, NC 1967. Ch 2, n 47; Ch 4, n 146; Ch 5, n 192;
    Ch 8, n 21.

Shea v. Phillips. 98 SE 2d 552, Ga 1957. Ch 5, n 39.

Shearin v. Lloyd, 98 SE 2d 508, NC 1957. Ch 5, n 4.

Shepherd v. McGinnis, 131 NW 2d 475, Iowa 1964. Ch 6, n 49.

Sheridan v. Quarrier, 16 A 2d 479, Conn 1940. Ch 12, n 47.

Sherman v. Board of Regents, 266 NYS 2d 39, NY 1966. Ch 11, n 60.

Sherman v. Hartman, 290 P 2d 894, Cal 1955, Ch 5, n 84.

Sherman v. McEntire, 179 P 2d 797, Utah 1947. Ch 11, n 27.

Shetter v. Rochelle, 409 P 2d 74, Ariz 1965. Ch 8, n 40.

Shiffman v. Manhattan Eye, Ear and Throat Hospital, 314 NYS 2d 823, NY 1970.
    Ch 11, n 144.

Shoemaker v. Friedberg, 183 P 2d 318, Cal 1947. Ch 9, n 38.

Sibert v. Boger, 260 SW 2d 569, Mo 1953. Ch 3, n 98.

Silver v. Castleman Memorial Hospital, 497 P 2d 564, Hawaii 1972. Ch 11, n 134;
    Ch 11, n 149.

Silverhart v. Mount Zion Hospital, 98 Cal Rptr 187, Cal 1971. Ch 6, n 27.

Silvers v. Wesson, 266 P 2d 169, Cal 1954. Ch 4, n 56.

Silverson v. Weber, 372 P 2d 97, Cal 1962. Ch 4, n 38.

Simmons v. Wilder, 169 SE 2d 480, NC 1969. Ch 10, n 87.

Simonsen v. Swenson, 177 NW 831, Neb 1920. Ch 9, n 32.

Simpkins v. Moses T. Cone Memorial Hospital, 323 F 2d 959, CCA 4, 1963. Ch 11, n 122.

Sims v. Callahan, 112 So 2d 776, Ala 1959. Ch 3, n 109.

Sinatra v. National X-ray Products Corporation, 141 A 2d 28, NJ 1958. Ch 6, n 75.

Sinclair v. Brunson, 180 NW 358, Mich 1920. Ch 12, n 23.

Singer v. Bossingham, 188 NW 155, Minn 1922. Ch 12, n 16.

Sinkey v. Surgical Associates, 186 NW 2d 658, Iowa 1971. Ch 3, n 93.

Sinz v. Owens, 205 P 2d 3, Cal 1949. Ch 2, n 66.

Sisler v. Jackson, 460 P 2d 903, Okla 1969. Ch 8, n 30.

Sivertson v. New York, 252 NYS 2d 623, NY 1964. Ch 6, n 40.

Skillings v. Allen, 180 NW 916, Minn 1921. Ch 4, n 124.

Skinner v. Oklahoma, 316 U.S. 535, 1942. Ch 8, n 111.

Skodge v. Hardy, 288 P 2d 471, Wash 1955. Ch 1, n 155; Ch 12, n 22; Ch 12, n 87.

Sligar v. Tucker, 267 So 2d 54, Fla 1972. Ch 12, n 104.

Smart v. Kansas City, 105 SW 709, Mo 1907, Ch 1, n 16.

In re Smith, 295 A 2d 238, Md 1972. Ch 1, n 135.

Smith v. Baker, 326 F Supp 787, DC Mo 1970. Ch 1, n 55.

Smith v. Beard, 110 P 2d 260, Wyo 1941. Ch 7, n 23.

Smith v. Children's Hospital of Michigan, 189 NW 2d 753, Mich 1971. Ch 1, n 39.

Smith v. DiCara, 329 F Supp 439, DC NY 1971. Ch 9, n 21.

Smith v. Kern County Medical Association, 120 P 2d 874, Cal 1942. Ch 11, n 100.

Smith v. Mallinckrodt Chemical Works, 251 SW 155, Mo 1923. Ch 2, n 33.

State ex rel Smith v. Schaffer, 270 Pac 604, Kans 1928. Ch 8, n 110.

Smith v. Schneckloth, 414 F 2d 680, CCA 9, 1969. Ch 1, n 52.

Smith, v. Seibley, 431 P 2d 719, Wash 1967. Ch 1, n 120; Ch 1, n 151.

Smith v. Shankman, 25 Cal Rptr 195, Cal 1962. Ch 3, n 21.

Smith v. Thornhill, 25 SW 2d 597, Tex 1930. Ch 1, n 1.

Smith v. Wharton, 154 SE 12, NC 1930. Ch 12, n 39.

Smith v. Wright, 305 P 2d 810, Kans 1957. Ch 3, n 33.

Smith v. Yohe, 194 A 2d 167, Pa 1963. Ch 3, n 30; Ch 3, n 50.

Snyder v. Pantaleo, 122 A 2d 21, Conn 1956. Ch 3, n 10.

Sobotta v. Vogel, 194 NW 2d 564, Mich 1971. Ch 10, n 83.

Solgaard v. Guy F. Atkinson Co. 491 P 2d 821, Cal 1971. Ch 1, n 36.

Solorio v. Lampros, 82 Cal Rptr 753, Cal 1969. Ch 3, n 70.

Somma v. United States, 180 F Supp 519, DC Pa 1960. Ch 10, n 26.

State ex rel Sorensen v. Lake, 236 NW 762, Neb 1931. Ch 11, n 13.

Sos v. Board of Regents, 281 NYS 2d 831, NY 1967. Ch 11, n 14.

Sosa v. Board of Managers of Va Verde Memorial Hospital, 437 F 2d 173, CCA 5, 1971. Ch 11, n 129.

Stokes v. Dailey, 85 NW 2d 745, ND 1957. Ch 3, n 10.

Stone v. Proctor, 131 SE 2d 297, NC 1963. Ch 5, n 205.

Stottlemire v. Cawood, 213 F Supp 897, DC DC 1963. Ch 5, n 194; Ch 6, n 60.

Stowers v. Wolodzko, 191 NW 2d 355, Mich 1971. Ch 8, n 101; Ch 9, n 89.

Strance v. New Mexico Board of Medical Examiners, 487 P 2d 1085, NM 1971. Ch 11, n 22; Ch 11, n 79.

Strnad v. Strnad, 78 NYS 2d 390, NY 1948. Ch 8, n 114.

People ex rel Strohsahl v. Strohsahl, 222 NYS 319, NY 1927. Ch 8, n 127.

Strunk v. Strunk, 445 SW 2d 145, Ky 1969. Ch 8, n 85.

Stuck v. Board of Medical Examiners, 211 P 2d 389, Cal 1949. Ch 11, n 27.

Stumper v. Kimel, 260 A 2d 526, NJ 1970. Ch 7, n 38.

Stundon v. Stadnik, 469 P 2d 16, Wyo 1970. Ch 4, n 89.

Suburban Hospital Association v. Mewhinney, 187 A 2d 671, Md 1963. Ch 1, n 3.

Sugaya v. Morton, 40 P 2d 581, Cal 1935. Ch 5, n 10.

Sukeforth v. Thegan, 256 A 2d 162, Maine 1969. Ch 1, n 154.

Sulack v. Miller Hospital, 165 NW 2d 207, Minn 1969. Ch 6, n 104.

Sullivan v. Montgomery, 279 NYS 575, NY 1935. Ch 1, n 113; Ch 1, n 120.

Sullivan v. O'Connor, 296 NE 2d 183, Mass 1973. Ch 4, n 93.

Sussman v. Overlook Hospital, 231 A 2d 389, NJ 1967. Ch 11, n 120.

Swank v. Halivopoulos, 260 A 2d 240, NJ 1969. Ch 1, n 108.

Swanson v. Hill, 166 F Supp 296, DC ND 1958. Ch 5, n 27; Ch 10, n 58.

Sweeny v. Erving, 228 US 233, 1913. Ch 5, n 99.

Swenson v. Swenson, 227 SW 2d 103, Mo 1950. Ch 1, n 117.

Swigerd v. Ortonville Hospital, 75 NW 2d 217, Minn 1956. Ch 6, n 19.

Swope v. Printz, 468 SW 2d 34, Mo 1971. Ch 10, n 136.

Sylvia v. Gobeille, 220 A 2d 222, RI 1966. Ch 1, n 107.

Synnott v. Midway Hospital, 178 NW 2d 211, Minn 1970. Ch 5, n 108.

Tabor v. Scobee, 254 SW 2d 474, Ky 1952. Ch 8, n 56.

Tadlock v. Lloyd, 173 Pac 200, Colo 1918. Ch 4, n 16; Ch 12, n 26.

Tady v. Warta, 196 NW 901, Neb 1924. Ch 5, n 34.

Tangora v. Matanky, 42 Cal Rptr 348, Cal 1964. Ch 3, n 11; Ch 5, n 182.

Tanner v. Espey, 190 NE 229, Ohio 1934. Ch 10, n 65.

Tarasoff v. Regents of the University of California, 108 Cal Rptr 878, Cal 1972. Ch 9, n 33.

Taylor v. Beekman Hospital, 62 NYS 2d 637, NY 1946. Ch 6, n 12.

Taylor v. Glotfelty, 201 F 2d 51, CCA 6, 1952. Ch 9, n 25.

Taylor v. Milton, 92 NW 2d 57, Mich 1958. Ch 5, n 43.

Taylor v. St. Vincent's Hospital, 369 F Supp 948, DC Mont, 1973. Ch 1, n 149.

Teig v. St. John's Hospital, 387 P 2d 527, Wash 1963. Ch 2, n 57.

Temple v. New York, 65 NYS 2d 50, 1946. Ch 9, n 9.

Terrill v. Harbin, 376 SW 2d 945, Tex 1964. Ch 8, n 66.

Tessier v. United States, 164 F Supp 779, DC Mass 1958, Ch 1, n 20.

Tveldt v. Haugen, 294 NW 183, ND 1940. Ch 1, n 2; Ch 2, n 31; Ch 2, n 69.

Unick v. Kessler Memorial Hospital, 257 A 2d 134, NJ 1969. Ch 12, n 103.

Union Carbide and Carbon Corporation v. Stapleton, 237 F 2d 229, CCA 6, 1956. Ch 1, n 82.

United States v. Doremus, 249 US 86, 1919. Ch 1, n 77.

United States v. Gray, 99 F 2d 239, CCA 10, 1952. Ch 4, n 103.

United States v. Morin, 229 F 2d 824, CCA 9, 1956. Ch 7, n 18; Ch 12, n 81.

United States v. Muniz, 374 US 150, 1963. Ch 1, n 61.

United States v. Ramzy, 446 F 2d 1184, CCA 5, 1971. Ch 1, n 76.

United States v. Warren, 453 F 2d 738, CCA 2, 1972. Ch 1, n 76.

Updegraff v. City of Ottumwa, 226 NW 928, Iowa 1939. Ch 10, n 23.

Urdang v. Mahrer, 158 NE 2d 902, Ohio 1959. Ch 6, n 85.

Urritia v. Patino, 297 SW 512, Tex 1928. Ch 1, n 158; Ch 12, n 85.

Usen v. Usen, 269 NE 2d 442, Mass 1971. Ch 8, n 124.

Uter v. Bone and Joint Clinic, 192 So 2d 100, La 1966. Ch 4, n 77.

Valdez v. Percy, 217 P 2d 422, Cal 1950. Ch 1, n 19; Ch 3, n 67; Ch 8, n 54; Ch 10, n 51.

Valentine v. Kaiser Foundation Hospitals, 12 Cal Rptr 26, Cal 1961. Ch 2, n 76.

Van Skike v. Potter, 73 NW 295, Neb 1897, Ch 5, n 53; Ch 12, n 50.

Vanaman v. Milford Memorial Hospital, 272 A 2d 718, Del 1970. Ch 7, n 77.

Vanderbilt University v. Henderson, 127 SW 284, Tenn 1938. Ch 10, n 156.

Vann v. Harden, 47 SE 2d 314, Va 1948. Ch 1, n 9; Ch 4, n 71; Ch 12, n 73.

Veals v. Ciccone, 281 F Supp 1017, DC Mo 1968. Ch 1, n 58.

Vergott v. Deseret Pharmaceutical Company, 463 F 2d 12, CCA 5, 1972. Ch 5, n 38; Ch 6, n 71.

Vidrine v. Mayes, 127 So 2d 809, La 1961. Ch 1, n 156; Ch 12, n 89.

Vigil v. Herman, 424 P 2d 159, Ariz 1967. Ch 3, n 60.

Vigil v. Rice, 397 P 2d 719, NM 1964. Ch 9, n 18.

Volk v. City of New York, 30 NE 2d 596, NY 1940. Ch 5, n 153.

Von Blumenthal v. Cassola, 3 NYS 2d 246, 6 NYS 2d 342, NY 1938. Ch 10, n 84.

Voss v. Bridwell, 364 P 2d 955, Kans 1961. Ch 7, n 58.

Vuitch v. Hardy, 473 F 2d 1370, CCA 4, 1973. Ch 11, n 29.

Waddle v. Sutherland, 126 So 201, Miss 1930. Ch 5, n 97.

Wade v. Bethesda Hospital, 337 F Supp 671, DC Ohio 1971. Ch 8, n 109.

Walker v. Distler, 296 P 2d 452, Idaho 1956. Ch 5, n 125.

Walker v. Rynd, 280 P 2d 259, Wash 1955. Ch 6, n 35.

Wall v. Brim, 138 F 2d 478, CCA 5, 1943. Ch 8, n 8.

People ex rel Wallace x. Labrenz, 104 NE 2d 769, Ill 1952. Ch 1, n 69.

Wallace v. LaVine, 97 P 2d 879, Cal 1940. Ch 2, n 8.

Wallace v. University Hospitals of Cleveland, 164 NE 2d 917, Ohio 1959. Ch 12, n 99.

Wallace v. Yudelson, 244 Ill App 320, 1927. Ch 2, n 35.

Wallstedt v. Swedish Hospital, 19 NW 2d 426, Minn 1945. Ch 6, n 21.

Wangel v. Pangman, Trial Court decision, Los Angeles County, Cal, Docket # WEC 9141, 1971. Ch 4, n 92.

Ware v. Culp, 74 P 2d 283, Cal 1937. Ch 6, n 20; Ch 7, n 62.

Warwick v. Bliss, 195 NW 501, SD 1923. Ch 12, n 69.

Washington v. Gile, 35 Pac 417, Wash 1894. Ch 11, n 164.

Washington v. Kuljis, 422 P 2d 480, Wash 1967. Ch 1, n 104.

Washington v. White, 433 P 2d 682, Wash 1967. Ch 12, n 112.

Wassermann v. Board of Regents, 182 NE 2d 264, NY 1962, Ch 11, n 52.

Waukesha Memorial Hospital v. Baird, 173 NW 2d 700, Wisc 1970. Ch 1, n 102.

Weary v. Baylor University Hospital, 360 SW 2d 895, Tex 1963. Ch 11, n 144.

Weatherman v. White, 179 SE 2d 134, NC 1971. Ch 3, n 99.

State ex rel Weathers v. Davis, 196 So 487, Fla 1940. Ch 11, n 12.

Webb v. Jorns, 488 SW 2d 407, Tex 1972. Ch 5, n 128.

Webb v. Texas, 467 SW 2d 449, Tex 1971. Ch 1, n 92.

Wecker v. Kilmer, 294 NE 2d 132, Ind 1973. Ch 10, n 89.

Weeks v. Latter Day Saints Hospital, 418 F 2d 1035, CCA 10, 1969. Ch 6, n 17.

Weiner v. Board of Regents, 158 NYS 2d 730, NY 1956. Ch 11, n 32.

Weintraub v. Rosen, 93 F 2d 544, CCA 7, 1937. Ch 10, n 61.

Weiser v. Hampton, 445 SW 2d 224, Tex 1969. Ch 8, n 16.

Weiss v. Board of Regents, 265 NYS 2d 314, NY 1965. Ch 11, n 30.

Weiss v. Rubin, 173 NE 2d 791, NY 1961. Ch 5, n 79.

Welch v. Frisbie Memorial Hospital, 9 A 2d 761, NH 1939. Ch 3, n 92; Ch 12, n 53.

Wellander v. Brooklyn Hospital, 174 NYS 2d 107, NY 1958. Ch 10, n 81.

Welsh v. Mercy Hospital, 151 P 2d 17, Cal 1944. Ch 6, n 37.

Wendland v. Wendland, 138 NW 2d 185, Wisc 1965. Ch 8, n 134.

West v. West, 170 So 2d 160, La 1964. Ch 8, n 134.

West Coast Hospital Association v. Hoare, 64 So 2d 293, Fla 1953. Ch 11, n 117.

Wheatley v. Heideman, 102 NW 2d 343, Iowa 1960. Ch 3, n 2.

Wheeler v. Barker, 208 P 2d 68, Cal 1949. Ch 8, n 51.

White v. Andrew, 197 Pac 564, Colo 1921. Ch 11, n 70.

White v. Matthews, 223 NYS 415, NY 1927. Ch 10, n 111.

White v. United States, 399 F 2d 813, CCA 8, 1968. Ch 1, n 76.

Whitfield v. Daniel Construction Co., 83 SE 2d 460, SC 1954. Ch 2, n 50; Ch 4, n 141; Ch 5, n 195.

Whitfield v. Whittaker Memorial Hospital, 169 SE 2d 563, Va 1969. Ch 2, n 87; Ch 5, n 114; Ch 5, n 135.

Whitree v. New York, 290 NYS 2d 486, NY 1968. Ch 3, n 90; Ch 4, n 117; Ch 9, n 95.

Wickham v. North American Rockwell Corporation, 87 Cal Rptr 563, Cal 1970. Ch 7, n 89.

Wilder v. Edwards, 173 SE 2d 72, NC 1970. Ch 12, n 115.

Willey v. Willey, 115 NW 2d 833, Iowa 1962. Ch 8, n 131.

Williams v. Chamberlain, 316 SW 2d 505, Mo 1958. Ch 2, n 57; Ch 5, n 31; Ch 5, n 49.

Williams v. Hospital Authority of Hall County, 168 SE 2d 336, Ga 1969. Ch 1, n 39.

Williams v. Marini, 162 Atl 796, Vt 1932. Ch 2, n 52; Ch 4, n 148; Ch 10, n 44.

Williams v. Menehan, 379 P 2d 292, Kans 1963. Ch 8, n 32.

Williams v. Orange Memorial Hospital Association, 202 So 2d 859, Fla 1967. Ch 6, n 34.

Williams v. Wurdemann, 128 Pac 639, Wash 1912. Ch 10, n 20.

Williams v. Vanderhoven, 482 P 2d 55, NM 1971. Ch 4, n 81.

Willis v. White, 310 F Supp 205, DC La 1970. Ch 1, n 47.

Wilkinson v. Harrington, 243 A 2d 745, RI 1968. Ch 5, n 91.

Wilkinson v. Vesey, 295 A 2d 676, RI 1972. Ch 8, n 38.

Wilson v. Corbin, 41 NW 2d 702, Iowa 1950. Ch 2, n 34.

Wilson v. Hungate, 434 SW 2d 580, Mo 1968. Ch 1, n 87; Ch 7, n 90; Ch 10, n 112.

Wilson v. Martin Memorial Hospital, 61 SE 2d 102, NC 1950. Ch 3, n 75; Ch 7, n 14; Ch 12, n 78.

Wilt v. McCallum, 253 SW 156, Mo 1923. Ch 5, n 119.

Wimer v. Miller, 383 P 2d 1005, Ore 1963. Ch 10, n 111.

Winik v. Jewish Hospital of Brooklyn, 293 NE 2d 95, NY 1972. Ch 3, n 120.

Winters v. Miller, 446 F 2d 65, CCA 2, 1971. Ch 8, n 103; Ch 9, n 4.

Winthral v. Callison Memorial Hospital, Cal Super Ct, San Francisco County, Docket #582565, 1972. Ch 6, n 31.

Wohlert v. Seibert, 23 Pa Sup Ct 213, 1903. Ch 2, n 30.

Wojcik v. Aluminum Company of America, 183 NYS 2d 351, NY 1959. Ch 4, n 122.

Wolfe v. Virusky, 306 F Supp 519, DC Ga 1969. Ch 10, n 147.

Wolfsmith v. Marsh, 337 P 2d 70, Cal 1959. Ch 5, n 138; Ch 7, n 19.

Woodard v. Porter Hospital, 217 A 2d 37, Vt 1966. Ch 11, n 144; Ch 11, n 157.

Woodbury v. McKinnon, 447 F 2d 839, CCA 5, 1971. Ch 11, n 148; Ch 11, n 154.

Woods v. Brumlop, 377 P 2d 520, NM 1962. Ch 5, n 200; Ch 8, n 19; Ch 9, n 64.

Wooten v. Curry, 362 SW 2d 820, Tenn 1961. Ch 4, n 133; Ch 12, n 59.

Woronka v. Sewall, 69 NE 2d 581, Mass 1946. Ch 4, n 48.

Wyatt v. Cerf, 149 P 2d 309, Cal 1944. Ch 11, n 71; Ch 11, n 106.

Wyatt v. Stickney, 325 F Supp 781, DC Ala 1971. Ch 4, n 120; Ch 8, n 94.

Yarborough v. Yarborough, 290 US 202, 1933. Ch 1, n 112.

Yeager v. Dunnavan, 174 P 2d 755, Wash 1946. Ch 5, n 131.

Yeargin v. Hamilton Memorial Hospital, 195 SE 2d 8, Ga 1972. Ch 1, n 26; Ch 11, n 132.

Yeates v. Harms, 401 P 2d 659, Kans 1965. Ch 8, n 48.

Yerzy v. Levine, 260 A 2d 533, NJ 1970. Ch 4, n 82.

In re Appointment of a Guardian of the Person of Maida Yetter, Docket #1973-533, Pa Ct Common Pleas, Northampton Co Pa, 1973. Ch 1, n 62; Ch 8, n 42.

Yorston v. Pennell, 153 A 2d 255, Pa 1959. Ch 3, n 10; Ch 5, n 181; Ch 7, n 37.

Yoshizawa v. Hewitt, 52 F 2d 411, CCA 9, 1931. Ch 11, n 93.

You Goo Ho v. Yee, 43 Hawaii 289, 1959. Ch 5, n 45.

Young v. Jordan, 145 SE 41, W Va 1928. Ch 12, n 18; Ch 12, n 34.

Younge v. State Board of Registration, 451 SW 2d 346, Mo 1969. Ch 11, n 6; Ch 11, n 28.

Youts v. St. Frances Hospital and School of Nursing, 469 P 2d 330, Kans 1970. Ch 1, n 121.

Zaman v. Schultz, 19 Pa D&C 309, 1933. Ch 1, n 114.

Zanzon v. Whittaker, 17 NW 2d 206, Mich 1945. Ch 5, n 53.

Zebarth v. Swedish Hospital Medical Center, 499 P 2d 1, Wash 1972. Ch 8, n 22.

Zeigler v. Illinois Trust &. Savings Bank, 91 NE 1041, Ill 1910. Ch 9, n 81; Ch 12, n 92.

Zimmerman v. Board of Regents, 294 NYS 2d 435, NY 1968. Ch 11, n 103.

Zipkin v. Freeman, 436 SW 2d 753, Mo 1968. Ch 1, n 5; Ch 9, n 17; Ch 9, n 84.

Zoterell v. Repp, 153 NW 692, Mich 1915, Ch 1, n 9.

CASES BY JURISDICTION

Alabama

Dabney v. Briggs, 121 So 394, Ala 1929. Ch 1, n 160; Ch 12, n 90.

Donald v. Swann, 137 So 178, Ala 1931. Ch 7, n 9.

Hester v. Ford, 130 So 203, Ala 1930. Ch 1, n 4.

Jackson v. Burton, 147 So 414, Ala 1933. Ch 12, n 41.

Moore v. Andalusia Hospital Inc., 224 So 2d 617, Ala 1969. Ch 11, n 115.

Norward Clinic v. Spann, 199 So 840, Ala 1941, Ch 6, n 90.

Piper v. Halford, 25 So 2d 264, Ala 1946. Ch 10, n 60.

Sellers v. Edwards, 265 So 2d 438, Ala 1972. Ch 10, n 118.

Sims v. Callahan, 112 So 2d 776, Ala 1959. Ch 3, n 109.

South Highlands Infirmary v. Camp, 180 So 2d 904, Ala 1965. Ch 6, n 52.

Stephens v. Druid City Hospital Board, 268 So 2d 824, Ala 1972. Ch 5, n 143.

Thaggard v. Vafes, 119 So 647, Ala 1928. Ch 12, n 31.

Alaska

Patrick v. Sedwick, 391 P 2d 453, 413 P 2d 169, Alaska 1964. Ch 4, n 86; Ch 10, n 2.

Arizona

Acton v. Morrison, 155 P 2d 782, Ariz 1945. Ch 10, n 134.

Arizona v. Marcus, 450 P 2d 689, Ariz 1969. Ch 1, n 76.

Arizona Osteopathic Medical Association v. Fridena, 457 P 2d 945, Ariz 1969. Ch 11, n 99.

Beeck v. Tucson General Hospital, 500 P 2d 1153, Ariz 1972. Ch 5, n 111.

DuVall v. Board of Medical Examiners of Arizona, 66 P 2d 1026, Ariz 1937. Ch 11, n 41; Ch. 11, n 70.

Falcher v. St. Luke's Hospital Medical Center, 506 P 2d 287, Ariz 1973. Ch 6, n 39.

Findlay v. Board of Supervisors, 230 P 2d 526, Ariz 1951. Ch 1, n 23; Ch 11, n 124.

Goedecke v. Price, 506 P 2d 1105, Ariz 1973. Ch 3, n 97.

Hall v. Delvat, 389 P 2d 692, Ariz 1964. Ch 5, n 20.

Kleinman v. Armour, 470 P 2d 703, Ariz 1970. Ch 3, n 40.

Maricopa County Medical Society v. Blende, 448 P 2d 68, Ariz 1968. Ch 11, n 95.

Purcell v. Zimbelman, 500 P 2d 335, Ariz 1972. Ch 7, n 82.

Shetter v. Rochelle, 409 P 2d 74, Ariz 1965. Ch 8, n 40.

Tiller v. Von Pohle, 230 P 2d 213, Ariz 1951. Ch 5, n 1.

Tucson General Hospital v. Russell, 437 P 2d 677, Ariz 1968. Ch 6, n 10.

Vigil v. Herman, 424 P 2d 159, Ariz 1967. Ch 3, n 60.

Arkansas

Arkansas Midland Railroad Co. v. Pearson, 135 SW 917, Ark 1911. Ch 10, n 156.

Arkansas State Medical Board v. Grimmett, 463 SW 2d 662, Ark 1971. Ch 11, n 16.

Brown v. Dark, 119 SW 2d 529, Ark 1938. Ch 12, n 52.

Caldwell v. Missouri State Life Ins. Co., 230 SW 566, Ark 1921. Ch 1, n 12.

Chudy v. Chudy. 420 SW 2d 401, Ark 1967. Ch 9, n 87.

Dollins v. Hartford Accident and Indemnity Co., 477 SW 2d 179, Ark 1972. Ch 10, n 54.

Feige v. State, 194 SW 865, Ark 1917. Ch 11, n 172.

Fort v. City of Brinkley, 112 SW 1084, Ark 1908, Ch 11, n 41.

Graham v. Sisco, 449 SW 2d 949, Ark 1970. Ch 4, n 61.

Hake v. Arkansas State Medical Board, 374 SW 2d 173, Ark 1964. Ch 11, n 86.

Lanier v. Trammell, 180 SW 2d 818, Ark 1944. Ch 4, n 32.

Martin v. Aetna Casualty and Surety Company, 387 SW 2d 334, Ark 1965. Ch 6, n 44.

Ragsdale v. Arkansas, 432 SW 2d 11, Ark 1968. Ch 1, n 105.

Routen v. McGehee, 186 SW 2d 779, Ark 1945. Ch 5, n 99.

Runyan v. Goodrum, 228 SW 397, Ark 1921. Ch 5, n 95.

State Medical Board v. Rodgers, 79 SW 2d 83, Ark 1935. Ch 11, n 33.

California

Agnew v. Larson, 185 P 2d 851, Cal 1947. Ch 3, n 10; Ch 5, n 190.

Agnew v. Parks, 343 P 2d 118, Cal 1959. Ch 1, n 23.

Ales v. Ryan, 64 P 2d 409, Cal 1936. Ch 5, n 4.

Armstrong v. Svoboda, 49 Cal Rptr 701, Cal 1966. Ch 2, n 7; Ch 4, n 99.

Armstrong v. Wallace, 47 P 2d 740, Cal 1935. Ch 5, n 4.

Ash v. Mortensen, 150 P 2d 876, Cal 1944. Ch 10, n 90.

Ballard v. Anderson, 484 P 2d 1345, Cal 1971. Ch 1, n 134.

Barham v. Widing, 291 Pac 173, Cal 1930. Ch 2, n 93.

Bauer v. Otis, 284 P 2d 133, Cal 1955. Ch 7, n 5.

Bellandi v. Park Sanitarium Association, 6 P 2d 508, Cal 1931. Ch 5, n 209, Ch 9, n 7.

Belshaw v. Feinstein, 65 Cal Rptr. 788, Cal 1968. Ch 10, n 101.

Bennett v. Los Angeles Tumor Institute, 227 P 2d 473, Cal 1951. Ch 5, n 102.

Berkey v. Anderson, 82 Cal Rptr 67, Cal 1969. Ch 8, n 20.

Bernstein v. Alameda-Contra-Costa Medical Association, 293 P 2d 862, Cal 1956. Ch 11, n 81.

Bernstein v. Board of Medical Examiners, 22 Cal Rptr 419, Cal 1962. Ch 11, n 62.

Black v. Caruso, 9 Cal Rptr 634, Cal 1960. Ch 2, n 86.

Black v. Dillon, 28 Cal Rptr 678, Cal 1963. Ch 10, n 109.

Blinder v. California, 101 Cal Rptr 635, Cal 1972. Ch 1, n 78.

Bowers v. Olch, 260 P 2d 997, Cal 1953. Ch 5, n 5.

Bowman v. Southern Pacific Corporation, 204 Pac 403, Cal 1921. Ch 7, n 92.

Brown v. Superior Court, 32 Cal Rptr 527, Cal 1963. Ch 13, n 43.

Burge v. City and County of San Francisco, 262 P 2d 6, Cal 1953. Ch 1, n 111.

Cadilla v. Board of Medical Examiners, 103 Cal Rptr 455, Cal 1972. Ch 11, n 23; Ch 11, n 61.

Cagle v. Bakersfield Medical Group, 241 P 2d 1013, Cal 1952. Ch 6, n 84.

California v. Anderson, 105 Cal Rptr 664, Cal 1972. Ch 1, n 78.

California v. Eckley, 108 Cal Rptr 52, Cal 1973. Ch 11, n 36.

California v. Kraft, 84 Cal Rptr 280, Cal 1970. Ch 1, n 97; Ch 1, n 98.

California v. Superior Court, 493 P 2d 1145, Cal 1972. Ch 1, n 99.

Campos v. Weeks, 53 Cal Rptr 915, Cal 1966. Ch 3, n 11; Ch 5, n 183.

Cavero v. Franklin General Benevolent Society, 223 P 2d 471, Cal 1950. Ch 5, n 127.

Champion v. Bennetts, 236 P 2d 155, Cal 1951, Ch 5, n 13.

Cobbs v. Grant, 502 P 2d 1, Cal 1972. Ch 8, n 37.

Coffee v. McDonnell-Douglas Corporation, 503 P 2d 1366, Cal 1972. Ch 7, n 96.

Coleman v. California Friends Church, 81 P 2d 469, 470, Cal 1938. Ch 2, n 1.

Collins v. Board of Medical Examiners, 105 Cal Rptr 634, Cal 1972. Ch 11, n 45; Ch 11, n 47.

Combs v. Combs, 327 P 2d 164, Cal 1958. Ch 8, n 131.

Costa v. Regents of the University of California, 254 P 2d 85, Cal 1953. Ch 5, n 96.

Crowe v. McBride, 152 P 2d 727, Cal 1944. Ch 6, n 5.

Cullum v. Seifer, 81 Cal Rptr 381, Cal 1969. Ch 3, n 64.

Custodio v. Bauer, 59 Cal Rptr 463, Cal 1967. Ch 1, n 153; Ch 4, n 6.

Dean v. Dyer, 149 P 2d 288, Cal 1944. Ch 5, n 144.

Deckard v. Sorenson, 2 Cal Rptr 121, Cal 1960. Ch 2, n 91.

Dees v. Pace, 257 P 2d 756, Cal 1953. Ch 4, n 36.

DeMartini v. Alexandria Sanitarium, 13 Cal Rptr 564, Cal 1961. Ch 4, n 105.

Dierman v. Providence Hospital, 188 P 2d 12, Cal 1948. Ch 5, n 117; Ch 6, n 9.

Donahoo v. Lovas, 288 P 698, Cal 1930. Ch 5, n 170.

Doyle v. Giuliucci, 401 P 2d 1, Cal 1965. Ch 13, n 62.

Dunlap v. Marine, 51 Cal Rptr 158, Cal 1966. Ch 4, n 41; Ch 10, n 56.

Fallis v. Department of Motor Vehicles, 70 Cal Rptr 595, Cal 1968. Ch 1, n 101.

Farber v. Olkon, 254 P 2d 520, Cal 1953. Ch 5, n 200.

Fay v. Mundy, 54 Cal Rptr 591, Cal 1966, Ch 10, n 144.

Fick v. Board of Medical Examiners for the State of California, 101 Cal Rptr 260, Cal 1973. Ch 11, n 41.

Fraser v. Sprague, 76 Cal Rptr 37, Cal 1969. Ch 4, n 88.

Furnish v. Board of Medical Examiners, 308 P 2d 924, Cal 1957. Ch 11, n 32.

Garlock v. Cole, 18 Cal Rptr 393, Cal 1962. Ch 9, n 70.

Gerber v. Day, 6 P 2d 535, Cal 1931. Ch 10, n 27.

Gerhardt v. Fresno Medical Group, 31 Cal Rptr 633, Cal 1963. Ch 4, n 84.

Gist v. French, 288 P 2d 1003, Cal 1955. Ch 3, n 69; Ch 4, n 97.

Glesby v. Hartford Accident and Indemnity Company, 44 P 2d 365, Cal 1935. Ch 7, n 12.

Gluckstein v. Lipsett, 209 P 2d 98, Cal 1949. Ch 1, n 10; Ch 4, n 91.

Gottsdanker v. Cutter Laboratories, 6 Cal Rptr 320, Cal 1960. Ch 6, n 61.

Grannis v. Board of Medical Examiners, 96 Cal Rptr 868, Cal 1971. Ch 11, n 44.

Guillen v. Martin, 333 P 2d 266, Cal 1958. Ch 4, n 82.

Hedlund v. Sutter Medical Service Co., 124 P 2d 878, Cal 1942. Ch 10, n 153.

Hewitt v. Board of Medical Examiners, 84 Pac 39, Cal 1906. Ch 11, n 2.

Hoffman v. Rogers, 99 Cal Rptr 455, Cal 1972. Ch 1, n 88.

Horace v. Weyrauch, 324 P 2d 666, Cal 1958. Ch 4, n 54.

Huffman v. Lindquist, 234 P 2d 34, Cal 1951. Ch 2, n 98; Ch 6, n 29.

Hundley v. St. Francis Hospital, 237 P 2d 131, Cal 1958. Ch 3, n 113; Ch 8, n 54.

Huntly v. Zurich Accident Ins. Co., 280 Pac 163, Cal 1929. Ch 8, n 59.

Inouye v. Black, 47 Cal Rptr 313, Cal 1965. Ch 5, n 42; Ch 6, n 54.

James v. Spear, 338 P 2d 22, Cal 1959. Ch 10, n 7.

Jessin v. County of Shasta, 79 Cal Rptr 359, Cal 1969. Ch 1, n 144.

Johnston v. Black Company, 91 P 2d 921, Cal 1939. Ch 6, n 4.

Jones v. Fakehany, 67 Cal Rptr 810, Cal 1968. Ch 12, n 107.

Kalmus v. Cedars of Lebanon Hospital, 281 P 2d 872, Cal 1955. Ch 5, n 156.

Kennedy v. Gaskell, 78 Cal Rptr 753, Cal 1969. Ch 7, n 55.

Key v. Caldwell, 104 P 2d 87, Cal 1940. Ch 5, n 7.

Kritzer v. Citron, 224 P 2d 808, Cal 1950. Ch 1, n 137.

Landsberg v. Kolodny, 302 P 2d 86, Cal 1956. Ch 5, n 6.

Langford v. Kosterlitz, 290 Pac 80, Cal 1930. Ch 2, n 22; Ch 5, n 162.

Lathrope v. Flood, 63 Pac 1007, Cal 1901. Ch 12, n 5.

Latson v. Zeiler, 58 Cal Rptr 436, Cal 1967. Ch 9, n 67.

Lorenz v. Board of Medical Examiners, 298 P 2d 537, Cal 1956. Ch 11, n 69; Ch 11, n 106.

Love v. Wolf, 38 Cal Rptr 183, 58 Cal Rptr 42, Cal 1967. Ch 5, n 194; Ch 6, n 60.

Maben v. Rankin, 358 P 2d 681, Cal 1961. Ch 3, n 22; Ch 9, n 93.

Maertins v. Kaiser Foundation Hospital, 328 P 2d 494, Cal 1958. Ch 3, n 61.

Magee v. Wyeth Laboratories, 29 Cal Rptr 322, Cal 1963. Ch 6, n 61.

Magit v. Board of Medical Examiners, 366 P 2d 816, Cal 1961. Ch 11, n 85.

Mangrum v. Union Pacific Railroad Company, 41 Cal Rptr 536, Cal 1964. Ch 7, n 101.

Marvin v. Talbott, 30 Cal Rptr 893, Cal 1963. Ch 1, n 9.

Marvulli v. Elshire, 103 Cal Rptr 461, Cal 1972. Ch. 7, n 56.

Matthews v. Atchison Topeka & Santa Fe Railroad Co., 129 P 2d 435, Cal 1942. Ch 10, n 96.

Mayers v. Litow, 316 P 2d 351, Cal 1957. Ch 4, n 86.

McBride v. Saylin, 56 P 2d 941, Cal 1936. Ch 3, n 58.

McLennan v. Holder, 36 P 2d 448, Cal 1934. Ch 5, n 9.

McNamara v. Emmons, 97 P 2d 503, Cal 1939. Ch 1, n 157; Ch 12, n 91.

McPheeters v. Board of Medical Examiners, 284 Pac 938, Cal 1930. Ch 11, n 76.

Meier v. Ross General Hospital, 67 Cal Rptr 471, Cal 1968. Ch 4, n 103.

Minaker v. Adams, 203 Pac 806, Cal 1921. Ch 11, n 27.

Mondot v. Vallejo General Hospital, 313 P 2d 78, Cal 1957. Ch 2, n 95; Ch 5, n 20.

Moore v. Belt, 212 P 2d 509, Cal 1949. Ch 4, n 55.

Moore v. Steen, 283 Pac 833, Cal 1929. Ch 5, n 103.

Morand v. Seaside Memorial Hospital, 264 P 2d 96, Cal 1953. Ch 6, n 45.

Morris v. Board of Medical Examiners, 41 Cal Rptr 351, Cal 1964. Ch 11, n 32.

Murray v. Thrifty Drug Store, *Trial Court Decision,* Sacramento, Cal Super Ct. Docket #209949, 1972. Ch 5, n 150.

O'Beirne v. Superior Court of Santa Clara County, Sup Ct. Cal, December 7, 1967. Ch 1, n 140.

O'Donnell v. Slack, 55 Pac 906, Cal 1899. Ch 8, n 78.

O'Reilly v. Board of Medical Examiners, 58 Cal Rptr 7, Cal 1967. Ch 7, n 11.

Patterson v. Marcus, 265 Pac 222, Cal 1928. Ch 3, n 40.

Pedesky v. Bleiberg, 59 Cal Rptr 294, Cal 1967. Ch 8, n 49.

People v. Hunt, 147 Pac 476, Cal 1915. Ch 11, n 173.

People v. Long, 96 P2d 354, Cal 1939. Ch 11, n 159.

People v. McCaughan, 317 P 2d 974, Cal 1957. Ch 9, n 12.

People v. Phillips, 75 Cal Rptr 720, Cal 1969. Appealed to Federal Court as Phillips v. Pitchess, 451 F 2d 913, CCA 9, 1971. Ch 11, n 177.

People v. Sorensen, 66 Cal Rptr 7, Cal 1968. Ch 8, n 113.

Pfeifer v. Pfeifer, 280 P 2d 54, Cal 1955. Ch 8, n 135.

Pinsker v. Pacific Coast Society of Orthodontists, 81 Cal Rptr 623, Cal 1969. Ch 11, n 95.

Puffinbarger v. Day, 24 Cal Rptr 533, Cal 1962. Ch 4, n 147; Ch 10, n 4.

Putensen v. Clay Adams, Inc., 91 Cal Rptr 319, Cal 1970. Ch 6, n 76; Ch 8, n 12.

Quintal v. Laurel Grove Hospital, 397 P 2d 161, Cal 1964. Ch 4, n 43; Ch 5, n 133.

Ragin v. Zimmerman, 276 Pac 107, Cal 1929. Ch 5, n 101.

Rainer v. Grossman, 107 Cal Rptr 469, Cal 1973. Ch 1, n 17.

Rannard v. Lockheed Aircraft, 157 P 2d 1, Cal 1945. Ch 1, n 83.

Reis v. Reinard, 117 P 2d 386, Cal 1941. Ch 2, n 52.

Rilcoff v. State Board of Medical Examiners, 203 P 2d 844, Cal 1949. Ch 1, n 34; Ch 11, n 85.

Rinaldo v. Board of Medical Examiners, 42 P 2d 724, Cal 1935. Ch 11, n 50.

Rosenberg v. Feigin, 260 P 2d 143, Cal 1953. Ch 1, n 137.

Rosner v. Eden Township Hospital District, 375 P 2d 431, Cal 1962, Ch 11, n 128.

Rosner v. Peninsula Hospital District, 36 Cal Rptr 332, Cal 1964. Ch 11, n 131.

Salgo v. Leland Stanford Board of Trustees, 317 P 2d 170, Cal 1957. Ch 4, n 53; Ch 8, n 11; Ch 8, n 32.

Sanchez v. Rodriguez, 38 Cal Rptr 110, Cal 1964. Ch 5, n 83; Ch 5, n 165.

Schessler v. Keck, 271 P 2d 588, Cal 1954. Ch 9, n 27.

In re Adoption of Schroetter, 67 Cal Rptr 819, Cal 1968. Ch 8, n 123.

Schwartz v. Thiele, 51 Cal Rptr 767, Cal 1966. Ch 9, n 25.

Scott v. McPheeters, 92 P 2d 678, Cal 1939. Ch 4, n 58.

Seneris v. Haas, 291 P 2d 915, Cal 1955. Ch 2, n 96; Ch 5, n 126.

Sherman v. Hartman, 290 P 2d 894, Cal 1955. Ch 5, n 84.

Shoemaker v. Friedberg, 183 P 2d 318, Cal 1947. Ch 9, n 38.

Silverhart v. Mount Zion Hospital, 98 Cal Rptr 187, Cal 1971. Ch 6, n 27.

Silvers v. Wesson, 266 P 2d 169, Cal 1954. Ch 4, n 56.

Silverson v. Weber, 372 P 2d 97, Cal 1962. Ch 4, n 38.

Sinz v. Owens, 205 P 2d 3, Cal 1949. Ch 2, n 66.

Smith v. Kern County Medical Association, 120 P 2d 874, Cal 1942. Ch 11, n 100.

Smith v. Shankman, 25 Cal Rptr 195, Cal 1962, Ch 3, n 21.

Solgaard v. Guy F. Atkinson Co., 491 P 2d 821, Cal 1971. Ch 1, n 36.

Solorio v. Lampros, 82 Cal Rptr 753, Cal 1969. Ch 3, n 70.

Stephenson v. Kaiser Foundation Hospital, 21 Cal Rptr 646, Cal 1962. Ch 3, n 39.

Stuck v. Board of Medical Examiners, 211 P 2d 389, Cal 1949. Ch 11, n 27.

Sugaya v. Morton, 40 P 2d 581, Cal 1935. Ch 5, n 10.

Tangora v. Matanky, 42 Cal Rptr 348, Cal 1964. Ch 3, n 11; Ch 5, n 182.

Tarasoff v. Regents of the University of California, 108 Cal Rptr 878, Cal 1973. Ch 9, n 33.

Tomei v. Henning, 431 P 2d 633, Cal 1967. Ch 4, n 83.

Tunkl v. Regents of the University of California, 383 P 2d 441, Cal 1963. Ch 10, n 98; Ch 13, n 70.

Valdez v. Percy, 217 P 2d 422, Cal 1950. Ch 1, n 19; Ch 3, n 67; Ch 8, n 54; Ch 10, n 51.

Valentine v. Kaiser Foundation Hospitals, 12 Cal Rptr 26, Cal 1961. Ch 2, n 76.

Wallace v. LaVine, 97 P 2d 879, Cal 1940. Ch 2, n 8.

Wangel v. Pangman, Trial Court decision, Los Angeles County, Cal, Docket No. WEC 9141, 1971. Ch 4, n 92.

Ware v. Culp, 74 P 2d 283, Cal 1937. Ch 6, n 20; Ch 7, n 62.

Welsh v. Mercy Hospital, 151 P 2d 17, Cal 1944. Ch 6, n 37.

Wheeler v. Barker, 208 P 2d 68, Cal 1949. Ch 8, n 51.

Wickham v. North American Rockwell Corporation, 87 Cal Rptr 563, Cal 1970. Ch 7, n 89.

Winthral v. Callison Memorial Hospital, Cal Super Ct., San Francisco County, Docket #582565, 1972. Ch 6, n 31.

Wolfsmith v. Marsh, 337 P 2d 70, Cal 1959. Ch 5, n 138; Ch 7, n 19.

Wyatt v. Cerf, 149 P 2d 309, Cal 1944. Ch 11, n 71; Ch 11, n 106.

Colorado

Adams v. Poudre Valley Hospital District, 502 P 2d 1127, Colo 1972. Ch 10, n 149.

Beadles v. Metayka, 311 P 2d 711, Colo 1957. Ch 7, n 40.

Bernandi v. Community Hospital Association, 443 P 2d 708, Colo 1968. Ch 5, n 169; Ch 7, n 274; Ch 12, n 105.

Bolles v. Kinton, 263 Pac 26, Colo 1928. Ch 12, n 83.

Brown v. Hughes, 30 P 2d 259, Colo 1934. Ch 2, n 93; Ch 8, n 145.

Doran v. State Board of Medical Examiners, 240 Pac 335, Colo 1925. Ch 11, n 30.

Glenn v. Colorado State Board of Medical Examiners, 284 P 2d 230, Colo 1955. Ch 11, n 41.

Graeb v. State Board of Medical Examiners, 139 Pac 1099, Colo 1913. Ch 11, n 57.

Hanley v. Spencer, 115 P 2d 399, Colo 1941. Ch 10, n 25.

Jackson v. Burnham, 39 Pac 577, Colo 1895. Ch 4, n 28.

Lowen v. Hilton, 351 P 2d 881, Colo 1960. Ch 9, n 92.

Maercklein v. Smith, 266 P 2d 1095, Colo 1954. Ch 3, n 15; Ch 4, n 47.

Mallett v. Pirkey, 466 P 2d 466, Colo 1970. Ch 8, n 47.

McKay v. State Board of Medical Examiners, 86 P 2d 232, Colo 1938. Ch 11, n 46; Ch 11, n 92.

Nitka v. Bell, 487 P 2d 379, Colo 1971. Ch 10, n 124.

Pearson v. Norman, 106 P 2d 361, Colo 1940. Ch 12, n 3.

Poltera v. Garlington, 489 P 2d 334, Colo 1971. Ch 10, n 65.

Poudre Valley Hospital District v. Heckart, 491 P 2d 984, Colo 1971. Ch 1, n 123.

Sams v. Curfman, 137 P 2d 1017, Colo 1943. Ch 10, n 65.

Sapero v. State Board of Medical Examiners, 11 P 2d 555, Colo 1932. Ch 11, n 73.

Schwalb v. Connely, 179 P 2d 667, Colo. 1947. Ch 8, n 74.

St. Luke's Hospital Association v. Long, 240 P 2d 917, Colo 1952. Ch 6, n 36.

Tadlock v. Lloyd, 173 Pac 200, Colo 1918. Ch 4, n 16; Ch 12, n 26.

White v. Andrew, 197 Pac 564, Colo 1921. Ch 11, n 70.

Connecticut

Bria v. St. Joseph's Hospital, 220 A 2d 29, Conn 1966. Ch 5, n 171.

Camp v. Booth, 273 A 2d 714, Conn 1970. Ch 6, n 38.

Edson v. Griffin Hospital, 144 A 2d 341, Conn 1958. Ch 11, n 125; Ch 11, n 150.

Giambozi v. Peters, 16 A 2d 833, Conn 1940. Ch 5, n 67.

Gibson v. Connecticut Medical Examining Board, 104 A 2d 890, Conn 1954. Ch 11, n 82.

Hally v. Hospital of St. Raphael, 294 A 2d 305, Conn 1972. Ch 6, n 26.

Jaffe v. State Department of Health, 64 A 2d 330, Conn 1949. Ch 9, n 91; Ch 11, n 56.

Kelly v. Sheehan, 259 A 2d 605, Conn 1969. Ch 12, n 111.

Lametta v. Connecticut Light & Power Co., 92 A 2d 731, Conn 1952. Ch 10, n 144.

Levett v. Etkind, 265 A 2d 70, Conn 1969. Ch 6, n 86.

Marchlewski v. Casella, 106 A 2d 466, Conn 1954. Ch 2, n 64.

McDermott v. St. Mary's Hospital, 133 A 2d 608, Conn 1957. Ch 6, n 21; Ch 10, n 161.

Page v. Brodoff, 169 A 2d 901, Conn 1961. Ch 10, n 11.

Sage-Allen Co., Inc. v. Wheeler, 179 Atl 195, Conn 1935. Ch 11, n 90.

Sheridan v. Quarrier, 16 A 2d 479, Conn 1940. Ch 12, n 47.

Snyder v. Pantaleo, 122 A 2d 21, Conn 1956. Ch 3, n 10.

State v. Clark, 261 A 2d 294, Conn 1969. Ch 1, n 73.

Delaware

Christian v. Wilmington General Hospital Association, 135 A 2d 727, Del 1957. Ch 10, n 62.

DiFillipo v. Preston, 173 A 2d 333, Del 1961. Ch 2, n 13; Ch 4, n 87; Ch 8, n 33.

Durney v. St. Francis Hospital, 83 A 2d 753, Del 1951. Ch 10, n 157.

Equitable Life Assurance Society v. Young & Revel, Inc., 250 A 2d 509, Del 1969. Ch 8, n 76.

Fischer v. Wilmington General Hospital, 149 A 2d 749, Del 1959. Ch 8, n 34.

Hornbeck v. Homeopathic Hospital Association, 197 A 2d 461, Del 1964. Ch 5, n 136.

Larrimore v. Homeopathic Hospital Associatoin, 181 A 2d 573, Del 1962. Ch 5, n 148.

Manlove v. Wilmington General Hospital, 169 A 2d 18, 174 A 2d 135, Del 1961. Ch 1, n 40.

Nigro v. Flinn, 192 Atl 685, Del 1937. Ch 10, n 144.

Schagrin v. Wilmington Medical Center, 304 A 2d 61, Del 1973. Ch 7, n 71.

Vanaman v. Milford Memorial Hospital, 272 A 2d 718, Del 1970. Ch 7, n 77.

District of Columbia

Application of President and Directors of Georgetown College, Inc., 331 F 2d 1000, CA DC 1964. Ch 1, n 65.

Alden v. Providence Hospital, 382 F 2d 163, CA DC 1967. Ch 3, n 1; Ch 10, n 5.

Barnett v. Bachrach, 34 A 2d 626, CA DC 1943. Ch 2, n 62; Ch 3, n 38; Ch 3, n 43; Ch 8, n 52.

In re Boe, 322 F Supp 872, DC DC 1971. Ch 1, n 133.

Bonner v. Conklin, 62 F 2d 875, CA DC 1932. Ch 12, n 40.

Bonner v. Moran, 126 F 2d 121, CA DC 1941. Ch 1, n 115.

Bryant v. District of Columbia Dental Society, 26 App DC 461, DC 1906. Ch 11, n 97.

Burke v. Washington Hospital Center, 475 F 2d 364, CA DC 1973. Ch 7, n 41.

Canterbury v. Spence, 464 F 2d 772, CA DC 1972. Ch 8, n 36.

Carr v. Shifflette, 82 F 2d 874, CA DC 1936. Ch 9, n 49.

In re Curry, 452 F 2d 1360, CA DC 1971. Ch 8, n 93.

Czarra v. Board of Medical Supervisors, 25 App DC 433, DC 1925. Ch 11, n 74.

Dixon v. Jacobs, 427 F 2d 589, CA DC 1970. Ch 4, n 114; Ch 8, n 95.

Doe v. General Hospital of the District of Columbia, 434 F 2d 423, CA DC, 1970. Ch 1, n 142; Ch 1, n 145.

Emmett v. Eastern Dispensary and Casualty Hospital, 396 F 2d 931, CA DC 1967. Ch 12, n 108.

Fletcher v. Hand, 358 F 2d 549, CA DC 1966. Ch 10, n 73.

Furr v. Herzmark, 206 F 2d 468, CA DC 1953. Ch 5, n 40; Ch 5, n 54.

Haven v. Randolph, 342 F Supp 538, DC DC 1972. Ch 8, n 39.

Hohenthal v. Smith, 114 F 2d 494, CA DC 1940. Ch 5, n 48.

Mattocks v. Bell, 194 A 2d 307, DC DC 1963. Ch 9, n 8.

Monk v. Doctors' Hospital, 403 F 2d 580, CA DC 1968. Ch 7, n 47.

Morse v. Moretti, 403 F 2d 564, CA DC 1968. Ch 2, n 84.

National Homeopathic Hospital v. Phillips, 181 F 2d 293, CA DC 1950. Ch 5, n 68.

President and Directors of Georgetown College v. Hughes, 130 F 2d 810, DC DC 1942. Ch 10, n 167.

Price v. Neyland, 320 F 2d 674, CA DC 1963. Ch 2, n 78; Ch 3, n 86; Ch 5, n 81.

Rogers v. Lawson, 170 F 2d 157, CA DC 1948. Ch 1, n 159; Ch 12, n 85.

Rotan v. Greenbaum, 273 F 2d 830, CA DC 1959. Ch 4, n 10; Ch 5, n 152; Ch 10, n 8.

Rouse v. Cameron, 373 F 2d 451, CA DC 1966. Ch 4, n 115; Ch 8, n 91.

Schulman v. Washington Hospital Center, 222 F Supp 59, DC DC 1963. Ch 11, n 45.

Schwartz v. United States, 226 F Supp 84, DC DC 1964. Ch 4, n 106.

Stottlemire v. Cawood, 213 F Supp 897, DC DC 1963. Ch 5, n 194; Ch 6, n 60.

Florida

Atkins v. Humes, 107 So 2d 253, Fla 1958. Ch 4, n 73.

Baldor v. Rogers, 81 So 2d 658, Fla 1955. Ch 2, n 15; Ch 4, n 9; Ch 5, n 151; Ch 8, n 148.

Bernstein v. Lilly Tulip Cup Corporation, 177 So 2d 362, Fla 1965. Ch 6, n 67.

Bess Ambulance Company, Inc. v. Boll, 208 So 2d 308, Fla 1968. Ch 6, n 38; Ch 10, n 35.

Bourgeois v. Dade County, 99 So 2d 575, Fla 1957. Ch 3, n 54.

Bowers v. Talmage, 159 So 2d 888, Fla 1963. Ch 4, n 53; Ch 9, n 64.

Brooks v. Serrano, 209 So 2d 279, Fla 1968. Ch 4, n 59.

C. R. Bard, Inc. v Mason, 247 So 2d 471, Fla 1971, Ch 6, n 73.

Carter v. Metropolitan Dade County, 253 So 2d 920, Fla 1971. Ch 5, n 176.

Cavenaugh v. South Broward Hospital District, 247 So 2d 769, Fla 1971. Ch 6, n 100.

Cawthon v. Coffer, 264 So 2d 873, Fla 1972. Ch 1, n 94.

Chappell v. Masten, 255 So 2d 546, Fla 1971. Ch 8, n 121; Ch 9, n 73.

Chew v. State Board of Medical Examiners, 265 So 2d 542, Fla 1972. Ch 11, n 15; Ch 11, n 56.

Cleaver v. Dade County, 272 So 2d 559, Fla 1973. Ch 6, n 45.

Crovella v. Cochrane, 102 So 2d 307, Fla 1958. Ch 2, n 78; Ch 3, n 34.

Ditlow v. Kaplan, 181 So 2d 226, Fla 1965. Ch 8, n 32.

Dohr v. Smith, 104 So 2d 29, Fla 1958. Ch 5, n 19; Ch 7, n 56.

Dunn v. Campbell, 166 So 2d 217, Fla 1964. Ch 4, n 68.

The Florida Bar v. Hefty, 213 So 2d 422, Fla 1968. Ch 11, n 66.

Florida Bar Association v. Kay, 232 So 2d 378, Fla 1970. Ch 11, n 68.

General Hospital of Greater Miami, Inc. v. Gager, 160 So 2d 749, Fla. 1964. Ch 10, n 17.

Gian-Cursio v. State, 180 So 2d 396, Fla 1965. Ch 11, n 175.

Hampton v. State, 39 So 421, Fla 1905. Ch 11, n 162.

Harwick v. Harris, 166 So 2d 912, Fla 1964. Ch 2, n 35; Ch 7, n 25.

Hine v. Fox, 89 So 2d 13, Fla 1956. Ch 6, n 74.

Hoder v. Sayet, 196 So 2d 205, Fla 1967. Ch 5, n 57.

Hofmann v. Blackmon, 241 So 2d 752, Fla 1970. Ch 4, n 121; Ch 9, n 36.

Jackson v. Anderson, 230 So 2d 503, Fla 1970. Ch 1, n 152.

Jackson v. Rupp, 228 So 2d 916, Fla 1969. Ch 8, n 61; Ch 8, n 72.

Jones v. Smith, 278 So 2d 339, Fla 1973. Ch 1, n 138.

Lane v. Cohen, 201 So 2d 804, Fla 1967. Ch 1, n 153.

LePrince v. McLeod, 171 So 2d 189, Fla 1965. Ch 2, n 92.

Levy v. Kirk, 187 So 2d 401, Fla 1966. Ch 4, n 17; Ch 12, n 28.

Martin v. Parks, 165 So 2d 220, Fla 1964. Ch 3, n 105.

Mizell v. North Broward Hospital District, 175 So 2d 583, Fla 1965. Ch 11, n 142.

Musachia v. Rosman, 190 So 2d 47, Fla 1966. Ch 10, n 16.

North Shore Hospital v. Luzi, 194 So 2d 63, Fla 1967. Ch 5, n 166.

O'Grady v. Wickman, 213 So 2d 321, Fla 1968. Ch 4, n 45.

Palm Springs Hospital v. Martinez, Fla Cir Ct, Dade Co. Docket #71-12687, 1971. Ch 1, n 63; Ch 8, n 42.

Pensacola Sanitarium v. Wilkins, 67 So 124, Fla 1914. Ch 6, n 14.

Reams v. Florida, 279 So 2d 839, Fla 1973. Ch 11, n 36.

Reeves v. North Broward Hospital, 191 So 2d 307, Fla 1966. Ch 1, n 29; Ch 3, n 26; Ch 7, n 60.

Russell v. Community Blood Bank, 185 So 2d 749, Fla 1966. Ch 5, n 61.

Ruvio v. North Broward Hospital District, 186 So 2d 45, Fla 1966. Ch 12, n 55.

Saunders v. Lishkoff, 188 So 815, Fla 1939. Ch 1, n 158; Ch 3, n 18.

Sligar v. Tucker, 267 So 2d 54, Fla 1972. Ch 12, n 104.

State v. Heines, 197 So 787, Fla 1940. Ch 11, n 171.

State Board of Medical Examiners v. Morlan, 3 So 2d 402, Fla 1941. Ch 11, n 48.

State ex rel Weathers v. Davis, 196 So 487, Fla 1940. Ch 11, n 12.

West Coast Hospital Association v. Hoare, 64 So 2d 293, Fla 1953. Ch 11, n 117.

Williams v. Orange Memorial Hospital Association, 202 So 2d 859, Fla 1967. Ch 6, n 34.

Georgia

Adams v. Ricks, 86 SE 2d 329, Ga 1955. Ch 5, n 211.

Albright v. Powell, 147 SE 2d 848, Ga 1966. Ch 3, n 84.

Andrews v. Lofton, 57 SE 2d 338, Ga 1950. Ch 12, n 55.

Bazemore v. Savannah Hospital, 155 SE 194, Ga 1930, Ch 9, n 53.

Bulloch County Hospital Association v. Fowler, 183 SE 2d 586, Ga 1971. Ch 7, n 75.

Butler v. Jones, 68 SE 2d 173, Ga 1951. Ch 6, n 81.

Buttersworth v. Swint, 186 SE 770, Ga 1936. Ch 1, n 18.

Caldwell v. Knight, 89 SE 2d 900, Ga 1955. Ch 9, n 3.

Candler General Hospital v. Purvis, 181 SE 2d 77, Ga 1971. Ch 6, n 105; Ch 10, n 158.

Carroll v. Griffin, 101 SE 2d 764, Ga 1958. Ch 12, n 22.

Cartwright v. Bartholomew, 64 SE 2d 323, Ga 1951. Ch 1, n 2.

Clark v. Piedmont Hospital, 162 SE 2d 468, Ga 1968. Ch 4, n 145; Ch 6, n 43; Ch 10, n 37.

Clary v. Hospital Authority of the City of Marietta, 126 SE 2d 470, Ga 1962. Ch 7, n 84.

Cochran v. Sears Roebuck & Co., 34 SE 2d 296, Ga 1945. Ch 9, n 37.

Cohran v. Harper, 154 SE 2d 461, Ga 1967. Ch 5, n 157.

Crawford v. McDonald, 187 SE 2d 542, Ga 1972. Ch 10, n 123.

Crawford Long Memorial Hospital v. Hardeman, 66 SE 2d 63, Ga 1951. Ch 6, n 95.

Creamer v. Georgia, 192 SE 2d 350, Ga 1972. Ch 1, n 92.

Dunbar v. Hospital Authority of Gwinnett County, 182 SE 2d 89, Ga 1971. Ch 11, 133.

Gay v. Greene, 84 SE 2d 847, Ga 1954. Ch 10, n 111.

Hipp v. Hospital Authority of the City of Marietta, 121 SE 2d 273, Ga 1961. Ch 10, n 162.

Hospital Authority of Emanuel County v. Gray, 181 SE 2d 299, Ga 1971. Ch 10, n 93.

Irwin v. Arrendale, 159 SE 2d 719, Ga 1967. Ch 1, n 55.

Joiner v. Mitchell County Hospital Authority, 186 SE 2d 307, 189 SE 2d 412, Ga 1972. Ch 7, n 79; Ch 10, n 164; Ch 11, n 111.

Keen v. Coleman, 20 SE 2d 175, Ga 1942. Ch 9, n 70.

Knight v. Lowery, 185 SE 2d 915, Ga 1971. Ch 10, n 86.

Louisville and Nashville Railroad Co. v. Blackmon, 59 SE 341, Ga 1907. Ch 8, n 75.

Lovett v. Emory University, 156 SE 2d 923, Ga 1967. Ch 5, n 63.

Massey v. State, 177 SE 2d 79, Ga 1970. Ch 1, n 93.

Mayo v. McClung, 64 SE 2d 330, Ga 1951. Ch 2, n 88.

McKinney v. Schaefer, 161 SE 2d 446, Ga 1968. Ch 5, n 172.

McLendon v. Daniel, 141 SE 77, Ga 1927. Ch 12, n 46.

Morton v. Savannah Hospital, 96 SE 887, Ga 1918. Ch 10, n 156.

Mull v. Emory University, 150 SE 2d 276, Ga 1966. Ch 8, n 46.

Mullins v. DuVall, 104 SE 513, Ga 1920. Ch 7, n 6.

Murphy v. Little, 145 SE 2d 760, Ga 1965. Ch 2, n 71.

Norton v. Hamilton, 89 SE 2d 809, Ga 1955. Ch 12, n 17.

Parker v. Vaughn, 183 SE 2d 605, Ga 1971. Ch 10, n 117.

Perry v. Hodgson, 148 SE 659, Ga 1929. Ch 8, n 54.

Piedmont Hospital v. Truitt, 172 SE 237, Ga 1933. Ch 10, n 74.

Pogue v. Hospital Authority of Dekalb County, 170 SE 2d 53, Ga 1969. Ch 7, n 69.

Porter v. Patterson, 129 SE 2d 70, Ga 1962. Ch 6, n 47.

Robinson v. Campbell, 97 SE 2d 544, Ga 1957. Ch 10, n 43.

Shea v. Phillips, 98 SE 2d 552, Ga 1957. Ch 5, n 39.

Starr v. Emory University, 93 SE 2d 399, Ga 1956. Ch 6, n 92.

Williams v. Hospital Authority of Hall County, 168 SE 2d 336, Ga 1969. Ch 1, n 39.

Yeargin v. Hamilton Memorial Hospital, 195 SE 2d 8, Ga 1972. Ch 1, n 26; Ch 11, n 132.

Hawaii

Gibo v. City and County of Honolulu, 459 P 2d 198, Hawaii 1969. Ch 6, n 102.

Nishi v. Hartwell, 473 P 2d 116, Hawaii 1970. Ch 1, n 137; Ch 8, n 17.

Silver v. Castleman Memorial Hospital, 497 P 2d 564, Hawaii 1972. Ch 11, n 134; Ch 11, n 149.

You Goo Ho v. Yee, 43 Hawaii 289, 1959. Ch 5, n 45.

Idaho

Billings v. Sister of Mercy of Idaho, 389 P 2d 224, Idaho 1964. Ch 10, n 148.

Estes v. Magee, 109 P 2d 631, Idaho 1940. Ch 10, n 94.

Hall v. Bacon, 453 P 2d 816, Idaho 1969. Ch 3, n 99.

Nash v. Meyer, 31 P 2d 273, Idaho 1934. Ch 1, n 158; Ch 12, n 86.

State v. McMahan, 65 P 2d 156, Idaho 1937. Ch 11, n 160.

Walker v. Distler, 296 P 2d 452, Idaho 1956. Ch 5, n 125.

Illinois

Anderson v. Martzke, 266 NE 2d 137, Ill 1970. Ch 10, n 76.

Barton v. Southwick, 101 NE 928, Ill 1913. Ch 10, n 106.

Beringer v. Lackner, 73 NE 2d 620, Ill 1947. Ch 8, n 54.

In Re Brooks' Estate, 205 NE 2d 435, Ill 1965. Ch 1, n 68.

Bruni v. Department of Registration, 290 NE 2d 295, Ill 1972. Ch 11, n 9; Ch 11, n 33.

Cunningham v. MacNeal Memorial Hospital, 266 NE 2d 897, Ill 1970. Ch 5, n 64.

Darling v. Charleston Community Memorial Hospital, 211 NE 2d 253, Ill 1965, 200 NE 2d 149, Ill 1964. Ch 1, n 43; Ch 2, n 39; Ch 7, n 73; Ch 10, n 161.

Doerr v. Villate, 220 NE 2d 767, Ill 1966. Ch 1, n 11; Ch 1, n 152; Ch 4, n 6; Ch 10, n 150.

Duvardo v. Moore, 98 NE 2d 855, Ill 1951. Ch 10, n 110.

Edgar County Bank & Trust Co. of Paris Hospital, Inc., 294 NE 2d 319, Ill 1973. Ch 10, n 91.

Felton v. Coyle, 238 NE 2d 191, Ill 1968. Ch 9, n 88.

Galesburg Sanitarium v. Jacobson, 103 Ill App 26, Ill 1902. Ch 5, n 210; Ch 9, n 9.

Gorman v. St Francis Hospital, 208 NE 2d 653, Ill 1965. Ch 5, n 99.

Grace v. Howlett, 283 NE 2d 474, Ill 1972. Ch 13, n 66.

Graham v. St Luke's Hospital, 196 NE 2d 355, Ill 1964. Ch 5, n 172.

Green v. Hussey, 262 NE 2d 156, Ill 1970. Ch 5, n 107.

Guth v. Vaughn, 231 Ill App 143, 1923. Ch 10, n 79.

Hoffman v. Wilkins, 270 NE 2d 594, Ill 1971. Ch 11, n 137.

Horwitz v. Michael Reese Hospital, 284 NE 2d 4, Ill 1970. Ch 6, n 28.

Hundt v. Proctor Community Hospital, 284 NE 2d 676, Ill 1972. Ch 7, n 84.

Illinois v. Frey, 294 NE 2d 257, Ill 1973. Ch 11, n 29.

Lipsey v. Michael Reese Hospital, 262 NE 2d 450, Ill 1970. Ch 3, n 66.

Lundahl v. Rockford Memorial Hospital Association, 235 NE 2d 671, Ill 1968. Ch 2, n 42.

McNevins v. Lowe, 40 Ill 209, Ill 1866. Ch 1, n 7.

People ex rel Nabstedt v. Barger, 121 NE 2d 781, Ill 1954. Ch 8, n 127.

Newman v. Spellberg, 234 NE 2d 152, Ill 1968. Ch 4, n 51.

People v. Lowe, 248 NE 2d 530, Ill 1969. Ch 1, n 93.

People to Use of State Board of Health v. McCoy, 17 NE 786, Ill 1888. Ch 11, n 72.

Pratt v. Davis, 79 NE 562, Ill 1906. Ch 8, n 3.

Pugh v. Swiontek, 253 NE 2d 3, Ill 1969. Ch 2, n 63; Ch 3, n 33.

Ritchey v. West, 23 Ill 329, Ill 1860. Ch 1, n 7.

Scardina v. Colletti, 211 NE 2d 762, Ill 1965. Ch 4, n 96.

Shireson v. Walsh, 187 NE 921, Ill 1933. Ch 11, n 49.

Schyman v. Department of Registration, 133 NE 2d 551, Ill 1956. Ch 11, n 20.

People ex rel Wallace v. Labrenz, 104 NE 2d 769, Ill 1952. Ch 1, n 69.

Wallace v. Yudelson, 244 Ill App 320, 1927. Ch 2, n 35.

Zeigler v. Illinois Trust & Savings Bank, 91 NE 1041, Ill 1910. Ch 9, n 81; Ch 12, n 92.

Indiana

Adams v. State of Indiana, 299 NE 2d 834, Ind 1973. Ch 1, n 92-A.

Adkins v. Ropp, 14 NE 2d 727, Ind 1938. Ch 2, n 6; Ch 4, n 1.

Ball Memorial Hospital v. Freeman, 196 NE 2d 274, Ind 1964. Ch 5, n 121.

Bence v. Denbo, 183 NE 326, Ind 1932. Ch 6, n 3.

Board of Medical Medical Registration v. Kaadt, 76 NE 2d 669, Ind 1948. Ch 11, n 58.

Board of Medical Registration and Education of Indiana v. Armington, 178 NE 2d 741, Ind 1961. Ch 11, n 41.

Carpenter v. Campbell, 271 NE 2d 163, Ind 1971. Ch 7, n 10.

County Department of Public Welfare v. Morningstar, 151 NE 2d 150, Ind 1958. Ch 9, n 75.

Eaglen v. State, 231 NE 2d 147, Ind 1967. Ch 1, n 73.

Funk v. Bonham, 183 NE 312, Ind 1932. Ch 5, n 8.

Gramm v. Boener, 56 Ind 497, 1877. Ch 10, n 49.

Hachat v. Hachat, 71 NE 2d 927, Ind 1947. Ch 1, n 112.

Hamilton County Hospital v. Andrews, 84 NE 2d 469, 85 NE 2d 365, Ind 1949. Ch 11, n 126.

Hess v. Lowery, 23 NE 156, Ind 1890. Ch 7, n 19.

Huber v. Protestant Deaconess Hospital Association of Evansville, 133 NE 2d 864, Ind 1956. Ch 7, n 53.

Hurley v. Eddingfield, 59 NE 1058, Ind 1901. Ch 1, n 24.

Meier v. Combs, 263 NE 2d 194, Ind. 1970. Ch 9, n 94.

Memorial Hospital of South Bend, Inc. v. Scott, 290 NE 2d 80, Ind. 1972. Ch 6, n 98; Ch 10, n 30.

Porter Memorial Hospital v. Harvey, 279 NE 2d 583, Ind 1972. Ch 11, n 125.

Shirey v. Schlemmer, 223 NE 2d 759, Ind 1967. Ch 10, n 18.

St. Vincent Hospital v. Stine, 144 NE 537, Ind 1924. Ch 10, n 161.

Wecker v. Kilmer, 294 NE 2d 132, Ind 1973. Ch 10, n 89.

Iowa

Barnes v. Bovenmyer, 122 NW 2d 312, Iowa 1963. Ch 2, n 75; Ch 4, n 136; Ch 12, n 54.

Beatty v. Armstrong, 73 NW 2d 719, Iowa 1955. Ch 10, n 95.

Beck v. The German Klinik, 43 NW 617, Iowa 1889. Ch 2, n 46; Ch 4, n 137.

Dickinson v. Mailliard, 175 NW 2d 588, Iowa 1970. Ch 7, n 70.

Frost v. Des Moines Still College, 79 NW 2d 306, Iowa 1956. Ch 10, n 78.

Gebhardt v. McQuillen, 297 NW 301, Iowa 1941. Ch 4, n 75.

Grosjean v. Spencer, 140 NW 2d 139, Iowa 1966. Ch 8, n 24.

Hollenbeck v. Ristine, 86 NW 377, Iowa 1901. Ch 9, n 22.

Iowa v. Bedel, 193 NW 2d 121, Iowa 1971. Ch 1, n 104.

Jackovach v. Yocom, 237 NW 444, Iowa 1931. Ch 8, n 51.

In re Karwath, 199 NW 2d 147, Iowa 1972. Ch 1, n 71.

Kastler v. Iowa Methodist Hospital, 193 NW 2d 98, Iowa 1971. Ch 6, n 99.

Lemon v. Kessel, 209 NW 393, Iowa 1926. Ch 4, n 142.

McGulpin v. Bessmer, 43 NW 2d 121, Iowa 1950. Ch 1, n 14; Ch 2, n 67; Ch 10, n 15.

Mucci v. Houghton, 57 NW 305, Iowa 1894. Ch 12, n 9.

Natale v. Sisters of Mercy of Council Bluffs, 52 NW 2d 701, Iowa 1952. Ch 11, n 116.

Paine v. Wyatt, 251 NW 78, Iowa 1933, Ch 10, n 110.

Phillips v. Werndorff, 243 NW 525, Iowa 1932. Ch 10, n 64.

Pitzenberger v. Schnack, 245 Iowa 745, 1932. Ch 8, n 126.

Porter v. Powell, 44 NW 295, Iowa 1890. Ch 1, n 112.

Poweshiek County National Bank v. Nationwide Mutual Insurance Co., 156 NW 2d 671, Iowa 1968. Ch 12, n 109.

Ramberg v. Morgan, 218 NW 492, Iowa 1928. Ch 2, n 28.

Sampson v. Holton, 185 NW 2d 216, Iowa 1971. Ch 8, n 122.

Shepherd v. McGinnis, 131 NW 2d 475, Iowa 1964. Ch 6, n 49.

Sinkey v. Surgical Associates, 186 NW 2d 658, Iowa 1971. **Ch 3, n 93.**
State v. Hanson, 207 NW 769, Iowa 1926. Ch 11, n 12.
Tomer v. Aiken, 101 NW 769, Iowa 1904. Ch 12, n 44.
Traer v. State Board of Medical Examiners, 76 NW 833, Iowa 1898. Ch 11, n 90.
Updegraff v. City of Ottumwa, 226 NW 928, Iowa 1929. Ch 10, n 23.
Wheatley v. Heideman, 102 NW 2d 343, Iowa 1960. Ch 3, n 2.
Willey v. Willey, 115 NW 2d 833, Iowa 1962. Ch 8, n 131.
Wilson v. Corbin, 41 NW 2d 702, Iowa 1950. Ch 2, n 34.

Kansas

Barnes v. St Francis Hospital, 507 P 2d 288, Kans 1973. Ch 5, n 160.
In re Estate of Bernatzki, 460 P 2d 527, Kans 1969. Ch 12, n 114.
Bernsden v. Johnson, 255 P 2d 1033, Kans 1953. Ch 5, n 51.
Brown v. Hassig, 15 P 2d 401, Kans 1932. Ch 11, n 54.
Bugg v. Security Benevolent Association,, 112 P 2d 73, Kans 1941. Ch 3, n 16.
Capps v. Valk, 369 P 2d 238, Kans 1962. Ch 5, n 14; Ch 7, n 36; Ch 12, n 6; Ch 12, n 79.
Collins v. Meeker, 424 P 2d 488, Kans 1967. Ch 3, n 13; Ch 12, n 14.
Emrie v. Tice, 258 P 2d 332, Kans 1953. Ch 5, n 105.
Feiser v. St. Francis Hospital and School of Nursing, Inc., 510 P 2d 145, Kans 1973. Ch 10, n 77.
Flentie v. Townsend, 30 P 2d 132, Kans 1934. Ch 12, n 32.
French v. Heibert, 262 P 2d 831, Kans 1953. Ch 6, n 87.
Hecht v. First National Bank & Trust Co., 490 P 2d 649, Kans 1971. Ch 10, n 124.
Kansas State Board v. Seasholtz, 504 P 2d 576, Kans 1972. Ch 11, n 51.
The Kansas State Board of Healing Arts v. Foote, 436 P 2d 828, Kans 1968. Ch 11, n 89.
Keown v. Young, 283 Pac 511, Kans 1930. Ch 10, n 72.
McCoy v. Wesley Hospital and Nurse Training School, 362 P 2d 841, Kans 1961. Ch 10, n 150.
Meffert v. State Board of Medical Registration, 72 Pac 247, Kans, 195 US 625, 1903. Ch 11, n 67.
Mickens v. Davis, 294 Pac 896, Kans 1931. Ch 9, n 23.
Natanson v. Kline, 354 P 2d 670, 350 P 2d 1093, Kans 1960. Ch 4, n 19; Ch 5, n 107; Ch 8, n 5; Ch 8, n 22; Ch 10, n 47.
Neely v. St. Francis Hospital and School of Nursing, 363 P 2d 438, Kans 1961. Ch 5, n 179.
Rule v. Cheeseman, 317 P 2d 472, Kans 1957. Ch 1, n 8; Ch 2, n 73.
Smith v. Wright, 305 P 2d 810, Kans 1957. Ch 3, n 33.
State ex rel Smith v. Schaffer, 270 Pac 604, Kans 1928. Ch 8, n 110.
Voss v. Bridwell, 364 P 2d 955, Kans 1961. Ch 7, n 58.
Williams v. Menehan, 379 P 2d 292, Kans 1963. Ch 8, n 32.
Yeates v. Harms, 401 P 2d 659, Kans 1965. Ch 8, n 48.

Younts v. St. Frances Hospital and School of Nursing, 469 P 2d 330, Kans 1970. Ch 1, n 121.

Kentucky

Beauchamp v. Davis, 217 SW 2d 822, Ky 1948. Ch 7, n 15.

Blair v. Eblen, 461 SW 2d 370, Ky 1970. Ch 2, n 67; Ch 10, n 29.

Boyd v. Wynn, 150 SW 2d 648, Ky 1941. Ch 9, n 29.

Burke v. Miners Memorial Hospital, 381 SW 2d 758, Ky 1964. Ch 2, n 53.

Burkhart v. Community Medical Center, 432 SW 2d 433, Ky 1968. Ch 11, n 118; Ch 11, n 147.

Doan v. Griffith, 402 SW 2d 855, Ky 1966. Ch 2, n 31; Ch 4, n 135; Ch 12, n 53.

Engle v. Clarke, 346 SW 2d 13, Ky 1961. Ch 1, n 162; Ch 4, n 95; Ch 12, n 1; Ch 12, n 82.

Forman v. State Board of Health, 162 SW 796, Ky 1914. Ch 11, n 74.

Hardman v. Hardman, 214 SW 2d 391, Ky 1948. Ch 8, n 133.

Hazelwood v. Stokes, 483 SW 2d 576, Ky 1972. Ch 8, n 77.

Holmes v. Powers, 439 SW 579, Ky 1969. Ch 8, n 109.

Hughes v. Good Samaritan Hospital, 158 SW 2d 159, Ky 1942. Ch 11, n 115.

Jarboe v. Harting, 397 SW 2d 775, Ky 1965. Ch 2, n 63; Ch 3, n 33.

Johnson v. Vaughn, 370 SW 2d 591, Ky 1963. Ch 4, n 15; Ch 4, n 129; Ch 12, n 29.

Meador v. Arnold, 94 SW 2d 626, Ky 1936. Ch 4, n 75.

Meimen v. Rehabilitation Center, Inc., 444 SW 2d 78, Ky 1969. Ch 10, n 97; Ch 11, n 39.

Merker v. Wood, 210 SW 2d 946, Ky 1948. Ch 4, n 12.

Miller v. Blackburn, 185 SW 864, Ky 1916. Ch 12, n 50.

Our Lady of Mercy Hospital v. McIntosh, 461 SW 2d 377, Ky 1970. Ch 10, n 38.

Piper v. Menifee, 51 Ky 465, 1851. Ch 4, n 125.

Quillen v. Skaggs, 25 SW 2d 33, Ky 1930. Ch 6, n 14.

Stacy v. Williams, 69 SW 2d 697, Ky 1934. Ch 10, n 14; Ch 12, n 66.

Steinmetz v. Humphrey, 160 SW 2d 6, Ky 1942. Ch 5, n 26; Ch 10, n 59.

Strunk v. Strunk, 445 SW 2d 145, Ky 1969. Ch 8, n 85.

Tabor v. Scobee, 254 SW 2d 474, Ky 1952. Ch 8, n 56.

Louisiana

Albritton v. Bossier City Hospital, 271 So 2d 353, La 1972. Ch 5, n 110.

Andrepont v. Ochsner, 84 2d 63, La 1955. Ch 5, n 118; Ch 6, n 9.

Burton v. Leftwich, 123 So 2d 766, La 1960. Ch 9, n 6.

Clovis v. Hartford Accident Company, 223 So 2d 178, La 1969. Ch 6, n 22.

Creighton v. Karlin, 225 So 2d 288, La 1969. Ch 10, n 150.

D'Antoni v. Sara Mayo Hospital, 144 So 2d 643, La 1962. Ch 6, n 42.

Favalora v. Aetna Casualty Co., 144 So 2d 544, La 1962. Ch 2, n 44.

Fontenot v. Aetna Casualty and Surety Company, 166 So 2d 299, La 1964. Ch 5, n 174.

Glenn v. Kerlin, 248 So 2d 834, La 1971. Ch 9, n 25.

Grant v. Touro Infirmary, 223 So 2d 148, La 1969. Ch 5, n 8; Ch 7, n 41.

Irwin v. Lorio, 126 So 669, La 1930. Ch 11, n 101.

Johnson v. St. Paul Mercury Insurance Company, 219 So 2d 524, La 1969. Ch 3, n 4.

Joyner v. Alton Ochsner Medical Foundation, 230 So 2d 913, La 1970. Ch 1, n 46.

Lauro v. The Travelers' Insurance Company, 261 So 2d 261, 262 So 2d 787, La 1972. Ch 6, n 32.

LeBlanc v. Midland National Insurance Company, 219 So 2d 251, La 1969. Ch 6, n 24.

Lindsey v. Michigan Mutual Liability Insurance Co., 156 So 2d 313, La 1963. Ch 11, n 39.

Louisiana State Board of Medical Examiners v. Heiman, 230 So 2d 405, La 1970. Ch 11, n 37; Ch 11, n 45.

Meynier v. DePaul Hospital, 218 So 2d 98, La 1969. Ch 5, n 201.

Norton v. Argonaut Insurance Company, 144 So 2d 249, La 1962. Ch 5, n 161.

State ex rel Paul v. Department of Public Welfare, 170 So 2d 549, La 1965. Ch 8, n 130.

Pennison v. Provident Life Insurance Co., 154 So 2d 617, La 1963. Ch 9, n 39.

Powell v. Fidelity Casualty Company, 185 So 2d 324, La 1966. Ch 5, n 85.

In re Richardson, 284 So 2d 185, La 1973. Ch 8, n 84.

Thibodeaux v. Aetna Casualty Insurance Company, 216 So 2d 314, La 1968. Ch 4, n 128.

Thomas v. Lobrano, 76 So 2d 599, La 1954. Ch 5, n 96.

Thompson v. Brent, 245 So 2d 751, La 1971. Ch 7, n 8.

Truxillo v. Gentilly Medical Building, Inc. 225 So 2d 488, La 1969. Ch 6, n 88.

Uter v. Bone and Joint Clinic, 192 So 2d 100, La 1966. Ch 4, n 77.

Vidrine v. Mayes, 127 So 2d 809, La 1961. Ch 1, n 156; Ch 12, n 89.

West v. West, 170 So 2d 160, La 1964. Ch 8, n 134.

Maine

Cyr v. Landry, 95 Atl 883, Maine 1915. Ch 5, n 15; Ch 10, n 42.

Dunbar v. Greenlaw, 128 A 2d 218, Maine 1956. Ch 1, n 154; Ch 9, n 91.

Emery v. Fisher, 148 Atl 677, Maine 1930. Ch 5, n 33.

Merrill v. Odiorne, 94 Atl 753, Maine 1915. Ch 2, n 52; Ch 10, n 19.

Miller v. Dore, 148 A 2d 692, Maine 1959. Ch 7, n 17; Ch 12, n 76.

Sukeforth v. Thegan, 256 A 2d 162, Maine 1969. Ch 1, n 154.

Maryland

Avery v. Maryland, 292 A 2d 728, Md 1972. Ch 9, n 13.

Coolahan v. Maryland, 270 A 2d 669, Md 1970. Ch 1, n 76.

Craig v. State, 155 A 2d 684, Md 1959. Ch 1, n 73; Ch 11, n 176.

Dashiell v. Griffith, 35 Atl 1094, Md 1896. Ch 7, n 16; Ch 12, n 4; Ch 12, n 69.

Grantham v. Board of County Commissioners for Prince George's County, 246 A 2d 548, Md 1968. Ch 10, n 92.

Lane v. Calvert, 138 A 2d 902, Md 1958. Ch 2, n 57; Ch 4, n 3.

Levin v. Sinai Hospital, 46 A 2d 298, Md 1946. Ch 11, n 144; Ch 11, n 156.

In re Smith, 295 A 2d 238, Md 1972. Ch 1, n 135.

Stevens v. Emergency Hospital, 121 Atl 475, Md 1923. Ch 11, n 146.

Suburban Hospital Ass'n v. Mewhinney, 187 A 2d 671, Md 1963. Ch 1, n 3.

Thomas v. Corso, 288 A 2d 379, Md 1972. Ch 12, n 12; Ch 12, n 56.

Massachusetts

Aurelio v. Laird, 223 NE 2d 531, Mass 1967. Ch 4, n 33.

Barrette v. Hight, 230 NE 2d 808, Mass 1967. Ch 7, n 31.

Berman v. Board of Registration, 244 NE 2d 553, Mass 1969. Ch 11, n 26.

Biancucci v. Nigro, 141 NE 568, Mass 1923. Ch 5, n 131.

Brune v. Belinkoff, 235 NE 2d 793, Mass 1968. Ch 2, n 80; Ch 5, n 115; Ch 5, n 129.

Butler v. Layton, 164 NE 920, Mass 1929. Ch 5, n 133.

Callahan v. Longwood Hospital, 208 NE 2d 247, Mass 1965. Ch 5, n 68.

Chesley v. Durant, 137 NE 301, Mass 1922. Ch 5, n 13.

Commonwealth v. Goldenberg, 155 NE 2d 187, Mass 1959. Ch 9, n 14.

Commonwealth v. Pierce, 138 Mass 165, 1885. Ch 11, n 168.

Commonwealth of Massachusetts v. Wiseman, 249 NE 2d 610, Mass 1969. Ch 9, n 59.

Curley v. McDonald, 160 NE 796, Mass 1928. Ch 5, n 112.

Delaney v. Rosenthall, 196 NE 2d 878, Mass 1964. Ch 7, n 1.

Dugdale v. Board of Registration in Medicine, 169 NE 547, Mass 1930. Ch 11, n 20.

Ernen v. Crofwell, 172 NE 73, Mass 1930, Ch 5, n 29.

Forman v. Wolfson, 98 NE 2d 615, Mass 1951. Ch 10, n 103.

Forziati v. Board of Registration in Medicine, 128 NE 2d 789, Mass 1955. Ch 11, n 78.

Gahn v. Leary, 61 NE 2d 844, Mass 1945. Ch 8, n 68.

Johnson v. Phillips, 223 NE 2d 677, Mass 1967. Ch 5, n 170.

Karjavinen v. Buswell, 194 NE 295, Mass 1935. Ch 1, n 154; Ch 9, n 91.

King v. Solomon, 81 NE 2d 838, Mass 1948. Ch 5, n 198; Ch 10, n 45.

Kudish v. Board of Registration in Medicine, 248 NE 2d 264, Mass 1969. Ch 11, n 27.

Linhares v. Hall, 257 NE 2d 429, Mass 1970. Ch 4, n 42; Ch 10, n 57.

Massachusetts v. Concepcion, 290 NE 2d 514, Mass 1972. Ch 12, n 113.

Massachusetts v. Miller, 282 NE 2d 394, Mass 1972. Ch 1, n 76.

McCarthy v. Boston City Hospital, 266 NE 2d 292, Mass 1971. Ch 5, n 100.

McDonald v. Massachusetts General Hospital, 120 Mass 432, 1876. Ch 10, n 152.

Muse v. DeVito, 137 NE 730, Mass 1923. Ch 10, n 69.

Nason v. Superintendent of Bridgewater State Hospital, 233 NE 2d 908, Mass 1968. Ch 8, n 92.

Pasquale v. Chandler, 215 NE 2d 319, Mass 1966. Ch 5, n 52.

Purchase v. Seelye, 121 NE 413, Mass 1918. Ch 10, n 75.

Riggs v. Christie, 173 NE 2d 610, Mass 1961. Ch 3, n 94; Ch 12, n 49.

Petition of Rohrer, 230 NE 2d 915, Mass 1967. Ch 8, n 90.

Shannon v. Ramsey, 193 NE 235, Mass 1934. Ch 12, n 43.

Sullivan v. O'Connor, 296 NE 2d 183, Mass 1973. Ch 4, n 93.

Thomas v. Ellis, 106 NE 2d 687, Mass 1952. Ch 3, n 74.

Usen v. Usen, 269 NE 2d 442, Mass 1971. Ch 8, n 124.

Woronka v. Sewall, 69 NE 2d 581, Mass 1946. Ch 4, n 48.

Michigan

Anderson v. Board of Trustees of Caro Hospital, 159 NW 2d 347, Mich 1968. Ch 11, n 139; Ch 11, n 143.

Bakker v. Welsh, 108 NW 94, Mich 1906, Ch 1, n 120.

Ballance v. Dunnington, 217 NW 329, Mich 1928. Ch 4, n 20; Ch 5, n 94.

Bishop v. Shurly, 211 NW 75, Mich 1926. Ch 1, n 120.

Bradshaw v. Blaine, 134 NW 2d 386, Mich 1965. Ch 4, n 40.

Bryson v. Stone, 190 NW 2d 336, Mich 1971. Ch 3, n 110; Ch 8, n 28.

Chase v. Clinton County, 217 NW 565, Mich 1928. Ch 12, n 11.

DeMay v. Roberts, 9 NW 146, Mich 1881. Ch 9, n 48.

Dyke v. Richard, 198 NW 2d 797, Mich 1972. Ch 10, n 141.

Facer v. Lewis, 40 NW 2d 457, Mich. 1950. Ch 10, n 46.

Fortner v. Koch, 261 NW 762, Mich 1935. Ch 3, n 81; Ch 4, n 29; Ch 8, n 145.

Gaertner v. Michigan, 187 NW 2d 429, Mich. 1971. Ch 12, n 100.

Haewsky v. St. John Hospital, Mich Cir Ct, Wayne Co. Docket 136-064 June 10, 1970. Ch 8, n 118.

Hand v. Park Community Hospital, 165 NW 2d 673, Mich 1968, Ch 6, n 14.

Harvey v. Silber, 2 NW 2d 483, Mich 1942. Ch 1, n 20.

Johnson v. Borland, 26 NW 2d 755, Mich 1947. Ch 3, n 27.

Jones v. Bouza, 160 NW 2d 881, Mich 1968. Ch 1, n 86; Ch 7, n 88.

Kaimowitz v. Department of Mental Health, Civil Action #73-19434-AW (Mich, Wayne Co. Cir Ct, 1973). Ch 8, n 136-A.

Kambas v. St. Joseph's Hospital, 189 NW 2d 879, Mich 1971. Ch 10, n 141.

Kopprasch v. Stone, 65 NW 2d 852, Mich 1954. Ch 9, n 78.

Loveland v. Nelson, 209 NW 835, Mich 1926. Ch 5, n 121.

Luka v. Lowrie, 136 NW 1106, Mich 1912. Ch 1, n 113; Ch 8, n 13.

McGarry v. J. A. Mercier Co., 262 NW 296, Mich 1935. Ch 12, n 93.

Michigan v. Bricker, 208 NW 2d 172, Mich 1973. Ch 11, n 36.

Miles v. Van Gelder, 137 NW 2d 292, Mich 1965. Ch 8, n 31.

Milford v. People's Community Hospital Authority, 155 NW 2d 835, Mich 1968. Ch 11, n 136; Ch 11, n 153.

Miller v. Toles, 150 NW 118, Mich 1914. Ch 2, n 19; Ch 4, n 28.

Morgan v. Engles, 127 NW 2d 382, Mich 1964. Ch 2, n 31.

Naccarato v. Grob, 180 NW 2d 788, Mich 1970. Ch 2, n 82; Ch 3, n 80.

Olepa v. Mapletoff, 141 NW 2d 350, Mich 1966. Ch 9, n 96.

Parker v. Port Huron Hospital, 105 NW 2d 1, Mich 1960. Ch 5, n 71; Ch 5, n 76.

Podvin v. Eickhorst, 128 NW 2d 523, Mich 1964. Ch 1, n 161.

Rauhe v. Langeland Memorial Chapel, Inc., 205 NW 2d 313, Mich 1973. Ch 8, n 80.

Rostron v. Klein, 178 NW 2d 675, Mich 1970. Ch 3, n 55.

Rytkonen v. Lojacono, 257 NW 703, Mich 1934. Ch 1, n 137.

Schneider v. Little Company, 151 NW 587, 588, Mich 1915. Ch 2, n 2.

In re Estate of Searchill, 157 NW 2d 788, Mich 1968. Ch 12, n 114.

Sinclair v. Brunson, 180 NW 358, Mich 1920. Ch 12, n 23.

Smith v. Children's Hospital of Michigan, 189 NW 2d 753, Mich 1971. Ch 1, n 39.

Sobotta v. Vogel, 194 NW 2d 564, Mich 1971. Ch 10, n 83.

Stewart v. Rudner, 84 NW 2d 816, Mich 1957. Ch 3, n 72.

Stowers v. Wolodzko, 191 NW 2d 355, Mich 1971. Ch 8, n 101; Ch 9, n 89.

Taylor v. Milton, 92 NW 2d 57, Mich 1958. Ch 5, n 43.

Troppi v. Scarf, 187 NW 2d 511, Mich 1971. Ch 4, n 7; Ch 5, n 149.

Zanzon v. Whittaker, 17 NW 2d 206, Mich 1945. Ch 5, n 53.

Zoterell v. Repp, 153 NW 692, Mich 1915. Ch 1, n 9.

Minnesota

Almquist v. Wilcox, 131 NW 796, Minn 1911. Ch 10, n 88.

Bang v. Charles T. Miller Hospital, 88 NW 2d 186, Minn 1958. Ch 8, n 44.

Christy v. Saliterman, 179 NW 2d 288, Minn 1970. Ch 2, n 81; Ch 4, n 140; Ch 5, n 213; Ch 12, n 53.

Couillard v. Charles T. Miller Hospital, 92 NW 2d 96, Minn 1958. Ch 10, n 90.

Gamradt v. DuBois, 230 NW 774, Minn 1930. Ch 12, n 33.

Harris v. Wood, 8 NW 2d 818, Minn 1943. Ch 5, n 128.

Henslin v. Wheaton, 97 NW 882, Minn 1904. Ch 5, n 94.

House v. Hanson, 72 NW 2d 874, Minn 1955. Ch 10, n 105.

Johnson v. Sterling Drug Co., 190 NW 2d 77, Minn 1971. Ch 10, n 120.

Jordahl v. Berry, 75 NW 10, Minn 1898. Ch 10, n 107.

Kingsley v. Forsyth, 257 NW 95, Minn 1934. Ch 8, n 73.

Korman v. Hagen, 206 NW 650, Minn 1925. Ch 4, n 59.

Larson v. Chase, 50 NW 238, Minn 1891. Ch 8, n 61.

Manion v. Tweedy, 100 NW 2d 124, Minn 1959. Ch 2, n 24; Ch 2, n 29.

Miller v. Hennepin County Medical Society, 144 NW 1091, Minn 1914. Ch 11, n 104.

Miller v. Raaen, 139 NW 2d 877, Minn 1966. Ch 5, n 137.

Minnesota v. Hodgson, 204 NW 2d 199, Minn 1973. Ch 11, n 29.

Minnesota State Board of Medical Examiners v. Schmidt, 292 NW 255, Minn 1940. Ch 11, n 59.

Moehlenbrock v. Parke-Davis and Company, 169 NW 541, Minn 1918, Ch 6, n 57.

Moeller v. Hauser, 54 NW 2d 639, Minn 1952. Ch 4, n 130; Ch 7, n 35; Ch 12, n 80.

Mohr v. Williams, 104 NW 12, Minn 1905. Ch 8, n 54.

Mulder v. Parke-Davis and Co., 181 NW 2d 882, Minn 1970. Ch 5, n 192.

Mulliner v. Evangelischer Diakonniessenversein of Minnesota District of German Evangelical Synod of North America, 175 NW 699, Minn 1920. Ch 10, n 159.

Nelson v. Farrish, 173 W 715, Minn 1919. Ch 12, n 45.

Nelson v. Swedish Hospital, 64 NW 2d 38, Minn 1954. Ch 6, n 11.

Ray v. Wagner, 176 NW 2d 101, Minn 1970. Ch 4, n 134.

Schulz v. Feigal, 142 NW 2d 84, Minn 1966. Ch 5, n 145; Ch 7, n 2.

Singer v. Bossingham, 188 NW 155, Minn 1922. Ch 12, n 16.

Skillings v. Allen, 180 NW 916, Minn 1921. Ch 4, n 124.

Staloch v. Holm, 111 NW 264, Minn 1907. Ch 2, n 58.

State v. Lester, 149 NW 297, Minn 1914. Ch 11, n 163.

Sulak v. Miller Hospital, 165 NW 2d 207, Minn 1969. Ch 6, n 104.

Swigerd v. Ortonville Hospital, 75 NW 2d 217, Minn 1956. Ch 6, n 19.

Synnott v. Midway Hospital, 178 NW 2d 211, Minn 1970. Ch 5, n 108.

Wallstedt v. Swedish Hospital, 19 NW 2d 426, Minn 1945. Ch 6, n 21.

Mississippi

Chapman v. Carlson, 240 So 2d 263, Miss 1970. Ch 5, n 86; Ch 10, n 55.

Copeland v. Robertson, 112 So 2d 236, Miss 1959. Ch 3, n 112.

Gulf and Ship Island RR Co. v. Sullivan, 119 So 501, Miss 1928. Ch 1, n 120.

Hill v. Stewart, 209 So 2d 809, Miss 1968. Ch 3, n 83.

Hood v. Moffett, 69 So 664, Miss 1915. Ch 12, n 16.

Long v. Sledge, 209 So 2d 814, Miss 1968. Ch 5, n 11; Ch 10, n 60.

Metropolitan Life Insurance Co. v. Evans, 184 So 426, Miss 1938. Ch 1, n 80.

Mississippi Baptist Hospital v. Holmes, 55 So 2d 142, Miss 1951. Ch 5, n 70; Ch 10, n 156.

New Biloxi Hospital v. Frazier, 146 So 2d 882, Miss 1962. Ch 1, n 28; Ch 12, n 57.

Prewett v. Philpot, 107 So 880, Miss 1926. Ch 5, n 17.

Ross v. Hodges, 234 So 2d 905, Miss 1970. Ch 8, n 32.

Waddle v. Sutherland, 126 So 201, Miss 1930. Ch 5, n 97.

Missouri

Baird v. National Health Foundation, 144 SW 2d 850, Mo 1940. Ch 12, n 30.

Barber v. Time, Inc., 159 SW 2d 291, Mo 1942. Ch 9, n 55.

Boyd v. Andrae, 44 SW 2d 891, Mo 1932. Ch 12, n 25.

Brown v. Scullin Steel Company, 260 SW 2d 513, Mo 1953. Ch 3, n 79.

Burns v. Owens, 459 SW 2d 303, Mo 1970. Ch 7, n 28.

Carter v. Ries, 378 SW 2d 487, Mo 1964. Ch 3, n 95.

Cazzell v. Schofield, 8 SW 2d 580, Mo 1928. Ch 12, n 27.

Crump v. Piper, 425 SW 2d 924, Mo 1968. Ch 7, n 25.

English v. Sahlender, 47 SW 2d 150, Mo 1932. Ch 6, n 89.

Ernst v. Schwartz, 445 SW 2d 377, Mo 1969. Ch 10, n 15.

Evans v. Clapp, 231 SW 79, Mo 1921. Ch 5, n 102.

Fausette v. Grim, 186 SW 1177, Mo 1916. Ch 9, n 68; Ch 12, n 62.

Gore v. Brockman, 119 SW 1082, Mo 1909. Ch 5, n 90.

Gross v. Robinson, 218 SW 924, Mo 1920. Ch 5, n 106.

Haase v. Garfinkel, 418 SW 2d 108, Mo 1967. Ch 4, n 100.

Hager v. Major, 186 SW 2d 564, Mo 1945. Ch 9, n 23.

Hales v. Raines, 141 SW 917, Mo 1911. Ch 4, n 20; Ch 5, n 106.

Hughes v. State Board of Health, 159 SW 2d 277, Mo 1942. Ch 11, n 84.

Ingram v. Poston, 260 SW 773, Mo 1924. Ch 5, n 28.

Jaime v. Neurological Hospital Association, 488 SW 2d 641, Mo 1973. Ch 10, n 146.

Johnston v. The Upjohn Company, 442 SW 2d 93, Mo 1969. Ch 6, n 65.

State ex rel Kerr v. Landwehr, 32 SW 2d 83, Mo 1930. Ch 11, n 10.

State ex rel Lentine v. State Board of Health, 65 SW 2d 943, Mo 1933. Ch 11, n 75.

Logan v. Field, 75 Mo App 594, Mo 1898. Ch 2, n 27.

State ex rel Mayfield v. St. Louis Medical Society, 91 Mo App 76, Mo 1901. Ch 11, n 107.

Mitchell v. Robinson, 334 SW 2d 11, Mo 1960. Ch 5, n 207; Ch 8, n 6; Ch 8, n 19.

Orphant v. St. Louis State Hospital, 441 SW 2d 355, Mo 1969. Ch 6, n 111.

Parkell v. Fitzporter, 256 SW 239, Mo 1923, Ch 10, n 71.

Raschelbach v. Benincasa, 372 SW 2d 120, Mo 1963. Ch 5, n 139.

Reed v. Laughlin, 58 SW 2d 440, Mo 1933. Ch 12, n 58.

Sibert v. Boger, 260 SW 2d 569, Mo 1953. Ch 3, n 98.

Smart v. Kansas City, 105 SW 709, Mo 1907. Ch 1, n 16.

Smith v. Mallinckrodt Chemical Works, 251 SW 155, Mo 1923. Ch 2, n 33.

Spain v. Burch, 154 SW 172, Mo 1913. Ch 5, n 130.

Staehlin v. Hockdoerfer, 235 SW 106, Mo 1921. Ch 10, n 83.

State v. Atkins, 292 SW 422, Mo 1926. Ch 9, n 14.

Steele v. Woods, 327 SW 2d 187, Mo 1959. Ch 2, n 48; Ch 4, n 144; Ch 10, n 34.

Swenson v. Swenson, 227 SW 2d 103, Mo 1950. Ch 1, n 117.

Swope v. Printz, 468 SW 2d 34, Mo 1971. Ch 10, n 136.

Tryon v. Casey, 416 SW 2d 252, Mo 1967. Ch 12, n 109.

Williams v. Chamberlain, 316 SW 2d 505, Mo 1958. Ch 2, n 57; Ch 5, n 31; Ch 5, n 49.

Wilson v. Hungate, 434 SW 2d 580, Mo 1968. Ch 1, n 87; Ch 7, n 90; Ch 10, n 112.

Wilt v. McCallum, 253 SW 156, Mo 1923. Ch 5, n 119.

Younge v. State Board of Registration, 451 SW 2d 346, Mo 1969. Ch 11, n 6; Ch 11, n 28.

Zipkin v. Freeman, 436 SW 2d 753, Mo 1968. Ch 1, n 5; Ch 9, n 17; Ch 9, n 84.

Montana

Doerr v. Movius, 463 P 2d 477, Mont 1970. Ch 3, n 107.

Ham v. Holy Rosary Hospital, Docket No. 14910 Mont Dist Ct, Custer County, February 13, 1973. Ch 1, n 150.

Hutchins v. Blood Services of Montana, 506 P 2d 449, Mont 1973. Ch 5, n 58.

Kober v. Stewart, 417 P 2d 476, Mont 1966. Ch 7, n 67.

Nebraska

Acker v. Sorensen, 165 NW 2d 74, Neb 1969. Ch 10, n 126.

Bailey v. Williams, 203 NW 2d 454, Neb 1973. Ch 12, n 48.

In re Cavitt, 157 NW 2d 171, Neb 1968. Ch 8, n 107.

Foley v. Bishop Clarkson Memorial Hospital, 173 NW 2d 881, Neb 1970. Ch 10, n 6.

In re Johnson's Estate, 16 NW 2d 504, Neb 1944, Ch 3, n 15; Ch 3, n 41.

Munk v. Frink, 116 NW 525, Neb 1908. Ch 11, n 10; Ch 11, n 27.

Munson v. Bishop Clarkson Memorial Hospital, 186 NW 2d 492, Neb 1971. Ch 10, n 52.

Simonsen v. Swenson, 177 NW 831, Neb 1920. Ch 9, n 32.

State ex rel Sorensen v. Lake, 236 NW 762, Neb 1931. Ch 11, n 13.

Stohlman v. Davis, 220 NW 247, Neb 1928. Ch 1, n 13; Ch 7, n 13; Ch 12, n 9; Ch 12, n 74.

Tady v. Warta, 196 NW 901, Neb 1924. Ch 5, n 34.

Van Skike v. Potter, 73 NW 295, Neb 1897. Ch 5, n 53; Ch 12, n 50.

Nevada

Bowell v. Board of Medical Examiners, 293 P 2d 424, Nev 1956. Ch 11, n 80.

Corn v. French, 289 P 2d 173, Nev 1955. Ch 8, n 27.

Lockart v. Maclean, 361 P 2d 670, Nev 1961. Ch 2, n 65.

Moore v. The Board of Trustees of Carson Tahoe Hospital, 495 P 2d 605, Nev 1972. Ch 11, n 155.

Nichter v. Edminston, 407 P 2d 721, Nev 1965. Ch 7, n 43; Ch 13, n 42.

Percifield v. Foutz, 285 P 2d 130, Nev 1955. Ch 5, n 43.

State v. Lung, 28 Pac 235, Nev 1891. Ch 9, n 15.

New Hampshire

Bricker v. Sceva Speare Memorial Hospital, 281 A 2d 589, NH 1971. Ch 11, n 151.

Carrigan v. Roman Catholic Bishop, 178 A 2d 502, NH 1962. Ch 2, n 88; Ch 3, n 45.

Hawkins v. McGee, 146 Atl 641, NH 1929. Ch 4, n 5.

Haynes v. Ordway, 58 NH 167, 1877. Ch 10, n 108.

Holland v. Metalious, 198 A 2d 654, NH 1964. Ch 8, n 79.

Leighton v. Sargent, 27 NH 460, 1853. Ch 2, n 59.

Mehigan v. Sheehan, 51 A 2d 632, NH 1947. Ch 12, n 34.

Michael v. Roberts, 23 A 2d 361, NH 1941. Ch 4, n 98.

Welch v. Frisbie Memorial Hospital, 9 A 2d 761, NH 1939. Ch 3, n 93; Ch 12, n 53.

New Jersey

Baptisa v. St. Barnabas Medical Center, 262 A 2d 902, 270 A 2d 409, NJ 1970. Ch 5, n 75.

Beadling v. Sirotta, 176 A 2d 546, NJ 1961. Ch 1, n 82; Ch 3, n 108.

Becker v. Eisenstodt, 158 A 2d 706, NJ 1960. Ch 5, n 144.

Bergen v. Miller, 250 A 2d 49, NJ 1969. Ch 7, n 87.

Brody v. Overlook Hospital, 296 A 2d 668, NJ 1972. Ch 5, n 65.

Bush v. Kallen, 302 A 2d 142, NJ 1973. Ch 12, n 102.

Carbone v. Warburton, 91 A 2d 518, 94 A 2d 680, NJ 1953. Ch 2, n 75.

Clark v. Wichman, 179 A 2d 38, NJ 1962. Ch 4, n 76; Ch 12, n 82; Ch 12, n 88.

Collopy v. Newark Eye and Ear Infirmary, 141 A 2d 276, NJ 1958. Ch 10, n 165.

Daily v. Somberg, 146 A 2d 676, NJ 1958. Ch 10, n 90.

Davis v. Morristown Memorial Hospital, 254 A 2d 125, NJ 1969. Ch 11, n 121.

Falcone v. Middlesex County Medical Society, 170 A 2d 791, NJ 1961. 75 *Harvard Law Rev* 1142, 1962. Ch 11, n 95.

Fernandez v. Baruch, 244 A 2d 109, NJ 1968. Ch 4, n 109.

Fleishmann v. Richardson Merrell, Inc., 226 A 2d 843, NJ 1967. Ch 12, n 51.

Flynn v. Stearns, 145 A 2d 33, NJ 1958. Ch 10, n 39.

Greisman v. Newcomb Hospital, 192 A 2d 817, NJ 1963. Ch 11, n 123.

Grove v. Seltzer, 266 A 2d 301, NJ 1970. Ch 13, n 56.

Hague v. Williams, 181 A 2d 345, NJ 1962. Ch 9, n 45.

Jackson v. Muhlenberg Hospital, 249 A 2d 65, NJ 1969. Ch 5, n 62.

Kelly v. Stern, 132 Atl 234, NJ 1926. Ch 5, n 30.

Kennedy Hospital v. Heston, 279 A 2d 670, NJ 1971. Ch 1, n 67.

Kent v. County of Hudson, 245 A 2d 747, NJ 1968. Ch 6, n 15; Ch 10, n 36.

Kern v. Kogan, 226 A 2d 186, NJ 1967. Ch 3, n 85.

Lewis v. Read, 193 A 2d 255, NJ 1963. Ch 2, n 73.

Lindroth v. Christ Hospital, 123 A 2d 10, NJ 1956. Ch 6, n 108.

Lopez v. Swyer, 300 A 2d 563, NJ 1973. Ch 9, n 72; Ch 10, n 133.

Magner v. Beth Israel Hospital, 295 A 2d 363, NJ 1972. Ch 6, n 51.

Marchese v. Monaco, 145 A 2d 809, NJ 1958. Ch 5, n 187.

Marsello v. Barnett, 236 A 2d 869, NJ 1967. Ch 13, n 55.

Martin v. Perth Amboy General Hospital, 250 A 2d 40, NJ 1969. Ch 5, n 9; Ch 7, n 41.

Myers v. Holborn, 33 Atl 389, NJ 1895. Ch 7, n 15.

Raleigh-Fitkin Memorial Hospital v. Anderson, 201 A 2d 537, NJ 1964. Ch 1, n 64.

Renrick v. City of Newark, 181 A 2d 24, NJ 1962. Ch 5, n 165.

Rose v. Raleigh-Fitkin Memorial Hospital, 57 A 2d 29, NJ 1948. Ch 6, n 109.

Rothman v. Silber, 216 A 2d 18, NJ 1966. Ch 10, n 127.

Sanzari v. Rosenfeld, 167 A 2d 625, NJ 1961. Ch 5, n 132.

Schireson v. State Board of Medical Examiners of New Jersey, 28 A 2d 879, NJ 1942. Ch 11, n 12; Ch 11, n 47.

Scott v. Salem County Memorial Hospital, 280 A 2d 843, NJ 1971. Ch 4, n 80.

Sinatra v. National Xray Products Corporation, 141 A 2d 28, NJ 1958. Ch 6, n 75.

State v. Perricone, 181 A 2d 751, NJ 1962. Ch 1, n 69.

State Board of Medical Examiners v. Weiner, 172 A 2d 661, NJ 1961. Ch 11, n 166.

Stumper v. Kimel, 260 A 2d 526, NJ 1970. Ch 7, n 38.

Sussman v. Overlook Hospital, 231 A 2d 389, NJ 1967. Ch 11 n 120.

Swank v. Halivopoulos, 260 A 2d 240, NJ 1969. Ch 1, n 108.

Tramutola v. Bortone, 304 A 2d 197, NJ 1973. Ch 7, n 23.

Unick v. Kessler Memorial Hospital, 257 A 2d 134, NJ 1969. Ch 12, n 103.

Yerzy v. Levine, 260 A 2d 533, NJ 1970. Ch 4, n 82.

New Mexico

Crockett v. Encino Gardens Care Center, Inc., 492 P 2d 1273, NM 1972. Ch 6, n 109.

Crouch v. Most, 432 P 2d 250, NM 1967. Ch 8, n 14; Ch 8, n 63.

Los Alamos Medical Center v. Coe, 275 P 2d 175, NM 1954. Ch 5, n 199; Ch 10, n 45.

Mantz v. Follingstad, 505 P 2d 68, NM 1972. Ch 10, n 115.

New Mexico v. Strance, 506 P 2d 1217, NM 1973. Ch 11, n 29.

Seidenberg v. New Mexico Board of Medical Examiners, 452 P 2d 469, NM 1969. Ch 11, n 3; Ch 11, n 51.

Strance v. New Mexico Board of Medical Examiners, 487 P 2d 1085, NM 1971. Ch 11, n 22; Ch 11, n 79.

Vigil v. Rice, 397 P 2d 719, NM 1964. Ch 9, n 18.

Williams v. Vanderhoven, 482 P 2d 55, NM 1971. Ch 4, n 81.

Woods v. Brumlop, 377 P 2d 520, NM 1962. Ch 5, n 200; Ch 8, n 19; Ch 9, n 64.

New York

New York Ex rel Abajian v. Dennett, 184 NYS 2d 178, NY 1958. Ch 8, n 114.

In re Adoption of Anonymous, 345 NYS 2d 430, NY 1973. Ch 8, n 114.

Amrieri v. St. Joseph's Hospital, 228 NYS 483, NY 1936. Ch 10, n 87.

Anonymous v. Anonymous, 246 NYS 2d 835, NY 1964. Ch 8, n 113.

Antowill v. Friedmann, 188 NYS 777, NY 1921. Ch 5, n 94.

Application of Howe, 295 NYS 2d 883, NY 1968. Ch 9, n 97.

Application of Shaw, 212 NYS 2d 701, NY 1961. Ch 11, n 52.

Arshanasky v. Royal Concourse Co., 283 NYS 2d 646, NY 1967. Ch 2, n 36.

B v. S., 335 NYS 2d 131, NY 1972. Ch 1, n 139.

Bach v. Long Island Jewish Hospital, 267 NYS 2d 289, NY 1966. Ch 1, n 116.

Bachrach v. Farbenfabriken Bayer AG, 344 NYS 2d 286, NY 1973. Ch 9, n 57.

Baidach v. Togut, 190 NYS 2d 120, NY 1959. Ch 7, n 31.

New York ex rel Baker v. Narcotics Addiction Control Commission, 297 NYS 2d 1018, NY 1968. Ch 1, n 52.

Barcia v. Society of the New York Hospital, 241 NYS 2d 373, NY 1963. Ch 1, n 27; Ch 12, n 55.

Barnes v. Gardner, 9 NYS 2d 785, NY 1939. Ch 1, n 7.

People ex rel Bartlett v. Medical Society, 32 NY 185, NY 1865. Ch 11, n 107.

Battistella v. Society of the New York Hospital, 191 NYS 626, NY 1959. Ch 1, n 80; Ch 7, n 95.

Becker v. Janinski, 15 NYS 675, NY 1891. Ch 12, n 36; Ch 12, n 64.

Bennett v. New York, 299 NYS 2d 288, NY 1969. Ch 8, n 96; Ch 10, n 33.

Benson v. Dean, 133 NE 125, NY 1921. Ch 2, n 27; Ch 4, n 8; Ch 5, n 25; Ch 5, n 50.

Berg v. New York Society for the Relief of the Ruptured and Crippled, 136 NE 2d 523, NY 1956. Ch 5, n 73.

Bernanke v. Board of Regents, 264 NYS 2d 399, NY 1965. Ch 11, n 45.

Bing v. Thunig, 143 NE 2d 3, NY 1957. Ch 7, n 45.

Birnbaum v. Seigler, 76 NYS 2d 173, NY 1948. Ch 9, n 70.

Blair v. Bartlett, 75 NY 150, 1878. Ch 10, n 104.

Boland v. New York, 333 NYS 2d 410, NY 1972. Ch 10, n 145.

Boll v. Sharpe and Dohme, Inc., 120 NE 2d 836, NY 1954. Ch 5, n 88.

Bowman v. American National Red Cross, 241 NYS 2d 971, NY 1963. Ch 5, n 89.

Brown v. Broome County, 170 NE 2d 666, NY 1960. Ch 8, n 69.

Burns v. Board of Regents, 233 NYS 2d 927, NY 1962. Ch 11, n 52.

Calvaruso v. Our Lady of Peace Roman Catholic Church, 319 NYS 2d 727, NY 1971. Ch 3, n 51.

Capuano v. Jacobs, 305 NYS 2d 837, NY 1969. Ch 1, n 22; Ch 3, n 89.

Carpenter v. Blake, 60 Barbour 488, NY 1871. Ch 4, n 22.

Clark v. Geraci, 208 NYS 2d 564, NY 1960. Ch 9, n 20.

Collins v. Davis, 254 NYS 2d 666, NY 1964. Ch 1, n 66.

Cox v. New York, 171 NYS 2d 818, NY 1958. Ch 12, n 110.

Cremonese v. City of New York, 215 NE 2d 157, NY 1966. Ch 8, n 68.

In re Culbertson's Will, 292 NYS 2d 806, NY 1968. Ch 12, n 95.

Curry v. Corn, 277 NYS 2d 470, NY 1966. Ch 9, n 40.

D'Alois v. Allen, 297 NYS 2d 826, NY 1969. Ch 11, n 11; Ch 11, n 53.

Darrah v. Kite, 301 NYS 2d 286, NY 1969. Ch 8, n 10.

Davie v. Lenox Hill Hospital, 81 NYS 2d 583, NY 1948. Ch 4, n 31.

Davis v. New York, 315 NYS 2d 82, NY 1970. Ch 4, n 27.

Davis v. New York, 322 NYS 2d 569, NY 1972. Ch 8, n 96; Ch 9, n 10.

Derby v. Prewitt, 187 NE 2d 556, NY 1962. Ch 10, n 80.

DiGiovanni v. Pessel, 250 A 2d 756, NY 1969. Ch 1, n 154; Ch 3, n 24.

Doe v. Roe, 345 NYS 2d 560, NY 1973. Ch 9, n 56.

Dunn v. New York, 312 NYS 2d 61, NY 1970. Ch 4, n 112.

Durfee v. Durfee, 87 NYS 2d 275, NY 1949. Ch 1, n 110.

Eisele v. Malone, 157 NYS 2d 155, 158 NYS 2d 761, NY 1957. Ch 5, n 204.

Erickson v. Dilgard, 252 NYS 2d 705, NY 1962. Ch 1, n 68.

Evans v. Newark - Wayne Community Hospital, 316 NYS 2d 447, NY 1970. Ch 6, n 25; Ch 10, n 31.

Falum v. Medical Arts Center Hospital, 160 *New York Law Journal* 2, 1968. Ch 12, n 101.

Feeney v. Young, 181 NYS 481, NY 1920. Ch 9, n 52.

Felis v. Greenberg, 273 NYS 2d 288, NY 1966. Ch 9, n 43.

Ferrara v. Galluchio, 152 NE 2d 249, NY 1958. Ch 3, n 119.

Fiorentino v. Wenger, 272 NYS 2d 557, NY 1966, rev'd on other grounds, 227 NE 2d 296, NY 1967. Ch 2, n 17; Ch 7, n 83; Ch 8, n 7; Ch 8, n 146.

Foxluger v. New York, 203 NYS 2d 985, NY 1960. Ch 2, n 12.

Frank v. Board of Regents, 264 NYS 2d 413, NY 1965. Ch 11, n 52.

Frankel v. Wolper, 169 NYS 15, NY 1918. Ch 10, n 150.

Gates v. Preston, 41 NY 113, 1869. Ch 10, n 104.

Gerken v. Plimpton, 70 NYS 793, NY 1901. Ch 12, n 67.

Gielskie v. New York, 200 NYS 2d 691, NY 1960. Ch 2, n 10.

Golia v. Health Insurance Plan of Greater New York, 166 NYS 2d 889, NY 1957. Ch 4, n 121; Ch 9, n 35.

Gorlin v. Master Contracting Corporation, 180 NYS 2d 84, NY 1958. Ch 5, n 185.

Graddy v. New York Medical College, 243 NYS 2d 940, NY 1963. Ch 5, n 128; Ch 7, n 22.

Griffin v. Medical Society of the State of New York, 11 NYS 2d 109, NY 1939. Ch 9, n 50.

Gursky v. Gursky, 242 NYS 2d 406, NY 1963. Ch 8, n 115.

Hammer v. Polsky, 233 NYS 2d 110, NY 1962. Ch 9, n 30.

Hammer v. Rosen, 165 NE 2d 756, NY 1960. Ch 9, n 5.

Higgins v. New York, 265 NYS 2d 254, NY 1965. Ch 4, n 110.

Hoerner v. Bertinato, 171 A 2d 140, NY 1961. Ch 1, n 69.

Hoff v. New York, 18 NE 2d 671, NY 1939. Ch 8, n 100.

Holtfoth v. Rochester General Hospital, 105 NE 2d 610, NY 1952. Ch 6, n 46.

Holzberg v. Flower and Fifth Avenue Hospitals, 330 NYS 2d 682, NY 1972. Ch 5, n 142.

Hubbell v. South Nassau Communities Hospital, 260 NYS 2d 539, NY 1965. Ch 5, n 59.

Hyman v. Jewish Chronic Disease Hospital, 206 NE 2d 338, NY 1965. Ch 8, n 141.

People ex rel Jacobs v. Worthing, 4 NYS 2d 630, NY 1938, Ch 8, n 100.

James v. Holder, 309 NYS 2d 385, NY 1970. Ch 5, n 82; Ch 7, n 68.

In re John Children, 306 NYS 2d 797, NY 1969. Ch 8, n 119.

Kaplan v. New York, 100 NYS 2d 693, NY 1950. Ch 5, n 41; Ch 5, n 47.

Kirschner v. Equitable Life Ass. Society, 284 NYS 506, NY 1935. Ch 1, n 4.

Kleber v. Stevens, 241 NYS 2d 497, NY 1963. Ch 1, n 154.

Koump v. Smith, 250 NE 2d 857, NY 1969. Ch 12, n 116.

Kraus v. Spielberg, 236 NYS 2d 143, NY 1962. Ch 3, n 121.

Kropp v. DeAngelis, 138 NYS 2d 188, NY 1955. Ch 10, n 79.

Laidlaw v. Andrew Freedman Home, 300 NYS 2d 979, NY 1969. Ch 6, n 95.

Leider v. Beth Israel Hospital, 182 NE 2d 393, NY 1962. Ch 11, n 117.

Lesyk v. Park Avenue Hospital, 289 NYS 2d 873, NY 1968. Ch 6, n 103.

MacPherson v. Buick, 111 NE 1050, NY 1916. Ch 6, n 66.

Malvica v. Blumenfield, 310 NYS 2d 329, NY 1970. Ch 10, n 82.

In re Mandel, 264 NYS 2d 867, NY 1964. Ch 11, n 52.

Mandelbaum v. Weil, 203 NYS 289, NY 1924. Ch 5, n 46.

Mascitelli v. Board of Regents, 299 NYS 2d 1002, NY 1969. Ch 11, n 28.

McCartney v. Austin, 298 NYS 2d 26, NY 1969. Ch 1, n 70.

McDermott v. Manhattan Eye, Ear and Throat Hospital, 228 NYS 2d 143, 203 NE 2d 469, NY 1964. Ch 4, n 90; Ch 8, n 41.

McQuinn v. St. Lawrence County Laboratory, 283 NYS 2d 747, NY 1967. Ch 3, n 68.

Meiselman v. Crown Heights Hospital, 34 NE 2d 367, NY 1941. Ch 12, n 60.

In re Estate of Mgurdichian, 291 NYS 2d 453, NY 1968. Ch 8, n 62.

Morgan v. New York, 319 NY 2d 151, NY 1970. Ch 9, n 5.

Morse v. Rapkin, 263 NYS 2d 428, NY 1965. Ch 10, n 10.

Morwin v. Albany Hospital, 185 NYS 2d 85, NY 1959. Ch 5, n 140.

Mulligan v. Wetchler, 332 NYS 2d 68, NY 1972. Ch 3, n 7.

Necolayff v. Genesee Hospital, 72 NE 2d 117, NY 1947. Ch 5, n 80.

New York v. Leyra, 98 NE 2d 553, rev'd 347 U. S. 556, 1951. Ch 9, n 29.

New York v. Seaman, 315 NYS 2d 743, NY 1970. Ch 1, n 100.

O'Connell v. Westinghouse Xray Company, 41 NE 2d 177, NY 1942. Ch 6, n 78.

O'Neil v. New York, 323 NYS 2d 56, NY 1971. Ch 2, n 55; Ch 3, n 13.

O'Neill v. Board of Regents, 74 NYS 2d 762, NY 1947. Ch 11, n 83.

O'Neill v. Montefiore Hospital, 202 NYS 2d 436, NY 1960. Ch 1, n 15; Ch 13, n 83.

O'Rourke v. Halcyon Rest, 117 NE 2d 639, NY 1954. Ch 5, n 202.

Peck v. Towns Hospital, 89 NYS 2d 190, NY 1949. Ch 5, n 154; Ch 6, n 30.

Pepe v. Board of Regents, 295 NYS 2d 209, NY 1968. Ch 11, n 77.

People v. Edwards, 249 NYS 2d 325, NY 1964. Ch 1, n 73.

People v. Pierson, 68 NE 243, NY 1903. Ch 1, n 73.

Perlmutter v. Beth David Hospital, 123 NE 2d 792, NY 1954. Ch 5, n 60.

Petterson v. Lynch, 299 NYS 2d 244, NY 1969. Ch 8, n 31.

Pike v. Honsinger, 49 NE 760, NY 1898. Ch 2, n 5; Ch 4, n 137.

Pindar v. Parke Davis and Co., 337 NYS 2d 452, NY 1972. Ch 12, n 106.

Public Administrator of New York County v. New York, 177 NYS 2d 95, NY 1958. Ch 6, n 45.

Rabasco v. New Rochelle Hospital, 44 NYS 2d 293, NY 1943. Ch 6, n 12.

Reddick v. Board of Regents, 297 NYS 2d 339, NY 1969. Ch 11, n 18; Ch 11, n 35.

Richardson v. Denneen, 82 NYS 2d 623, NY 1947. Ch 7, n 33.

Robins v. Finestone, 127 NE 2d 330, NY 1955.

Rodriguez v. Columbus Hospital, 326 NYS 2d 439, NY 1971. Ch 5, n 159.

Safian v. Aetna Life Ins. Co., 24 NYS 2d 92, NY 1940. Ch 1, n 10.

In re Sampson, 317 NYS 2d 641, NY 1970. Ch 1, n 72.

Sawyer v. Jewish Chronic Disease Hospital, 234 NYS 2d 372, NY 1962. Ch 5, n 134.

Schloendorff v. Society of New York Hospital, 105 NE 92, NY 1914. Ch 8, n 4.

Sherman v. Board of Regents, 266 NYS 2d 39, NY 1966. Ch 11, n 60.

Shiffman v. Manhattan Eye, Ear and Throat Hospital, 314 NYS 2d 823, NY 1970. Ch 11, n 144.

Sivertson v. New York, 252 NYS 2d 623, NY 1964. Ch 6, n 40.

Sos v. Board of Regents, 281 NYS 2d 831, NY 1967. Ch 11, n 14.

Soto v. New York, 333 NYS 2d 588, NY 1972. Ch 4, n 107.

St. Pierre v. New York, 48 NYS 2d 613, NY 1944. Ch 9, n 9.

Stammer v. Board of Regents, 39 NE 2d 913, NY 1942. Ch 11 n 58.

Stewart v. Long Island College Hospital, 296 NYS 2d 41, 1968. Ch 1, n 143; Ch 8, n 23.

Strnad v. Strnad, 78 NYS 2d 390, NY 1948. Ch 8, n 114.

People ex rel Strohsahl v. Strohsahl, 222 NYS 319, NY 1927. Ch 8, n 127.

Sullivan v. Montgomery, 279 NYS 575, NY 1935. Ch 1, n 113; Ch 1, n 120.

Taylor v. Beekman Hospital, 62 NYS 2d 637, NY 1946. Ch 6, n 12.

Temple v. New York, 65 NYS 2d 50, 1946. Ch 9, n 9.

Tompkins v. Board of Regents, 87 NE 2d 517, NY 1949. Ch 11, n 45.

Toth v Community Hospital at Glen Cove, 239 NE 2d 368, NY 1968. Ch 2, n 77.

Tropp v. New York, 290 NYS 2d 612, NY 1968. Ch 5, n 178.

Volk v. City of New York, 30 NE 2d 596, NY 1940. Ch 5, n 153.

Von Blumenthal v. Cassola, 3 NYS 2d 246, 6 NYS 2d 342, NY 1938. Ch 10, n 84.

Wassermann v. Board of Regents, 182 NE 2d 264, NY 1962. Ch 11, n 52.

Weiner v. Board of Regents, 158 NYS 2d 730, NY 1956. Ch 11, n 32.

Weiss v. Board of Regents, 265 NYS 2d 314, NY 1965. Ch 11, n 30.

Weiss v. Rubin, 173 NE 2d 791, NY 1961. Ch 5, n 79.

Wellander v. Brooklyn Hospital, 174 NYS 2d 107, NY 1958. Ch 10, n 81.

White v. Matthews, 223 NYS 415, NY 1927. Ch 10, n 111.

Whitree v. New York, 290 NYS 2d 486, NY 1968. Ch 3, N 90; Ch 4, n 117; Ch 9, n 95.

Winik v. Jewish Hospital of Brooklyn, 293 NE 95, NY 1972. Ch 3, n 120.

Wojcik v. Aluminum Company of America, 183 NYS 2d 351, NY 1959. Ch 4, n 122.

Zimmerman v. Board of Regents, 294 NYS 2d 435, NY 1968. Ch 11, n 103.

North Carolina

Belk v. Schweizer, 149 SE 2d 565, NC 1966. Ch 2, n 74.

Brawley v. Heymann, 191 SE 2d 366, NC 1972. Ch 6, n 2.

Brewer v. Valk, 167 SE 638, NC 1933. Ch 8, n 110.

Childers v. Frye, 158 SE 744, NC 1931. Ch 1, n 13; Ch 12, n 21.

Davis v. Wilmerding, 24 SE 2d 337, NC 1943. Ch 2, n 18.

Davis v. Wilson, 143 SE 2d 107, NC 1965. Ch 5, n 69.

Galloway v. Lawrence, 145 SE 2d 861, NC 1966. Ch 4, n 70; Ch 10, n 84.

Goldman v. Kossove, 117 SE 2d 35, NC 1960. Ch 6, n 80.

Gray v. Weinstein, 42 SE 2d 616, NC 1947. Ch 12, n 42.

Groce v. Myers, 29 SE 2d 553, NC 1944. Ch 12, n 9.

Gurganious v. Simpson, 197 SE 163, NC 1938. Ch 8, n 71.

Habuda v. Trustees of Rex Hospital, Incorporated, 164 SE 2d 17, NC 1968. Ch 7, n 63.

In re Hawkins, 194 SE 2d 540, NC 1973. Ch 11, n 51.

Hawkins v. McCain, 79 SE 2d 493, NC 1954. Ch 1, n 9.

Helms v. Williams, 166 SE 2d 852, NC 1969. Ch 7, n 64.

Jackson v. Joyner, 72 SE 2d 589, NC 1952. Ch 7, n 50.

Jackson v. Mountain Sanitarium, 67 SE 2d 57, NC 1951. Ch 5, n 133.

Kennedy v. Parrott, 90 SE 2d 754, NC 1956. Ch 8, n 53.

Koury v. Follo, 158 SE 2d 548, NC 1968. Ch 1, n 108; Ch 5, n 177; Ch 8, n 21.

Lippard v. Johnson, 1 SE 2d 889, NC 1939. Ch 5, n 121.

Long v. Methodist Home, 187 SE 2d 718, NC 1972. Ch 6, n 110.

Nance v. Hitch, 76 SE 2d 461, NC 1953. Ch 5, n 93.

Nash v. Royster, 127 SE 356, NC 1925. Ch 12, n 71.

Pendergraft v. Royster, 166 SE 285, NC 1932. Ch 2, n 98; Ch 5, n 16.

Rabon v. Rowan Memorial Hospital, 152 SE 2d 485, NC 1967. Ch 10, n 166.

Sharpe v. Pugh, 155 SE 2d 108, NC 1967. Ch 2, n 47; Ch 4, n 146; Ch 5, n 192; Ch 8, n 21.

Shearin v. Lloyd, 98 SE 2d 508, NC 1957. Ch 5, n 4.

Simmons v. Wilder, 169 SE 2d 480, NC 1969. Ch 10, n 87.

Smith v. Wharton, 154 SE 12, NC 1930. Ch 12, n 39.

Stetson v. Easterling, 161 SE 2d 531, NC 1968. Ch 4, n 60.

Stone v. Proctor, 131 SE 2d 297, NC 1963. Ch 5, n 205.

Thornburg v. Long, 101 SE 99, NC 1919. Ch 9, n 26.

Weatherman v. White, 179 SE 2d 134, NC 1971. Ch 3, n 99.

Wilder v. Edwards, 173 SE 2d 72, NC 1970. Ch 12, n 115.

Wilson v. Martin Memorial Hospital, 61 SE 2d 102, NC 1950. Ch 3, n 75; Ch 7, n 14; Ch 12, n 78.

North Dakota

Benzmiller v. Swanson, 117 NW 2d 281, ND 1962. Ch 4, n 127.

Hanson v. Thelan, 173 NW 457, ND 1919. Ch 4, n 70.

Stokes v. Dailey, 85 NW 2d 745, ND 1957. Ch 3, n 10.

Tveldt v. Haugen, 294 NW 183, ND 1940. Ch 1, n 2; Ch 2, n 31; Ch 2, n 69.

Ohio

Bartolas v. Coleman, 161 NE 20, Ohio 1927. Ch 12, n 70.

Belcher v. Carter, 234 NE 2d 311, Ohio 1967. Ch 8, n 22; Ch 8, n 30.

Bird v. Pritchard, 291 NE 2d 769, Ohio 1973. Ch 10, n 22.

Bradshaw v. Wilson, 94 NE 2d 706, Ohio 1950. Ch 4, n 78.

Champs v. Stone, 58 NE 2d 803, Ohio 1944. Ch 10, n 12.

In re Clark, 185 NE 2d 128, Ohio 1962. Ch 1, n 69.

Clary v. Christiansen, 83 NE 2d 644, Ohio 1948. Ch 6, n 53.

Cooper v. Sisters of Charity of Cincinnati, 272 NE 2d 97, Ohio 1971. Ch 1, n 45; Ch 3, n 53; Ch 7, n 76.

Couch v. Rice, 261 NE 2d 187, Ohio 1970. Ch 1, n 100; Ch 1, n 105.

Dorsten v. Lawrence, 253 NE 2d 804, Ohio 1969. Ch 12, n 111.

Gillette v. Tucker, 65 NE 865, Ohio 1902. Ch 12, n 20.

Haines v. Ebert, 187 NE 2d 522, Ohio 1961. Ch 4, n 85.

Jeswald v. Hutt, 239 NE 2d 37, Ohio 1968. Ch 6, n 82.

Jones v. Stanko, 160 NE 456, Ohio 1928. Ch 4, n 123.

Kuhn v. Banker, 13 NE 2d 242, Ohio 1938. Ch 2, n 88.

Lacey v. Laird, 139 NE 2d 25, Ohio 1956. Ch 1, n 120; Ch 1, n 122.

Lundberg v. Bay View Hospital, 191 NE 2d 821, Ohio 1963. Ch 1, n 21; Ch 3, n 87; Ch 7, n 65.

Mainfort v. Giannestras, 111 NE 2d 692, Ohio 1951. Ch 4, n 21; Ch 10, n 48.

Melnyk v. The Cleveland Clinic, 290 NE 2d 916, Ohio 1972. Ch 10, n 119.

Modrzynski v. Lust, 88 NE 2d 76, Ohio 1949. Ch 4, n 37.

Morgan v. Sheppard, 188 NE 2d 808, Ohio 1963. Ch 2, n 43.

Morris v. Monterey-Yorkshire Nursing Inn, 278 NE 2d 686, Ohio 1971. Ch 10, n 142.

Oberlin v. Friedman, 213 NE 2d 168, Ohio 1965. Ch 5, n 122.

Ohio v. Tims, 224 NE 2d 348, Ohio 1967. Ch 12, n 112.

Oleksiw v. Weidener, 207 NE 2d 375, Ohio 1964. Ch 5, n 32; Ch 5, n 47.

Paulson v. Stocker, 4 NE 2d 609, Ohio 1935. Ch 3, n 42.

Rice v. Rinaldo, 119 NE 2d 657, Ohio 1951. Ch 1, n 23.

Robinson v. Gatti, 184 NE 2d 509, Ohio 1961. Ch 3, n 46.

Tanner v. Espey, 190 NE 229, Ohio 1934. Ch 10, n 65.

Thackery v. Helfrich, 175 NE 449, Ohio 1931. Ch 10, n 21.

Urdang v. Mahrer, 158 NE 2d 902, Ohio 1959. Ch 6, n 85.

Wallace v. University Hospitals of Cleveland, 164 NE 2d 917, Ohio 1959. Ch 12, n 99.

Oklahoma

Aderhold v. Bishop, 221 Pac 752, Okla 1923. Ch 7, n 44.

Barrow v. Oklahoma, 188 Pac 351, Okla 1920. Ch 11, n 174.

Choate v. Oklahoma, 232 P 2d 634, Okla 1951. Ch 11, n 30.

Clinton v. Miller, 186 Pac 932, Okla 1919. Ch 9, n 80.

Duke Sanitarium v. Hearn, 13 P 2d 183, Okla 1932. Ch 12, n 3.

Greenwood v. Harris, 362 P 2d 85, Okla 1961. Ch 3, n 35.

King v. Carney, 204 Pac 270, Okla 1922. Ch 8, n 55.

Masonic Hospital Association v. Taggart, 43 P 2d 142, Okla 1935. Ch 5, n 163.

McBride v. Roy, 58 P 2d 886, Okla 1936. Ch 3, n 96.

McPosey v. Sisters of the Sorrowful Mother, 57 P 2d 617, Okla 1936. Ch 8, n 63.

Nutt v. Carson, 340 P 2d 260, Okla 1959. Ch 10, n 134.

Orthopedic Clinic v. Hanson, 415 P 2d 991, Okla 1966. Ch 6, n 6; Ch 7, n 3.

Rhodes v. Lamar, 292 Pac 335, Okla 1930. Ch 5, n 21.

Seanor v. Browne, 7 P 2d 627, Okla 1932. Ch 10, n 150.

Sisler v. Jackson, 460 P 2d 903, Okla 1969. Ch 8, n 30.

Tulsa Hospital Association v. Juby, 175 Pac 519, Okla 1918. Ch 6, n 93.

Oregon

Allen v. Allen, 330 P 2d 151, Ore 1958. Ch 9, n 74.

Austin v. Sisters of Charity of Providence, 470 P 2d 939, Ore 1970. Ch 5, n 109.

Board of Medical Examiners of the State of Oregon v. Mintz, 378 P 2d 945, Ore 1963. Ch 11, n 73.

Brockman v. Harpole, 444 P 2d 25, Ore 1968. Ch 10, n 50.

Carruthers v. Phillips, 131 P 2d 193, Ore 1942. Ch 2, n 99.

Cook v. Oregon, 495 P 2d 768, Ore 1972. Ch 8, n 108.

Eckleberry v. Kaiser Foundation Northern Hospitals, 359 P 2d 1090, Ore 1961. Ch 2, n 59.

Getchell v. Mansfield, 489 P 2d 953, Ore 1971. Ch 8, n 25.

Gwynn v. Wilhelm, 360 P 2d 312, Ore 1961. Ch 10, n 106.

Livingston v. Portland General Hospital Association, 357 P 2d 543, Ore 1960. Ch 4, n 14; Ch 12, n 72.

May v. Broun, 492 P 2d 776, Ore 1972. Ch 7, n 46.

Mayor v. Dowsett, 400 P 2d 234, Ore 1965. Ch 5, n 124.

Orendino v. Clarke, 402 P 2d 527, Ore 1965. Ch 4, n 146.

Rhodes v. Moore, 398 P 2d 189, Ore 1965. Ch 6, n 42.

Rockhill v. Pollard, 485 P 2d 28, Ore 1971, Ch 1, n 33.

State v. Blum, 463 P 2d 367, Ore 1970. Ch 8, n 128.

Wimer v. Miller, 383 P 2d 1005, Ore 1963. Ch 10, n 111.

Pennsylvania

Alexander v. Knight, 177 A 2d 142, Pa 1962. Ch 9, n 24.

Cameron, to use of Cameron v. Eynon, 3 A 2d 423, Pa 1939. Ch 1, n 12.

Collins v. Hand, 246 A 2d 398, Pa 1968. Ch 5, n 203.

Cooper v. Roberts, 286 A 2d 647, Pa 1971. Ch 8, n 35.

Demchuck v. Bralow, 170 A 2d 868, Pa 1961. Ch 4, n 50.

Frick v. McClelland, 122 A 2d 43, Pa 1956. Ch 8, n 73.

Grantham v. Goetz, 164 A 2d 225, Pa 1960. Ch 5, n 165.

Gray v. Grunnagle, 223 A 2d 663, Pa 1966. Ch 2, n 97; Ch 8, n 50.

Henderson v. National Drug Company, 23 A 2d 743, Pa 1942. Ch 5, n 189.

Hirko v. Reese, 40 A 2d 408, Pa 1945. Ch 8, n 69.

Hoffman v. Misericordia Hospital, 267 A 2d 867, Pa 1970. Ch 5, n 66.

Incollingo v. Ewing, 282 A 2d 206, Pa 1971. Ch 2, n 42; Ch 5, n 193; Ch 6, n 63.

Kelly v. Yount, 7 A 2d 582, Pa 1939. Ch 6, n 8.

Marcus v. Frankford Hospital, 283 A 2d 69, Pa 1971. Ch 6, n 112.

McCandless v. McWha 22 Pa 261, Pa 1853. Ch 4, n 35.

McConnell v. Williams, 65 A 2d 243, Pa 1949. Ch 7, n 39.

Pennsylvania State Board v. Schireson, 61 A 2d 343, Pa 1948. Ch 11, n 50.

Powell v. Risser, 99 A 2d 454, Pa 1953. Ch 4, n 34; Ch 5, n 208.

Robinson v. Wirts, 127 A 2d 706, Pa 1956. Ch 8, n 51.

Rockwell v. Stone, 173 A 2d 48, Pa 1961. Ch 7, n 57.

Smith v. Yohe, 194 A 2d 167, Pa 1963. Ch 3, n 30; Ch 3, n 50.

State Board of Medical Education v. Ferry, 94 A 2d 121, Pa 1953. Ch 11, n 83.

Thomas v. Hutchinson, 275 A 2d 23, Pa 1971. Ch 7, n 48.

Thompson v. Fox, 192 Atl 107, Pa 1937. Ch 10, n 65.

Tonsic v. Wagner, 289 A 2d 138, Pa 1972. Ch 7, n 48.

Wohlert v. Seibert, 23 Pa Sup Ct 213, 1903. Ch 2, n 30.

In re Appointment of a Guardian of the Person of Maida Yetter, Docket No 1973-533, Pa Ct. Common Pleas, Northhampton County, Pa 1973. Ch 1, n 62; Ch 8, n 42.

Yorston v. Pennell, 153 A 2d 255, Pa 1959. Ch 3, n 10; Ch 5, n 181; Ch 7, n 37.

Zaman v. Schultz, 19 Pa D & C 309, 1933. Ch 1, n 114.

Rhode Island

Board of Examiners in Medicine v. Jacobson, 42 A 2d 887, RI 1945. Ch 11, n 49.

Knoop v. State Board of Health, 103 Atl 904, RI 1918. Ch 11, n 41.

Morrell v. Lalonde, 120 Atl ⅍35, RI 1923. Ch 12, n 61.

Nolan v. Kechijian, 64 A 2d 866, RI 1949. Ch 9, n 69.

Sylvia v. Gobeille, 220 A 2d 222, RI 1966. Ch 1, n 107.

Wilkinson v. Harrington, 243 A 2d 745, RI 1968, Ch 5, n 91.

Wilkinson v. Vesey, 295 A 2d 676, RI 1972. Ch 8, n 38.

South Carolina

Burke v. Pearson, 191 SE 2d 721, SC 1972. Ch 6, n 29.

Crawford v. Davis, 134 SE 247, SC 1926. Ch 7, n 92.

Hodge v. Shea, 168 SE 2d 82, SC 1969. Ch 9, n 79.

State Board of Medical Examiners v. Gandy, 188 SE 2d 846, SC 1972. Ch 11, n 17; Ch 11, n 43.

Whitfield v. Daniel Construction Co., 83 SE 2d 460, SC 1954. Ch 2, n 50; Ch 4, n 141; Ch 5, n 195.

South Dakota

Bennett v. Murdy, 249 NW 805, SD 1933, Ch 5, n 22.

Block v. McVay, 126 NW 2d 808, SD 1964. Ch 8, n 46.

Hinkle v. Hargens, 81 NW 2d 888, SD 1957. Ch 9, n 65.

Kelly v. Hollingsworth, 181 NW 959, SD 1921. Ch 3, n 106.

State v. Still, 202 NW 479, SD 1925. Ch 9, n 16.

Warwick v. Bliss, 195 NW 501, SD 1923. Ch 12, n 69.

Tennessee

Ball v. Mallinkrodt Chemical Works, 381 SW 2d 563, Tenn 1964. Ch 4, n 26.

Blankenship v. Baptist Memorial Hospital, 168 SW 2d 491, Tenn 1942. Ch 2, n 14; Ch 2, n 60; Ch 5, n 92.

Boyd v. Coca Cola Bottling Works, 177 SW 80, Tenn 1915. Ch 2, n 3.

Burnett v. Layman, 181 SW 157, Tenn 1915. Ch 12, n 7.

Calhoun v. Fraser, 126 SW 2d 381, Tenn 1938. Ch 4, n 18.

French v. Fischer, 362 SW 2d 926, Tenn 1962. Ch 5, n 5; Ch 7, n 42.

Gresham v. Ford, 241 SW 2d 408, Tenn 1951. Ch 2, n 41.

Harrison v. Wilkerson, 405 SW 2d 649, Tenn 1966. Ch 5, n 25.

Haskins v. Howard, 16 SW 2d 20, Tenn 1929. Ch 9, n 70.

Henderson v. City of Knoxville, 9 SW 2d 697, Tenn 1928. Ch 11, n 117.

Hill v. Travelers' Insurance Co., 294 SW 1097, Tenn 1927. Ch 8, n 65.

Hughes v. Hastings, 469 SW 2d 378, Tenn 1971. Ch 5, n 141.

Johnson v. Ely, 205 SW 2d 759, Tenn 1947. Ch 5, n 18.

Lewis v. Casenburg, 7 SW 2d 808, Tenn 1928. Ch 5, n 98.

Martin v. Carbide and Carbon Chemical Co., 197 SW 2d 798, Tenn 1946. Ch 11, n 40.

Methodist Hospital v. Ball, 362 SW 2d 475, Tenn 1961. Ch 1, n 44.

Osborne v. Frazor, 425 SW 2d 768, Tenn 1968. Ch 2, n 25.

Poor Sisters of St. Francis v. Long, 230 SW 2d 659, Tenn 1950. Ch 4, n 63.

Quinley v. Cocke, 192 SW 2d 992, Tenn 1946. Ch 5, n 202.

Ray v. Scheibert, 484 SW 2d 63, Tenn 1972. Ch 10, n 138.

Rural Educational Association v. Busch, 298 SW 2d 761, Tenn 1956. Ch 5, n 9.

Vanderbilt University v. Henderson, 127 SW 2d 284, Tenn 1938. Ch 10, n 156.

Wooten v. Curry, 362 SW 2d 820, Tenn 1961. Ch 4, n 133; Ch 12, n 59.

Texas

Allison v. Blewett, 348 SW 2d 182, Tex 1961. Ch 9, n 66.

Axcell v Phillips, 473 SW 2d 554, Tex 1971. Ch 10, n 117.

Barker v. Heaney, 82 SW 2d 417, Tex 1935. Ch 1, n 137.

Bell v. Umstattd, 401 SW 2d 306, Tex 1966. Ch 5, n 139.

Borden v. Sneed, 291 SW 2d 485, Tex 1956. Ch 10, n 65.

Brown v. Harris County Medical Society, 194 SW 1179, Tex 1917. Ch 11, n 102.

Brown v. Shannon West Texas Hospital, 222 SW 2d 248, Tex 1949. Ch 5, n 87; Ch 5, n 155.

Callison v. Red, 149 SW 2d 153, Tex 1941. Ch 6, n 83.

Cannon v. Pearson, 383 SW 2d 565, Tex 1964. Ch 10, n 66.

Charrin v. Methodist Hospital, 432 SW 2d 572, Tex 1968. Ch 10, n 53.

Chasco v. Providence Memorial Hospital, 476 SW 2d 385, Tex 1972. Ch 2, n 54.

Constant v. Howe, 436 SW 2d 115, Tex 1968. Ch 5, n 214.

Cooper v. Texas State Board of Medical Examiners, 489 SW 2d 129, Tex 1972. Ch 11, n 24; Ch 11, n 42.

Cudmore v. Richardson-Merrell, 398 SW 2d 640, Tex 1965. Ch 6, n 65.

Floyd v. Michie, 11 SW 2d 657, Tex 1928. Ch 2, n 37; Ch 7, n 23.

Frazier v. Levi, 440 SW 2d 393, Tex 1969. Ch 8, n 109.

Goelz v. Wadley Institute, 350 SW 2d 573, Tex 1961. Ch 5, n 75.

Gorden v. State, 90 SW 636, Tex 1904. Ch 11, n 161.

Gravis v. Physicians' and Surgeons' Hospital, 415 SW 2d 674, Tex 1967. Ch 5, n 123.

Gulfway General Hospital v. Pursley, 397 SW 2d 93, Tex 1965. Ch 6, n 91.

Hart v. Van Zandt, 399 SW 2d 791, Tex 1965. Ch 2, n 53.

Hays v. Hall, 477 SW 2d 402, Tex 1972. Ch 10, n 131.

Hess v. Rouse, 22 SW 2d 1077, Tex 1929. Ch 5, n 91.

Houston Clinic v. Busch, 64 SW 2d 1103, Tex 1933. Ch 5, n 31.

Howe v. Citizens Memorial Hospital, 426 SW 2d 882, Tex 1968. Ch 5, n 201.

Jacobi v. Board of Medical Examiners, 308 SW 2d 261, Tex 1957. Ch 11, n 108.

Kaster v. Woodson, 123 SW 2d 981, Tex 1938. Ch 5, n 155.

Korndorffer v. Texas State Board of Medical Examiners, 460 SW 2d 879, Tex 1970. Ch 11, n 21.

Lee v. Dewbre, 362 SW 2d 900, Tex 1962. Ch 12, n 7; Ch 12, n 77.

Levermann v. Cartall, 393 SW 2d 931, Tex 1965. Ch 3, n 101.

Lotspeich v. Chance Vought Aircraft Corporation, 369 SW 2d 705, Tex 1963. Ch 1, n 81; Ch 10, n 110.

Love v. Aetna Casualty & Surety Co., 99 SW 2d 646, Tex 1936. Ch 8, n 64.

Maclay v. Kelsey-Seybold Clinic, 456 SW 2d 229, 466 SW 2d 716, Tex 1971. Ch 7, n 20; Ch 9, n 85.

Martin v. Eschelman, 33 SW 2d 827, Tex 1930. Ch 5, n 104.

Martinez v. Texas State Board of Medical Examiners, 476 SW 2d 400, Tex 1972. Ch 9, n 2; Ch 11, n 64.

Martisek v. Ainsworth, 459 SW 2d 679, Tex 1970. Ch 4, n 138.

McKinney v. Tromly, 386 SW 2d 564, Tex 1964. Ch 5, n 120; Ch 7, n 49.

McMillen v. Klingensmith, 467 SW 2d 193, Tex 1971. Ch 10, n 85.

Medical and Surgical Memorial Hospital v. Cauthorn, 229 SW 2d 932, Tex 1949. Ch 6, n 33.

Miles v. Harris, 194 SW 839, Tex 1917. Ch 12, n 2.

Morris v. Rousos, 397 SW 2d 504, Tex 1965. Ch 9, n 42.

Nichols v. Nichols, 247 SW 2d 143, Tex 1952. Ch 8, n 131.

Nichols v. Smith, 489 SW 2d 719, Tex 1973. Ch 10, n 139.

Penaloza v. Baptist Memorial Hospital, 304 SW 2d 203, Tex 1957. Ch 5, n 147.

Pendleton v. Burkhalter, 432 SW 2d 724, Tex 1968. Ch 9, n 86.

Rockett v. Texas State Board of Medical Examiners, 287 SW 2d 190, Tex 1956. Ch 11, n 83.

Rose v. Friddell, 423 SW 2d 658, Tex 1967. Ch 4, n 72.

Ross v. Sher, 483 SW 2d 297, Tex 1972. Ch 7, n 24.

Schooler v. Tarrant County Medical Society, 457 SW 2d 644, Tex 1970. Ch 11, n 96.

Scott v. Wilson, 396 SW 2d 532, Tex 1965. Ch 8, n 31.

Smith v. Thornhill, 25 SW 2d 597, Tex 1930. Ch 1, n 1.

Terrill v. Harbin, 376 SW 2d 945, Tex 1964. Ch 8, n 66.

Texas State Board of Medical Examiners v. Haynes, 388 SW 2d 258, Tex 1965. Ch 11, n 63.

Texas State Board of Medical Examiners v. Koepsel, 322 SW 2d 609, Tex 1959. Ch 11, n 63.

Texas State Board of Medical Examiners v. McClellan, 307 SW 2d 317, Tex 1957, Ch 11, n 41.

Texas State Board of Medical Examiners v. Scott, 377 SW 2d 104, Tex 1964. Ch 11, n 20.

Thomas v. Pugh, 6 SW 2d 202, Tex 1928. Ch 6, n 77.

Thompson v. Texas, 493 SW 2d 913, Tex 1973. Ch 11, n 29.

Tuscany v. United States Standard Products Company, 243 SW 2d 207, Tex 1951. Ch 6, n 58.

Urritia v. Patino, 297 SW 512, Tex 1928. Ch 1, n 158; Ch 12, n 85.

Weary v. Baylor University Hospital, 360 SW 2d 895, Tex 1963. Ch 11, n 144.

Webb v. Jorns, 488 SW 2d 407, Tex 1972. Ch 5, n 128.

Webb v. Texas, 467 SW 2d 449, Tex 1971. Ch 1, n 92.

Weiser v. Hampton, 445 SW 2d 224, Tex 1969. Ch 8, n 16.

Utah

Anderson v. Nixon, 139 P 2d 216, Utah 1943. Ch 3, n 29.

Berry v. Moench, 331 P 2d 814, Utah 1958. Ch 9, n 19.

Dibblee v. Groves Latter Day Saints Hospital, 364 P 2d 1085, Utah 1961. Ch 5, n 75.

Joseph v. Groves Latter Day Saints Hospital, 348 P 2d 935, Utah 1960. Ch 5, n 72.

Parker v. Rampton, 497 P 2d 848, Utah 1972. Ch 1, n 144.

Passey v. Budge, 38 P 2d 712, Utah 1934. Ch 5, n 35.

Paull v. Zions First National Bank, 417 P 2d 759, Utah 1966. Ch 10, n 28.

Peterson v. Richards, 272 Pac 229, Utah 1928. Ch 6, n 50.

Ricks v. Budge, 64 P 2d 208, Utah 1937. Ch 12, n 37.

Sherman v. McEntire, 179 P 2d 797, Utah 1947. Ch 11, n 27.

Vermont

Domina v. Pratt, 13 A 2d 198, Vt 1940. Ch 1, n 108; Ch 3, n 19.

Largess v. Tatem, 291 A 2d 398, Vt 1972. Ch 2, n 21.

In re Rathburn, 266 A 2d 423, Vt 1970. Ch 8, n 129.

Williams v. Marini, 162 Atl 796, Vt 1932. Ch 2, n 52; Ch 4, n 148; Ch 10, n 44.

Woodard v. Porter Hospital, 217 A 2d 37, Vt 1966. Ch 11, n 144; Ch 11, n 157.

Virginia

Carroll v. Richardson, 110 SE 2d 193, Va 1959. Ch 5, n 175.

Corbett v. Clarke, 46 SE 2d 327, Va 1948. Ch 10, n 74.

Danville Community Hospital v. Thompson, 43 SE 2d 882, Va 1947. Ch 6, n 16.

Jefferson Hospital v. Van Lear, 41 SE 2d 441, Va 1947. Ch 6, n 101; Ch 10, n 153.

Khoury v. Community Memorial Hospital, 123 SE 2d 533, Va 1962. Ch 11, n 143.

Powell v. Troland, 183 SE 2d 184, Va 1971. Ch 10, n 113.

Reed v. Church, 8 SE 2d 285, Va 1940. Ch 2, n 40; Ch 4, n 34; Ch 5, n 186.

Vann v. Harden, 47 SE 2d 314, Va 1948. Ch 1, n 9; Ch 4, n 71; Ch 12, n 73.

Whitefield v. Whittaker Memorial Hospital, 169 SE 2d 563, Va 1969. Ch 2, n 87;
   Ch 5, n 114; Ch 5, n 135.

Washington

Adams v. State, 429 P 2d 109, Wash 1967. Ch 4, n 104.

Benjamin v. Havens, Inc., 373 P 2d 109, Wash 1962. Ch 12, n 117.

Clampett v. Sisters of Charity, 136 P 2d 729, Wash 1943. Ch 6, n 18.

Conrad v. Lakewood General Hospital, 410 P 2d 785, Wash 1966. Ch 5, n 12.

Dahl v. Wagner, 151 Pac 1079, Wash 1915. Ch 2, n 11.

Derr v. Bonney, 231 P 2d 637, Wash 1951. Ch 4, n 2.

Dickerson v. St. Peter's Hospital, 432 P 2d 293, Wash 1967. Ch 5, n 36.

DiNike v. Mowery, 418 P 2d 1010, Wash 1966. Ch 10, n 79.

Dinner v. Thorp, 338 P 2d 137, Wash 1959. Ch 2, n 73; Ch 3, n 73.

Douglas v. Bussabarger, 438 P 2d 829, Wash 1968. Ch 2, n 70; Ch 5, n 125.

Ericson v. Ericson, 195 Pac 234, Wash 1921. Ch 8, n 132.

Foster v. Brady, 86 P 2d 760, Wash 1939. Ch 9, n 82.

Gile v. Kennewick Public Hospital District, 296 P 2d 662, Wash 1956. Ch 5, n 75.

Gonzales v. Peterson, 359 P 2d 307, Wash 1961. Ch 3, n 49; Ch 4, n 13.

Gray v. Davidson, 130 P 2d 341, Wash 1942. Ch 12, n 38.

Gross v. Partlow, 68 P 2d 1034, Wash 1937. Ch 1, n 13; Ch 12, n 63.

Harris v. Fireman's Fund Indemnity Co., 257 P 2d 221, Wash 1953. Ch 1, n 6;
   Ch 6, n 7.

In re Hendrickson, 123 P 2d 322, Wash 1942. Ch 8, n 110.

Hoglin v. Brown, 481 P 2d 458, Wash 1971. Ch 2, n 61; Ch 3, n 36.

Horner v. Northern Pacific Benevolent Association Hospitals, 382 P 2d 518, Wash
   1963. Ch 4, n 64.

Hubbard v. Washington State Medical Disciplinary Board, 348 P 2d 981, Wash 1960.
   Ch 11, n 86.

Hunter v. Brown, 484 P 2d 1162, Wash 1971. Ch 8, n 35.

Hutter v. MacKay, 293 P 2d 766, Wash 1956. Ch 3, n 102.

Just v. Littlefield, 151 Pac 780, Wash 1915, Ch 3, n 14.

Kaiser v. Suburban Transportation System, 398 P 2d 14, Wash 1965. Ch 2, n 51;
   Ch 4, n 141; Ch 5, n 196.

Kelly v. Carroll, 219 P 2d 79, Wash 1950. Ch 2, n 9.

Kemalyan v. Henderson, 277 P 2d 372, Wash 1954. Ch 5, n 135; Ch 7, n 51.

In re Kindschi, 319 P 2d 824, Wash 1958. Ch 11, n 32.

Koenig v. Group Health Cooperative, 491 P 2d 702, Wash 1971. Ch 10, n 122.

Martin v. Cunningham, 161 Pac 355, Wash 1916. Ch 10, n 69; Ch 10, n 79.

Miles v. Hoffman, 221 Pac 316, Wash 1923. Ch 2, n 46; Ch 4, n 131.

Olson v. Weitz, 221 P 2d 537, Wash 1950. Ch 4, n 74.

Peddicord v. Lieser, 105 P 2d 5, Wash 1940. Ch 2, n 10.

Pederson v. Dumouchel, 431 P 2d 2d 976, Wash 1967. Ch 1, n 43; Ch 2, n 68; Ch 7, n 74; Ch 12, n 19.

Peterson v. Hunt, 84 P 2d 999, Wash 1938. Ch 3, n 40.

Riste v. General Electric Corporation, 289 P 2d 338, Wash 1955. Ch 1, n 80.

Russell v. Jackson, 221 P 2d 516, Wash 1950. Ch 8, n 57.

Ruth v. Dight, 453 P 2d 631, Wash 1969. Ch 10, n 125.

Skodje v. Hardy, 288 P 2d 471, Wash 1955. Ch 1, n 155; Ch 12, n 22; Ch 12, n 87.

Smith v. Seibly, 431 P 2d 719, Wash 1967. Ch 1, n 120; Ch 1, n 151.

State v. Karsunky, 84 P 2d 390, Wash 1938. Ch 11, n 170.

State v. McFadden, 93 Pac 414, Wash 1908. Ch 11, n 176.

State v. Parmenter, 444 P 2d 680, Wash 1968. Ch 8, n 117.

State Board of Medical Examiners v. Macy, 159 Pac 801, Wash 1916. Ch 11, n 74.

Teig v. St. John's Hospital, 387 P 2d 527, Wash 1963. Ch 2, n 57.

Walker v. Rynd, 280 P 2d 259, Wash 1955. Ch 6, n 35.

Washington v. Gile, 35 Pac 417, Wash 1894. Ch 11, n 164.

Washington v. Kuljis, 422 P 2d 480, Wash 1967. Ch 1, n 104.

Washington v. White, 433 P 2d 682, Wash 1967. Ch 12, n 112.

Williams v. Wurdemann, 128 Pac 639, Wash 1912. Ch 10, n 20.

Yeager v. Dunnavan, 174 P 2d 755, Wash 1946. Ch 5, n 131.

Zebarth v. Swedish Hospital Medical Center, 499 P 2d 1, Wash 1972. Ch 8, n 22.

West Virginia

State ex rel Bronaugh v. City of Parkersburg, 136 SE 2d 783, W Va 1964. Ch 11, n 124.

Browning v. Hoffman, 111 SE 492, W Va 1922. Ch 12, n 65.

Howell v. Biggart, 152 SE 323, W Va 1930. Ch 12, n 68.

Hundley v. Martinez, 158 SE 2d 159, W Va 1967. Ch 2, n 79; Ch 9, n 71; Ch 10, n 137.

Jones v. Laird Foundation, Inc., 195 SE 2d 821, W Va 1973. Ch 7, n 94.

Lawson v. Conaway, 16 SE 564, W Va 1892, Ch 10, n 104.

Mier v. Yoho, 171 SE 535, W Va 1933. Ch 10, n 65.

State v. Comstock, 70 SE 2d 648, W Va 1952. Ch 11, n 165.

Young v. Jordan, 145 SE 41, W Va 1928. Ch 12, n 18; Ch 12, n 34.

Wisconsin

Allen v. Voje, 89 NW 924, Wisc 1902. Ch 4, n 28.

Beaudoin v. Watertown Memorial Hospital, 145 NW 2d 166, Wisc 1966. Ch 4, n 66.

Hartley v. St. Francis Hospital, 129 NW 2d 235, Wisc 1964. Ch 10, n 70.

Heimlich v. Harvey, 39 NW 2d 394, Wisc 1949. Ch 7, n 9.

Jacobs v. Grigsby, 205 NW 394, Wisc 1925. Ch 5, n 23.

Jaeger v. Stratton, 176 NW 61, Wisc 1920. Ch 3, n 117.

Johnson v. City of Ripon, 47 NW 2d 328, Wisc 1951. Ch 11, n 135; Ch 11, n 152.

Kosak v. Boyce, 201 NW 757, Wisc 1925. Ch 3, n 57.

Kuglich v. Fowle, 200 NW 648, Wisc 1924. Ch 6, n 20.

Maniaci v. Marquette University, 184 NW 2d 168, Wisc 1971. Ch 8, n 88; Ch 9, n 34; Ch 9, n 98.

Margoles v. Wisconsin State Board of Medical Examiners, 177 NW 2d 353, Wisc 1970. Ch 11, n 18; Ch 11, n 32.

McManus v. Donlin, 127 NW 2d 22, Wisc 1964. Ch 12, n 8.

Newman v. Anderson, 217 NW 306, Wisc 1928. Ch 4, n 139.

Olson v. St. Croix Valley Memorial Hospital, 201 NW 2d 63, Wisc 1972. Ch 5, n 74; Ch 10, n 132.

Peterson v. Roloff, 203 NW 2d 699, Wisc 1973. Ch 10, n 116.

Retelle v. Sullivan, 211 NW 756, Wisc 1927. Ch 10, n 72.

Schuster v. St. Vincent Hospital, 172 NW 2d 421, Wisc 1969. Ch 6, n 96; Ch 10, n 32.

Waukesha Memorial Hospital v. Baird, 173 NW 2d 700, Wisc 1970. Ch 1, n 102.

Wendland v. Wendland, 138 NW 2d 185, Wisc 1965. Ch 8, n 134.

Wyoming

Govin v. Hunter, 374 P 2d 421, Wyo 1962. Ch 8, n 31.

Smith v. Beard, 110 P 2d 260, Wyo 1941. Ch 7, n 23.

Stundon v. Stadnik, 469 P 2d 16, Wyo 1970. Ch 4, n 89.

FEDERAL

COURT

DECISIONS

United States Supreme Court

Barsky v. Board of Regents, 347 US 442, 1954. Ch 11, n 1.

Buck v. Bell, 274 US 200, 1927. Ch 8, n 105.

DeZon v. American President Lines, 318 US 660, 1943. Ch 1, n 90; Ch 7, n 98.

Doe v. Bolton, 410 US 179, 1973, Ch 1, n 132.

Eisenstadt v. Baird, 405 US 438, 1972. Ch 1, n 129; Ch 1, n 146.

Griswold v. Connecticut, 381 US 479, 1965. Ch 1, n 128; Ch 1, n 146; Ch 9, n 46.

Gunning v. Cooley, 281 US 90, 1930. Ch 5, n 144.

Hayman v. City of Galveston, 273 US 414, 1927. Ch 11, n 114.

Jackson v. Indiana, 406 US 715, 1972. Ch 4, n 118.

Jefferson v. United States, 77 F Supp 706, 1948, 340 US 135, 1950. Ch 5, n 2.

Roe v. Wade, 410 US 113, 1973. Ch 1, n 132.

Schmerber v. California, 384 US 757, 1966. Ch 1, n 96.

Skinner v. Oklahoma, 316 US 535, 1942. Ch 8, n 111.

Sweeny v. Erving, 228 US 233, 1913. Ch 5, n 99.

United States v. Doremus, 249 US 86, 1919. Ch 1, n 77.

United States v. Muniz, 374 US 150, 1963. Ch 1, n 61.

Yarborough v. Yarborough, 290 US 202, 1933. Ch 1, n 112.

United States Circuit Courts of Appeals
(Excluding the District of Columbia)

Abbott Laboratories v. Lapp, 78 F 2d 170, CCA 7, 1935. Ch 6, n 56.

Alexandridis v. Jewett, 388 F 2d 829, CCA 1, 1968. Ch 7, n 34; Ch 12, n 11; Ch 12, n 35.

Ayers v. Parry, 192 F 2d 181, CCA 3, 1951. Ch 5, n 123.

Basko v. Sterling Drug Inc., 416 F 2d 417, CCA 2, 1969. Ch 6, n 59.

Beaumont v. Morgan, 427 F 2d 667, CCA 1, 1970. Ch 9, n 96.

Bowles v. Zimmer Manufacturing Company, 277 F 2d 868, CCA 7, 1960. Ch 6, n 68.

Brinkley v. Hassig, 83 F 2d 351, CCA 10, 1936. Ch 11, n 58.

Brown v. Moore, 247 F 2d 711, CCA 3, 1957. Ch 5, n 212; Ch 10, n 100.

Campbell v. Oliva, 424 F 2d 1244, CCA 6, 1970. Ch 8, n 45.

Campbell v. Wainwright, 416 F 2d 949, CCA 5, 1969. Ch 8, n 82.

Cates v. Ciccone, 422 F 2d 926, CCA 8, 1970. Ch 1, n 59.

Caylor v. Virden, 217 F 2d 739, CCA 8, 1955. Ch 5, n 113.

Chaparro v. Jackson & Perkins Co., 346 F 2d 677, CCA 2, 1965.

Chiaffitelli v. Dettmer Hospital, 437 F 2d 429, CCA 6, 1971. Ch 11, n 137.

Church v. Hegstrom, 416 F 2d 449, CCA 2, 1969. Ch 1, n 53.

Clark v. United States, 402 F 2d 950, CCA 4, 1968. Ch 3, n 31.

Coleman v. Johnston, 247 F 2d 273, CCA 7, 1957. Ch 1, n 49.

Colley v. Canal Bank and Trust Co., 159 F 2d 153, CCA 5, 1947. Ch 10, n 144.

Correia v. United States, 339 F 2d 596, CCA 1, 1964. Ch 2, n 65.

Davis v. Wyeth Laboratories, 399 F 2d 121, CCA 9, 1968. Ch 6, n 59.

Don v. Okmulgee Memorial Hospital, 443 F 2d 234, CCA 10, 1971. Ch 11, n 130.

Donnelly v. Guion, 467 F 2d 290, CCA 2, 1972. Ch 8, n 70.

Duby v. American College of Surgeons, 468 F 2d 364, CCA 7, 1972. Ch 11, n 109.

Dunham v. Wright, 423 F 2d 940, CCA 3, 1970. Ch 8, n 17; Ch 8, n 43.

Edwards v. Duncan, 355 F 2d 993, CCA 4, 1966. Ch 1, n 48.

Flagler Hospital v. Hayling, 344 F 2d 950, CCA 5, 1965. Ch 1, n 41.

Foster v. Mobile County Hospital Board, 398 F 2d 227, CCA 5, 1968. Ch 11, n 127.

Gault v. Poor Sisters of St. Frances, 375 F 2d 539, CCA 6, 1967. Ch 5, n 146.

Geddes v. Daughters of Charity, 348 F 2d 144, CCA 5, 1965. Ch 4, n 113.

United States ex rel Gittlemacker v. County of Philadelphia, 413 F 2d 84, CCA 3, 1969. Ch 1, n 55.

Hall v. United States, 136 F Supp 187, DC La 1955, aff'd 234 F 2d 811, CCA 5, 1956. Ch 5, n 123.

Harris v. Fall, 177 Fed 79, CCA 7, 1910. Ch 12, n 46.

Hathaway v. Worcester City Hospital, 475 F 2d 701, CCA 1, 1973. Ch 1, n 148.

Heryford v. Parker, 396 F 2d 393, CCA 10, 1968. Ch 8, n 89.

Hicks v. United States, 368 F 2d 626, CCA 4, 1966. Ch 3, n 20.

Hill v. James Walker Memorial Hospital, 407 F 2d 1036, CCA 4, 1969. Ch 6, n 94.

Hirons v. Patuxent Institution, 351 F 2d 613, CCA 4, 1965. Ch 1, n 48.

United States ex rel Hyde v. McGinnis, 429 F 2d 864, CCA 2, 1970. Ch 1, n 57.

Insurance Company of North America v. Prieto, 442 F 2d 1033, CCA 6, 1971. Ch 7, n 66.

Iverson v. Frandsen, 237 F 2d 898, CCA 10, 1956. Ch 9, n 41.

Jeanes v. Milner, 428 F 2d 598, CCA 8, 1970. Ch 3, n 91.

Jines v. General Electric Corporation, 313 F 2d 76, CCA 9, 1962. Ch 1, n 80; Ch 7, n 86.

Kershaw v. Sterling Drug Inc., 415 F 2d 1009, CCA 5, 1969. Ch 6, n 59.

Kozan v. Comstock, 270 F 2d 839, CCA 5, 1959. Ch 10, n 99.

Krusilla v. United States, 287 F 2d 34, CCA 2, 1961. Ch 2, n 49; Ch 4, n 143.

Landon v. Kansas City Gas Co., 10 F 2d 263, CCA 8, 1926. Ch 1, n 12.

Landsdown v. Worthey, 458 F 2d 485, CCA 8, 1972. Ch 1, n 54.

Lester v. Aetna Casualty and Surety Co., 240 F 2d 676, CCA 5, 1957. Ch 8, n 15.

Liberatore v. National Cylinder Gas Company, 193 F 2d 429, CCA 2, 1952, Ch 6, n 79.

Martinez v. Mancusi, 443 F 2d 921, CCA 2, 1970. Ch 1, n 50.

Mazer v. Lipschutz, 327 F 2d 42, 360 F 2d 275, CCA 3, 1966. Ch 5, n 77. Ch 10, n 68.

McBride v. United States, 462 F 2d 72, CCA 9, 1972. Ch 7, n 61.

Meredith v. Allen County War Memorial Hospital Commission, 397 F 2d 33, CCA 6, 1968. Ch 11, n 138; Ch 11, n 152.

Metzger v. Western Maryland Railway Company, 30 F 2d 50, CCA 4, 1929. Ch 7, n 91.

Moore v. Guthrie Hospital, 403 F 2d 366, CCA 4, 1968. Ch 5, n 158.

Moore v. Tremelling, 78 F 2d 821, CCA 9, 1935. Ch 2, n 88.

Morey v. Thybo, 199 Fed 760, CCA 7, 1912. Ch 7, n 59.

Murray v. United States, 329 F 2d 270, CCA 4, 1964. Ch 1, n 30.

O'Brien v. Stover, 443 F 2d 1013, CCA 8, 1971. Ch 3, n 63.

Olsen v. Royal Metals Corporation, 392 F 2d 116, CCA 5, 1968. Ch 6, n 107.

Orthopedic Equipment Company v. Eutster, 276 F 2d 455, CCA 4, 1960. Ch 6, n 70.

Panko v. Consolidated Mutual Insurance Co., 423 F 2d 41, CCA 3, 1970. Ch 9, n 44.

Parke, Davis and Company v. Stromstadt, 411 F 2d 1390, CCA 8, 1969. Ch 6, n 62.

Previn v. Tenacre, 70 F 2d 389, CCA 3, 1933. Ch 9, n 9.

Putnam v. Erie City Manufacturing Company, 338 F 2d 911, CCA 5, 1964. Ch 6, n 72.

Reder v Hanson, 338 F 2d 244, CCA 8, 1964. Ch 2, n 85.

Rewis v. United States, 369 F 2d 595, CCA 5, 1966. Ch 3, n 5.

Rivers v. Union Carbide Corporation, 426 F 2d 633, CCA 3, 1970. Ch 12, n 115.

Rudick v. Prineville Memorial Hospital, 319 F 2d 764, CCA 9, 1963. Ch 2, n 89.

Sams v. Ohio Valley General Hospital Association, 413 F 2d 826, CCA 4, 1969. Ch 11, n 119.

Sas v. Maryland, 334 F 2d 506, CCA 4, 1964. Ch 4, n 120.

Sawyer v. Sigler, 445 F 2d 818, CCA 8, Ch 1, n 50.

Simpkins v. Moses H. Cone Memorial Hospital, 323 F 2d 959, CCA 4, 1963. Ch 11, n 122.

Smith v. Schneckloth, 414 F 2d 680, CCA 9, 1969. Ch 1, n 52.

Sosa v. Board of Managers of Val Verde Memorial Hospital, 437 F 2d 173, CCA 5, 1971. Ch 11, n 129.

Taylor v. Glotfelty, 201 F 2d 51, CCA 6, 1952. Ch 9, n 25.

Thompson v. Lillehei, 273 F 2d 376, CCA 8, 1959. Ch 7, n 54.

Tinnerholm v. Parke Davis and Company, 411 F 2d 48, CCA 2, 1969. Ch 6, n 62.

Toal v. United States, 438 F 2d 222, CCA 2, 1971. Ch 10, n 135.

Tolbert v. Eyman, 434 F 2d 625, CCA 9, 1970. Ch 1, n 48.

Union Carbide and Carbon Corporation v. Stapleton, 237 F 2d 229, CCA 6, 1956. Ch 1, n 82.

United States v. Gray, 199 F 2d 239, CCA 10, 1952. Ch 4, n 103.

United States v. Morin, 229 F 2d 824, CCA 9, 1956. Ch 7, n 18; Ch 12, n 81.

United States v. Ramzy, 446 F 2d 1184, CCA 5, 1971. Ch 1, n 76.

United States v. Warren, 453 F 2d 738, CCA 2, 1972. Ch 1, n 76.

Vergott v. Deseret Pharmaceutical Company, 463 F 2d 12, CCA 5, 1972. Ch 5, n 38; Ch 6, n 71.

Vuitch v. Hardy, 473 F 2d 1370, CCA 4, 1973. Ch 11, n 29.

Wall v. Brim, 138 F 2d 478, CCA 5, 1943. Ch 8, n 8.

Weeks v. Latter Day Saints Hospital, 418 F 2d 1035, CCA 10, 1969. Ch 6, n 17.

Weintraub v. Rosen, 93 F 2d 544, CCA 7, 1937. Ch 10, n 61.

White v. United States, 399 F 2d 813, CCA 8, 1968. Ch 1, n 76.

Winters v. Miller, 446 F 2d 65, CCA 2, 1971. Ch 8, n 103; Ch 9, n 4.

Woodbury v. McKinnon, 447 F 2d 839, CCA 5, 1971. Ch 11, n 148; Ch 11, n 154.

Yoshizawa v. Hewitt, 52 F 2d 411, CCA 9, 1931. Ch 11, n 93.

United States District Courts
(Excluding the District of Columbia)

Akins v. Novinger, 322 F Supp 1205, DC Tenn 1970. Ch 2, n 24.

Amdur v. Zim Israel Navigation Company, 310 F Supp 1033, DC NY 1969. Ch 7, n 99.

Banks v. King Features Syndicate Inc., 30 F Supp 352, DC NY 1939. Ch 9, n 54.

Baum v. Turel, 206 F Supp 490, DC NY 1962. Ch 9, n 70.

Bishop v. Cox, 320 F Supp 1031, DC Va 1970. Ch 1, n 55.

Booth v. United States. 155 F Supp 235 (Ct Cl 1957). Ch 3, n 1.

Bruce v. United States, 167 F Supp 579, DC Cal 1958. Ch 2, n 14; Ch 4, n 25.

Carter v. Taylor Diving and Salvage Co., 341 F Supp 628, DC La 1972. Ch 1, n 37.

Chitta v. Delaware Valley Hospital, 313 F Supp 301, DC Pa 1970. Ch 11, n 141.

Ciccarone v. United States, 350 F Supp 554, DC Pa 1972. Ch 10, n 121.

Coe v. Gerstein, Case no. 72-1842-Civ JE (DC Fla. Aug. 14, 1973). Ch. 1, n 141.

Corson v. United States, 304 F Supp 155, DC Pa 1969. Ch 5, n 37.

Cotter v. United States, 279 F Supp 847, DC NY 1968. Ch 8, n 97; Ch 9, n 11; Ch 10, n 160.

Cullen v. Grove Press, Inc., 276 F Supp 727, DC NY 1967. Ch 9, n 58.

Dietze v. King, 184 F Supp 944, DC Va 1960. Ch 2, n 90; Ch 3, n 48; Ch 5, n 25; Ch 5, n 52; Ch 8, n 32; Ch 10, n 58.

Felber v. Foote, 321 F Supp 85, DC Conn 1970. Ch 1, n 79.

Frederic v. United States, 246 F Supp 368, DC La 1965. Ch 4, n 106.

Geiger v. Jenkins, 316 F Supp 370, DC Ga 1970. Ch 11, n 4; Ch 11, n 45.

Hall v. Ferry, 235 F Supp 821, DC Va 1964. Ch 3, n 47.

Hammonds v. Aetna Casualty & Surety Co., 327 F Supp 96, DC Ohio 1965. Ch 4, n 44.

Hendriksen v. Roosevelt Hospital, 297 F Supp 1142, DC NY 1969. Ch 8, n 67.

Jackson v. United States, 182 F Supp 907, DC MD 1960. Ch 5, n 44.

Johnson v. United States, 271 F Supp 205, DC Ark 1967. Ch 10 n 24.

Karp v. Cooley, 349 F Supp 827, DC Tex 1972. Ch 4, n 23; Ch 8, n 7; Ch 8, n 149; Ch 10, n 3.

Keene v. Methodist Hospital, 324 F Supp 233, ND Ind 1971. Ch 1, n 20.

Kopa v. United States, 236 F Supp 189, DC Hawaii 1964. Ch 6, n 97.

Lane v. United States, 225 F Supp 850, DC Va 1964. Ch 4, n 46.

Lange v. United States, 179 F Supp 777, DC NY 1960. Ch 4, n 102.

Larrabee v. United States, 254 F Supp 613, DC Cal 1966. Ch 4, n 62.

Leech v. Bralliar, 275 F Supp 897, DC Ariz 1967. Ch 10, n 67.

Lemonovich v. Klimoski, 315 F Supp 1288, DC Pa 1970. Ch 7, n 93.

McCollum v. Mayfield, 130 F Supp 112, DC Cal 1955. Ch 1, n 48.

McHugh v. Audet, 72 F Supp 394, DC Pa 1947. Ch 2, n 11; Ch 3, n 6; Ch 8, n 147.

Merchants National Bank v. United States, 272 F Supp 409, DC ND 1967. Ch 2, n 56; Ch 3, n 28; Ch 4, n 111.

Morgan v. Aetna Casualty Company, 185 F Supp 20, DC La 1960. Ch 3, n 122.

Mulvihill v. Butterfield Memorial Hospital, 329 F Supp 1020, DC NY 1971. Ch 11, n 144.

Pearce v. United States, 236 F Supp 431, DC Okla 1964. Ch 3, n 1.

Penn Tanker Company v. United States, 310 F Supp 613, DC Tex 1970. Ch 7, n 80; Ch 11, n 111.

Prosch v. Baxley, 345 F Supp 1063, DC Ala 1972. Ch 11, n 5; Ch 11, n 34.

Rahn v. United States, 222 F Supp 775, DC Ga 1963. Ch 2, n 31.

Ramsey v. Ciccone, 310 F Supp 600, DC Mo 1970. Ch 1, n 47; Ch 1, n 56.

Redding v. United States, 196 F Supp 871, DC Ark 1961. Ch 5, n 68.

Roberts v. Wood, 206 F Supp 579, DC Ala 1962. Ch 8, n 16; Ch 12, n 51.

Rogers v. United States, 216 F Supp 1, DC Ohio 1963. Ch 3, n 116.

Schwartz v. United States, 230 F Supp 536, DC Pa 1964. Ch 3, n 13; Ch 4, n 11.

Shaffer v. Jennings, 314 F Supp 588, DC Pa 1970. Ch 1, n 51.

Smith v. Baker, 326 F Supp 787, DC Mo 1970. Ch 1, n 55.

Smith v. DiCara, 329 F Supp 439, DC NY 1971. Ch 9, n 21.

Somma v. United States, 180 F Supp 519, DC Pa 1960. Ch 10, n 26.

Steeves v. United States, 294 F Supp 446, DC SC 1968. Ch 2, n 23; Ch 3, n 14; Ch 3, n 76.

Swanson v. Hill, 166 F Supp 296, DC ND 1958. Ch 5, n 27; Ch 10, n 58.

Taylor v. St. Vincent's Hospital, 369 F Supp 948, DC Mont 1973. Ch 1, n 149.

Tessier v. United States, 164 F Supp 779, DC Mass 1958. Ch 1, n 20.

Veals v. Ciccone, 281 F Supp 1017, DC Mo 1968. Ch 1, n 58.

Wade v. Bethesda Hospital, 337 F Supp 671, DC Ohio 1971. Ch 8, n 109.

Willis v. White, 310 F Supp 205, DC La 1970. Ch 1, n 47.

Wolfe v. Virusky, 306 F Supp 519, DC Ga 1969. Ch 10, n 147.

Wyatt v. Stickney, 325 F Supp 781, DC Ala 1971. Ch 4, n 120; Ch 8, n 94.

OTHER
REFERENCES

"Law and Medicine" Series. *Journal of the American Medical Association*

"Abandonment" Parts I–IV, 225 JAMA No. 9, page 1157, August 27, 1973; 225 *JAMA* No. 10, page 1285, September 3, 1973; 225 *JAMA* No. 11, page 1429, September 10, 1973; 225 *JAMA* No. 12, page 1511, September 17, 1973; Ch 4, n 15; Ch 12, n 13; Ch 12, n 24; Ch 12, n 75; Ch 12, n 65; Ch 12, n 84.

"Administration of Wrong Drugs," 204 *JAMA* No. 11, page 225, June 10, 1968, Ch 5, n 3.

"Adult Jehovah's Witnesses and Blood Transfusions," 219 *JAMA* No. 2, page 273, January 10, 1972. Ch 1, n 68.

"Alternative Medical Procedures," 212 *JAMA* No. 2, page 385, April 13, 1970. Ch 2, n 16; Ch 8, n 147; Ch 4, n 24.

"Analysis of Fee-splitting Statutes," 208 *JAMA* No. 6, page 1083, May 12, 1969 Ch 11, n 18.

"Angiograms," 213 JAMA No. 2, page 349, July 13, 1970. Ch 4, n 52.

"Appointment of Independent Medical Expert," 216 *JAMA* No. 1, page 207, April 15, 1971. Ch 1, n 91.

"Arbitration of Medical Liability," 211 *JAMA* No. 1, page 175, January 5, 1970. Ch 13, n 59.

"Authorization for Autopsies," 203 *JAMA* No. 5, page 199, January 29, 1968. Ch 8, n 58.

"Biopsies," Parts 1 and 2, 223 *JAMA* No. 12, page 1429, March 19, 1973 and No. 13, page 1573, March 26, 1973. Ch 1, n 19; Ch 3, n 62.

"Birth Injuries," 219 *JAMA* No. 1, page 129, January 3, 1972. Ch 4, n 57.

"Breast Cancer," 222 *JAMA* No. 13, page 1713, December 25, 1972. Ch 3, n 65.

"Cardiac Arrest," 216 *JAMA* No. 13, page 2217, June 28, 1971. Ch 4, n 39.

"Charitable Immunity," 197 *JAMA* No. 9, page 201, August 29, 1966. Ch 10, n 151.

"Child Abuse and the Physician," 222 *JAMA* No. 4, page 517, October 23, 1972. Ch 1, n 73; Ch 8, n 116.

"Civil Liability for Patient's Addiction," 212 *JAMA* No. 9, page 1573, June 1, 1970, Ch 5, n 197.

"Classification of Medical Defendants," 219 *JAMA* No. 13, page 1833, March 27, 1972. Ch 13, n 5.

"Common Law and Clinical Investigation," 203 *JAMA* No. 6, page 231, February 5, 1968. Ch 8, n 137.

"Compulsory Psychiatric Examination," 220 *JAMA* No. 9, page 1277, May 29, 1972. Ch 1, n 93.

"Compulsory Sterilization," 221 *JAMA* No. page 229, July 10, 1972. Ch 8, n 106.

"Consent in Clinical Investigation," 203 *JAMA* No. 7, page 281, February 12, 1968. Ch 8, n 137.

"Contributory Negligence," Parts I, II and III, 218 *JAMA* No. 5, page 785, November 1, 1971; No. 6, page 933, November 8, 1971; No. 7, page 1109, November 15, 1971; Ch 10, n 10; Ch 10, n 28; Ch 10, n 40.

"The Courts and Fee-Splitting," 208 *JAMA* No. 7, page 1241, May 19, 1969. Ch 11, n 78.

"Criminal Prosecution for Patient's Death," 222 *JAMA* No. 10, page 1341, December 4, 1972. Ch 10, n 158.

"Critical Areas in Clinical Investigation," 203 *JAMA* No. 8, page 241, February 19, 1968. Ch 8, n 147.

"The Darling Case," 206 *JAMA* No. 7, page 1665, November 11, 1968. Ch 1, n 43; Ch 7, n 73.

"The Darling Case Revisited," 206 *JAMA* No. 8, page 1875, November 18, 1968. Ch 1, n 43; Ch 7, n 73.

"Delay of Surgery," 216 *JAMA* No. 9, page 1527, May 31, 1971. Ch 3, n 100.

"Desertion, Abandonment & Neglect of Patient," 199 *JAMA* No. 8, page 245, February 20, 1967. Ch 4, n 15.

"Diabetes," Parts I and II, 223 *JAMA* No. 4, page 471, January 22, 1973; No. 5, page 591, January 29, 1973; Ch 3, n 82.

"Disciplinary Proceedings," Parts I, II, III, IV, V and VI, 000 *JAMA* No. 000, 000. Ch 11, n 4; Ch 11, n 7; Ch 11, n 55; Ch 11, n 19.

"Disclosure of Confidential Information," 216 *JAMA* No. 2, page 385, April 12, 1971, Ch 9, n 28.

"Discretion in Disciplinary Hearing," 209 *JAMA* No. 4, page 611, July 28, 1969. Ch 11, n 25.

"Drug Induced Aplastic Anemia," 222 *JAMA* No. 3, page 405, October 16, 1972. Ch 5, n 191. Ch 6, n 64.

"Drug Reactions," 197 *JAMA* No. 8, page 221, August 22, 1966. Ch 5, n 188.

"Due Process in the Disciplinary Hearing," 208 *JAMA* No. 11, page 2229, June 16, 1969. Ch 11, n 8.

"Duty to Consult," 226 *JAMA* No. 1, page 111, October 1, 1973. Ch 2, n 20.

"Duty to Refer Patient to Medical Specialist," 204 *JAMA* No. 8, page 281, May 20, 1968; Ch 2, n 26.

"Duty to Refer Patient to Orthopedic Specialist," 204 *JAMA* No. 7, page 249, May 13, 1968. Ch 2, n 31.

"Duty to Refer to Larger Hospital," 224 *JAMA* No. 12, page 1687, June 18, 1973. Ch 2, n 32.

"Effects of Increased Litigation," 215 *JAMA* No. 6, page 1043, February 18, 1971, Ch 13, n 35.

"Electroshock Therapy," 210 *JAMA* No. 3, page 631, October 20, 1969. Ch 5, n 214.

"Electrosurgical Instruments," 223 *JAMA* No. 1, page 111, January 1, 1973. Ch 6, n 48.

"Emergency Room Liability," 220 *JAMA* No. 5, page 761, May 1, 1972. Ch 1, n 38. Ch 7, n 72.

"Erroneous Commitment," 219 *JAMA* No. 10, page 1389, March 6, 1972. Ch 1, n 154; Ch 3, n 23; Ch 9, n 90.

"Expanding Statutes of Limitations," 210 *JAMA* No. 13, page 2467, December 29, 1969. Ch 10, n 124.

"Expulsion from Medical Society," Parts I and II, 229 *JAMA* No. 11, p. 1502, September 9, 1974. Ch 11, n 105; 229 *JAMA* No. 12, p. 1656, September 16, 1974.

"Failure to Diagnose Infection," 220 *JAMA* No. 2, page 321, April 10, 1972. Ch 3, n 25.

"Failure to Diagnose Ectopic Pregnancy," 202 *JAMA* No. 9, page 213, November 27, 1967. Ch 3, n 37.

"Failure to Diagnose Normal Pregnancy," 202 *JAMA* No. 8, page 375, November 20, 1967. Ch 3, n 32.

"Failure to 'keep up' as Negligence," 224 *JAMA* No. 10, page 1461, June 4, 1973. Ch 2, n 38.

"Failure to Make Diagnostic Tests," 210 *JAMA* No. 1, page 213, October 6, 1969. Ch 3, n 30.

"Failure to Take Medical History," 226 *JAMA* No. 4, page 509, October 22, 1973. Ch 2, n 53. Ch 3, n 17. Ch 10, n 4.

"Failure to Transmit Medical Information," 213 *JAMA* No. 13, page 2351, September 28, 1970. Ch 3, n 88.

"Follow-up Procedures," 212 *JAMA* No. 1, page 223, April 6, 1970. Ch 2, n 45; Ch 4, n 26.

"Foreign Bodies in the Eye," 218 *JAMA* No. 3, page 495, October 18, 1971. Ch 3, n 25; Ch 3, n 56.

"Foreign Objects Left in the Patient," 195 *JAMA* No. 4, page 275, January 24, 1966. Ch 5, n 3.

"Fraud and Duress," (in press).

"Government Liability for Negligent Treatment," Parts I, II, and III, 224 *JAMA* No. 1, page 163, April 2, 1963; No. 2, page 279, April 9, 1973; No. 3, page 443, April 16, 1973; Ch 10, n 155.

"Guarantee of Medical Results," 219 *JAMA* No. 3, page 431, January 17, 1972. Ch 4, n 4; Ch 1, n 9.

"Healthy Subjects in Clinical Investigation," 203 *JAMA* No. 9, page 369, February 26, 1968. Ch 8, n 136.

"Heart Attacks," 223 *JAMA* No. 3, page 365, January 15, 1973. Ch 3, n 25.

"Hip Fractures," 219 *JAMA* No 5, page 659, January 31, 1972. Ch 3, n 49.

"Homicide by Quackery," 222 *JAMA* No. 9, page 1219, November 27, 1972. Ch 3, n 169.

"Hospital Burns," 214 *JAMA* No. 3, page 653, October 19, 1970. Ch 6, n 13.

"Hospital Emergency Room Liability Cases," 208 *JAMA* No. 2, page 423, April 14, 1969. Ch 7, n 72.

"Hospital Fires," 223 *JAMA* No. 9, page 1073, February 26, 1973. Ch 6, n 23.

"Hospital Liability for Physician Negligence," 214 *JAMA* No. 9, page 1755, November 30, 1970. Ch 1, n 43; Ch 7, n 81; Ch 11, n 110.

"Hospital Liability for Staff Negligence," 224 *JAMA* No. 8, page 1225, May 21, 1973. Ch 1, n 43; Ch 11, n 110.

"Hospital Obligation to Nonemployee Personnel," 224 *JAMA* No. 9, page 1329, May 28, 1973. Ch 6, n 106.

"Hospital Staff Privileges," Parts II, III, VI and VI, 000 *JAMA* No. 000. Ch 11, n 118; Ch 11, n 127; Ch 11, n 140; Ch 11, n 156.

"Hospital Staff Privileges," 213 *JAMA* No. 7, page 1233, August 17, 1970. Ch 11, n 112.

"Hospital's Right to Refuse Admission," 213 *JAMA* No. 4, page 673, July 27, 1970. Ch 1, n 38.

"How to Avoid Malpractice Claims," 211 *JAMA* No. 13, page 2233, March 30, 1970. Ch 13, n 18.

"Hysterectomies," 217 *JAMA* No. 10, page 1439, September 6, 1971, Ch 3, n 114.

"Iatrogenic Disorders," 200 *JAMA* No. 13, page 237, June 26, 1967. Ch 3, n 118.

"The Importance of Medical Records," 228 *JAMA* No. 1, page 118, April 1, 1974. Ch 10, n 1.

"Improper Release from Mental Hospital," 220 *JAMA* No. 6, page 897, May 8, 1972. Ch 3, n 25; Ch 4, n 108.

"Incompetence as Unprofessional Conduct," 208 *JAMA* No. 5, page 927, May 5, 1969. Ch 11, n 90.

"Informed Consent," Parts I, II and III, 214 *JAMA* No. 6, page 1181, November 9, 1970; No. 7, page 1383, November 16, 1970; No. 8, page 1611, November 23, 1970. Ch 8, n 1.

"Injections by Office Assistants," 204 *JAMA* No. 4, page 193, April 22, 1968. Ch 7, n 4.

"Irregular Assistants and Legal Risks," 207 *JAMA* No. 5, page 1027, February 3, 1969. Ch 7, n 7.

"Jehovah's Witnesses and Blood Transfusions," 195 *JAMA* No. 6, page 303, February 7, 1966, Ch 1, n 68.

"Joint Screening Panels," 215 *JAMA* No. 10, page 1715, March 8, 1971. Ch 13, n 37.

"Keeping the Patients' Secrets," 195 *JAMA* No. 5, page 227, January 31, 1966. Ch 9, n 29.

"Lawsuits and Quality of Patient Care," 215 *JAMA* No. 7, page 1211, February 15, 1971. Ch 13, n 32.

"Legal Implications of Photographing Surgical Operations," 198 *JAMA* No. 13, page 221, December 26, 1966. Ch 9, n 51.

"Legal Risks of Electroshock Therapy," 196 *JAMA* No. 6, page 331, May 9, 1966. Ch 5, n 214.

"Liability for Administering Blood Test," 217 *JAMA* No. 1, page 119, July 5, 1971. Ch 1, n 95.

"Liability for Cesarean Section," 214 *JAMA* No. 4, page 809, October 26, 1970. Ch 3, n 71.

"Liability for Esophageal Perforation," 216 *JAMA* No. 8, page 1399, May 24, 1971. Ch 4, n 49.

"Liability for Gas Gangrene," 221 *JAMA* No. 9, page 1083, August 28, 1972. Ch 4, n 79.

"Liabiltiy for Mental Anguish," 217 *JAMA* No. 6, page 869, August 9, 1971. Ch 1, n 106.

"Liability for Obstetrical Injuries," 217 *JAMA* No. 7, page 1015, August 16, 1971. Ch 4, n 57.

"Liability for Patient's Suicide," 215 *JAMA* No. 11, page 1879, March 15, 1971. Ch 4, n 101.

"Liability for Penicillin Reactions," 212 *JAMA* No. 11, page 2015, June 15, 1970. Ch 5, n 180; Ch 3, n 9.

"Liability for Resident's Negligence," 213 *JAMA* No. 1, page 181, July 6, 1970. Ch 8, n 30; Ch 1, n 42.

"Liability for Transfusion Hepatitis," 211 *JAMA* No. 8, page 1431, February 23, 1970. Ch 5, n 55.

"Liability for Unauthorized Treatment," 196 *JAMA* No. 10, page 293, June 6, 1966. Ch 8, n 29; Ch 8, n 9.

"Liability for Vesicovaginal Fistula," 212 *JAMA* No. 6, page 1113, May 11, 1970. Ch 4, n 36.

"Liability in Dilation and Curettage Cases," 218 *JAMA* No. 12, page 1873, December 20, 1971, Ch 4, n 65.

"Liability Insurance for Slander and Libel," 206 *JAMA* No. 13, page 2985, December 23, 1968. Ch 9, n 28.

"Liability in 'Tight Cast' Cases," 217 *JAMA* No. 12, page 1767, September 20, 1971. Ch 4, n 69.

"Liability of Company for Ship's Surgeon," 215 *JAMA* No. 8, page 1381, February 22, 1971. Ch 1, n 90; Ch 7, n 99.

"Liability of Referring Physician," 204 *JAMA* No. 3, page 273, April 15, 1968. Ch 2, n 35; Ch 7, n 23.

"Lost or Broken Teeth," 221 *JAMA* No. 1, page 119, July 3, 1972. Ch 5, n 141.

"Lung Cancer," 222 *JAMA* No. 7, page 877, November 13, 1972. Ch 3, n 25.

"Manufacturer's Liability for Drug Reaction," 213 *JAMA* No. 11, page 1975, September 14, 1970, Ch 6, n 55.

"Mediation of Liability Claims," 222 *JAMA* No. 2, page 241, October 9, 1972. Ch 13, n 52.

"Medical Arbitration Experiments," 211 *JAMA* No. 2, page 351, January 12, 1970. Ch 13, n 60.

"Medical Premises Liability," Parts I and II, 226 *JAMA* No. 5, page 597, October 29, 1973; No. 6, page 717, November 5, 1973, Ch 6, n 1.

"Medical Treatment Without Consent," 200 *JAMA* No. 5, page 229, May 1, 1967. Ch 8, n 2.

"Mental Illness and Parental Rights," 216 *JAMA* No. 3, page 575, April 19, 1971. Ch 8, n 125.

"Minors and Contraception," 216 *JAMA* No. 12, page 2059, June 21, 1971. Ch 1, n 127.

"Misdiagnosis of Appendicitis," 212 *JAMA* No. 10, page 1763, June 8, 1970. Ch 3, n 77; Ch 3, n 115.

Misdiagnosis of Pregnancy," 218 *JAMA* No. 13, page 2013, December 27, 1971. Ch 3, n 32.

"Misdiagnosis of Tuberculosis,'" 219 *JAMA* No. 4, page 561, January 24, 1972. Ch 3, n 59.

"Misdiagnosis Without Fault," Parts I and II, 219 *JAMA* No. 7, page 967, February 14, 1972; No. 8, page 1127, February 21, 1972. Ch 3, n 3.

"Mistaken Diagnosis of Pregnancy," 202 *JAMA* No. 10, page 249, December 4, 1967. Ch 3, n 32.

"Mistaken Identity," 221 *JAMA* No. 7, page 747, August 14, 1972. Ch 4, n 44; Ch 3, n 111.

"Mistaken Procedures," 226 *JAMA* No. 8, page 1053, November 19, 1973. Ch 4, n 44.

"More About Informed Consent," Parts I and II, 224 *JAMA* No. 13, page 1831, June 25, 1973, 225 *JAMA* No. 1, page 95, July 2, 1973. Ch 8, n 35.

"Mother's Right to Consent," 213 *JAMA* No. 8, page 1393, August 24, 1970. Ch 1, n 109.

"Negligence of Office Assistants," 204 *JAMA* No. 2, page 257, Aprli 8, 1968, Ch 7, n 1.

"Negligence of Patient Subsequent to That of Physician," 205 *JAMA* No. 2, page 161, July 8, 1968. Ch 10, n 13.

"Negligent Selection of Hospital Staff," 223 *JAMA* No. 7, page 833, February 12, 1973. Ch 1, n 43; Ch 10, n 163; Ch 7, n 78; Ch 11, n 94; Ch 11, n 110.

"Non-Negligent Failure to Take Xray Films," 219 *JAMA* No. 9, page 1259, February 28, 1972. Ch 3, n 44.

"Nurse Anesthetists," 211 *JAMA* No. 9, page 1591, March 2, 1970. Ch 7, n 49.

"Organ Donation by Incompetent," 213 *JAMA* No. 3, page 513, July 20, 1970. Ch 8, n 86.

"Package Inserts as Evidence," 208 *JAMA* No. 3, page 589, April 21, 1969. Ch 5, n 188.

"Paralysis Following Injection," 199 *JAMA* No. 7, page 251, February 13, 1967. Ch 4, n 167.

"Parental Consent to Treatment of a Minor," 200 *JAMA* No. 1, page 273, April 3, 1967. Ch 1, n 108.

"Patients Who Faint During Office Visits," 195 *JAMA* No. 3, page 261, January 17, 1966. Ch 5, n 173.

"Personal Character and Licensure," 207 *JAMA* No. 13, page 2517, March 31, 1969. Ch 11, n 65.

"The Physician and Adoption," 222 *JAMA* No. 8, page 953, February 19, 1973. Ch 8, n 120.

"The Physician as Fellow Servant," 223 *JAMA* No. 10, page 1203, March 5, 1973. Ch 1, n 84.

"The Physician as Rescuer," 223 *JAMA* No. 6, page 721, February 5, 1973. Ch 1, n 35.

"Physicians Employed by Physicians," 204 *JAMA* No. 1, page 257, April 1, 1968. Ch 7, n 11.

"Physician's Liability for Acts of Hospital Nurses," 209 *JAMA* No. 11, page 1791, September 15, 1969. Ch 7, n 26.

"Physician's Liability for Drug Reaction," 213 *JAMA* No. 12, page 2143, September 21, 1970. Ch 5, n 188, Ch 3, n 8.

"Physician's Liability for Improper Disclosure," 198 *JAMA* No. 7, page 331, November 14, 1966. Ch 9, n 29.

"Physician's Records and the Chiropractor," 224 *JAMA* No. 7, page 1071, May 14, 1973. Ch 12, n 97.

"Physician Risk in Blood Transfusions," 205 *JAMA* No. 10, page 177, September 2, 1968. Ch 5, n 78.

"Prenatal Injuries," 214 *JAMA* No. 11, page 2105, December 14, 1970. Ch 1, n 106.

"Prisoner's Right to Medical Treatment," 216 *JAMA* No. 7, page 1253, May 17, 1971. Ch 1, n 47.

"Problems of Malpractice Insurance," 215 *JAMA* No. 3, page 529, January 18, 1971. Ch 13, n 35.

"Professional Corporations," 207 *JAMA* No. 10, page 1983, March 10, 1969. Ch 7, n 21.

"Professional Negligence in Hospital Emergency Rooms," 208 *JAMA* No. 1, page 231, April 7, 1969. Ch 7, n 72.

"Profiles of Medical Defendants," 219 *JAMA* No. 12, page 1687, March 20, 1972. Ch 13, n 5.

"Proximate Cause," Parts I, II and III, 218 *JAMA* No. 9, page 1479, November 29, 1971; No. 10, page 1617, December 6, 1971, No. 11, page 1761, December 13, 1971; Ch 2, n 83.

"Psychiatric Procedures and Their Legal Effects," 201 *JAMA* No. 2, page 235, July 10, 1967. Ch 5, n 206.

"Radiation Therapy," 220 *JAMA* No. 13, page 1807, June 26, 1972, Ch 8, n 22; Ch 5, n 91.

"Recent Decisions on Transfusion Hepatitis," 228 *JAMA* No. 6, p. 786, May 6, 1974. Ch 5, n 55.

"Recent Decisions on Unnecessary Surgery," 222 *JAMA* No. 12, page 1593, December 18, 1972. Ch 3, n 104.

"Recent Decisions on Statutes of Limitations," Parts I and II, 227 *JAMA* No. 11, page 1336, March 18, 1974; 227 *JAMA* No. 12, page 1500, March 25, 1974. Ch 10, n 143; Ch 10, n 140.

"Referral to a Specialist," 211 *JAMA* No. 11, page 1911, March 16, 1970. Ch 2, n 26.

"Release of Original Wrongdoer," 196 *JAMA* No. 12, page 217, June 20, 1966. Ch 10, n 65.

"Res Ipsa Loquitur," Parts I–VII, 211 *JAMA* No. 5, page 537, July 31, 1972; 221 *JAMA* No. 6, page 633, August 7, 1972; 221 *JAMA* No. 10, page 1201, September 4, 1972; 221 *JAMA* No. 11, page 1329, September 11, 1972; 221 *JAMA* No. 12, page 1441, September 18, 1972; 221 *JAMA* No. 13, page 1587, September 25, 1972; 222 *JAMA* No. 1, page 121, October 2, 1972. Ch 2, n 94.

"Responsibility for Future Medical Care," 199 *JAMA* No. 9, page 253, February 27, 1967. Ch 4, n 132.

"Restriction of Hospital Privileges," 215 *JAMA* No. 9, page 1547, March 1, 1971. Ch 11, n 113.

"Revocation of License for Professional Incompetence," 208 *JAMA* No. 4, page 751, April 28, 1969. Ch 11, n 89.

"Right to Refuse Necessary Treatment," 221 *JAMA* No. 3, page 335, July 17, 1972. Ch 1, n 62; Ch 8, n 42.

"Right to Release from Mental Hospital," 220 *JAMA* No. 10, page 1405, June 5, 1972. Ch 4, n 116.

"Right to Sterilization," 226 *JAMA* No. 9, page 1151, November 26, 1973. Ch 1, n 147.

"The Right to Treatment," 220 *JAMA* No. 8, page 1165, May 22, 1972. Ch 8, n 87; Ch 4, n 119.

"The Rise of Medical Liability Suits," 215 *JAMA* No. 5, page 843, February 1, 1971. Ch 13, n 17.

"Roentgenograms of Head Injuries," 222 *JAMA* No. 5, page 613, October 30, 1972. Ch 3, n 52.

"Sciatic Nerve Damage from Injection," 219 *JAMA* No. 6, page 807, February 7, 1972. Ch 5, n 168.

"The Standard of Care," Parts I, II, and III, 225 *JAMA* No. 6, page 671, August 6, 1973; No. 7, page 791, August 13, 1973; No. 8, page 1027, August 20, 1973. Ch 2, n 5.

"Standard of Care for Specialists," Parts I and II, 226 *JAMA* No. 2, page 251, October 8, 1973; No. 3, page 395, October 15, 1973. Ch 2, n 72.

"Statutes of Limitations: Discovery Rule," 210 *JAMA* No. 10, page 1983, December 8, 1969. Ch 10, n 124.

"Surgeons and Anesthesiologists,'" 211 *JAMA* No. 10, page 1753, March 9, 1970. Ch 7, n 52.

"Surgical Assault and Battery," 198 JAMA No. 11, page 299, December 12, 1966. Ch 8, n 26; Ch 9, n 1.

"Surgical Hemorrhage," 220 *JAMA* No. 3, page 453, April 17, 1972. Ch 4, n 94.

"Surgical Infections from the Standpoint of Statute of Limitations," 197 *JAMA* No. 5, page 221, August 1, 1966. Ch 10, n 114.

"Tetanus Antitoxin Reactions," 224 *JAMA* No. 4, page 559, April 23, 1972. Ch 3, n 9; Ch 5, n 184.

"Therapeutic Restraint," 197 *JAMA* No. 1, page 205, July 4, 1966. Ch 9, n 9; Ch 5, n 208.

"Tissue Damage from Life-Saving Drug," 202 *JAMA* No. 6, page 317, November 6, 1967. Ch 5, n 164.

"Transplant Problems," 223 *JAMA* No. 11, page 1315, March 12, 1973. Ch 8, n 81.

"Treating a Minor for Veneral Disease," 214 *JAMA* No. 10, page 1949, December 7, 1970. Ch 1, n 124.

"Twelve Months of Medicine in Court," 217 *JAMA* No. 9, page 1287, August 30, 1971. Ch 13, n 4.

"Unauthorized Autopsies," 214 *JAMA* No. 5, page 967, November 2, 1970. Ch 8, n 58.

"Unlicensed Treatment," 214 *JAMA* No. 1, page 209, October 5, 1970. Ch 11, n 38; Ch 7, n 11.

"Unnecessary Mastectomies," 206 *JAMA* No. 1, page 199, September 30, 1968. Ch 3, n 103.

"Unnecessary Surgery," 213 *JAMA* No. 10, page 1755, September 7, 1970. Ch 3, n 104.

"Use of Bed Rails," 220 *JAMA* No. 1, page 163, April 3, 1972. Ch 6, n 41.

"Vasectomies," 217 *JAMA* No. 13, page 1943, September 27, 1971. Ch 1, n 153; Ch 4, n 67.

"Voluntary Sterilization," 225 *JAMA* No. 13, page 1743, September 24, 1973. Ch 1, n 147.

"Who Should Provide Emergency Care?," 210 *JAMA* No. 4, page 775, October 27, 1969. Ch 7, n 72.

Other References from the *Journal of the American Medical Association*

"Answers to Editorial Inquiries," 180 *JAMA,* page 706, May 26, 1962; 189 *JAMA* No. 5, page 390, August 3, 1964. Ch 1, n 32.

"The Public Wants a Doctor When They Want Him," Editorial, 136 *JAMA,* page 695, March 6, 1948. Ch 1, n 25.

Federal Statutes, Federal Regulations and Executive Orders

Federal Employer's Liability Act 45 USC Section 51. Ch 7, n 100; Ch 1, n 89.

Federal Food, Drug and Cosmetic Act 21 USC Sections 301–392, Sections 355, 1964, Ch 8, n 138; 21 USC Sections 301–392. Ch 1, n 75; Ch 6, n 69.

Federal Tort Claims Act, 28 USCA Section 1346 et seq. Ch 10, n 154.

Food and Drug Administrative Regulation 21 C.F.R. Section 130.37. Ch 3, n 139.

Food and Drug Administration Policy Statement on Consent in Clinical Investigation, 31 Fed Reg 11415 (1966). Ch 8, n 140.

Harrison Narcotics Act, 26 USCA, Sections 4701–4736, 4773. Ch 1, n 74.

Health Maintenance Organization and Resources Development Act of 1972, Section 3327, 92nd Congress, 2nd Session, 1972. Ch 13, n 77.

Jones Act, 46 USC, Section 688. Ch 1, n 90, Ch 7, n 97.

Presidential Health Message, February 18, 1971. Ch 13, n 2.

State Statutes

Alabama Code Title 7, Section 25 (1). Ch 10, n 129.

Arizona Rev Statute 44-132, 44-133. Ch 1, n 119.

California Welfare & Institutions Code Section 5325, 1968, Ch 8, n 104.

Conn. General Statute Section 52-584. Ch 10, n 130.

Illinois Rev Statutes C. 83 Section 22.1. Ch 1, n 128.

Indiana Statutes Ann Section 35-4407. Ch 1, n 119.

Louisiana Civil Code Art 1489. Ch 9, n 83.

Michigan Stat Ann Section 14.533. Ch 9, n 31.

Mississippi Code 7129-81 et seq. Ch 1, n 119.

Nevada Rev Statute Section 129.030. Ch 1, n 119.

New Hampshire Revised Statutes Annotated, Section 519-A: 1-519: A 10, 1971. Ch 13, n 57.

New Jersey Supreme Court Rule 425 B Adopted February 21, 1966. Ch 13, n 54.

New Mexico Statutes Annotated, Section 12-12-1 et seq. Ch 1, n 119.

Newspapers, News Magazines and Popular Periodicals

TheAlbuquerque Journal, December 7, 1969. Ch 13, n 51.

The Charlotte Observer, July 17, 1973, page 4A. Ch 9, n 62.

Crile, George, M.D. "Breast Cancer: A Patient's Bill of Rights," *Ms,* September 1973, page 66, at page 94. Ch 13, n 25.

Newsweek, December 24, 1973, pages 104–105, at page 105. Ch 13, n 34.

New York Times, page 30 Col 1, June 25, 1972. Ch 13, n 52.

New York Times, May 9, 1973, page 54, Ch 4, n 30.

New York Times, "Report of Ad Hoc Committee," June 13, 1973, page 21, Col 3. Ch 8, n 142.

New York Times, June 27, 1973, page 44, Col. 3. Ch 9, n 76.

New York Times, June 28, 1973, page 14. Ch 9, n 76.

New York Times, June 29, 1973, page 28. Ch 9, n 76.

New York Times, July 2, 1973, page 10. Ch 9, n 76.

New York Times, July 8, 1973. Sec. 4, page 4 Col 4. Ch 9, n 77.

New York Times, July 13, 1973, page 43, Col 4. Ch 9, n 60.

New York Times, July 22, 1973, page 30, Col 4. Ch 9, n 61.

New York Times, August 1, 1973, page 27, Col 1. Ch 9, n 61.

United States Government Documents
Reports of Congressional Hearings

Constitutional Rights of the Mentally Ill, Hearing before the U.S. Senate Committee on the Judiciary, 91st Congress 1969–70, Washington, D. C. Printing Office. Ch 13, n 99.

Medical Malpractice: The Patient Versus the Physician, Subcommittee on Executive Reorganization Committee on Government Operations, United State Senate, 91st Congress, 1st Session, Released November 20, 1969, U. S. Government Printing Office, Washington, D. C. Ch 13, n 1.

Report of Executive Department

Medical Malpractice, Report of the Secretary's Commission on Medical Malpractice, Department of Health, Education and Welfare, Washington, D. C. (DHEW Publication No. (05) 73-88), Ch 13, n 3.

Pages 5–6. Ch 13, n 8; Ch 13, n 7.

Page 8. Ch 13, n 10.

Pages 9–11. Ch 13, n 12; Ch 13, n 13; Ch 13, n 9.

Page 12. Ch 13, n 30; Ch 13, n 14.

Page 15. Ch 13, n 33.

Page 18. Ch 8, n 36.

Page 24. Ch 13, n 15.

Page 31. Ch 13, n 19.

Page 32. Ch 13, n 20.

Page 33. Ch 13, n 21.

Pages 34–35. Ch 13, n 22; Ch 13, n 23.

Page 52. Ch 11, n 31.

Page 69. Ch 13, n 86.

Page 70. Ch 13, n **16.**

Pages 73–88. Ch 11, n 87; Ch 11, n 88.

Page 91. Ch 13, n 45; Ch 13, n 58.

Page 92. Ch 13, n 63.

Page 93. Ch 13, n 75; Ch 13, n 64.

Pages 96–97. Ch 13, n 78; Ch 13, n 76.

Pages 100–102. Ch 13, n 81; Ch 13, n 84.

Chapter 2 "Magnitude and Impact of the Medical Malpractice Problem." Ch 13, n 6.

Chapter 6, "The Human Dimension." Ch 13, n 24.

Appendix to the Report of the Secretary's Commission on Medical Malpractice

Adams, Charles C., Jr. and Bell, Alexander, "Alternatives to Litigation, II, Constitutionality of Arbitration Statutes," Appendix, pages 315–325. Ch 13, n 67; Ch 13, n 65.

Baird, C. Bruce, Munsterman, G. Thomas and Stevens, Julian P., "Alternatives to Litigation, I: Technical Analysis," Appendix pages 214–314. Ch 13, n 41; Ch 13, n 49; Ch 13, n 44; Ch 13, n 47; Ch 13, n 38; Ch 13, n 50.

Bernstein, Arthur H., "No-Fault Compensation for Personal Injury in New Zealand," Appendix, pages 836–848. Ch 13, n 79.

Bernzweiz, Eli P., "Defensive Medicine," Appendix pages 38–40. Ch 13, n 31.

Byrnes, Michael, "The Media and Medical Malpractice," Appendix pages 653–657 at page 657. Ch 13, n 16.

Dietz, Stephen, Baird, C. Bruce and Berul, Lawrence, "The Medical Malpractice Legal System," Appendix pages 87–167. Ch 13, n 26; Ch 13, n 28; Ch 13, n 29.

Helfman, Denis, Jarrett, Glenn, Lutzker, Susan, Schneider, Karen, and Stein, Peter, "Access to Medical Records," Appendix, pages 177–213. Ch 12, n 98.

Henderson, Stanley D., "Alternatives to Litigation III: Contractual Problems in the Enforcement of Agreements to Arbitrate Medical Malpractice," Appendix pages 326–345. Ch 13, n 68. Ch 13, n 69.

Mirabella, Meyers and Rudor, "Medical Malpractice Insurance Claims Files Closed 1970," pages 1–25, Appendix at page 17. Ch 13, n 11.

Roth, Edwin and Rosenthal, Paul, "Non-Fault Based Medical Injury Compensation Systems," Appendix, pages 450–493. Ch 13, n 82; Ch 13, n 85.

Rubsamen, David, "The Experience of Binding Arbitration in the Ross-Loos Medical Group," Appendix, pages 424–449. Ch 13, n 61; Ch 13, n 74.

Thompson, Fango, Lupton, Andrew and Feldesman, James, "Patient Grievance Mechanisms In Health Care Institutions," Appendix, Pages 758–835. Ch 13, n 88.

Legal and Medical Journals

American Law Institute, *Restatement of the Law of Torts,* Section 463, Ch 10, n 9.

American Medical Association *News,* April 17, 1967, page 4. Ch 1, n 125.

"Are Malpractice Screening Panels the Answer?," *Medical Economics,* March 1, 1971, page 112. Ch 13, n 48.

Barnett, F. J., "Liability for Adverse Drug Reactions," 1 *J Leg Med* No. 2, page 47, May/June 1973. Ch 5, n 188.

The Bulletin, King County Medical Society, February 1969, page 45. Ch 13, n 40.

Busek, Linda C., "Where Malpractice Suits Have Been Cut to Zero," *Med Econ,* April 2, 1973, page 91. Ch 13, n 51.

"Contributory Negligence in Malpractice," 12 *Cleveland-Marshall Law Rev* 455, 1963. Ch 10, n 44.

"Contributory Negligence in Malpractice," 21 *Cleveland State Law Rev* 58, January 1972. Ch 10, n 44.

43 *Colorado Law Rev* 629, 1943. Ch 13, n 69.

Dienes C. Thomas, "Artificial Donor Insemination: Perspectives on Legal and Social Change," 54 *Iowa Law Rev* 253, October 1958. Ch 8, n 112.

Dornette, William H. L .M.D., "Medical Injury Insurance—A Possible Remedy for the Malpractice Problem," *J Legal Med,* March/April 1973, page 28. Ch 13, n 80.

Dorsey, J. S., "Release of Tortfeasor, Release of Physician," 15 *NC Law Rev.* 293, 1937. Ch 10, n 102.

"Effect of Release of Given Tortfeasor Causing Initial Injury and Later Action for Malpractice Aganist Treating Physician," 40 *NC Law Rev* 88, 1961. Ch 10, n 102.

"Family Planning and the Law," *Family Law Quart,* December 1967, pages 103–108. Ch 1, n 126.

"For the Defense," Defense Research Institute Newsletter, March 1967, pages 1 and 2. Ch 13, n 39.

Forbes, Peter R., "Voluntary Sterilization of Women as a Right," 18 *DePaul Law Review,* Nos. 2 and 3, page 560, Summer 1969. Ch 1, n 147.

Fry, Robert M.D., "The Demise of Charitable Immunity," in *Legal Medicine Annual: 1970,* at page 115, Cyril H. Wecht, Ed. Appleton-Century-Crofts, New York 1970. Ch 10, n 166.

Gelfand, Leo, "Modern Concepts of Property in a Dead Body," in *Legal Medicine Annual: 1971,* page 229, Cyril H. Wecht, Ed. New York, Appleton-Century-Crofts, 1971. Ch 8, n 60.

Gibbs, Richard F., M.D. "Malpractice Screening Panels and Arbitration in Medical Liability Disputes," *J Legal Med,* May/June 1973, page 30. Ch 13, n 53; Ch 13, n 71; Ch 13, n 72.

Gibbs, Richard F., "Therapeutic Abortion and the Minor," 1 *J Legal Med,* No. 1, page 36, March/April 1973. Ch 1, n 136.

Guttmacher, Alan F., "Artificial Insemination," 18 *DePaul Law Rev* 566, Summer 1969. Ch 8, n 112.

74 *Harvard Law Rev* 448, 1961. Ch 13, n 63.

Hershey, Nathan, "The Defensive Practice of Medicine—Myth or Reality?" *Milbank Memorial Fund Quarterly,* January 1972, pages 69–97. Ch 13, n 31.

Holder, James B., M.D., "Serum Hepatitis," 6 *Lawyers' Med J* 79, May 1970. Ch 5, n 56.

"Hospital Emergency Services and the Open Door," 66 *Michigan Law Rev* 1455, 1968. Ch 1, n 39.

Karcher, Joseph T., "Malpractice Claims Against Doctors, New Jersey's Screening Procedure," 53 *American Bar Assoc J*, page 328, April, 1967. Ch 13, n 54.

McCord, Allen H., "The Care Required of Medical Practitioners," pages 39–45 in *Professional Negligence*, Roody and Anderson, Eds, Vanderbilt University Press, Nashville 1960. Ch 4, n 35.

McIntire, Leon L., "The Action of Abandonment in Medical Malpractice Litigation," 36 *Tulane Law Review* 834, 1962. Ch 12, n 9.

"Malpractice Suits: Is the End in Sight?," *Med Econ*, June 7, 1971, page 27. Ch 13, n 80.

"The Malpractice Threat," A Study of Defensive Medicine," *Duke Law J*, December 1971, pages 939–993. Ch 13, n 31.

Miller, Frank R., "Does Release of the Original Tortfeasor Release the Subsequently Negligent Physician,?" 36 *Insurance Counsel J*, No. 3, page 360, July 1969. Ch 10, n 83.

New Eng J Med 270, No. 19, page 1003, May 7, 1964. Ch 1, n 32.

Nuremburg Trials 2 *The Medical Case*, pages 181–183, U. S. Printing Office 1947. Ch 8, n 143.

"A Physician's Defense Panel is a Must," *Med Econ*, March 1, 1971, page 103. Ch 13, n 39.

Pilpel, Harriet F. and Wechsler, Nancy F., "Birth Control, Teenagers and the Law," 1 *Family Planning Perspectives*, page 29, 1969. Ch 1, n 131.

Principles of Medical Ethics, American Medical Association, 1960, page 14. Ch 8, n 144.

Proceedings of the Conference on Malpractice, Center For the Study of Democratic Institutions, Santa Barbara 1971. Ch 13, n 34.

Report, Medical–Legal Committee, Annual Meeting, House of Delegates, New Mexico Medical Association May 1970. Ch 13, n 46.

Report on Family Planning, Family Law Section, 1968, *Family Law Quart,* December, 1967, pages 103–108, American Bar Association, 1155 60th Street, Chicago, Illinois. Ch 1, n 130.

"The Right to Treatment," 57 *Georgetown Law J,* March 1969. Ch 4, n 119.

Sadler and Sadler, "Recent Developments in the Law Relating to Transplantation," in *Legal Medicine Annual, 1971,* page 243, Cyril H. Wecht, Ed., New York, Appleton-Century-Crofts, 1971.

151 *Science,* pages 663–666, 1963. Ch 8, n 141.

Smith, George, "Through a Test-Tube Darkly: Artificial Insemination and the Law," 67 *Michigan Law Rev* 127, November 1968. Ch 8, n 112.

Sneidman, B. "Prisoners and Medical Treatment: Their Rights and Remedies," 4 *Criminal Law Bull* 450, October, 1968. Ch 1, n 60.

Swartz, Edward M., "Products Liability: Manufacturer's Responsibility for Defective or Negligently Designed Medical and Surgical Equipment," in *1970 Legal Medicine Annual,* page 131, Cyril H. Wecht, Ed., Appleton-Century-Crofts, New York, 1970. Ch 4, n 55.

Wadlington, Walter, "Artificial Insemination: The Dangers of a Poorly Kept Secret," 64 *Northwestern Law Rev,* page 777, January–February, 1970. Ch 8, n 112.

Warren, Charles and Branders, Louis D., "The Right to Privacy," *Harvard Law Rev* 4 (1890), 193. Ch 9, n 47.

Wasmuth, Carl E., "Organ Transplantation," in *Legal Medicine Annual 1969*, page 391, Cyril H. Wecht, Ed., New York, Appleton-Century-Crofts, 1969. Ch 8, n 83.

Welch, Williams J., "Pity the Poor Devils With Pains," *Prism*, November 1973, page 32. Ch 13, n 89.

Zimmerly, James G., M.D., "Is Arbitration the Answer?," *J Legal Med*, March/April 1973, page 48. Ch 13, n 73.

Books

American Medical Association Law Division, *Disciplinary Digest*, Chicago, 1967. Ch 11, n 3.

Brakel and Rock, eds, *The Mentally Disabled and the Law*, Rev. ed., University of Chicago Press, Chicago 1971. Ch 8, n 98; Ch 8, n 102.

Chayet, Neil L., *Legal Implication of Emergency Care*, Appleton-Century-Crofts, New York, 1969. Ch 1, n 31, n 34, n 38, n 103; Ch 11, n 38.

Hayt, Emanuel and Hayt, Jonathan, *Legal Aspects of Medical Records*, Physicians' Record Co. Berwyn, Illinois 1964, Ch 12, n 94; Ch 12, n 96.

Herbert, A. P., *Misleading Cases in the Common Law*, pages 12–16, Methuen Press, London, 1972. Ch 2, n 4.

Louisill, David W. and Williams, Harold, *Medical Malpractice*, Matthew Bender Co., New York, 1960 and Annual Supplements. Ch 13, n 49; n 69; Ch 8, n 18.

Sagall, E. L., and Reed, B. C., *The Heart and the Law*, MacMillan Co., New York, 1968. Ch 3, n 78.

Shartel, Burke and Plant, Marcus, L., *The Law of Medical Practice*, C. C. Thomas, Springfield, Illinois, 1959. Ch 1, n 25, n 28.

Wasmuth, C. E. and Wasmuth, C. E., Jr., *Law and the Surgical Team*, Baltimore, Williams and Wilkins Co., 1960, Chapter 8. Ch 8, n 83.

INDEX